OXFORD EARLY CHRISTIAN STUDIES

General Editors
Gillian Clark   Andrew Louth

THE OXFORD EARLY CHRISTIAN STUDIES series includes scholarly volumes on the thought and history of the early Christian centuries. Covering a wide range of Greek, Latin, and Oriental sources, the books are of interest to theologians, ancient historians, and specialists in the classical and Jewish worlds.

The Doctrine of Deification in the Greek Patristic Tradition

NORMAN RUSSELL

OXFORD

UNIVERSITY PRESS

OXFORD
UNIVERSITY PRESS

Great Clarendon Street, Oxford OX2 6DP

Oxford University Press is a department of the University of Oxford.
It furthers the University's objective of excellence in research, scholarship,
and education by publishing worldwide in

Oxford New York

Auckland Bangkok Buenos Aires Cape Town Chennai
Dar es Salaam Delhi Hong Kong Istanbul Karachi Kolkata
Kuala Lumpur Madrid Melbourne Mexico City Mumbai Nairobi
São Paulo Shanghai Taipei Tokyo Toronto

Oxford is a registered trade mark of Oxford University Press
in the UK and in certain other countries

Published in the United States
by Oxford University Press Inc., New York

First published 2004

British Library Cataloguing in Publication Data

Data applied for

Library of Congress Cataloging in Publication Data

Data available

ISBN 0–19–926521–6

1 3 5 7 9 10 8 6 4 2

Typeset in Garamond MT by
RefineCatch Limited, Bungay, Suffolk

Printed in Great Britain by
Biddles Ltd, King's Lynn

To the memory of
Elizabeth Moraitis Russell
1916–1983

Preface

It is becoming less necessary in the English-speaking world to apologize for the doctrine of deification. At one time it was regarded as highly esoteric, if it was admitted to be Christian at all. But since the appearance in 1957 of the English version of Lossky's brilliant book on the Eastern Church's mystical theology, steady progress in the translation of modern Greek theologians such as Mantzaridis, Nellas, and Yannaras, as well as the publication in English of studies by John Zizioulas and the Romanian theologian Dumitru Stăniloae, have brought the importance of deification (or theosis) in Orthodox soteriology to the attention of a wide readership. In recent years a succession of works on deification in individual Fathers from Irenaeus to Maximus the Confessor has confirmed the patristic basis of the doctrine. Since the 1950s several studies have shown how deification, in a more muted way, is also at home in the Western tradition.

The present work, based on an Oxford doctoral dissertation submitted in 1988, is the fruit of nearly twenty years of study and research. During that time I have incurred a number of debts. The first is to my former colleagues at the London Oratory who generously gave me leave of absence and shouldered the additional burdens that arose for them in consequence. I must also record my deep gratitude to the friends and relations who funded my doctoral studies, especially Ursula Hand and Shirley Thorp. Of my early mentors I mention with affection and gratitude Father Louis Bouyer, who first pointed me in the direction of theosis, and Bishop Kallistos of Diokleia, who supervised my initial research. I owe a number of insights and improvements to my examiners, Rowan Williams and Anthony Meredith. Since beginning the work of revision I have also benefited from the erudition and kindness of many others. I am especially grateful to Sebastian Brock, Henry Chadwick, and Lucas Siorvanes, who responded generously to my enquiries about deification in the Syriac Fathers, St Augustine, and Proclus, respectively. I should also like to thank Judith Herrin and Andrew Louth for inviting me to present portions of the work to their graduate students at the Universities of London and Durham, and Mother Nikola OSB for inviting me to conduct a study day on theosis at Minster Abbey.

My thanks are due to Lucy Qureshi of Oxford University Press and the editors of the Oxford Early Christian Studies series, Gillian Clark and Andrew Louth, for accepting the book for the series. I am grateful, too, to

Linda Bartlett and Andrea Rafferty for their expertise in putting a hand-written manuscript into the form required by the Press. Andrew Louth and Richard Price, who read the entire typescript, saved me from numerous errors and made many valuable suggestions. I am very grateful to them both. I am also much indebted to Charles Lomas for his help on points of style.

Finally, the dedication of this book to my mother reflects more than customary *pietas*. My mother not only taught me Greek in my earliest childhood but also nurtured in me a love of the Fathers and Byzantine civilization. May her memory be eternal.

Norman Russell

Sunday of the Holy Fathers, 2004

Contents

Abbreviations

ACW	Ancient Christian Writers
ANF	Ante-Nicene Fathers
Ath. Mitt.	*Mitteilungen des deutschen archäologischen Instituts, Athenische Abteilung*, Berlin
BJRL	*Bulletin of the John Rylands Library*, Manchester
CBQ	*Catholic Biblical Quarterly*, Washington, DC
CCSG	Corpus christianorum, series graeca, Turnhout
CCSL	Corpus christianorum, series latina, Turnhout
CH	*Corpus Hermeticum*
CIG	A. Boeckh (ed.), *Corpus Inscriptionum Graecarum*, Berlin, 1828–77
CPG	M. Geerard and F. Glorie (eds), *Clavis Patrum Graecorum*, 5 vols, CCSG, Turnhout, 1974–87; supplementary vol., M. Geerard and J. Noret (eds), 1998
CR	*Classical Review*, Oxford
CSCO	Corpus scriptorum christianorum orientalium, Louvain
CSEL	Corpus scriptorum ecclesiasticorum latinorum, Vienna
CSS	Cistercian Studies Series
CWS	The Classics of Western Spirituality
DOP	*Dumbarton Oaks Papers*, Washington, DC
DS	M. Viller *et al.* (eds), *Dictionnaire de Spiritualité*, Paris, 1932–95
GCS	Die griechischen christlichen Schriftsteller der ersten drei Jahrhunderte, Berlin
GNO	Gregorii Nyseni Opera
HTR	*Harvard Theological Review*, Cambridge, Mass.
ICC	International Critical Commentary
IGR	R. Cagnat *et al.* (eds), *Inscriptiones Graecae ad res Romanas pertinentes*, vols i, iii, and iv, Paris, 1906–27
JBL	*Journal of Biblical Literature*, New Haven, Conn.
JEH	*Journal of Ecclesiastical History*, London
JHS	*Journal of Hellenic Studies*, London
JRS	*Journal of Roman Studies*, London
JTS	*Journal of Theological Studies*, Oxford
LCC	Library of Christian Classics
LCL	Loeb Classical Library

LSJ	H. G. Liddell and R. Scott, *A Greek-English Lexicon*, revised by H. S. Jones, with a supplement, Oxford, 1968
LXX	Septuagint
NHL	*Nag Hammadi Library*
NPNF	Nicene and Post-Nicene Christian Fathers
n.s.	new series
OCA	Orientalia christiana analecta, Rome
OCP	*Orientalia christiana periodica*, Rome
OCT	Oxford Classical Texts
ODCC[3]	E. A. Livingstone and F. L. Cross (eds), *The Oxford Dictionary of the Christian Church* (3rd edn), Oxford, 1997
OECT	Oxford Early Christian Texts
OGI	W. Dittenberger (ed.), *Orientis Graeci Inscriptiones Selectae*, Leipzig, 1903–5
PBSR	*Papers of the British School at Rome*, Rome
PG	J.-P. Migne (ed.), Patrologia Graeca, Paris, 1857–66
P. Genev.	J. Nicole (ed.), *Les Papyrus de Genève*, Geneva, 1896, 1900
PGL	G. W. H. Lampe, *A Patristic Greek Lexicon*, Oxford, 1961–70
P. Graec. Mag.	K. Preisendanz (ed.), *Papyri Graecae Magicae*, Leipzig and Berlin, 1928, 1931
PL	J.-P. Migne (ed.), Patrologia Latina, Paris, 1844–64
P. Lond.	F. G. Kenyon and H. I. Bell, *Greek Papyri in the British Museum*, London, 1893–
PO	Patrologia Orientalis, Paris and Turnhout
P. Oxyr.	B. P. Grenfell and A. S. Hunt, *Oxyrhynchus Papyri*, London, 1898–
P. Tebt.	B. P. Grenfell *et al.* (eds), *Tebtunis Papyri*, London and New York, 1902–38
RechSR	*Recherches de science religieuse*, Paris
SBL	Society of Biblical Literature
SC	Sources Chrétiennes, Paris
SIG[3]	W. Dittenberger (ed.), *Sylloge Inscriptionum Graecarum* (3rd edn), Leipzig, 1915–24
SJT	*Scottish Journal of Theology*, Edinburgh
StPat	*Studia Patristica*, Louvain
TU	Texte und Untersuchungen zur Geschichte der altchristlichen Literatur, Berlin
VigChr	*Vigiliae Christianae*, Amsterdam
ZNTW	*Zeitschrift für die neutestamentliche Wissenschaft*, Giessen and Berlin

Introduction

1. The Metaphor of Deification

All the earlier patristic writers who refer to deification, although sometimes conscious of the boldness of their language, took it for granted that their readers understood what they meant. Clement of Alexandria was first to use the technical vocabulary of deification, but he did not think it necessary to explain it. No formal definition of deification occurs until the sixth century, when Dionysius the Areopagite declares: 'Deification ($\theta\acute{\epsilon}\omega\sigma\iota\varsigma$) is the attaining of likeness to God and union with him so far as is possible' (*EH* 1. 3, PG 3. 376A). Only in the seventh century does Maximus the Confessor discuss deification as a theological topic in its own right.

The reason for this is that deification language is most often used metaphorically.[1] The implications of the metaphor were clear to its first hearers or readers and did not need to be spelled out, the context of the utterance enabling them to construe its meaning. But by the sixth century the metaphorical sense was fading. Deification was becoming a technical term susceptible of definition.[2] That is to say, the same truth which was originally expressed in metaphorical language came in the early Byzantine period to be expressed conceptually and dogmatically.

The subject of this book is Christian deification from its birth as a metaphor to its maturity as a spiritual doctrine. The early Fathers use deification language in one of three ways, nominally, analogically, or metaphorically. The first two uses are straightforward. The nominal interprets the biblical application of the word 'gods' to human beings simply as a title of honour. The analogical 'stretches' the nominal: Moses was a god to Pharaoh as a wise man is a god to a fool; or men become sons and gods 'by grace' in relation to Christ who is Son and God 'by nature'.[3] The metaphorical use is more

---

[1] On the role of metaphor in theological discourse the best study is Soskice 1985. See also McFague 1983.

[2] 'Metaphorical usages which begin their careers outside the standard lexicon may gradually become lexicalized' (Soskice 1985: 83).

[3] When attached to the word 'gods', the phrase 'by grace' ($\kappa\alpha\tau\grave{\alpha}\ \chi\acute{\alpha}\rho\iota\nu$) functions, in Aristotelian terms, as a 'negative addition' (Aristotle, *Poet.* 21. 1457^{b}30–32) denying the attribute of uncreatedness. It indicates that 'gods' is not to be taken literally.

complex. It is characteristic of two distinct approaches, the ethical and the realistic. The ethical approach takes deification to be the attainment of likeness to God through ascetic and philosophical endeavour, believers reproducing some of the divine attributes in their own lives by imitation. Behind this use of the metaphor lies the model of *homoiosis*, or attaining *likeness* to God. The realistic approach assumes that human beings are in some sense transformed by deification. Behind the latter use lies the model of *methexis*, or *participation*, in God.

Homoiosis and *methexis* are two key terms used by Plato with long and distinguished careers in later Platonic thought. Their meanings are distinct, but their spheres of reference overlap. Although the latter is the stronger term, they both seek to express the relationship between Being and becoming, between that which exists in an absolute sense and that which exists contingently. *Methexis* has been defined in the following way: ' "Participation" is the name of the "relation" which accounts for the togetherness of elements of diverse ontological type in the essential unity of a single instance. In this sense it is a real relation, one constitutive of the nexus qua nexus which arises from it' (Bigger 1968: 7). In other words, participation occurs when an entity is defined in relation to something else. For example, a holy person is an entity distinct from holiness, but is defined as holy because he or she has a share in holiness. Without holiness there is no holy person, but the holy person has a separate existence from holiness. To say that the holy person 'participates' in holiness conveys a relationship which is (a) substantial, not just a matter of appearance, and (b) asymmetrical, not a relationship between equals. 'Likeness' is the name of another 'relation' which accounts for the togetherness of elements of diverse ontological type, but in a weaker, non-constitutive way, closer to analogy than to participation. Likeness occurs when two entities share a common property. For example, two holy people resemble each other because they both possess holiness. The boundaries between these distinctions, however, are not rigid. 'Participation' can be strong or weak depending on whether it is used properly (κυρίως) or figuratively (καταχρηστικῶς).[4]

Analogy, imitation, and participation thus form a continuum rather than express radically different kinds of relationship. Furthermore, the realistic approach, which is based on the participation model, has two aspects, one ontological, the other dynamic. The ontological aspect is concerned with human nature's transformation in principle[5] by the Incarnation, the dynamic with the individual's appropriation of this deified humanity through the

---

[4] The best study of participation in Plato is still Bigger 1968; see also Allen 1965. The later Platonic tradition explores the mechanics of the whole system, taking in Aristotelian insights.

[5] Here and elsewhere I use the expression 'in principle' as a convenient way of referring to God's action in the Incarnation before the benefits accomplished by it come to be internalized by the believer through the life of faith.

sacraments of baptism and the Eucharist. These four basic approaches, nominal, analogical, ethical, and realistic (in both its ontological and dynamic aspects) will be used as a framework for much of what follows.

2. The Need for the Study

Metaphors, as Andrew Louth has observed, 'disclose a way of looking at the world, a way of understanding the world. If we wish to understand the way in which any of the ancients understood their world, we must pay heed to their use of metaphors'.[6] But Western scholars have rarely given the metaphor of deification sympathetic attention. The tone was set by Adolf von Harnack. Towards the end of the nineteenth century he correctly identified deification as a leading theme in Irenaeus of Lyons that found ready acceptance among his contemporaries because it not only surpassed the Gnostic conception of salvation but also accorded with Christianity's eschatological tendencies and the mystical currents of Neoplatonism. Moreover, it came close but 'in a very peculiar way' to Pauline theology (1896–9: ii. 240–1). But in Harnack's view the 'exchange formula' encapsulating this doctrine (God became man that man might become god) was fundamentally derived from the mystery cults and was consequently to be deplored: 'when the Christian religion was represented as the belief in the incarnation of God and as the sure hope of the deification of man, a speculation that had originally never got beyond the fringe of religious knowledge was made the central point of the system and the simple content of the Gospel was obscured' (1896–9: ii. 10, 318). More precisely, deification presented redemption as 'the abrogation of the natural state by a miraculous transformation of our nature'; it distinguished the supreme good from the morally good; it excluded an atonement; and it called for christological formulas which contradicted the picture of Jesus in the Gospels (1896–9: iii. 164–6).

Biblical scholars today are less confident about the simplicity of the Gospel, but Harnack's judgement on deification has endured. In 1960 Benjamin Drewery declared: 'I must put it on record that deification is, in my view, the most serious aberration to be found not only in Origen but in the whole tradition to which he contributed, and nothing that modern defenders of ἀποθέωσις . . . have urged has shaken in the slightest my conviction that here lies the disastrous flaw in Greek Christian thought' (1960: 200–1). Drewery's protest is not to be dismissed lightly. In 1975 he published a brief but well documented study of deification which may still serve as a good, if provocative, introduction. After reviewing the relevant texts, his evaluation was still negative. He considered the doctrine unbiblical and irrational, its modern

---

[6] Louth 1983*a*: 19, summarizing a central idea of Giambattista Vico's.

champions being 'guilty of pushing a paradox into the realms of the non-sensical' (1975: 52).

Drewery's hostility is partly to be explained by the fact that he was reacting against the confident and somewhat polemical accounts of deification put forward by three Orthodox writers, Myrrha Lot-Borodine, Vladimir Lossky, and Philip Sherrard. It was Lot-Borodine who first drew the attention of Western readers to the doctrine's centrality in the Eastern Orthodox tradition in a series of articles entitled 'La doctrine de la "déification" dans l'Église grecque jusqu'au XIᵉ siècle' published in the *Revue d'histoire des religions* in 1932–3 and subsequently reissued with a preface by Cardinal Daniélou in 1970. Daniélou says that when he first read them, the articles had a profound effect on him: 'They crystallized for me something for which I had been searching, a vision of man transfigured by the divine energies' (Lot-Borodine 1970: 10). They were to exercise a powerful influence on his important work of 1944 on the mystical theology of Gregory of Nyssa. Lot-Borodine's articles, however, had appeared without a full scholarly apparatus. In Daniélou's words, they abounded instead 'with something more precious', with a profound sense of the Byzantine spiritual tradition (Lot-Borodine 1970: 11). At the same time this Byzantine interpretation of the early Greek Fathers could be seen as a weakness. Even a sympathetic reader like Daniélou could not accept an account of early patristic theology couched in the language of Gregory Palamas. This seemed to him to fall into an error mirroring that of Western scholasticism. Nor did he accept Lot-Borodine's neat opposition between Eastern and Western theology.

A similar polemical tendency is also evident in the work of Vladimir Lossky, who has perhaps done more than anybody else to explain Orthodox spirituality to a Western public. His *Essai sur la théologie mystique de l'Église d'Orient* of 1944, translated into English in 1957, made the doctrine of deification widely known as the crowning achievement of Byzantine mystical theology. Deification is the final end of humankind, the fullness of mystical union with God, seen in terms of a participation in the divine and uncreated energies which can begin even in this life. Lossky draws a strong contrast between the dynamic theology (in the strict sense) of the East, as represented by the later Fathers and St Gregory Palamas, and the static theology of the West, as embodied in the writings of St Augustine and St Thomas Aquinas. His polemical tone has attracted adverse comment even from fellow Orthodox. 'As a controversialist and apologist', John Meyendorff writes, 'Vladimir Lossky was sometimes intransigent and harsh' (Lossky 1963: 5). The intransigence was not all one-way. At the time, Orthodox theology was often treated by Western writers in a hostile or patronizing manner, as the writings of Martin Jugie, for example, witness. Lossky's reaction is understandable: 'In the present state of dogmatic difference between East and West it is essential, if one wishes to study the mystical theology of the Eastern Church, to choose between two possible standpoints. Either, to place oneself on western dogmatic ground and to examine the eastern tradition across that of the West—that is, by way of criticism—or else to present that tradition in the light of the dogmatic attitude of the Eastern Church. This latter course is for us the only possible one' (Lossky 1957: 12).

Philip Sherrard's influential study, *The Greek East and the Latin West* (1959, 2nd edn 1992) also deemed Lossky's course the only possible one. Disenchanted with Western attitudes—'the spiritual dereliction, not to say slump into systematic barbarity, of the modern western world' (1992: v)—Sherrard came to Orthodoxy in later life. Convinced that Christianity is a 'Way of salvation', not a system of thought, he presents the Greek theological tradition from a soteriological perspective in which man's conscious participation in the divine 'realizes' his own spiritual principle with consequences for all creation (Sherrard 1992: 43–4). As with Lossky and Lot-Borodine, the patristic doctrine of deification is viewed from a Palamite perspective with a strong colouring, in Sherrard's case, of Christian Platonism.[7]

In the meantime, the investigation of the doctrine of deification according to modern notions of impartial scientific study was advancing steadily. The first tentative survey was a brief general account by V. Ermoni, published in French in 1897. A much more thorough treatment in Russian by I. V. Popov appeared in 1906, but had little impact outside the Russian-speaking world. An ambitious attempt to cover the same ground in German was begun by Louis Baur in 1916. In the difficult conditions prevailing in Germany after the First World War, however, his monograph remained unfinished. There were only two further articles of a general nature by O. Faller (1925) and M.-J. Congar (1935), the latter responding to Lot-Borodine, before Jules Gross published his landmark study in 1938.[8]

Gross set out to answer Harnack. He denied that deification was an importation from Hellenism, claiming instead that it was a biblical idea in Greek dress, the equivalent of the Western doctrine of sanctifying grace (1938: vi). Inspired by Leipoldt (1923) and Faller (1925), he saw the doctrine of deification fundamentally as the re-expression by the Greek Fathers in the language of their own culture of two themes already present in the New Testament, namely, the Pauline teaching on mystical incorporation into

---

[7] It may be mentioned that Greece at this time was dominated by an academic theological tradition that did not pay much attention to deification. The important work by Greek theologians since 1960 is discussed in Chapter 9. 5, below.

[8] Appearing on the eve of the Second World War, this book, despite its importance, survives in very few copies. The welcome publication of an English translation in 2000 came too late for me to refer to, but fortunately the translator, for ease of reference, has included the page numbers of the French edition in the margins.

Christ, and the Johannine idea of the incarnate Logos as the source of divine life (1938: 105–6). To prove his thesis, Gross first examines the analogues to deification in contemporary pagan culture, then discusses the beginnings of deification in the Old and New Testaments, and finally reviews the entire Greek patristic tradition from the Apologists to John Damascene. The results are impressive. For the first time all the evidence is examined in great detail, and a wealth of material adduced to prove the ubiquity of the doctrine of deification, particularly in writers of the Alexandrian tradition. But there are a number of weaknesses. First, Gross does not study the vocabulary. He treats deification as a concept that is embodied in different writers as it is transmitted from one generation to another, without looking closely at the terminology that was developed to express it. Secondly, he does not examine the questions to which the patristic discussions of deification were the answers. The doctrine is presented simply as it appears from time to time in various Fathers. Thirdly, although the different aspects of deification are not ignored, he focuses perhaps too strongly on incorruptibility and immortality: 'All the Greek doctors insist that to participate in the divine nature is to participate in incorruptibility. In effect they often identify the terms "to deify" and "to immortalize" ' (1938: 350). Close attention to the context of patristic discussions of deification suggests a broader range of meanings.

A brief response to Gross by A.-J. Festugière was published in 1939. After the war, however, the emphasis changed. Two remarkable studies, one of Maximus the Confessor by Hans Urs von Balthasar (1941), the other the study of Gregory of Nyssa by Jean Daniélou already mentioned (1944), inspired deeper investigation of the spiritual teaching of individual Fathers. Walther Völker, after his monograph on the ideal of human perfection in Origen of 1931, resumed his work with a series of important studies of Greek spiritual writers from the second to the fourteenth century.[9] Subsequently there have been a number of significant monographs specifically on the doctrine of deification in Gregory of Nazianzus (Winslow 1979), Athanasius of Alexandria (Norman 1980), Irenaeus of Lyons (de Andia 1986), Maximus the Confessor (Larchet 1996), and Cyril of Alexandria (Keating 2004). The findings of these studies have not yet been incorporated into an overview. The last general surveys of deification were undertaken in the early 1950s, the fruits of which were I.-H. Dalmais' expert summary, which appeared in the third volume of the *Dictionnaire de Spiritualité* (1954–7), and A. Theodorou's fine dissertation, arranged on a systematic rather than a historical basis, which was published in Athens in 1956. While these remain

---

[9] These are on Clement of Alexandria (1952), Gregory of Nyssa (1955), Dionysius the Areopagite (1958), Maximus the Confessor (1965), John Climacus (1968), Symeon the New Theologian (1974), and Nicholas Cabasilas (1977).

very useful, there is a need for a new evaluation of deification in the light of later research.

3. Scope and Method

The section Eric Osborn devotes to deification in his book, *The Beginning of Christian Philosophy* (1981: 111–20) is one of the liveliest of the more recent contributions to the debate. Osborn stresses the importance of method in any discussion of deification, the available methods he lists being the cultural, the polemical, the doxographical, and the problematic. The cultural method presents deification as an integral part of the Eastern Christian ethos, treating it as the expression of a homogeneous tradition with each patristic author adding his stone to the edifice. The polemical method attacks it as wrong from the standpoint that truth is univocal and any proposition which does not accord with that truth (which is to be found in one's own tradition) must be erroneous. The doxographer simply collects the opinions of each writer. The problematic method seeks to identify the problems to which deification was the solution. Osborn considers this the only method which, with the help of the cultural and doxographical approaches, can really shed much light on deification. Indeed, 'it is a waste of time writing on deification unless some attempt is made to elucidate the problem' (Osborn 1981: 113).

Osborn identifies an important but previously neglected aspect of deification. A problematic approach investigates the questions that arose from the need to demonstrate the rational coherence of the faith of the New Testament in language which had to take cognizance of Greek categories of thought. An early difficulty arose from the very notion of immortality. If immortality was a fundamental divine attribute—which no one disputed—in what sense did believers attain it without blurring the distinction between themselves and God? In this connection Psalm 82: 6, 'I said, you are gods and all of you sons of the Most High', needed to be reconciled with the biblical insistence on the transcendence of God. As solutions were suggested, these in turn gave rise to new problems. For example, after Athanasius' successful struggle against Arianism, Origen's account of how the soul ascended to God was no longer acceptable in its original form. The problem now became one of reconciling the ascent of the soul and its attainment of likeness to God with the profound gulf which was perceived to exist between the 'genetic' and 'agenetic' orders of reality.

Another difficulty arose from the doctrine of the Incarnation. Many Fathers, particularly of the Alexandrian tradition, considered the concepts of the Incarnation of God and the deification of man to be correlative to one another. The opponents of Arianism could therefore use the doctrine of deification as an argument for the fully divine nature of Christ: human beings could be deified only if Christ was indeed God. As has often been pointed out, soteriological concerns lay behind the christological disputes of the fourth century and later. If salvation was seen in terms of an inter-penetration of the human and the divine, christological doctrine needed to reflect this. Conversely, the development of christology had implications for the development of the doctrine of deification.

The problematic approach, however, is not exhaustive, because deification is more than a conceptual term, the fruit simply of intellectual analysis. As a widely accepted metaphor, it had become part of tradition and had some-how to be accommodated in theological discourse. Even a writer such as Augustine, whose cast of mind was different from that of his Greek con-temporaries, accepted their exegesis of Psalm 82: 6, with its sacramental implications. The Fathers were much more aware than we are today of the unity of theology and spirituality, and also of the unity of divine revelation. According to the Alexandrian exegetical tradition, the whole of Scripture at its deepest level is about the mystery of Christ—both the Old and New Testaments in their entirety, not just the New with the Messianic prophecies of the Old. All of Scripture concerns the divine economy, and in ways not immediately obvious.

The present study confirms Gross's thesis that the deification metaphor has biblical roots and that during the second and third centuries it came to be expressed in the language of Hellenism. After examining the first Christian ideas about deification and their relationship to pagan and Jewish parallels, I trace how successive writers gave different meanings and connotations to deification and show how they arose according to the specific philosophical, theological, or exegetical problems they addressed. Unlike Gross, however, who concludes with John Damascene, I take my account up to Maximus the Confessor, whose teaching on deification represents the true climax of the patristic tradition. Finally, I describe briefly the concept as inherited by the Byzantine Church.

I am aware of the limitations of word studies, but as the vocabulary of deification has not yet been examined in detail, I list and discuss almost every instance of θεοποιέω—ἀποθεόω—θεόω and θεοποίησις—ἀποθέωσις—θέωσις in context until the end of the fourth century, together with signifi-cant examples from the fifth to the eighth centuries. Usage determines meaning. Deification's meaning cannot be established a priori or by general-izing from a few examples. The full range of usages must be considered. Appendix 2 summarizes my lexical findings. Briefly, the Christian usage of deification terms expressing the soul's ascent to God precedes the pagan usage rather than the other way round, as is often assumed.

Heeding Osborn's advice, I look at the problems that each writer was addressing. In what sense may human beings (on the authority of Psalm 82: 6) be called gods? How is the destiny of the Christian related to the divine economy of the Incarnation? How does the Christian philosopher (not to be outdone by his pagan rival) attain 'likeness to God so far as possible' (Plato, *Theaet.* 176b)? How is the soul's ascent to God to be reconciled with the distinction between 'genetic' and 'agenetic', created and uncreated? How does a human being 'participate' in God and still remain a creature? What is the role of the sacraments and the moral life? Few writers confront all these problems simultaneously. With each author it is necessary to identify the problems he was trying to solve, and place them in their context.

At the risk of over-schematization, I use my classification of the various approaches to deification as nominal, analogical, ethical, and realistic as a key for analysing the historical development of the doctrine. The earliest approaches are the nominal and the analogical, both of which are used by Philo, from whom they pass into the Christian tradition. The next is the realistic, which also, surprisingly, has Jewish antecedents. Inspired by Rabbinic exegesis, Justin Martyr laid claim to the 'gods' of Psalm 82: 6 for the Church, as a consequence of which Irenaeus takes it for granted that Christians may be called 'gods' on the authority of Scripture because they have been incorporated into Christ through baptism, thereby attaining a potential immortality. A new approach appears alongside this in Clement of Alexandria and Hippolytus of Rome, who are the first to use the verb θεοποιέω. The Christian philosopher may be called a 'god' because he has become like God through the attainment of gnosis and dispassion. By the fourth century all four approaches are well developed, with the realistic, expressed in the language of participation and relating to the sacraments of baptism and the Eucharist, and the ethical, expressed in the language of imitation and relating to the ascetic and contemplative life, predominating. Many writers use both approaches, though the realistic is especially character- istic of the Alexandrian tradition, the ethical of the Cappadocian. The two approaches are successfully integrated by Cyril of Alexandria and, most impressively, by Maximus the Confessor.

This study aims to be as comprehensive as possible within reasonable limits, which would have been exceeded if the scope of the book had not been confined to the Greek Fathers. As no mention at all of the Syriac and Latin Fathers, however, would have left the reader with an incomplete view of the role of deification in patristic thought and spirituality, a summary account of their teaching is included in Appendix 1.

4. Overview

Before Constantine, Christians lived as a minority in a strongly polytheistic environment in which the deification of human beings was commonplace.

Not only were there numerous temples to gods who had once been men, but in every city pride of place was given to the cult of the emperor. Deceased emperors had been deified from the time of Augustus. Since Domitian the reigning emperor was also regarded as a god. How were Christians to react? With regard to pagan religion in general, Christian intellectuals readily adopted a Euhemeristic approach. If all the gods had once been human, polytheism did not present a threat. The imperial cult was more difficult to fit into a Christian perspective. Under persecution, Christians may have been determined not to render to the emperor the worship due to God alone, but in times of peace they were more flexible. Throughout the Graeco-Roman world the imperial cult excited popular devotion. Indeed, it played a vital role in unifying society. It is no surprise that the cult survived the transition to a Christian empire by more than a century. Christians in practice could be very tolerant of it. Moreover, the deification conferred by the imperial funeral rites became available by a process of 'democratization' to ordinary citizens, so that by the second century 'apotheosis' could mean no more than solemn burial.

For an approach to deification connected with the religious development of the individual, we need to turn to the mystery cults and Orphism, and ultimately to antiquity's most noble expression of the religious instinct in the Platonic philosophical tradition. Philosophical religion was based on the conviction that the attainment of the divine was fundamentally the realization of something within oneself. A significant number of Christians could accept the aspirations of philosophical religion with very few reservations. A pupil of Origen's, for example, could refer to the dictum 'Know thyself' as a sublime method 'for attaining a kind of apotheosis'. Alongside the high philosophy practised by the educated elite, however, there was also a 'demoticized' version available to the students of Hermes Trismegistus. Hermetists aimed to return to God through spiritual awakening under the guidance of an experienced teacher in a manner that dispensed with the need for serious philosophical study. Christian writers do not refer to Hermetic texts until the fourth century. But the verb θεοποιέω in a spiritual context is first attested in Clement of Alexandria and the Hermetic corpus more or less simultaneously. Perhaps this is not a coincidence.

If we leave aside later exegesis, there is no evidence of deification in the Old Testament. But the canon of the Hebrew Scriptures was the product of Rabbinic Judaism, the successor to only one of the forms of Judaism which flourished at the time when Christian convictions were taking shape. Of the other forms, the Hellenistic and Enochic were particularly influential and made fundamental contributions to the development of the doctrine of deification.

A Jewish idea of blessed immortality is first encountered in Hellenistic Judaism. The author of the Book of Wisdom is the first Jewish writer to conceive of human fulfilment in terms of the destiny of the immortal soul.

This approach is taken much further by Philo of Alexandria with the help of Platonism. Philo identifies four different ways in which the soul ascends to God. The first is the religious, when the soul abandons idolatry and turns to the true faith; the second is the philosophical, raising the mind from sensible to intelligible objects of contemplation; the third is the ethical, for the virtues confer immortality by making the soul like God; and the fourth is the mystical, enabling the true philosopher to go out of himself and come as close to the divine as a human being can in so far as he has become pure *nous*. Moses was such a man. As an embodiment of wisdom, he occupied a mediating position between God and man. But even he can be called a god only figuratively in the sense that he came to share in the divine attributes of incorporeality and immortality.

Enochic Judaism is less accessible to us today but may be studied in the earlier parts of 1 Enoch and in the writings of the breakaway Essene sect that established itself at Qumran. This form of Judaism also had a doctrine of a transcendent life beyond the grave that had developed independently of Hellenism. The righteous were predestined to transcend death and be promoted to a community of life with the angels. The leader of the Qumran community was a new Moses who would lead his fellow sectaries to the fulfilment of the angelic life, which was to be identified with the life of the 'gods' of the psalmist's heavenly court. This divine life could already be anticipated in the liturgical worship of Qumran.

Even Rabbinic Judaism had its own version of deification. Merkabah mysticism—a spiritual approach that grew out of meditation on Ezekiel's vision of the throne-chariot of God—offered a rich alternative, expressed in anthropomorphic terms, to the intellectualizing Platonic version of the ascent to God. Even more important, from the Christian point of view, was the Rabbinic exegesis of Psalm 82: 6. The teaching that the 'gods' of the psalm were those who had won immortality through the faithful observance of the Torah was, in its Christian form, to exercise a decisive influence on the development of the doctrine of deification.

Did Paul have an idea of deification? He uses various expressions for participatory union—'in Christ', 'with Christ', 'Christ in us', 'sons of God', and so on, but does not isolate 'participation' for special consideration. Moreover, these expressions are images. 'Deification' as a technical term only emerged later when Paul's metaphorical images were re-expressed in conceptual language. The same may be said with regard to the Johannine writings, which reveal an approach to participatory union with Christ not unlike that of Paul.

Among Christian authors contemporary with the last New Testament writers, only Ignatius of Antioch takes up the theme of participatory union. He does not use the terminology of deification but prepares the way for it by speaking of Christ as God. If participation in Christ is participation in God, it will not be long before the Christian who is christified will be said to be deified.

The earliest explicit discussion of deification in a Christian writer arose from a consideration of Psalm 82: 6. Who is it that Scripture is addressing as gods? In around 160 Justin Martyr, drawing on the Rabbinic exegesis already mentioned, put forward the view that as the people of Christ were the new Israel, the gods were those who were obedient to Christ. Justin's younger contemporary, Irenaeus of Lyons, went on to draw out the implications of the conjunction of 'gods' with 'sons' and claim that the gods were the baptized. Through baptism they had recovered their lost likeness to God and therefore had come to participate in the divine life which that likeness entailed. God had come to dwell within them, making them sons of God and gods. This status was not secure, for it was vulnerable to loss through sin—we are gods but can die like men, according to the next verse of the Psalm—but nevertheless the fundamental transition from death to life, from mortality to immortality, had been made, enabling the baptized to be called 'gods'.

Towards the end of the century Clement of Alexandria also taught that the gods are those whom God has adopted through baptism. But alongside this he brought in a new philosophical dimension. The 'gods' are at the same time those 'who have detached themselves as far as possible from everything human' (*Strom.* 2. 125. 5). Through mastery of the passions and the contemplation of intelligibles they have transcended their corporeal state and come to participate in the divine attributes themselves. Clement links these two approaches, the ecclesiastical and the philosophical, through his teaching on the attainment of the divine likeness, which, although requiring intellectual effort, is at its deepest level 'the restoration to perfect adoption through the Son' (*Strom.* 2. 134. 2). Origen was also interested in the philosophical ascent of the soul to God but in a different way from Clement. Deification for him was not the perfection of the Christian Gnostic through ethical purification but the participation of the rational creature, through the operation of the Son and the Holy Spirit, in a dynamic divinity that derives ultimately from the Father. His emphasis was less on ethics, though it was by no means neglected, than on the nature of the dynamic relationship which connects the contingent with the self-existent. Life, goodness, and immortality are attributes which do not originate in the contingent order but belong properly to the Father alone. The rational creature is deified as these attributes are progressively communicated to it through its responding to the active reaching-out of the second and third Persons of the Trinity. Athanasius took this aspect of the dynamic participation in God further. But because his approach to God was more apophatic than that of Origen, it was only possible in his view for human beings to participate directly in the deified flesh of the incarnate Logos. Through participation in the body of Christ believers participate in the divinity with which that body was endowed, which leads them to participate in incorruption and immortality, and ultimately in the resurrected life and eschatological fulfilment of heaven.

The Cappadocians took the doctrine of deification from the Alexandrians and adapted it to a Platonizing understanding of Christianity as the attainment of likeness to God so far as was possible for human nature. Only the body of Christ, the ensouled flesh which the Logos assumed, is deified in the sense of being 'mingled' with the divine. Human beings are not deified in accordance with a realistic approach, the emphasis being as much on the ascent of the soul to God as on the transformation of the believer through baptism. This is because of the centrality of the concept of imitation: Christianity is essentially the imitation of the incarnate life of Christ, who deified the body which he assumed in order to enable us to return to the likeness we have lost. But such imitation is not simply external. Although it consists largely in overcoming the passions and freeing the soul from the constraints of corporeal life, it is also a putting on of Christ in baptism. We imitate God through the practice of virtue; we also imitate him by clothing ourselves in Christ. But we can never become gods in the proper sense; that is to say, we can never bridge the gap between the contingent and the self-existent orders of reality. For the Cappadocians, deification never went beyond a figure of speech. Gregory of Nazianzus made extensive use of it in his discussion of the Christian life. Gregory of Nyssa, by contrast, while accepting it in the case of the physical body of Christ and, by extension, of the bread of the Eucharist, was unwilling to apply it to the believer.

The fifth century marks the beginning of new developments. The Alexandrian theological tradition came to full maturity with Cyril, who developed his ideas on deification in the context of his polemics against Judaism, Apollinarianism, and Nestorianism. The technical terminology of deification became problematic for him even before his struggle with Nestorius. He uses it in those of his early works that are heavily influenced by Athanasius but subsequently drops it. In its place 'partakers of the divine nature' (2 Pet. 1: 4) comes to the fore for the first time. This Petrine phrase, used previously (but very sparingly) only by Origen, Athanasius, and Theophilus of Alexandria is quoted or alluded to by Cyril with great frequency. In Cyril's usage *physis*, or nature, seems to have a more dynamic sense than *ousia*, or substance, representing not the divine essence but that aspect of the divine which is communicable to humanity. Accordingly, the deification of human beings is seen less in terms of an Athanasian transformation of the flesh than as a recovery of the divine likeness in our inner life. In Cyril's scheme, in which the moral life and the reception of the sacraments are well integrated for the first time, participation in the divine nature implies our regaining of the divine image or likeness, which in turn finds expression in our sanctification, our filiation, and our attainment of incorruptibility.

Deification entered the Byzantine tradition, however, not through Cyril but through Dionysius the Areopagite and Maximus the Confessor. Theosis for Dionysius was primarily the attaining of unity and likeness. In his treatment of deification he took his language and his conceptions from both Gregory of Nazianzus and the Neoplatonist Proclus, combining Gregory's ascent of the soul with Proclus' thrust towards unity. Deification is the condition of the saved, which begins with baptism and is nurtured by participation in the holy *synaxis*, by reception of the Eucharist, by opening the mind to divine illumination. For Maximus it was not the problem of oneness and multiplicity that was central, but how a mortal human being can participate in a transcendent God. He took up the Gregorian and Dionysian approach but supplied a major corrective, for Dionysius has little to say about the Incarnation. In Maximus God is operative in the world through his divine energies. By virtue of the Incarnation the believer can participate in these. Theosis is God's gift of himself through his energies. On analogy with Maximus' christology, in the believer the human and the divine interpenetrate without confusion. The eschatological fulfilment of this deification is summed up in the following definition: 'Theosis, briefly, is the encompassing and fulfilment of all times and ages, and of all that exists in either' (*Var. Cent.* 4. 19; trans. Palmer, Sherrard, and Ware).

In summary, until the end of the fourth century the metaphor of deification develops along two distinct lines: on the one hand, the transformation of humanity in principle as a consequence of the Incarnation; on the other, the ascent of the soul through the practice of virtue. The former, broadly characteristic of Justin, Irenaeus, Origen, and Athanasius, is based on St Paul's teaching on incorporation into Christ through baptism and implies a realistic approach to deification. The latter, typical of Clement and the Cappadocians, is fundamentally Platonic and implies a philosophical or ethical approach. By the end of the fourth century the realistic and philosophical strands begin to converge. In Cyril the realistic approach becomes more spiritualized through the use he makes of 2 Peter 1: 4; in Maximus the philosophical approach comes to be focused more on ontological concerns under the influence of his post-Chalcedonian christology.

The Antiochene fathers are different. They speak of men as gods only by title or analogy. When the Antiochenes are compared with the Alexandrians, the correlation between deification and christology becomes clear, the contrast between the metaphysical union of the Alexandrians and the moral union of the Antiochenes in their christology being reflected in their respective attitudes to deification. For the Alexandrians the transformation of the flesh by the Word is mirrored in the transformation of the believer by Christ. For the Antiochenes the deliberate and willed nature of the union of the human and the divine in Christ finds its counterpart in the moral struggle that human beings need to experience before they can attain perfection. Just as without Platonism there is no philosophical approach to deification, so without a substantialist background of thought in christology there is no basis for a realistic approach.

Through Dionysius and Maximus the Confessor deification became established in the Byzantine monastic tradition as the goal of the spiritual life. The two most influential teachers of this final phase, Symeon the New Theologian of the late tenth and early eleventh centuries and Gregory Palamas of the fourteenth, emphasized the experiential side of deification. The controversies in which Palamas became involved were the result of his conviction that the hesychast was transfigured both spiritually and physically by the immediate vision, in prayer, of the divine light. The distinction between the imparticipable essence of God and his participable energies was passionately defended by Palamas as the theoretical basis of a strongly realistic view of participation in the divine. In the last phase of the controversy deification as a merely nominal or analogous term was expressly excluded. It was in this form that deification was handed on to the Orthodox Church of today.

2

Deification in the Graeco-Roman World

1. The Origins of Deification

When Paul and Barnabas were visiting Lystra in the province of Galatia, their healing of a man who had been a lifelong cripple provoked an enthusiastic response from the local population: 'When the crowds saw what Paul had done, they lifted up their voices, saying in Lycaonian, "The gods have come down to us in the likeness of men!" Barnabas they called Zeus, and Paul, because he was the chief speaker, they called Hermes. And the priest of Zeus, whose temple was in front of the city, brought oxen and garlands to the gates and wanted to offer sacrifice with the people' (Acts 14: 11–13). Despite the scepticism of biblical scholars, historians have detected in this story the ring of authenticity (Lane Fox 1986: 99–100). Pagans could provoke the same reaction; Apollonius of Tyana did so on several occasions, according to Philostratus (*V. Apoll.* 4. 31; 5. 24). The divine and human worlds were not separated by an impenetrable barrier. Ordinary people met the gods in their dreams or as apparitions in their sleep; natural disasters were unexpected visitations of divine power. If someone gave evidence of superhuman power, it was natural to assume that he must really be a god in disguise.

Evidence of superhuman power could suggest a human being who had joined the gods as well as a god in human form. This is why Paul was credited with divine power in Malta when he was bitten by a viper without coming to any harm (Acts 28: 1–6) or why Apollonius of Tyana was worshipped as a god at Ephesus for having banished the plague (Philost. *V. Apoll.* 7. 21). The awarding of divine honours to human beings was relatively new. Originally the human recipients of cult were clearly distinguished from the gods. We know of over eighty historical persons who were worshipped in the Greek world from classical times to the Roman period (Farnell 1921: 420–6). These subjects of heroic cult were the founders of cities, soldiers killed in the wars against the Persians, statesmen, legislators, athletes, poets, and philosophers—in short, anyone who was a benefactor of his city-state and therefore deserved the gratitude of his fellow citizens. The first to have received a specifically divine cult was Lysander, whose victories at the end of the Peloponnesian War had raised him to a position of unprecedented power (Plutarch, *Lysander* 18. 4; Habicht 1970: 3–6, 243–4). Divine honours were not the result of the devaluation of heroic honours, as was formerly thought. They arose through the need, as S. R. F. Price has argued, 'to come to terms with a new kind of power' (1984*b*: 29). The power exercised by the Hellenistic kings after Alexander was of a completely new order. It could no longer be accommodated within the legal and social structure of the city-state. Divine cult was rendered to the ruler on analogy with the cult rendered to the gods in order to give expression to the new relationship of power which had come to exist between the ruler and the cities. We do not need to appeal to 'oriental influences' to account for the voting of divine honours to their rulers by citizens of Hellenistic cities. 'The cults of the gods were the one model that was available to them for the representation of a power on whom the city was dependent which was external and yet still Greek' (Price 1984*b*: 30).

The divine cult rendered to Hellenistic rulers probably inspired Euhemerus (fl. 300 BCE) to suggest in his travel romance, the *Sacred History*, that all the gods of popular worship had once been rulers or heroes. This view was taken up by Diodorus Siculus, who explains in his *World History*, written in Alexandria between 60 and 30 BCE, how Ouranos, the inventor of urban life, was accorded immortal honours after his death because the accurate way in which he predicted the movements of the heavenly bodies convinced his subjects that he 'partook of the nature of the gods' (3. 57. 2). Euhemerism attained its greatest influence in the second and third centuries. Sextus Empiricus (fl. 200 CE) says approvingly that 'Euhemerus declared that those considered gods were certain men of power, which is why they were deified by the rest and reputed to be gods' (*Adv. Math.* 9. 51). He gives the Stoic sage as an example of a man who 'was in all respects considered a god because he never expressed a mere opinion' (*Adv. Math.* 7. 423). Sextus' Christian contemporary, Clement of Alexandria, also found Euhemerism helpful. Unlike the Apologists, he does not see why Euhemerus and other rationalists should be regarded as atheists, for even if they did not see the full truth at least they stripped away error, leaving the field clear for the one supreme God who is the Father of the Lord Jesus Christ. All the gods that are not the personifications of inanimate forces or qualities, he insists, had once been men (*Prot.* 2. 29. 1; 2. 38. 1). This is proved by the existence of their tombs, such as those of Ares, Hephaestus, and Asclepius, by the human passions characteristic of their lives, and by the relative newness of their worship. Among recently invented gods Clement lists Eros, Serapis, Demetrius, and Antinous (*Prot.* 3. 44. 2; 4. 48. 1–6; 4. 49. 1–2; 4. 54. 6). The many benefactors who have been accorded divine status include the Buddha, whom the Indians 'have honoured as a god on account of his great sanctity' (*Strom.* 1. 71. 6). Clement's lead is followed by Origen and Athanasius, who adopt the same Euhemeristic perspective.[1]

Clement not only accounts for pagan religion in terms of deification but is the first to speak of the deification of the Christian. G. M. Schnurr has noted in a suggestive article that Christian deification comes to the fore after Greek myth language has become secularized: 'Without giving any ontological sanction to the old myths, which were already secularized, mythological categories can provide a descriptive shorthand for the end and goal of Christian life' (1969: 103). In Clement's case it was more precisely the secularization implicit in Euhemerism that enabled him to appropriate the language of deification and put it to Christian use without at the same time taking over the content of pagan religion. If those whom the pagans called gods had been men who were able to achieve immortality, at least in the popular estimation, how much better a claim to the title had perfected Christians, who enjoyed a direct relationship with the source of immortality, Jesus Christ.

2. The Ruler-Cult

In the imperial period the men of power par excellence were the emperors. The emperor was the Roman paterfamilias writ large: the holders of the chief 'secretarial' posts were his freedmen; his subjects were his extended family over whom, like any paterfamilias, he had the power of life and death. Although in the provinces his rule was mediated by the local *ordo*, the notables who ran the cities as autonomous units, on occasion whole communities could feel his wrath, as Alexandria did in 215 with Caracalla or in 298 with Diocletian. On the latter occasion the emperor swore to punish the rebellious Alexandrians by plunging the city in blood up to his horse's knees. When the animal stumbled on entering the city, the citizens in their gratitude honoured it with a statue (Bowman 1996: 45). For the inhabitants of the empire the emperor was a figure of absolute power on a colossal scale. Moreover, he was present everywhere through his portrait, to which honour had to be paid as if to the emperor in person. The office of a priest of the imperial cult was one of the most prestigious to which a local notable could aspire. And the *sebasteia*, the temples of the cult, occupied the most prominent sites in the cities. The ruler-cult was not simply a fiction or a formality. For his Greek-speaking subjects in particular, the emperor was a living god who stirred feelings of fear, gratitude, and devotion.

---

[1] Origen: *Hom. Jer.* 5. 3, GCS iii. 33. 21; *C. Cels.* 4. 59, GCS i. 331. 19; Athanasius: *CG* 9. 34–42, Thomson 24; *De Inc.* 49. 4–11, Thomson 256–8.

The origins of the imperial cult go back to the practices of the Hellenistic kingdoms. Since the time of the *diadochoi* the peoples of the Greek East had been accustomed to giving their rulers divine honours. The most extravagant of these, the honours awarded to Demetrius Poliorcetes at Athens, are also the most Greek (Scott 1928: 164–6). Demetrius was honoured as incarnate power, as present and manifest might at the service of the Athenian state. An insight into popular sentiment is provided by the ithyphallic song with which the Athenians greeted him in 290 BCE when he brought home his bride Lanassa from Sicily:

> Other gods are either far away,
> or they have no ears,
> or they do not exist, or pay no attention to
> us, not in the least;
> but you we see before us,
> not made of wood or stone but real.
> (Athenaeus, *Deipnosoph.* 6. 253e)

Once Demetrius' power began to wane, however, the Athenians turned against him and all his divine honours evaporated overnight. His divinity belonged to his role, not his person.

The Ptolemaic version of the ruler-cult was similarly Greek in inspiration but was shaped in a distinctive manner by the Egyptian milieu in which it developed, that is to say, by a centrally organized 'state church' and the tradition of regarding the dead pharaoh as an Osiris.[2] Ptolemy I did nothing more than institute a cult of Alexander. The Ptolemaic dynastic cult dates from 271 BCE when images of Ptolemy II and Arsinoe were incorporated into the temple of Alexander next to the *sema* as the Brother and Sister Gods. On Arsinoe's death in July 270, her statue in the form of a ram was placed in every temple in Egypt, an unprecedented distinction indicative both of the awe in which Arsinoe was held in her lifetime and of the control which Ptolemy II had acquired over temple worship. It is this remarkable development that Callimachus celebrates in his poem *The Deification of Arsinoe*. The cult of Arsinoe became immensely popular, helped no doubt by her assimilation to Isis and Aphrodite, and before long had spread to the Aegean islands and beyond.

The state cult of the next royal couple, Ptolemy III and Berenice, the Benefactor Gods, did not follow immediately upon their accession. It seems to have been added to the cults of Alexander and the Brother and Sister Gods after Ptolemy's victorious return from his Syrian campaign in 241 (Bevan 1927: 207–8). Three years later the Benefactor Gods, together with their recently deceased daughter Berenice, were incorporated by a formal

---

[2] Nock 1930: 16; Cerfaux and Tondriau 1957: 209. On the Pharaonic ruler-cult see Morenz 1973: 36–41.

assembly of the entire priesthood of Egypt into all the temples of the country, as is recorded by the Canopus Decree of March 238 BCE.[3] This decree, which records the first dated instances of ἀποθέωσις and ἐκθέωσις, reveals an interesting blend of Greek and Egyptian elements. The assumption that death for the princess is a transition to the gods, the ceremonies of deification to be carried out on analogy with the deification of Apis and Mnevis, and the form of the prescribed annual festival are clearly Egyptian. On the other hand, the awarding of divine honours to the rulers in gratitude for their achievements, the voting of a decree of deification by an assembly (in this case of priests rather than of citizens), the form of the decree, and the sharing of a temple with a high god are all fundamentally Greek.

The Egyptian precedent was followed in Syria but developed there along rather different lines (Bikerman 1938: 256–7). Syria, unlike Egypt, had no state religion. Each autonomous city therefore honoured the sovereign in its own way. By the end of the third century a state-organized dynastic cult had been initiated by Antiochus III (Welles 1934: no. 36; Bikerman 1938: 247), but this had no relation to the municipal cults, which maintained an independent existence. In the Hellenistic period there were thus two kinds of royal cult, that of the living ruler, which was fundamentally a municipal cult by which the citizens sought to represent to themselves the majesty of the royal power, and that of the dynasty, which was initiated by the rulers themselves and sought to overcome the threats to security and stability inherent in the mortality of kings. Both these forms were to prove useful under the Roman empire.

The Roman imperial cult was not simply a continuation of the Hellenistic royal cult.[4] Indeed, just as the cult of Demetrius Poliorcetes had ceased when he fell from power, so the dynastic cults came to an end along with the dynasties they sustained. There is, however, a connection between the Hellenistic and Roman forms of the cult. The same motivation that had prompted the one also gave rise to the other, the Greeks adapting their traditional cults as they 'attempted to represent to themselves first the Hellenistic kings and then the power of Rome' (Price 1984*b*: 47).

This power began to be experienced by the Greeks at the end of the third century BCE. Their response was to award temples and cult to the goddess Roma, the people of Rome, and individual Roman officials who had impressed them with their authority and just administration.[5] The cults of individuals died away in due course to be replaced by the cult of the

---

[3] *OGI* 56. There are four surviving exemplars of the decree, which was set up in temple precincts in Greek, Egyptian (i.e. hieroglyphics), and demotic. The text is given in translation in Bevan 1927: 208; and Bowman 1996: 169–70.

[4] For the history of the ruler-cult in the Roman empire see Nock 1928, 1930, and 1957; Charlesworth 1935 and 1939; Cerfaux and Tondriau 1957; and esp. Price 1984*b*.

[5] The earliest was probably Marcellus, who received a cult at Syracuse in 212 BCE (Cicero, *Ver.* 2. 51).

emperors. Julius Caesar himself took active steps to promote his cult, building a Caesareum at Alexandria and starting another at Antioch (Weinstock 1971: 296–9), and under Augustus the imperial cult rapidly acquired its permanent characteristics (Price 1984*b*: 53–77).

After the deification of Julius Caesar by the Senate in 42 BCE, Octavian, as he then was, became known as *divi filius*. As his power grew so did the honours accorded to him. In 30 BCE, after his victory at Actium, the Senate decreed that libations should be offered to his genius. In 27 BCE he received from the Senate the title of Augustus (*Sebastos*), which though not divine gave him the aura of divinity, and the month Sextilis was renamed after him. Moreover, the reorganization of the city into 265 wards (*vici*) in 12 to 7 BCE enabled him to introduce his genius among the *Lares compitales* of each ward. But this was as far as the cult of the living ruler went in the capital. Constitutionally the position of Augustus and his successors was different from that of the Hellenistic kings. The Roman *princeps* was in theory the elected leading citizen of the empire. Such was Augustus' skill in endowing his unique position with the appearance of constitutional legality that in Rome itself any of the trappings of a Hellenistic monarch, such as temples and cult, would have been out of place. On the provincial level, however, steps were taken by Augustus to foster the ruler-cult through the provincial assemblies. The oldest of these was the Assembly of the Greeks of Asia, an institution which had been inherited from the Attalids. As a consultative council which met annually, it had from Hellenistic times included among its duties the regulation of cult and the awarding of honours to benefactors. It was found to be a useful means of communication between Rome and the local population which could report on the activities of bad governors, but its religious duties soon became the most important ones. In 29 BCE the assembly was entrusted with the cult of Augustus and Roma at Pergamon (Magie 1950: 447–9; Price 1984*b*: 56). Besides instituting a sacrifice, it also announced a prize for the person who could propose the greatest honours for the god (i.e. Augustus). Roman citizens had separate arrangements. They worshipped Roma and Divus Julius in their own temple at Ephesus (Dio Cassius, *Hist.* 51. 20; cf. Tacitus, *Ann.* 4. 37). The Greek emphasis, however, as in earlier times was on the living ruler. Other provinces that had also been Hellenistic kingdoms, such as Bithynia, also had assemblies and these too were authorized to worship Augustus in conjunction with Roma. Such an institution was too useful not to be transferred to the West. By the time of the Flavians every province with the exception of Egypt had its *concilium*. The native Egyptians, of course, already worshipped the emperor as their pharaoh.[6]

---

[6] Reliefs portrayed the reigning emperor as pharaoh engaged in traditional Egyptian rituals. See Bowman 1996: 168–70.

On the municipal level the imperial cult was purely a matter for local initiative. An interesting insight is provided by an inscription from Mytilene which records one of the first uses of the verb θεοποιέω (*OGI* 456; cf. Price 1980: esp. 34–5). The citizens of Mytilene were happy to assimilate Augustus as closely as possible to Zeus. They decreed that the prizes at the quadrennial games in honour of Augustus should be the same as those specified for games in honour of Zeus, and also that a monthly sacrifice should be made to Augustus at which the animals should be distinguished from those offered to Zeus only by the fact that they should be ἐφελιομένοι, which probably means 'with a spot on the brow' (i.e. with a small differentiation from animals considered suitable for sacrifice to a high god). Finally they decreed that 'if anything more distinguished than these [honours] should be discovered in later times, the zeal and piety of the city will not fail to carry out anything that can deify him further'. There is no mistaking the profound sense of gratitude that people felt towards Augustus. While there are some elements of continuity with the past, there is a new dimension of universality. The benefits that Augustus had brought to the whole Mediterranean world merited his assimilation to Zeus himself.

When Augustus died in 14 CE, the Senate voted him divine honours, declaring him a *divus* as they had done with Julius Caesar. This time the comet that had accompanied Caesar's funeral could not be expected, so at the funeral an eagle was released from the pyre to represent the soul soaring to the heavens. Subsequently the eagle became a regular feature of the *consecratio*. The funeral was an important rite in Rome which initiated the cult of the *divus*.[7] The Greek East, by contrast, had no special ceremony to mark an imperial funeral but focused its attention on the living ruler. Unlike the Italians, the Greeks did not distinguish between *deus* and *divus*. The *divus* was a *theos* like the living ruler. In the Latin West there was a contrast in terminology between the living emperor and a deceased predecessor, and between such a deceased predecessor and the high gods, that was absent in the East.

The pattern established by Augustus proved enduring. The only significant change before the reign of Constantine was brought about by Domitian. This emperor began his reign in a constitutional way, refusing the title *dominus* and preferring *princeps*. Then in 85/6 there occurred a change of policy. From that year Domitian wished to be addressed as *dominus* and *deus*. This did not mark the onset of megalomania but was a deliberate decision to have the state fully represented in the emperor's person. The living emperor was henceforth to be exalted and worshipped even in Rome as a focus of unity and loyalty (Scott 1936: 103–10).

The characteristics of the Roman imperial cult may therefore be summed up as follows: it was popular, being not only a creation of Augustus but also a

---

[7] On the imperial funerary ceremony and Christian attitudes towards it see MacCormack 1981: 93–144.

response to initiatives from below; it was based on the traditional way the Greeks had of defining their relationship to royal power; and it aroused strong feelings of devotion. In illustration of this one may compare the ithyphallic song sung for Demetrius (quoted above) with a panegyric celebrating Diocletian's crossing of the Alps in 291:

When you were seen more closely . . . altars were lit, incense was burned. People did not invoke gods whom they knew from hearsay, but Jupiter close at hand, visible and present: they adored Hercules, not a stranger but the emperor himself. (*Panegyrici Latini* iii (11) 10)

Although this is the composition of a court orator, we are probably not wrong in assuming that it reflects popular feeling. Like the Athenians six centuries previously, the citizens of the Roman empire saw their ruler as the visible manifestation of divine power.

3. Jewish and Christian Attitudes to the Ruler-Cult

It is commonly assumed that there was a dual attitude towards the ruler-cult, the mass of people taking it at face value, while the educated elite regarded it with a certain amount of scepticism (Bowersock 1973; Price 1984*b*: 114–17). The evidence for this lies in the critical comments of moralists such as Plutarch, Seneca's satirical *Apocolocyntosis*, Vespasian's wry deathbed remark, 'Vae, puto deus fio' ('Oh dear, I think I'm becoming a god'), and the absence of treatises on the significance of the cult. Such evidence, however, may be interpreted differently. Plutarch objected not to the imperial cult itself but to the grandiose titles of Hellenistic kings. Power, along with incorruption and virtue, was one of the divine characteristics in which a human being could participate. But of the three it occupied the lowest rank. It was when power went with moral attainment that a human being could most readily be described as divine. Insofar as these remarks may be applied to the imperial cult, they urge emperors to become worthy of devotion in their moral lives as well as in their exercise of power (Plutarch, *Aristides* 6). Seneca's *apocolocyntosis* (or 'pumpkinification') of Claudius reflects personal malice towards the emperor rather than cynicism with regard to the imperial funerary ceremonies. Vespasian's remark was probably an expression of modesty or may just have been a nervous joke.[8] Nor is the absence of technical treatises significant, for they would only have been needed to explain the cult to outsiders. Herodian's account of the apotheosis of emperors for a Greek readership (*c.*240) demonstrates this, for he dwells precisely on that aspect of

---

[8] Suetonius (*Vespasian* 23. 4) takes it to have been a joke although he himself documents Vespasian's unassuming manner and simplicity of life.

the cult which was not known in the Greek East, the solemn funeral of the deceased emperor (*History* 4. 2).

The assumption that the educated elite formed a superior level of society with a more 'rational' approach to such matters as the ruler-cult is anachronistic. The educated elite were not outsiders, nor were they alienated from the imperial cult through adherence to a sceptical attitude. As Price says, we cannot determine whether the symbols of the cult evoked different responses in the educated and the uneducated, but we can say with confidence that both participated in the cult with equal enthusiasm (1984*b*: 116–17). Educated outsiders, on the other hand, notably Jews and Christians, may be thought to have experienced some difficulty. In fact they were able to accommodate the imperial cult with relative ease. The Jews did not find a certain degree of participation in it problematic except in times of particular stress. There were two reasons for this. First, unlike the Christians, the Jews were respected as a people with an old and venerable religion, and therefore were not coerced into offering sacrifices to the gods. Nor were they perceived to be especially disloyal, in spite of the bitter Jewish wars of the first and second centuries. Indeed, there is evidence that in the third century Jews played a prominent part in the civic life of a number of Greek cities (Lane Fox 1986: 429–30). Secondly, until the destruction of Jerusalem, animal sacrifice played an important part in Jewish religious practice, a part which was readily intelligible to the pagans and could accommodate the imperial cult up to a point. Sacrifices could be offered 'on behalf of' the emperor rather than directly to him. This accommodation goes back to Hellenistic Alexandria, where inscriptions have been found recording the dedications of synagogues 'on behalf of' the reigning Ptolemy (Fraser 1972: i. 283, 298–9).

Philo's comments on the imperial cult illustrate these points. In 39 CE he was chosen by the Jewish community of Alexandria to travel with an embassy to Rome in order to make representations against Gaius' proposal to set up a statue of himself in the Temple at Jerusalem. The Jews had a record of assisting the spread of Roman power in the eastern Mediterranean. In keeping with this, Philo remarked in the presence of the emperor that the Jewish Temple had been the first to offer sacrifices on behalf of Gaius' rule. He pointed out, furthermore, that since Gaius' accession there had been two further occasions when sacrifices had been offered, once in thanksgiving for his escape from the plague, and again for victory in his German war (*Leg. ad Gaium* 45, 356). In the *In Flaccum* he stresses the law-abiding nature of the Jewish community and reports a speech in which the Jews ask the authorities how they are going to show their religious veneration for the imperial house if the synagogues are destroyed, leaving them with no place or means for paying their homage (*In Flac.* 49). The normal Jewish attitude was one of loyalty and accommodation. Only under pressure does

Philo insist on the merely human nature of the emperor in comparison with the one God who is 'the Father and Maker of the world'.

The apparent disloyalty of Christians, on the other hand, attracted the attention of the authorities early on. In response the Apologists took pains to explain the Christian attitude and protest their loyalty. Justin (*c.*150) is the first of several Christian authors to discuss the cult, but the only one to venture any criticism of the apotheosis of deceased emperors: 'And what shall we say of the emperors who when they die among yourselves are always deemed worthy of deification (ἀεὶ ἀπαθανατίζεσθαι ἀξιοῦντες) and you produce someone who swears that he has seen the cremated Caesar ascending from the pyre to heaven?' (1 *Apol.* 21). Justin is here generalizing for polemical effect. Not all the emperors had been deified after death; Gaius, Nero, and Domitian had suffered *damnatio*. Nor, after the funeral of Augustus, did someone swear every time that he had seen the soul of the dead Caesar rise to heaven. But it is not the details he is objecting to; it is the whole notion that just because men have been emperors they could be declared by rescript to have transcended the limitations of their human status (1 *Apol.* 55). The emperors, insists Justin, were simply men like everyone else: 'they died the death common to all' (1 *Apol.* 18).

These are bold comments but they echo contemporary, and particularly Middle Platonist, sentiments. Plutarch had rejected the bodily translation to heaven of Romulus and others because 'this is to ascribe divinity to the mortal features of human nature as well as the divine' (*Romulus* 28. 4–6). Philo, combining his Platonism with his Jewish piety, had declared with reference to Gaius' self-deification that nothing could have been more offensive than 'when the created and corruptible nature of man was made to appear uncreated and incorruptible by a deification which our nation judged to be the most grievous impiety, since sooner could God change into a man than man into a god' (*Leg. ad Gaium* 16, 188; trans. Colson, LCL). Even a pagan historian, Justin's younger contemporary, Dio Cassius, could assert that it was impossible for a man to become a god merely through a show of hands (*History* 52. 35. 5). Yet all these could admit that virtue deifies. Justin himself goes on to use ἀπαθανατίζομαι for 'those who have lived a holy and virtuous life close to God', contrasting the immortality conferred by decree of the Senate with that won by virtue (1 *Apol.* 21).

In their attitude to the living emperor the Christian Apologists follow the Jews. Justin says that they acknowledge his authority and pray for him (cf. Tit. 3: 1; 1 Tim. 2: 2) but they will not worship him: 'We worship God alone' (1 *Apol.* 17). The later Apologists repeat Justin's views. His pupil Tatian says that he pays the taxes which the emperor imposes but he will honour him only as a human being (*Orat.* 4. 1; cf. 1 Pet. 2: 7). Athenagoras assures Marcus Aurelius that Christians pray for his reign, for the peaceful succession of the imperial power from father to son, and for the extension of the imperial authority (*Legat.* 37. 2). Theophilus says that he will pay honour to the emperor not by worshipping him but by praying for him. The emperor is a man appointed by God and entrusted with a stewardship, but worship must be given to God alone (*Ad Aut.* 1. 11).

Although the attitude of the early Christians was similar to that of the Jews, the newness of their sect did not entitle them to the same respect from the Roman authorities. The imperial cult, however, did not play an important role in the persecution and martyrdom of Christians (Beaujeu 1973; Millar 1973; Price 1984*b*: 220–2). In times of crisis arising from natural or political disasters it was the anger of the gods that was held to blame and the 'atheism' of Christians that was believed to have provoked it. When Christians refused to sacrifice to the gods, sacrifice to the emperor was often offered by the judge as an easy way out: 'at least' sacrifice to the emperor, defendants were told. The authorities simply wanted a gesture of respect for tradition and of loyalty to the emperor (Lane Fox 1986: 425–6). The imperial cult itself was not the main issue. Indeed, in the Eastern empire it survived the official adoption of Christianity with only the most essential modifications. Under Constantine temple and cult were allowed to continue provided there were no sacrifices. Theodosius finally closed the temples in 392 but the *consecratio* went on for much longer (Bowersock 1982; MacCormack 1981: esp. 121–32). None of these developments provoked any expressions of outrage from Christian writers. Insofar as they comment on them at all it is with a voice scarcely distinguishable from that of educated pagans. Writing in about 320, Athanasius objects to the *consecratio*, in a manner reminiscent of Dio Cassius as much as Justin Martyr, on the grounds that the Senate has no authority to deify when its members are merely human: 'those who make gods should themselves be gods' (*CG* 9, Thomson 27). In an oration delivered towards the end of 380 Gregory of Nazianzus apostrophizes the Christian emperors, telling them like Plutarch before him to become gods to those under them by exhibiting virtue and beneficence (*Or.* 36. 11; cf. Winslow 1979: 184–5). Christian intellectuals by the fourth century were no longer outsiders.

4. The 'Democratization' of the Ruler's Apotheosis

The ruler-cult, giving expression as it did to a popular religious sentiment, came to be very widely disseminated. It is therefore not surprising in an era of social mobility and change to find it affected by a process of 'democratization'. What was originally reserved to the emperor and his immediate family, namely, the ascent after death to a divine destiny among the stars, came in the age of the Antonines to be appropriated by the less exalted. The earliest private deification for which we have evidence is that carried out by Cicero of his beloved daughter, Tullia (*Ad Att.* XII. 18. 1, 12. 1, 36. 1). Cicero was rather self-conscious about the prominence of his daughter's shrine on the Appian Way, but by the second century deification could be taken for granted as following upon death without any implied claim to high social status. Indeed, a number of inscriptions from the Greek cities of Asia Minor use the word ἀποθέωσις with reference to ordinary citizens simply as an expression for solemn burial (Keil and von Premerstein 1908: 85. no. 183; Waelkens 1983: 259–307; *CIG* ii. 2831–2).

In Egypt this process of 'democratization' had been going on for many centuries. In the Old Kingdom only the pharoah, by virtue of his divine office, was ranked with the gods.[9] During his lifetime his role was to mediate between the divine and the human worlds; on his death he became one with Osiris, the Lord of the Underworld.[10] Gradually the privilege of Osirian burial was appropriated by great officials and eventually by the population at large, at least by those who could afford it, for the required mummification and the provision of the customary funerary goods always remained expensive. By preserving the body intact as an earthly anchor for the *ka* (the life-force) and the *ba* (the soul) and burying it with the proper ritual even the ordinary Egyptian could be assured assimilation to Osiris, who as an ancient vegetation god had himself been raised from the dead. This development is reflected in the evolution of the mortuary texts, the magical formulae that enabled the *ba* to avoid judgement and achieve a satisfactory transition to the next world. In the earliest period they were incised on the chamber walls of the royal tombs and are known as Pyramid Texts. Later, when they no longer applied solely to the king, they were painted on the coffins of private persons, so becoming Coffin Texts. Finally, when Osirian burial became widespread, they were inscribed on papyrus rolls and buried with the mummy, sometimes being inserted into the wrappings themselves, turning thus into Books of the Dead. These texts refuse to accept the finality of death: 'Rise alive,' they proclaim, 'you did not die; rise to life, you did not die' (Morenz 1973: 205). Osiris long before Ptolemaic times could encompass everyone.[11]

Amongst the most haunting surviving artefacts of the ancient world are the mummy portraits of Roman Egypt. Something of how their subjects perceived themselves and how they conceived of the afterlife can be deduced from the fusion of Roman, Greek, and Egyptian elements in these skilfully rendered images. The clothing, the hairstyles, the techniques of portraiture are Roman, providing striking evidence of the uniformity of culture among

---

[9] The one notable exception is Imhotep, author of wisdom literature and architect of the Stepped Pyramid of Djoser, who was raised to the pantheon at some point after his death. Evidence for his cult, however, only dates from the New Kingdom, when he was joined in the pantheon by his fellow architect and scribe, Amenhotep. The cult of both deified sages lasted well into Graeco-Roman times. See further Wildung 1977: 31–110.

[10] Only outstanding kings, however, were the recipients of cult after their death (Wildung 1977: 1–30).

[11] On the 'democratization' of Osirian burial and the widening of access to immortality see Morenz 1973: 54–5; Griffiths 1986a: 20–9.

the upper classes of the empire. A number of the mummies in which the portraits are inserted are inscribed with standard Greek funerary valedictions: 'Farewell! Be happy!' (Walker and Bierbrier 1997: no. 32, no. 99). But the religious context is thoroughly Egyptian. Apart from mummification itself (the rhomboid pattern of bandaging intending to recall the mummy of Osiris), the Egyptian Lord of the Underworld is often explicitly represented or invoked. A linen shroud of the Antonine period, for example, shows a young man in Hellenistic dress and pose being guided by a jackal-headed Anubis towards Osiris represented as a mummy (Walker and Bierbrier 1997: no. 105). A beautiful young woman, dressed in the fashionable style of the Trajanic period, carries an inscription across her throat in demotic: 'Eirene, daughter of S . . . May her soul rise before Osiris-Sokar, the Great God, Lord of Abydos, for ever' (Walker and Bierbrier 1997: no. 111). Many of the subjects of these portraits were contemporaries or near-contemporaries of Clement of Alexandria. Whether Greeks of pure descent or Hellenized native Egyptians, they bear witness to the widespread belief in Egypt amongst people of Greek culture and high social standing that after death, like the kings of the past, they would become one with Osiris.

5. The Mystery Cults

Concern for the afterlife, so far as we can tell from funerary art, seems to have been particularly intense in Egypt. Elsewhere in the empire funerary art, as evidence for religious belief, should be used with caution (Veyne 1987: 232–3). Mythological motifs on sarcophagi, for example, with their scenes of voluptuous enjoyment have more to do with dispelling the fear of death than with evoking a bliss beyond the grave. And inscriptions, for all their occasional references to ἀποθέωσις, are more concerned to proclaim the status and achievements of the deceased in this life than to make any statement about their fate in the next. A remarkable second-century verse inscription by Titus Flavius Secundus from the mausoleum of the Flavii at Cillium in Roman North Africa brings out well the ambiguities of the Roman attitude to death. Secundus is not sure if the dead still have feelings but he is confident that his father is immortal because of the rectitude of his earthly life and the fact that his mausoleum is more a temple than a memorial. From its pinnacles the dead man can continue to survey the woods and vines of his estate and enjoy the familiar skyline of the mountains.[12] There can be little doubt that most people, as Clement said, 'clinging to the world as certain seaweeds cling to the rocks of the sea', held immortality of little account (*Prot.*

---

[12] For an English translation with full references see Davies 1999: 221–4. For a general survey of Roman beliefs in the afterlife and their connection with funerary practice see Toynbee 1971.

9. 71; cf. Plato, *Rep.* 611d). Indeed, insouciant statements such as 'I was not, I was, I am not, I don't care'—in its Latin form, 'non fui, fui, non sum, non curo', often abbreviated simply to N.F.F.N.S.N.C.—were not at all uncommon (Cagnat 1914: 291; cf. Bowman 1996: 187). What, then, are we to make of the mysteries? Did they not offer to initiates from all social classes solace in this life and the hope of a blissful immortality in the next?

Apart from a few autobiographical statements emanating from a tiny cultural elite, the mysteries are the nearest that we can get to a genuinely personal religion in antiquity. Yet the documentary evidence is scanty. Initiates were sworn to secrecy about everything but the preliminaries to the rites. And although profanations occurred from time to time, the vow was well kept. We have only one first-person account of an initiation, the famous narrative of Apuleius of Madaura in Book XI of the *Metamorphoses*, and even that does not reveal the secrets of the climax of the rite. But if the details of what occurred are not known to us, we have ample testimonies to the effects of the rites on initiates. The most celebrated of these is that of Plato, who in the *Phaedrus* compares the philosopher's joy at the vision of true Being with the elation and sense of liberation that comes to the initiate at the climax of the mystery, the moment of final revelation (250bc).

The mystery to which Plato was referring was that of Eleusis, the oldest and most venerated of them all. Even Socrates bathed with his sacrificial piglet in the Saronic gulf and underwent the other prescribed purifications before being initiated into the mystery in the hall at Eleusis. Many distinguished people followed him over the centuries. Cicero came (*De leg.* 2. 36), so did Plutarch, who speaks of the joy and confusion mixed with hope that initiates experience (*De aud. poet.* 47a). Eleusis retained its power to move and inspire right up to its destruction in 395 CE. Writing in the fifth century, the Neoplatonist Proclus gives us the last testimony to the effects of the rites, which he had received from the daughter of one of the last hierophants:

They cause sympathy of the souls with the ritual in a way that is unintelligible to us, and divine, so that some of the initiands are stricken with panic, being filled with divine awe; others assimilate themselves to the holy symbols, leave their own identity, become at home with the gods and experience divine possession. (*In Remp.* ii. 108. 17–30, cited by Burkert 1987: 113–14)

The experience of initiation is everything. There is no salvation from sin, no theology of death and rebirth, no higher spirituality. The emphasis is always on 'blessedness', an intense feeling which carries with it the hope of a better life in the next world.

The other great mystery cult of the classical period, the Dionysiac, was different in many respects from the Eleusinian. It was not attached to a great sanctuary but, in the early days at least, initiation was administered by

itinerant priests and charismatics. Another difference is that it did endow
initiates with a group identity, which in Italy drew hostility from outsiders
with catastrophic results. In 186 BCE the Roman Bacchanalia were bloodily
suppressed by the Roman Senate in an action which cost 6,000 lives. Finally,
it had a much more developed doctrine of the afterlife than did the other
mysteries. For Bacchic views on the afterlife we have not only literary evidence but inscribed gold leaves from the fourth century BCE that have been
found in tombs in southern Italy, Thessaly, and Crete. The oldest, the
Hipponion *lamella*, which was discovered in 1969, maps out the journey of the
soul after death (Vermaseren 1976; Burkert 1985: 293–5). The initiate is to
say to the guardians at the spring flowing from the Lake of Recollection that
he is the son of the earth and the starry sky. He will then be allowed to drink
and sent along a sacred way to a blessed eternity. Other similar gold leaves
from Thurii in southern Italy speak of the dead person as the child of earth
and heaven but really of the heavenly race alone. 'Happy and blessed one,' he
is told, 'a god you will be instead of a mortal' (Zuntz 1971: 301. 8).

The overcoming of mortality was also characteristic of Orphism. It has
been disputed whether Orphism was any more than a collection of writings
attributed to a mythological singer (Linforth 1941: 291–9). Certainly with the
appearance of *Orphica* literacy became important for the first time. And this
new form of transmission gave rise to a new kind of authority, that of the
written text. Plato mentions itinerant priests who 'produce a bushel of books
of Musaeus and Orpheus' (*Rep.* 364e), which, like medieval pedlars of indul-
gences, they use to carry out rites for the remission of sins and the deliverance from evils in the next life. Modern scholarship, encouraged by the texts
discovered on the gold leaves, is more inclined to see Orphism as a unified
spiritual movement akin to that of the Pythagoreans. At its centre lay a
distinctive anthropology. The human race was created from the ashes of the
Titans, who had been destroyed by Zeus because they had devoured
Dionysus, the Divine Child. As a result of its creation from matter that was
at once both Dionysian and Titanic, human nature had a dual character. The
Titanic element was the body ($\sigma\tilde{\omega}\mu\alpha$) or prison ($\sigma\tilde{\eta}\mu\alpha$) of the soul. The
Dionysian element was the soul, the divine spark or $\delta\alpha\acute{\iota}\mu\omega\nu$ trapped in
the body until it could be released through a life of asceticism and purifica-
tion, or rather, through several lives, for only thus could the soul realize its
true divinity and mount upwards never to return.

The Orphics were not an organized cult, but their honouring of Orpheus,
the singer of hymns and rescuer of Dionysus' mother Eurydice from the
Underworld, and their belief in the divine destiny of their immortal
$\delta\alpha\acute{\iota}\mu\omega\nu\epsilon\varsigma$ gave them a distinct group identity. The 'Pythagoreans' as
described by Plato were a similar group distinguished by their devotion to
Apollo rather than Dionysus, but holding the same views on immortality and
the transmigration of the soul. Unlike the Orphics the Pythagoreans were

founded by a historical figure whom later generations revered as a 'divine man' (θεῖος ἀνήρ).[13] Pythagoras was a charismatic figure, a philosopher with shamanistic powers who left behind him a reputation as a wonderworker. His belief in metempsychosis is well-attested (Xenophanes, fr. 7; Heraclitus, frs. 40, 129; Empedocles, fr. 129; Ion of Chios, fr. 4; Herodotus, *Hist.* 4. 95) as is his learning and cultivation of Apolline purity. These beliefs and pursuits were characteristic of the religious society that Pythagoras established at Croton in southern Italy, a society dedicated to the practice of an ascetic way of life (which included abstinence from meat) and to the pursuit of an esoteric study of nature with the aim ultimately of escaping from the cycle of rebirth. Like the Bacchic groups in Italy, however, it provoked hostility and was eventually ruthlessly suppressed.

A notable figure in the Orphic-Pythagorean tradition was Empedocles of Acragas in Sicily, who in his work entitled *On Nature*[14] proclaimed to his fellow-citizens: 'I go about among you as an immortal god, now no longer mortal, honoured by all as is fitting, crowned with fillets and luxuriant garlands' (fr. 102 [112]).[15] Evidently in Empedocles' view his soul had arrived at the last of its embodied lives. After death it would return no more to the 'roofed-over cave' (fr. 115 [120]) of this world as 'an exile from the gods and a wanderer' (fr. 107 [115]) but enjoy immortality for ever in the abodes of the blessed. It was Plato, however, who gave this tradition its definitive expression (Claus 1981: 183). In his hands the idea of the soul as the essential self that can exist independently of the body (*Laws* 12. 959b) rapidly reached its full development with profound consequences not only for the Platonic philosophical tradition but also for Judaism and Christianity. Pythagorean metempsychosis serves to underline the soul's independent existence. It is striking that in two of Plato's more important discussions of the soul the mysteries are mentioned as paradigms of the soul's primeval vision of blessedness when it was still free of the prison-house of the body (*Phaedo* 81a; *Phaedr.* 250b). All human souls have experienced that vision at one time or else they would have descended not into human bodies but into some lower form of animal life. The philosopher's soul alone, however, is able to recover that vision, to reverse the effects of the fall and flee to a realm which, like itself, is divine and immortal never to return.

In imperial times Pythagoreanism was revived as a mystical and ascetical

---

[13] The term is applied to Pythagoras by his Neoplatonist biographer, Iamblichus. Pythagoras' thaumaturgic ability was regarded as proof of his sharing in one of the chief attributes of divinity, that of power. Iamblichus himself, however, is the first philosopher 'whom posterity conventionally rather than exceptionally referred to as "divine" ' (Fowden 1982: 36).

[14] The following fragments are still printed by Wright as belonging to the *Katharmoi*, but recent scholarship believes that the supposed fragments from the *Katharmoi* all belong to Empedocles' main work, *Peri Physeos*.

[15] Cf. Pythagoras, of whom Iamblichus says, 'It is generally agreed that as a result of his exhortatory addresses he procured that no one should refer to him by his own name but that all should address him as "divine" (θεῖον)' (*V. Pyth.* 10 [53]).

tradition within Platonism. The mysteries also benefited from the renewed interest in religion characteristic of the age. The Eleusinian continued to hold its ground, as we have seen, but newer mysteries also flourished. One of the most successful was that of Isis. We know something of the rites through the remarkable account of them given in the late second century by Apuleius of Madaura in Book XI of the *Metamorphoses*. Although the *Metamorphoses* is a work of fiction, the eleventh book is generally believed to be based on personal experience. Isis, a Hellenized Egyptian deity, was a saviour goddess who had delivered her consort Osiris from the underworld and could similarly deliver her devotees once they had been initiated into her mysteries. At the climax of the rites the hero, Lucius, baptized and fasting, is led to the innermost part of the temple of Isis, where on the appointed holy night he says he 'saw the sun flashing with bright effulgence' and 'approached close to the gods above and the gods below and worshipped them face to face' (ch. 23, trans. Griffiths). After the rites are over, Lucius is given special robes and presented to the crowd outside in the guise of an Osiris, wearing 'a crown of gleaming palm' with the leaves pointing outwards like rays. To the onlookers he appears 'adorned like the sun and set up in the manner of a divine statue' (ch. 24, trans. Griffiths). The identification with the god, even if temporary, is complete. Thereafter he will carry with him the promise of a blissful union with Isis after death (Griffiths 1986*b*: 46–59).

The cult of Isis was widespread throughout the Mediterranean world. Another new cult that enjoyed a following in the Roman period was that of Mithras (Burkert 1987: 84–7; Martin 1987: 113–18). This, too, had an Eastern, syncretistic origin, but in this case Iranian rather than Egyptian. With its cult of *deus invictus* it appealed especially to soldiers. In fact it was entirely masculine. No women were admitted, nor were there itinerant priests or *thiasoi* or temples, as with the other mysteries. Groups of men met in windowless chapels—'caves' they were called, although the imagery of Mithraic myth is astral rather than chthonic—where their worship seems to have aimed at a transcending of the world. There were seven grades of initiation, corresponding to an ascent through the seven planetary spheres. The goal of the worshipper was to become one with the cosmos. 'I alone', says a fragment of a Mithraic liturgy, 'may ascend into heaven as an enquirer and behold the universe' (*P. Graec. Mag.* iv. 434–5, cited by Martin 1987: 118).

Perhaps the most remarkable of these new cults was that of Antinous (Lambert 1984: esp. 177–97). In 130 CE during an imperial visit to Egypt the young *eromenos* of the Emperor Hadrian was drowned in the Nile, either by accident or, perhaps, as was popularly believed, as a voluntary sacrifice to restore the emperor to health and avert evil to the empire. Hadrian was inconsolable after the death of his beloved. He lingered in Egypt while the body of Antinous was prepared for Osirian burial. In October 130 he founded the city of Antinoopolis in his honour and instituted annual games.

Without promulgating any official decrees, he immediately set about promoting the cult of Antinous-Osiris in Egypt and throughout the empire. In the eight years until his death the cult grew rapidly. Temples were constructed, notably at Antinoopolis, the chief centre of the cult, at Bithynion, Antinous' birthplace, and at Mantinea, Bithynion's mother city. Mysteries were organized at Antinoopolis and Bithynion. Coins, medallions, and domestic busts were produced in large numbers. Plaques were manufactured for fixing to coffins. In spite of his origins, or rather, because he had died for love, Antinous became the god of triumph over death, as a number of dedications witness (Lambert 1984: 191–2). In Egypt he was enthroned in the temples with the other gods in the manner initiated by the enthronement of Arsinoe three and a half centuries earlier. Elsewhere he was assimilated to Hermes or Dionysus. The high-minded might censure the cult, but popular devotion endowed the worship of Antinous with a real vitality: having conquered death himself he offered to others the prospect of eternal life.

The 'sacred nights' of Antinous that were celebrated at Antinoopolis very soon became notorious (Clem. Alex. *Prot.* 4. 43). Other mysteries, however, were much more sedate. The Dionysiac, which in the imperial period was re-established in Italy, had very little to do with the ecstatic *orgia* represented by Euripides, the details of which in any case are more literary than historical. The later mystery drew on the aspect of Dionysus as a god connected with the Underworld that was prominent among the Orphics. But the surviving evidence does not convey the impression of an intense Orphic spirituality. An inscription of 176 CE, for example, gives us a detailed account of a meeting of an Athenian Bacchic society called the Iobacchi (*SIG*³ 1109, discussed by Lane Fox 1986: 85–8). The inscription lays down rules of conduct and procedure at meetings rather than express the religious aims of the society. Members were to elect various officers, pay subscriptions for the wine consumed at monthly meetings, and discipline those who behaved badly or did not attend. Yet the religious side was also present. There were theological speeches, ceremonies honouring the presence of Dionysus, and the choosing by lot of a member as 'Dionysus'. But whether this indicates an identification with the god we do not know.

The Christian attitude to the mysteries was one of disgust and contempt. The most detailed denunciation of them, Clement of Alexandria's (*Prot.* 2. 11–19), holds nothing back in condemning them as savage, obscene, and deceitful. And yet in his peroration to the *Protrepticus* Clement clothes the true mysteries of the Logos in the very imagery of their pagan counterpart:

O truly sacred mysteries! O pure light! In the blaze of the torches I have a vision of heaven and of God.[16] I become holy by initiation. The Lord reveals the mysteries; he

---

[16] δᾳδουχοῦμαι τοὺς οὐρανοὺς καὶ τὸν θεὸν ἐποπτεῦσαι. These are technical terms of initiation into the mysteries. Δᾳδουχοῦμαι is to be illuminated, and alludes to δᾳδοῦχος (lit: 'torch-bearer') the holder of a hereditary office at Eleusis. Ἐποπτεύω is to be admitted to the highest grade of the mysteries.

marks the worshipper with his seal, gives light to guide his way, and commends him, when he has believed, to the Father's care, where he is guarded for ages to come. These are the revels of my mysteries! If you will, be initiated too, and you shall dance with angels around the unbegotten and imperishable and only true God, the Logos of God joining with us in our hymn of praise.   (*Prot.* 12. 93, trans. Butterworth)

Clement woos his audience, capitalizing on the longing for illumination and assurance that the mysteries sought to satisfy and trumping the pagan version with his own images of joy and self-forgetful union with God. We shall observe a similar desire to go one better than paganism in his use of the vocabulary of deification.

6. Philosophical Religion

By imperial times many of the mysteries had become 'socially acceptable and legally recognized religious clubs that required membership and functioned in accordance with laws governing spiritual meetings' (Filoramo 1990: 27–8). For an expression of a more intense quest for union with the divine we must turn to the small groups that in the second and third centuries gathered round charismatic spiritual teachers (Fowden 1982; Brown 1988: 103–5). These teachers were leaders of *didaskaleia*, or study circles, dedicated to the deepening of spiritual life through intellectual enquiry. They could be Platonists or Christians or Gnostics or Hermetists but they had a number of things in common. One was the intense devotion they inspired in their disciples. Towards the end of the second century Clement, for example, made a number of journeys to different centres of learning before arriving in about 180 at Alexandria and discovering in Pantaenus an inspired lecturer 'who engendered in the souls of his hearers a deathless element of knowledge' (*Strom.* 1. 1. 11). Some fifty years later in the same city Plotinus experienced a similar elation when he was directed to the lectures of Ammonius Saccas after having been bitterly disappointed by other philosophers. 'This is the man I was looking for,' he exclaimed and spent the next eleven years studying with him. While Plotinus was attending lectures at Alexandria, Origen, who had also studied with Ammonius Saccas, was conducting similar classes at Caesarea in Palestine. One of his students, Gregory Thaumaturgus, has left us an account in a panegyric delivered in 238 of what it was like to sit at Origen's feet. To him Origen was 'the pattern of the wise man', or rather, 'one who vehemently desires to imitate the perfect pattern' (*Pan.* 11, PG 10. 1081D–1084A). He taught his students in the early stages of his course of studies how to put into practice the precept 'Know thyself'. By looking into their souls they may see reflected there an image of the divine mind, which Gregory, as already noted, describes as a sublime method 'for attaining a kind of apotheosis' (1084C).

Six years after the delivery of this panegyric Plotinus, 'the philosopher of our times' (*V. Plot.* 1), arrived in Rome, where he began to hold classes attended by a learned circle that included a number of medical men and members of the Senate. Among those who came, 'fired by a real enthusiasm for philosophy' (*V. Plot.* 7), was Porphyry, who studied with Plotinus for six years and became his biographer and literary executor. He describes Plotinus at work, sweating gently with concentration, answering questions courteously and never losing his patience or train of thought in spite of the fact that Porphyry once questioned him relentlessly for three days—to the annoyance of other members of the group—on the soul's relationship with the body (*V. Plot.* 13). The fruits of these lectures and discussions were formally set out in the treatises arranged and edited by Porphyry. Plotinus' interests were almost entirely metaphysical: they were centred on the nature of ultimate reality and on how the soul was to come into contact with it. In this as in all things his supreme authority was Plato. But Plato himself discusses problems rather than provide solutions. The Platonism which Plotinus inherited had undergone a long period of systematization and development under Stoic, Peripatetic, and Neopythagorean influences.

One of the key figures in the revival of Platonism in the first century BCE was Eudorus of Alexandria. It was he who established 'likeness to God' as the *telos* of human life for all the Platonists who came after him. Previously the Stoic 'conformity to nature' had prevailed in the Academy. Eudorus' formula, from the *Theaetetus* (176b), marks a return to Plato and the adoption of a more spiritual perspective. In Middle Platonism it becomes a central concern but its meaning is not immediately evident. What is the nature of the God whom we are to resemble? What aspect of us can become like him? And how can we achieve this? Let us take each of these questions in turn.

As commentators have often pointed out, the English word 'god' does not adequately express the Greek *theos*. Without the article *theos* means 'a god', or used as a predicate it can simply mean 'divine', 'more than human' (Jones 1913; Skemp 1973; Grube 1980: 150–1). On the philosophical level the divine was equivalent to true 'being' (Kenney 1991: xvii–xviii, 3–32). We are accustomed to thinking of 'being' in terms of existence: something either exists or does not exist. But for the Greeks 'being' was contextual. Things did not just exist; they existed in a particular way. 'Being' was thus bound up with evaluative judgements, which enabled the Greeks to conceive of degrees of being or degrees of reality. That which was most real was divine in an absolute sense. Conversely, whatever was deficient in 'being' (i.e. was on a lower level of reality) was in certain respects deficient in divinity. In Plato's thought the highest level of reality (and therefore of divinity) was occupied by the Forms, 'the immutable divine paradigms of order and value' (Kenney

1991: 22). In the mature dialogues the One of the *Parmenides* or the Form of the Good of the *Republic* are especially representative of this transcendent aspect of the divine which is the ultimate cause of all lesser degrees of being, not through any kind of activity but by exemplifying their quality or value. Below them the dynamic or cosmogonic aspect of God is represented mythologically by the demiurge of the *Timaeus*. And below him come the gods of cultic polytheism. In the earlier dialogues Plato portrays them in a conventional way as manifestations of powers that are more than human. But in the *Euthyphro* he establishes that the gods are not free to do as they will but must conform to a higher moral reality. This hierarchical arrangement of the divine in Plato's writings was to be fundamental for later Platonic theology.

Aristotle's concept of God is fundamentally that of Plato, though by discarding the doctrine of Forms and the Platonic mythology Aristotle is able to give a more coherent and systematic account of God. In *Metaphysics* XII. 6–7 God is described as immaterial, eternal substance whose only activity is a direct intuitive knowledge not of anything external, because that would imply change, but of himself. His dynamic aspect is represented by his role as the unmoved mover and first cause, a role which he exercises solely by being the supreme object of desire, for any physical causation would involve a change in him through being acted upon by the moved. Yet he is not thereby reduced to a dry abstraction. Aristotle represents him as a perfect, living and intelligent being (1072^b26–30). Below God in this absolute sense are the heavenly bodies, the 'moved movers', which are also alive and divine. And below them on a descending scale are the gods, human beings, animals, and plants, though divine intelligence does not extend below the human level.

With the revival of Platonism in the Roman empire, the emphasis, which through Stoic influence had moved to a monistic pantheism, was again placed on a transcendent God who was the unmoved source of the stability and order of all that existed. This transcendent God clearly owed something to Aristotle's criticism. In a typical representative of early Middle Platonism such as Plutarch of Chaeronea, the Forms and the demiurge are brought together to make a supreme intellective principle, the 'really real' (τὸ ὄντως ὄν), whose intellection is the divine Forms. Thus the primary divine principle is not only a self-orientated mind but is a paradigm for the world of 'becoming' whose effect is felt on lower levels of reality as 'the object of striving for all Nature' (Dillon 1996: 199–202; Kenney 1991: 43–54).

Under the stimulus of Neopythagorean dualism a further important development took place which is associated particularly with Numenius of Apamea, who through Ammonius Saccas exercised an influence on Plotinus. This development is characterized by the demotion of the demiurge, who because of his contact with recalcitrant matter had to be separated from the first principle of the cosmos. The first principle is a *nous* engaged in self-intellection, the content of which is the Forms. It is, indeed, the totality of the Forms, 'being' in itself, which may be thought of as a mind to which the whole of reality is simultaneously present. The second principle is also *nous* but its intellection is extrinsic. It is directed 'upwards' as it contemplates the first principle, and 'downwards' as it exercises its demiurgic function. The latter causes it to be divided into the second and third gods, the further division being made because matter is now the Pythagorean dyad. By coming into contact with the dyad, the demiurge endows it with unity but is himself divided on account of the instability of matter. Numenius thus proposes a triad of gods: the One, the demiurge as an intellective principle, and the demiurge as a cosmogonic principle. There is no discontinuity in these three gods. They are simply modes of divine being as the deity unfolds progressively down the scale of reality (Dillon 1996: 366–72; Kenney 1991: 59–74).

With Plotinus the final step is taken of placing the first principle, the One, actually beyond 'being' and intellection as the inexhaustible source of life on which all finite things depend for their existence. The second hypostasis, the intellective principle (*nous*), emerges out of the first without changing or affecting it in any way, the One producing it only because perfection is necessarily productive. The third hypostasis, an inferior but still rational principle (*psyche*), emerges from the second as the second does from the first. At its lowest level *psyche* becomes Nature, the immanent power of life and growth. All the time it seeks to turn back on its source, as the *nous* does upon *its* source. There is therefore not only a procession *from* the One but a movement back towards it, for these principles are not separate, hierarchically ordered divinities, but modes of the One's disclosure at different levels of reality (Rist 1962; 1967*b*: 21–129; Armstrong 1970: 236–49; Wallis 1972: 47–61; Kenney 1991: 91–156).

That *nous* and *psyche* are replicated within each human being is one of the fundamental tenets of later Platonism. In Plato himself we can discern a development in his understanding of the soul. In the *Phaedo*, the dialogue set on the last day of Socrates' life, it is a unitary model of the soul which is discussed. Drawing on Orphic and Pythagorean ideas, Plato has Socrates present the soul as not simply a life force, which according to conventional wisdom perished upon death, but as the true self, the inner man 'chained hand and foot in the body, compelled to view reality not directly but only through its prison bars' (82e). Less metaphorically, the soul is the directing principle that controls the body and its passions (94d). Its unity is proved by its immortality, for only that which is not composite is indestructible (78c). And its immortality is proved by a series of converging arguments, notably the way learning is fundamentally recollection based on memory of a previous life (91e), the inability of the cause of life to participate in death (105de) and above all by the soul's ability to apprehend the Forms, which makes it akin to the divine (100b). The tripartite division of the soul first appears in the *Republic* and the *Phaedrus*. This elaboration marks a great advance on what had gone before because the passions and desires are now included within the soul, allowing for struggle and conflict within the human psyche. The famous image of the charioteer and the two horses appears in the *Phaedrus* (246a) as Plato explains how the intellect struggles to bring the unruly faculties of the soul into line with the more tractable ones. The whole theory is restated mythologically in the creation story of the *Timaeus*. There the demiurge himself does not create human beings because if they received life at his hands they 'would be on an equality with the gods' (41c). The creative movement initiated by the demiurge comes down to men at one remove through the gods created by him, thus ensuring that human beings are mortal. A divine element, the soul, is provided by the demiurge but the rest is the work of the gods. It is when the soul becomes incarnate in the body that it acquires its tripartite character. The noblest part is the intellect (*nous*), which is 'a god to each person' (90a), and it is the purpose of philosophy to cultivate this part, for only the *nous* is immortal, the incensive and appetitive parts perishing with the body (90cd).

Aristotle, while despising the doctrine of reincarnation, retained the kernel of Plato's psychology, that is to say, the immortality of at least some part of the soul. In Book II of the treatise *On the Soul* he sets out his position in terms of his favourite principles of matter and form, potentiality and actuality. He equates the soul with the form and the body with the matter of animals, and then goes on to define the soul as 'the first actuality of a natural body that potentially has life' (412ª27–8). Form and actuality are different ways of saying that the soul is that which makes a living being what it is. By implication the soul would then perish with the body upon death, for body and soul form a composite whole. But Aristotle, unable to break entirely with his Platonist formation, makes an important qualification with regard to the intellect. 'It seems', he says, 'that this is another kind of soul, and that this alone may be separable, as that which is eternal from that which is perishable' (413ᵇ25–7). In Book X of the *Nicomachean Ethics* he speaks more confidently of the intellect as something if not absolutely divine at least the most divine element in us which makes us immortal when we strive to live in accordance with it (1177ª16; 1177ᵇ27–35).

Aristotle's reinforcement of the fundamental duality of the soul in the *Dialogues* had repercussions for later Platonism. Alcinous, for example, in his reaction to the Stoic unitary view of spiritual reality (all human souls as 'parts'—*apospasmata*—of the World Soul), separates the rational and irrational parts of the soul so strongly that they tend to become two distinct souls. The irrational part was created by the young gods, as in the *Timaeus*, but does not participate in *nous* and is not immortal. The embodiment of this composite soul is regarded as a kind of fall, the result fundamentally of a wilful desire for pleasure. Alcinous has an ambivalent view of the world which strengthens the dualistic tendencies of Platonism. We find this ambivalence turning into downright hostility towards the world in Numenius. For him the descent of the soul is a complete disaster, for Matter exists independently of Good and is identified with Absolute Evil. Numenius represents human souls as congregating in the Milky Way before descending through the planetary spheres to earthly bodies, drawn down by the lure of pleasure. As a result of the acquisition of accretions on the way down and finally of embodiment, the rational soul now finds itself with an irrational counterpart. The human being is thus dominated not by different aspects of a single soul but by two distinct and warring souls. Plotinus, although influenced by Numenius, is much less radical in his dualism. The soul's descent is the result of metaphysical necessity, not moral evil. Evil comes from matter after the soul's embodiment, or rather, after the embodiment of that part of the soul which descends into the material world. Plotinus usually works with a twofold division of the soul, in which the rational level is identified with discursive reason and the irrational with sense perception, the emotions and so on. But sometimes the problems he is considering lead him to use a threefold division. In such contexts the highest level is the unfallen soul which has not descended into matter and remains in contemplation of *Nous*. The second level then becomes discursive reason and the third the irrational soul (Wallis 1972: 73–4). There are no sharp divisions, however. All soul forms a continuum but the different levels reflect a fact of experience. We feel drawn in different directions but we can choose on which level to live, whether the contemplative, the rational, or the irrational, and our choice assimilates us to that level and defines our identity.

Eudorus, as already mentioned, had made 'likeness to God' the *telos* of human life. The relevant passage in the *Theaetetus* has Socrates say that because of the evils in 'this region of our mortal nature . . . we should make all speed to take flight from this world to the other, and that means becoming like the divine so far as we can' (176b; trans. Cornford). The phrase hitherto understood as 'so far as we can'—κατὰ τὸ δυνατόν—is now taken to mean 'according to that part which is able'. It is only the higher, rational soul that can become like God and flee to the other world. The irrational soul must be trained to accept the guidance of reason and can then be ignored until it is discarded.

The fullest account by a Middle Platonist of the soul's return is given in Sulla's myth at the end of Plutarch's essay *On the Face in the Moon* (*Mor.* 943–4). There are in fact two deaths which human beings must undergo before they can achieve their *telos*. The first separates the body from the rest and takes place here on earth. The soul then ascends to the region between the earth and the moon, where 'the unjust and licentious souls pay penalties for their offences' (943c). The just arrive at the moon, where they enjoy the pleasant life of Elysium, having now become daemons. They are not entirely pure, nor is their state permanent, because they have not yet been freed from the influence of irrationality. After further improvement the best daemons undergo a further death separating the intellect, which alone is capable of immortality, from the lower soul. With the freeing of the intellect by this second death the last vestiges of irrationality are left behind. The intellect ascends to the sun, returning to the gods, from whom it originally came, under the impulse of a yearning in which all nature shares.

With Plotinus we encounter a different approach, couched in metaphysical rather than mythological terms and concentrating more on this earthly life. The beginning of the return to our source for Plotinus consists in turning inwards. 'If you are amazed at the soul in something else,' he says, 'be amazed at yourself' (*Enn.* v. 1. 2. 50–1). Divinity is already within us by virtue of our being ensouled: we are gods at the furthest that the divine descends from its source and archetype, the One. The first thing we must do is to purify our lower soul by stripping away everything alien to it so that it can be totally one with our higher soul, which does not need to be purified because it has not descended into the body. Purification, however, is not enough on its own: 'Our concern . . . is not to be out of sin but to be a god' (*Enn.* 1. 2. 6. 2–3). The attainment of the good necessitates reaching up to the divine world where the archetype of the good is to be found.

Since all soul is one *ousia*, or substance, there is no inherent difficulty in becoming one with *psyche* once the lower part of our souls has been fully subjected to the higher part. There is no sin to overcome; we simply have to decide to be guided by what is immediately prior to us. The world soul is like the higher individual soul in that it is not affected by the material world, while it differs from it in its direct control of the entire cosmos. When the individual soul becomes one with it, it shares in the direction of the universe (*Enn.* IV. 8. 2. 19–30).

Purification prevents us from being dragged down to sub-human, and consequently sub-divine, levels. But it is contemplation that enables us to rise to the intelligible world. This is because thinking and the object of thought ultimately become the same: the human soul is assimilated to the things it contemplates as it presses on towards the *nous*.[17] When the soul has become one with the *nous*, it can be said unequivocally to have become a god, for henceforth it lives on the level of the eternal (*Enn.* II. 9. 9. 50–1; VI. 4. 14. 16–22). But there still remains a further step, union with the One. This is different in kind from union with the *nous*, which requires in the soul a process of abstraction and purification in order to revert to its prior. This further step is described by Plotinus as requiring a leap towards the One (*Enn.* v. 5. 4. 8; cf.

---

[17] The key text is *Enn.* III. 8. 8. 1–9, in which Plotinus, alluding to Parmenides fr. B3DK, declares that at the end of the soul's ascent the objects of knowledge become one with the knower, not by mere appropriation or the attaining of moral likeness (οἰκειώσει), as in the case of the outstandingly virtuous, but substantially (οὐσίᾳ), because 'thinking and being are the same'. Cf. Siorvanes' summary of Proclus' theory of knowledge quoted below (p. 257).

Rist 1967*b*: 220). It is the ultimate stage of the soul's journey, the final annihilation of all duality. The soul becomes one with the object of its search, and yet is not absorbed into it. This causes fear, for the soul must open itself to the infinite, and pain, for the soul loses its familiar points of orientation. The union is described as vision, but 'vision' is not an adequate term because it still implies duality—a seer and the seen (*Enn.* III. 9. 10. 11–13; VI. 9. 11. 4–7; cf. VI. 9. 11. 22–5). It is also described as touch, as blending, as self-surrender, as ecstasy, as erotic mingling (*Enn.* VI. 9. 9. 33–44 and 44–6). A striking analogy is that of the superimposed centres of two circles. The centres are then indistinguishable from each other and yet they are still seen to be two points when they move apart (*Enn.* VI. 9. 8. 11–16). In spite of the union with the One being a dizzy leap into the infinite – 'the mind reels before something thus alien to all we know' (*Enn.* VI. 9. 7. 1–3)—it is not a leap into anything outside ourselves. Plotinus stresses that the journey is an inward one: 'we must ascend to the principle within ourselves' (*Enn.* VI. 3. 3. 20–1); 'when the soul begins again to mount, it comes not to something alien, but to its very self' (*Enn.* VI. 9. 11. 38–40). It is at that point, says Plotinus, that a man has become a god—but he at once corrects himself: 'or rather, is one' (*Enn.* VI. 9. 9. 58). We are already gods in our true, higher selves. We do not need to *become* gods but simply to realize what we are, which we attain in its fullness through union with the One: 'for a god is what is linked to that centre' (*Enn.* VI. 9. 8. 8–9; cf. Armstrong 1976).

All this was not merely a matter of philosophical theory to Plotinus. The quest for union with the divine dominated his life. Porphyry testifies that on several occasions Plotinus became rapt in ecstasy in his presence:

To Plotinus 'the goal ever near was shown': for his end and goal was to be united to, to approach the God who is over all things. Four times while I was with him he attained that goal, in an unspeakable actuality and not in potency only. (*V. Plot.* 23. 14–18; trans. Armstrong)

What this 'unspeakable actuality' felt like is described by Plotinus himself in the following words:

Often I have woken up out of the body to my self and have entered into myself, going out from all other things; I have seen a beauty wonderfully great and felt assurance that then most of all I belonged to the better part; I have actually lived the best life and come to identity with the divine; and set firm in it I have come to that supreme actuality, setting myself above all else in the realm of Intellect. Then after that rest in the divine, when I have come down from Intellect to discursive reasoning, I am puzzled how I ever came down, and how my soul has come to be in the body when it is what it has shown itself to be by itself, even when it is in the body. (*Enn.* IV. 8. 1. 1–11; trans. Armstrong)

The experience of going out of the body (which for Plotinus means ascending to the highest part of one's being), of beholding an incomprehensible beauty, of feeling deflated on returning to the body will be repeated by other Neoplatonists and not only pagans.[18] That these transitory ecstasies were only a foretaste of a union with God after death was confirmed for Porphyry by the oracle uttered at Delphi in response to a question put by another member of Plotinus' inner circle, Amelius. The soul of Plotinus, Amelius was told, having left the tomb of the body and become a daemon, had joined the company of Minos and Rhadamanthus, Plato and Pythagoras and 'all who have set the dance of immortal love and won kinship with spirits most blessed' (*V. Plot.* 22. 45–60; 23. 15–17).

As long as the Platonists maintained the doctrine of the undescended soul, deification in a technical sense was not possible. A major change comes with Iamblichus, for Iamblichus could not believe in the existence of an undescended element in the human person. In his view the Plotinian notion that the higher soul always remained in the intelligible world whether we were aware of it or not contradicted not only experience but the fundamental principle (going back to Aristotle) that the nature of a substance could be inferred from its acts. He could appeal to Platonic authority for his refusal to accept the doctrine of the undescended soul, for the charioteer in the Phaedrus myth does not continue on an uninterrupted course with the gods but sometimes rises and sometimes sinks (*Phaedr.* 248a). Moreover, the Plotinian doctrine cannot account for the existence of sin or unhappiness. If the higher soul is unaffected by the passions, how does the free will, which belongs to the ruling faculty, come to be seduced by the images of the sensible world? And if the highest part of the soul is constantly engaged in contemplation, with the bliss of fulfilment which that activity would bring, then the whole of our being ought to enjoy uninterrupted happiness, which is not the case (Proclus, *In Tim.* 3. 334–5; cf. Steel 1978: 40–4).

The result of Iamblichus' criticism of the higher soul was for the first time to turn the hypostases into a hierarchical series of different essences. These essences were connected with each other by the Law of Mean Terms, which resolved all beings into unparticipated terms, participated terms, and participants.[19] This law, formulated by Iamblichus himself, proved to be very influential. It enabled lower principles to be affected by higher ones and to move up the scale 'by participation' without compromising the transcendence of the latter.

---

[18] The only comparable personal testimony in a Christian writer is that of Augustine, *Confessions* 7. 17 (23) and 9. 10 (24) (Chadwick 1991: 127, 171). But Gregory of Nyssa attributes similar experiences to David (*De Virg.*, PG 46. 361B) and to Abraham (*C. Eun.* 12, PG 45. 940A–941B) (Musurillo 1961: 105, 119). Cf. also *The Book of the Holy Hierotheos*, discussed in Appendix 1.

[19] Our informant is Proclus (*In Tim.* 2. 105, 240, 313), who develops this principle in a systematic way (cf. *El. Theol.* 23 and 24). Its purpose is to solve the problem of the relationship between the transcendent and the immanent, the Form and the particular. For discussions of the concept of participation in the later Neoplatonists see Lloyd 1982; Niarchos 1985; Siorvanes 1996: 71–86; Siorvanes 1998.

Some foreshadowing of this Iamblichean development is already apparent in Plotinus' pupil, Porphyry, who is accordingly the first Platonist to use the technical language of deification (*c.*300). In a letter to his wife Marcella he presents a simplified version of his view of the purpose of philosophy:

He who practises wisdom practises knowledge of God, not by constantly offering prayers and sacrifices but by showing piety towards God through his deeds. For no one could become pleasing to God either through the opinions of men or through the empty words of rhetoricians. On the contrary, he makes himself pleasing to God and deifies himself (ἑαυτὸν ... ἐκθεοῖ) by assimilating his own condition to that which is blessed through incorruptibility.   (*Ad Marcellam* 17)

It has rightly been pointed out that 'in his ethical consideration Porphyry starts from the *distance* that separates the soul from the higher levels of being' (Steel 1978: 32). In other words, in his ethical writings he is nearer to the Iamblichean position than to the Plotinian, as his use of ἐκθεόω in this instance suggests. Normally in Porphyry's writings gods, daemons, and the souls of human beings are in essence the same, differing only in how much of the sensible world they control (the human soul controlling only the human body) and in the extent to which they participate in the passions. Here through practical philosophy a person is said to become like God in one of his most important attributes, that of incorruptibility, and this attainment of likeness is said to deify him.

With Iamblichus, Porphyry's pupil, the conditions that make deification in the proper sense possible become firmly established. As long as the human soul is considered to be part of the same essence as that of the gods in whole or in part, the realization of the human *telos* consists in waking up to what we really are: transcendent beings trapped in the world of sense. But once the notion of the undescended soul has been rejected and the soul of a human being is conceived of as essentially different from that of a god, some ontological transformation is needed before the soul can ascend to the divine life. This transformation is the result of theurgy, a concept which entered into Platonism from the *Chaldean Oracles*. 'Doing philosophy' could no longer in itself raise the soul to the level of the divine because the divine essence transcends the essence of the human soul to such a degree. It is therefore necessary for the divine to descend by a 'providential love' before the lower reality can be perfected through participation in the characteristics of the higher. Iamblichus speaks of theurgy as taking place through wordless symbols beyond the act of thinking. But his insistence on theurgy is accompanied by an extension of the term to cover intellectual activity as well as ritual. While we are still unpurified and weighed down by the body we still need material ritual; but this does not mean that all embodied souls need it. The few more perfect souls practise an intellectual and incorporeal kind of theurgy. It was the transformation wrought by theurgy, by 'the power of the wordless symbols intelligible to the gods alone', that enabled Pythagoras, for example, 'to be deified in a way surpassing human understanding' (*V. Pyth.* 23. 103).

These are almost the only instances of the use of the terminology of deification in philosophical writings before the fifth century (cf. also *De Myst.* 10. 5). It is only with Proclus that we meet with it frequently. Proclus' chief concern is to clarify the relationship between self-existent reality and the material world. Self-existent reality is 'that which is beyond all things and to which all things aspire' (*El. Theol.* 113). It is 'the One', 'the Good', or simply 'God'. The character of divinity is unity. Only the One possesses unity without any privations or contradictions. But unity can be shared. The participable 'ones' are the henads. Every entity in the world possesses unity in the manner appropriate to it through its relationship with its head-principle, or henad. Thus:

Every divine body is such through the mediation of a deified soul, every divine soul through a divine intellect, and every divine intellect by participation in a divine henad; the henad is natively (αὐτόθεν) a god, the intellect most divine, the soul divine, and the body deisimilar.   (*El. Theol.* 129; trans. Dodds, modified)

Deification in this late development is central to an understanding of how God is simultaneously detached from and present in the world. Proclus does not separate the One's ineffable aspect from its causal aspect. As Siorvanes has put it, God is both apophatic and the first positive term of existence. The principle of deification explains how this can be so (Siorvanes 1998, esp. 16–18).

7. The Egyptian Hermetists

In the new spiritual climate of the second and third centuries the intimate contact with the One God that could be attained by members of a cultural elite after years of rigorous intellectual training was not going to be confined to the tiny minority that had the necessary wealth and education to qualify for membership. There was a demand for such teaching amongst the many merchants, artisans, and government officials who thronged the major cities of the empire and to cater for their needs there was a new class of men— 'orators, lecturers, teachers who constitute a sort of turbulent, lively intellectual proletariat'.[20] Among these 'new men' were the teachers of Gnosis. Thanks to the polemics of their ecclesiastical adversaries brief details have come down to us of the leading Christian Gnostic teachers. Nothing is

---

[20] Filoramo 1990: 36. This new class, of course, only constituted a proletariat from the supreme vantage point of the intellectual elite. For the social context of Gnosticism see Filoramo 1990: 34–7, 173–8, and for that of Hermetism, Fowden 1993: 186–95.

known, however, of their pagan counterparts other than what we can deduce from their writings. These have survived in two forms, the philosophical, which are concerned with theology and the fate of the soul, and the technical, which are magical texts. The philosophical collection known as the Hermetic Corpus was probably made in late antiquity, although our earliest attestation is from the eleventh century and in its present form is a selection probably reflecting the tastes of its Byzantine compiler. The technical texts, which can seem bizarre to the modern eye, are not likely to have been considered different in kind by the Egyptian Hermetists themselves. A fascinating insight into how Hermetic works circulated in the middle of the fourth century is provided by Codex VI of the Gnostic library discovered at Nag Hammadi, which contains extracts from three Hermetic tractates. After the Prayer of Thanksgiving towards the end of the codex the scribe has added a note saying that although a large number of discourses had come to him, he was only copying the one he had just set down and was sending it on to his correspondents because he did not want to burden them, as they probably already had copies of the same texts (*NHL* VI. 7a).

The character of the Hermetic groups responsible for the tractates has been disputed. Against Reitzenstein and Cumont, Festugière insisted on the fundamentally Hellenic character of the Corpus (Festugière 1943–54: ii, xiii). More recently, however, scholarly opinion has tended to see the Corpus as primarily of Egyptian inspiration.[21] The Egyptian atmosphere is certainly strong. The teacher at the centre of the tractates is not a philosopher engaged in intellectual debate with his disciples in the Graeco-Roman manner. He is more like a priest imparting ancient wisdom within the precincts of a great temple. Indeed, the setting for the *Perfect Discourse* is such a temple filled with a numinous divine presence (*Ascl.* 1). The appropriate attitude of the hearer is one of hushed reverence: the teacher—often Hermes Trismegistus himself—expounds; the disciples listen in awe. Prayers or hymns sometimes conclude the tractates (*CH* I. 31; XIII. 18; *Ascl.* 41) because the highest expression of wisdom is worship: true philosophy is 'to adore the Godhead with simple mind and soul' (*Ascl.* 13). The physical presence of Egypt is strong in other ways too. Egypt is seen as an image of heaven, as 'the temple of the whole world' (*Ascl.* 24). Pride is expressed in the Egyptian language in which 'the very quality of the speech and sound of Egyptian words have in themselves the energy of the objects they speak of' (*CH* XVI. 2). Yet Egypt is in decline. One of the most moving passages in the Corpus is a lament for departed glory as the gods (perhaps under pressure from

---

[21] Cf. Dillon 1996: 213: 'the whole thought-world of the Hermetic Corpus is alien to that of Plato'. Fowden 1993: 73: Hermetism according to Mahé is 'mythical Egyptian thought translated into Greek'. Frankfurter 1998: 240: The Hermetic Corpus was composed by 'some shadowy conventicles of Greek-proficient [Egyptian] priests'.

Christian laws against pagan worship) withdraw from Egypt, leaving her desolate, with every sacred voice silenced (*Ascl.* 24, 25; *NHL* VI. 8. 70–3).

It is not only the local colour, however, that is of Egyptian provenance. There is evidence that such central themes as the spiritual father/son relationship, the filiation of man to the divine, and the deification of the initiand's soul are native Egyptian ideas (Daumas 1982: 13–16; Théodoridès 1982: 30–5; Griffiths 1986*b*: 56–9). But the expression of these is Greek. And the view of God as a triadic *nous*, demiurge, and world soul, to whom the individual soul is assimilated in successive stages, owes much to the standard themes of Platonism.

The Hermetic Corpus presents a God who is at once both transcendent and immanent. Some tractates stress one aspect, some the other. On the one hand God is beyond words and beyond the imagination (*CH* I. 32; V. 1). He is the first of all entities, eternal, unbegotten, creator of all that is (*CH* VIII. 2). He is the source of eternity and being (*CH* XI. 4; III. 1). He is master and father (*CH* IX. 7; XVIII. 12; *Ascl.* 22), light and life (*CH* I. 21), energy and power (*CH* XII. 20). He cannot be detected in anything in the cosmos (*CH* VI. 4). On the other hand, in the pantheistic fifth tractate he is reflected in the entire cosmos (*CH* V. 2). He is both 'invisible and wholly visible' (*CH* V. 10). He is the source of all things and yet there is nothing in the cosmos that he is not. All things that exist are in him; nothing is outside him and he is outside nothing (*CH* V. 9). God as *nous* gives birth to a second god, the demiurge in the *Poemandres* (*CH* I. 9) or the sun in the *Perfect Discourse* (*Ascl.* 29). It is worth noting that there is very little dualism in the Corpus. The demiurge, about whom there is nothing evil or shameful (*CH* XIV. 7), made the whole cosmos. In other versions the cosmos itself is the second god. Humankind then comes into being as the third god (*CH* VIII. 3; X. 14; *Ascl.* 10).

At the heart of Hermetism is a sense of wonder at the astonishing range of the human mind. In the twinkling of an eye the mind can travel to India or shoot up to the heavenly bodies (*CH* XI. 19). It is not bound by place or time. It can imagine itself in any place or before its own birth or even after its own death (*CH* XI. 20). It is truly capable of anything. This wonder at the godlike qualities of the mind finds mythical expression in the Hermetic anthropogony (which draws on Jewish *midrashim* on the book of Genesis) (*CH* I. 12–15). Anthropos was created in the image of the father as a 'brother' of the demiurge, the second god. He broke through the vault of heaven and looked down through the cosmic framework, 'thus displaying to lower nature the fair form of god'. Anthropos saw the beauty of his own form reflected in the water and reached down to take Nature into an erotic embrace. He wished to inhabit nature and 'wish and action came at the same moment'. Because of these origins the progeny of Anthropos possess a mortal body but an immortal inner self (*CH* I. 15). One part of ourselves is οὐσιώδης, our essential being, the other ὑλικός, our material outer form

(*Ascl.* 7). Some tractates, perhaps under Pythagorean influence, take a negative view of the body: it is 'the garment of ignorance, the foundation of vice, the bonds of corruption, the dark cage, the living death, the portable tomb' (*CH* VII. 2; cf. IV. 6). Others, and not only the more pantheistic, avoid such language. Looking within oneself and even at the marvellous way in which the body is constructed draws one to God.[22] There is a kinship, a community of being, with God: earthly man is a mortal god and the celestial God an immortal man (*CH* X. 25; XII. 1).[23]

In the *Perfect Discourse* man is said to have been created 'good and capable of immortality through his two natures, divine and mortal' (*Ascl.* 22). In fact the possession of mortality as well as divinity makes men better than the gods, who only possess a single nature. This superiority is developed in a striking way. The reciprocity that exists between man and the supreme God means that just as God has made the heavenly gods (the stars and planets), so man has made the temple gods. Man is not only deified but he also deifies. 'Not only is he god but he also creates gods,' as the Coptic version puts it (*NHL* VI. 8. 68; cf. *Ascl.* 23). Some sections further on Trismegistus makes it clear what he means. In Egypt there are three kinds of earthly gods: the images that are made of matter but animated by the theurgic drawing-down of a daemonic soul; the human benefactors like Asclepius' ancestor, the discoverer of medicine, who have been deified after death; and the holy animals, which have been deified while still alive (*Ascl.* 37, 38). Here we have a combination of Hellenistic and ancient Egyptian belief (cf. Mahé 1982: 98–102, 224, 315, 385). This human fashioning of the earthly gods far from diminishing their stature only points to the divine nature of human beings themselves. The whole thrust of this teaching is summed up in the final Prayer of Thanksgiving: 'While we were in the body you made us divine through your knowledge' (*NHL* VI. 7. 18–19; *Ascl.* 41).

The return to God, the 'way of immortality' (*NHL* VI. 6. 63), has been described as a journey with three stages: *gnôsis*, the awakening; *logos*, the process of attaining maturity; and *nous*, the vision of the divine intellect (Mahé 1991: 351). Gnosis is a spiritual awakening that is stimulated by amazement at the powers of the human mind. Consciousness is divinity itself (*Ascl.* 18). To become fully conscious is to become aware of the divine within oneself, for divine consciousness is found only in God and human beings (*Ascl.* 7, 32). The opposite to gnosis is ignorance, which is likened to drunkenness or sleep (*CH* VIII. 1). Ignorance is the worst evil (*CH* VIII. 2; x. 8). For the ignorant soul is blind and a slave to the body. The soul which attains gnosis, however, can begin the ascent of Olympus (*CH* x. 15); or, less metaphorically, 'He who has understood himself advances towards God' (*CH* I. 21).

---

[22] *CH* v. 6; cf. Job 34: 13; 38: 4–38, and the Egyptian Hymn to Khnum cited in Mahé 1982: 293–5, 279.
[23] On *CH*'s anthropology see most recently Mazzanti 1998.

The second stage is that of the acquisition of knowledge and the attaining of maturity through revelatory discourse. It involves, in Mahé's words, the spiritualization of popular piety. Death is merely an illusion (*CH* VIII. 1). Upon death there is a general dissolution of the physical and psychic elements which releases the essential man. The material body is given over to corruption, the form becomes invisible, the habitual character (*êthos*) is given over to one's personal daemon, the bodily senses return to their sources, becoming again parts of the astral energies, and the incensive and appetitive faculties return to irrational nature. The essential man then rises through the planetary spheres, stripping away certain powers at each level—at the first the power of increasing or diminishing, at the second the power of doing evil, at the third the delusion of desire, at the fourth ambition, at the fifth presumption, at the sixth the appetites that come from wealth, and at the seventh falsehood—until he enters into the eighth sphere 'possessing his own power' and is able to sing hymns to the Father in the company of the other Powers that inhabit that sphere, because at last he has become like them. Those who have achieved this state 'ascend towards the Father in order, and surrender themselves to the Powers, and having become Powers themselves, come to be in God. This is the blessed end of those who possess gnosis, to be deified (θεωθῆναι)' (*CH* I. 26; cf. *NHL* VI. 6. 59–60; Festugière 1943–54: iii. 124–52).

The final stage is the vision of *nous* that draws one up like a magnet (*CH* IV. 11). The rapture of seeing the beauty of God culminates in deification as the pure *nous*, separated progressively from the bodily senses, the psychic faculties, and the vices, is able to share a community of being with the Father and all his celestial powers. Such deification is not the exclusive prerogative of the elect but is open in principle to all. It is only necessary for human beings to be awakened for the return to become possible.

The discussion of deification in *CH* x introduces the term μεταβολαί, the transformations which the soul undergoes after death. Asclepius says to his disciple Tat that it is impossible 'for a soul that has contemplated the beauty of the Good to be deified (ἀποθεωθῆναι) while in a human body' (*CH* x. 6). He goes on to explain that all souls in the world are from one universal soul, and the transformations they have undergone distribute them among various kinds of creatures. Then in a passage reminiscent of Plutarch he says: 'Human souls begin to enter into immortality by transforming themselves into daemons and then in the same way into the choir of the gods' (*CH* x. 7; cf. *Mor.* 943–4). Gnosis and moral effort together produce a good soul, which after death undergoes a transformation and 'becomes entirely *nous*' (*CH* x. 6). The bad soul remains as it is and punishes itself.

When Poemandres is asked whether all human beings do not possess *nous*, he evades the question (*CH* x. 6). In the fourth tractate, however, it is stated categorically that *nous* is not distributed to all. God keeps it, as it were, in a great mixing-bowl and gives it as a reward to those who respond to the proclamation of gnosis (*CH* IV. 3–4). The response to gnosis is a fundamental orientation towards the invisible rather than the visible, the divine rather than the mortal. The author recognizes the difficulty of this. It is hard to abandon the familiar and to set aside the delights of the visible world. Yet this is necessary, for although the world is the work of God, and whoever contemplates it can recognize its maker, it is inimical to spiritual progress: 'If you do not first hate your body, my son, you will not be able to love yourself; but when you have come to love yourself, you will have *nous*, and having come to possess *nous* you will participate in knowledge' (*CH* IV. 6). It is this correct choice which deifies human beings, though not before they have departed from the body and passed through choirs of daemons and the orbits of the planets as they press on towards the One (*CH* IV. 7). The choice of gnosis brings about baptism in *nous* and is the beginning of the pursuit of the good. The opposite choice enmeshes human beings in bodily pleasures and leads to destruction.

In *CH* XIII the essential core of humanity similarly needs to be made divine through being endowed with *nous*. In this context a further term is introduced, that of παλιγγενεσία, or regeneration. Hermes teaches Tat that regeneration means a new birth ἐν νῷ or ἐν θεῷ—equivalent expressions because the *nous* belongs to the divine world—which results in a change from a life that is mortal to one that is immortal and therefore divine. Although the agent of regeneration is another human being who has become a god, regeneration is not taught but is the result of God's mercy (*CH* XIII. 3, 10). It comes about when the corporeal senses are set aside and the twelve punishments or vices (ignorance, sorrow, unchastity, desire, injustice, greed, deceit, envy, fraud, anger, rashness, and malice) are driven out by the ten divine powers or virtues (knowledge of God, knowledge of joy, chastity, endurance, justice, sharing, truth, and finally the Good, Life, and Light) (*CH* XIII. 7–9). 'You know, my child,' concludes Hermes, 'the manner of regeneration. When the Decad is present, my child, a spiritual generation has been contrived and it drives out the Dodecad, and we have been deified by this generation' (*CH* XIII. 10; cf. Grese 1979: 133–45). It is striking that in this tractate deification is not postponed until the end of the journey through the spheres after death. It comes about when a human being no longer lives a corporeal existence but through the coming together of the ten divine powers acquires *nous* and is thus able to transcend the limitations of the physical world.

These differing anthropologies seem to imply at least two distinct senses of the term 'deification', the one signifying the reduction of human beings to their divine core, the immortal *nous*, the other their endowment with a divine *nous* which they did not previously possess. These distinct senses, however, do not imply rival doctrines of the soul's ascent. The Hermetists were not particularly anxious about consistency. What we have here is a difference of emphasis rather than a difference of doctrine (cf. Fowden 1993: 108). Each tractate is able to present a different emphasis without compromising the whole. Thus a fall and a corresponding ascent are central to the teaching of the *Poemandres*. Deification in this tractate is described as a stripping away to the bare *nous*, which can only reach its fulfilment in the divine pleroma. *CH* x implies the same doctrine, glossing it by explaining the ascent as a series of transformations first into a daemon and then into a god. *CH* iv recognizes a pre-existent man who is sent down by God not as a punishment for sin but to adorn the Earth. He is endowed with *logos* but not with *nous*, which is only given to him when he commits himself to gnosis. It is this gift of *nous* that deifies human beings by enabling them to wing their way up to the One. In *CH* xiii there is neither a primordial fall nor an ascent. There is no innate divinity in humankind waiting to be recovered. Rather, human beings are deified by regeneration, which really changes them, transforming them into *nous* so that they can know God. This is not just an eschatological possibility but a present reality. The divine life can begin now and the body and earthly concerns be left behind.

The technical Hermetica do not contradict this teaching; they simply dispense with the need for a teacher. Through the use of the right magical formulae a spiritual initiation could be effected on one's own which would lead to ascent, rebirth, and the vision of the divine. In one early fourth-century papyrus the entire rite, which leads through lesser experiences to the vision of the supreme God, Aion, is called an ἀπαθανατισμός—an 'immortalization' or 'deification' (*P. Graec. Mag.* iv. 741, 747; Fowden 1993: 82–4). But in this case the effects are not permanent: the ἀπαθανατισμός 'can be performed three times a year'. For its purpose is not to effect an escape from the body but to obtain an oracle directly from the god, which can only be done if the human mind is raised to the level of the divine.

8. Interaction with Christianity

The Graeco-Roman environment of the first three centuries CE was not simply the background against which the early Church developed, either keeping itself free from contamination or succumbing to 'Hellenization'. Christians were part of the Graeco-Roman world and interacted with it. They were familiar with the idea of deification from the beginning, not only from the philosophical schools but also from the ruler-cult, the mysteries, and the study circles of popular teachers. Even if they repudiated it, they lived on intimate terms with it.

The figure of the philosopher commanded immense respect. But whether he was viewed as a θεῖος ἀνήρ, or 'divine man', before the third century CE is doubtful.[24] Philostratus' publication of the life of the Pythagorean thaumaturge, Apollonius of Tyana, in the 220s set an example in this respect, followed by biographies of Pythagoras himself by Porphyry and Iamblichus at the beginning of the fourth century. The Christian portrayal of Origen as a θεῖος ἄνθρωπος may have been partly in response to such literary activity.[25]

After Iamblichus the philosopher acquires a more deeply religious character, allowing modern scholars to refer to him as 'the pagan holy man'. The most enthusiastic admirer of the pagan θεῖοι ἄνδρες (although he does not use the expression) was Eunapius, whose *Lives of the Sophists* appeared in the last decade of the fourth century. But by then pagan holy men had become marginalized. In an aggressively Christian empire they survived only by leading lives of philosophical contemplation and theurgical worship in quiet seclusion. Yet when the true Christian philosopher is described, it is in the exact terms of his pagan counterpart. Writing in the 430s, Cyril of Alexandria claims:

In reality a sage is, and is described by us as being, a man who has been enriched by clear and unambiguous doctrine relating to the God of all things, and has made as careful an enquiry as possible into the matters that concern him, I mean as far as is permissible to human beings, and has acquired along with this a perfect knowledge of all necessary things, so as to be in a position to enable those who follow his teaching with righteousness to conceive a desire for adorning themselves with the splendours of virtue.   (*C. Jul.* 5, PG 76. 773AB)

On a more popular level, the Hermetic texts also had their Christian readers. We know from the contents of the sixth codex of the Nag Hammadi library that the spiritual teaching of Hermetism appealed to fourth-century Christian Gnostics. Amongst catholic Christians Hermes figures chiefly as a pagan prophet foretelling the triumph of Christianity (Fowden 1993: 179–80). In Egypt the first catholic Christian to quote from the Hermetica is Didymus the Blind (*c.*313–98). The next is Cyril of Alexandria, who quotes Hermes at some length in his attack on Julian's *Contra Galilaeos* to show that the very teacher relied upon by Julian was really a prophet of Christ (*C. Jul.* 1, PG. 76. 552D–553B). The Hermetica passed very early through Latin translation into Roman Africa (Fowden 1993: 198). Tertullian

---

[24] The idea of the θεῖος ἀνήρ was taken up in Germany between the wars by members of the History of Religions School, notably Ludwig Bieler (1935), who developed it as a way of linking the New Testament to the wider Roman world. Bieler conceived of the θεῖος ἀνήρ as an *allgemeine Typus*, an inclusive category, which could explain how Jesus fitted into his ancient milieu as a sage and wonderworker. Although the expression θεῖος ἀνήρ is first attested in Pindar and Plato (LSJ s.v. θεῖος (A)3), the evidence for its early use is rather meagre. Opponents of the History of Religions School such as Carl Holladay (1977) have disputed whether a Hellenistic concept of the 'divine man' ever really existed at all. In fact the θεῖος ἀνήρ as a recognizable figure only comes into prominence in the later Roman empire. For the debate on Bieler's *Typus* see Corrington 1986.

[25] For the late antique flowering of pagan holy men, and the part played by their biographies in the rivalry between paganism and Christianity, see Fowden 1982 and Cox 1983.

mentions 'the Egyptian Mercury' as a teacher of belief in the transmigration of souls (*An.* 33. 2). Lactantius, who was of African origin, and Augustine both appeal to Hermes as a pagan prophet of Christianity. This became his established role in the Christian world, in spite of Marcellus of Ancyra's attacking him (along with Plato and Aristotle) as the inspirer of all heresies (Fowden 1993: 209). The spiritual and theurgical side of Hermetism did not make its full impact on Christianity until much later. In the third century it was taken up enthusiastically by Iamblichus, who passed it on to the later Neoplatonists. It was thus through Proclus and Ps.-Dionysius that Hermetism influenced the Christian mystical tradition. Nevertheless it is curious that the use of the verb θεοποιέω in a spiritual sense appears for the first time in the second century, very possibly simultaneously, both in the Hermetic Corpus and in Clement of Alexandria. There is no evidence that Clement had direct knowledge of the Hermetic tractates, though of course he had certainly studied Gnostic texts at first hand for polemical purposes. Yet the declaration in the *Poemandres* that the blessed end of those who possess gnosis is to be deified (*CH* 1. 26) resonates with Clement's assertion that the teaching of Christ, which is true gnosis, deifies the believer (*Paed.* 1. 98. 3).

What is beyond doubt is Clement's and his successors' debt to Platonism. The definition of likeness to God as the goal of the spiritual life, the concept of participation, the metaphor of the soul's ascent, and the notion of reaching out to God in ecstasy are all of Platonic origin. But in the development of the idea of deification and its distinctive vocabulary, it was Christianity that led the way. By the time Porphyry first wrote of the philosopher deifying himself, Christians had already been speaking of deification for more than a century.

3

The Jewish Paradigm

From Ezekiel to the *yored merkavah*

1. Ancient Israel

Rabban Johanan ben Zakkai's flight to Jamnia (Yabveh) just before the Romans captured Jerusalem in 70 CE marks the beginning of a new era in Judaism. Not only was the Second Temple destroyed, bringing to an end the sacrificial system, but Messianic eschatology suffered a blow to its credibility that was to be compounded sixty-five years later by the failure of the Bar Kokhba revolt. The expected Kingdom, in which the faithful would find spiritual fulfilment in the personal reign of God, now receded into the distant future. In its place there developed, alongside the study of the Torah (for the few, at least, who were fortunate enough to find a suitable teacher) a spirituality of assimilation to the life of the angels, an angelification or deification (for the angels were the 'gods') that could be anticipated even in this life, at least in the imagination, by an ecstatic ascent to the vision of the throne-chariot of God.

Little of this is discernible in the canonical books of the Bible. In the earliest period of Hebrew religion we are aware much more of the profound gulf which separates the Creator from the created world. Nor does there seem to be any escape from the common fate which all the dead were believed to experience as shades in Sheol. The first elements of a belief that will come to resemble that of deification may be observed in the post-exilic Book of Ezekiel, in the visions of the dry bones (37: 1–14) and the throne-chariot of God (1: 1–28; 10: 1–22; 43: 1–5). These elements become more plentiful in the later Wisdom and Apocalyptic literature, most notably in such features as the multiplication of grades of angels and demons connecting God with his creation, the development of ideas of immortality and resurrection, and the translation of the heroes of the faith to heaven.

Angels probably derive from the ancient Canaanite gods. Ancient Hebrew religion was monolatrous rather than monotheistic. It was not until Jeremiah and Deutero-Isaiah that the pagan gods were declared to be 'nothings', mere empty idols (Jer. 2: 11; 10: 7–8; 16: 20, etc.; Isa. 41: 29; 43: 10; 44: 8, etc.). This is because Jewish monotheism developed not from philosophical speculation but as a result of the awful encounter with a majestic, personal God, a God who could be worshipped only in fear and trembling. This exalted experience of Yahweh eventually annihilated the other gods. But before they became 'nothings' they were fitted into Yahwism by being dethroned and set in a heavenly court ruled over by Yahweh, where they simply carried out the decrees of his will (Albright 1968: 166–8).

Yahweh himself is commonly called *elohim* in the Old Testament. This is an 'abstract plural' or a 'plural of intensity' signifying the totality of divine power as a personal unity (Eichrodt 1967: i. 185–7; cf. Johnson 1942: 19–23). Alongside this the word is also used as a true plural for the lower beings in the heavenly court, the former gods that were later to be called angels (Pss. 29: 1; 89: 7; Gen. 6: 2, 4; Job 1: 6; 2: 1; 38: 7). The difference between these *elohim* and Yahweh is revealed with especial clarity in Psalm 82, where Yahweh, enthroned in the midst of the heavenly council, pronounces judgement on those gods which have not upheld divine justice: 'But now I say: though you are gods, all of you sons of the Most High, yet you shall die as men must die, shall perish like the (earthly) princes' (vv. 6–7) (Mowinckel's translation 1967: i. 150). Following a tradition that goes back to the Targum, the older generation of exegetes often took these 'gods' to represent corrupt human judges. But in their original context they were literally the pagan gods who were set over the other nations by Yahweh (cf. Deut. 32: 8) on the model of the Ugaritic divine council (Mullen 1980: 175–209). For their failure to prevent oppression and injustice they were condemned to suffer the fate of mortal men. Even the 'gods' can die if they are not obedient to Yahweh and do not exercise their rule in conformity with his moral demands (Weiser 1962: 51, 556–7; Mowinckel 1967: i. 150-1).

In the pre-exilic writings of the Hebrew Bible no one, whether king or commoner, had any expectation of a life beyond the grave. The human person was seen not in analytical terms as a combination of body and soul, or of body, spirit, and soul, but as a 'unit of vital power' which can only express itself through the body and ebbs away at death (Johnson 1964: 87–8). The final state of the *nefesh*, the 'soul', was as a silent shade in the underworld, where it had no communication with God or with the living, no real consciousness. At the end of this early period, however, there are two apparent exceptions. How are the bodily translations to heaven of Enoch (Gen. 5: 24) and Elijah (2 Kgs. 2: 11) to be understood? It has long been recognized that the Priestly redactor of Genesis 5 was acquainted with Babylonian mythological traditions. Commentators have often drawn attention to the parallel between Enoch, the seventh of the antediluvian patriarchs, and Emmeduranki, the seventh of the primeval Babylonian kings, who was similarly carried off to the gods. (cf. VanderKam 1984: 33–51). Claus Westermann, however, in his monumental study of Genesis has argued that the parallel between the Babylonian list and Genesis 5 is superficial (1984: 351–4, 388–9). The salient point for the Hebrew author is that Enoch had a particularly close relationship with God. His departure is described in the words: 'and he was not', then are added: 'for God took him', the verb *laqah* being a technical term for translation. This second expression, according to Westermann, is a gloss which attempts to 'rational-ize' Enoch's disappearance (ibid: 358), without implying any view of a mythological place for him to inhabit beyond this world. 'Only gradually did the notion of removal as a state enter into the narrative of removal as an event' (ibid: 359).

The reference to Enoch in Genesis 5 is exilic if not later (von Rad 1972: 72; cf. Westermann 1984: 358–9). The story of Elijah's translation is also from the same period (Gray 1970: 472). It has been suggested that this awesome vision is either an elaboration of the title 'the chariotry of Israel and the horsemen thereof' or the result of the association of the story of Elijah with an old solar cult-legend (ibid: 476). There may be some truth in this, but as in the case of Enoch's translation nothing is said about the place to which Elijah was transported. The translations of Enoch and Elijah are thus comparatively late accounts of extraordinary events which did not in any way affect the expectations of the ordinary Israelite. Life was a gift from God, which presupposed living in obedience to him; death was the with-drawal of that gift, to be accepted with resignation. There is no cult of the dead in the Old Testament: 'The dead praise not the Lord' (Ps. 115: 17). By death they leave the covenant community, lose their relationship with Yahweh, and are of no concern to the living.[1] At this stage in Israel's religious development there is no suggestion of belief in resurrection or immortality, still less of belief in deification. Even for the *elohim* in the heavenly court, life is a gift which depends on obedience.

2. The Impact of Hellenism

When Jesus ben Sira's grandson went to stay in Egypt in the thirty-eighth year of Ptolemy VIII Euergetes II (126/5 BCE), he discovered a flourishing Jewish community with an established tradition of learning based on the Greek Torah (Sir. Prol.). His contact with the Diaspora encouraged him to translate his grandfather's book into Greek 'for those living abroad who wished to gain learning' so that they could live according to the Law even if

---

[1] The eighth-century prophet Amos is the first to attempt to bring Sheol within God's domain (Amos 9: 2) but his is a lone voice.

they had no Hebrew.[2] The tradition of wisdom that the younger Ben Sira brought to the Egyptian Jewish community was an old one with roots going back to the scribal schools of the ancient Near East. Although originally *hokmah*, or wisdom, was the practical knowledge that enabled one to carry out skilled tasks, by the Hellenistic age it had come to be identified with the culture of the educated elite. Ben Sira sets out the benefits of such a culture: a man who devotes himself to the study of the Law, the wisdom of ancient texts, and the discourses of famous men with the subtleties of their parables and proverbs will be a counsellor to the great and travel widely. His international outlook, however, will be balanced by a judicious moral sense and fidelity to the Law (Sir. 39: 1–5). For worldly success will not be his primary aim. All his life he will hunger and thirst after wisdom (24: 21) and when he has found her he will share her with those who seek instruction (24: 34). Although Ben Sira did not found a school, as a Jewish sage he would have had his disciples. This is reflected in his advice to the reader to attach himself to a teacher of wisdom if he can find one (6: 36) and also in his confidence that a lasting reputation will win him immortality (39: 9).

Wisdom is first personified in the Book of Proverbs, where, betraying her mythological origins, she appears as God's companion in the work of creation (8: 1–36). With Ben Sira the figure of Wisdom becomes the personification of the Torah (Sir. 24: 1–24). The benefits she confers are those of the Law—and she confers them not just on her professional exponents but on all who love her. She exalts her sons (4: 11), fills with joy those who seek her (4: 12) and bestows glory on those who hold fast to her (4: 13). She also showers material rewards on the homes of the righteous (1: 17). But there is nothing in Ben Sira's teaching about rewards after death. Death is final: the dead do not return (38: 21). Immortality consists simply in leaving behind a son as a replica of oneself (30: 4) or in attaining a reputation that will outlast one (39: 9). By the time of the composition of the Book of Wisdom, however, in the first century BCE, there has been a fundamental change. Wisdom is now no longer a personification of the religion of Israel but a figure much closer to God himself. She is 'a breath of the power of God', 'a pure emanation of the glory of the Almighty', 'an image of his goodness' (Wisd. 7: 25, 26). People are said to be saved by her, for she is no longer distinct from God (9: 18). Images of light abound: Wisdom is 'brilliant and unfading' (6: 12); her 'radiance never ceases' (7: 10); she is 'a reflection of eternal light' (7: 26); she is 'more beautiful than the sun and excels every constellation of the stars' (7: 29). Through this luminous emanation God reaches out to humankind. And the righteous respond with fidelity, trust, and love. Death will no longer cut them off from God.

---

[2] At this time the only education available for Jews living abroad was a Greek one. Educated Jews of the Diaspora 'necessarily became alienated from the civilization of their ancestors' (Bickerman 1988: 303).

Endowed now with immortality, the dead live for ever in the presence of God (3: 1; 5: 15).

Ben Sira wanted to encourage Diaspora Jews to stay faithful to the Law and resist the seductive attractions of their Hellenistic education. The temptation to infidelity for the anonymous author of the Book of Wisdom was more specific. The question now was: granted the shortness of life and the finality of death, should we not enjoy the good things of this world to the full regardless of moral constraints? The Book of Wisdom's reply was to put human life in an eternal perspective: 'the righteous live for ever and their reward is with the Lord' (5: 15).

If the author of the Book of Wisdom predates Philo, he is the first Hellenistic Jewish writer to posit an immortal soul. He attacks the old notion of Sheol as a belief that encourages a *carpe diem* mentality (1: 16–2: 11). Immortality or, rather, incorruption is the state for which humanity was created. The term ἀθανασία, 'immortality', appears in a parabiblical text for the first time. But it has been adapted somewhat to a Hebrew perspective. The human soul, whether *in toto* or in part, is not immortal by nature; it wins immortality through obedience to the Law. Immortality is thus a gift from God bestowed on each soul according to its merits. Another word which appears for the first time is ἀφθαρσία, or 'incorruption'. This is not just a synonym for immortality (*contra* Kolarcik 1991). It had been used originally by Epicureans to explain how the gods differed from human beings (Reese 1970: 65–8; Winston 1979: 121). In the Book of Wisdom this attribute is transferred from the gods to men, because by creating man in his own image God gave him a share in his own eternity (2: 23).[3] Incorruption has an ontological dimension: the Spirit of God is incorrupt (ἄφθαρτον), like the light of the Law (12: 1; 18: 4). Immortality, on the other hand, is a human quality: it is righteousness (1: 15), remembrance of virtue (4: 1), kinship to wisdom (8: 17), knowledge of the power of God (15: 3). Another striking Greek borrowing is the designation of the manna in the wilderness as 'ambrosial food' (19: 21). In the Book of Wisdom the pagan food of the immortal gods becomes the food of immortality, falling to humanity as a divine gift.

The kinship which the human soul enjoys with Wisdom, the emanation of divine glory, enables the devout to attain a new intimacy with God. Wisdom makes them 'friends of God' (7: 27), an expression applied to Abraham in the Bible (Isa. 41: 8; 2 Chr. 20: 7; Jas. 2: 23), and to virtuous men by the philosophers (Plato, *Rep.* 621c; *Tim.* 53d; Epictetus 2. 17. 29; 4. 3. 9, etc.), and akin to the Hellenistic 'friends of the king' attested in Ptolemaic Egypt (*OGI* 100.1; LSJ s.v. φίλος; cf. Winston 1979: 188–9), which suggests a role as counsellors at the court of heaven. A similar royal setting lies behind the idea that for the just man, union with Wisdom makes her a 'throne-partner'

---

[3] Or 'his own identity' if one reads ἰδιότητος with Vaticanus, Sinaiticus, and Alexandrinus against the αἰδιότητος of the *textus receptus*. Winston translates: 'his own proper being' (1979: *ad loc.*).

(πάρεδρος) with him (6: 14). 'Throne-partner' is also used to express Wisdom's relationship with God (9: 4), implying that the just man who has united himself with Wisdom can take his place in the divine council. It is tempting to think that the Ptolemaic enthroning of the images of Pharaoh and his consort in the temples of the gods might have contributed to the idea of Wisdom as πάρεδρος, but the term used for the Ptolemies is σύνναοι θεοί ('gods sharing the same temple'). The immediate antecedents of the enthroning of Wisdom are in fact biblical, the verb παρεδρεύω already being found in the Septuagint version of Prov. 8: 3 (cf. 1 Enoch 84: 3). A non-biblical influence, however, has been detected in one further image, the most intimate of them all. Union with Wisdom is described at 8: 2 in nuptial terms that have been shown to owe something to the language of Hellenistic hymns to Isis (Reese 1970: 46–9). That is not to say that the Isis cult had any appeal for the author of the Book of Wisdom himself, although we know that there were Jews in the Hellenistic period who were attracted to the pagan mysteries (Bickerman 1988: 254–5). Rather, we may guess that the language and imagery of the Isis cult satisfied a yearning which called for something equivalent in Judaism.

The author of the Book of Wisdom was not the only writer of the Jewish Diaspora to be influenced by Greek thought. There were apostates such as the Dositheus who became a priest of Alexander and the deified Ptolemies towards the end of the third century BCE (Bickerman 1988: 87), but there were others who adopted Greek culture without in any way discarding their Jewish faith. Nobody managed this with greater skill or versatility than Philo of Alexandria. Born in about 20 BCE of a distinguished Jewish family,[4] he received a liberal Greek education which brought him into contact with the revived Platonism of Eudorus and Posidonius. He was not, however, a systematic philosopher. His main concern was to comment on the Pentateuch in a way that would commend the teaching of Moses to Gentile proselytes and Jews who were looking for an intellectually satisfying expression of their faith in modern (i.e. Hellenistic) dress. A most useful tool in achieving this aim was the technique of allegorical interpretation, which had already been developed by Alexandrian scholars in relation to Homer. It was axiomatic to Philo that the Bible could contain nothing unworthy of God. Therefore any attribution of jealousy or anger, for example, to God had to have a deeper meaning. Yet in spite of not being a systematic philosopher, Philo marshalls his arguments coherently and effectively. He elaborates a chain of being that bridges the gap between God and man—while still maintaining a supremely transcendent God—and introduces the possibility of the ascent of the soul to God even in this life through the practice of philosophy. As with the

---

[4] His brother was Alabarch, or head of the Jewish community of Alexandria, and rich enough to lend Herod Agrippa 200,000 talents; his apostate nephew, Julius Alexander, was the first non-Roman prefect of Egypt (Josephus, *Ant.* 20.100).

pagan Platonists, however, this ascent is not called deification. In spite of the application of the term θεός to a broad spectrum of beings, man does not become a god in any real sense.

Philo frequently refers to the personal God of the Bible as ὁ θεός, but θεός in his usage, as in Greek writers generally, is a predicate with a wide application, not a term confined to the supreme deity alone.[5] Occasionally the personal name of God, ὁ ὤν, the Septuagint translation of YHWH, is contrasted with θεός and κύριος, which represent the creative and providential powers of God, respectively, and is set above them (*V. Mos.* 2.99).[6] It is unclear how far these powers are to be thought of as hypostatized. They are the Stoic *logoi*, the Platonic Forms, which Philo equates with the thoughts of God.[7] He also represents them in a more personal way as the angels, ruled by the two cherubim who guard the gates of paradise or who are set over the ark of the covenant.

The sum of all the Forms is the Logos, who is the supreme mediator between the transcendent uncreated God and the created world (Chadwick 1970: 143–5; Dillon 1977: 159–61). In relation to the 'first God' he is the 'second God', the first-born son of God, the wisdom and image of God (*QG* 2.62; *Agr.* 51; *Fuga* 109; *Conf.* 147). In relation to humankind he is the Archetype, the heavenly Adam, into whom God 'breathed a share of his own deity' (*Det.* 86) (Philo takes the two descriptions of the creation of man in Gen. 1: 27 and 2: 7 to refer to two distinct events). Other beings also mediate between God and humanity. The heavenly bodies are said to be visible gods because they are the purest of corporeal things (*Gig.* 8; *Opif.* 27, 55). Between the heavens and the earth the air is inhabited by its own incorporeal beings. Some of these descend into human bodies and become souls; Philo equates the remainder with the daemons of the Greeks and the angels of the Bible (*Gig.* 6, 16). (Like many of the Rabbis, he believed in the pre-existence of souls but not in the cycle of reincarnation.)

Earthly man, the product of a second human creation (Gen. 2: 7) and the last creature in the chain of being to participate in immortality, is a mixture of rational soul created directly by God and clay into which God has breathed life, the divine breath rendering the invisible part immortal (*Opif.* 135). The body, which with the irrational soul was created not directly by God but by the powers, is simply a dwelling-place for the higher, rational soul, which is 'a holy image, of all images the most godlike' (*Fuga* 69; *Spec. Leg.* 1. 329; *Opif.* 137; cf. Wolfson 1947: i. 387). It is an image of the

---

[5] Wolfson 1947: i. 173–80; Holladay 1977: 153–4. Philo's distinction between the articular and anarthrous use of θεός for God and the Logos was to be taken up by Origen.

[6] Philo associates θεός with the creative power of God because of an etymological connection which he sees between θεός and τίθημι.

[7] Chadwick 1970: 142; Dillon 1996: 158–66. This identification was probably the work of Antiochus of Ascalon (Dillon 1996: 95).

Archetype, the Logos, 'a fragment (ἀπόσπασμα) of that divine and blessed soul' (*Det.* 90; *Opif.* 146). This should not be taken in a Stoic sense to mean that the human soul is the same as the divine primary substance. There is no cosmic soul in Philo, nothing outside the primal God that is divine *per se*. Wolfson claims that the designation of the human soul as a 'fragment' means that it is 'an image of the idea of rational soul, which is as immaterial as its pattern' (Wolfson 1947: i. 390; cf. Holladay 1977: 192). In Runia's judgement, however, Philo reflects a lack of clarity endemic in contemporary Platonism—only with Plotinus is the question of whether 'the rational part is related to the divine in a model/copy or a part/whole relation' finally resolved (Runia 1988: 68). The intellect is the ruling element of the soul, and because the human intellect 'evidently occupies a position in men precisely answering to that which the great Ruler occupies in all the world', 'it is as it were a god to him who carries and enshrines it as an image' (*Opif.* 69). The human intellect is a god not in fact but by analogy. There is a gulf between the human and the divine which is never fully transcended in Philo. The first man is not the same thing as God but simply 'of near kin to the Ruler, since the divine spirit had flowed into him in full current' (*Opif.* 144).

Philo discusses the soul's ascent to God on four levels: the religious (which is the flight from idolatry), the philosophical, the ethical, and the mystical (Billings 1919: 11). The philosophical level may be studied conveniently in the treatise *On the Migration of Abraham*. First after relinquishing astrology, which according to Philo identifies the universe with the primal God, the intellect must come to know itself and its abode, the body. Then rising from the sensible to the intelligible world, it will be able to soar to the contemplation of Him that Is (*Migr.* 194–5). The passage from self-knowledge to the knowledge of God, however, is not achieved through intellectual effort alone. 'The first aim of knowledge', says Philo, drawing on his Jewish piety as well as Socrates, 'is to hold that we know nothing, he alone being wise who is also alone God' (*Migr.* 134). The heights above the earth are too exalted to be reached by the powers of thought: 'One would need to become a god—something which is impossible—in order to be able to apprehend God' (*Frg. from QE* 2.258; trans. Marcus). Wisdom, faith, piety, the practice of the virtues—these are the things which raise the intellect to God.

On the ethical level, the search for wisdom begins with the examination of the sovereign function of the intellect within the microcosm of man (*Migr.* 218). This leads to a decision to escape from the body—the 'foul prison-house'—and its pleasures and lusts, and provides the motivation for the cultivation of the virtues (*Migr.* 9; *Leg. Alleg.* 1.108; *Abr.* 52–4; cf. Dillon 1996: 149). The successful practice of the virtues enables the person who is on the way to perfection to attain μετριοπάθεια ('moderation of passion'), but the perfect human being strives to eradicate the passions altogether and arrive at ἀπάθεια ('absence of passion') (*Leg. Alleg.* 3. 132; cf. Dillon 1996: 151–2).

The virtues, being immortal, themselves confer immortality, for the soul is not immortal in its own right. The winning of immortality is described by Philo as παλιγγενεσία ('rebirth') (*Cher.* 114), which simply means that virtuous souls after death become pure *noes* (cf. *QE* 2.46 and *CH* XIII 3 and 10). This enables them to live for ever with the angels (cf. Wolfson 1947: i. 405–6). But not all appear to be capable of this. Evil people, Philo seems to imply in a discussion of Gen. 2: 17, having preserved no part at all of the true life (i.e. having lived entirely in the lower soul, which perishes with the body) vanish utterly (*QG* 1. 16; cf. Wolfson 1947: i. 407–13). The notion that the souls of the wicked perish is a philosophical idea that appears to go back to Chrysippus (Dillon 1996: 177–8). The goal of the moral life is the Platonic likeness to God, which Philo sees as equivalent to the Stoic *telos* of living in conformity with nature (*Migr.* 131) (Dillon 1996: 145–6; Nikiprowetzky 1977: 127). Both are equated with the teaching of Moses, for humankind was created originally in the image and likeness of God, and to follow nature is to keep the Law and follow the God of the Hebrew Scriptures. Philo recognizes, however, that here too human effort alone is insufficient. If we lift ourselves towards heaven without divine supervision, we will incur shipwreck (*Migr.* 171; cf. *Leg. Alleg.* 3.136). The achievement of the *telos* is only possible when God himself 'grants to the worthy a share of his own nature, which is repose' (*Post. C.* 28). It should be noted that 'nature' here refers not to the essence of God, which is incommunicable, but to one of his key attributes: the attainment of *apatheia* enables one to receive the gift of divine immutability (*Post. C.* 27). The soul, however, still remains a created entity. Participation in God does not therefore imply becoming God, or even a god. The separate identity of the individual is retained through becoming *like* God rather than being changed essentially.

The mystical level is expressed in Philo's description of an encounter between the human and the divine which is possible only out of the body—in this life in a state of ecstasy, in the next when a person has become pure *nous*. An intellect possessed by divine love forgets itself utterly (*Somn.* 2.232). It is 'drawn and seized' and 'led by the attractive force of sovereign existences' (*QG* 4.140). It is 'possessed by a sober intoxication like those seized with Corybantic frenzy, and is inspired, filled by another sort of longing and a more fitting desire . . . the eye of the understanding spins with dizziness' (*Opif.* 70–1; cf. *Heres.* 68–70; Lewy 1929; Winston 1985: 358 n. 341). In more philosophical language Philo says:

When the prophetic intellect becomes divinely inspired and filled with God, it becomes like the monad, not being at all mixed with any of those things associated with duality. But he who is resolved into the nature of unity is said to come near God in a kind of family relation, for having given up and left behind all mortal kinds, he is changed into the divine, so that such men become kin to God and truly divine. (*QE* 2. 29; trans. Marcus)

One should not read into this more than Philo intended. 'He who is resolved into the nature of unity' is exemplified elsewhere by the emaciated ascetic who has virtually become a disembodied intellect, or by Moses after death, who ascends to God as pure *nous* (*Mut.* 33; *V. Mos.* 2. 288). It is this reduction to incorporeality, rather than any essential transformation, which is signified by the expression 'changed into the divine' (cf. Holladay 1977: 155–60).

The supreme example of a man who has attained the *telos* and become 'truly divine' is Moses.[8] Even in his youth Moses was not like an ordinary human being. His intellect, which 'dwelt in his body like an image in its shrine', was so dazzling that his contemporaries did not know 'whether it was human or divine or a mixture of both' (*V. Mos.* 1. 27; cf. *Gig.* 24). It was not Moses' natural attributes alone which brought him close to the divine. Through his virtues and his entry on Mount Sinai into the darkness where God was, he became for his people a god and a king. Having come into contact with 'the unseen, invisible, incorporeal and archetypal essence of existing things', he became himself 'a piece of work beautiful and godlike, a model for those who are willing to copy it' (*V. Mos.* 1. 158).

The scriptural basis on which Philo is able to call Moses a god is Exodus 7: 1: 'See, I gave you as a god to Pharaoh' (LXX). In many passages in which this text is cited or alluded to Philo is quick to point out that Moses is described as a god by analogy: he is a god to Pharaoh in the same way that the *nous* is a god to the soul, or that a wise man is a god to a fool (*Leg. Alleg.* 1.40; *Det.* 162). Or alternatively, he is 'a god to men, not to the different parts of nature, thus leaving to the Father of all the place of King and God of gods' (*Prob.* 43). Yet in other passages Philo seems to go beyond a merely analogous use of the term. In a discussion of the role of the high-priest when he enters the Holy of Holies, Philo describes him as neither a man nor a god, because he unites the two extremes in his own person, being contiguous with each. He will not call him a god because 'this name is a prerogative assigned to the chief prophet, Moses, while he was still in Egypt' (*Somn.* 2.189). Moses is granted the title because of 'his partnership with the Father and Maker of all' (*V. Mos.* 1. 158). He is 'deemed worthy of divine rank' because he is a friend of God possessed by divine love (*Prob.* 44). After death he did not take his place among the angels like most ordinary virtuous men, nor even among the Forms like Isaac and Enoch, but was advanced even higher above the heavens to stand beside God himself (*Sacr.* 6, 8; *QG* 1.86).

Was Moses, then, as E. R. Goodenough asks, θεός in Philo's mind? (Goodenough 1935: 229). Goodenough's answer is yes and no. He saw Moses as a bridge between God and man, as something approaching the

---

[8] The main studies of Philo's treatment of Moses as a god are Goodenough 1935: 195–230; Meeks 1967: 100–31; Meeks 1968; Holladay 1977: 103–98; and Runia 1988.

Pythagorean 'third race', the result of Philo's vacillating 'between the mono-theism on the one hand which [he] had from his Jewish ancestry and from the Neo-Pythagorean and Platonic traditions in philosophy, and on the other hand the popular tendency to deify great figures and heroes' (Goodenough 1935: 223–4). Wayne Meeks later confirmed Goodenough's overall judge-ment but attempted to set Philo's views in a more Jewish context by suggest-ing that he made use of an existing midrash on Moses which already connected Exodus 7: 1 with the ascent of Mount Sinai (1967: 104–5; 1968: 355–7). The next response came from Carl Holladay, who demonstrated in a study of the key texts that Philo never calls Moses a god in a literal sense, his use of *theos* being either titular—distinguishing Moses in the Bible from any other personage—or allegorical (1977: 136–54). Even *On the Sacrifices of Abel and Cain* 8–10, the most important passage cited as evidence of the literal deification of Moses, turns out on close analysis to have an ethical-allegorical significance. It was Moses' 'sovereignty over the passions of the soul' that enabled him to be appointed a god. Accordingly, 'his being appointed θεός merely testifies to how successfully he has enslaved all the somatic passions and thus exemplifies the one in whom νοῦς rules the σῶμα, as it should be in the ideal virtuous man' (Holladay 1977: 139). A more recent commentator, David Runia, reaches a conclusion close to that of Holladay: 'The fact . . . that Moses is given the same title as God is certainly a great honour, but it does not imply a kind of deification in which Moses comes to share in the same nature as God' (1988: 60). Runia sees Philo's interpretation of Exod. 7: 1 as an amplification of Deut. 33: 1. Moses is a mediating figure, transmitting divine blessings to the people through his own person. His mediating role, however, does not hypostatize him as a divine power. His status as a σοφός, a perfectly wise man, grants him a 'privileged position, strictly speaking neither God nor man but rather occupying a midway position' (1988: 62–3).

Behind Philo's characterization of Moses lies the Greek application of θεός to the sage, the ruler, and the benefactor. These three applications are closely connected. Indeed, the sage had long since taken over the attributes of the ideal king as both philosopher and world ruler. Among the Stoics the wise man, according to Diogenes Laertius, was θεός καὶ βασιλεύς (Diog. Laert. 7.117 ff.). On the authority of Exodus 7: 1, Moses, the supremely wise man, could be called θεῖος καὶ βασιλεύς, ruling first over his body and his passions, then over the fool, and finally over the whole of nature through sharing in God's cosmic rule (*Sacr.* 9; *Mut.* 128; *Det.* 162; *V. Mos.* 1. 158; cf. Runia 1988: 55). Elsewhere Philo also appeals to the view that a benefactor may be reckoned as a god to his beneficiaries:

For one must be content if it be granted to him to follow right reasoning himself, but to procure the good gift for others is what only a greater, more perfect, truly God-inspired soul can promise, and the possessor of such a soul will with good reason be called a god . . .[9] The chief characteristic of a god is to be a benefactor. (*Mut.* 128–9; trans. Colson, modified)

This influence, however, should not be given undue weight. Set against it is Philo's implacable hostility to pagan deification, which is the only context—with one possible exception—in which he uses the relevant technical terms.[10] He protests against the deification of the heavenly bodies, of the four primary principles, even of reason itself (*Conf.* 173; *Dec.* 53; *Spec. Leg.* 1. 344). He ridicules the Egyptian deification of animals (*Dec.* 79). And he attacks the 'most godless deification' of Gaius with a passion worthy of a Maccabee (*Leg. ad Gaium* 77). Under the influence of Euhemerism, however, he does at least find it intelligible that the Egyptians should have deified the Nile, and he is sympathetic to the honours which were accorded to Augustus in view of his enormous benefactions to mankind (*V. Mos.* 2. 195; *Leg. ad Gaium* 143 ff.). Nevertheless, it is clear that he saw nothing in pagan deification or its terminology which could be used to illuminate the religion of the Jews.

In conclusion we may say that in spite of a doctrine of the soul which is thoroughly Greek, and in spite of a predicative use of the word θεός, which is also thoroughly Greek, Philo is unwilling to say that Moses is a god except by title or analogy. And without biblical authority he would not have ventured to say even that—so eager is he to qualify the statement—even though Moses shared in the kingship and glory of God through his ascent of Mount Sinai. The rational soul, having been created in the image of the Image, has a natural kinship with God. It can reach up towards him through philosophy, which raises the mind from the sensible to the intelligible, through the moral struggle, which strives to attain ἀπάθεια, and through mysticism, which seeks to free the *nous* from the shackles of the body by means of ecstasy in this life or by soaring up beyond the heavens after death. Yet Philo stresses repeatedly that although human beings can attain divinity in the sense of incorporeality or immortality, it is impossible for them to become gods. For all his Platonism he maintains the biblical gulf between the human and the divine, depreciating the ability of intellectual and moral effort on their own to raise the soul to God. There is a suggestion that through God's grace human beings can be given a share in the divine attributes in so far as they are

---

[9] θεός is the reading of the manuscripts but is printed by Cohn and Wendland with some hesitation. Colson and Whitaker (LCL) read θεοῦ – 'man of God'. Philo, however, as he shows in his discussion of the title 'man of God' (*Mut.* 126–9), finds it to be more or less equivalent to 'god'. Cf. Goodenough 1935: 227; Meeks 1968: 357.

[10] In *QE* 2. 40, R. Marcus (LCL, Philo Suppl. 2) translates from the Armenian: 'This (i.e. Exod. 24: 12) signifies that a holy soul is divinised by ascending not to the air or to the ether or to a region (which is) higher than all but to (a region) above the heavens. And beyond the world there is no place but God,' and notes in respect of 'divinised': 'Arm. *astouacanal* usually renders θεοῦσθαι, a word that seems not to occur elsewhere in Philo. Perhaps the original here was θεοφορεῖσθαι.' It seems to me more likely to have been θειοῦσθαι, which Philo does use once (*Ebr.* 110) to signify participation in incorruption.

capable of receiving them.[11] There is also a mention of the unending concord and union that come from cleaving to God (*Post. C.* 12). But this is as far as Philo is prepared to go.[12]

3. Palestinian Judaism

While Philo was composing his commentaries and treatises in Alexandria for the Greek-speaking Diaspora, other writers in Palestine were producing a different kind of literature. There was, of course, no rigid distinction between the Judaism (or rather, Judaisms) of Palestine and that of the Hellenized Diaspora. On the one hand, Jewish writers in Greek had no wish for the most part to break with their religious tradition; on the other, the Palestinian homeland itself was not immune to the penetration of Greek culture and ideas. Nevertheless, since the fourth century BCE certain circles in Palestine had been responsible for a number of developments which owed very little to Hellenism, namely, the peopling of heaven with the angelic orders, the revelation of divine mysteries to a representative human figure, and the participation of the elect in a new exalted life beyond the grave. These are the developments that we encounter in Apocalyptic literature and the sectarian writings of Khirbet Qumran.

Apocalyptic originated in the pluralistic age of the Second Temple, the age of Middle Judaism. In the early years of this period the two main forms of Palestinian Judaism were the Zadokite and the Enochic.[13] Zadokite Judaism, the product of the reforms of Ezra and Nehemiah, was centred on the worship of the Temple at Jerusalem and was controlled by the priestly elite. Enochic Judaism first appears in the third century BCE among the same elite, perhaps as a reaction to the Hellenization of the Zadokite priesthood. The name Enochic has been given to it because of the importance it attached to a number of ancient traditions which accorded a central role to Enoch as a mediator between heaven and earth. These traditions were collected in the five separate works which together came to make up 1 Enoch.[14] After the

---

[11] Dillon (1983: 223) sees a foreshadowing in Philo of the doctrine of 'suitability for reception' which we find in the later Neoplatonists.

[12] So Dodd 1953; Chadwick 1970; Holladay 1977; Runia 1988; Helleman 1990. *Contra:* Goodenough 1935; Meeks 1968; Tiede 1972.

[13] I have drawn my sketch of Middle Judaism from Boccaccini 1998 (cf. the useful diagram on p. xxii) and Sacchi 1994. Note, however, Adler's warning about the difficulty of locating Apocalyptic literature in any particular kind of Judaism: 'Because most of the Jewish apocalypses received a generally unfavourable reception in post-70 Judaism, there does not exist a developed tradition of Jewish interpretation to contextualize these documents or provide a framework for their analysis' (VanderKam and Adler 1996: 1).

[14] In chronological order (as given by VanderKam in VanderKam and Adler 1996: 33) these works are: (i) The Astronomical Book (1 Enoch 72–8), 3rd cent. BCE; (ii) The Book of the Watchers (1 Enoch 1–36), 3rd cent. BCE; (iii) The Epistle of Enoch (1 Enoch 91–108), 2nd cent. BCE; (iv) The Book of Dreams (1 Enoch 83–90), 2nd cent. BCE; (v) The Book of Parables (1 Enoch 37–71), 1st cent. BCE/CE.

Maccabean crisis, Zadokite Judaism divided into Sadduceeism and Pharisaism, while Enochic Judaism gave rise to Essenism.

The relationship of Qumran Judaism to these is disputed. The majority of scholars see Khirbet Qumran as an Essene settlement, perhaps even the headquarters of the movement, but there are a number of difficulties to this view. Although the teachings of the Qumran library share the anti-Zadokite character and dualist world view of the Essenes (many fragments of 1 Enoch were found in Cave 4), they differ markedly in emphasizing both an individual predestination and an inaugurated eschatology. Perhaps the most satisfactory explanation is that the Qumranites were indeed Essenes, but a marginal community that had broken away from mainstream Essenism (Boccaccini 1998: esp. 187–8).

Recent studies have shown that the doctrine of a transcendent life beyond the grave developed surprisingly early in Judaism, owing little, if anything, to Hellenism (Sacchi 1994: 402–14). Already in the Book of the Watchers (third century BCE) Enoch is shown the place of the dead, where the spirits of the righteous, separated from the spirits of sinners, dwell near 'a bright spring of water' (1 Enoch 22: 2, 9). Indeed, it seems to have been the hope of immortality held out by Enochic Judaism, rather than any ideas drawn from Hellenism, that provoked the scornful claim of Qoheleth that 'man has no advantage over the beasts . . . all go to one place . . . all turn to dust again' (Eccles. 3: 19–20; cf. 9: 10). But Qoheleth's was a voice from the past, whose old-fashioned conviction that human life ended in annihilation would survive only among the Sadducees. By the time of the Book of Parables, the latest part of 1 Enoch (turn of the CE), Enochic Judaism held that the righteous dead would share in the divine life itself. Their faces would shine with the light of God (1 Enoch 38: 4) and they would be clothed with the garments of glory (1 Enoch 62: 16). This was different in its corporate emphasis from the immortality of Hellenistic Judaism, which was a reward bestowed by God on an individual basis. It was different, too, from the idea of bodily resurrection which became a characteristic doctrine of Pharisaism.

The doctrine of angels also has its roots in primitive Hebrew religion. From their origins as members of the council of the gods which surrounded Yahweh, the angels, under the influence partly of Greek daemonic theory, but even more of Persian angelology, underwent a remarkable elaboration in Apocalyptic literature (Russell 1964: 235–62). In the heavenly court, or temple, they performed a priestly role, rendering worship to God. With regard to men, their function was twofold. First, they acted as a bridge between God and his creation, governing the world with a delegated power; secondly, they served as an explanation of suffering, either as angelic ministers who tested human beings (in the Zadokite tradition), or as fallen demons who warred against them (in Enochic Judaism). In the Hellenistic and Roman periods their mediatorial role was expanded further. Enoch, Moses, and other heroes of the faith were represented as ascending to heaven to participate with the angels in the heavenly liturgy. In their wake they drew up the faithful remnant of Israel, the promotion of the resurrected righteous to a community of life with the angels coming, in a non-philosophizing Jewish milieu, to form a parallel to Christian deification with important implications for both Christianity and Rabbinic Judaism.

Among the most powerful eschatological images in Apocalyptic literature are those of God on his heavenly throne surrounded by his angelic throng, or even more awesomely in his fiery chariot, the Merkabah, which are first met with in the vision of Micaiah (1 Kgs. 22: 19–22) and can be traced through Isaiah 6 and Ezekiel 1 to Daniel 7 and the theophanies of 1 Enoch 14, 46, and 71 (Black 1976: 57–73; Himmelfarb 1993: 9–28). In 1 Kings, Isaiah, and Ezekiel the theophany is the setting for the commissioning of the prophet. But in Daniel 7 the vision itself becomes an integral part of the prophet's message, which focuses on the destiny of the faithful remnant who have endured persecution. These will 'receive the kingdom and possess the kingdom for ever, for ever and ever' (7: 18). But there is mention, too, of 'one like a son of man' who comes to the Ancient of Days with clouds of heaven and is also given 'dominion and glory and kingdom' (7: 13–14). The identity of this figure is disputed. He has been seen variously as symbolizing Michael, the guardian angel of Israel (Collins 1995), or the historic Jewish people (Di Lella in Hartman and Di Lella 1978: 90–2), or both simultaneously (Collins 1974*b*) or in successive stages. Matthew Black goes so far as to say that 'what Daniel was contemplating was nothing less than the *apotheosis* of Israel in the end-time, a "deification", as it were, of the "saints of the Most High" ' (Black 1976: 61). The simplest explanation, however, is the most satisfactory.[15] The 'one like a son of man' is an angel, probably Michael, entrusted with the protection of the people of Israel. Only later, in Christian tradition and in the Book of Parables (1 Enoch 37–71) does he become a Messianic figure, the Elect of God.

Ezekiel and Daniel are models for later Apocalyptic writers of scenes set in the heavenly court. The mysterious figure of Enoch, who was rapt to heaven in Gen. 5: 24, came to play a central role. In the Book of the Watchers (1 Enoch 1–36) he is portrayed as lifted up into heaven (14: 8) into the presence of the Merkabah (14: 18–25) to mediate between angels and God (15: 1 to 16: 4; cf. Gen. 6: 1–4). In the Book of Parables, which draws on Daniel 7, his role is extended. He no longer performs a merely mediatory function but is invested with Messianic authority. The climax comes in chapter 71, where Enoch, having ascended into the heavens and seen the sons of the holy angels treading on flames of fire, is identified with the Son of Man. At the end of time, seated on the throne of his glory, Enoch will judge both

---

[15] It might be added that the discrediting of the notion of 'corporate personality' (Rogerson 1970) has made the idea of the Son of Man as a representative figure one that must be treated cautiously.

angels and men (69: 29). In other texts other patriarchs and heroes, though not cast in the Messianic role, will also have thrones in heaven. Isaac is told by an angel that a throne has been set up for him close to his father Abraham and that his son Jacob's lot 'will surpass that of all the others in the whole of God's creation' (*Test. of Isaac* 2: 5–6). Job silences Elihu and his companions with the boast that he will show them his throne with all 'its glory and its splendour at the right hand of the Father' (*Test. of Job* 33: 2–3).

   One of the most remarkable of these ascents is found not in an Apocalyptic text but in a Jewish Hellenistic play on the life of Moses, entitled *Exagoge*, which was written in Greek verse in the second century BCE by an Alexandrian Jew called Ezekiel (Jacobson 1983: lines 68–82; cf. Runia 1988: 48–52; Collins 1995: 50–3). In this case it is a dream that is recounted rather than a real ascent (which, as Runia says, demythologizes the account) but when Moses arrives before the throne of God, God does not simply set him on a throne but actually descends from his own throne and puts Moses on it in his place (lines 74–6). The whole cosmos then spreads itself before him and the stars fall on their knees and adore him (lines 79–80). 'The implication', as Runia points out, 'is that Moses is actually deified' (1988: 51). Neither Philo nor any of the Apocalyptic texts goes quite so far as this in their exaltation of a biblical personage, although the heroes, enthroned in glory, do share in the rule of God. In Apocalyptic literature, however, it is not only the great men of the past who will be assigned heavenly thrones. Enoch says that each of those who love God's holy name 'will be set on the throne of his honour' (108: 12). The righteous, admitted into the heavenly court, will also be enthroned with the patriarchs and heroic figures of Israel.

   The association of the righteous with the heavenly liturgy of the angels is a particularly striking feature of the sectarian writings of the Qumran community. One of the central tenets of the community was that its members were predestined to transcend death: 'For God has chosen them for an everlasting covenant and the glory of Adam shall be theirs' (1QS 4: 24; cf. 1QH 3: 5).[16] The glory awaiting the Qumranites was not a new state but a continuation of the life of the community. Each member under the Teacher of Righteousness and the sages of the community had been 'shaped from dust for the everlasting Council'. His spirit had been cleansed 'that it may stand with the host of the Holy Ones, and that it may enter into a community with the congregation of the Sons of Heaven' (1QH 3: 5; cf. 1QH 11: 7 and 4Q181). These Sons of Heaven are the angels who constitute the heavenly court. On a number of occasions they are called 'gods' (*elohim* or *elim*) after Psalm 82: 1: 'ELOHIM has taken his place in the divine council; in the midst of the gods he holds judgement' (11Q13. 10). As 'gods' they are organized under Michael or Melchizedek (1QM18) for the service of God

---

[16] Only one text out of 813 testifies to belief in the resurrection (Vermes 1995: 63).

(4Q400), for combat in the coming Messianic war, and for the praise and adoration of God (4Q403 1. i. 30–46; 4Q405 19ABCD). And those who have been elected to the community participate with them in each of these activities.

For the Qumran congregation the boundaries between heaven and earth are permeable. Indeed, on occasion they dissolve away entirely, as some of the hymns, in particular, make explicit:

> My eyes have gazed on that which is eternal,
> on wisdom concealed from men,
> on knowledge and wise design (hidden) from the sons of men;
> on a fountain of righteousness and on a storehouse of power,
> on a spring of glory (hidden) from the assembly of flesh.
> God has given them to His chosen ones as an everlasting possession,
> and has caused them to inherit the lot of the Holy Ones.
> He has joined their assembly to the Sons of Heaven
> to be a Council of the Community,
> a foundation of the Building of Holiness,
> and eternal Plantation throughout all ages to come.

So proclaims the hymn that concludes the Community Rule (1QS 11: 5–9; trans. Vermes 1995: 87). Another liturgical text takes up the same theme:

> Thou hast cleansed a perverse spirit of great sin
> that it may stand with the host of the Holy Ones,
> and that it may enter into community
> with the congregation of the Sons of Heaven.
> Thou hast allotted to man an everlasting destiny
> amidst the spirits of knowledge . . .
> (1QH 3: 21–2; trans. Vermes 1995: 198)

The inaugurated eschatology of these passages is characteristic of the liturgical worship of the Qumran community.[17] This is accompanied by a keen sense of the glorious destiny of the sectaries in contrast with that of the wicked. The latter will suffer everlasting damnation and eternal torment (1QS 4). But with regard to themselves: 'He caused some of the sons of the world to draw near (Him) . . . to be counted with Him in the com[munity of the "g]ods" as a congregation of holiness in service for eternal life and (sharing) the lot of His holy ones' (4Q181; trans. Vermes 1995: 183). One figure, however, seems called to an even more glorious destiny above that of his fellows. In a text which the editor, Maurice Baillet, called 'The Song of Michael and the Just' (4QMᵃ; Vermes 1995: 147; cf. Smith 1990; Collins 1995; Abegg 1997) the speaker claims confidently: 'my glory is incomparable, and apart from me none is exalted. None shall come against me, for I have taken

---

[17] See, too, the Songs for the Holocaust of the Sabbath (4Q400–407; Vermes 1995: 254–63).

my seat . . . in the heavens . . . I shall be reckoned with gods and established in the holy congregation.'[18] Who is this speaker? Vermes repeats Baillet's attribution without comment. Morton Smith, however, rightly argues against the speaker's being Michael (1990). It is clearly a human being who claims to have been raised to a seat in the heavens, a human being plausibly identified either with the Teacher of Righteousness himself, the founder of the Qumran community (Abegg 1997), or with 'a teacher of the first century BCE who saw himself, like Moses, enthroned in the heavens and issuing teachings and rulings of irresistible power' (Collins 1995: 55).

If the leader of the Qumran community is seen as a new Moses, it is so that he can lead others to the fulfilment of the angelic life. The theme of light is closely connected with this. In the Book of Daniel the writer had said that the wise ones, the *maskilim* or spiritual elite, 'shall shine like the brightness of the firmament. . . like the stars for ever' (12: 3). This motif, which perhaps draws on Greek ideas of astral immortality, reappears frequently in later writings. The Epistle of Enoch, echoing Daniel, says that the righteous will 'shine like the lights of heaven' (1 Enoch 104: 2; cf. 108: 12–15). In 2 Baruch, which was composed in about 100 CE, shortly after the destruction of the Qumran community, those who are justified 'will be transformed so that they will look like angels' (51: 5):

> For in the heights of the world shall they dwell,
> And they shall be made like the angels,
> And be made equal to the stars;
> And they shall be changed into whatever form they will,
> From beauty into holiness,
> And from light into the splendour of glory.
> (51: 10)

Indeed, their splendour will even exceed that of the angels (51: 12). For it is nothing short of a sharing in the glory of God. According to the Book of Parables, 'the righteous will be in the light of the sun, and the chosen in the light of eternal life' (1 Enoch 58: 3). The author of the Dead Sea Hymns Scroll expresses the confidence at the end of his work that he will 'stand [before Thee for ever] in the everlasting abode, illumined with perfect Light for ever' (1QH 18: 29; trans. Vermes 1995: 236).

Insofar as we can use the term 'deification' with regard to Apocalyptic literature and the writings of the Qumran community, it expresses the assimilation of the elect to the life of the 'gods' of the heavenly court. There is no innate divinity in any part of the human person simply waiting to be discovered. We are nothing but clay and dust (1QH 10: 6; 18: 26). But the elect, through obedience to the Covenant and participation in the cosmic liturgy,

---

[18] The translation draws on Vermes 1995 and Collins 1995.

can come to share with the angels in the glory of God. The disasters of the first and second centuries, however, were to sweep away not only the fragile communities of the Essenes but even the great Hellenistic Jewish community of Alexandria itself. The literature of Hellenistic and Enochic Judaism therefore came to be preserved by the Christian Church (which had its origin in these versions of Judaism) rather than by the Rabbinic tradition, which grew out of Pharisaism. Yet amongst the teachers of the new Rabbinic age there were a few who continued to be deeply influenced by stories of heavenly journeys and visionary experiences encountered in Apocalyptic.

4. The Rabbinic Tradition

Since Gershom Scholem's influential book on Jewish mysticism (1955), the heavenly journey of the *yored merkavah*, the seer who ascends to the vision of the throne-chariot of God, has dominated the study of that body of mystical writings of the Talmudic period known as the *Hekhalot* literature.[19] Scholem opposed those who wanted to see a Gnostic influence in Merkabah mysticism. The *yored merkavah*, in his view, was not, like the Gnostic, assimilated to the object of his contemplation but simply beheld the vision. The gulf between man and God therefore remained profound. Scholem, in turn, was opposed by Elliot Wolfson (1974), who agreed that *Hekhalot* mysticism was not Gnostic in character, but argued that Scholem was assuming a Neoplatonic idea of union with the divine as the only model of unitive spiritual experience and was therefore making too strong a divide between the mystic and God. In the *Hekhalot* model 'the enthronement of the mystic should be understood as a form of quasi-deification or angelification, in line with the older tradition expressed in apocalyptic literature concerning the transformation of individuals into angelic beings' (Wolfson 1974: 84–5). The gap between the human and the divine was thus much narrower than Scholem would allow.

More recently, Peter Schäfer has drawn attention to several hitherto neglected aspects of *Hekhalot* mysticism (1992). First, the *yored merkavah's* heavenly journey, the 'Himmelsreise der Seele', actually occupies a very small part in the literature. A more important aspect is magical adjuration. The reality of God resides in his name. Whoever knows the names of God therefore knows the Torah and, by manipulating the names, in some way has God in his power. The same is true with regard to the angels. By means of adjuration the angels are made to appear on earth and reveal their secrets to men.

---

[19] These writings, described by Gruenwald as 'short technical guides for mystics' (1988: 99), include *Hekhalot Rabbati* ('The Greater Palaces'), *Hekhalot Zutarti* ('The Lesser Palaces'), *Ma'aseh Merkavah* ('The Working of the Chariot'), *Merkavah Rabbah* ('The Great Chariot') and the Third or Hebrew Book of Enoch, properly called *Sefer Hekhalot*.

Magical adjuration thus 'allows the *yored merkavah* to dismantle the borders between heaven and earth' (Schäfer 1992: 166).[20] Secondly, the purpose of the heavenly journey is not just the vision of the Merkabah but participation in the cosmic liturgy. That is why the *yored merkavah* is set on a throne of glory. But he does not simply remain there rapt in adoration. By returning from heaven and reporting his experience to his companions, he unites angels and human beings in a single liturgy of praise.

The reasons for the appearance of this type of mysticism in the Tannaitic period (the first two centuries CE) have been the subject of some speculation. Ithamar Gruenwald sees Merkabah mysticism as a parallel development to Gnosticism, both of them drawing on Jewish Apocalypticism (with its hostility to the Jerusalemite priesthood) and both seeking to satisfy the desire of their adherents for an immediate experience of the divine through an anticipation (transitory in the case of the *yored merkavah*) of the blessed life to come. Gruenwald is not persuaded that the cultic changes brought about by the destruction of the Second Temple are sufficient to account for the appearance of Merkabah mysticism, although he does suspect that initially it may have arisen as a reaction against the prevailing eschatology (1988: 122). 'It is no mere coincidence', he suggests, 'that the first rabbinic sage about whom it is reported that he discussed matters relating to the *res mysticae* with his students (R. Johanan ben Zakkai) also symbolizes in his personality and activity the break with the priestly halakhic tradition which prevailed in Jerusalem' (1988: 141). Schäfer posits a loss of confidence in Merkabah circles in the ultimate revelation of God that was supposed to come about through the study of the Torah. More direct means were sought to induce the immediate experience of God. The Holy Name was invoked and by theurgic adjuration 'the unbearable period of time between the revelation at Sinai and the time to come is abolished' (Schäfer 1992: 163). Thus the whole of revelation, in both its realized and its future stages, 'is concentrated in the immediate experiencing by the *yored merkavah* of the simultaneously hidden and revealed God' (ibid.).

A recent contributor to the debate, Nathaniel Deutsch, identifies the central problem as that of how both Gnostics and Merkabah mystics encountered the *sacred* (1995: 75–9). He believes (*contra* Scholem) that Merkabah mysticism was in fact extremely rich in attempts to bridge the 'gulf' between the human and the divine, and that for the appreciation of these attempts a typological approach is more helpful than cut-and-dried

---

[20] This should be distinguished from Kabbalah, the other type of Jewish mysticism which emerged some centuries after Merkabah and shows evidence of Gnostic and Neoplatonic influence. In Kabbalah the central place is taken not by the 'Himmelsreise der Seele' but by 'the contemplation of the ten metaphysical *sefirot*, or ten emanations which comprise in metaphysical realms the fullness (technically the Pleroma) of the revealed Deity' (Gruenwald 1988: 133). The intention of such contemplation is to effect the reunification of the soul with its divine origin. On this see Idel 1988.

philosophical categorization (1995: 153). In Merkabah mysticism the types and images of union with God are anthropomorphic, because God and man share the same anthropomorphic form: the image of God is found in the human body, not in the soul alone. Hence the corporeal imagery of bodily ascent, of sitting on thrones, of wearing crowns, of being clothed in garments of light, which provides a vivid alternative to the intellectualizing Neoplatonic model of unitive experience.

The implications of the anthropomorphic image of God in Rabbinic Judaism are evident in the exalted status of Adam and Eve, and consequently in the potentially exalted status of the human race as a whole. An important text in this connection is Psalm 82: 6–7, which by this time is understood to have been addressed not to angels or corrupt human judges but to the entire people of the Covenant. The only Tannaitic discussion of the text is the following passage from *Sifre to Deuteronomy*: [21]

> R. Simai[22] used to say further: Both the soul and the body of creatures created from heaven are from heaven; both the soul and body of those creatures created from the earth are from earth, except for that one creature, man, whose soul is from heaven and whose body is from the earth. Therefore, if man lives by the Torah and performs the will of his Father in heaven, he is like the heavenly creatures, as it is said, 'I said, Ye are godlike beings, and all of you sons of the Most High' (Ps. 82: 6). But if he does not live by the Torah and does not perform the will of his Father in heaven, he is like the creatures of the earth, as it is said, 'Nevertheless ye shall die like Adam' (Ps. 82: 7). (*Sifre Deut.* 306; trans. Hammer)

The author, like many Rabbis, took the pre-existence of the soul for granted, but what entitles human beings to be called 'godlike beings', or literally, 'gods', is not the heavenly origin of one part of their nature; it is their observance of the Torah. Obedience to the Law confers immortality; disobedience brings death. And as with Jewish writers in Greek, immortality is properly a divine state which conforms human beings to the angelic life.

A similar emphasis is found in the Amoraic period (third to fifth centuries CE). The *amoraim* generally interpret Psalm 82: 6–7 as originally addressed to the Israelites in the desert on the occasion of their worshipping the golden calf. If they had not sinned, they would have remained immortal, for had they not eaten the manna which made them like the angels? But their sin of idolatry made them subject to death.[23] One of the earlier collections of midrashim, however, *Leviticus Rabbah*, applies verse 6 to Adam and Eve: ' "On the wings of the heights of the city" refers to the fact that the Holy

---

[21] *Sifre* (from the plural of Aramaic *sifra*, 'writing', or 'book') is a Tannaitic midrash on Numbers and Deuteronomy. It was a product of the school of R. Akiba.

[22] R. Simai was a teacher of the early second century CE.

[23] *Abod Zarah* 5a; *Midrash Rabbah* on Exod. 32: 1; 32: 7; *Midrash Rabbah* on Lev. 4: 1; *Midrash Rabbah* on Num. 7: 4; *Midrash Rabbah* on Deut. 7: 12; *Midrash Rabbah* on Eccles. 3: 16. 1. Cf. *Midrash Rabbah* on Ruth, Proem. 1; *Midrash Rabbah* on Song of Songs 1: 2, 5.

One, blessed be He, enabled them to fly, and attributed to them divine qualities, as it is said, "And I said: Ye are godlike beings" ' (Midrash Rabbah on Lev. 11: 1 and 3). The point the author makes, however, is similar. Adam and Eve were created to be like the angels, if not superior to them, but fell through sin.

The effects of the fall are reversed by the observance of the Torah, which gives the righteous a share in the holiness of God so that they can even be called by his name. More than one sage is reported to have said: 'The righteous will in time come to be called by the name of the Holy One, blessed be He' (*Babra Bathra* 75b). Morton Smith has suggested that the Roman ruler-cult might have had some influence in encouraging such deification by name (1958: 475–81). But this seems unlikely. It is not necessary to go outside the Jewish tradition to find the bestowal on the righteous of a special name incorporating the name of God.[24] Man had been created with a share in the divine glory: in one tradition the angels were actually commanded to worship Adam (*Life of Adam and Eve* 14). He fell from this eminence but even in the mainstream tradition the study of the Torah (which in Rabbinic piety is not simply a means to an end but communicates the personal experience of God) enables him to recover that share of divine glory which was lost through the Fall, that is, to assimilate himself to the life of the angels or the 'gods'.

In Merkabah circles the study of the Torah could be short-circuited; the promised assimilation to the life of the 'gods' could be anticipated. By magical adjuration and heavenly ascent the *yored merkavah* could ascend in a state of ecstasy through six magnificent halls or palaces (the *hekhalot*) to the vision of God's throne-chariot (the *merkavah*) in the seventh hall. The vision did not result in any inappropriate familiarity with God. The response evoked by the sight of his transcendent glory was rather one of prostration, fear, and worship. For the unprepared it was even dangerous. The famous story of the four Rabbis who entered Paradise to the detriment of three of them, only R. Akiba returning unharmed and in his right mind, may belong to this tradition.[25] But for those who were morally and spiritually attuned to the heavenly world, the prostration and fear brought about by contact with the sacred was accompanied by a sense of exaltation and joy.

Merkabah mysticism was nourished above all by the Enochic literature that was so central to Apocalyptic. From the period of the *amoraim* comes the *Third* or *Hebrew Book of Enoch*, which Odeberg dated to the latter half of the third century (1928: 45) but which is now thought to belong to the fifth

---

[24] Cf. Jer. 23: 6; 33: 16; Amos 9: 12. What is true of Israel may be extended to apply to the Rabbinic saint.

[25] On this see Halperin 1988: 1–37 and Schäfer 1988: 238–43. Both scholars argue that this was originally a Rabbinic parable, and only much later was taken to refer to ecstatic journeys to the third or seventh heaven in the manner of St Paul.

or sixth century. It is cast in the form of an account of R. Ishmael's ascent to the seventh heaven. On the way he is met by Enoch (now also called Metatron), who guides him to the throne of God. Enoch's glorification in this work is carried to even greater lengths than in the earlier Enochic literature. God has made him 'a garment of glory' (12: 1); he wears a crown 'like unto the light of the globe of the sun' (12: 3). These signify the transformed nature of those who are admitted into the presence of God and find parallels in the elect generally. R. Nathan ha-Bavli, for example, a *tanna* of the middle of the second century, is reported to have described the righteous in the world to come sitting with crowns on their heads and 'nourished by the effulgence of the *Shekinah*'.[26] But Enoch is associated even more closely than this with the divine glory. He says to R. Ishmael: 'And he called me THE LESSER YHWH in the presence of His heavenly household; as it is written (Exod. 23: 21): "For my name is in him"' (12: 5). The dwelling of the divine name in Enoch-Metatron makes him God's representative, even a manifestation of the *Shekinah*, so that he becomes almost a divine hypostasis to be worshipped by the angels (*3 Enoch* 14: 5). Later Rabbinic prohibition of the worship of Enoch suggests that some Jewish groups actually did treat him as a manifestation of Yahweh.[27]

Another hero who was called by the name of God was Moses. In the *Tanhuma*, which belongs to the second half of the fourth century, it is said that Moses was called a god (cf. Exod. 7: 1) because God 'apportions some of his glory to those who fear him according to his glory'.[28] A text from the Talmud says that it was as a man that Moses ascended to God on Mount Sinai and as a 'god' that he descended, his face shining, to communicate the law to the people[29] and another text that when he went up Mount Sinai, 'he ascended from human status to that of the angels'.[30] In Moses was restored the glory that had been lost by Adam. He was, as it were, the prototype of a new humanity.

Rabbinic Judaism in the Roman period struggled with a number of problems made all the more acute by the loss of the Temple sacrifices and the failure of Messianic expectations. How do you approach a transcendent God? How do you encounter the sacred? How do you attain the blessedness of the just? The answer to these in mainstream Rabbinic Judaism was through the study and observance of the Torah. Obedience to the Torah could restore in the believer the community of life with God which Adam had once possessed. Amongst the Rabbis there were some, however, who

[26] *Abot de R. Nathan* i. 8, quoted by Moore 1927: ii. 392–3; cf. Rabbah, a Babylonian *amora* of the early fourth century, *Berakhoth* 17a.

[27] On Metatron see Segal 1977: 64–73 and Gruenwald 1988: 240–8.

[28] *Tanhuma* on Num. 10: 1–2, quoted by Meeks 1968: 356.

[29] *Pesikta R. K.* 32f. 1986, quoted by Meeks 1968: 357.

[30] *Memor Marqah*, trans. Macdonald 206, quoted by Meeks 1968: 360.

looked to more esoteric means in order to overcome the divide which separated the human from the divine. To what extent Merkabah mysticism was based on personal ecstatic experience is a matter for debate. Scholem took it as axiomatic that the literature must have developed from the actual experience of ecstatic ascent. C. R. A. Morray-Jones, who accepts Scholem with modifications, sums up this position in the following words:

These traditions were associated with exegesis of Scriptural accounts of visions of the enthroned deity (Daniel 7, Isaiah 6 and, pre-eminently, Ezekiel 1) but it is probable that visionary-mystical practices were also involved. Such traditions were inherited from apocalyptic circles and enthusiastically developed by some Tannaim, but were opposed by others, mainly because the same traditions were being developed by groups whom they regarded as heretical, including the various forms of Christianity and Gnosticism. The Hekhalot writings represent the development of these traditions within rabbinism. (1992: 1)

Attractive as this is, the evidence for it is slight. The only personal account we have of a mystical ascent is that of St Paul (2 Cor. 12: 1–5) until Hai Gaon's instructions 800 years later on how to induce the experience with the aid of posture and breathing techniques (Segal 1995; cf. J. M. Scott 1997). The existence of Apocalyptic circles deeply immersed in spiritual practices in the first centuries of the Common Era is largely conjectural. A recent study of Jewish and Christian Apocalyptic regards the production of Apocalyptic works as primarily a literary endeavour (Himmelfarb 1993: 95–114). David Halperin and Peter Schäfer are equally sceptical about the experiential basis for Merkabah mysticism. In Halperin's view the Merkabah in the Tannaitic period was the subject of synagogue sermons, not the stimulus for mystical practice. It was only in Babylonia in the fourth century that 'expounding the Merkabah stopped being a matter of bible study alone' and 'took on overtones of ecstatic experience, of journeys to realms filled with strange and dangerous sights' (Halperin 1988: 37). Schäfer suggests a liturgical setting in the synagogue for the accounts of heavenly ascent: 'Like adjuration, the heavenly journey is a ritual, a liturgical act' (Schäfer 1988: 294). In his view it was the very recitation of the narratives that produced a sense of communion with God. Whether literary fiction or spiritual journals of mystical ascent, however, these texts were to have a profound influence on the esoteric tradition of Rabbinic Judaism.

5. Influence on Christianity

The Jewish paradigm is extremely rich and varied, ranging from the ethical/allegorical ascents of the Hellenists to the accounts of heavenly journeys and angelic liturgies of Enochic Judaism. Its influence on Christianity is indisputable. Not only Philo but also the apocalypses 'owe their survival almost entirely to early Christianity' (VanderKam and Adler 1996: 1). The legacy of the Hellenists to the Church may be summed up as four philosophical propositions: (i) immortality is a gift from God, not an innate property of the soul; (ii) the human soul has a kinship with the divine glory, yet the gulf between man and God is never fully transcended; (iii) through moral progress the human soul may nevertheless come to participate in some of the divine attributes; (iv) on rare occasions the human mind even in this life may attain to an ecstatic encounter with God. The legacy of Enochic Judaism, by contrast, lends itself to summary more as a series of visual images: (i) the gifted seer may ascend to the awesome vision of the throne-chariot of God; (ii) the righteous dead will share in the divine life itself, clothed in the radiant garments of glory; (iii) the elect will be assimilated to the life of the angels, worshipping God and serving him in his immediate presence. These twin legacies were to be of fundamental importance in shaping the Christian approach to deification.

Amongst Christians, the Platonizing theoreticians of the spiritual life were especially influenced by Hellenistic Judaism. Clement, Origen, and Gregory of Nyssa, in particular, each owe a direct debt to Philo (Runia 1993: 132–83, 243–61). Through their treatises and biblical commentaries, Philo's association of the creation of the human race in the image and likeness of God (Gen. 1: 26) with the Platonic doctrine of likeness to God as the goal of the moral life (*Theaet.* 176b), his presentation of Moses as the perfect man mediating between the human and the divine, and his teaching on the philosophical, ethical, and mystical ascents of the mind to God became naturalized within the Eastern Christian spiritual tradition. The influence of Enochic Judaism, appealing as it did to a less learned audience, was more diffuse. Indeed, through its Apocalyptic literature it was, along with Daniel, the source of much of the fundamental imagery not only of deification but of Christian eschatology in general (cf. VanderKam and Adler 1996: 24–6). In connection with our narrower theme, Jewish Apocalyptic and its Christian derivative popularized within the early Church the idea of dream-visions and heavenly journeys, along with the notion of the assimilation of the righteous to the angelic life and their participation in divine glory. Through the passions of the martyrs of the second and third centuries and the lives and apophthegmata of the monastic saints of the fourth and fifth centuries these motifs became part of the stock-in-trade of the perfect Christian, for in the martyr and the monk the eschatological age is already anticipated here on earth.

One of the most striking examples from this genre is Perpetua's dream of her entry into a radiant place where she beheld a boundless light and heard the angels singing the Sanctus (*Passio Perpet.* 4. 2). The martyrs are shown such things, claims the author of this earliest account of a Christian martyrdom, 'because they are no longer human beings but already angels' (*Mart. Polycarp.* 2. 3). In monastic literature assimilation of the perfect monk to the angelic life becomes a commonplace. Pachomius, for example, is credited with a heavenly visit during an ecstasy in which he witnessed Christ expounding the parables of the Gospel from a raised throne. Thereafter he was a man endowed with supernatural power. Whenever 'he repeated the words and their commentary which he had heard from the Lord's mouth, great lights would come out in his words, shooting out brilliant flashes' (*V. Pach.* 86, trans. Veilleux, cited Frankfurter 1996: 178). Pachomius and those like him were men who had seen for themselves, who spoke with personal authority of the things of heaven. In the words of David Frankfurter:

We can see the legacy of Jewish apocalyptic literature both in the character of the visions and the notion that the *living* holy man speaks from heaven itself. In this predominantly non-literate rural society the revelatory *text* has been replaced by the revelatory *voice*—indeed often under the same heroic name as the legendary seers of apocalypses: Elijah, Enoch, Daniel, Isaiah, Ezekiel, Abraham.   (1996: 175)

And beyond the revelatory *voice* of the holy man lay simply his revelatory *appearance*. A number of the desert fathers were seen transfigured by a radiant light, inspiring fear and awe in the beholder.[31] Merely to have beheld these men was to have encountered the divine. It is no coincidence that in the later Byzantine period the teachers and transmitters of the doctrine of deification were the hesychastic monks of Mount Athos, whose spiritual practices were directed specifically towards attaining the vision of the divine light.

---

[31] For example, Pambo (*Apoph. Pat.* Pambo 12), Sisoes (*Apoph. Pat.* Sisoes 14), Silvanus (*Apoph. Pat.* Pambo 12), Joseph of Panephysis (*Apoph. Pat.* Joseph Pan. 7), and Onnuphrius (*V. Onnuphrii* 20).

4

The Earliest Christian Model

Participatory Union with Christ

1. Pauline Christianity

Paul is a unique figure. As a Diaspora Jew from a Romanized family, who had received a good Greek education yet was proud of his Jewishness and knew the Septuagint well, he resembles Philo.[1] But in around 15 CE, when he was about twenty, he moved from Tarsus to Jerusalem, where he joined a circle of Pharisees, studying, according to Luke, under the great Rabbi Gamaliel (Acts 22: 3).[2] For the next fifteen years or so he applied himself zealously to acquiring a detailed knowledge of the Torah, both written and oral. At some stage he also conceived a strong antipathy to the new sect of 'Christians' or 'Messianists'.

The turning-point in his life came in about 33 CE when, for some unknown reason,[3] he went to Damascus. There the appearance to him in a vision of the risen Christ produced in him a complete *volte-face*. The enemy of Christ became his most ardent propagandist. From that time Paul devoted himself to missionary work, first in the client kingdom of the Nabataean Arabs,[4] and then in the eastern provinces of the Roman empire proper. Although he continued to regard himself as a devout Jew faithful to the covenant,[5] his conviction that the Torah could only be interpreted correctly in the light of Christ,[6] and that Christ was the new Adam who had

---

[1] Not only in his background but also in some aspects of his scriptural exegesis. See Chadwick 1965.

[2] My sketch of Paul's early life is based on the reconstruction by Jerome Murphy-O'Connor (1996).

[3] Murphy-O'Connor discounts Luke's version of the circumstances (Acts 9: 1–2) on the grounds of historical implausibility (1996: 65–70).

[4] Murphy-O'Connor presents a persuasive argument (1996: 81–5) for not regarding Paul's period in Arabia as a withdrawal for quiet reflection.

[5] Bockmuehl points out that nowhere does Paul characterize his Damascus experience as a 'conversion', though some of his contemporaries may have viewed it differently (1990: 130–2).

[6] Bockmuehl puts it well when he says that Christ became for Paul the 'hermeneutical key' or 'ground rule' 'for the understanding of all revelation: whether in the gospel, in Scripture, or in creation' (1990: 153).

re-established an authentic humanity for the benefit of the whole human race, led him from the outset to direct his efforts towards the Gentiles.

It is difficult to categorize the Christian communities that Paul founded in the cities of the eastern Mediterranean. The models available from the contemporary Graeco-Roman world include the private household, the voluntary cultic association, the Jewish synagogue and the philosophical or rhetorical school (Meeks 1983: 75–84). Pauline groups certainly met in private houses – the ἐκκλησία κατ᾽ οἶκον of so-and-so was the fundamental unit.[7] With their initiatory rite and ritual meal they operated like voluntary associations.[8] They had certain features in common with the Jewish communities in their cities, although they did not adopt the terminology and offices of the synagogue. In many respects they were also like the circles that gathered around charismatic teachers. Paul does not appear to have run a formal *didaskaleion* in the manner of Valentinus or Justin a century later, but it is reported by Luke that when faced with expulsion from the synagogue at Ephesus, Paul withdrew with his group and continued his teaching for two years in the lecture-hall of a certain Tyrannus (Acts 19: 9).[9] For their social composition the Pauline groups drew on a wide cross-section of society. They may not have included the distinguished citizens and philosophers who at about the same time were attending the lectures of Musonius Rufus, the Stoic moralist, at his school in Rome, but neither were they the nonentities that Paul for rhetorical effect made them out to be (cf. 1 Cor. 1: 27–8). Among their number in Corinth was the patroness (προστάτις) Phoebe, the synagogue leader (ἀρχισυνάγωγος) Crispus, and the municipal treasurer (οἰκονόμος τῆς πόλεως) Erastus.[10] Such 'upwardly mobile' people were probably not uncommon in early Christian circles. In Rome, for example, some of Paul's people were members of the 'household of Caesar' (Phil. 4: 22), slaves or freedmen no doubt, but very likely important figures in the administration of the empire.

Although Paul may originally have felt that he could leave the communities he had founded to the care of the Spirit while he moved on to new urban centres, problems soon arose which required his intervention either in person or through letters of instruction and admonition. All Paul's writings are occasional. But although he responds to particular situations, he does not develop his ideas haphazardly. There is an underlying coherence in the letters which derives from the strongly christological and soteriological orientation

---

[7] Meeks 1983: 75, citing H. Gülzow, 'Die sozialen Gegebenheiten der altchristlichen Mission', in H. Frohnes and U. W. Knorr (eds), *Kirchengeschichte als Missionsgeschichte*, vol. i, 1974, 198.

[8] Cf. the cult association of the Iobacchi, Lane Fox 1986: 85–8.

[9] Meeks 1983: 82. Paul's letters show familiarity with the style and methods of professional rhetoricians; see Malherbe 1989.

[10] Rom. 16: 2, 24; Acts 18: 8. On the prosopography of Paul's communities see Meeks 1983: 55–63. A Latin inscription found at Corinth honouring an aedile named Erastus may refer to Paul's Erastus.

of his thinking. A fundamental theme that reflects this coherence is that of participatory union with Christ.[11]

The striking parallel Paul draws between Adam and Christ in Romans and 1 Corinthians has led some New Testament scholars to speak of an Adamic christology. Adam was a type of Christ (Rom. 5: 14), Christ the second Adam (1 Cor. 15: 45), in the sense that what was wrought by each had consequences for the entire human race. Solidarity in Adam is mirrored by solidarity in Christ, death 'in Adam' balanced against life 'in Christ' (1 Cor. 15: 22, 45). Christ inaugurated a new beginning for humankind, a new mode of human existence: 'if anyone is in Christ, he is a new creation' (2 Cor. 5: 17).

Another typological comparison drawn by Paul, focusing this time on inclusivity in terms of the covenant rather than our common humanity, is that between Christ and Abraham. In the letter to the Galatians he offers an exegesis of the promise given in Genesis to Abraham (Gen. 12: 7). Abraham was reckoned righteous through his faith in God, thus proving that the Law was not indispensable. God then made a promise that the land would be given to his seed (*sperma*). Paul lays great emphasis on the singular number of *sperma*. That single descendant who was to be the recipient of the divine promise was Christ. Those who would benefit from the promise can now do so through Christ. For Christ is not isolated from those who believe in him. 'In Christ', the unique son, all believers are 'sons of God' by faith. They have 'put on' Christ through baptism. They have become 'one in Christ Jesus' and share through him in the promise made to Abraham (Gal. 3: 26–9).

The first to refer to the eschatological community as 'sons of the living God' was the eighth-century prophet, Hosea (Hos. 1: 10). The phrase expresses the intimacy with God enjoyed by members of the restored covenant relationship. Paul, although the first Jewish writer to use the term 'adoption' (υἱοθεσία), builds on these biblical foundations.[12] Baptism into Christ is a new Exodus leading the people of God out of slavery to demonic powers and into the freedom of the heir to the promises that were made to Abraham and David. By adoption they become fellow-sons and fellow-heirs with Christ and consequently can address God as 'Abba, Father!'

When Paul returns to the same image in Romans 8: 12–17, he brings to it some further insights. The agent of adoption is the Spirit, who is called the spirit of adoption in contrast with the spirit of slavery, and the joy of adoption is tempered by a contrast between present suffering and eschatological fulfilment. Participation in Christ is shown to have successive

---

[11] The theme of participatory union in Paul was first given prominence by Deissmann 1957 (=1926) and Schweitzer 1957 (=1931) and its implications have been further drawn out by Bouttier 1966 (= 1962), Sanders 1977 and 1991, and Ziesler 1990. Its soteriological significance, however, has been denied or played down by Bultmann (1952), Conzelmann (1969), and Bornkamm (1971), for a critique of whose views see Sanders 1977: 453–4.

[12] J. M. Scott (1992) has shown that Paul's teaching on adoption owes nothing (apart from the word itself) to the Graeco-Roman background.

stages: liberation from demonic powers, sharing in the sufferings of Christ, and finally sharing in his glory (Scott 1992: 221–66). This is brought out a little further on where Paul says: 'We know that the whole creation has been groaning in travail together until now; and not only the creation but we ourselves, who have the firstfruits of the Spirit, groan inwardly as we wait for adoption as sons, the redemption of our bodies' (Rom. 8: 22–3). Believers are not only adopted sons but heirs too. The sonship that they possess is only a firstfruit of the Spirit. For they share in the vanity and corruption to which the whole of creation is subject. The full manifestation of their sonship will only take place at the resurrection, when they will be liberated from vanity and corruption. The sonship of believers is therefore both a present reality and a future hope.

The aspect of future hope is especially prominent in 1 Corinthians 15: 42–58, where Paul sets out the destiny of the believer with poetic power and intensity. In response to the question: 'How is the resurrection possible after the body has dissolved in the grave?' he says that its dissolution, far from being a difficulty, is necessary before the resurrected body can be brought into being. The earthly body contributes nothing. This is underlined by the total contrast between the first Adam and the last, the former becoming 'a living soul' (ψυχὴν ζῶσαν) 'from the dust of the earth', the latter 'a life-giving spirit' (πνεῦμα ζωοποιοῦν) 'from heaven'. If believers take their character from the last Adam, they too 'shall bear the image of the heavenly'. The next question is: 'What kind of body will we have?' The answer is a body like that of Christ. 'A body conditioned by ψυχή, derived from Adam, will be transformed into a body conditioned by πνεῦμα, derived from Christ' (Robertson and Plummer 1914: 374). Finally, in reply to the question: 'What will happen to those who are still alive at the Second Coming?' Paul asserts that the transition from *psychikon* to *pneumatikon* will be instantaneous and radical (cf. 1 Thess. 4: 13–17). Elsewhere Paul speaks of what is mortal being 'swallowed up' by life, suggesting vividly the irresistible power of life-in-itself (2 Cor. 5: 4). Here he uses the metaphor (derived from the baptismal rite) of putting on clothes, what is mortal 'putting on' immortality and incorruption in a way that implies the continuity of the human person in spite of the far-reaching effects of the change experienced.

Paul speaks with confidence about the details of the eschatological life. Did he have access to Jewish esoteric traditions? The Gnostics certainly thought so.[13] And Paul's account of his ascent to the third heaven (2 Cor. 12: 2–4) lends support to their claims.[14] But Paul only refers to his own experi-

---

[13] Scott 1997: 107; Pagels 1975; Stroumsa 1996: 4–5, 38, 68, 70.

[14] The first to draw attention to a possible connection between Paul and the Merkabah tradition was Scholem 1960: 14–19. Modern scholarship is divided, opinion ranging from the very cautious (Schäfer 1986) to the confident assertion that Paul was a Merkabah mystic (Scott 1997: 118). For a review of the debate see Scott 1997: 106–9.

ence, in an extreme situation, to trump his opponents' claim to be recipients of 'visions and revelations of the Lord' (2 Cor. 12: 1). It is not something he would have used as a normal pastoral strategy to establish his credentials as an apostle and teacher. Markus Bockmuehl is right to conclude, without denying its reality, that its place was in Paul's private spiritual life (1990: 175–7). But even if it does not prove that Paul was 'the revelatory mediator of a Merkabah experience', mediating 'the glory of God in the midst of the Corinthians' (*pace* Scott 1997: 118), it does suggest that in hinting that he had glimpsed the beatitude of the saints and shared in the angelic worship of heaven, Paul was not unaware of the traditions of Qumran (cf. Fitzmyer 1999).

In the letters issued in Paul's name by members of his circle there is a shift of emphasis. We find here the characteristically Pauline word 'adoption' (Eph. 1: 5), the adoption of believers as sons through Jesus Christ being part of God's plan 'to sum up (ἀνακεφαλαιώσασθαι) all things in Christ' (Eph. 1: 10). But although believers are incorporated into Christ by baptism, Christ is the head of the body rather than the body itself (Eph. 1: 22; 4: 15; 5: 23; Col. 1: 18). This grows naturally out of Paul's hierarchal image of Christ as the head of every man just as a man is a woman's head (1 Cor. 11: 3; cf. Eph. 5: 23), but nevertheless points to a new perspective. Christ as the head of the body clarifies the status of the believer who is 'in Christ' as one who is under the power and authority of Christ. But Christ does not exercise power and authority for its own sake. He gives his adopted brothers and sisters free access (παρρησία) to the Father (Eph. 3: 12). Paul had urged his spiritual children to imitate Christ through him (1 Cor. 4: 16; 11: 1; 1 Thess. 1: 6); the author of Ephesians says boldly, 'Be imitators of God' (5: 1). Christ takes them right to the fountainhead. Through him they are to be 'filled with all the fullness of God' (Eph. 3: 19). That is not to say that the imitation of God can be undertaken easily. Although the new humanity created after the likeness of God has been put on and salvation is assured,[15] there is still need for development and growth. The new humanity needs nurturing; it is to be built up through the work of the different orders of ministry until it reaches the full stature of Christ, until it grows into him who is the head of the body (Eph. 4: 11–14). The final fulfilment is set in an eschatological future, which no longer seems to have the same urgency as in Paul's undisputed letters. The life of believers is now 'hid with Christ in God' (Col. 3: 3). When Christ appears, they will appear with him in glory (Col. 3: 4). This glory is represented in traditional Apocalyptic imagery. Christ has risen through the spheres (Eph. 4: 10) and is now seated at the right hand of God (Eph. 1: 20; Col. 3: 1). Those who have been renewed in Christ will be enthroned with him, or rather, have already been enthroned with him (Eph. 2: 6).

---

[15] The perfect tense of 'saved' (σεσωσμένοι) in Eph. 2: 5 is not found in the genuine letters of Paul.

Both in the genuinely Pauline letters and in those of his circle it is evident that a real change is brought about by participation in the new creation (Sanders 1991: 74). This is not a purely subjective matter, to be located in the Christian's self-understanding, as Bultmann (1952: 268–9) and Conzelmann (1969: 208–10) have maintained. Paul's exhortations against idolatry and sexual immorality, for example, are not based simply on the fact that they are transgressions against the moral law. As transgressions they represent a participatory union which is in conflict with the union with Christ that comes through participating in his body and blood (cf. 1 Cor. 10: 1–7) (Sanders 1977: 454–6). Participatory union is real, not just a figure of speech, although the precise category of reality is difficult to determine.[16] In Ziesler's words, 'Christ is still an individual and there is no confusion of identity between Him and those who are in Him, but because He is a power-centre He can no longer be thought of in isolation from His people' (1990: 64). With Christ as their power-centre Christians really are transformed as they are renewed inwardly (2 Cor. 4: 16), really do advance in union with Christ from one glory to another (2 Cor. 3: 18).

This dynamic relationship with Christ is expressed in a variety of images. 'In Christ' all shall be made alive (1 Cor. 15: 22) and sanctified (1 Cor. 1: 2), shall become a new creation (2 Cor. 5: 17), and have eternal life (Rom. 6: 23). Alternatively, Christ must be formed 'in us' (Gal. 4: 19), and it is only when Christ is within us that our spirits are alive (Rom. 8: 10). In a particularly striking image Paul sees himself as a woman in labour struggling to bring forth his spiritual children until Christ is formed in them (Gal. 4: 19; cf. 1 Cor. 4: 15; Philem. 10). Believers are sons of God by adoption (Rom. 8: 14–15; Gal. 4: 5; cf. Eph. 1: 5). They are 'heirs of God and fellow-heirs with Christ' (Rom. 8: 17; Gal. 3: 29; cf. Eph. 1: 14. They 'put on' Christ in baptism, clothing themselves in life and incorruption (Rom. 13: 14; 1 Cor. 15: 53; Gal. 3: 27; cf. Eph. 4: 24 and Col. 3: 10). They become one body, the body of Christ, because they share in the one eucharistic bread (1 Cor. 10: 17). As Sanders has said, 'the very diversity of the terminology helps to show how the general conception of participation permeated his thought' (1977: 456).

To what extent, then, can we speak of a doctrine of deification already present in Paul? Albert Schweitzer, in spite of his insistence that 'the fundamental conception of the Pauline mysticism is that the Elect and Christ partake of the same corporeity' (1957: 121), was quite sure that the conception of deification had no place in Pauline teaching, rightly pointing out that while Paul stresses the union of the believer with Christ, he 'never speaks of being one with God' (1957: 3, 26). Several writers on deification have

---

[16] D. E. H. Whiteley has suggested that the term 'secondary literal sense' might be used to express a union with Christ that is in between the magical and the metaphysical (1964: 132–3).

disagreed.[17] But there are strong arguments on Schweitzer's side. First, Christ is not called 'God' unequivocally before the second century. Until that step is taken, union with Christ is not the same as union with God. Secondly, Paul did not isolate 'participation' for special consideration. He did not have a fixed technical term for participatory union with Christ, the various expressions which he uses – 'in Christ', 'with Christ', 'Christ in us', 'sons of God' and so on – reflecting different aspects of that union or being utilized in different contexts. Thirdly, we should not forget that these expressions are metaphorical images. 'Deification' as a theological term only emerges when the Pauline metaphors are re-expressed in metaphysical language. Paul simply gives us a hint of what is to come in the writings of Clement, Origen, and their successors.

Imitation is less important than participatory union in Paul. In his undisputed letters it is mostly linked with obedience.[18] When he says, 'Be imitators of me as I am of Christ' (1 Cor. 11: 1), Paul is admonishing his hearers as their 'father' (cf. 1 Cor. 4: 15–16), calling on them to submit to his authority. Imitation is also connected with copying an example. Believers imitate Paul and the Lord by sharing in suffering and thus becoming themselves a model ($\tau \acute{\upsilon} \pi o \nu$) of discipleship (1 Thess. 1: 6; 2: 14). In Ephesians, alongside the idea of following an example, there is a further, ethical emphasis. Believers are exhorted to be 'imitators of God' in a moral sense, to forgive one another as God in Christ forgave them (Eph. 5: 1). Ignatius of Antioch takes up the expression of Ephesians, 'be imitators of God' but links imitation with sacrificial discipleship more in the manner of Paul himself (cf. section 4, below). It is only towards the end of the second century that 'imitation' becomes a mystical term in Christian usage when Clement of Alexandria, guided by Philo, takes the momentous step of connecting the imitation of God with the Platonic goal of attaining likeness to God as far as humanly possible (*Theaetetus* 176b).

2. Jewish Christianity

The familiarity of the author of Hebrews with Jewish worship has led many commentators to suppose that his addressees were Christians with a Jewish background, but attempts to connect them specifically with the Hellenistic Judaism of Philo or the Enochic Judaism of Qumran have not been convincing (Attridge 1989: 28–9). The most we can say is that the Jewish heritage of Christianity is more pronounced in the author of Hebrews than in any other New Testament writer.

---

[17] e.g. Lattey 1916: 257; Theodorou 1956: 21; and Bilaniuk 1973: 347.
[18] On Paul's relationship to the philosophical idea of imitation see Malherbe 1989, esp. 56–8.

Hebrews was not ascribed to Paul until the end of the second century. It is easy to see why the ascription was made, for there are a number of similarities with Pauline thought, among which is the designation of believers as 'sons of God' and 'partakers of Christ'. God is described as 'bringing many sons to glory' (2: 10), and believers are designated 'Christ's brethren', 'for he who sanctifies and those who are sanctified have all one origin' (2: 11). Yet Christ is greater than his brethren, for they are also 'the children that God has given' him (2: 13). The author then elucidates the nature of Christ's solidarity with the human race. First Christ 'partook of the same nature' as men (παραπλησίως μετέσχεν τῶν αὐτῶν) (2: 14), that is, flesh and blood, so as to be able to conquer death and the devil and become a high priest in expiation of the sins of the people, setting himself alongside those who are tempted in order to help them. Believers in turn participate in Christ through becoming 'sharers in a heavenly calling' (κλήσεως ἐπουρανίου μέτοχοι) (3: 1), which makes them God's house, over which the Father has set his Son. It is this that enables us to be 'partakers of Christ' (μέτοχοι τοῦ Χριστοῦ) 'if only we hold our first confidence firm to the end' (3: 14).

Our participation in Christ thus begins when we become members of his household and share in his destiny, entering into the heavenly sanctuary. The emphasis differs from what we find in Paul. To be a son sets the believer alongside Christ rather than 'in him'. Christ is the brother who is also the leader, the pioneer of salvation (ἀρχηγὸς τῆς σωτηρίας) (2: 10), the high priest of blessings to come (9: 11), the mediator of the new covenant (9: 15) and 'the source of eternal salvation for all who obey him' (5: 9), not the saviour in whom we are 'clothed', with whose life we actually live (Gal. 2: 20). According to Hebrews, participating in Christ as a son brings one into the Father's presence. A comparable use of μετέχω and related words is also found in phrases expressing the reception of a share of milk (ὁ μετέχων γάλακτος) (5: 13), of the Holy Spirit at baptism (μετόχους γενηθέντας Πνεύματος Ἁγίου) (6: 14) – which is to taste of the heavenly gift – and of the blessings of God (μεταλαμβάνει εὐλογίας ἀπὸ τοῦ θεοῦ) (6: 7). For the author of Hebrews, to participate in something means having access to a source. To participate in Christ is therefore to have access through him to the Father, the ultimate source of salvation and sanctification.[19]

---

[19] J. Moffat, like many older commentators, gives an inadequate interpretation of μέτοχοι τοῦ Χριστοῦ when he says that the author 'means no more than their membership in the household of God over which Christ presides' (1924: liv–lv). H. W. Attridge recognizes the metaphysical connotations: 'The basic structure of the comment replicates that of 3: 6, although the emphasis on the conditional quality of the addressees' relationship to Christ is stressed more firmly. That relationship is described not in terms of the metaphor of God's house, but with the suggestive language of "participants" (μέτοχοι) in Christ. That this participation is a reality is also more strongly affirmed in the note that "we have become" (γεγόναμεν) partakers, at the same time that its conditional quality is reemphasized. The notion of participation in Christ recalls the Pauline and deutero-Pauline image of the church as the body, although the philosophical conceptuality is distinctive' (1989: 117–18).

Hebrews develops the Pauline idea of sonship in the context of an over-riding liturgical imagery. Christ mediates between man and God. He entered the heavenly sanctuary in his human nature and made expiation for our sins. The result is παρρησία, a key expression in the Epistle (3: 6; 4: 16; 10: 19; 10: 35). Being a son implies our solidarity with Christ and our access, through him and the expiation made by him, to the Father. This is what it means to be a 'partaker of Christ' – a different concept from the Pauline participatory union with Christ which transforms believers and makes them like him.

3. Johannine Christianity

Ephesus, which may have been the centre of a Pauline 'school',[20] is also the traditional home of the circle which at the end of the first century produced the Fourth Gospel and the Epistles of John. The Johannine community is more anonymous and less easy to profile than the Pauline groups. Only in the third Epistle, where the 'presbyter' writes to Gaius, commending Demetrius and complaining of the attitude of Diotrephes, are we able to put names to any of its members. But from a careful analysis of the Johannine documents it is possible to reconstruct, as R. E. Brown has done (1979), a plausible history of the community.

The pre-Gospel community had strong Palestinian connections rooted in the eyewitness testimony of the Beloved Disciple. The Gospel was written in about 90 CE, when the community had been expelled from the synagogues (John 9: 22), 'the Jews' were its opponents, and 'the world' stood for those who preferred darkness to light. The divided Johannine community por-trayed in the Epistles belongs to a third stage. There were now two groups who were interpreting the christology and ethics of the Gospel differently. The secessionists drew on the Fourth Gospel's high christology, with its emphasis on the pre-existence of God's Son. They were convinced they were sinless and already enjoyed intimacy with God. As a corrective, the author of 1 John stresses the need for ethical behaviour and for following the teaching of the earthly Jesus. His pessimistic remark that the world is paying heed to his opponents (1 John 4: 5) suggests that the secessionists were enjoying greater success. Finally the Johannine community was dis-solved. The secessionists moved in the direction of Gnosticism, taking the Fourth Gospel with them, while the remainder was absorbed into the Great Church.

The merit of such a reconstruction is that it accounts for the subsequent history of the Fourth Gospel. With the corrective of 1 John, the Gospel was accepted early into the canon of the New Testament, but it is not much

---

[20] First suggested by Conzelmann (1965); cf. Meeks 1983: 82.

referred to by proto-orthodox writers. The Gnostics make more explicit use of it: the earliest commentary we know is by the Valentinian Heracleon. It was only in the third century, when Heracleon was answered by Origen, that the Fourth Gospel was reclaimed by the Great Church.[21]

The destiny of the Christian as represented in the Fourth Gospel has features which encourage the further development of the believer's exalted status as we encounter it amongst the secessionists of 1 John. In his valedictory prayer Jesus promises his unity with the Father to those who believe in him, that they might receive his glory and be 'brought to perfection as one' (John 17: 22–3). This unity originates in the Father and the Son and flows down from them to believers. Two characteristic motifs running right through the Gospel which express this gift of unity with God are those of life and light.

In the synoptic Gospels the righteous expect to inherit eternal life in the future. In John all who believe in Christ possess it here and now (John 3: 16). This is because Jesus Christ not only has this life from the Father (John 5: 26); he actually *is* life (John 11: 25; 14: 6; 1 John 1: 2; 5: 11; Rev. 1: 18). All who participate in him by believing in him and sharing in baptism (John 3: 15) and the Eucharist (John 6: 54) participate in eternal life: 'He who has the Son has life' (1 John 5: 12; cf. John 3: 36). Possessing a supernatural life which originates in the Father and was made manifest by the Son (1 John 1: 2) is analogous to children receiving biological life from their earthly father (cf. John 1: 13). Accordingly, believers are called 'children of God'. Unlike Paul, John never calls them 'sons of God'. The phrase υἱὸς τοῦ θεοῦ is reserved for the unique Son; believers are τέκνα τοῦ θεοῦ – perhaps John's equivalent to the distinction between Son and sons which Paul expresses by his image of adoption. These children of God are a new spiritual creation. As God breathed natural life into Adam's nostrils when he was created from the dust of the earth (Gen. 2: 7), so Christ imparted supernatural life to his disciples when he breathed on them and said: 'Receive the Holy Spirit' (John 20: 22). Through the Spirit given by the glorified Christ believers already possess an eternal life which death cannot destroy. Even more emphatically than Paul, John teaches an eschatology that has already been inaugurated. A future fulfilment still awaits believers at the resurrection, but John's treatment of it is cursory and conventional (John 5: 28–9). His personal conviction is that we enjoy the fullness of life, even the fullness of the knowledge of God, *now*: 'He who has seen me has seen the Father' (John 14: 9).

John associates life with light (John 1: 4; 8: 12). Again, Jesus Christ does not just resemble light; He *is* light (John 8: 12; cf. 1: 7; 3: 19). Light is a

---

[21] On the Gnostic use of John see Pagels 1973. The first orthodox writer generally recognized to have quoted John is Theophilus of Antioch, but both Ignatius and Justin appear to have been familiar with Johannine themes.

particularly powerful image for John's purposes. It was the first product of God, created on the first day of the week (Gen. 1: 3). It provides the necessary conditions for life. It was already established in the Old Testament (and even more strongly in the writings of the Qumran community) as a symbol of good in contrast with the darkness of evil. Just as participation through faith and the sacraments in the life of God makes believers 'children of God', so participation in the light of God makes them 'sons of Light' (John 12: 36). Possession of the light is associated, moreover, with knowledge and vision. This is connected by the author of 1 John with the future aspect of Johannine eschatology that is neglected by the secessionists: 'Beloved, we are God's children now; it does not yet appear what we shall be, but we know that when he appears we shall be like him, for we shall see him as he is' (1 John 3: 2). It is not certain whether our being like him is consequent to the vision or a precondition for it, but what is clear is the a fortiori argument that if we have already been raised to the status of 'children of God', 'how much greater transforming power shall there be in the vision of Him as He is, no longer veiled by the conditions of earthly life!' (Brooke 1912: 83).

The author of 1 John is correcting a one-sided Johannine spirituality that minimizes the significance of the earthly life of Jesus. The eschatological state of the Christian may have already been inaugurated but it has not yet been consummated. Believers may be 'children of God' and 'sons of light'. They may have received the Spirit (John 20: 22) and may enjoy a share of the fullness of God (John 1: 16). But if they give credence to those who deny that Christ came in the flesh or that his death has any salvific meaning (1 John 4: 2; 5: 6), if they believe that they have already attained perfection (1 John 1: 8), if they do not put the commandment of love into practice in their moral conduct (1 John 2: 3; 2: 9; 3: 4), they do not possess eternal life (1 John 5: 11; 5: 20). The views criticized by the author of 1 John clearly tend towards a docetic christology and a 'divine spark' anthropology characteristic of Gnostic forms of Christianity. It is not surprising that the Fourth Gospel found an appreciative readership amongst the Valentinians and others like them.[22]

4. Ignatius of Antioch

A decade or so after the Johannine community's dissolution, Ignatius of Antioch passed through the province of Asia on his way under military

---

[22] The Nag Hammadi Library testifies to the popularity of John in Gnostic circles, e.g. *The Tripartite Tractate*, *The Apocryphon of John* (in two versions) and the *Trimorphic Protenoia*, all of which probably belong to the mid-second century CE.

escort to martyrdom in Rome. Modelling himself on Paul,[23] he wrote five letters to the churches of Asia on various theological and pastoral issues, one to Polycarp of Smyrna on the role of the bishop, and one to the church of Rome to prepare it for his arrival and prevent it from using its influence to thwart his longing for a martyr's death. His letters have style and fervour. Although in the highly mannered rhetorical tradition known as 'Asianism', they are intensely personal. Ignatius was in a delicate position. He was bishop of Antioch but seems to have had a difficult relationship with an important faction of the Antiochene church. He may even have lost control of the church, and suffered humiliation as a consequence (Schoedel 1985: 10). His letters appeal for recognition and support in his struggle to resolve the situation at Antioch. With the re-establishment of peace in his church, his anxieties subside (*Polyc.* 7. 1).[24] He could now go forward to his martyrdom confident that it would seal and consummate his episcopate.

The spiritual themes of the letters – participation in God, the Eucharist, martyrdom, unity, attaining God, imitation – have been taken to imply a major departure from biblical eschatology, the replacement, under Gnostic influence, of the resurrection of the faithful by the Hellenistic ascent of the soul to immortality.[25] But throughout Ignatius' letters the ecclesiastical dimension is paramount. Against the individualism of docetic 'false teachers' he stresses the need to show love for widows and orphans and those in distress (*Smyrn.* 6. 2; *Polyc.* 4. 1). True Christians are not those who follow their own will but those who are united with their fellow worshippers under the leadership of their bishop (*Eph.* 5. 1 to 6. 1). Their final state is not as bodiless spirits but as participants in the resurrection with Christ (*Smyrn.* 2). If the letters are thought to have a mystical tone, this comes from the intensity which Ignatius' impending martyrdom lends to his arguments. Yet he is more interested in common Christian solidarity than his personal destiny.

The keynote of all that Ignatius writes is unity. The unity of the Church, which implies obedience to the bishop, is one of the fundamental marks of authentic Christianity (*Philad.* 3). Because obedience to the bishop is equivalent to obedience to God, Ignatius can say that the union which God offers is himself (*Trall.* 11. 2). This expression has been thought to indicate a conception of the Church as something resembling the Gnostic divine pleroma (Schlier 1929: 90). But comparison with similar passages shows that Ignatius is not identifying union with the Church with union with God. The emphasis is rather on the obedience to the Church's teachers that gives one access to

[23] *Rom.* 6. 3, 9. 2, cf. 1 Cor. 4: 16; 11: 1; 15: 8. Ignatius, however, is closer than Paul to Hellenistic epistolary models (Schoedel 1985: 7, 35).

[24] Very likely because he had heard that hostility between rival factions of Christians at Antioch had ceased. Trevett suggests that Ignatius might have given himself up voluntarily to the authorities to bring about such a peace (1992: 59–66).

[25] Preiss 1938; cf. Tinsley 1957 and especially Swartley 1973.

God. In one image the bishop presides on the model of God, with the presbyters seated on the model of the college of Apostles (*Magn.* 6. 1).[26] In another the presbyterate is seen as attuned to the bishop like the strings of a (twelve-stringed) cithara, with the faithful, all singing with one voice, forming the chorus (*Eph.* 4. 1). The true Christian, then, is in perfect concord and harmony with the Church gathered round the bishop.

Such unity leads to participation in God (*Eph.* 4. 2). In keeping with his readiness to call Christ God without any qualification (*Eph.* 7. 2; *Smyrn.* 1. 1; *Polyc.* 8. 2), Ignatius goes further than any New Testament author in speaking of the believer's intimacy with God. Christians are 'God-bearers' (*Eph.* 9. 2) and 'God-runners' (*Philad.* 2. 2). They 'participate in God' (*Eph.* 4. 2), 'are wholly of God' (*Eph.* 8. 1) 'are full of God' (*Magn.* 14. 1) and 'have God in themselves' (*Rom.* 6. 3). These phrases, however, imply only that their subjects are authentic Christians obedient to the will of God as expressed by the bishop. They do not carry the sense of a warm relationship with a personal God. Their mystic possibilities, as Schoedel says, are not exploited by Ignatius (1985: 19).

Where we do find personal warmth and fervour is in passages expressing the imitation and the attainment of God, particularly where Ignatius applies these terms to himself (Swartley 1973: 98–103; Schoedel 1985: 28–31). Instances of the latter, however, are rare. It is mostly the recipients of the letters, not the author himself, who are called imitators of God. The Ephesians are such (*Eph.* 1. 1) because they display love in sending a delegation led by bishop Onesimus to greet Ignatius on his arrival in Smyrna. The Trallians are also 'imitators of God' because they have acted similarly under their bishop, Polybius (*Trall.* 1. 2). Moreover, the Ephesians are exhorted to be imitators of God (i.e. Christ) in their patient endurance of wrongs (*Eph.* 10. 3), while the Philadelphians are urged to be imitators of Jesus Christ in their love of union and obedience to the bishop (*Philad.* 7. 2). Only on one occasion does Ignatius apply the theme of imitation to himself, when he beseeches the Roman church to allow him to be an imitator of the suffering of his God (*Rom.* 6. 3). This does not indicate an individualistic preoccupation with his own salvation. He longs to exemplify in his own life the obedience to Christ and the acceptance of suffering which he recommends to other Christians. Indeed, in his diffidence he sees others as already 'imitators of God' (*Eph.* 1. 2) while he himself will only become an imitator through his martyrdom.[27]

---

[26] This passage is sometimes cited as evidence of an ecclesiology that sees the Church on earth as representing the order of heaven. The archetype for perfect ecclesial relations, however, is not the heavenly communion of saints but the historical example of the perfect obedience to God exhibited by Christ and the Apostles during their life on earth. As Schoedel observes, Ignatius treats the Apostles 'basically as figures from the past', rather than members of some heavenly hierarchy (1985: 113).

[27] It is noteworthy that Ignatius only once refers to himself as a bishop (*Rom.* 9. 1). It was in virtue of his coming martyrdom that he could speak with authority to churches other than his own.

The same diffidence may be observed in connection with attaining God. This ultimate spiritual fulfilment is not a present reality for the Christian but a future possibility, a communion with God which is realized at the moment of death. Every Christian is thought to attain God as a reward for endurance (*Smyrn.* 9. 2). But Ignatius does not take his own salvation for granted. He asks for the prayers of the Magnesians that he may attain God (*Magn.* 14). Such an achievement is the fruit of true discipleship (*Eph.* 10. 1), a discipleship which he hopes to consummate in the arena.

Even those who are inclined to maximize Ignatius' mystical side do not consider him a proponent of deification (Corwin 1960: 265–7). Certainly he has little in common with the Platonizing intellectuals of Alexandria. He places himself in the tradition of Paul, but there are also discontinuities with Pauline thought. He lacks, for example, Paul's sense of participatory union with Christ; nor do we find that characteristically Pauline phrase, 'in Christ'. Yet he does envisage a transformation that is brought about in the believer through his being a true disciple of the Lord. We can see this most vividly in the language which he uses about his impending martyrdom. Some of this admittedly has Gnostic overtones. He implores the Romans not to deceive him with matter but to let him receive pure light (*Rom.* 6. 2). But this does not amount to a Gnosticizing view of salvation. The closest parallels are with Paul. He feels that the pangs of birth are upon him (*Rom.* 6. 1; cf. Rom. 8: 23): his material longing has been crucified (*Rom.* 7. 2; cf. Gal. 6: 14); he wants no longer to live in a human fashion (*Rom.* 8. 1; cf. Gal. 2: 20) but to become an authentic human being (*Rom.* 6. 2). 'I am the wheat of God', he says, 'and I am ground by the teeth of wild beasts that I may be found pure bread' (*Rom.* 4. 1). The allusion is probably not eucharistic (Schoedel 1985: 175–6). The emphasis is rather on the transformation of a natural product into something greatly superior. Through martyrdom Ignatius will attain to the new humanity inaugurated by Christ, a pure white bread produced from the humble raw material of grains of wheat.

5. Valentinian Christianity

Ignatius appears to have had a rhetorical training but at the same time was thoroughly rooted in the ecclesiastical tradition. The Christian intellectuals of the first half of the second century came from a different background. They were perhaps more highly educated, certainly more at home in the philosophical culture of their day. Although not detached from the Christian congregations gathered around their bishop, they set up independent *didaskaleia* in the great urban centres on the model of the philosophical schools. People who wanted deeper, more spiritual insights than could be found at the Sunday *synaxis*[28] went to the lectures and seminars of such teachers. After all, had not Paul himself said, 'Yet among the mature . . . we impart a secret and hidden wisdom of God which God decreed before the ages for our glorification. . . . And we impart this in words not taught by human wisdom but taught by the Spirit, interpreting spiritual truths to the spiritual' (1 Cor. 2: 6–13)? Those who saw themselves as successors of the Apostle in this respect included Basilides and Carpocrates in Alexandria, Aristides in Athens, and Marcion, Valentinus, and Justin in Rome. Some accepted the authority of the bishops and presbyters of ecclesiastical Christianity; others relied on a more esoteric tradition, using subjective qualitative criteria to define true membership of the Church. For the latter the real Christians were those who had come to know God through the application of the maxim 'Know thyself'. By looking within and exploring their own experience they could discover a divine principle which would lead them up out of this world of illusion to unity with the very source of divine life.

One of the most influential of such teachers was Valentinus (*c.*100–175 CE). He was born in the Nile delta and received his education at Alexandria. He may have met the Gnostic Basilides, who was teaching in Alexandria at the time, but there are no reports of this. To furnish him with apostolic credentials his followers claimed that he had studied under a disciple of St Paul called Theudas. Shortly before 140 he moved to Rome, where he founded a successful school. He seems to have been an outstanding teacher who could expound his doctrines with poetic and rhetorical power. His successors continued his teaching for several generations and in the second and third centuries were ecclesiastical Christianity's most formidable opponents.

Valentinus' undisputed writings survive only in a few fragments quoted by ecclesiastical writers, chiefly Clement and Hippolytus. *The Gospel of Truth*, however, which we have in Coptic translation thanks to the discovery at Nag Hammadi, is attributed by many to Valentinus on stylistic grounds. Its genre is not that of a Gospel but of a homily, its title coming from its *incipit*. Bentley Layton calls it 'the earliest surviving sermon of Christian mysticism', and 'one of the most brilliantly crafted works of ancient Christian literature' (1987: 250). If not by Valentinus himself, it is at least the work of a brilliant pupil. It is a call to the spiritually minded to turn inwards in order to attain true understanding and through Christ return to the primordial source of their being.

The Gospel of Truth begins with an analysis of the situation in which we find ourselves. This material world is not reality; it is illusory, 'the modelled form of deception' (16. 24–5), whereas reality, or truth, is unchangeable,

---

[28] The Sunday sermon was well-established by the second century. For an account of liturgical preaching see Justin, 1 *Apol.* 67.

imperturbable, supreme beauty. Not everyone can appreciate this. Those in the 'middle' (i.e. ordinary Christians) are beguiled and taken captive by error, which is the result of forgetfulness, the soul's obliviousness to its previous heavenly existence. Thus far *The Gospel of Truth* follows the standard tenets of Platonism. But the proposed solution parts company with Platonic doctrine. The remedy for ignorance is *gnôsis*—a knowledge or understanding which is not philosophical but personal and experiential. Knowledge of reality is not taught in a discursive way but is communicated by a person, Jesus Christ, who is the *gnôsis* of the Father, or rather, who was persecuted by Error and nailed to a tree so that he became the fruit of the Father's *gnôsis*. Those who eat of this tree can discover truth within themselves. The metaphor of eating underlines the experiential nature of the knowledge of truth. It also points to its reciprocal character: he who created the pleroma is contained within the person who has eaten, even though the person who has eaten is part of the pleroma. Truth is personal: to have *gnôsis* is to know and be known, to be glorified and to give glory (18. 11 to 19. 30).

Responding to the invitation to *gnôsis* is like coming to oneself after a period of drunkenness (22. 16–18) or waking up from a nightmare (30. 2–14). Through the Son, who 'put off the corrupt rags of the body and put on immortality', the elect are enrolled in the book of the living and gain understanding (20. 10 to 21. 24). They learn that they came from the Father and must return to him (22. 23; 33. 30), that they are 'children of interior understanding' (32. 38–9), that they are 'the day that is perfect' in whom 'there dwells the star that does not set' (32. 32–4), that they are 'unsheathed intelligence' (33. 9), the 'fragrance', or emanation, of the Father (34. 1). Those who are moved to seek truth must therefore turn inwards: 'Focus your attention upon yourselves' (33. 11), says the author. They should not be concerned with others except to raise up those who wish to rise and awaken those who sleep. For the return to the Father is essentially a solitary path of self-discovery (Pagels 1979: 125–8).

Those who strain up towards salvation find that it reaches down towards them, for the pleroma naturally strives to fill all deficiencies. The final goal of the elect is repose in the Father. All who have emanated from the Father will return to him. Not that their knowledge of him will be total. The Father remains 'the one who is hidden' (37. 38); he is unnameable and indescribable (40. 16–17). The elect will return to the place from which they emanated and there they will still continue to develop, 'tasting of it and being nourished and growing' (41. 10–11). In the repose of the Father they become identified with ultimate reality though without exhausting its meaning. Yet they themselves *are* the truth, and the Father is within them and they are in the Father, being perfect (42. 25–8; cf. John 17: 21; 1 John 2: 24). In a striking simile the author says, 'they hold themselves close to him so that, as it were, they receive from his face something like kisses' (41. 32–4). In another tender image the elect strain 'towards the solitary and perfect, him who is mother to them' (42.15–17). They become his perfect children, worthy of his name, dwelling in the place of repose in true and eternal life and continually occupied with the father of the pleroma (43).

Other Valentinian texts fill out this destiny of the elect, not so much in terms of philosophical or theological analysis as in the development of suggestive images. Although the successors of Valentinus soon split into two traditions, the eastern restricting salvation to the pneumatics while the western allowed an intermediate form also to the psychics,[29] both traditions speak of the spirits of the elect entering the bridal chamber, overcoming the male–female divide, and participating as angels or brides of angels in the Father's pleroma (Irenaeus, *AH* 1. 7. 5; Clem. Alex. *Exc. Theod.* 64. 1; 79). The sexual imagery of the bridal chamber draws on two fundamental sources, the synoptic evangelists' presentation of the kingdom of heaven as a wedding feast (Matt. 22: 1–14; 25: 1–13) and Aristophanes' myth of the original androgynous unity of human nature, the 'primeval wholeness' of which the urge to sexual union seeks to recapture (Plato, *Symp.* 189c–193d). In *The Gospel of Philip* the separation of Eve from Adam (Gen. 2: 21–2) is interpreted against this background as the source of death, which Christ came to rectify by reuniting the two components of male and female (*Gos. Phil.* 63, 70). Final union amongst the Valentinians takes place in the heavenly realm. According to the reports of both Irenaeus and Clement, the pneumatics shed the soul and become pure *noes*, or spiritual selves, or 'angels' (which is always masculine in Greek), or 'brides' swallowed up in the masculinity of the angels (*AH* 1. 7. 1; *Exc. Theod.* 64. 1). Alternatively, 'the seed of light' is seen as female which when formed (i.e. trained) becomes male and a son of the heavenly bridegroom. Having become male it enters the pleroma and unites with the angels (*Exc. Theod.* 79). Such union, however, can be anticipated in this world. With their emphasis on symbolism and imagery, the Valentinians had a developed sacramental system: 'truth did not come into the world nakedly; rather it came in prototypes and images: the world will not accept it in any other form' (*Gos. Phil.* 59). Baptism, the first of their sacraments, was nothing short of a symbolic appropriation of the resurrection. There is no raising of bodies at some future date. Those who have separated themselves from the bondage of the body and attained an interior unity 'already possess the resurrection' (*Treat. Res.* 49. 9–23). And if they 'do not first receive resurrection when they are alive, once they have died they will receive nothing' (*Gos. Phil.* 79). For the vital thing is the resurrection of the spirit, 'which

---

[29] This division was the result of christological disagreement, the western branch, under Ptolemy, holding that Christ had a psychic body, while the eastern branch, under Theodotus, restricted his body simply to the pneumatic. Consequently for Theodotus only the spirituals enter the pleroma as brides of the angels, but for Ptolemy 'the souls of the just also (i.e. the psychics) will gain repose in the place of the midpoint' (Irenaeus, *AH* 1. 1. 12).

swallows up the resurrection of the soul along with the resurrection of the flesh' (*Treat. Res.* 46. 1). The resurrection of the spirit is the first stage of the return to the Father. The last stage before death is marked by the sacrament of the bridal chamber, which endows the recipient, through chrismation, with a 'garment of light' (*Gos. Phil.* 59, 69, 90, 107), the wedding garment with which he or she will be able to enter into union with the angels and become spiritual aeons (Clement, *Exc. Theod.* 64. 1; cf. Eusebius, *HE* 4. 11. 5).

The Valentinians exercised an enormous influence on contemporary Christians, not only negatively—orthodox ecclesiastical Christianity defining itself largely in reaction to Gnostic groups—but positively, too. Their writings were keenly studied by such speculative theologians as Clement of Alexandria and Origen who, unlike the heresiologists, were able to adapt some of their insights to orthodox use.[30] Origen in particular skilfully exploited the Valentinian myth of the soul's descent and ascent, 'demythologizing' it and integrating it into a more orthodox scheme of salvation. The fruits of this adaptation of Gnostic teaching will be seen in the intellectualist spirituality of some of Origen's successors, especially Evagrius Ponticus and Gregory of Nyssa (Rudolph 1987: 369).

6. Justin Martyr

One of Valentinus' proto-orthodox rivals, who conducted his own *didaskaleion* in Rome in the late 150s 'above the baths of a certain Martinus' (Musurillo 1972: 49), was Justin Martyr. His meetings with his disciples, who included Tatian and possibly Irenaeus, have not been described for us, but it is not unlikely that they included the kind of questioning mentioned by Porphyry in his account of Plotinus' school in the following century. Justin himself tells us that he was led to Christianity by the questions put to him by a mysterious old man he met while walking on the seashore at Ephesus as a young student. He had considered the claims of the Stoics, the Peripatetics, and the Pythagoreans, but for different reasons was put off them all. For a while the Platonists satisfied his thirst for 'the science of being and the knowledge of truth' (*Dial.* 3). For the *telos* of man in Platonism, as Justin says, is to see God, the supreme cause of all things (*Dial.* 2). Yet he doubted whether Platonism in itself could achieve this *telos*. The key question was put to him by the old man on the seashore: 'What affinity is there between us and God? Is the soul divine and immortal and a part of that royal intellect [which

---

[30] Clement made an annotated collection of passages from various Gnostic writers, the *Excerpta ex Theodoto*, amongst whom is the leading member of the eastern branch of the Valentinian school who gives the collection its name. Origen, in the course of his commentary on St John's Gospel, reproduces and discusses forty-eight passages from a commentary on the same Gospel by the western Valentinian, Heracleon.

Plato describes]?' (*Dial.* 4). The answer is no: the affinity we have with God is moral, not ontological. No one will see God 'except he who shall have lived righteously, purified by righteousness and every other virtue'. Justin supports this assertion with a neat syllogism. If the soul were immortal, it would be unbegotten (i.e. if it had no end, it could have had no beginning). And if it were unbegotten, there would be a multiplicity of unbegotten beings. But there can only be one unbegotten being—who is by definition God— otherwise there is no escape from the problem of infinite regression. There- fore the soul is not immortal of its own nature. The old man goes on to point out that neither is the soul of its own nature alive. Either it is life or it possesses life. If it is life, it would be able to move other beings. As it cannot do so, it only participates in life, and 'that which participates in anything is distinct from that which is participated in'. The soul therefore participates in life for as long as God wishes it to live. It does not live of itself as God does; when the life-giving spirit withdraws from it, it ceases to exist.

Both these arguments derive from Aristotle (Grant 1956: 246–8). They prove that Platonism cannot deliver what it promises: because the soul has no natural powers of vision arising from an innate immortality or ontological affinity with the divine, the human intellect cannot see God 'unless adorned by the Holy Spirit'. It therefore needs the prophets of the Old Testament and ultimately Christ himself, who opens 'the gates of light' and grants wisdom to the understanding. The old man uses philosophical arguments simply as a preparation for the response of faith to the message of the prophets and the illumination which follows as a gift from God.

This is precisely the approach that Plotinus was to find so contemptible a century later. Justin was aware, however, that presenting Christ as the fulfil- ment of the prophets was not going to mean much to a pagan audience. In his two *Apologies*, addressed to the Emperor Antoninus Pius (138–61 CE),[31] he therefore tries a different approach. To counter the objection that Christi- anity is a recent and arbitrary innovation he argues for the universal signifi- cance of Christ through the operation of the divine *logos*. The fullness of the *logos* is Christ, in whom people have shared in part throughout human history by the operation of the *logos spermatikos*, the 'sowing *logos*' who disseminates the 'seeds of truth' (1 *Apol.* 46).[32] This enables those who have 'lived with the *logos*', such as Socrates (2 *Apol.* 10), Heraclitus (1 *Apol.* 46), and Musonius (2 *Apol.* 8), to be regarded as honorary Christians, 'for each person spoke well, according to the part present in him of the divine *logos*' (2 *Apol.* 13;

---

[31] Fergus Millar believes that Justin's *Apology* or *Apologies* (it is not clear whether the second, which lacks a formal address, was originally independent of the first) may well have been a real petition, a *libellus*, presented to the emperor (1992: 562–3).

[32] *Logos spermatikos* is a term with a background in Stoicism which was used by Justin in an entirely original way. For a good discussion of its meaning, with a review of the scholarly literature, see Barnard 1997: 196–200.

trans. Barnard). But to live by the knowledge and contemplation of the whole *logos*, who is Christ, is a different matter. In Justin's view, the philosophers and poets may have known Christ in an imperfect way, but the full possession of the divine *logos* can only take place through the personal knowledge of the *incarnate logos* that comes by grace, especially via baptism and the Eucharist (1 *Apol.* 61; 2 *Apol.* 10).

Baptism is 'the bath of repentance and knowledge' because it cleanses the soul from the sins which preclude knowledge of God—anger, avarice, envy, and hatred (*Dial.* 14). Knowledge of God is not an external knowledge, such as people might have of music, arithmetic, or astronomy (*Dial.* 3). It is an intimate, personal knowledge that comes from living the life of Christ through participating in it. Although initiated by the new birth (ἀναγέννησις) and illumination (φωτισμός) of baptism, this knowledge needs to be nurtured by the Eucharist. For the Eucharist is not received as common bread and wine; it is Christ's flesh and blood, nourishing our own flesh and blood 'by a transformation' (κατὰ μεταβολήν) (1 *Apol.* 23, 61). Such an inward conformation to Christ of the whole human person in the Pauline manner is equivalent to the believer's restoration to the Adamic state, which, according to Justin, Scripture shows to have been divine.

The *Dialogue with Trypho* purports to be the record of a two-day debate between Justin and a Jewish scholar and his companions, presumably in Ephesus.[33] It is unlikely to mirror an actual debate: Justin was writing in Rome in the 160s, some twenty years after the supposed event, and in any case the Dialogue was a well-established fictional genre. But the Jewish milieu that Justin portrays has many convincing features. Trypho is not simply a two-dimensional figure set up to prove the superiority of the Christian position. He may be too ready to concede some of Justin's points, but he stands firm on the characteristic features of Diaspora Judaism, circumcision, the sabbath, festivals, and the observance of new moons, and makes some telling points, such as the observation that Christians claim to be pious but do not distinguish themselves sufficiently from the Gentiles (*Dial.* 10. 3). In spite of not offering a sustained counter-argument, he is no pushover for Justin but remains courteous, though unconvinced, to the end. We can safely say that Justin is drawing on real experience of Christian–Jewish debate for the *Dialogue*. Such experience would account for the accurate knowledge of Jewish practice and biblical exegesis which he displays.

Toward the end of the *Dialogue* the debate turns to who is the true Israel. Justin argues that the Christians have supplanted the Jews as the true Israel because they have inherited the divine promises: Christians are related to the Messianic Israel of Isaiah 42: 1–4 (LXX) by a spiritual birth just as Jews are related to the Hebrew patriarch of Genesis 35: 10–11 by physical descent.

---

[33] On the setting of the *Dialogue* see Lieu 1996: 103–9.

Because Christ 'begot us in regard to God, like Jacob and Israel and Judah and Joseph and David, we are called the true children of God and are such (cf. 1 John 3: 1), for we keep the commandments of Christ' (*Dial.* 123). Trypho's objection to the claim that Christians are the children of God causes Justin to embark on a detailed justification of it. By a standard technique of Jewish exegesis he appeals to another passage in Scripture where a similar expression occurs in order to illuminate the Johannine verse (1 John 3: 1) to which he has alluded.[34] The passage is Psalm 82: 6, 'I said, you are gods, and all of you sons of the Most High'. The verse which follows, 'You shall die like men, and you shall fall like one of the princes' shows, Justin says, that these words were addressed originally to Adam and Eve, who had once been immortal but after their transgression had become subject to death and had fallen 'like one of the princes', namely, Satan. In verse 7 'the Holy Spirit reproaches human beings, who were made dispassionate and immortal like God, if they had kept his commandments, and were deemed worthy by him to be called his sons, and yet made themselves like Adam and Eve and worked death for themselves'. In Psalm 82, Justin concludes, 'it is proved that all human beings are deemed worthy of becoming gods and of having the power to become sons of the Most High, and will be judged and condemned on their own account like Adam and Eve' (*Dial.* 124).

This is the first appearance of Psalm 82: 6 in Christian literature as a proof-text supporting the notion of deification.[35] The background to Justin's use of the text lies in the increased interest of second-century Christians in Jewish Messianic testimony sources.[36] The New Testament's testimonies had concentrated on what was novel, even shocking, in the Christian claims for Jesus' Messiahship, namely, his suffering, death, and resurrection. By the second century, when Christians and Jews were competing for converts

---

[34] Justin's καὶ θεοῦ τέκνα ἀληθινὰ καλούμεθα καὶ ἐσμέν (*Dial.* 123) seems to echo 1 John's ἵνα τέκνα θεοῦ κληθῶμεν καὶ ἐσμέν (3: 1) rather more closely than Paul's ὅτι ἐσμὲν τέκνα θεοῦ (Rom. 8: 16), even though Justin has a direct relationship with Paul and certainly makes use of Romans in the *Dialogue*. If this is an allusion to John, it is one of the earliest in an orthodox writer. On Justin's relationship to Paul see Skarsaune 1987: 92–100, where full reference is made to the literature. On his more problematic relationship to John see Chadwick 1966: 4, 124–5 and Skarsaune 1987: 105–6.

[35] The reference to Psalm 82: 6 in John 10: 34 serves a different purpose, though the exploration of its meaning given there also owes a debt to Rabbinic exegesis. When accused of making himself equal to God, Jesus resorted to a method of argument characteristic of Rabbinic hermeneutics. He clearly accepted one of the learned views current among the Tannaim (see above, Chapter 3. 4) that Ps. 82: 6 referred to corrupt human judges, or perhaps even to the Israelites who worshipped the golden calf at Sinai. The implication of his quoting Ps. 82: 6 was (i) that if men would be referred to as gods in Scripture without blasphemy, why should it be blasphemous for him to call himself the (or a) Son of God, and (ii) if human beings who received the word of God but were later sentenced to death for wrongdoing could be called gods, a fortiori how much more worthy of the title was he who was the recipient of God's word in a unique way, or indeed was the Word of God himself? (cf. R. E. Brown 1966–70: 409–10).

[36] In what follows I rely on Skarsaune 1987. It should also be noted that the Rabbinic interpretation of Ps. 82: 6–7 discussed in Chapter 3 above may have its context in a general concern to respond to Christian claims that Christians had superseded the Jews as the favoured people of the covenant. See further Hammer 1986: 17–20.

amongst sympathetic Gentiles, Christians had to address the mainstream Jewish Messianic testimonies. Justin uses material which exploits such testimonies—a 'recapitulation' source and a 'kerygmatic' source have been identified (Skarsaune 1987: 425–7)—and supplements it with Old Testament quotations taken directly from Romans and Galatians. In these letters, which Justin seems to have known well, Paul had claimed that Christians were the true seed of Abraham and therefore inheritors of God's promise. This view had been attacked by Rabbis who had pointed out that not all the descendants of Abraham were inheritors of the promise but only the descendants of Jacob/Israel. After all, Hagar and Esau were the ancestors of people not encompassed by the promise. Justin counter-attacks by claiming that Christ is the new Jacob/Israel and that Christians inherit the promise as his true spiritual descendants.

At this point Oskar Skarsaune, who has made a detailed study of Justin's use of the Old Testament, detects a change of source (1987: 187–8). The logic of Justin's argument would seem to require his saying that as Christ is the Messianic Israel, so those begotten by him are the true spiritual Israel. The reference to the children of God does not flow from the preceding discussion. Moreover, the text to which Justin appeals, Psalm 82: 6, does not prove that Christians are the children of God; it proves, rather, that all human beings have failed in their vocation to become sons of the Most High. Skarsaune believes that *Dial.* 124 fits better thematically with *Dial.* 125 than with the preceeding section, the argument being that 'Christ conquers (*Dial.* 125) where Adam (and Eve) failed' (*Dial.* 124). The etymology in *Dial.* 125 of the name Israel, he suggests, is the link which in Justin's mind connects the otherwise disparate *Dial.* 124–5 with *Dial.* 123 (1987: 188).

Can we identify Justin's source? Skarsaune adduces *Sifre to Deuteronomy*, a halakhic midrash from the school of Rabbi Akiba, as illustrative of the views counter-attacked by Justin at *Dial.* 120–1, namely, that the election of Israel began with Jacob (1987: 346–7). *Sifre to Deuteronomy* also provides a parallel to Justin's interpretation of Psalm 82: 6 (see above, Chapter 3. 4). We find there the same application of the psalm to Adam and Eve together with an episodic approach to sin in which the process of alienation from God that began with the Fall is reversible in principle through obedience. Justin, or more probably the testimony source on which he relies,[37] was almost certainly familiar with *Sifre to Deuteronomy*. As a testimony, its interpretation of Ps. 82: 6 provided the setting for the Christian kerygma: Adam and Eve's failure was reversed by the success of Christ. What Justin seems to have contributed himself is the connection with the Johannine or Pauline children

---

[37] The evidence for Justin's testimony source lies in the textual criticism of Ps. 82: 6–7 which he offers. He quotes from the Jewish version of the psalm, which appears to have said 'you will die like a man (ὡς ἄνθρωπος)', and then corrects it from his own source, which has the LXX reading: 'you will die like men (ὡς ἄνθρωποι)'. On this see Skarsaune 1987: 34–5.

of God. The destiny which was intended for Adam and Eve is attainable by Christians because they have become children of God through obedience to the commandments of Christ.

Justin Martyr turned Judaism's obedience to the Torah into obedience to the commandments of Christ. Such obedience is made possible by our being 'begotten' with regard to God by Christ. But the baptismal implications of his interpretation of Psalm 82: 6 are not brought out by Justin. The identification of the 'gods' with those who have been incorporated into Christ through baptism would only be made explicit by Irenaeus some decades later.

7. Two Anonymous Contemporaries

Before we pass to Justin's pupil, Tatian, two anonymous writers of the late second or early third century deserve attention for their mention of men as gods without reference to Psalm 82: 6. The *Epistle to Diognetus* and the *Discourse to the Greeks* are works which demonstrate the untroubled interpenetration of Hellenic culture and biblical religion characteristic of many Christian apologists of the age of the Antonines.[38]

The tenth chapter of the *Epistle to Diognetus* urges the imitation of God through knowledge and love of the Father. Loving God makes us imitators of his goodness. For the imitation of God does not lie in the acquisition of power or wealth. We must show love to the weak and the needy: 'whoever takes on himself the burden of his neighbour, whoever wishes to benefit another in some matter in which he is better provided, whoever supplies to the needy what he has received himself from God becomes a god to those who receive from him; such a man is an imitator of God' (θεὸς γίνεται τῶν λαμβανόντων, οὗτος μιμητής ἐστι θεοῦ).[39] This combines the Christian virtue of almsgiving with the traditional Hellenistic view that a man is a god to his beneficiaries; through being a benefactor he becomes a god by analogy.

An even bolder idea is expressed in the *Discourse to the Greeks*. At the end of this work the author urges the Greeks to partake of incomparable wisdom, be instructed by the divine Logos, and acquire knowledge of the incomparable King. For the power of the Logos does not make poets or philosophers or orators, 'but by educating them makes mortals immortal,

---

[38] Both the *Epistula ad Diognetum* and the *Oratio ad Graecos* were traditionally attributed to Justin Martyr, and are printed in Otto's edition of Justin's works (i. 2–12; ii. 464–506). Many authors have been suggested for *Ad Diognetum*, among the more plausible of whom are an anonymous disciple of Aristides (Christou 1978a: 618–21) or Clement's teacher Pantaenus (Lightfoot, *Apostolic Fathers* (1926) and Marrou, SC 33 bis (1965) cautiously supported by Chadwick (1966) 138 n. 6).

[39] *Ad Diogn.* 10; cf. Justin, 1 *Apol.* 10, where Christians are those who imitate the attributes of God, particularly σωφροσύνη, δικαιοσύνη, and φιλανθρωπία.

mere human beings gods (ἀλλὰ παιδεύουσα ποιεῖ τοὺς θνητοὺς ἀθάνατους, τοὺς βροτοὺς θεούς), and transfers them to realms whose bounds are beyond Olympus' (*Orat.* 5). In its vocabulary this echoes the staple school authors, Homer and Euripides (cf. *Andromache* 1196); in its content it resembles the passage in the *Stromateis* where Clement says that as Isomachus makes his pupils farmers, Demosthenes orators, and Plato philosophers, so the Lord makes them gods (*Strom.* 7. 101. 4). The operative principle is that as a cause produces a like effect, so pupils acquire the attributes of their teachers. In the case of the Logos the attribute in which people participate is that of immortality.

These expressions may be much less complex than the syntheses we find in Clement and Origen but they indicate how perfectly unexceptionable it had become for Christian authors addressing a pagan or mixed readership to speak metaphorically of human beings as gods.

8. Tatian

Tatian, who, according to Irenaeus, as reported by Eusebius (*HE* 4. 29. 3), had been a pupil of Justin's, may have repudiated his teacher's Hellenism when he returned to his native Mesopotamia, but he still viewed the purpose of the Christian life as the recovery of the immortality lost by Adam. In his *Discourse to the Greeks* he rejects the Greek definition of man as 'a rational animal capable of receiving *nous* and knowledge' and proposes that man is a being made in the image and likeness of God (cf. Gen. 1: 26) 'who has advanced far beyond his humanity towards God himself' (*Orat.* 15. 2). This advance is not achieved through shedding the body and the lower part of the soul as in Hellenism, but through the spiritualization of both body and soul. Tatian holds that the human person is constituted of a body, a material spirit (the soul), and a spiritual spirit (the *pneuma*), which alone is made in the image and likeness of God (*Orat.* 12. 1). This *pneuma*, being immortal and therefore divine, is not easily distinguished from the Spirit of God. The first human beings were endowed with both a material and a spiritual *pneuma* and therefore enjoyed immortality. For the Logos made man 'in imitation of the Father who begot him, so that just as incorruptibility belongs to God, man might in some way participate in God's portion and possess immortality' (*Orat.* 7. 1). The soul is thus not immortal in its own right but only in virtue of participation through the *pneuma* in the attributes of God (*Orat.* 13. 1).

The present human condition is the result of the Fall, in which the soul lost through sin its union with the spirit. Yet some glimmer of the spirit's power remains, not enough for one to see one's way clearly, but enough to enable those souls obedient to wisdom to attract to themselves the kindred spirit (*Orat.* 13. 3). For our task is now 'to search for what we once had and have lost' (*Orat.* 15. 1). Although formerly defeated in Adam, we can win another time if we reject the human constitution that produces death.

The way of return entails the recovery of immortality through union with the Holy Spirit (*Orat.* 15. 1). When we bring the soul into conjunction with the spirit, we 'can obtain the heavenly garment of mortality, which is immortality', and 'return to our ancient kinship', that is, to the unity of soul and spirit (*Orat.* 20. 3). It is this which enables man to advance 'far beyond his humanity to God himself' (*Orat.* 15. 2). Fallen angels are 'robbers of the divine' because they have seized divinity for themselves (*Orat.* 12. 2). But human beings transcend their humanity because they receive as a gift from God a participation in the immortality that belongs properly to him alone. This gift is appropriated not only by the soul but also by the body: through the resurrection 'the piece of flesh joined to the soul is immortal too' (*Orat.* 25. 2). It is thus that we recover the divine image and likeness in which we were created.

Tatian's latest editor calls this return an 'intellectual soteriology' (Whittaker, xvi). But although it is knowledge (ἐπίγνωσις) that enables the soul to reunite itself with the *pneuma* and participate in the incorruption and immortality of God in a manner reminiscent of the Gnostics, this is not an esoteric knowledge reserved to an educated elite. Everyone who reads the Scriptures can, like Tatian, become a 'theodidact' and once the power which makes souls immortal has come upon him can 'easily apprehend the divine' (*Orat.* 29. 2). Nor is the intellect released to soar up to God in the Hellenic manner. Quite the contrary, Tatian teaches in a thoroughly Semitic way that the human person is raised to immortality through the transformation of his or her entire being by the living God. Far from being 'intellectual' his soteriology may more accurately be termed 'pneumatological' and 'physicalist'. Hence his Encratite stance. In practical terms, the embodied soul's greatest obstacle to regaining the Holy Spirit is the marital intercourse that accompanied Adam's fall and brought him close to the beasts. Sexual union together with the eating of meat and the drinking of wine had to be renounced if the entire human person was to be re-spiritualized.

9. Theophilus of Antioch

A similarly Semitic anthropology is evident in the writings of Tatian's contemporary fellow-Syrian, Theophilus of Antioch. The creation of man in the image and likeness of God, says Theophilus, reveals simply his dignity as the only work of God's 'hands', and his sovereignty over nature.[40] Man was not created immortal, even if most people think he was (*Ad Aut.* 2. 19). After

---

[40] *Ad Aut.* 2. 18. This was to become the standard Antiochene interpretation of Gen. 1: 26.

creating him, God transferred him from the earth out of which he was made to a paradise between heaven and earth, 'giving him an opportunity for progress so that by growing and becoming mature, and furthermore having been declared a god, he might also ascend into heaven (for man was created in an intermediate state, neither entirely mortal nor entirely immortal, but capable of either state . . .)' (*Ad Aut*. 2. 24; trans. Grant). The reason for this intermediate state is that if man had been made mortal, God would have been responsible for his death; and if he had been made immortal, God would have made him a god. He was therefore between the two: by keeping God's commandments, 'he would win immortality as a reward from him and become a god'; by disobeying God, 'he would be responsible for his own death' (*Ad Aut*. 2. 27).

The affinities between this and the exegesis of Psalm 82: 6 which we have noted in the Rabbinic *Sifre to Deuteronomy* and in Justin Martyr's *Dialogue with Trypho* are striking. In all three cases obedience to God enables a human being to be called a god; disobedience brings death. Although not cited explicitly, Psalm 82: 6 appears to lie behind Theophilus' account. Man had the opportunity to become a god through the divine gift of immortality, bestowed as a reward for obedience, not through the separation of the soul from the body and its ascent to the divine realm. Such an approach is in keeping with the close Jewish links which scholars have already noted in Theophilus (Grant 1970: xvii–xix).

Adam's failure to grow into his full divine maturity, however, did not doom the whole human race. God by a gift of grace bestows on those obedient to him the immortality which the first human being forfeited. 'For God gave us a law and holy commandments; everyone who performs them can be saved and, attaining to the resurrection, can attain incorruptibility' (*Ad Aut*. 2. 27; trans. Grant; cf. 1 Cor. 15: 50). The emphasis, as in contemporary Judaism, is on obedience to the Law. Baptism is described with Paul as a 'bath of regeneration' (cf. Tit. 3: 5) but there is no development of the Pauline or Ignatian idea of incorporation into Christ (*Ad Aut*. 2. 16). Indeed, although the Logos is described as a 'hand' of God, and 'innate' in God (ἐνδιάθετος), no mention is made of Christ the incarnate Logos (*Ad Aut*. 2. 10). Baptism is simply a rebirth which enables the recipient to receive the divine grace which in turn enables him to obey God. The reward for such obedience is the immortality which humankind will enjoy after death.

Although immortality is said to accompany the human person's ascent into heaven, this is not an escape of the soul from the material world. On the contrary, immortality is expressed in the complete reforming of the person after death by means of the resurrection of the body. Man is shattered and resmelted like some faulty metal pot 'so that in the resurrection he may be found sound, I mean spotless and righteous and immortal' (*Ad*

Aut. 2. 26; trans. Grant). It is this immortality through righteousness to be enjoyed at the resurrection which constitutes the human person's becoming a 'god'.

10. Irenaeus of Lyons

While Tatian and Theophilus were grappling with pagan and Jewish beliefs in the East, a thousand miles to the West Irenaeus, the bishop of Lyons, was struggling with very different problems. His opponents were the enemies within, the Gnostic teachers who claimed to preserve an esoteric tradition representing true Christianity. In his polemic against the Gnostics Irenaeus develops the baptismal implications contained in the interpretation of Psalm 82: 6 put forward by Justin and Theophilus. In Irenaeus' case his purpose is not to outbid Jewish claims, but to demonstrate the possibility of the attainment of incorruption by all Christians, not just a spiritual elite. If the rank and file of the Church can attain immortality and become 'gods', it is by virtue of the Incarnation and the sacraments of baptism and the Eucharist. Irenaeus does not use any of the technical terms of deification, and even the word 'gods' is applied to human beings only within the context of his exegesis of Psalm 82: 6. But in countering Gnostic claims concerning the spirituals he presents a 'realist' account of salvation which will provide a number of later writers—and Athanasius in particular—with the content of their doctrine of deification.[41]

In his great work, *Against Heresies*, Irenaeus discusses Psalm 82: 6 on three occasions. He uses the text to oppose a Gnostic argument for more than one God, to provide evidence for the divinity of the Son, and to support the assertion that human beings advance in spiritual maturity.[42] In these arguments we find a remarkable advance on Justin and Theophilus.

In the third book of *Against Heresies* Irenaeus says that he will adduce proofs against the Valentinians from Scripture. One of the fundamental doctrines of the Valentinian school was that there is a transcendent God distinct from the God of the Old Testament, the latter corresponding to the Gnostic Demiurge who has created the world in opposition to the transcendent God. Irenaeus argues vigorously against this (*AH* 3. 6. 1). There is no God, he insists, 'except God the Father ruling over all and his Son who has received dominion from his Father'. What then should we make

---

[41] The first to discuss the significance of deification for Irenaeus' realistic view of redemption was Harnack 1896–9: ii. 239–44. The conception of deification is the starting-point for d'Alès 1916, who followed this with another study centred on the Spirit (1924). The attaining of likeness to God is the main theme for Gross 1938: 147–59. The aspect of participation in incorruptibility has been studied by Aubineau 1956; Theodorou 1956: 66–71; and de Andia 1986.

[42] *AH* 3. 6. 1; 3. 19. 1; 4. 38. 4. Aubineau (1956: 30) characterizes *AH* 4. 38 as the best introduction to Irenaeus' thought on deification. Cf. de Andia 1986: 127–45; 170–84.

of Psalm 82: 1: 'God stood in the congregation of God, he judges in the midst of gods' (Symmachus' version)? This refers to the Father, the Son, and those who have received adoption, namely, the Church, for the congregation of God is the congregation of the Son which he has gathered to himself. Psalm 50: 1 also refers to 'the God of gods'. Who are these gods? 'They are those to whom God says, "I said, you are gods and all of you sons of the Most High" (Ps. 82: 6), that is to say, those who have received the grace of adoption, through which we cry, "Abba, Father!" ' (Rom. 8: 16). Therefore no one is properly called God except the one who revealed himself to Moses as 'I am who I am' (cf. Exod. 3: 14).

Psalm 82: 6 had been discussed in a similar way before by Justin Martyr. But Justin is still close to the Rabbinic exegesis which understood men to become gods through obedience to the Law. Irenaeus is the first to dwell on the baptismal implications which Justin indicates but does not develop. Whereas Justin had linked the text with the Johannine 'children of God', Irenaeus links it with the Pauline 'adoption'. This interpretation was to become very influential. Men become 'gods' through baptism, which makes them adopted sons of God in the Pauline manner.

The second discussion of Psalm 82: 6 occurs in a passage in which Irenaeus counters the christological heresy of those who assert that the Son of God was a mere man (*AH* 3. 19. 1). Such people remain in the slavery of the ancient disobedience and die in it, 'not yet having been mingled with the Word of God, nor having participated in the freedom of the Son'. Not knowing the incarnate God, 'they deprive themselves of his gift, which is eternal life; and not having received the Word of incorruption, they remain in the mortal flesh'. The verses, 'I have said, you are gods and all of you sons of the Most High; nevertheless you shall die like men,' are addressed to them, that is, to 'those who have not received the gift of adoption'. They fail to honour the incarnation of the Word and 'deprive man of his ascent to God'.

This passage marks a development of the conviction that the gods are to be understood a sons by adoption. Here we see Irenaeus moving towards the *tantum-quantum* or 'exchange' formula, namely, that the Son of God 'became what we are in order to make us what he is himself' (*AH* 5. Praef.). The Incarnation is an essential prerequisite for our journey to God, for we need to be mingled with the Logos through the adoption of baptism in order to participate in immortality and incorruption. These attributes belong to God alone; we can only participate in them if God first unites himself to the human race through the incarnation of the Logos. Individual human beings may then be united with Christ through filial adoption, which enables them to participate in the divine attributes of incorruption and immortality. As a result of the Incarnation Christians have access to a divine dignity which heretics fail to attain: the latter are gods and sons of the Most High but die like men.

The third reference to Psalm 82: 6 occurs in an important discussion of why humanity was not made perfect from the beginning (*AH* 4. 38. 3). Created things, says Irenaeus, must be inferior to him who created them. Being inferior to God, we could not have endured Christ if he had come to us in his immortal glory. He therefore accommodated himself to our infant state so as to enable us to grow and mature until we reach the stage when we can accept God's gratuitous gift of eternal existence, for 'the permanence of incorruption is the glory of the Uncreated'. People who complain about the present weakness of human nature are ignorant, ungrateful, and insatiable. Before becoming human beings, that is, before overcoming the passions, they want to become like God, abolishing the difference between the uncreated God and his recent human creation. 'We reproach him because we were not made gods from the beginning, but first men and only then gods.' That is why God says to us: 'I have said, you are gods and sons of the Most High,' but adds at once: 'Nevertheless, you shall die like men.' The second verse was added because 'we could not carry the power of divinity'. It expresses our weakness in the face of God's gift, and our freedom to accept it or reject it.

On this occasion Irenaeus develops his interpretation of Psalm 82: 6 in response to Christians who wish to advance too quickly. The bridging of the gap between created and uncreated has been achieved historically by the Incarnation and potentially by the individual Christian through baptism, but the reality of human experience remains. We actually find ourselves a long way from the vision of God which produces incorruption, and are very limited in our ability to attain it rapidly. Irenaeus therefore brings in the idea of moral progress. Human beings must attain to the divine likeness before they can overcome their mortality and realize the immortality that they possess potentially through baptism. This involves the exercise of moral choice. Theophilus had already spoken of man's growing to maturity so that he becomes a 'god', probably, as we have seen, with reference to Psalm 82: 6. Irenaeus connects this growth explicitly with attaining the image and likeness of Genesis 1: 26 which Adam had forfeited.

In the last book of *Against Heresies* and the *Proof of the Apostolic Preaching*, which represent the mature expression of his thought, Irenaeus makes a distinction between image and likeness.[43] The image of the as yet invisible Son was manifested in Adam's body; the likeness was communicated by the Spirit and was manifested in Adam's participation in the Son's divine life and freedom. Of the two supreme gifts conveyed by the divine likeness, the first is life. Like Justin, Irenaeus teaches that man does not possess life but only participates in it, the continuance of his existence depending on the grace of

---

[43] *AH* 5. 6. 1; 5. 11. 2; 5. 16. 2; *Proof* 11. On the image and likeness in Irenaeus see Daniélou 1973: 398–9; Regnault 1971: 1938–69; de Andia 1986: 68–74; Osborn 2001: 211–16.

God.[44] The other great gift is freedom. Man was created free with a good will and the power of choice. But this is not the same as licence. Man exercises his freedom in willingly submitting to the will of God. It is this free choice of the good which maintains his likeness to God. Through obedience he possesses life and the freedom of a son; through disobedience he loses these and is reduced to slavery and death.[45]

The Fall was the result not of malice but of immaturity: 'Man was a little one, and his discretion still undeveloped, wherefore he was easily misled by the deceiver' (*Proof* 12). Nevertheless, the Fall had an effect on the whole of subsequent humanity, not so much in condemning it as in providing a new setting for its growth to maturity through education and training. In fact the Fall is turned to humanity's advantage. Besides introducing death as a limitation to the effects of sin, it enables us to gain a deeper understanding of good through experience of the contrary, and also teaches us the limitations of our nature and thus the 'true comprehension of existent things, that is, of God and man' (*AH* 5. 2. 3). Human beings are prepared in this way for the coming of the Son of God.

Against the docetism of the Gnostics, Irenaeus taught that the Incarnation was a true union of God with man, of created with uncreated. Without this ontological basis the soteriological purpose of the Incarnation could not have been made effective. The Incarnation took place in order to recover what was lost in Adam and to complete humanity's growth to full maturity. It therefore has two aspects, the first being summed up in the idea of recapitulation, Christ realizing in his own person the humanity that Adam and his descendants had failed to attain, and the second consisting in the access to the divine life which Christ affords to individual believers by being 'the mediator between God and men' (1 Tim. 2: 5).[46] As the mediator, he both accommodates God to men and accustoms men to receiving God (*AH* 3. 18. 7; 3. 20. 2; 4. 28. 2). Or alternatively, 'because of his infinite love he became what we are in order to make us what he is himself' (*AH* 5. Praef.).

The 'exchange formula' has its roots in Pauline thinking: though Christ was rich, 'yet for your sake he became poor, so that by his poverty you might become rich' (2 Cor. 8: 9; cf. Phil. 2: 6–8). The 'exchange' signifies precisely that: an exchange of properties, not the establishment of an identity of essence. He who was Son of God by nature became a man in order to make us sons by adoption (*AH* 3. 19. 1). Our sonship by adoption, which is effected by baptism, endows us with one supreme property in particular: the Son's immortality and incorruption.

There is nothing automatic, however, about our progress towards incor-

---

[44] Cf. Justin, *Dial.* 6. Irenaeus, however, is less optimistic than Justin about freedom. On this see Osborn 1981: 94–5; 2001: 232–7.

[45] Cf. Theophilus, *Ad Aut.* 2. 27, and the comments of Regnault 1971: 1946.

[46] *AH* 3. 18. 1; cf. 5. 1. 2. On this see Harnack 1896–9: ii. 292–3; Altermath 1975: esp. 64–5.

ruption and immortality. It depends on our moral behaviour and on our participation in the sacraments, which together attain the divine likeness, morality being linked with the freedom and the sacraments with the life of the divine likeness.

Baptism is the means by which we begin to avail ourselves of the divine life of the Son. Through his divine sonship a human being is 'mingled with the Logos' and becomes a dwelling-place of God (*AH* 3. 19. 1; 3. 20. 2). He recovers the likeness to God, which brings him both the freedom to do good and communion with the immortal and incorrupt life of God (*AH* 3. 18. 7). Adoption as sons makes human beings gods because it relates them by participation to the source of life. The progressive nature of this participation is frequently stressed. One of the images which Irenaeus uses to convey this is that of increasing clarity of vision: God was 'seen formerly through the Spirit in the prophetic mode, is seen now through the Son in the adoptive mode, and will be seen in the kingdom of heaven in the paternal mode, the Spirit preparing human beings for the Son of God, the Son leading them to the Father, and the Father granting them incorruption and eternal life, which for those who see God results from the vision of him' (*AH* 4. 20. 5). In this scale of progress people become gods at the stage of adoption, for this is when they regain the divine likeness and begin to participate in the freedom and immortality that belong to the Father and his Logos.

The Spirit is at work throughout this process, not merely in inspiring the prophets and preparing the way for the Incarnation. In the present life we possess a portion of the Spirit to prepare us for incorruption by gradually making us accustomed to receive and bear God (*AH* 5. 8. 1).[47] The Spirit is the Pauline 'guarantee of our inheritance' (Eph. 1: 14). It effects our adoption as sons by enabling us to cry 'Abba, Father!' It swallows up mortality by immortality, for 'flesh and blood cannot inherit the kingdom of God' (1 Cor. 15: 50) unless united with the soul and the Spirit. Against the Gnostics Irenaeus insists that the body, as an integral part of the human person, is capable of incorruption. The seed of incorruption is possessed here below but the full fruit is only harvested with the resurrection. At that time, through the Spirit, incorruptibility will penetrate the whole of the human person, body and soul. In the case of Enoch and Elijah this has already been anticipated through their bodily assumption (*AH* 5. 5. 1). But for most people the process will only be consummated at the general resurrection.

Moral behaviour and the reception of the Eucharist are the two complementary ways in which the Spirit is nurtured in the believer. On the moral level obedience to God produces the fruits of the Spirit, for spiritual actions 'vivify man, that is, engraft the Spirit on to him' (*AH* 5. 11. 1). Conversely, immoral behaviour impoverishes people by banishing the Spirit and renders

---

[47] On the Spirit see d'Alès 1924; de Andia 1986: 205–53.

them the mere flesh and blood that will not inherit the kingdom of heaven (cf. 1 Cor. 15: 50). On the sacramental level the union with the Spirit initiated by baptism is maintained by the Eucharist. Through being nourished by the body and blood of the Lord the body does not go to corruption but partakes of Life (*AH* 4. 18. 5; cf. 5. 2. 3). Just as the bread is transformed spiritually by the prayers of the Eucharist, so are our bodies when they receive communion. In both cases the two realities, heavenly and earthly, are mingled (*AH* 4. 18. 5). Irenaeus expands this thought when he returns to it in Book V. The destiny of our bodies resembles that of the vine cutting and the grain of wheat, which though 'dying' in the ground in winter grow in the spring and become the wine and bread which receive the Word of God and finally become the Eucharist. Our bodies, nourished by the Eucharist, are similarly put in the ground, and rising at the appointed time are granted resurrection by the Word of God 'to the glory of the Father' (Phil. 2: 11), 'who procures immortality for what is mortal, and grants incorruption to what is corruptible' (*AH* 5. 2. 3; cf. 1 Cor. 15: 53). This is to show us that everlasting life is a gift from God and does not belong to our own nature. God's power is demonstrated magnificently in our weakness.

11. Hippolytus of Rome

Hippolytus (d. 235) is remarkable for using the expression γίγνεσθαι θεόν without reference to Psalm 82: 6 and also for being one of the first writers to use the term θεοποιεῖν in a Christian context (*Ref.* 10. 34 (GCS iii. 292–3); cf. Gross 1938: 186–91; Ritschl 1959). His older contemporary, Clement of Alexandria, had already given the term a Christian meaning, but Hippolytus seems not to have been aware of this.[48] As a biblical exegete and controversialist, it was the Asiatic Greeks, Justin, Melito of Sardis, Theophilus of Antioch, and, above all, Irenaeus, who influenced him most. Indeed, if there is a connection between Hippolytus and Clement in their use of deification language, it is in their common dependence on Irenaeus.[49]

Like Irenaeus, Hippolytus develops the idea of Christian deification not in a speculative context but in the course of a kerygmatic presentation of the destiny of humanity. Against the Gnostics he insists that a human being is not a failed god: 'If God had wished to make you a god, he could have done so' (*Ref.* 10. 33 (GCS iii. 290. 3)). But a human being can become a god

---

[48] Hippolytus' fame extended to Alexandria – Origen, according to Eusebius (*HE* 6. 14. 10) and Jerome (*De viris illustr.* 61), heard him preach during his visit to Rome in 229. But Clement was apparently not known to Hippolytus. In Daniélou's view 'Alexandria is the only place with which Hippolytus certainly had no contact' (Daniélou and Marrou 1964: 148).

[49] Christou 1978a: 724; Simonetti 1994: 27–31. According to Photius, Hippolytus had been a disciple of Irenaeus (*Bibl.* 121).

through obedience in virtue of Christ's renewal of mankind. Because he is found faithful in small things, he can be entrusted with great things. These great things are no less than the attributes of the Father, which have been granted to the Son and are promised to the believer in the life to come:

And having been instructed in knowledge of the true God, you will escape these [torments], and your body will be immortal and incorruptible like your soul, and you will receive the kingdom of heaven, since you lived on earth and gained knowledge of the heavenly king, and you will be a companion of God and a co-heir with Christ, since you are not enslaved by desires or passions and diseases. For you have become a god. Whatever sufferings you endured, being a man, these he gave you because you are a man, but whatever is connected with God, these God promised to bestow on you, because you have been deified and born immortal (ὅτι ἐθεοποιήθης, ἀθάνατος γεννηθείς). This is the meaning of 'Know thyself', to have known the God who made you. For to know yourself is concomitant with being known by him by whom you have been called. Do not be at enmity with one another, O men, nor hesitate to return (τὸ παλινδρομεῖν). For Christ is God who is over all things, who has arranged to wash away sin from men, since he has made the old man new, having called him an image from the beginning, and proving his love for you through a type. When you have obeyed his solemn precepts, and have become a good imitator of him who is good, you will be like him, for you will have been honoured by him. For God is not impoverished by also making you a god to his glory.   (*Ref.* 10. 34 (GCS iii. 292–3))

Becoming a god is an eschatological event. The foundations for it are laid in this life, for it is necessary first that one should attain *gnosis* and *apatheia*, but divine status is only bestowed in the world to come with the resurrection of the body. To be deified is presented as the equivalent of being born into immortality. This rebirth refers not to baptism but to resurrection. The knowledge and dispassion that lead to this event are summed up in the attaining of the divine likeness. Knowledge is to know God and be known by him. This implies some kind of likeness, which cannot be ontological but only moral. Through obedience to the precepts of Christ, through imitation of his goodness, the believer becomes like God, for Christ is God. This attainment of likeness to God will manifest itself as participation in the glory of God.

Some elements in this sketch indicate that we are already moving towards a new stage in the Christian appropriation of Greek thought. Knowledge of self leading to knowledge of God, and assimilation to the divine through the mastery of passion, are Greek themes that we find more fully developed in Clement of Alexandria (cf. *Paed.* 3. 2. 1; *Strom.* 7. 20. 7). The 'gods' are those who have attained immortality; no longer are they linked exclusively with the 'sons' of Psalm 82: 6.[50] The intensity of participation in Christ that is found

---

[50] Pitra, *Analecta Sacra* iv. 335; cf. *Ad Aut.* 2. 27. The only other reference to Psalm 82: 6 by Hippolytus is at the end of *Ref.* 5. 2, where he refutes its Gnostic use to support the idea of the generation of gods and men from the same source.

in Irenaeus is not present in Hippolytus. The emphasis in the latter is more on the eschatological fulfilment of resurrection than on the divine status which is brought about in principle by the adoption of baptism. Elsewhere Hippolytus says that we could not imitate Christ if he were not of the same nature as ourselves (*Ref.* 10. 33). The Logos took upon himself the flesh of Adam in order to renew mankind, restoring immortality to us by uniting his power to our mortal body (*Ref.* 10. 33; *C. Noet.* 17; *De Anti.* 4). As in the case of Irenaeus, our imitation of Christ is no external emulation. Yet the incorporation of the believer into Christ by baptism is not emphasized by Hippolytus. Could this be connected with his rigorist view of the Church as the society of the perfect? As D. Ritschl says, 'Irenaeus's conception of the importance of the humanity of Christ was better and more radically understood by Athanasius than by Hippolytus, whose ecclesiology was in many ways separated from his christology' (1959: 339). The welding together of soteriology, christology, and Hellenic thought into a coherent structure was to be the great achievement of the Alexandrian tradition.

12. The Early Christian Approach to Deification

The idea of human beings becoming 'gods' entered Christian thought from Rabbinic Judaism, perhaps initially through a testimony source which borrowed a Rabbinic exegesis of Psalm 82: 6, as a way of contrasting the failure of Adam and Eve, who were called to be gods but died like men, with the success of Christ, who through his victory over death recapitulated human history as God had intended it to be. Justin uses this exegesis in an environment in which Christians are in sharp competition with Jews for Gentile converts to suggest that it is the Christians and not the Jews who are the true people of God because only the former are able to participate in God's great plan for humanity through obedience to the commandments of Christ and thus benefit from verse 6 ('I said, "you are gods" ') while avoiding the condemnation of verse 7 ('You shall die like men'). Irenaeus develops the Christian use of this exegesis in a different context in which the opponents claiming to be the people of God were the Valentinian Gnostics rather than the Jews. Surprisingly, perhaps, the Gnostics themselves do not seem to have appealed to Psalm 82: 6. This may be because of their predilection for intermediaries between humanity and God. Irenaeus, by contrast, holds that God himself has intervened directly in human life through the Incarnation in order to bring the created realm into a close relationship with the divine. The sons of the Most High who are 'gods' are those who have received the grace of adoption. This is then used by Irenaeus as an argument to support the reality of the Incarnation. If Christ had not really become human, there could be no true baptism with its bestowal of incorruption and immortality.

The inward renewal and transformation of the Christian was only possible if the Incarnation was real. Moreover, the following verse 7 shows, in Irenaeus' view, that human beings could not of themselves carry the power of divinity. They are totally dependent on Christ for the avoidance of death. There is no ontological affinity with God, no escape from the corruption and illusion of the material world through the discovery of any divinity within oneself. The application of the word 'gods' to human beings, then, only serves to emphasize their dependence on the incarnate Christ.

A further point may be made. In both Justin and Irenaeus becoming a 'god' is a way of expressing a realized and internalized eschatology. Participation in immortality and incorruption is not postponed to the eschaton but attained in principle as a result of the believer's incorporation into Christ through baptism. The technical language of participation is rarely used. Justin quotes with approval the principle (so fruitful in later Neoplatonism) that 'that which participates in anything is distinct from that which is participated in' (*Dial.* 4) but it is only because he sees participation in negative terms as indicating lack of completeness. When he alludes to the principle again ('a seed and imitation of the *logos* . . . is one thing, and the thing itself another' (2 *Apol.* 13)), it is only to emphasize the partial nature of that which participates.[51] Irenaeus, writing for ecclesiastical Christian readers to inoculate them against those he regards as theological innovators, has no use for Justin's *logos* theory. The notion if not the language of participation, however, is fundamental to him.[52] For Irenaeus, created things are necessarily inferior to the Creator. But in Christ the created is united with the uncreated, and we in turn are related to the uncreated through Christ. The Incarnation is part of a larger economy that enables us to participate in the divine attributes of immortality and incorruption and attain the *telos* which had been intended for Adam. This is why the development of the doctrine of deification in its realistic aspect will be closely linked to the development of christology.

Irenaeus' theological heirs were to take up his insights into the reciprocal relationship between the Incarnation and deification and develop them in a fruitful way. In this respect Hippolytus is disappointing. His relegation of deification to an eschatological fulfilment does not mark any advance on Irenaeus. The real development, in fact, was to take place not in Rome but in Alexandria.

Finally, the ethical and mystical approaches to deification are not significant at this stage. There is no linking as yet of Genesis 1: 26 with *Theaetetus* 176b. Nor is there any yearning for an ecstatic experience of God. Nor, in

---

[51] In 2 *Apol.* 13 Justin links 'participation' with 'part'. Barnard rightly translates μετουσία as 'part possession' (1997: 84).

[52] As Osborn observes, 'participation defines Irenaeus' account of the life which will grow to all eternity' (2001: 230). But Irenaeus does not use it in a technical philosophizing way.

orthodox Christian theology, is deification described in terms of the ascent of the soul, or its highest part, the *nous*, to a God who is utterly remote from the material world. The task of adapting these strands of thought to Christian use was also to fall to the Christian Platonists of Alexandria and their Cappadocian successors.

5

The Alexandrian Tradition I

Christian Schools and Study Circles

The doctrine of deification as the Byzantine Church knew it was in its origins essentially an Alexandrian *theologoumenon*. Justin and Irenaeus may have laid the foundations, but the devising of a technical vocabulary, the elaboration of a philosophical framework, the borrowing of motifs from Hellenistic and Enochic Judaism, the enlargement of biblical support through the allegorical exegesis of Scripture, and the development of a correlative christology all took place in Alexandria, shaped by the unique character of Alexandrian Christianity.

The key figures are Clement and Origen. Clement was the innovator, Origen the brilliant teacher and biblical scholar who, building on Clement, established deification as one of the Church's most striking metaphors of salvation. Most writers who mention deification as the goal of the Christian life were influenced by them. But before we consider their intellectual achievements, we must look at the Christian community to which they belonged.

1. Alexandrian Christianity

The Church in Egypt has left no archaeological evidence dating from before the fourth century to help us trace its rise and development.[1] Written sources are also few. Eusebius offers no information for the period before the last decade of the second century beyond a bare list of bishops with an indication of their date.[2] It is only with Bishop Demetrius (189–232), in whose

---

[1] The origins and early development of the Egyptian Church have been studied by Bell (1953: 78–105); Roberts (1979); Pearson (1986 and 1990: 194–213); Bagnall (1993: 278–89). See now also Jakab (2001).

[2] Eusebius' list in his *Ecclesiastical History* of ten names up to Demetrius, succeeding each other at approximately ten-year intervals, has all the appearance of being fictitious. The names, which are distributed throughout the narrative, are: Annianus (*HE* 2. 24), Abilius (3. 21), Cerdo (3. 21), Primus (4. 1), Justus (4. 4), Eumenes (4. 5), Marcus (4. 11. 6), Celadion (4. 11. 6), Agrippinus (4. 20) and Julian (5. 9).

episcopate Pantaenus, Clement, and Origen were active, that Eusebius has reliable material to draw on.

The near-invisibility of the early Egyptian Church may be explained by the vicissitudes of the once large Jewish community that in the earliest years must have formed the Church's matrix. The Jewish revolt of 115–117 resulted in the destruction of Jewish life and property on such a scale that Egyptian Jewry never fully recovered. The Church in this period was probably insufficiently differentiated from Judaism not to be affected by its eclipse (Roberts 1979: 55–8). At any rate, it lost the matrix that would have enabled it to spread rapidly in the nome capitals (Bagnall 1993: 278). This is a more plausible explanation of the lack of early evidence than Bauer's theory that Christianity's original form in Egypt was what was later judged to be heretical, with the result that its history was suppressed out of embarrassment once ecclesiastical Christianity had established itself in the course of the third century (Bauer 1934, trans. 1971; cf. Roberts 1979: 49–54; Pearson 1986 and 1990: 196–8; Jakab 2001: 58–61).

The Church's recovery between 117 and 200 was slow. Although its original foundation had probably been from Palestine, in the second phase of its development there is evidence of help from the West. For example, the parish organization that was now established at Alexandria resembles the Roman. Moreover, second-century fragments of the *Shepherd* of Hermas and the *Adversus Haereses* of Irenaeus discovered in the Fayyum point to close contacts with the West at precisely this period (Roberts 1979: 12, 23, 53, 59). By the end of the second century the Alexandrian Church had recovered its strength and was already exhibiting two of its characteristic features: centralized episcopal government and a Platonizing intellectualist tradition.

In the development of the episcopacy, Bishop Demetrius is a key figure. He has been described as 'clearly the first "monarchical bishop" in Alexandria' (Pearson 1990: 209), or even 'the Second Founder of the Church in Alexandria' (Telfer 1952: 2). Later tradition reports that at the start of his episcopate he was the only bishop in Egypt. By his death he had appointed three suffragans. His successor, Heraclas, consecrated a further twenty (Pearson 1990: 211 no. 64). These suffragans enhanced the power of the bishops of Alexandria. In the neighbouring regions of Syria and Asia Minor, the provincial metropolises became in the third century the seats of metropolitan bishops enjoying considerable independence. In Egypt, by contrast, the only metropolis (except in Libya) was Alexandria. The nome capitals lacked autonomy, and therefore, when Christian communities came to be established in them, so did their bishops. All power, both civil and ecclesiastical, resided in the city of Alexandria.

The Platonizing intellectualist tradition of the Alexandrian Church was the product of its interaction with its cultural environment. Second-century Alexandria was one of the foremost intellectual centres of the Roman world.

The library of the Museum had been open to the public since the time of Augustus. There was also the Serapeum, with its significant 'daughter library', and many schools, both public and private, which attracted students from all over the Mediterranean. The excavations which have been conducted in the Alexandrian quarter of Kôm el-Dikka have revealed an impressive series of lecture-halls, each with a seating capacity of sixty to eighty students (Haas 1997: 155, 191–3). These halls date from the reconstruction of the quarter in the early fourth century, but earlier buildings were probably similar. Alexandria was famous for the teaching of medicine, mathematics, and rhetoric, but the crowning subject was philosophy. Galen, for example, who came in the 150s to study medicine, claims that any doctor worthy of the name must also be a philosopher (*Med. Phil.* 3. 60). No merely vocational training should be allowed to take precedence over the acquisition of wisdom. For wisdom leads to the attaining of perfection, which is to cease to be human (with all the failings that being human entails) and become like God (*Anim. Pass.* 3. 11).

The search for God began with an inward journey. Ever since Plato, 'Know thyself' had been the starting-point of wisdom (cf. *Charm.* 164d; *Ep.* 7. 341–2). To embark upon a programme of spiritual development, however, one did not need to belong to the educated elite. Any 'literate but not especially learned' person who wanted to investigate 'his actual or potential relationship with God' (Fowden 1993: xxi) could always find a suitable teacher. Before Clement began to receive students, the ecclesiastically minded Christian seeker might have attended the school of Pantaenus, or, if he was attracted by a more esoteric brand of Christianity, the rival school of Basilides' son, Isidore. His non-Christian counterpart had access to a broad range of schools and study circles dedicated to the purification and perfection of the soul and its ascent to God. The teachers of these *didaskaleia* included Hermetists, Gnostics, and fringe members of the philosophical establishment such as the ex-Christian (according to Porphyry) Ammonius Saccas. Ammonius is described by Dillon as 'a charismatic purveyor of Numenian Neopythagoreanism' whom one 'did not come upon . . . in the normal academic round, but had to be put on to . . ., almost initiated into his circle' (1996: 381, 383). This did not prevent his attracting to his lecture hall first-rate minds such as Plotinus and Origen. In Alexandria the pursuit of wisdom could transcend sectarian boundaries.

The popular literature that circulated among Alexandrian Christians in the pre-Constantinian era reflected these interests. It has long been known that apocryphal gospels and apocalypses were widely read (Gamble 1995: 236). The discovery in 1945, however, of the Nag Hammadi texts, a collection of spiritual writings hidden in the late fourth or early fifth century in response to the changed cultural conditions of the times, has given us a more precise appreciation of the yearning of at least one group of educated Christians for the transcendent.[3] The sixty-two tractates of the cache, distributed among thirteen codices, comprise a wide variety of genres. There is, for example, a passage from Plato (*Republic* 588a–589b), a Hermetic text (*Asclepius* 21–9), a collection of Neopythagorean maxims (*The Sentences of Sextus*), and an example of Christian wisdom literature (*The Teachings of Silvanus*), besides a number of Gnostic works of apocalyptic ascent (such as *Marsanes*, *Allogenes*, and *Zostrianos*) and other writings of a more wildly esoteric nature. *The Teachings of Silvanus* and the apocalyptic tractates are of particular interest to us, for in these works Jewish elements blend with popular Platonism to produce a powerful teaching centred on the notion of self-transcendence.

The earliest is probably *The Teachings of Silvanus*. A master urges his disciple to discover the divine element within himself: 'From now on, then, my son, return to your divine nature' (*NHL* VII. 4. 90). 'Do not bring grief or trouble to the divine which is within you' (*NHL* VII. 4. 92). The mind is in the image of God. To live by the mind is to become assimilated to the angelic life. Indeed, divine reason raises man above the angels (*NHL* VII. 4. 116). Christ is essential to this process because one cannot know God except through Jesus Christ, who has the Father's image (*NHL* VII. 4. 100). In a passage strongly reminiscent of Clement, Silvanus says that through Christ the rational man makes himself like God, even while still living on earth (*NHL* VII. 4. 108; cf. *Strom.* 7. 101. 4). For Christ 'who has exalted man became like God, not in order that he might bring God down to man, but than man might become like God' (*NHL* VII. 4. 111).

The stories of Gnostic heavenly ascent also assume a divine kernel in the human make-up, at least of the elect. 'Awaken your divine part to God,' says Zostrianos (*NHL* VIII. 1. 130), for the ascent is primarily inward. 'Understand yourself as you really are,' says Allogenes (*NHL* XI. 3. 59). 'Withdraw to reality and you will find it standing at rest and still' (ibid.). Zostrianos, in his vision, rises by a series of purificatory baptisms through successive grades of angelic being (*NHL* VIII. 1. 6) until his soul is eventually reintegrated with the divine (*NHL* VIII. 1. 53), anticipating thus in the inward journey the soul's ascent to the heavenly world after death.

These works were known and studied in serious intellectual circles. Plotinus encountered them in Rome in the mid-third century in the possession of Christians (Porphyry, *V. Plot.* 16), and no doubt they also circulated in Alexandria. When Clement arrived there in about 180, drawn by the reputation for learning of its Christian teachers, particularly Pantaenus, he would have been aware of schools claiming a superior, arcane wisdom. The most important of these had been founded by Valentinus and Basilides in the generation before Clement. Valentinus had transferred his establishment to

---

[3] For a discussion of the possible identity of this group see Rousseau 1999: 26–8.

Rome in about 136. Basilides had died soon afterwards. But they left behind them disciples who continued their traditions. One of these was Basilides' son, Isidore, who succeeded his father as head of his school.

2. The School of Basilides

Basilides is usually considered a Gnostic teacher in the opposite camp to Pantaenus and Clement. Too strong a contrast, however, is misleading. Basilides' intellectual background, like that of Clement, was the standard mix of Stoic ethics and Pythagorean theology that used to be labelled 'eclecticism' but is now regarded as characteristic of the Platonist philosophy of the Hellenistic age (Dillon and Long 1988: 1–13). Against this background Basilides expounded a sophisticated version of Christianity, drawing on an esoteric tradition that he claimed had come down through Matthias, which sought to satisfy the religious and intellectual concerns of his Alexandrian audience. None of his writings has survived, but from the accounts given by Irenaeus and Hippolytus and the fragments preserved by Clement and Origen the main lines of his approach may be established.[4]

Basilides' anthropology was correlative to a cosmology in which all that is descends from a supreme source and returns to it. There is a tripartite division in the original mixture of all the elements (the *panspermia*), which Hippolytus, in his account of Basilides' system, describes as fine particles, particles needing purification, and dense particles (*Ref.* 7. 22; Osborne 1987: 289). The finest particles quickly ascend and return to their source. This is the first sonship. The second sonship ascends once it has been equipped with a wing provided by the Holy Spirit. The third sonship is left behind to correct and perfect the souls below (*Ref.* 7. 25; Osborne 1987: 297–9). There is thus a movement from initial confusion first towards segregation and then towards restoration. Jesus is the first-fruit of the segregation. The *pneumatikoi*, revealed by the Gospel as the children of God, follow Jesus and, after purification, ascend and become like the most fine-particled. They leave their psychic selves behind and put on a new individual soul. For the elect are transcendent by nature. Among the rest, ignorance prevails to prevent the lower souls from longing for what they cannot have, 'like fish yearning to graze with the sheep on the mountains' (*Ref.* 7. 27; Osborne 1987: 305). Everything finds its proper place in the end, the purified elements above, and the denser mass below.

---

[4] Irenaeus, *AH* 1. 24; Hippolytus, *Ref.* 7. 14–28, Greek text with English trans. conveniently in Osborne 1987: 274–309. The fragments (seven from Clement and one from Origen) are collected in Layton 1987: 427–44. Hippolytus' account has been thought to sit awkwardly with that of Irenaeus and the fragments from Clement, but Obsorne (1987: 52–67) has demonstrated that it is based on a close reading of Basilides. Cf. Grant (1979), who defends the originality of Irenaeus' account.

Clement studied Basilides' and his son Isidore's writings carefully.[5] What he objected to was not Basilides' speculative cosmology but the deterministic character of his scheme of salvation and the implied ethical consequences. If the elect are transcendent by nature, the commandments are rendered redundant and moral effort becomes superfluous (*Strom.* 4. 165. 3; 5. 3. 3). Basilides' scheme, however, offered a neat solution to the problem of innocent suffering. By means of successive reincarnations the souls of the elect might pass through several life cycles before being purified. Their suffering in this life balances sins committed in a previous one. As for the tribulations of the martyrs, Basilides thought the suffering of noble souls was a consequence of the sinfulness of being human; martyrs were not punished for sins committed, which was why they sometimes seemed not to feel any pain at all. Clement refutes this at some length on the grounds that it denies divine providence. Indeed, it leads to the logical absurdity that if martyrdom is regarded as punishment, even in attenuated form, then faith and doctrine co-operate in punishment and the devil is deified (*Strom.* 4. 81–3).

3. The School of Pantaenus

It was therefore not the school founded by Basilides that attracted Clement but the lecture hall of the former Stoic (or Pythagorean), Pantaenus.[6] In his apologia at the beginning of the *Stromateis* Clement lists his teachers without naming them (*Strom.* 1. 1. 11). The last and best was his Alexandrian mentor, 'the true Sicilian bee', who inspired all who heard him with a thirst for *gnosis*. It is Eusebius who gives us Pantaenus' name and adds the further information that he directed the education of the faithful at Alexandria at 'a school of sacred learning' that had existed 'from ancient custom' and was still extant in Eusebius' own time (*HE* 5. 10). This has often been thought to refer to the Alexandrian 'Catechetical School' that is described in greater detail by the fifth-century historian Philip of Side.[7] Most probably, however, the schools of Pantaenus, Clement, and even Origen were never more than private *didaskaleia*, even though they seem to have worked closely with the bishop. Eusebius appears to have run them together and institutionalized them under episcopal control, projecting into earlier times, perhaps, the more formal arrangements that existed in his own day. The Catechetical School proper dates from the time when Bishop Demetrius asked Origen, who was

---

[5] Basilides is quoted by Clement at *Strom.* 4. 81. 2–4. 83. 2; 4. 86. 1; 4. 153. 3; 4. 162. 1; 4. 165. 3; 5. 3. 2–3; 5. 74. 3; Isidore at *Strom.* 2. 20. 113; 2. 114. 1; 3. 1. 2; 6. 6. 53. On Isidore see Christou 1978*a*: 152.

[6] On Pantaenus see most recently Jakab 2001: 107–15.

[7] Fragment published by Dodwell 1689: 488; reproduced in Christou 1978*a*: 757–8. On Philip see *ODCC*[3], s.v. Philip Sidetes.

already running his own *didaskaleion*, to undertake the teaching of catechumens (Eusebius, *HE* 6. 3. 3). Later Origen appointed a deputy, Heraclas, to teach these beginners while he devoted himself to directing more advanced studies. It is doubtful whether Origen's school of higher learning survived his transfer to Caesarea. The Catechetical School, however, appears to have been maintained under successive bishops until the end of the fourth century, when it was probably closed in the wake of the Origenist crisis soon after the death of its last known head, Didymus the Blind.[8]

4. Clement of Alexandria

Clement of Alexandria (*c.*150 to *c.*215) was the first ecclesiastical writer to apply the technical terms of deification to the Christian life. Some of his expressions are startling to Western ears (Tollinton 1914: ii. 91–2; Dodds 1965: 74). According to Clement, the Christian is deified by a heavenly teaching (*Prot.* 11. 114. 4); when fully perfected after the likeness of his teacher, he 'becomes a god while still moving about in the flesh' (ἐν σαρκὶ περιπολῶν θεός) (*Strom.* 7. 101. 4); and at the end of his life he is enthroned 'with the other gods' in the heavenly places. Tollinton felt that 'some reduction in our conception of the godhead is certainly involved in such phraseology', but suggests that with regard to the spirit's progress in the higher life 'we should rather envy [Clement's] optimism than criticise his terms' (1914: ii. 92). Others have not been so generous. Benjamin Drewery, Clement's fiercest critic, dismisses with contempt his 'absurd picture of the perfect Christian as ἐν σαρκὶ περιπολῶν θεός' (1975: 61).

Such polemical remarks at least highlight one of the central problems. Clement teaches a supremely transcendent God, in whom participation is not a 'natural relation, as the founders of the heresies declare' (*Strom.* 2. 16. 73), yet his doctrine of man has divinity as its *telos*. How is his apophatic theology to be reconciled with such an optimistic anthropology?[9] Alexandrians were to struggle with this question until Cyril's time. A satisfactory solution requires a christology which does justice to both the human and the divine in Christ. For a transcendent God can only be approached by human beings in an intimate way if he has first united himself to human nature in the person of Christ. But it was not until the Arian controversy that the problem was formulated in those terms. Clement's task was to determine how a human being could become sufficiently like a God who was beyond all

---

[8] On the Catechetical School as a late development see Bardy 1937 and 1942. This view is opposed by Méhat (1966: 62–70), who argues that Pantaenus and Clement must have undertaken their teaching with the encouragement of the bishop. Runia (1993: 133 n. 3) regards Méhat's refutation as convincing. But Jakab (2001: 91–106) sides with Bardy. Cf. also Le Boulluec 1987.

[9] This point is well brought out by Osborn 1981: 116–18.

human knowledge and virtue to enjoy a community of being with him. His attempt to harmonize two approaches, one philosophical, linking Genesis 1: 26 with *Theaetetus* 176b in the Philonic manner, the other ecclesiastical, centred on the idea of participatory union with Christ in the Pauline and Irenaean manner, may lack final coherence, but at least it set the agenda for his successors.

(a) Vocabulary

Clement's originality is strikingly evident in his vocabulary. He is the first ecclesiastical writer to speak of the θεοποιούμενοι, if not of θεοποίησις— the noun does not appear until the fourth century. His favourite word for pagan deification is ἐκθειάζω,[10] which usually means 'to treat as divine' or 'to ascribe divinity to' without any implication of personal commitment. Next come θειάζω,[11] ἀποθέωσις,[12] θεοποιέω,[13] and ἐκθεόω,[14] with one instance each of ἀποθεόω (*Prot.* 10. 96. 4) and θεοποιός (*Prot.* 4. 51. 6). In a Christian context there is only one instance of ἐκθειάζω—one of the virtues of Christian philosophy is that it recognizes the divinity of the Creator: ἡ γὰρ ἀκόλουθος Χριστῷ διδασκαλία καὶ τὸν δημιουργὸν ἐκθειάζει (*Strom.* 1. 52. 3). For the deification of the Christian Clement uses: θεοποιέω (three times— *Prot.* 209. 87. 1; 11. 114. 4; *Strom.* 6. 125. 4), and more rarely, θεόω (*Strom.* 4. 152. 1), ἐκθεόω (*Paed.* 1. 98. 3) and θεοποιός (*QDS* 19).[15] Θεοποιέω is thus a key term which is used in both pagan and Christian contexts, but with different meanings. In the context of pagan deification θεοποιέω never refers to human beings. Like the apologists Aristides, Tatian, and Athenagoras, Clement uses this verb solely for the deification of inanimate things. In a Christian context θεοποιέω was therefore available for the deification of human beings without too close an association with the deification celebrated by polytheistic cults. Indeed, the application of θεοποιέω to human beings is not at all common even in pagan philosophical writers. The only examples of a usage close to Clement's come from his contemporary, the Sceptical philosopher Sextus Empiricus, who uses θεοποιέω for the deification of Pythagoras (*Adv. Math.* 7. 94) and the Stoic sage (*Adv. Math.* 7. 423), and also from the Hermetic Corpus, which has one instance of θεόω in an eschatological context for the soul that after acquiring *gnosis* and becoming

---

[10] There are twelve instances of its use: *Prot.* 1. 3. 1; 2. 26. 1; 2. 31. 1; 4. 63. 5; 5. 64. 1; 5. 64. 3; 10. 102. 3; *Strom.* 1. 50. 6; 1. 94. 1; 2. 58. 2; 5. 69. 6; 5. 108. 1.

[11] Seven instances: *Prot.* 1. 2. 1; 2. 13. 4; 4. 49. 1; 4. 51. 3; *Strom.* 2. 119. 4; 4. 85. 1; 7. 4. 3.

[12] Five instances: *Strom.* 1. 105. 1; 1. 105. 3; 1. 105. 4; 1. 137. 3; 3. 5. 2.

[13] Four instances: *Prot.* 2. 26. 3; 3. 44. 24; *Strom.* 6. 146. 3; 7. 31. 2.

[14] Two instances: *Prot.* 2. 26. 5; *Strom.* 1. 105. 1.

[15] Apart from these terms Clement frequently calls the perfected Christian θεός. The following is, so far as I am aware, a complete list: *Prot.* 12. 123. 1 (quoting Ps. 82: 6); *Paed.* 1. 26. 1 (quoting Ps. 82: 6); 3. 2. 1 (quoting Heraclitus); *Strom.* 2. 125. 4–5 (quoting Ps. 82: 6); 4. 149. 8–150. 1 (quoting Ps. 82: 6 and Empedocles); 4. 155. 2 (quoting Plato); 6. 113. 3; 6. 146. 1 (alluding to Ps. 82: 6); 7. 3. 6; 7. 56. 6; 7. 95. 2; 7. 101. 4.

pure *nous* has become a power in God (*CH* I. 26), and another for the soul that has been transformed into *nous* by a regeneration in this life (*CH* XIII. 10). None of these, however, provides an exact parallel with Clement.[16] Furthermore, he not only found new uses for the term θεοποιέω, but is also the first Greek writer to endow ἐκθεόω with the meaning 'to deify' and the first to make θεοποιός mean 'deifying'.

(b) Cultural Background

Clement was also inventive on the doctrinal level. He was a Platonist, a Philonist, and a Euhemerist, a close student of the Bible, of Gnostic masters, and of ecclesiastical writers, and a well-informed commentator on mystery cults and Egyptian religion, but his teaching is more than simply a blending of these influences. He presents a coherent Christian anthropology which has subsumed elements from his background and transformed them into a noble vision of the destiny of the true Christian.[17]

A rapid survey of the rich cultural milieu in which Clement worked will help us to place his achievement in context. Before becoming a Christian, Clement had been a Platonist. His knowledge of Plato was not mediated through any Jewish or Christian writer but was extensive and first-hand. More precisely, he was a Middle Platonist, the modern term for a philosopher who professed the amalgam of Platonic and Pythagorean theology, Stoic ethics, and Aristotelian logic that school Platonism had been since the time of Eudorus of Alexandria. The goal of this Platonism was to become like God so far as possible (Dillon 1996: 115–35). Clement's pursuit of it brought him to Christianity even before he got to Egypt. At Alexandria he studied scriptural exegesis ('the spoil of the flowers of the apostolic and prophetic meadow') with Pantaenus, but probably pursued his philosophical studies with other teachers too. Salvatore Lilla thinks it very likely that Clement had a close relationship with Ammonius Saccas (1971: 5).

At Alexandria Clement also discovered Philo, whose works had survived Hadrian's destruction of Alexandrian Jewry through having been deposited in a Christian library, in all probability the library of the school of Pantaenus (Runia 1993: 22, 135). Clement mentions Philo four times but draws on him

---

[16] Mondésert (1944: 192) and Lilla (1971: 124–7) have also noted linguistic parallels between Clement and Sextus Empiricus, though none of them proves Clement's dependence on Sextus. It is also doubtful whether Clement was acquainted with any Hermetic texts.

[17] Estimates of the Christian character of Clement's doctrine of deification vary. Butterworth (1916: 163) and Lattey (1916: 257–62) see in the doctrine a Hellenic form with a Christian content. This is also the view of Gross, who says that Clement adopted 'l'idéal hellénique de la divinisation . . . mais en lui infusant une âme chrétienne' (1938: 161). Baert (1965: 473–4) and Lilla (1971: 186–7) believe that deification is basically Platonic and Gnostic. Völker (1952: 606–8) and Osborn (1981: 113–18), on the other hand, maintain that it is fundamentally Christian, a metaphor for the attaining of immortality. My own view, like that of Völker and Osborn, is that Clement has integrated Platonic and Philonic elements into a profoundly Christian perspective.

more extensively than these citations would imply.[18] The fundamental lesson he learned from him was how to bring his Platonism to bear on biblical thought and exegesis (Runia 1993: 155). In this connection, Philo's exegesis of the relationship between Sarah and Hagar was important, Sarah standing for faith, while Hagar, her handmaid, represented philosophy.[19] The figure of Moses was also of fundamental significance, but Clement adapts Philo's treatment of Moses to a Christian perspective. The true Law-giver is now the only-begotten Son. Moses is simply the perfect man who has attained gnosis and therefore is the paradigm for every Christian Gnostic. As David Runia remarks, Clement is 'constantly in dialogue with his source' (1993: 142), giving his material a new thrust in accordance with his Christian convictions.

These convictions were shaped by his Christian contemporaries. But he refers to them by name only when he disapproves of them, so that their influence must be inferred from the way he handles his principal theological themes. Two figures, in particular, stand out. Henry Chadwick believes that Clement knew Justin, because he reproduces Justin's teaching that all wisdom is summed up in Christ: 'Both the Old Testament and Greek philosophy are alike tutors to bring us to Christ and are both tributaries of the one great river of Christianity' (1966: 40; cf. *Strom.* 1. 28. 3; 1. 29. 1). The evidence of Clement's dependence on Irenaeus is even stronger. L. G. Patterson has shown that it was from Irenaeus that Clement derived the basic lines of his anthropology (1997*a*). The underlying incarnational scheme that we find in Clement (the divine became human that the human might become divine), the distinction between image and likeness (the former congenital, the latter acquired through progress in virtue), and the doctrine of a 'soft' Fall (Adam created like a child for the reception of virtue) with the implication that the task of all Christians is to advance from imperfection to perfection, are all Irenaean themes.

We know that Clement also studied non-ecclesiastical Christian writers. His close examination of Basilidean and Valentinian texts has already been mentioned (cf. 4. 5 and 5. 2 above). The careful notes he made on Theodotus illustrate his method: excerpting, commenting, reusing the vocabulary so that it is often difficult to separate quotation from commentary. He was able to do this because he was secure in his basic ecclesiastical perspective. Gnostic elements are integrated into an orthodox (or 'proto-orthodox')

---

[18] All four citations are in the first two books of the *Stromateis*: 1. 31. 1; 1. 72. 4; 1. 151. 2; 2. 100. 3 (Runia 1993: 135–6). The last is on Plato's *telos* (becoming like God) being the same as that of Moses. The absence of any citation or even approximate quotation in Books VI and VII of the *Stromateis* lends support to the view that the work was finished after Clement had left Alexandria, when he no longer had access to Philo (Runia 1993: 144). The works of Philo which Clement made most use of are: *Post. C., Congr., V. Mos.* and *Virt.* On Clement's debt to Philo, besides Runia's magisterial survey (1993: 132–56) see Chadwick 1966 and 1970, and Van den Hoek 1988.

[19] Sarah and Hagar are also allegorized by Paul, but differently (Gal. 4: 21–31). In the Pauline version (the only use of ἀλληγορέω in the NT) they stand for the two covenants. Clement reports Philo's etymology of Sarah and Hagar at *Strom.* 1. 31. 1 (Runia 1993: 85–6, 135).

scheme with the confidence of one who was certain how they related to ecclesiastical Christianity (cf. Lilla 1971: 181–9). Secular literature and pagan religion were treated in the same way. The Greek philosophers and poets are seen as often divinely inspired because everything of value they taught had been plagiarized from Moses and the prophets (cf. *Strom.* 5. 14). The mysteries and the impressive processions that issued on the appointed days from Egyptian temples are observed accurately and without animus (*Strom.* 6. 4; cf. Mondésert 1944: 33). Clement may castigate some of the religious practices of his non-Christian contemporaries, but he does not feel threatened by them. His Euhemerism gave him an overall unifying theory which enabled him to see all manifestations of polytheism in rationalist terms as the fruit of human deification.

(c) Texts and Themes

Clement first refers to Christian deification in the *Protrepticus*. After mentioning the kenotic action of the Logos in becoming man, he echoes Irenaeus' 'exchange formula', saying that the Word now speaks to us 'having become man in order that you too may learn from a man how it is even possible for a man to become a god' (ὁ λόγος ὁ τοῦ θεοῦ ἄνθρωπος γενόμενος, ἵνα δὴ καὶ σὺ παρὰ ἀνθρώπου μάθῃς, πῇ ποτε ἄρα ἄνθρωπος γένηται θεός)[20] How do we learn from him? Through the Scriptures. Hence the Scriptures are sanctifying and deifying (τὰ ἱεροποιοῦντα καὶ θεοποιοῦντα γράμματα), for through them God conforms human beings to his own likeness (*Prot.* 9. 87. 1). Speaking through the Scriptures Christ manifests himself as the light and life of the world who transplants 'corruption to the soil of incorruption', granting us the Father's divine portion and 'making men divine by a heavenly teaching' (οὐρανίῳ διδασκαλίᾳ θεοποιῶν τὸν ἄνθρωπον), 'putting laws into their minds and writing them upon the heart' (*Prot.* 11. 114. 4; cf. Jer. 31: 33 and Heb. 8: 10).

Through the Scriptures Christ's teaching is implanted in our hearts, assimilating us to God and making us divine. The way this happens is set out in a passage in the sixth book of the *Stromateis*. According to Plato the truth can only be learned from God or from his progeny (*Tim.* 40de). In the Scriptures we are taught the truth by the Son of God himself, first through the prophecies and then more clearly in the Gospels. Even in the Gospels, however, the truth is veiled, for Christ always expressed the divine mysteries

---

[20] *Prot.* 1. 8. 4, trans. Butterworth. Butterworth's interpretation is also that of Bigg (1913: 106), Bouyer (1968: 273), Dalmais (1954–7: 1378), and Floyd (1971: 87). C. Mondésert, however, in the Sources Chrétiennes edition of the *Protrepticus* renders the passage thus: 'le Logos de Dieu devenu homme, afin qu'à vous encore ce soit un homme qui apprenne comment un Dieu est devenu homme' (SC 2 *bis*: 63). Mondésert's translation is a possible one, but unlikely in the context. We know from a papyrus fragment (*P. Oxyr.* iii. 405) that Irenaeus' *Adversus Haereses* circulated in Egypt at a very early date, perhaps as early as the end of the second century (Roberts 1979: 23). It is noteworthy that a version of the 'exchange formula' is also found in *The Teachings of Silvanus* (*NHL* VII. 4. 111) from the same period (see 5. 1 above).

in parables. The Scriptures do not yield their meaning without an authoritative guide, and that guide is the Church's rule of faith (τὸν ἐκκλησιαστικὸν
κανόνα). Interpreting Scripture in accordance with the Church's rule reveals
the truth taught by Christ, which is divine knowledge (γνῶσιν θείαν), leading
to prudence or practical wisdom (φρόνησιν). Divine knowledge and
practical wisdom are roughly equivalent, says Clement, 'and are found in
those who are being deified' (ἐν τοῖς θεοποιουμένοις). They are divine and
contemplative, unlike self-control (σωφροσύνη), for example, which is merely
human—an imperfect practical wisdom, so to speak—and therefore render a
person like God (*Strom.* 6. 125. 4).

In the seventh book of the *Stromateis* Clement again advocates the need
for sound criteria in interpreting the Scriptures. Without the Church's rule
of faith—'the canon of truth' received 'from the truth itself' (*Strom.* 7.
94. 5)—the reader of the Scriptures will go astray; with it he will attain
perfection:

As if, then, one were to become a beast instead of a man, like those who were
changed by Circe's drugs (*Odyssey* 10. 235–47), so it is with him who has spurned the
tradition of the Church and has suddenly taken up with the fancies of human
sects; he has lost the character of a man of God, and of enduring trust in the Lord.
But he who has returned from this deceit, after hearing the Scriptures, and has
turned his life to the truth, such a person becomes in the end as it were a god
instead of a man.   (*Strom.* 7. 95. 1–2; trans. Mayor/Chadwick)

This threefold division into beasts, men, and gods reflects Clement's threefold distinction between perfect actions (κατορθώματα), which raise a man
to the highest glory, intermediate actions, which are sufficient to enable
believers to be saved, and sinful actions, which lead to condemnation (*Strom.*
6. 111. 3). Those guilty of sinful actions lose their human dignity and become
like the beasts; those who have achieved perfection through being taught by
Christ augment it and become 'as it were' gods. As so often, Clement
qualifies the word 'god', drawing attention to its analogous character.

It is divine *gnosis* received in accordance with the ecclesiastical rule of faith
that deifies. We attain it by imitating Christ, for Christ, like any teacher, makes
his disciples like him:

And just as Isomachus will make those who attend to his instructions husbandmen,
and Lampis sea-captains, and Charidemus commanders, and Simon horsemen, and
Perdix hucksters, and Crobylus cooks, and Archelaus dancers, and Homer poets, and
Pyrrho wranglers, and Demosthenes orators, and Chrysippus logicians, and Aristotle
men of science, and Plato philosophers, so he who obeys the Lord and follows
the prophecy given through him is fully perfected after the likeness of his teacher,
and thus becomes a god while still moving about in the flesh (τελέως ἐκτελεῖται
κατ᾽ εἰκόνα τοῦ διδασκάλου ἐν σαρκὶ περιπολῶν θεός). (*Strom.* 7. 101. 4; trans.
Mayor/Chadwick)

Other passages also emphasize the deifying effect of imitating Christ. In the first book of the *Paedagogus* Clement says that Christ came to transform 'earth-born man into holy and heavenly man'. We can realize this destiny in our own lives through the imitation of Christ, which is brought about by listening to the Word and 'meditating on the Saviour's heavenly mode of life by which we are deified' (τὴν ἐπουράνιον μελετῶντες πολιτείαν, καθ' ἥν ἐκθεούμεθα) (*Paed.* 1. 98. 3). Christ's mode of life is a 'model of incorruption' and moral excellence. By participating in this incorruption and moral excellence we are assimilated to God and therefore deified.

Imitating Christ also enables the believer to appropriate true beauty:

That person with whom the Logos dwells and who does not put on paint or make-up but keeps the form of the Logos and is made like God, that person is beautiful as opposed to beautified. There is a true beauty which is God; and that person becomes a god because God wishes it.[21] Heraclitus was therefore right to say: 'Men are gods and gods men' (frg. 66, Diels). It is the same Logos. This is a manifest mystery: God is in man, and man is a god, and the mediator fulfils the will of the Father. For the Logos common to both is a mediator, and at the same time Son of God and Saviour of men, God's servant and our pedagogue.   (*Paed.* 3. 2. 1)

A beautiful person imitates the Logos, the image of the Father, who dwells within the soul and has become incarnate in Jesus Christ. In ordinary people there is a beauty of soul, which is the understanding (διάνοια) and a beauty of body, which is self-restraint (σωφροσύνη). In the Lord's case his beauty of soul is beneficence (τὸ εὐεργετικόν) and his beauty of body immortality (τὸ ἀθάνατον). By exercising self-control corporeally, and imitating the incarnate Logos spiritually, the serious Christian acquires the beauty of the Logos, that is to say, his beneficence and his immortality, which make him a god. At the same time these attributes are divine gifts; the Christian 'becomes a god because God wishes it'.

Clement supports this assertion not with a biblical text but—in keeping with his conviction that the Greek philosophers elaborate and refine the teaching which they first found in the Hebrew Scriptures—with a quotation, or rather, an adaptation of a quotation, from Heraclitus.[22] Heraclitus is notoriously obscure, but this quotation, which in its original form asserted that immortals are mortal and mortals immortal, is similar to others in which he states that opposites are two sides of the same reality. Mortals and immortals form a continuum. In the words of his latest editor, 'the opposites are "one" because they *condition* each other' (Marcovich 1967: 241). Mortality has meaning only in relation to immortality, and vice versa. Clement,

---

[21] Following the reading of the Sources Chrétiennes edition. Marrou notes: 'Même dialectique dans l'*A Diognète*, 10, 4. Et c'est ce texte de l'*A Diognète* qui nous fait garder la leçon du manuscrit P: ὁ θεός (ὁ θεός, Bernays, Stählin)' (SC 158: 14).

[22] The original form of the fragment is given by Hippolytus: ἀθάνατοι θνητοί, θνητοὶ ἀθάνατοι (*Ref.* 9). On Clement's adaptation of it see Wheelwright 1959: 74–5, 132–3, 147.

however, gives the quotation a different thrust. It is generally agreed that the
phrase, 'It is the same Logos', is Clement's own comment and not part of the
quotation (Wheelwright 1959: 147; Marcovich 1967: 241). 'Logos' is indeed a
term Heraclitus uses for the underlying unity of things, but Clement uses it
in an entirely different way. The Logos that is common to both God and man
in Clement is both the Word that took the form of a servant, namely, the
flesh, and set it free from corruption, endowing it with incorruption and
immortality, and also the Word that dwells within man, guiding his *logistikon*.
The remark, 'God is in man, and man is a god', is ambiguous, but is probably
Clement's restatement in more monotheistic terms of Heraclitus' saying.
The notion that the Logos has a dual aspect, both indwelling the human
mind and transcending it, may have been derived from Justin.[23] It is the
indwelling Logos that enables a human being to be called a god.

If participation in moral excellence is attained by imitating Christ on the
ethical level, participation in incorruption requires the experience of
baptism. In the first book of the *Paedagogus*, in a passage clearly dependent on
Irenaeus (see 4. 10 above), Clement sets out the effects of the sacrament on
the believer. Christ, he says, was perfected by the bath of baptism alone and
sanctified by the descent of the Holy Spirit:

> The same also takes place in our case, whose exemplar Christ became. Being
> baptized, we are illuminated; illuminated, we become sons; being made sons, we
> become perfect; being made perfect, we become immortal. 'I said,' says Scripture,
> 'you are gods and all of you sons of the Most High'. (*Paed.* 1. 26. 1; Ps. 82: 6)

There has been some discussion whether Clement intends us to understand
that baptism makes us gods at once, or at the end of a process involving
several stages.[24] In my view Clement thought baptism also brought illumination, adoption, perfection, and immortality not successively but all at once,
for God's gifts 'lack nothing'. At the same time their final fulfilment has not
been attained. Perfection is simultaneously both realized and unrealized. For
'the future is anticipated by the power of God's will' (*Paed.* 1. 26. 3). Faith and
regeneration bring perfection, 'for God is never weak', but perfection is only
consummated at the end, when 'what is generated in time' is 'secured for
eternity' (*Paed.* 1. 28. 5). Baptism makes us adopted sons or gods and therefore perfect and immortal in principle, but our perfection and immortality
need to be brought to fulfilment in eternity.

Clement's exegesis of Ps. 82: 6 in this passage recalls that of Justin and
Irenaeus (see 4. 6 and 4. 10 above). The explicit link with baptism, the
inaugurated eschatology coupled with the idea of moral progress, are found

---

[23] Cf. 2 *Apol.* 8 (where Heraclitus is also mentioned) and 2 *Apol.* 13, with Barnard's note *ad loc.* (1997:
196–200 no. 71).

[24] Butterworth (1916: 160) and Dalmais (1954–7: 1378) favour deification by stages, Lattey (1916: 260)
as an immediate consequence of baptism.

in *Adversus Haereses* 3. 6. 1; 3. 19. 1; and 4. 38. 3 (see 4. 10 above). Elsewhere his exegesis of Ps. 82: 6, however, goes beyond Irenaeus in the development of the moral aspect and, moreover, brings into play the Philonic connection of Gen. 1: 26 with *Theaetetus* 176b (see 3. 2 above). At the end of the *Protrepticus* Clement declares that man is beloved of God, with the result that everything that belongs to God also belongs to man:

It is time then for us to affirm that only the devout Christian is rich and of sound mind and well-born (*Theaet.* 176b), and therefore the image together with the likeness of God (cf. Gen. 1: 26); and to say and believe that when he has been made by Christ Jesus 'righteous and holy with the help of practical wisdom' (*Theaet.* 176b), he also becomes in the same degree already like God. Accordingly, the prophet openly reveals this gracious favour when he says, 'I said you are gods and all of you sons of the Most High' (Ps. 82: 6). Now we, I say, we are those whom God has adopted, and of us alone he is willing to be called Father, not of the disobedient. (*Prot.* 12. 122. 4–123. 1; trans. Butterworth, modified)

Clement maintains that only a Christian can be a true philosopher, fulfilling not only the ideal of the Stoic sage, who was held to be truly rich and noble, but also the Platonic precept of *Thaeatetus* 176b to become like God so far as possible through the acquisition of righteousness with the help of practical wisdom. The Platonic 'likeness to God' is considered equivalent to the 'image and likeness' of Genesis 1: 26, which only Christ can restore because only he can impart righteousness. This recalls the Christian exegesis of Psalm 82: 6 already established by Justin and Irenaeus. Those who become like God are those whom the Scriptures call 'gods' because they have been baptized.

When Clement returns to Psalm 82: 6 in the *Stromateis*, however, he leaves the baptismal associations behind. The gods who are sons of the Most High are now perfected Christians who have conquered the passions:

'God stood in the congregation of the gods; in their midst he judges gods' (Ps. 82: 1). Who are these gods? They are those who are superior to pleasure, who rise above the passions, who have a precise knowledge of everything that they do, who are gnostics, who transcend the world. Then comes: 'I said you are gods and all of you sons of the Most High' (Ps. 82: 6). To whom is the Lord speaking? To those who have detached themselves as far as possible from everything human. (*Strom.* 2. 125. 4–5)

Later in the *Stromateis* the Christian Gnostic is again called a god with reference to Psalm 82: 6:

By this means it is possible for the Gnostic to have become a god. 'I said, you are gods and all of you sons of the Most High' (Ps. 82: 6). And Empedocles says that the souls of the wise become gods in this life, when he writes: 'But in the end they come among men on earth as prophets, bards, doctors and princes; and thence they arise as gods mighty in honour'. (frg. 146 Diels, 132 Wright; *Strom.* 4. 149. 8–4. 150. 1)

The Gnostic becomes a god by controlling his soul's lower faculties, for in this way he comes to resemble God, who is 'free from passion, from anger and from desire' (*Strom.* 4. 151. 1). Deification by imitation is corroborated by quotations from Psalm 82 and Empedocles, both of which are used in a way peculiar to Clement. Psalm 82: 6 is no longer cited as evidence for the deifying effect of baptism. The passage from Empedocles, which was taken by Clement's contemporaries to refer to escape from the cycle of reincarnation,[25] is made to support deification through imitating God. God's freedom from passion, anger, and desire is expressed by his oneness. When human beings overcome the passions and cease to have conflicting forces at work within them, they replicate within themselves the divine unity and thus come to be gods by analogy, even in this life.[26]

There is a final allusion to Psalm 82: 6 in an allegorical exposition of the Ten Commandments in the sixth book of the *Stromateis*. Here Clement calls believers 'gods' in relation to the first cause of divinity:

The fifth in the sequence is the commandment on the honour of father and mother. This clearly describes God as Father and Lord. It therefore also calls those who know him sons and gods. Accordingly, the Lord and Father is the Creator of the universe, and the mother is not, as some say, the substance from which we were made, nor, as others have taught, the Church, but the divine knowledge and wisdom, as Solomon says when he calls wisdom the mother of the just.[27]

The linking of sons and gods clearly refers to Psalm 82: 6. Just as we are sons in relation to God as Father, so we are gods in relation to God as Lord. Human beings are again 'gods' by analogy.

Almost immediately after this, Clement describes the deifying power of contemplation:

'Blessed is he who has been trained in scientific observation, and has no hostile intent against his fellow citizens, nor any urge to commit unjust actions, but studies the undecaying order of immortal nature to perceive how it came into existence and in what way and what manner it subsists. The practice of shameful deeds never adheres to such men' (Euripides, frg. 910). Plato therefore rightly says too that he who devotes himself to the contemplation of the ideas will live as a god among

---

[25] Cf. Diog. Laert. 7. 62 and 7. 77; Aelian, *De nat. animal.* 12. 7. Empedocles himself, according to Wright (1995: 74–5) seems to have thought of the final 'divine' state as the ultimately *permanent* union of the four elements.

[26] Cf. Philo, *QE* 2. 29. It is no coincidence that 'prophets, bards, doctors and princes' are categories of benefactors. There are two further passages which emphasize the connection between dispassion and deification: In the *Stromateis* Clement says that the passions pull us in different directions. When we eradicate them we replicate within ourselves one of the supreme divine attributes, that of unity: εἰς τὴν ἀπάθειαν θεούμενος ἄνθρωπος ἀχράντως μοναδικὸς γίνεται (*Strom.* 4. 152. 1). In his only surviving sermon he adds that paradoxically when we detach ourselves from possessions we become rich with another kind of wealth that deifies us and supplies us with eternal life (ἕτερον πλοῦτον θεοποιὸν καὶ ζωῆς χορηγὸν αἰωνίου) (*QDS* 19. 5).

[27] *Strom.* 6. 146. 1–2. The allusion to Solomon has not been identified.

men.[28] The intellect is the place of ideas, and the intellect is God. He therefore called him who contemplates the invisible God a living god among men. And in the *Sophist* Socrates called the stranger of Elea, who was a dialectician, a god (216ab): such are 'the gods who like foreign guests' frequent cities (*Odyssey* 17. 485). For when the soul has transcended the created world and is alone by itself and associates with the Ideas, like the 'coryphaeus' in the *Theaetetus* (173c), it has already become like an angel and will be with Christ, since it has become contemplative and always contemplates the will of God, in truth 'alone wise, while the rest flit like shadows' (*Odyssey* 10. 495). (*Strom.* 4. 155)

In this passage Clement's Middle Platonist, or more specifically Philonic, assumptions are very clearly set out. Like Philo, Clement sees the Forms as the thoughts of God (cf. Philo, *De Cher.* 49). A man who separates himself from the corporeal world and contemplates the Forms therefore assimilates himself to God. This is the standard philosophical ascent to God through the contemplation of intelligibles which we find in Philo and other Middle Platonists. Clement, however, adapts it to his own Christian perspective. Plato had reckoned that every philosopher was in a sense divine, for in this life he was preparing for the release of his inner self, his *nous*, from the cycle of rebirth and its return to its heavenly home (*Sophist* 216b). Philo is much more reserved. He is able to call Moses a god while on earth, but only in the sense that the intellect is a god to the soul or a wise man a god to a fool. In heaven Moses is a god by analogy because he has been separated from the body and has become pure *nous* (cf. *Leg. Alleg.* 1. 40; *Det.* 162; *V. Mos.* 2. 288). Clement follows Philo, but extends the category to which Moses belongs by calling any man a god who has transcended the corporeal state and become 'like an angel'. Contemplation begins to deify a man even in this life by removing him from the created world, from corporeity, and making him like God. It is an anticipation of life after death.

In the last two books of the *Stromateis*, which were probably written after Clement's departure from Alexandria (Méhat 1966: 42–54; Runia 1993: 144), the eschatological dimension of deification comes into greater prominence. In the sixth book Clement returns to the connection between dispassion, knowledge, and deification. Although salvation is one and is for all believers, there are nevertheless 'degrees of glory' (cf. 1 Cor. 15: 41) in heaven. For there are 'the more chosen among the chosen, who by reason of perfect knowledge are culled even from the Church itself and honoured with the most majestic glory' (*Strom.* 6. 107. 2). These are the twenty-four elders of Revelation 4: 4, who are seated on thrones clad in white garments with golden crowns on their heads. With them are 'the philosophers of God', who 'through the beneficence of assimilation to God' are promoted to the

---

[28] This is implied rather than stated by Plato. Stählin notes that here and in the following sentences are three versions of the same thought derived from the *Sophist*.

highest level of contemplation (*Strom.* 6. 108. 1). Below them are 'other
sheep' who are ordinary believers. These must put off the passions in order
to be saved. But 'just as to know is more than to believe, so to be dignified
with the highest honour after being saved is a greater thing than being saved'
(*Strom.* 6. 109. 2). A person who is simply saved is saved as a result of
'intermediate' actions. The Gnostic is saved through perfect actions and
attains to a higher status in heaven.[29] The performance of perfect actions
requires intelligence, knowledge, a good conscience, and divine grace:

> This good conscience preserves holiness towards God and justice towards men,
> and keeps the soul pure with serious thoughts, pure words and just deeds. By
> receiving the Lord's power in this way the soul studies to be a god ($\mu\epsilon\lambda\epsilon\tau\hat{q}$ $\epsilon\hat{i}\nu\alpha\iota$
> $\theta\epsilon\acute{o}s$), regarding nothing as evil except ignorance and action contrary to right reason,
> and always giving thanks to God for all things by righteous hearing and divine
> reading, by true inquiry, by a holy sacrifice, by blessed prayer, singing praises and
> hymns and blessings and psalms. Such a soul is never at any time separated from
> God.   (*Strom.* 6. 113. 2–3)

Through attaining moral perfection and through the Christian sacrifice of
worship and praise, the soul strives with the help of the Lord's power to
attain the highest possible degree of glory, above that of ordinary believers.
This is what it is doing when it 'studies to be a god'. It wants to be classed
with the 'philosophers of God' in the closest proximity to the twenty-four
elders. To attain this, the highest perfection open to human beings, is to
attain likeness to God.

It is in the seventh book of the *Stromateis* on spiritual perfection that
Clement calls believers gods with the least reservation. Clement begins the
book by stating that his purpose is to prove that only the Gnostic is truly
devout. The Gnostic alone worships the true God as befits him, and this
includes loving God and being loved by him. His service of God consists in
his constant close attention to his soul, and in his preoccupation with that
which is divine in himself (the indwelling Logos?) by showing unceasing love
(*Strom.* 7. 3. 1).

This love imitates that of the angels, for just as the angels worship God
and see to his earthly administration, so the Gnostic serves God and sets his
philosophy before men. Alluding perhaps to his own work in culling
passages from pagan Greek authors, Clement says that the true Gnostic
gathers the fruits of all who have come to believe in God and sets them
before his hearers to endow them with knowledge and bring them to the way
of salvation. This is true reverence towards God.

---

[29] *Strom.* 6. 111. 3. These classes of action by which a person is saved are derived from the Stoic division
of actions into good, evil, and indifferent. On Clement's adaptation of this scheme see Bradley 1974: 57–
9. Bradley shows how the Stoics were greater rigorists than Clement, for had he applied their definitions
strictly, simple believers could not have been saved.

If reverence is a habit of mind which preserves that which is fitting towards God, only the reverent man is dear to God. And such would be he who knows what is fitting both in theory and in life with regard to how a man should live who will become a god, and indeed is already being made like God.   (*Strom.* 7. 3. 6)

To become a god is to resemble the angels in their dual service of God and man, on the one hand offering 'silent worship in holy awe', and on the other instructing the faithful in the knowledge of God. In this life he 'studies to be a god', as Clement has already said. But he will become a god only in eternity.

In the tenth chapter Clement discusses the believer's steps to perfection from faith through knowledge to love. Knowledge is 'the perfection, so to speak, of man as man, brought to completion through the science of divine things' (*Strom.* 7. 55. 1). Faith confesses the existence of God but knowledge, the deposit handed down by tradition, provides the content of faith. Faith and love cannot be taught, but the middle stage, knowledge, can be taught, and indeed requires rigorous training:

This knowledge leads us on to that perfect end which knows no end, teaching us here the nature of the life we shall hereafter live with gods according to the will of God, when we have been delivered from all chastisement and punishment, which we have to endure as salutary chastening (cf. Heb. 12: 7) in consequence of our sins. After this deliverance rank and honours are assigned to those who are perfected, who have done now with purification and all other ritual, though it be holy among the holy; until at last, when they have been made pure in heart (cf. Matt. 5: 8) by their closeness to the Lord, the final restoration attends on their everlasting contemplation of God. And the name of gods is given to those that shall hereafter be enthroned with the other gods, who first had their stations assigned to them beneath the Saviour (καὶ θεοὶ τὴν προσηγορίαν κέκληνται, [οἳ] σύνθρονοι τῶν ἄλλων θεῶν, τῶν ὑπὸ τῷ σωτῆρι πρώτων τεταγμένων, γενησόμενοι). (*Strom.* 7. 56. 3–6; trans. Mayor/Chadwick)

If knowledge is the perfection of man as man, love is the perfection of man as god. The pure in heart will see God and love him in perfect contemplation. To be enthroned with the other gods does not refer to assimilation to the angels, as Chadwick notes (Oulton and Chadwick 1954: 129 no. 88a), nor is it Lattey's 'reminiscence of the Ptolemies, gods themselves while alive, and on their death to be tacked on in pairs as synthronoi to the preceding Ptolemies' (1916: 261–2). It refers to the enthroned twenty-four elders of Revelation 4: 4 whom Clement has already mentioned in a similar context.[30] Christians who have attained perfection will be enthroned in glory with the highest grade of the saved, but still on a lower level than Christ. As

---

[30] *Strom.* 6. 107. 2. Baert alone recognizes the possible influence of Apocalyptic in this passage but he still judges the main inspiration to be Greek: 'L'idée d'une réunion avec les dieux exprimée par la formule "μετὰ (τῶν) θεῶν" est Hellénistique' (1965: 473–4). If the gods are never the angels but always human beings who have become like Christ, the case for a Greek model is weakened.

Butterworth points out, this shows 'how careful Clement is to distinguish between the most exalted men or angels and Christ' (1916: 161). The divinity of the perfect is a divinity by title or analogy.

The twelve passages in which the perfect are called gods complement those in which θεοποιεῖν or a related term is used. In Justin and Irenaeus human beings are called gods only in connection with Psalm 82: 6; that is to say, they become gods in principle through participatory union with Christ in baptism. We find this usage in Clement's first reference to men as gods at the end of the *Exhortation*. But a new note is also sounded. Besides being those whom God has adopted, the gods are also those who have become *like* God. This second aspect becomes more and more important in Clement's writings. In the *Stromateis*, Psalm 82: 6 is applied on its first appearance not to the baptized but to those who have risen above the passions. In the rest of the work these perfected Christian Gnostics are called gods for the most part without reference to Psalm 82. Their divine status is not postponed to the next life but begins here and now.

A god, then, is a person who turns to truth after hearing the Scriptures, who becomes like Christ his teacher by imitating the beauty of the Logos. He must be baptized and obedient to the Church's teaching. But he must also be capable of striving for perfection in contemplation and the ethical life. Through the contemplation of intelligibles, he must transcend the corporeal state, so that when he has attained the highest level of contemplation he may finally be 'enthroned with the other gods'. Through the mastery of the passions he must attain an interior unity and freedom from desire which resembles the unity and autonomy of God. This is not for the ordinary Christian.

Clement's model of deification is that of the imitation of God. In other words, the Christian Gnostic becomes a god through reproducing within himself, by moral and intellectual effort with the help of divine grace, the divine attributes of unity, freedom from passion, and incorporeality. As a result of these he is granted immortality and admitted to the highest rank of the saved.

(d) The Attainment of Likeness to God

The Alexandrian philosopher Eudorus established 'likeness' or 'assimilation to God' from *Theaetetus* 176b as the *telos* for Platonism (Dillon 1996: 44). Philo also adopted it as the goal of human life but it was probably already part of Clement's Platonism before he encountered Philo.[31] Likeness to God meant living according to virtue. The Christian Gnostic did this 'by practising self-restraint and endurance, by living righteously, by ruling over the passions, by sharing his possessions as far as possible, and by doing good in

[31] On Clement's teaching on 'likeness' the fundamental study is Merki 1952: 45–60.

both word and deed' (*Strom.* 2. 97. 1). He became like God by imitating his freedom from passion, self-sufficiency and beneficence. He also imitated God's kingly rule, reigning over both the exterior and the interior worlds — 'the wild beasts without and the wild passions within' (*Strom.* 6. 115. 2).

For Clement freedom from passion, *apatheia*, is primarily a divine attribute. Only Christ, as the incarnate divine Logos, is 'absolutely without passion' (ἀπαξαπλῶς ἀπαθής) (*Strom.* 6. 9. 71). In attaining *apatheia* the perfect Christian becomes godlike in his freedom from all needs and desires (*Strom.* 6. 71–7), even to the point of not desiring, as his principal goal, his own salvation (*Strom.* 4. 135–6). This is a condition brought about fundamentally by the operation of grace. Clement's conception of *apatheia* as divine gift, differing both from the Stoic *apatheia* (arising simply from the use of right reason), and the Platonic *metriopatheia* (the result of restraining the passions), reveals a profound debt to Philo.[32]

'Likeness to God', of course, as Philo saw, could also refer to the biblical creation of man 'in the image and likeness of God' (Gen. 1: 26). Usually Clement distinguishes between image and likeness, man being created in the image of God but only receiving the likeness when he has attained perfection (*Strom.* 2. 131. 5; cf. Mayer 1942, and Mortley 1973). Both image and likeness refer not to the First Cause—God's utter transcendence precludes this—but to the Logos. Man is an image of the image. In the Gnostic 'the divine image is now beheld in a third embodiment, assimilated as far as possible to the Second Cause' (*Strom.* 7. 16. 6). This has affinities with Alcinous, who taught that men attain likeness only to the Second God, because 'the First God is far too transcendent for man to assimilate himself to him' (*Didaskalikos* 28; cf. Dillon 1996: 299–300).

Plato's 'likeness to God' accords well with Christianity. But what of the body? In Platonism it had always been a hindrance to be discarded. Eudorus refined the *Theaetetus* precept by teaching that to become like God κατὰ τὸ δυνατόν meant not 'as far as possible' but 'according to that part which is capable', that is to say, it was only the *nous* or highest part of the soul which could become like God (Dillon 1996: 122–3). Clement is in sympathy with this: 'Conformity with the image and likeness does not refer to the body, for it is not right that the mortal should be assimilated to the immortal; it refers to the *nous* and its intellectual processes, on which the Lord appropriately impresses the seal of his likeness, with regard to doing good (τὸ εὐεργετεῖν) and exercising rule' (τὸ ἀρχεῖν) (*Strom.* 2. 102. 6; cf. Plutarch, *Romulus*, 28. 6). On the other hand, he also says that by the Incarnation God freed the flesh from corruption and endowed it with immortality (*Paed.* 3. 2. 3). How is this immortality communicated to the flesh of believers?

---

[32] On Philo's approach to *apatheia* see Chapter 3. 2 above. The Stoic contribution to Clement's thinking is discussed by Bradley (1974: 53–4), who rightly stresses that while the Stoic sage achieves virtue without any help, 'the Gnostic is self-sufficient because he has been given grace and knowledge'.

The answer is through an imitation which is more personal than the Platonic, an imitation expressed by the adoption which makes us brothers and joint heirs of Christ:

Correctly interpreted, assimilation as far as possible is the *telos* and restoration to perfect adoption through the Son, a restoration which ever glorifies the Father through the great High Priest, who has deigned to call us 'brethren' and 'fellow heirs'. (*Strom.* 2. 134. 2; cf. Rom. 8: 14–17)

Adoption links the believer with God in a particularly intimate way, for only those whom God has adopted can call him Father (*Prot.* 12. 123. 1; cf. *QDS*, 9. 2). The Gnostic illustrates this. Not only is he a son of God but also a temple of God (cf. 1 Cor. 3: 16): 'The Gnostic is therefore already holy and divine, carrying God within him and being carried by God' (θεοφορῶν καὶ θεοφορούμενος) (*Strom.* 7. 82. 2). He who has God enthroned within him lives perfectly. He is translated from servitude to sonship, knowing God and being known by him. Sonship imitates the unity of God:

Let us, who are many, hasten to be gathered together into one love corresponding to the union of the One Being [. . .]. And the union of many into one, bringing a divine harmony out of many scattered sounds, becomes one symphony, following one leader and teacher, the Word, and never ceasing till it reaches the truth itself with the cry 'Abba, Father'. (*Prot.* 9. 88. 2–3; trans. Butterworth)

Adoption also leads to immortality, for incorruption and immortality can only be attained through Christ. Clement often expresses this by allusion to 1 Cor. 15: 53: 'We are children of God who have put aside the old man and stripped off the garments of wickedness and put on the incorruption of Christ' (*Paed.* 1. 32. 4). This is not simply a spiritual incorruption referring only to the soul: 'Christ wishes to save my flesh by enveloping it in the robe of incorruption' (*Paed.* 1. 84. 3). The flesh rendered incorrupt by Christ provides the soul with its immortal envelope, its 'undefiled vesture', in heaven (*Paed.* 2. 109. 3).

Clement takes over the Platonic *telos* in its Eudorian form, but adapts it in important ways, adding an ethical content which appears to owe something to an independent study of Stoicism, and presenting Christian adoption as its most profound expression, because only God can conform a man to his own likeness. It is beyond the power of human beings to imitate the transcendent First Cause. The imitation of God is the imitation of Christ, the incarnate Logos, who makes his adopted brethren like God, endowing them with immortality.

(e) How is an Apophatic Theology Combined with an Optimistic Anthropology?

Although Clement willingly calls the perfected Christian a god, only the Creator is truly God (*Prot.* 4. 63. 3). He is so utterly transcendent that he has no natural relationship with us (*Strom.* 2. 74. 1; cf. Witt 1931: 197). He is beyond our capacity for knowledge and our powers of expression: 'We know not what God is but what he is not' (*Strom.* 5. 71. 3). Only the Logos knows the divine essence (*Strom.* 5. 66. 3). The knowledge we have of God is a divine gift (*Strom.* 5. 83–4). We know God only through Christ by the gift of the Holy Spirit, 'but it is not as a portion of God that the Spirit is in each of us' (*Strom.* 5. 88. 3).[33] The ontological difference between human beings and God is profound. So too is the moral difference: we cannot be perfect in the same way that God is perfect (*Strom.* 6. 88. 6; 6. 114. 5). In what sense, then, can the Gnostic become a god?

While the Father as the First Cause is utterly transcendent, the Logos as the Second Cause does come into contact with the material world. Through the Incarnation two different orders of reality are brought into relationship with one another. On the one hand, although he descends into the flesh, as Clement puts it, the Logos still retains his transcendence (*Strom.* 5. 105. 4).[34] On the other, the Logos becomes an αἰσθητὴ παρουσία, 'a presence accessible to the senses' (*Strom.* 5. 38. 6). The Incarnation is the Son's assumption of visibility; he becomes the *prosopon* of the Father, 'by whom God is made visible and manifest' (*Paed.* 1. 57. 2; *Strom.* 5. 34. 1). Such a christology does not given equal weight to both the human and the divine elements in Christ.[35] Christ has no πάθη of the soul, no automatic bodily functions (*Strom.* 6. 9. 71; 3. 6. 49). Christ's human soul is not denied, but his 'inner man' is the Logos, which fulfils the role of the ἡγεμονικόν wrapped in the soul, which is in turn wrapped in the flesh.

The human implications of this christology are not ontological—human nature per se is not transformed by the Logos—but exemplary. The incarnate Logos is 'a model of incorruption and moral excellence' (*Paed.* 1. 98. 3). Christ is above all a mediator and a teacher, a high priest and a pedagogue. But he does not simply call forth an intellectual response. Knowledge of God must be personal, for to know the Father 'is eternal life through participation in the power of the Incorrupt; and to be free from corruption is to participate in divinity' (*Strom.* 5. 63. 8). This personal knowledge of Christ, the incarnate Logos, which brings participation in incorruption and hence divinity, is acquired through the sacraments of baptism and the Eucharist.

Clement does not often dwell directly on the sacraments, but their role in bringing the Gnostic to perfection is indispensable, for they are the means by

---

[33] This is an anti-Valentinian statement; cf. A. Le Boulluec, *Stromate* v. ii (SC 279) 284–5.

[34] On Clement's christology see Grillmeier 1975: 133–8.

[35] In Grillmeier's judgement, Clement 'consistently maintains the reality of the human nature of Christ, though at the same time his tendency to spiritualize seems to make the reality of the incarnation merely relative' (1975: 136).

which the Gnostic actually lays hold of incorruption.[36] Baptism is described as the healing medicine (Παιώνιον φάρμακον) that dissolves away sin (*Paed.* 1. 6), or the bath (λουτρόν) that brings salvation and illumination (*Prot.* 10. 76). Illumination, as we have seen, implies also adoption, perfection, and the attainment of immortality (*Paed.* 1. 26. 1).[37] The Eucharist is a mystery transcending reason (μυστήριον παράδοξον) (*Paed.* 1. 6. 43). In the second book of the *Paedagogus* (*Paed.* 2. 19. 4; cf. 1. 51. 2 and *QDS* 29) Clement explains it on two different levels, literally as the wine and the water making a feast 'unto faith', and spiritually as the 'divine mixture' of water, wine and Logos analogous to 'man mixed with Spirit and Logos mystically by the Father's will'. To 'drink of the blood of Jesus is to participate in the Lord's incorruption' because on the spiritual level the Spirit and the Logos make the soul and the flesh, respectively, like themselves.

This ecclesiastical dimension tends to mitigate Clement's intellectualism. Indeed, the supreme example of the man or woman who has attained perfection is not the philosopher but the martyr. Clement condemns Basilides' opinion that martyrdom may be an expiation of sin committed in a previous life (*Strom.* 4. 83. 2). He censures those Christians who deliberately seek martyrdom to attain to the joys of heaven (*Strom.* 4. 76. 1–4. 77. 3). The genuine martyr does not court persecution, but accepts it as the price of discipleship. Martyrdom thus exhibits 'the perfect work of love' (*Strom.* 4. 14. 3). It is 'to philosophize without being learned' (*Strom.* 4. 58. 3). Like Ignatius, Clement held that the martyr's death assimilates him to Christ in the most complete way possible. But the life of the true Gnostic may also be called a martyrdom, for it involves a struggle to live by the Gospel and overcome the passions (*Strom.* 4. 15. 4). Therefore 'anyone who ascends to love is a blessed and true martyr' and becomes a son of God and a brother of the Lord (*Strom.* 4. 75. 4).

Clement connects an apophatic theology with an optimistic anthropology through the mediation of the incarnate Logos. Christ came not so much to undo the effects of the Fall as to consummate the Father's love for humankind (*Paed.* 1. 8. 2; *Prot.* 11. 116. 1). By becoming like Christ as fully as possible the Gnostic has access to the Father. The acquisition of *gnosis* and *apatheia* are indispensable but in themselves insufficient. The aspirant to the divine life must also participate in the Church's sacramental life.

---

[36] The sacraments have not received much attention from writers on Clement. Tollinton's chapter on Sacraments and Worship is still worth consulting (1914: ii. 135–64); see also Bigg 1913: 136–42; Marsh 1936; Völker 1952: 598–600.

[37] See also Clement's collection of passages on baptism from Theodotus (*Exc. Theod.* 76–86) together with Sagnard's discussion in SC 23, Appendix F. The address *To the Newly Baptized* in Stählin iii and LCL 92 is not by Clement. It has been shown to be a paraphrase of one of Gregory Nazianzen's poems; see *CPG* i. 1391.

(f) Conclusion

Clement is innovative on both the linguistic and the conceptual levels. He does not use θεοποιέω as a philosophical term. On each of the three occasions on which he uses the word in a Christian context it denotes the effect of the communication of Christ's teaching through the Scriptures. Θεόω and θεοποιός, however, *are* used in a philosophical sense for the attaining of dispassion. Deification is thus twofold: it has an ecclesiastical aspect in so far as it is brought about by Christ, and a philosophical aspect in so far as it is the product of intellectual and moral effort. Clement's use of the word *theoi* reflects this dual approach. The gods are the baptized in whom the Logos dwells, and also those who through the practice of philosophy have mastered the passions and become like God. Clement links these two approaches by presenting the attainment of the divine likeness, at its deepest level, as 'the restoration to perfect adoption through the Son'.

Lilla has seen in Clement's use of the term *theoi* 'a blending of Gnostic and Platonic conceptions', in which Clement has filtered out the elements most obviously incompatible with Christianity 'but has retained the typically Gnostic and Platonic idea of the deification of the perfect soul' (1971: 186–7). I would say that Clement attempts to harmonize two traditions, the one ecclesiastical, the other Philonic. The identification of the gods of Psalm 82: 6 with those who have become adopted sons of God through baptism had been established by Justin and Irenaeus and is accepted by Clement as one possible interpretation. Deification in this sense represents an inaugurated eschatology which begins in principle in this life but awaits its fulfilment in heaven. The other approach, the ascription of divinity to those who have attained an eminent degree of virtue, belongs to the Platonic tradition, and indeed goes back to Plato himself, although the application of the term 'gods' to them is in fact rare.[38] Such an approach is found in a pagan Middle Platonist such as Plutarch, but it is from Philo that Clement has drawn his fundamental ideas.

Philo had already done much of the groundwork for Clement, connecting the biblical image and likeness of God in which man was created with the Platonic *telos* of likeness to God, and presenting contemplation and the attainment of dispassion as the means by which the soul ascends towards God so that it becomes 'kin to God and truly divine' (*QE* 2. 29). Clement adapts Philo, however, in two important respects, namely, in his negative attitude to the body and his restriction of the title of 'god' to Moses.

For Philo, the journey towards God can be undertaken only by escaping from the body. This can be anticipated before death through the experience of ecstasy, when the soul encounters God outside the body in a state of intoxicated frenzy. The ecstatic approach, which in Philo accompanies the

---

[38] Cf. *Laws* 904d; Clement reads the term 'gods' for men of virtue back into Plato.

philosophical and ethical modes of ascent, is entirely lacking in Clement. Escape from the body is replaced by Clement with the immortalization of the body through becoming an adopted brother and fellow heir of the incarnate Logos.

The other important difference is that in Philo only Moses is called a god, and even Moses is a god by title or analogy only, for Philo thought it impossible for a man to become a god in a literal sense. Moses' special title was granted to him because he enslaved the passions so successfully that he received the gift of immortality and a unique place in the immediate presence of God above that of anyone else. Clement, by contrast, is able to call every Christian who has attained perfection a god. This is because he has inherited a Christian interpretation of Psalm 82: 6 (a text never quoted by Philo) which enables him to say that those who have become adopted sons of God by baptism may also be called gods. Clement is thus able to expand the category represented in Philo by the word 'god' to include all perfected Christians.

The title 'gods' comes to Clement primarily from Christian and Jewish biblical exegesis, although it is coloured by Hellenic associations with immortality, beneficence, and power. Human beings may become gods by title (the name of gods being given in heaven to those enthroned with the other gods), or by analogy (men being gods to God as Lord as they are sons to him as Father), or by participation in the divine attributes, in an external sense through reproducing in themselves the unity and freedom from passion characteristic of God, or more intimately through the grace and immortality imparted by Christ.

5. Origen

Although he never mentions Clement by name and only rarely cites him, Origen (*c.*185–*c.*253) takes up Clement's terminology of deification, adapting it to his own soteriology.[39] Considering the bulk of his writings, his references to deification are relatively few. Moreover, they always have some christological reference. As Andrew Louth remarks, Origen 'was not a convert from philosophy like Justin Martyr or Clement of Alexandria, and he had none of their welcoming attitude towards philosophy, which, for him,

---

[39] The first author to discuss Origen's doctrine of deification as his spiritual goal was Völker (1931: 117–44, esp. 121–2). This pioneering work was followed by Lieske 1938: 126–31; Gross 1938: 174–85; Dalmais 1954–7: 1379; and Crouzel 1956: 160–79. The linking of deification with Origen's trinitarian theology as a whole began with Nemeshegyi 1960: 168–74, 199–202; and continued with Crouzel 1961: esp. 102; Rius-Camps 1970*b*: esp. 304–5, 388, 401–10; and Balás 1975: esp. 269–70. A hostile assessment of Origen's treatment of deification has been presented by Drewery 1975: 44–6 (cf. Drewery 1960: 200–1). Several more recent studies mention deification as an aspect of the soul's journey to God (Torjesen 1986: 32–4; 70–2; 85; Scott 1991: 72, 158–64), as transition from sin to holiness (Alviar 1993*b*: 68–9, 95), or as participation in divine glory (Trigg 1998: 103–4, 233, 237–8).

was simply a useful study for the Christian theologian as a training in dialectic, and something he justifies by the example of the Israelites' "spoiling of the Egyptians" at the Exodus' (1981: 53–4). The Origen of the texts examined in this section is the man of the Church rather than the systematic thinker—the ardent biblical exegete who pored over the 'divine oracles' late into the night in the company of his convert and patron, Ambrosius, neglecting meals and sleep through their absorption in their common task.[40] The study of the Scriptures was the work of transcending their humanity, a work not to be undertaken without prayer. 'Do not be content with knocking and seeking,' Origen wrote to his former pupil, Gregory Thaumaturgus,

for prayer is most necessary for the understanding of divine things. And the Saviour urged us to this when he said not only, 'Knock and it will be opened to you,' and 'Seek and you will find,' but also, 'Ask, and it will be given you' (Matt. 7: 7). I have ventured to say this out of my fatherly love for you. If I have done well or not in venturing, God and his Christ know, and anyone who partakes of the Spirit of God and the Spirit of Christ. May you too be a partaker and ever increase the participation, that you may say not only, 'We have become partakers of Christ' (Heb. 3: 14), but also, 'We have become partakers of God.' (*Philocalia* 13. 4; trans. Lewis, modified)

(a) Vocabulary

Origen's vocabulary of deification is narrower than Clement's. Unlike his predecessor, he does not use ἀποθέωσις or θεόω. On the other hand, he does use ἀποθεόω, a term avoided by Clement, dividing its four instances equally between pagan and Christian contexts.[41] Ἐκθεόω appears only once and ἐκθειάζω, a favourite term of Clement's, only twice, in each case with a pejorative sense.[42] As in Clement, however, the most common term by far for the deification of the Christian is θεοποιέω, which Origen uses eight times in a Christian context and nine times with a pejorative metaphorical sense.[43] Like Clement, too, he also has a single instance of θεοποιός in the new Christian sense which Clement has given it (*Sel. in Ez.* 1. 3, PG 13. 769B). Christians are also frequently called θεοί, often with reference to Psalm 82: 6.[44]

---

[40] Origen gives this picture in a fragment of a letter quoted by Lawlor and Oulton in their translation of Eusebius' *Ecclesiastical History* 2: 213–14 (cited by Trigg 1983: 147). Cf. Eusebius, *HE* 6. 23.

[41] Pagan contexts: *Hom. Jer.* 5. 3; GCS iii. 33. 21; *C. Cels.* 4. 59, GCS i. 331. 19. Christian contexts: *In Matt.* 16. 29, GCS x. 574. 7; *In Psalm.* 81, Pitra, *Analecta Sacra* iii. 140. 25. The last, however, is doubtfully attributed to Origen.

[42] Ἐκθεόω: *Hom. Jer.* 5. 2, GCS iii. 33. 4. Ἐκθειάζω: *In Jo.* 10. 34, GCS iv. 207. 36; *Hom. Jer.* 7. 3, GCS iii. 53. 26.

[43] Christian context: *In Jo.* 2. 2 (twice), GCS iv. 54. 30. 55. 1; *In Jo.* 32. 27 (twice), GCS iv. 472. 30 and 34; *Mart.* 25, GCS i. 22. 27; *Orat.* 25. 2; 27. 13, GCS ii. 358. 22 and 372. 2; *In Matt.* 17. 32, GCS x. 686. 2; cf. deifico—*In Matt.* 24. 4, GCS xi. 61. 7. Pejorative context: *In Jo.* 13. 13, GCS iv. 237. 21; *Hom. Jer.* 5. 2 (twice), GCS iii. 33. 2–3; *Hom. Jer.* 7. 3 (four times), GCS iii. 53. 25 and 33–5; *In Matt.* 11. 12 and 14, GCS x. 53. 30 and 56. 1.

[44] See the list of references to Ps. 82: 6 in *Biblia Patristica* iii, and also *In Jo.* 20. 29, GCS iv. 367. 2 and *Hom. Luc.* 29. 7, GCS ix. 171. 7–19.

Origen's first use of the vocabulary of deification in a Christian context is in his anti-Valentinian *Commentary on John*, which was begun in Alexandria in 231 with the encouragement of Ambrosius. In Book II he discusses the significance of the anarthrous use of θεός in the Johannine prologue, and concludes that with the article θεός is the uncreated cause of all things, i.e. the Father, but without it is the Logos or Son. The Father is αὐτόθεος, the Son is god only by participation in the source of divinity, and is therefore θεοποιούμενος: 'everything that is deified (θεοποιούμενον) by him who is αὐτόθεος through participation in his godhead should not be called ὁ θεός but more properly θεός' (*In Jo.* 2. 2. 17, GCS iv. 54. 32–4). The Son is thus 'the first-born of all creation' (Col. 1: 15), in that he alone is able ceaselessly to contemplate the Father's depths. Other rational beings can become gods through the Son, 'who has drawn from God the power that enables them to be deified' (εἰς τὸ θεοποιηθῆναι αὐτούς) (*In Jo.* 2. 2. 17, GCS iv. 55. 1 f.). Yet these gods are not on the same level as the Son, for the Son, while an image of God, is himself the archetype for all the other images. As the Father is αὐτόθεος in relation to the divinity of the Son and his brethren, so the Son is αὐτολόγος in relation to the *logos* in each rational being (*In Jo.* 2. 3. 204, GCS iv. 55. 17–20).

The realization of this potential divinity calls for a life of prayer and the practice of the virtues undertaken within a framework of right belief. The virtues are fundamental. Those who won't practise them are 'those who don't wish to be deified' (τοῖς μὴ βουλομένοις ἀποθεωθῆναι) and become sons of the Most High (*In Matt.* 16. 29, GCS x. 574. 3–9). But right belief is also important. Origen emphasizes this in his exegesis of the passage in Deuteronomy about the woman whose deceased husband's brother will not raise up seed for her (Deut. 25: 7–10), where he offers no fewer than three spiritual meanings. According to the second, the first brother is the old law, the second brother—who is the child of the same Logos—is the new law of Christ, and the woman is the soul under the law. As the first brother dies on the advent of the second brother, the latter is obliged to make the woman fruitful and constitute the true Israel. A second brother who refuses to do this is one who 'does not wish to be deified by bearing fruit' (οὐ βουληθέντι θεοποιηθῆναι ἐκ τοῦ καρποφορῆσαι) (*In Matt.* 17. 32, GCS x. 686. 2 f.). He belongs to those heresies which divide the Godhead by denying the divinity of Christ, and separate the law from the Gospel. That is why one sandal is removed from his foot (cf. Deut. 25: 9).

If one perseveres in the moral struggle and adheres to ecclesiastical Christianity, the life of prayer is one of infinite progress towards an ever-deepening perfection. Origen explains why this must be so in his analysis of the Lord's Prayer. When he turns to the phrase, 'Thy kingdom come,' the question arises how a person can continue to make this petition if in his case the kingdom—which Origen suggests is 'the blessed state of the ruling faculty and the ordered condition of wise thoughts' (*Orat.* 25.1, GCS ii. 357. 9 f.)—has already come. The answer is that progress towards perfection continues as a person goes on receiving 'more and more intuitions (θεωρήματα) of wisdom and knowledge' (*Orat.* 25. 2, GCS ii. 358. 7 f.) until Christ delivers up the kingdom to the Father (cf. 1 Cor. 15: 24). 'Therefore "praying without ceasing" (1 Thess. 5: 17) with a disposition that is being deified by the Logos (μετὰ διαθέσεως τῷ λόγῳ θεοποιουμένης), let us say to our Father in heaven, "Hallowed be thy name; thy kingdom come" '(*Orat.* 25. 2, GCS ii. 358. 21–4). Deification is presented as a process in which the intellect, through the power of the Logos, becomes more and more conformed to God.

A little later in the same treatise Origen investigates the use of the word ἐπιούσιος in the Lord's Prayer (Matt. 6: 11). The normal English translation, 'daily', obscures the uncertainty of its meaning in Greek. Origen connects ἐπιούσιος with οὐσία ('reality' or 'substance') and thus understands the bread that the Father gives as 'super-real' or 'suprasubstantial' (cf. Noel 1992: 484–5). This spiritual bread communicates divine power to the intellect and the soul. It 'imparts a share of its own immortality (for the Logos of God is immortal) to him who eats of it' (*Orat.* 27. 9, GCS ii. 369. 21 f.). He who partakes of the ἐπιούσιος bread becomes a son of God (*Orat.* 27. 12, GCS ii. 370. 28 f.). It surpasses all other food. We therefore 'ought to pray that we may be deemed worthy of it, and by feeding on 'God the Word' who was 'in the beginning with God' may be deified (καὶ τρεφόμενοι τῷ 'ἐν ἀρχῇ' 'πρὸς θεὸν' θεῷ λόγῳ θεοποιηθῶμεν) (*Orat.* 27. 13, GCS 11. 372. 1 f.). Again deification takes place through a spiritual participation in the Logos.

The way in which such deification is manifested is through participation in divine glory, which may begin even in this life. This is a theme which Origen develops in his *Commentary on John* in his exegesis of the verse: 'Now is the Son of Man glorified, and in him God is glorified' (John 13: 31). He reviews the occasions in the Old Testament when the glory of the Lord was manifested, the most significant being when Moses came down from the mountain after speaking to God, his face shining with divine radiance (Exod. 34: 29):

According to the literal sense, a more divine manifestation took place in the tabernacle, and in the temple when it was completed, and in the face of Moses, when he conversed with the divine nature. According to the anagogical sense, an exact knowledge of the things of God and their contemplation by an intellect made fit through utter purity may be described as the vision of the glory of God, since an intellect which has been purified and has transcended all material things is deified by what it contemplates (ἐν οἷς θεωρεῖ θεοποιεῖται) in order that it may perfect the contemplation of God. Such a state may be said to be the glorification of the face of him who has contemplated God and conversed with him and spent time in such a vision, since this is represented figuratively by the glorified face of Moses, when his intellect had been deified by God (θεοποιηθέντος αὐτῷ τοῦ νοῦ). (*In Jo.* 32. 27. 338–9, GCS iv. 472. 24–34)

This transforming contemplation which enables one to participate in the divine is available through Christ to the Christian believer. For just as the dispensation of the Spirit transcends the dispensation of death, so the transfiguration of Christ transcends that of Moses (cf. Luke 9: 29–38; 2 Cor. 3: 7–11). Paul shows how this will relate to the believer when he says: 'And we all, with unveiled face, beholding the glory of the Lord, are being changed into his likeness from one degree of glory to another' (2 Cor. 3: 18). Far from being static, contemplation is a dynamic activity, leading to an ever greater participation in the glory of God. It is a divine gift, conforming the recipient to the divine likeness, enabling him to know God and be known by him, and therefore deifying him (cf. Crouzel 1956: 233; Louth 1981: 73; Trigg 1998: 233–40).

It is significant that the language of deification occurs not in the more speculative *De Principiis*, but in works which are concerned with the exegesis of biblical texts. Θεοποιέω and its cognates are not used as philosophical terms. They express the relationship of the believer through the Logos to the source of all being and life. There are similarities with Clement in the characterization of the deified as those to whom the Word of God has come, and also in the description of Moses as an intellect deified by moral purity and philosophical ascent (cf. above, p. 124). But there are also differences. First, the Son, although divine by nature, is himself deified in relation to the Father who alone is *autotheos*. Origen has a strong sense of the hierarchy of being, even within the Godhead. Secondly, he is less apophatic than Clement and more intellectualist. Deification is more often participation in the eternal rather than the incarnate Logos, the intellect through such participation ascending the hierarchy of being in response to the descent of divine grace. Thirdly, his interpretation of the 'gods' of Psalm 82: 6 is more biblical than Clement's. In Clement the gods are often those who have attained dispassion; in Origen they are the saints who follow Christ. Irenaeus had equated them with those who had become sons by adoption. Origen, more concerned with the practical consequences of baptism, is equally Pauline but in a different way. The gods are those who have put to death the deeds of the body and live by the Spirit. They have transcended their human nature through the operation of the Son and the Spirit. This is not the only interpretation, however, which Origen offers of the gods of Psalm 82: 6.

(b) In What Sense May Christians be called Gods?

The general philosophical issues raised by the term 'god' are discussed by Origen in the preface to his *Commentary on the Psalms* (*Sel. in Psalm.* Praef., PG

12. 1053B). Drawing on the Stoic philosopher Herophilus,[45] he distinguishes between that which is divine in a dependent sense through participating in divinity and that which is divine in its own right. Thus in the most general sense every being which is living, immortal, and rational ($\zeta\hat{\omega}ον\ \dot{α}θ\dot{α}νατον\ λογικόν$) that is to say, every human soul, is a god. But from another point of view our souls are not gods because only a being which is living, immortal, and rational of itself ($\zeta\hat{\omega}ον\ \dot{α}θ\dot{α}νατον\ λογικὸν\ καθ'\ αὑτὸ\ \ddot{ο}ν$) is a god. The same may be said with respect to virtue and the exercise of sovereignty. A fundamental distinction should be made between that which is immortal, rational, good, etc. of itself and that which merely participates in these attributes, although the term 'god' may be predicated equally of both.

This is a distinction which Origen adopts himself and uses in his biblical exegesis. In his *Commentary on John*, as we have already noted, the appearance in the Johannine Prologue (John 1: 1) of $θεός$ with the article for the Father and without it for the Logos leads him to suggest that $θεός$ with the article is the appropriate term for the Father as the source of all being, the uncreated cause of the whole universe, while the use of $θεός$ as a predicate of the Logos conveys the derivative character of the Son's divinity (*In Jo.* 2. 2. 14, GCS iv. 54. 15–17). Ὁ $θεός$ is equivalent to $αὐτόθεος$ while $θεός$ on its own is synonymous with $θεοποιούμενος$ (*In Jo.* 2. 2. 17, GCS iv. 54. 32–4; cf. Balás 1975: 269–70). In the *Dialogue with Heraclides* the predicative use of $θεός$ helps Origen to explain how the Father and the Son are two Gods in one sense and one God in another. They are two in so far as they are distinct from one another: the Father is not the Son and the Son is not the Father. At the same time they are one God in the same way that Adam and Eve are one flesh and Christ and the righteous man are one spirit. Flesh, spirit, and god are predicates in ascending order of honour and importance (*Her.* 126). $Θεός$ is predicated of the Logos in a similar way in the *Commentary on John*.

Once it has been established that the Logos is God in a subordinate sense, the question arises: How does he differ from the other beings that are called gods in the Scriptures? The solution to this problem lies in the unique, mediating role of the Logos. The divinity which he has received from the Father he communicates to those who accept him, making them images of God, or rather, images of himself, who is the archetypal image of God (*In Jo.* 2. 2. 18, GCS iv. 55. 3–5). Although like the Logos they are recipients of divinity, they are much further removed from God. The Logos alone abides intimately with God in ceaseless contemplation of the Fatherly depths (ibid., GCS iv. 55. 7 f.).

These different senses of the word 'god' are summed up in the Prologue to the *Commentary on the Song of Songs*. There in Rufinus' translation Origen

---

[45] Origen cites Herophilus by name. He is mentioned by Chrysippus (von Arnim, *Stoicorum Veterum Fragmenta* iii. 440) but nothing survives of his work.

says that the term refers properly (principaliter = κυρίως) to him 'ex quo omnia et per quem omnia et in quo omnia' (cf. 1 Cor. 8: 6), an expression which he (Origen or Rufinus?) takes to signify the Trinity. From this point of view the Logos and the Spirit are therefore also God in a proper sense. It refers inexactly or relatively (abusive = καταχρηστικῶς) to those human beings 'to whom the word of God came' (cf. John 10: 35), and also to the angelic powers. The difference is thus underlined again between the Logos and the *logikoi*. Finally, it refers falsely (falso = ψευδῶς) to the pagan gods, for these are simply demons (cf. Ps. 95: 6; *In Cant.* Prol. 2. 34, GCS viii. 71. 4–13).

According to this scheme, references to gods in the relative sense are found in the Bible in the 'God of gods' of Psalms 50: 1 (LXX) and 136: 2, in the 'gods and sons of the Most High' of Psalm 82: 6 and John 10: 35, and in the 'many gods and many lords' of 1 Cor. 8: 5. Origen first discusses the identity of these gods in the *Commentary on John* 1. 31. Here the key to understanding the Psalmist's 'God of gods' is Matt. 22: 32, where God is described as the God not of the dead but of the living. The 'gods' are therefore those who are truly alive. They form a class alongside the thrones, dominions, principalities, and authorities of Col. 1: 16. Indeed, they head the order of classes of rational beings, being followed immediately by the thrones, then the dominions, and so on, until man is reached, the last of the *logikoi* (*In Jo.* 1. 31. 216, GCS iv. 38. 26–30).

The angelic orders thus form a continuum extending from the gods down to men. This enables Origen to interpret the 'gods' of Scripture sometimes as angels but more often as human beings who have been promoted to the angelic life.[46] The gods are 'those to whom the Word of God came' (John 10: 35).[47] They are the saints,[48] the perfect,[49] those who live in beatitude.[50] Through participation in God they have ceased to be men;[51] having ascended to the supreme God, they have been transformed from men into angels or gods.[52]

In comparison with Clement, Origen is much more willing to bridge the gulf between man and God. Clement does not call the angels

---

[46] On the angels as gods, see *C. Cels.* 5. 4 and *Hom. Exod.* 8. 2, GCS vi. 220. 14–20. For the full list of the 26 references to Ps. 82: 6 in Origen, see *Biblia Patristica* iii. 177.

[47] *Sel. in Psalm.* 135, PG 12. 1656A; *Cat. in Psalm.* 81, Pitra, *Analecta Sacra* iii. 141; *Sel. in Ez.* 1. 3, PG 13. 769B; *In Cant.* Prol. 2. 34, GCS viii. 71. 8; *In Matt.* A 24, GCS xi. 40. 6 f.; the reference is to John 10: 35.

[48] *Sel. in Psalm.* 4. 3, PG 12. 1137D; *Cat. in Psalm.* 81, Pitra, *Analecta Sacra* iii. 140.

[49] *Hom. Ez.* 13. 1, GCS viii. 440. 26–441. 10; *C. Cels.* 4. 29, GCS i. 298. 13.

[50] *In Jo.* 32. 18, GCS iv. 456. 30–457. 12.

[51] *In Jo.* 20. 27, GCS iv. 364. 3 f.; *In Jo.* 20. 29, GCS iv. 367. 2; *Sel. in Psalm.* 4. 3, PG 12. 1137D; *In Rom.* 3. 1, PG 14. 925C; *In Matt.* 17. 19, GCS x. 638. 12–639. 3; *In Matt.* 17. 32, GCS x. 679. 6–26.

[52] *Hom. Lev.* 9. 11, GCS vi. 439. 1–10 and 440. 9–14; *Sel. in Psalm.* 23. 6, PG 12. 1268BC; *Hom. Jer.* 16. 1, GCS iii. 132. 18; *Hom. Luc.* 29. 7, GCS ix. 171. 7–19; *In Matt.* 17. 30, GCS x. 671. 22–34; *C. Cels.* 8. 3, GCS ii. 233. 1–8; *C. Cels.* 8. 74, GCS ii. 291. 17–29.

'gods'.[53] Nor does he hold divine virtue to be the same as human virtue. But Origen maintains that men are virtuous in a contingent sense by participation in a goodness which is self-subsistent. They are similarly rational, immortal, and alive in dependence on him who is rationality, immortality, and life in itself. The key to Origen's understanding of the concept of deification is the concept of participation.

(c) How is the Self-Subsistent related to the Contingent?

Participation, or μετοχή, was, as we have noted, mentioned in passing as a philosophical term by Justin Martyr. Origen is the first to integrate the concept into a coherent structure of Christian thought. In other words, he is the first to give the Pauline image of participatory union in Christ a metaphysical rationale.[54]

Although Origen does not offer a definition of participation, he does discuss the implications of the concept at some length, particularly in the first and fourth books of *De Principiis* and the second book of the *Commentary on John*. These implications may be grouped under three headings: (i) the non-corporeal nature of participation; (ii) the fundamental kinship between participant and participated; (iii) the distinction between a participation which is natural or ontological and one which is supernatural or dynamic.[55] Let us take each of these in turn.

First, participation expresses a relationship which is metaphysical, not corporeal. Partaking of the Logos, for example, does not localize him or diminish him (*De Prin.* 4. 4. 2, GCS v. 351. 7 ff., *In Jo.* 13. 10, GCS iv. 234. 23–5). Nor does partaking of the Spirit imply that he is apportioned like a material substance. The Spirit is a 'sanctifying power', the saints participating in him in the way that physicians participate in the art of healing (*De Prin.* 1. 1. 3, GCS v. 18. 20 ff.). On the other hand, more physical images can be used to express the dynamic effect of participation. The Logos is the leaven that transforms *logikai* souls into itself (*Fragm.* 302 Matt. 13. 33, GCS xii. 135).

[53] In Clement the gods form a hierarchy of the saved parallel to the angelic one. Book VII of the *Stromateis* is particularly rich in examples; cf. 5. 6; 13. 1 (where the 'blessed abodes of the gods' should be compared not only with *Phaedrus* 246d, as in Hort and Mayor, but also with 1 Enoch 39: 4); 20. 1; 56. 1. Only once are the gods one of the orders of angels, and this is in a Valentinian source which Clement notes in *Exc. Theod.* 43.

[54] The centrality of the philosophical notion of participation to Origen's doctrine of deification has been recognized by Crouzel 1956: 173–7; Dupuis 1967: 97–8; Rius-Camps 1968, 1970a, 1972, and 1970b; and Balás 1975.

[55] The two different levels of participation are distinguished by Gruber 1962 (in relation to 'life'); Dupuis 1967: 257; Rius-Camps 1968; 1970a (esp. 214–24); 1970b (esp. chs 1 and 5); 1972; and Balás 1975 (esp. 265). Dupuis speaks of participation according to being and according to activity. Rius-Camps contrasts the 'ser primero, contingente, commun a todos los seres creados' with the 'ser divino, participado solamente a los santos'. Balás distinguishes between natural and supernatural levels, i.e. 'that of being and nature in general and that of salvation (including moral and religious perfection)', and proposes a further level for participations within the Trinity. My own preference is for the terms 'ontological' and 'dynamic', which correspond to Balás's first two levels.

The Spirit is also called a heavenly leaven that changes an earthly man into a heavenly or spiritual man (*Schol. in Luc.* 13. 21, PG 17. 357CD). When the Holy Spirit is 'mingled' (ἀνακέκραται) with the soul, it transfuses it with its qualities, making the recipient of salvation *pneumatikos* (*In Jo.* 1. 28, GCS v. 36. 12–14; cf. Dupuis 1967: 94–6).

Secondly, participation implies some kind of kinship both among co-participants and between participant and participated. It has, as it were, both a horizontal and a vertical dimension. In the horizontal dimension it is axiomatic that all the participants in something must be of the same nature. Accordingly, the human soul must be immortal and incorruptible like the heavenly powers because it shares with them in the contemplation of the intellectual light (i.e. the divine nature) (*De Prin.* 4. 4. 9). In the vertical dimension it also follows 'logically and of necessity' that 'since the nature of Father, Son and Holy Spirit, to whom alone belongs the intellectual light in which the universal creation has a share, is incorruptible and eternal, . . . every existence which has a share in that eternal nature must itself also remain for ever incorruptible and eternal' (ibid.; trans. Butterworth). While the participated must be superior to the participant (cf. *Frag. in Eph.* 25, p. 561. 11–12), it is nevertheless also true that the two terms must be similar in nature, for 'the participated can only produce in the participant an effect similar to himself' (Dupuis 1967: 98). At the time of the first Origenist Controversy, Origen was accused of holding that man and God shared the same nature.[56] But what his critics missed was that while the participant, through a fundamental similarity of nature, can share in the attributes of that in which he participates, the two terms remain distinct, and must do so, otherwise there would be no relationship of participation: 'Just as the substance of ointment is one thing and its odour another, so Christ is one thing and his participants another' (*De Prin.* 2. 6. 6, GCS v. 146. 2–3; cf. Plotinus, *Enn.* vi. 4. 13).

The third implication is a distinction between a participation which is natural and is concerned with beings qua beings, and one which is supernatural and is concerned with the activity of beings. The term participation, as we have seen, had been used in the Platonic tradition, both pagan and Christian, to indicate how the specific is related to the universal, or how that which exists in a contingent sense is related to that which exists of itself. Origen uses it in this way to express what may be called a natural or onto-logical participation. All creatures that exist (οἱ ὄντες) do so because they participate in Him who Is (ὁ ὤν) (*In Jo.* 2. 13, GCS iv. 69. 25–8; cf. *De Prin.* 1. 3. 6, GCS v. 57. 1–5). All that are alive are so because they participate in Life itself (*In Jo. fragm.* 2, GCS iv. 485. 24–6; cf. Gruber 1962). All that are rational

---

[56] See Theophilus of Alexandria, Festal Letter for 402 (= Jerome, *Ep.* 98), CSEL 55. 198. 25–6: 'ut nostras animas non alterius a deo naturae esse contendat'; also Jerome, *Ep.* 124 *ad Avitum* 14; cf. Butterworth 1973: 326 n. 1; Russell 2004*b*.

are *logikoi* because they participate in the Logos (*De Prin.* 1. 3. 6, GCS v. 56. 19–57. 1). In this sense all human beings share a similarity with God and partake of him by their very nature. But there is also a supernatural participation which is the result of the free human response to the operations of the Trinity and has the power to transform. In this narrower sense only the saint is *logikos*, only the Christian is alive.[57] By a parallel process of filiation, which is participation in the Son, and spiritualization, which is participation in the Spirit, the Christian can arrive at deification, which is ultimately participation in the Father.[58]

This dynamic, supernatural participation is wholly trinitarian. 'It is impossible', says Origen, 'to become a partaker of the Father or of the Son without the Holy Spirit'.[59] Participation in the Holy Spirit makes a person holy and spiritual, enabling him to receive the gifts of wisdom and knowledge. Several times Origen says that only the saints participate in the Holy Spirit. On one occasion, however, he expresses the opinion that every rational creature receives a share in the Holy Spirit, just as it does in the Logos (*De Prin.* 1. 3. 8, GCS v. 61. 3 ff.). Butterworth harmonizes these passages by supposing that 'the Spirit is given potentially to all, but his effective working is confined to the saints' (1973: 117 n. 1). An alternative way of putting it is to distinguish between a natural participation in the Spirit which all men enjoy through possession of a dormant created *pneuma*, and a supernatural participation which is limited to those whose *pneuma* has been awakened (cf. Dupuis 1967: 31–3; Crouzel 1955: 565). The supernatural participation begins to be active after baptism, when those who have received their existence from the Father, their rationality from the Logos, and their holiness from the Spirit 'become capable of receiving Christ afresh in his character of the righteousness of God' (*De Prin.* 1. 3. 8, GCS v. 61. 3 ff.). Once they have been illuminated, they become partakers of the Spirit in a new way (*In Jo.* 20. 12, GCS iv. 341. 25–9; cf. 28. 7, GCS iv. 397. 32). They now receive from the Spirit those particular gifts which they need (*De Prin.* 2. 7. 3, GCS v. 150. 1–10). Through their participation in the Spirit they are transformed progressively as they attain higher degrees of perfection until they are no longer ἄνθρωποι but πνευματικοί (*In Jo.* 2. 21, GCS iv. 78. 2–6). The *pneuma*, quickened by the Holy Spirit and suffused by him, becomes the dominant element in their constitution. By living in the *pneuma* they are able to turn away from the flesh and open themselves to the treasures of Christ.

---

[57] *In Jo.* 2. 16; cf. *In Gen.* 16. 1: He who dies to sin and the world is made alive by the Logos and receives another life.

[58] Cf. *Frag. in Is.*, PG 13. 217A–218A. Deification relates the believer specifically to the Father because he alone is αὐτόθεος. On filiation and spiritualization see Nemeshegyi 1960: 161–202; Dupuis 1967: 7; and Rius-Camps 1970*b*: 406–8. Rius-Camps sees the Holy Spirit as an inferior form of the Spirit of adoptive filiation.

[59] *De Prin.* 1. 3. 5, GCS v. 54. 20–55. 2. Cf. *In Rom.* 4. 9, PG 14. 997C, where Origen says that the grace of the Trinity makes us participants in the divine nature through the ministration of the Holy Spirit.

Participation in Christ in the supernatural or dynamic sense is made possible by his *epinoiai*. For Christ alone is wise, righteous, and rational, men being such only by sharing in his attributes (*De Prin.* 1. 3. 8; 4. 4. 5; *In Jo.* 2. 10). Indeed, Christ is the whole of wisdom, the whole of righteousness and the whole of rationality. These belong to his essential nature and cannot be alienated from him. Men are wise, righteous, or rational only accidentally. They acquire these attributes through personal effort and merit in proportion to their earnestness and intellectual capacity, and can lose them through sin. Other *epinoiai* are those of Christ as the Son, the Life and the Light of God. Men are adopted as God's sons through participation in Christ as the Son of God; they possess life and light through participation in him as the Life and Light of God.

Through Christ men also participate in the Father. Not that there are any further attributes, or *epinoiai*, for them to share in by participating in the Father. It simply follows from the fact that the Father is the source of everything that the Son is, the Father alone not living by participation. If the Son is Logos, the Father is αὐτολόγος; if the Son is Wisdom, the Father is αὐτοσοφία (*C. Cels.* 5. 39, GCS ii.44. 1; 7. 17, GCS ii. 168. 27). If the Son is θεός, the Father is ὁ θεός and αὐτόθεος.[60] Human beings come to participate in *logos*, wisdom, and divinity at a much further remove. In the Son these, although participated, reside essentially; in human beings they are possessed only accidentally.

When Origen's use of participation is compared with that of his contemporary, Plotinus, it is striking that while they both share the same understanding of the ontological aspect of participation, the dynamic aspect is found only in the Christian writer.[61] Plotinus illuminates the nature of participation with the image of the circle. The radii cannot exist without the central point. They take from it their origin and being and therefore 'participate in the point' (*Enn.* IV. 1. 1. 25–30). The point itself, however, remains 'in itself' and without division. In one sense it is the end of each radius; in another it is independent of the radii without extension or place. The One is analogous to this. It is not part of any being but 'rides, so to speak, on all beings at once' (*Enn.* IV. 1. 1. 21–2). Everything as a series of 'ones' participates in the undivided One in accordance with its capacity, so that the One can be said to be omnipresent by participation (*Enn.* III. 8. 9. 22–4). The goal of the philosophical life is ascent to the One that is not one by participation (*Enn.* V. 5. 4. 1–5). That is to say, philosophy prepares the individual intellect to receive the One not as a dim reflection in accordance with the intellect's

---

[60] *In Jo.* 2. 2, GCS iv. 54. 32–4. On the *auto-* compounds see Balás 1975: 263. All can also be applied to the Son in relation to the *logikoi* with the exception of αὐτόθεος and τὸ αὐταγαθόν. These belong to the Father alone.

[61] Cf. Crouzel 1956: 173. Plotinus' main discussions of participation are in *Enn.* I. 1. 1; I. 6. 2; III. 6. 11–14; III. 8. 9; VI. 4. 13; VI. 5. 8.

capacity but in its fullness and entirety. The One, however, is totally detached from human affairs and takes no initiative in the process.

The additional presence of a dynamic participation in Origen is to be attributed to the *personal* nature of the Christian divine hypostases. As Crouzel has suggested, 'the "gods" do not merely receive into themselves something of the reality of the Father and of the Word, the sons and the *logika* are not merely the reflections of the Unique Son and the Logos, but they are made gods and sons and *logika* by the voluntary action of the two divine Persons' (Crouzel 1956: 173). God 'procures' men's becoming gods, giving them bountifully a share in his own goodness (*In Jo.* 2. 2. 17, GCS iv. 54. 36–55. 2). The Lord by 'mingling' himself with beings gives them a share of his divinity and raises them to the right hand of the Father (*In Jo.* 19. 4, GCS iv. 303. 5–11). By falling into *logikai* souls, the Logos, like leaven, transforms them wholly into himself (*Frag.* 302 Matt. 13. 33, GCS xii. 135). The divine initiative calls for a human response. The Holy Spirit sanctifies those who choose to participate in him by faith, enabling them as they make progress in wisdom to participate more and more in Christ. By proceeding along 'the steep path of virtue' they become through imitation of Christ 'partakers of the divine nature' (2 Pet. 1: 4).

Origen is the first writer to quote 2 Peter 1: 4, a text he is able to use because of his concept of a dynamic or supernatural participation in God.[62] The Second Epistle of Peter, a pseudepigraphical work of the end of the first century, begins with a statement of the main theme couched in metaphysical language not encountered elsewhere in the New Testament. Through his 'glory and virtue' Christ bestows on us his 'precious and magnificent promises' which enable us to 'escape from the corruption which is in the world' and 'become partakers of the divine nature' (θείας κοινωνοὶ φύσεως). This is not 'naturalizing within Christian theology a widely diffused mystical tradition' as has often been thought, but a declaration that the destiny of believers is to share in Christ's divine attributes, which are his virtue, power, incorruptibility, and glory. A thorough study of 2 Peter 1: 4 has recently been made by James Starr (2000), who shows how Paul's idea of participating in Christ has been restructured through the juxtaposition of κοινωνός with θεία φύσις. The Christian takes on a new identity through sharing in Christ's nature, *now* by taking on his moral excellence, and *after the parousia* by sharing in his eternal life. Starr argues convincingly that 2 Peter's perspective is fundamentally Pauline, though there are also continuities with popular philosophical thought. In Origen's writings those who participate in the divine nature do so because they receive a share of the personal life of God through the action of the Trinity. There is no confusion between the

---

[62] Cf. *C. Cels.* 3. 37; *De Prin.* 4. 4. 4, GCS v. 355. 1–7; *Hom. Lev.* 4. 4, GCS vi. 319. 16–17; *In Rom.* 4. 9, PG 14. 997C; the last three texts survive only in Rufinus' Latin translation.

essence of God and that of the human soul because the relationship of participation ensures that the lower reality must be distinct from the higher as the term of the latter's action (cf. Dupuis 1967: 108–9). Thus Origen can say that the one God makes those in whom he dwells gods, the one Christ makes his adopted brethren christs, and the one Holy Spirit makes the saints holy spirits (*Frag. in Is.*, PG 13. 217A–218A; *In Jo.* 6. 3, GCS iv. 115. 17; cf. Dupuis 1967: 100–1). For through participation in the Holy Spirit the Christian becomes holy and spiritual. Through participation in *the* Son of God he becomes *a* son of God replete with wisdom, righteousness, and *logos*. And in this way he shares in the divinity—and with it the goodness, immortality, and incorruption—which has its principle of origin in the Father alone, becoming a god by participation (κατὰ μετουσίαν) as distinct from the unique Saviour, who is God by nature (κατ᾽ οὐσίαν) (*Sel. in Psalm.* 135, PG 12. 1656A).

(d) What is the role of Christ?

It has rightly been pointed out that Origen's christology is built on economic rather than ontological considerations (Grillmeier 1975: 141). The Logos undertook the Incarnation in order to heal the wounds in our souls caused by the Fall and restore us to friendship with God. The purpose of the Incarnation, in other words, is primarily the bridging of the gulf between the created and the uncreated, the Logos mediating between God and the rational creation (*De Prin.* 2. 6. 1), and the soul of Christ in turn mediating between the Logos and the flesh (*De Prin.* 2. 6. 3). Put in another way, the Logos is the image of God and the soul is the image of the Logos (*De Prin.* 1. 2. 6; 4. 4. 1). There is thus a hierarchy of elements even within Christ. The Logos remains dominant, for the lower reality participates in the higher, acquiring its attributes. The flesh is deified by the soul, and the soul is deified by the Logos, just as the Logos himself is deified by the Father (*C. Cels.* 3. 41; *De Prin.* 2. 6. 3; *In Jo.* 2. 2. 17, GCS iv. 54. 32–4; *In Matt.* ser. 33, GCS xi. 61. 7–8).

In the *Dialogue with Heraclides* Origen says that the whole man would not have been saved unless the Saviour had taken the whole man upon himself (*Her.* 137). Yet at the same time there is a tendency in Origen's christology for the human element to be swamped as the lower realities are subsumed into the higher. On the lowest level is the body, which is really corporeal, for 'they do away with the salvation of the human body when they say that the body of the Saviour is spiritual' (ibid.). This corporeality, however, is relative. In reply to pagan critics of the Incarnation, Origen asserts that Christ's body and human soul were deified from the beginning 'not only by communion but by union and intermingling, so that by sharing in His divinity he was transformed into God' (*C. Cels.* 3. 41; trans. Chadwick). It does not seem remarkable to Origen that 'the mortal quality of Jesus' body should have been changed into an ethereal and divine quality' (ibid.). The soul of Christ, which plays a vital part as the medium which makes the God-man possible (*De Prin.* 2. 6. 3), is nevertheless on a higher level than the body. It is of the same nature as other souls but different in that it is sent by God (*In Jo.* 20. 19), is not susceptible to sin (*De Prin.* 2. 6. 5), and is free from death (*In Jo.* 1. 20; 19. 16). In other words, it is an unfallen soul without the unruly lower faculties. On the highest level of all is the Logos. As the divine *hegemonikon* it forms the basis for the unity of Christ. Yet the *nous* is also the *hegemonikon* of the human nature. Are there then two centres of activity in Christ? The soul is united with the Logos, says Origen, as the Son is with the Father (*De Prin.* 4. 4. 4). Yet Origen is also able to call the Father and the Son two gods (*Her.* 124). Grillmeier is right in saying that Origen does not succeed in establishing a real ontic unity—there is a defective sense of the person of Christ.[63] But the person of Christ is not as important to Origen as his soteriological function. As the mediator between the simplicity of the Father and the multiplicity of the created world, the divine nature of Christ is from one point of view simple and from another multiple (*In Jo.* 1. 20). The multiplicity of Christ lies in his *epinoiai*, or titles, as the wisdom, power, might, Logos, and life of God (*De Prin.* 1. 2. 4; *In Jo.* 1. 20; *Hom. Jos.* 7. 7, GCS vii. 335). It is through participation in these that the perfect gain access to the Father.

Origen's christology has repercussions for his anthropology, the relationship of the human nature in Christ to the Logos providing a model for the relationship of the lower elements of the human constitution to the *nous*. As the soul and the flesh in Christ are subsumed by the Logos, so the human soul, led by the *pneuma*, will become entirely *nous*, enabling the human person to move up the scale of *logika* from 'man' to 'god'.[64] Although this transformation is effected by the Holy Spirit, Christ is the model and paradigm in whom we participate through his *epinoiai*, for by sharing in the name we participate in the reality. Yet Christ himself always remains distinct from men; he is God by nature whereas men are gods by grace. It is this unique aspect of his constitution that makes him the perfect mediator between the simplicity of God and the multiplicity of the world.

The sacramental dimension of deification is not given much prominence by Origen. Baptism is the point of departure for becoming a son, a christ, and a god by adoption, but its role is not discussed except incidentally. The Eucharist likewise is in the background rather than presented as a means of transformation. This reflects Origen's ambivalent attitude to the body. In his discussion of the *epiousios* bread Origen speaks of an intellectual nourishment by the Word without mentioning specifically its sacramental reception. In our becoming gods the material world is left behind.

---

[63] 1975: 146; but cf. Stead 1981: 170–91, who warns against our trying to impose modern notions of personality on Origen.

[64] On humanity's place in the scale of *logika*, see Rius-Camps 1970b: 304, 401–2.

(e) Conclusion

Deification in Origen's writings means the participation of rational creatures through the operation of the Son and the Holy Spirit in the divinity that derives ultimately from the Father. Only ὁ θεός, the Father, is αὐτόθεος. Every other being who is θεός is θεοποιούμενος. The Son is unique, for he is θεοποιούμενος in relation to the Father but θεοποιός in relation to men. He is thus the prime agent of deification, the Holy Spirit making men holy and spiritual so that the divine Son can make them sons and gods. They need to become gods because only like can know like. Only as gods who have recovered the divine likeness can human beings contemplate the source of divinity, the Father, and partake of the life, goodness, immortality, and incorruption that are properly his alone. Participation is the means by which such a deification is effected. The term denotes not merely the ontological dependence of the contingent on the self-existent, but also the dynamic reaching out of the Persons of the Trinity to rational creatures in order to endow them with their attributes. The divine initiative meets with a human response when the lower levels in the hierarchy of rational being participate by free choice in the higher, undergoing a progressive transformation as they acquire the attributes of the Spirit and the Son.

Although Origen adopts Clement's vocabulary, his more ontological and dynamic participation through the Logos in God's very life is new. Clement's use of 'participation' is close to that of Plato and Philo (cf. above, p. 127) It expresses the way in which creatures come to possess attributes which belong properly to a higher level of being. Participation in the attributes of God is the means by which likeness to God is brought about. Origen uses participation in a more dynamic way to signify 'living with the life of God'.[65] God reaches out actively to human beings whose response, through participation in the life of the Trinity, makes them spirits, christs, and gods. Indeed Origen's doctrine may be said to be the re-expression in metaphysical terms of the Pauline metaphors of participatory union with Christ. This is fitted into a highly speculative spiritual anthropology, but nevertheless was to prove highly influential.

6. Didymus the Blind

One of Origen's most influential successors was Didymus the Blind (c.313–98). Didymus, however, lived and taught in a cultural environment very different from Origen's more than a century before him. He was the last great teacher of Alexandria who was not also its bishop. Born at about the

---

[65] Clement just begins to hint at this when he suggests that imitation is equivalent to adoption (*Strom.* 2. 134. 2); cf. above 5. 4 (c).

time of Constantine's triumph, when the intellectual life of the Christian community was still centred on the private or Church-sponsored *didaskaleion*, he died at the age of eighty-five in the new era of powerful bishops and militantly Christian official policies inaugurated by the Emperor Theodosius I. The chief priority was now doctrinal orthodoxy. Speculative thought had become highly suspect and Origen could only be used with discretion. It is probably no coincidence that after Didymus we hear no more of a Church or Catechetical School. From the time of Theophilus' episcopate (385–412) the formerly separate roles of educator of the faithful and guardian of the doctrinal traditions of the Church coalesce in the person of the bishop.

Didymus belongs to the earlier world of the charismatic teacher. He had an international reputation as an ascetic and a biblical scholar which was all the more remarkable for his having been blind since the age of four. His visitors included the Westerners Rufinus, who attended his lectures regularly between 370 and 380 (*Apol. in Hier.* 2. 8; *HE* 11. 7), and Jerome, who frequently pays tribute to his scholarship in his prefaces (e.g. *In Gal., In Matt., In Osee, In Is., In Dan.*). Rufinus, who knew him well, describing himself as 'in some sense' a disciple, says that 'he became the master of the church school, having won the esteem of Bishop Athanasius' (*HE* 11. 7; trans. Amidon). It is probable that Didymus enjoyed some kind of official status, but whether he was director of an institution of higher education (the 'Catechetical School') is difficult to say. For most of his life he seems to have taught in his private *didaskaleion*, which may have been nothing grander than his monastic cell. Rufinus gives us a sketch of his method of study, describing how he used to turn over in his mind during his long hours of nocturnal wakefulness the material which his assistants had read to him earlier in the night (*HE* 11. 7). A visit to his cell was obligatory for any admirer of Origen. Jerome came to consult him in 386 before his quarrel with Rufinus. (Later he was to call Didymus a *doctor perversus*.) Palladius visited him several times in the 390s during his stay in Egypt (*HL* 4), no doubt on the recommendation of his mentor, Evagrius Ponticus, who regarded Didymus as 'the great Gnostic teacher' (*Gnostikos* 4. 8).

Didymus died just before Theophilus launched his campaign against Origenism, but that did not save him from eventual condemnation. Along with Origen and Evagrius Ponticus he was anathematized by the Fifth Ecumenical Council of 553. As a result, most of his immense literary production has perished. For centuries nothing much more was known of Didymus' works than his *De Spiritu Sancto* (in Jerome's translation) and fragments of his commentaries preserved in the *catenae*. Then in 1769 L. Mingarelli identified a mutilated Greek manuscript as Didymus' *De Trinitate* (*CPG* ii. 2570). Since that time several other texts have been claimed for Didymus, most notably ps.-Basil's *Adversus Eunomium* IV and V (*CPG* ii. 2837). The most spectacular discovery, however, came in 1941, when some workmen clearing a cave at Tura, near Cairo, for use as a munitions dump came across a jar containing several papyrus codices, including a representative sample of Didymus' biblical commentaries. It is these commentaries, the authorship of which is not in doubt, that provide us with our best evidence for Didymus' approach to deification.[66]

The most important of the Tura commentaries for our purpose are those on Zechariah and Genesis. It is striking in these works how close Didymus is to Origen, even though Origen is never mentioned. Becoming a 'god' for both authors is the product not of philosophical study but of Christian discipleship. For both of them, too, a key text is John 10: 34–6, where Christ is reported as saying: 'Is it not written in your law, "I said, you are gods"? If he called them gods to whom the word of God came . . .'. Receiving the word (or Word) of God and making it fruitful enables us to transcend our human nature.[67] Didymus, however, avoids the more speculative aspects of Origen's anthropology. He does not venture beyond saying that those are deified who have received the Word of God, first the prophets and holy personages of the Bible, and then all who through participation in the Word have the deity dwelling within them.

(a) Vocabulary

The vocabulary of deification is comparatively rare in Didymus. In his extant biblical commentaries he uses θεοποιέω seven times (*In Zach.* 1. 4; 267. 5, 11; *In Gen.* 248. 7, 8, 15; *In Psalm.* 81, PG 39. 1447D), and θεοποίησις once (*In Gen.* 109. 12) to signify participation in the Word of God (*In Zach.* 1. 4; 267. 5, 11; *In Gen.* 248. 7, 8, 15), in the virtues (*In Psalm.* 81, PG 39, 1447D), or in immortality (*In Gen.* 109. 12). The angels, in virtue of their immortality, and human beings who have come to participate in the Word may also be called 'gods'.[68]

The *De Trinitate* also uses θεοποιέω, but in a different way, more in the manner of Athanasius, to indicate the effects of baptism and prove the divinity of the Holy Spirit (2. 4, 25; 3. 2, 16). Besides θεοποιέω the *De Trinitate*, remarkably, also uses ἀποθεόω. The verb ἀποθεόω had only been used twice before in a Christian context, once by Origen for the immortalizing power of the virtues (*In Matt.* 16. 29, GCS x. 574. 7) and once

---

[66] The commentaries on Zechariah and Genesis have been published in Sources Chrétiennes (nos. 83, 84, 85 and nos. 233, 234) in 1962 and 1976–9. Three further commentaries, on Job, the Psalms, and Ecclesiastes, have appeared in the series Papyrologische Texte und Abhandlungen (1969–80). The Tura find also included the text of Origen's hitherto unknown debate with Heraclides, published in Sources Chrétiennes (no. 67) in 1960.

[67] For Origen and Didymus, of course, the 'word of God' of John 10: 35 (lower case in the RSV and other modern versions) which came to the prophets was the eternal Logos. The One Word of God underlay the many words of Scripture, giving Scripture its unity (Young 1997: 25–6).

[68] *In Zach.* 94. 25, 28; 95. 2; *In Gen.* 109. 12; 159. 3, 5; 230. 14; 246. 11; 277. 26.

by Apollinarius for the deification of the flesh by the Logos (frag. 98, Lietzmann 230. 6). Its appearance in the *De Trinitate* is the first time it is used with reference to baptism.

(b) Texts and Themes

The constantly reiterated theme in the passages in which Didymus refers to deification is that human beings can be said (on the basis of John 10: 35) to be deified when the Word of God comes to dwell within them. If they can be called 'gods' it is because the state implied by the word is a divine gift, not an element of their natural make-up:

> The Word is described not as *being* in men inspired by the Spirit (τοὺς πνευματοφόρους ἄνδρας) but as *coming* to them. It is not until then that it comes to be in them. For it is then that they will be 'gods', when the Word of God has come to dwell in them, as the Saviour says in the Gospel to those who find it difficult to accept that he called himself Son of God. For the text says: 'If he called them gods to whom the Word of God came, whom the Father consecrated and sent into the world'—myself who am speaking these words—'do you say that he blasphemes because he said. "I am the Son of God" ' (John 10: 35–6)? And since those to whom the Word of God came are proved to be gods, it is appropriate to understand and accept as sayings of God those things which the blessed prophets announced when they were inspired.   (*In Zach.* 94. 23–95. 5)

The different ways in which this insight can illuminate biblical texts may be illustrated by two passages, one from the *Commentary on Genesis* on Hagar's flight into the desert (Gen. 16: 12–14), the other from the *Commentary on Zechariah* on the homecoming of the exiled Israelites to Gilead and Lebanon (Zech. 10: 8–10). In the first passage Hagar, having fled from Sarah, is visited by an angel of the Lord. She receives the prophecy that she will have a son who will be called Ishmael. Reflecting on her experience, she says, 'Have I really seen God and remained alive after seeing him?' (cf. Gen. 16: 13). Didymus suggests why Hagar should refer to the angel as 'God'. An angel, he says, is at the service not of his own words but of those of God, just as the prophets were. 'The name "angel" represents an activity, not a substance, as does also the name "prophet" ' (*In Gen.* 247. 11–12). The angel that spoke to Hagar was called 'God' because of the One who dwelt in him. It is the same with the prophets. Isaiah, for example, sometimes speaks in his own person, and sometimes in the person of God, introducing the latter passages with the formula, 'the Lord says':

> We say this to show that the words of Isaiah are not all spoken as if he was only an intermediary, but because participation in God also conferred the authority of God and because as a result of the dwelling of God in them, those who participate in him are called 'gods'.   (*In Gen.* 247. 24–7)

Didymus then lists other angelic messages to demonstrate that 'with regard to their ministry, the words are those of angels, but with regard to their meaning they are the words of God' (*In Gen.* 248. 1–3). He follows this statement with two spiritual applications. The first is no longer legible. The second is as follows:

There is another similar meaning for the beginner. It is that there are many 'gods' and many 'lords' in heaven and on earth (cf. 1 Cor. 8: 5) and it is not the idols or demons that are 'gods' but those to whom he who has deified them has come (cf. John 10: 35). If the Word of God comes to people, those people are deified ([θ]εοποιοῦνται) . . . They are called 'gods' in the phrase, 'God of gods, the Lord, has spoken', that is to say, he is God of those who have become gods by participation (κατὰ μετουσίαν). (*In Gen.* 248. 4–12)

This is the same exegesis as Origen had proposed in the prologue to his *Commentary on the Song of Songs* (cf. 5. 5(b) above), set out here with particular clarity for the spiritual novice.

The second passage from the *Commentary on Zechariah* supports this:

Those who have been brought by God into Gilead are also brought into Lebanon, since they have been deified (θεο[π]οιηθέντες). For Lebanon signifies divinity in what was said by the divine bridegroom to the divine bride, which is the divine soul and 'the Church in splendour' abundantly sanctified 'since it is without spot or wrinkle or any such thing' (Eph. 5: 27). 'The scent of your garments is like the scent of Lebanon' (Song 4: 11). This could have been addressed to each of those who have been deified by participation in the Word of God (θεοποιηθέντων μετοχῇ τοῦ θεοῦ λόγου), about whom it was said by the Lord, 'He called them gods to whom the Word of God came' (John 10: 35). (*In Zach.* 267. 4–13)

Those 'to whom the Word of God came' include the patriarchs, such as Noah and Abraham, the prophets, such as David, Isaiah, and Zechariah, and finally any holy person who may be considered even in this life to be a citizen of the heavenly Jerusalem.

Like Origen—and many non-Christian Middle Platonists—Didymus regards spiritual progress as an ascent from the human to the divine. Noah, for example, was not entirely a human being (οὐ καθόλου ἄνθρωπο[ς ἦν]). He had risen above the human condition on account of his having been a recipient of the Word of God (*In Gen.* 158. 26–159. 4). At this point another biblical text is brought into play, David's declaration: 'I said in my ecstasy, every man is a liar' (Ps. 116: 11 = 115. 2 LXX). A person who is truthful is therefore no longer a man but a god. He is 'one who through virtue has transcended the appellation "man", in accordance with the text: "For where there is jealousy and strife, are you not men and behave as such?" ' (cf. 1 Cor. 3: 3) (*In Gen.* 159. 9–11).

The same texts are cited in Didymus' exegesis of Genesis 15: 12: 'At about the setting of the sun an ecstasy fell on Abraham' (*In Gen.* 230. 2–25). An ecstasy, Didymus explains, is not a derangement but a wonderment and a removal of the mind from things visible to things invisible. We are transported by contemplation to a realm beyond the human:

That is why David said, 'I said in my ecstasy, every man is a liar' (Ps. 116: 11). For having entered into an ecstasy and become a god, he says with regard to men that they are liars, since he was no longer a man on account of his sharing in the Holy Spirit (διὰ τὴν τοῦ ἁγίου πνεύματος κοινωνίαν), but was different from them. Of the latter it was said: 'For where there is jealousy and strife are you not men and behave as men?' (cf. 1 Cor. 3: 3). (*In Gen.* 230. 13–18)

Ecstasy is pre-eminently a Philonic theme. Indeed Philo has influenced Didymus deeply. He is cited seven times by name in the *Commentary on Genesis,* and his presence may be detected at other points too (Runia 1993: 200–4). On the subject of ecstasy, however, the emphasis of the two exegetes differs. In Philo, 'when the prophetic intellect becomes divinely inspired' the ecstatic is changed into the divine through escaping from the duality of mind and body (*QE* 2. 29). In Didymus, the ecstatic goes out from his human state through the indwelling of the divine Persons. Zechariah was a seer in this mould:

Since the eye of his understanding was illuminated and since he was deified (θεοποιηθείς) by the Word which came to him, he saw great visions and proclaimed the prophetic word in many ways and in many forms. (*In Zach.* 1. 3–6)

But it is not only the patriarchs and prophets who have been deified. Serious Christians who have made some progress in the spiritual life may also, in a nominal sense, be said to have become gods. Didymus develops this theme in his exegesis of Genesis 16: 12, where in the Septuagint version it is said of Esau: 'He will be a rustic man':

It is appropriate to say that he is not only 'a rustic' but also 'a man'. For participation in the Word of God occurs in a person not while he is still a beginner but after he has made some progress—for those are called gods to whom the Word of God came (cf. John 10: 35)—and this is how he will be a citizen of the heavenly city. For it is concerning such people that the wise Paul says in his epistle to the Hebrews: 'In Mount Zion and the city of the living God, the heavenly Jerusalem, there you will be enrolled' (cf. Heb. 12: 22–3). (*In Gen.* 246. 9–15)

The rusticity of the merely human is contrasted with the urbanity of the divine. As the Christian enters the heavenly city through his participation in the divine Word, he acquires the appellation of 'god'. This does not involve any ontological change. It is simply a restatement in a Christian context of the Platonist theme that the person approaching perfection ceases to be human and becomes like God—with the difference that it is participation in Christ that makes moral excellence possible.[69]

The authenticity of the *De Trinitate* since Mingarelli attributed it to Didymus has been much debated. Most scholars today agree that Didymus is the author.[70] From the point of view of deification, however, it must be said that the difference between the commentaries, whose authorship is not disputed, and the *De Trinitate* is striking. In the first place the author of the *De Trinitate* sees deification as the work of the Trinity as a whole without any separation of function: the Father creates, sanctifies, justifies, and deifies just as the Son and the Spirit do (*De Trin.* 3. 16, PG 39. 868c). The attribution of a deificatory role directly to the Father is unprecedented and points to a developing sense of the one divine nature of the Godhead. As Athanasius had already hinted in his *First Letter to Serapion*, however, deification is especially associated with the Holy Spirit: 'the divine Spirit makes us sons of God and deifies us' (*De Trin.* 2. 25, PG 39. 749c). With an eye perhaps on Arianism, the author also states that the angels are created and not from the substance of the Father. They therefore 'do not regenerate us, they do not deify, they do not forgive sins, they do not vivify, they do not create, they do not sanctify, they do not judge' (*De Trin.* 2. 4, PG 39. 481c). The power to deify is a function that belongs exclusively to the 'agenetic' deity, and the absence of such a power in the angels proves that they belong to the 'genetic' order of reality.

In the *De Trinitate* the power of the Spirit to deify through baptism is brought out explicitly in a new way. Two passages are of especial interest. The first, anticipating Cyril, connects the Spirit closely with the Father and the Son in the work of restoring the divine image by adopting us as sons and gods: 'If the Holy Spirit at the same time as the Father and the Son restores us to our original image through baptism, and is the cause by participation of our adoption and our becoming sons, and no creature has the power to adopt or deify in this way, how is he not truly God? (*De Trin.* 3. 2, PG 39. 801D–804A). The second expresses the deifying property of baptism differently: 'If the baptism which once took place in shadow (i.e. Noah's flood) was able to save, how much more so that which immortalizes us and deifies (ἀποθεοῖ) us in truth' (cf. 1 Pet. 3: 21–2) (*De Trin.* 2. 14, PG 39. 716 A). The novelty of the verb ἀποθεόω in such a context points to the growing importance of the sacraments as a means of appropriating the fruits of Christ's deification of his flesh.

---

[69] See also *In Zach.* 101. 1–7, where Didymus says that those who are imitators (μιμηταί) of Christ through the acquisition of the virtues are also called 'christs' because they have become partakers (μέτοχοι) of him. In this, too, Didymus follows Origen, who makes a similar point in his commentary on Isaiah (*Frag. in Is.* (PG 13. 217A–218A); cf. 5. 5 (c) above).

[70] *CPG* ii. 2570 notes that Doutreleau, having earlier denied Didymus' authorship, changed his mind.

In the *Commentary on Genesis* the gods of Psalm 82: 6 are the angels. In the *De Trinitate* they are those who have been granted the title through the gift of adoption (*De Trin.* 3. 24, PG 39. 937B). In a note on Psalm 82 which is also attributed to Didymus, the gods are those who have been deified by virtue (τοῖς κατ᾽ ἀρετὴν θεοποιηθεῖσι) (*In Psalm.* 81, PG 39. 1477D). The fact that different interpretations are suggested does not necessarily mean the passages are by different authors. In the *Commentary on Genesis*, however, deification is by participation in the eternal Logos in the style of Origen. The *De Trinitate*, with its emphasis on the deifying power of all three Persons of the Trinity, betrays the influence of Athanasius and looks forward to Cyril. If both works are by the same author, they show him capable of two different approaches, the one transmitting the teaching of Origen, the other responding to the new challenge in the latter part of the fourth century presented by the opponents of the *homoousion* of the Spirit.

7. The Alexandrian Concept of Deification

Of the two aspects of the Alexandrian concept of deification, the ecclesiastical and the philosophical, the former has priority. Even with Clement, discussions of deification generally arise out of the exegesis of biblical texts, or refer to the product of their study. The verb θεοποιέω is not used in philosophical contexts. It expresses the bringing about of a change in the believer by Christ, a promotion from the fallen condition of humanity to a state freed from subjection to death. Christ's teaching is all-sufficient. According to Clement the very words of Scripture are deifying. For Origen and Didymus the 'gods', on the authority of the Lord himself, are 'those to whom the word (= Word) of God came' (John 10: 35). Θεοποίησις is therefore fundamentally a product of Christian discipleship. This is because to be deified is to attain immortality, and immortality is not an innate human characteristic but a gift from God. It does not come about through the realization of the essential self, as in Platonism, but is granted as a result of fidelity to the teaching of Christ and his Church.

From the philosophical point of view, however, deification is the result of intellectual and moral effort, not in isolation from Christian discipleship but as part of it. This aspect of deification borrows from Platonism the metaphor of the soul's ascent, an ascent which is achieved through mastery of the passions and is accompanied by the recovery of the divine likeness. Another important Platonic borrowing is the concept of participation, which Origen develops in a new way to encompass not only an ontological participation of the human in the divine qua being, but also a dynamic participation qua active agent. The believer reaches up to the divine in response to the filiating and sanctifying operations of the Son and the Spirit, becoming a god by participation (κατὰ μετουσίαν), in contrast to the Son, who is God by nature (κατ᾽ οὐσίαν), through coming to share by means of the Son and the Spirit in the very source of life, which is the Father.

The deification of the believer is closely related to an Alexandrian christology in which the humanity of Christ is exalted and spiritualized. Origen's Christ is the mediator between the created and the uncreated, the Word being deified in relation to the Father, but deifying in relation to the soul and the flesh which he assumed. Through the Word the lower levels of reality in Christ participate in the higher, receiving in this way the Word's attributes. The soul of ordinary human beings is similarly deified by the Word, as it is drawn up into higher levels of reality, or in more pictorial terms, as it rises up through the angelic orders to the vision of God. Origen concedes that this teaching might be considered 'esoteric and mysterious'.[71] It is not for those whom later writers called the *simpliciores* but for those for whom the humanity of Christ was important only as an illustration of deification, not as the principal channel by which they gained access to divine life.

Deification also expresses an inaugurated eschatology. The soul's participation in divine glory can begin even in this life (hence Clement's talk of the Christian who has attained the perfect likeness of his heavenly teacher being a god while still moving about in the flesh, or Origen's claim that the intellect which has been purified and has transcended all material things is glorified and deified by what it contemplates), but its consummation is experienced in the next, when it is 'enthroned with the other gods', worshipping the Father with them in silent awe. In this approach there is little room for a literal understanding of resurrection.

From Clement to Didymus the concept of deification undergoes a gradual narrowing and focusing. Clement took over Irenaeus' exegesis of the 'gods' of Psalm 82: 6 as the baptized but quickly moved to a position in which the gods are those who have become *like* God. Human beings referred to as gods are those who have imitated Christ in the highest degree possible, who have conquered the passions, who have reproduced within themselves the attributes of God. In Origen the gods are those to whom the word of God has come, who participate in the divine attributes of the Father through the Son and the Spirit. In Didymus the emphasis is almost entirely on divine action, on the indwelling of God in the believer.

The trajectory of this development reflects the apologetic or polemical concerns of each writer. Both Clement and Origen were anxious to define

---

[71] *C. Cels.* 3. 37. The passage deserves quotation in full: 'There are some who because of their great simplicity do not know how to explain their actions, although it is with good reason that they observe the traditions which they have received. But there are others who explain their actions with arguments which may not be lightly regarded but which are profound and, as a Greek might say, esoteric and mysterious. They believe a profound doctrine about God and about those beings who through the only-begotten divine Logos have been so honoured by God that they participate in the divine nature [cf. 2 Pet. 1: 4], and for this reason are also granted the name (cf. Ps. 82: 6)' (trans. Chadwick).

the Christian goal (and the means of attaining it) in relation to the sophisticated and seductive claims of Basilidean and Valentinian Gnosticism. By the time of Didymus, however, there was already a question mark over Origen. Didymus took over Origen's vocabulary and general approach but did not make use of his distinctive anthropology. Although he defended Origen in his lost commentary on the *De Principiis* (Socrates, *HE* 4. 25), and appears to have believed in the pre-existence of souls and the *apocatastasis* (Jerome, *Adv. Ruf.* 1. 6; 2. 16), he has nothing to say in his discussions of deification about the descent and ascent of the human soul through the scale of the *logika*. All his points are firmly grounded in biblical exegesis.

No doubt the biblical basis of the concept of deification was one of the factors that prevented it from being included amongst the Origenist propositions condemned by Theophilus in 400.[72] In any case, Athanasius had already made extensive use of it in his anti-Arian polemics. By 400 it was already too well established to be affected by the Origenist crisis.

The approaches to deification used by Clement, Origen and Didymus are the ethical, analogous and titular. The realistic or sacramental approach, which envisages an ontological transformation of the believer by the incarnate Christ, was to be developed during the christological debates of the fourth and fifth centuries by Athanasius and Cyril.

---

[72] On Theophilus' study of the *De Principiis* and his list of condemned propositions, see Clark 1992: 105–21; cf. Russell 2004*b*. Theophilus' principal target seems to have been the teaching of Evagrius Ponticus.

6

The Alexandrian Tradition II

The Imposition of Episcopal Control

1. The Eclipse of the Independent Teacher

Pantaenus, Clement, and Origen (in his Alexandrian period) seem to have worked closely with Bishop Julian and his successor Demetrius (Eusebius, *HE* 5. 10. 4; 6. 3. 3; 6. 6. 1). But in spite of apparently undertaking the instruction of catechumens, they were all essentially independent teachers. Indeed, Origen lost no time in assigning the supervision of catechumens to a deputy, Heraclas, while he himself concentrated on higher studies with more advanced pupils (Eusebius, *HE* 6. 15). For Origen spiritual authority lay in the attainment of virtue and philosophical insight. Such attainment, in his view, did not always grace the occupant of the episcopal throne, the *cathedra doctoris* (Origen, *Hom. in Num.* 2. 1; Williams 1987: 83; Brakke 1995: 62). It was inevitable that sooner or later tension would arise between the bishop presiding over the eucharistic community on the one hand, and the charismatic teacher surrounded by his pupils on the other. Such tension came to a head in the dispute that erupted in 231 over Origen's ordination to the priesthood.

Some years previously Demetrius had angrily recalled Origen from Palestine on hearing that he was preaching in the churches there. On that occasion he complained to his Palestinian confrères that it was unheard of 'that laymen should preach in the presence of bishops' (Eusebius, *HE* 6. 19. 17). He was in any case uneasy about some aspects of Origen's speculative theology. The storm broke when Origen, during a visit to Caesarea, was ordained to the priesthood by his friend Bishop Theoctistus. Demetrius was not unnaturally outraged by Origen's advancement to the presbyterate without his leave. Adding an accusation of heterodox teaching to that of insubordination, he called an Alexandrian council which deposed Origen and banished him from Egypt. This action gave notice that henceforth the intellectual life of the Church of Alexandria would be subject to episcopal control.

A generation after Origen the problem of two parallel kinds of authority, the one hierarchical, the other charismatic, arose again in a particularly acute form. By the time of Bishop Alexander (312–28) Alexandria had a fully developed system of parishes, each with a priest who enjoyed a considerable amount of independence. The priest of the suburban parish of Baucalis was an ascetic teacher called Arius, who appears to have given public lectures every Wednesday and Friday to a devoted following of serious-minded Christians (Brakke 1995: 64). It has been argued persuasively that the old tradition of the *didaskaleia* lingered on in the fourth century in Baucalis and the other parish churches of Alexandria (Williams 1987: 85–91). Certainly Arius saw himself as an inspired teacher, a *theodidaktos*, after the manner of Clement or Origen (*Thalia*, in Athanasius, *CA* 1. 5). In about 318, when he heard his bishop propounding the co-eternity of the Son with the Father, he protested publicly that Alexander was teaching Sabellianism (Socrates, *HE* 1. 5). Alexander in turn, subjecting Arius' biblical exegesis to close scrutiny, found its denial of the Son's eternity grossly heretical, and had its author condemned and deposed as an apostate by an Alexandrian council.

The conflict embodied the old tension between the 'academic' tradition of the charismatic spiritual teacher and the 'catholic' tradition of the episcopal guardian of apostolic doctrine (Williams 1987: 91). It may even at first have also reflected intercommunal rivalries between the different topographical divisions of Alexandria.[1] But Arius' appeal to other Eastern bishops, particularly Eusebius of Caesarea and Eusebius of Nicomedia, soon raised the profile of the dispute. International support for Arius was organized by Eusebius of Nicomedia, whose campaign against the bishop of Alexandria and his theology forged an alliance between Arius and former pupils of Lucius of Antioch (like Eusebius himself) that was to divide the Church for many decades.

Alexander's difficulties in imposing his authority extended far beyond the confines of the city of Alexandria. During the episcopate of Peter I (300–11), Melitius of Lycopolis, objecting to the lenient terms on which Peter had received back those who had lapsed during the Diocletianic persecution, set up a rival hierarchy to minister to the needs of the 'church of the confessors'. In Alexander's time Melitius had some twenty-eight bishops besides a number of ascetic communities that acknowledged his leadership.[2]

The Council of Nicaea (325) attempted to resolve these problems. Alexander's condemnation of Arius was upheld and he was sent into exile in Illyria together with two Libyan bishops who continued to support him. Melitius was treated much more leniently. Although forbidden to carry out

---

[1] Haas 1997: 268–71. Though Haas's ideas of inter-communal conflict are to be treated with caution.

[2] On the Melitian schism see Martin 1996: 217–98. Martin suggests that the penitential question was only a pretext. The dispute, in her view, really reflects the tension between Alexandria and the rest of Egypt.

further ordinations, he was allowed to remain in his see. His priests and bishops were to be received back into the catholic Church but with a status inferior to that of the non-schismatic clergy. These arrangements, however, did not last long. The creed produced by the council met with widespread resistance on account of its non-traditional language and was soon dropped by the imperial government. In Egypt the council's canonical decisions regarding the Melitians depended on their co-operation and were never enforced. When Athanasius, who had accompanied Alexander to Nicaea as his deacon, succeeded to the episcopal throne on 8 June 328, it was a deeply divided Alexandrian Church that he inherited.[3]

2. Athanasius

Athanasius was the first of a formidable series of ecclesiastical politicians that was to dominate the Church of Alexandria until the middle of the fifth century. In Melitius, however, he met his match. In spite of his efforts to bring the Melitians under his control by violent means, the bishop of Lycopolis outmanoeuvred him. Melitius' intrigues with pro-Arian bishops hostile to Alexandria resulted several years later in the deposition of Athanasius by the Council of Tyre (335) and his banishment by Constantine to Trier. Athanasius' earliest work, and the first to mention Christian deification, his two-part apology, *Contra Gentes—De Incarnatione*, probably belongs to this first phase of his episcopate. Written perhaps between 328 and 335, just before his first exile, its purpose was to present an authoritative defence of the Christian faith befitting the incumbent of one of the greatest sees of the Roman empire.[4]

On Constantine's death in 337, Athanasius returned to Alexandria to a hero's welcome. Two years later he was forced out again by Constantius II under pressure from a group of bishops led by Eusebius of Nicomedia. Athanasius fled to Rome, where he was received by Pope Julius I. It was there that he wrote the *Orations against the Arians* and the *First Epistle to Serapion* (Barnes 1993: 53–5), the works which contain the bulk of his references to deification.

Athanasius returned from his second exile in 346 as a result of political pressure from the Western emperor, Constans, and ruled his diocese in

---

[3] On Athanasius' episcopal career Barnes 1993 (though often criticized for its negative and one-sidedly political evaluation of its subject) is fundamental. See also Arnold 1991 and esp. Martin's well-documented study (1996), which sets Athanasius authoritatively in his Egyptian milieu.

[4] The dating of *CG* has been much disputed, the proposed dates ranging from 318 to 350. For summaries of the arguments and references to their proponents see Barnes 1993: 12–13 and Anatolios 1996: 26–30. Barnes suggests that Athanasius wrote the work between Nicaea and his becoming bishop (i.e. 325–8) 'to establish his credentials as a worthy successor of Alexander' (1993: 13). Anatolios, noting the author's 'subtly magisterial tone', argues persuasively for 328–35 (1996: 29 and 215 n. 17).

comparative peace for ten years. In 356 he fled again when Constantius tried to have him arrested and disappeared into the desert monasteries until the accession of Julian in 361. This third exile was the most productive period of his life in literary terms, but references to deification are sparse, occurring only in *De Decretis* and *De Synodis*. From the final phase of his life, when he was once again in possession of his see, we have brief mentions of deification in the two anti-Arian letters addressed to Adelphius and Maximus.

Statistically, Athanasius uses the technical terms of deification much more frequently than any previous writer.[5] The works in which the terms appear, however, occupy a narrow range: those writings directed specifically against the opponents of Nicaea, whom Athanasius lumps together as 'Ariomaniacs'. Deification is primarily a weapon in Athanasius' dogmatic armoury against Arianism. It does not appear in his more general soteriological writings, such as his *Festal Letters*, or in any of his works of a more spiritual nature, such as the *Life of Antony*. That is not to say that deification is of minor importance. Athanasius' primary task throughout his episcopate was to overcome the divisions besetting his diocese. His christology was fundamental to this programme. Even though deification is referred to in comparatively few texts, it underlies his christological model and therefore constitutes a vital aspect of his struggle to unify the Alexandrian Church.

(a) Vocabulary

Athanasius' preferred term for deification is the verb θεοποιέω. He uses it no fewer than fifty times, twenty times in a pagan context and thirty in a Christian one.[6] The pagan instances, however, nearly all occur in his earliest work, the *Contra Gentes*. After the first appearance of θεοποιέω with a Christian sense in *De Incarnatione* 54, the word is used with a pagan sense only on two further occasions. (*Ep. Serap.* 4. 18, PG 26. 665B; *V. Ant.* 76, 949B). Ἐκθειάζω and θεοποιΐα are used with a pagan sense alone—the former

---

[5] No writer on Athanasius as a theologian, or on the development of the doctrine of deification in general, has neglected this aspect of his thought. Older studies which give prominence to Athanasius' doctrine of deification include Newman 1881: ii. 88–90, 424–5; Sträter 1894; Bornhäuser 1903: 13–48; Gross 1938: 201–18; Bernard 1952; Demetropoulos 1954: 116–23; Dalmais 1954–7: 1380–1; Theodorou 1956: 75–8; Roldanus 1968: 162–9, 192–5; Bilaniuk 1973; Scurat 1973; Stăniloae 1974; Norman 1980; Kolp 1982; Strange 1985. Among more recent studies Hess (who accepts Kannengiesser's argument that *CA* 3 is not by Athanasius) argues that divinization was not the central issue in Athanasius' theology (1993); Pettersen provides the best short summary (1995: 105–7); and Anatolios offers some very suggestive reflections on the role of deification in bridging the gulf between God and creation (1998: 133–63).

[6] Pagan: *CG* 9. 24, 33, 57, 58, 65, Thomson 24–6; 12. 7, 36, Thomson 34; 13. 18, Thomson 36; 18. 33, Thomson 50; 20. 17, Thomson 56; 21. 25, Thomson 58; 24. 20, Thomson 66; 27. 21, Thomson 72; 29. 7, Thomson 78; 40. 6, Thomson 110; 45. 42, Thomson 126; 47. 18, Thomson 132; *De Inc.* 49. 5, Thomson 256; *Ep. Serap.* 4. 18, PG 26. 665B; *V. Ant.* 76, PG 26. 949B. Christian: *De Inc.* 54. 11, Thomson 268; *De Decret.* 14 (twice), PG 26. '448' [440]D; *CA* 1. 9, Bright 9; 1. 38, Bright 40; 1. 39 (twice), Bright 40 and 41; 1. 42, Bright 44; 1. 45, Bright 47; 2. 47, Bright 117; 2. 70 (three times), Bright 140; 3. 23, Bright 178; 3. 33, Bright 187; 3. 34, Bright 189; 3. 38, Bright 192; 3. 39, Bright 194; 3. 48, Bright 202; 3. 53, Bright 206; *Ep. Serap.* 1. 24 (twice), PG 26. 588A; 25 (three times), 589B; *De Syn.* 26, PG 26. 729C; 51 (three times), 784B; *Ep. Adelph.* 4, PG 26. 1077A; *Ep. Max.* 2, PG 26. 1088C.

twice (*CG* 8. 30, Thomson 22; 9. 29, Thomson 24) and the latter three times (*CG* 12. 8, Thomson 34; 21. 23, Thomson 58; 29. 38, Thomson 80)—both of them in the *Contra Gentes*. There is a single instance of θεοποιός in the *De Synodis* with the Christian meaning that Clement gave it (*De Syn.* 51, PG 26. 784A). The noun θεοποίησις makes its first appearance in a Greek writer in the *Orationes contra Arianos* (*c.*340), on each of its three occasions in a Christian context (*CA* 1. 39, Bright 40; 2. 70, Bright 140; 3. 53, Bright 206). Athanasius couples it twice with an explanatory synonym—once with σωτηρία (*CA* 2. 70, Bright 140) and once with χάρις (*CA* 3. 53, Bright 206). Finally, it may be noted that ἀποθεόω and ἀποθέωσις are terms which Athanasius does not use at all.

Unlike Origen, Athanasius very rarely refers to human beings as 'gods'. When he does, it is either to emphasize the glorious destiny originally intended for the human race (*De Inc.* 4. 30–3, Thomson 144), or to explain that the biblical references to 'gods' do not encroach upon the uniqueness of the Word made flesh (*CA* 1. 9 and 1. 39, Bright 9 and 40).

In comparison with Clement and Origen, Athanasius narrows the range of the vocabulary applied to Christian deification. He uses only a single verb, θεοποιέω, in a Christian context. The only noun he uses with a Christian sense is his own coinage, θεοποίησις, reserving θεοποιΐα exclusively for pagan deification. Athanasius thus goes further than his predecessors in distinguishing even linguistically between pagan deification and its Christian counterpart.

(b) Pagan Deification

In his discussions of pagan deification Athanasius reproduces the arguments already familiar from the apologetic writings of his predecessors. The fundamental error of the pagans is to worship the creature rather than the Creator (*CG* 8 and 40; *V. Ant.* 76). God is incorporeal, invisible, inaccessible to touch, and all-powerful. 'How can those who deify creation', he asks, 'not see that it does not fall within such a definition of God?' (*CG* 29; trans. Thomson 79). The heavenly bodies do not meet this criterion (*CG* 27). The popular gods whom the pagans worship are, moreover, exponents of adultery and other crimes (*CG* 12). Like other apologetic writers, Athanasius found Egyptian religion ludicrous.[7] He also takes up the standard subject of the deification of Antinous, which only serves to prove that all idolatry was invented by men for the satisfaction of their passions.[8] Indeed in reality the gods are all non-existent (*CG* 9, 45, and 47). Athanasius appeals to Euhemeristic arguments to show that the gods have simply been invented by men.

---

[7] *CG* 24; cf. Origen, *C. Cels.* 3. 17–19. Origen is more subtle than Athanasius, for he recognized (as did Celsus) the symbolic nature of the Egyptian theromorphic gods.

[8] *CG* 9; cf. Justin, 1 *Apol.* 29; Tatian, *Discourse* 10. 2; Athenagoras, *Legat.* 30. 2; Clement of Alexandria, *Prot.* 4. 29. 1–2; Origen, *C. Cels.* 3. 36.

Asclepius, for example, was deified as a benefactor of humanity because he practised healing (*De Inc.* 49; cf. *CG* 18).

Athanasius' discussion of the imperial cult is interesting because its key idea is not unconnected with the fundamental principle of Christian deification. His objection to the cult is specifically that the senate has no authority to deify when its members are merely human: 'those who make gods should themselves be gods' (*CG* 9; trans. Thomson 27). By dying they prove their decrees of deification to be false. Here we have a foreshadowing of the argument which was to be advanced by Athanasius to prove the true deification of the Christian, for the Son can deify precisely because he *is* God.

Finally, it is worth noting, in view of Athanasius' reputed emphasis on the physical aspect of redemption, that unlike Origen he hardly ever uses deification terms in a pagan context in a metaphorical sense.[9]

(c) Christian Deification

Athanasius' first use of θεοποιέω in a Christian theological context is in his famous enunciation of the 'exchange formula' in *De Incarnatione* 54: 'he became human that we might become divine' (αὐτὸς γὰρ ἐνηνθρώπησεν, ἵνα ἡμεῖς θεοποιηθῶμεν) (Thomson 268. 11–12). The dependence of this on Irenaeus was pointed out more than a century ago (Sträter 1894: 40). It is a restatement in more technical language of Irenaeus' 'he became what we are in order to make us what he is himself' ('factus est quod sumus nos, uti nos perficeret esse quod et ipse') (*AH* 5, Praef.). Like Irenaeus, Athanasius sees salvation in terms of a reorientation of fallen humanity towards the divine (cf. Torrance 1995: 179). There is in his thought a fundamental polarity between God who is uncreated and the world which was brought into being from nothing. As a result of the Fall humanity is drawn towards the pole of createdness with a tendency to return to nothingness. The Incarnation has reversed the direction of gravitational pull. Through the convergence of the uncreated and the created in Christ, through his simultaneous 'otherness' and 'nearness' in relation to us, humanity is now drawn towards the opposite pole of the uncreated (Anatolios 1998: 35–8). Athanasius goes on to say by way of explanation: 'he revealed himself through a body that we might receive an idea of the invisible Father; and he endured insults from men that we might inherit incorruption' (trans. Thomson 269). The fruits of the deification of the representative humanity assumed by the Word are knowledge of God and freedom from corruption.

It is this christological model that Athanasius brings to his anti-Arian polemic. In the *Discourses against the Arians*, which were written in Rome

---

[9] From the Christian point of view all pagan deification is non-literal because the gods do not exist. But the deification to which Athanasius refers implies actual worship, with the sole exception of *Ep. Serap.* 4. 18, where he accuses the Pharisees of having deified Beelzebub rather than the Lord.

during his second exile, deification is one of his chief weapons against his opponents. First he argues against the Arian contention that the Son is himself a participant in divinity and therefore deified: καὶ οὐκ ἔστιν ἀληθινὸς θεὸς ὁ Χριστὸς ἀλλὰ μετοχῇ καὶ αὐτὸς ἐθεοποιήθη (*CA* 1. 9, Bright 9, quoted from the *Thalia*, frg. 3). Origen's distinction between the Son as deified in relation to the Father but as deifier in relation to men has no place in the light of the radical division now made between the 'agenetic' Godhead and the 'genetic' created order, the ἀγένητος and the γενητά. If to be deified by participation must be contrasted with true divinity, then the Logos is certainly not deified. He is not a son by adoption, or grace, or participation, or title. Such a son would not be the Wisdom and Word of the Father with a perfect knowledge of him amounting to comprehension.

Later in the first *Discourse* Athanasius begins to answer the Arian objections from Scripture to the eternity and uncreatedness of the Son. Philippians 2: 9–10 is a favourite Arian text, but it does not imply that the Son himself was promoted. He did not receive the name of Son and God

but rather he himself has made us sons of the Father, and deified men by becoming himself man (καὶ ἐθεοποίησε τοὺς ἀνθρώπους, γενόμενος αὐτὸς ἄνθρωπος). Therefore he was not man and then became God, but he was God and then became man, and that to deify us (ἵνα μᾶλλον ἡμᾶς θεοποιήσῃ). (CA 1. 38–39, Bright 40; trans. Newman/Robertson)

If the Old Testament makes mention of Moses and others as sons and gods (cf. Exod. 7: 1; Ps. 82: 1), that implies that the true Son and God in whom they participate must have pre-existed them. Adoption and deification are, according to Athanasius, scripturally attested before the coming of Christ. That means that there must have already been a Son and God who could effect this. For 'how can there be deification apart from the Logos, and anterior to him?' (πῶς δὲ καὶ θεοποίησις γένοιτ' ἂν χωρὶς τοῦ Λόγου, καὶ πρὸ αὐτοῦ) (*CA* 1. 39, Bright 40). Christ himself bears witness that the ancestors of his hearers 'to whom the Word came' were called gods (cf. John 10: 35; Ps. 82: 6).

And if all that are called sons and gods, whether in earth or in heaven, were adopted and deified through the Word (διὰ τοῦ Λόγου, υἱοποιήθησαν καὶ ἐθεοποιήθησαν), and the Son himself is the Word, it is plain on the one hand that they are all sons and gods through him, and on the other that he pre-exists them all, or rather that he alone is a true Son . . . by nature and according to essence. (CA 1. 39, Bright 41; trans. Newman/Robertson, modified)

That certain human beings had been deified in the past is taken for granted. For deification itself was not a point of contention with the Arians, seeing that they held Christ himself to have been deified. Athanasius therefore uses deification to prove the existence of the deifying power, and consequently the full divinity, of the Son. But the argumentation is biblical rather than philosophical. The existence of sons and gods in the Bible implies the existence of adoption and deification. The agent of this must be the pre-existent Son, who is contrasted with the sons who have come into being in time. The recipients of adoption and deification have simply received the name of sons and gods; Christ, however, is Son and God 'by nature and according to essence'.

The remaining instances of θεοποιέω in the first and second *Discourses against the Arians* are all concerned primarily with the deification of the body which the Logos assumed.[10] In *Contra Arianos* 1. 42–5 Athanasius is at pains to explain in what sense God 'exalted' the Son and 'bestowed' the name of Jesus on him (cf. Phil. 2: 9). 'The Word was not diminished in receiving a body, that he should seek to receive a grace, but rather he deified that which he put on (ἐθεοποίησεν ὅπερ ἐνεδύσατο), and moreover bestowed it freely on the human race' (*CA* 1. 42). It was the human body that was exalted, the Word not needing any exaltation, and not being diminished by the assumption of a body. We too are exalted with Jesus by becoming sons of God so that he dwells within us. As a result we share in the deified flesh which he put on, for it was our own fallen flesh. We are redeemed from sin, raised from the dead, and exalted to heaven (*CA* 1. 43). What is 'bestowed' on the Son only touches his humanity, and is the exaltation and grace which he himself gives to believers. This exaltation of human nature in Christ, Athanasius says later, constituted its deification: ὕψωσις δὲ ἦν τὸ θεοποιεῖσθαι αὐτόν (*CA* 1. 45, Bright 47). The created body of Christ was prepared 'that in him we might be capable of being renewed and deified' (ἵν' ἐν αὐτῷ ἀνακαινισθῆναι καὶ θεοποιηθῆναι δυνηθῶμεν) (*CA* 2. 47, Bright 117).

In these passages Athanasius introduces the key idea of the solidarity of the human race. Exactly how this solidarity is to be conceived is difficult to determine.[11] As Pettersen says, Athanasius is interested in 'the "why" rather than the "what" of Christ's humanity' (1995: 109). A fruitful approach is perhaps to see Christ's humanity as having a *representative* significance (cf.

[10] On the body in Athanasius' thought the perceptive remarks of Anatolios deserve quotation (1998: 64): 'The body . . . seems to represent for Athanasius what most immediately belongs to humanity, as its own, and thus what is primarily to be transcended. The soul is not conceived in the same way—as that which is to be transcended—not because it is naturally superior to the body or more "divine", but simply because the soul is supposed to be the organ which actually effects this self-transcendence. In other words, the soul is conceived more as the subject of self-transcendence and the body as what has to be transcended. Moreover . . . the body is not the object of this self-transcendence because it is evil, but precisely because it is what is "closest to humanity". Surprisingly then, and in a striking departure from a prevailing Platonic identification of humanness with the soul (which is basically the position of Origen), it seems that for Athanasius the "selfness" of being human resides particularly in the body.'

[11] Earlier scholars thought they could detect in Athanasius' conception of Christ's humanity a universal reality in the Platonic mould (Harnack 1896–9: iii. 295–303; Gross 1938: 208–9; Kelly 1977: 378–9; Norman 1980: 98–100). More recent scholars, while not denying a critical acceptance by Athanasius of certain Platonic themes, interpret his view of Christ's human nature in terms of a representative humanity (Pettersen 1995: 132–3; Anatolios 1996: 284; 1998: 70–8, 140–5).

Torrance 1995: 192–3). The incarnate Word took our nature into himself in
order to save it. Thus, according to Torrance, Athanasius understood
redemption 'as taking place within the mediatorial life and person of the
Incarnate Son. Just as he thought of the *Logos* as internal to the being of
God, so he thinks of our salvation as taking place in the *inner relations of the
Mediator* (μεσίτης), and not simply in Christ's external relations with sinners'
(1995: 193). Or, as Anatolios puts it, 'our whole salvation and deification are
rooted in our human condition's being "ascribed" to the Word, for that is
what essentially constitutes our own being "Worded" '(1998: 143). Human
nature becomes the Word's 'own' (ἴδιον), so that we are all, in some sense,
incorporated into the incarnate Word and benefit from the 'giving' and 'receiving', the *communicatio idiomatum*, or exchange of attributions, between God and
created nature (Anatolios 1996 and 1998: 155; cf. Roldanus 1968: 180–1).

The most important passage in this connection is *Contra Arianos* 2. 70,
where Athanasius, now moving on to objections from Proverbs 8: 22,
explains at some length how the new creation could not have been brought
about if Christ had been a creature. The Logos assumed a created human
body

> that having renewed it as its creator, he might deify it in himself (ἐν ἑαυτῷ
> θεοποιήσῃ), and thus might bring us all into the kingdom of heaven in his likeness.
> For man would not have been deified if he had been united with a creature, or if the
> Son had not been true God, nor would man have been brought into the Father's
> presence unless he who had put on the body had been his natural and true Word.
> And just as we would not have been delivered from sin and the curse, if it had not
> been natural flesh which the Word put on (for we should have had nothing in
> common with that which was foreign), so also man would not have been deified (οὐκ
> ἂν ἐθεοποιήθη ὁ ἄνθρωπος) unless the Word who became flesh had been by nature
> from the Father and true and proper to him. For that is why the union was of this
> kind, that he might unite what is naturally man to what is naturally of the Godhead,
> and his salvation and deification (θεοποίησις) be made sure.   (*CA* 2. 70, Bright 140;
> trans. Newman/Robertson, modified)

Here Athanasius moves easily from the deification of a body to the deification of humanity as a whole. As Roldanus notes, 'his conception of salvation
depends in effect as much on the community of the human *sarx* of Christ
with that of our own as on the community of his divine nature with that of
the Father' (1968: 164). The renewal of the human race is like a second
creation carried out by the Creator, but this time from within. The unity of
humankind, which Athanasius takes for granted, means that the whole of
human nature is deified in principle when the human nature which the Logos
assumed is deified by him. A Pauline influence has rightly been seen in this
presentation of the solidarity of believers with the body of Christ (cf. Rom.
6: 4) (Sträter 1894: 175; Norman 1980: 99–100). But Athanasius' fundamental
conception of humanity seems to be one of likeness rather than corporate

identity (Pettersen 1995: 133). The deification of humanity in principle, however, still leaves salvation to be appropriated by individuals.

Reference to deification occurs eight times in the third Discourse, on the first occasion in the course of an exegesis of John 17.[12] The work which the Lord 'perfected' (John 17: 4) is the abolition of death and corruption, which he accomplished through 'having borne their body and become man'.

And the work is perfected because men, having been redeemed from sin, no longer remain dead; but having been deified (θεοποιηθέντες), have in each other, by looking at me, the bond of love. (*CA* 3. 23, Bright 178; trans. Newman/Robertson, modified)

It is instructive to compare this with Eusebius' handling of the same text (*De eccles. theol.* 3. 18, PG 24. 1041BC). In the older man the perfection achieved is a moral one which enables men to participate in the divine splendour. In Athanasius the same perfection is the transcendence of mortality and corruption which the Lord achieved first in his own person. Once this has been communicated to men, they are able, by contemplating the Son, to share in his unity with the Father, a unity constituted by the bond of love.

Later in the third *Discourse* Athanasius returns to the *communicatio idiomatum* of the Logos and the flesh:

For if the works of the Word's divinity had not taken place through the body, humanity would not have been deified (οὐκ ἂν ἐθεοποιήθη ἄνθρωπος); and again, if the properties of the flesh had not been ascribed (ἐλέγετο) to the Word, men would not have been delivered completely from them. (*CA* 3. 33, Bright 187; trans. Newman/Robertson, modified)

The ascription or attribution of divinity to Christ's human nature and of humanity to his divine nature is fundamental to Athanasius' understanding of how the 'agenetic' and the 'genetic' converge in Christ. It is in this convergence that our salvation is rooted, for the 'humanity' that is deified in this passage is both the body of Christ and the human race.

Shortly afterwards, emphasizing the benefits that have accrued to human beings through the *communicatio idiomatum*, Athanasius says that the Word's assumption of the form of servitude entails human nature's riddance of corruption:

For just as the Lord became man by putting on the body, so we men are deified by the Word, having been assumed through his flesh (παρὰ τοῦ Λόγου τε θεοποιούμεθα προσληφθέντες διὰ τῆς σαρκὸς αὐτοῦ), and henceforth we inherit eternal life. (*CA* 3. 34, Bright 189)

---

[12] The Athanasian authorship of *CA* 3 has been questioned by Kannengiesser, who has proposed Apollinarius as the true author (1983). The aspect of deification developed in *CA* 3, however, namely, the deification of the human race as a whole through the deification of the flesh assumed by the Logos, is an Athanasian theme which has already appeared in *CA* 1 and 2 but is not prominent in Apollinarius. Cf. Stead's criticism of Kannengiesser's thesis (1985).

Again Athanasius stresses the solidarity of the whole human race with the body which the Logos assumed, so that *we* can be said to have been assumed, with the result that we now have access to eternal life.

This is a point that Athanasius hammers home. In the person of Christ the human and the divine are held together in a state of creative tension. The Word did not cease to be God when he became man. 'But rather, being God, he has assumed the flesh, and being in the flesh, he deified the flesh' (καὶ ἐν σαρκὶ ὢν ἐθεοποίει τὴν σάρκα) (*CA* 3. 38, Bright 192). The Incarnation, Athanasius reiterates, took place not to promote the Logos but to promote the body: 'the Word came to dwell among us in order to redeem the human race, and the Word became flesh in order to sanctify them and deify them' (καὶ ἵνα αὐτοὺς ἁγιάσῃ καὶ θεοποιήσῃ) (*CA* 3. 39, Bright 193–4). If the flesh was deified through the Incarnation, its deification was reaffirmed through the Resurrection: 'For now the flesh had arisen and put off its mortality and been deified' (ἦν ἡ σὰρξ ἀναστᾶσα, καὶ ἀποθεμένη τὴν νέκρωσιν, καὶ θεοποιηθεῖσα) (*CA* 3. 48, Bright 202).

The final reference to deification in the third *Discourse* develops the idea of the transcendence of human nature. In reply to the Arian objection from Luke 2: 52 that Jesus 'advanced in wisdom' Athanasius rejects the idea of development or advance (προκοπή) in the case of the Son, but he does allow it for human beings.

What is this advance that is spoken of other than, as I have said, the deification and grace (θεοποίησις καὶ χάρις) imparted by Wisdom to men, the sin and corruption that is in them having been obliterated according to their likeness to the flesh of the Word and their kinship with it?   (*CA* 3. 53, Bright 206)

But does not this imply, because of the solidarity of all human flesh, that the flesh of the incarnate Son also advanced? Yes, it does. Wisdom himself did not advance,

but the human element advanced in Wisdom, transcending by degrees human nature, and being deified (ὑπεραναβαῖνον κατ᾽ ὀλίγον τὴν ἀνθρωπίνην φύσιν, καὶ θεοποιούμενον), and becoming and appearing to all the organ of Wisdom for the operation and shining forth of the Godhead. (*CA* 3. 53, Bright 206; trans. Newman/Robertson, modified)

In Christ humanity transcended its own nature, and this is communicated to believers through their 'likeness to the flesh of the Word and their kinship with it'.

In the *First Letter to Serapion*, which also belongs to the period of his second exile, Athanasius uses θεοποιέω in two passages to prove the divinity of the Holy Spirit.

If by participation in the Spirit, we become 'partakers of divine nature' (2 Pet. 1: 4), it would be insane to say that the Spirit belongs to created nature and not to God.

For that is why those in whom he comes to dwell are those who are deified (ἐν οἷς γίνεται, οὗτοι θεοποιοῦνται). And if he deifies there is no doubt that his nature is of God (εἰ δὲ θεοποιεῖ, οὐκ ἀμφίβολον, ὅτι ἡ τούτου φύσις Θεοῦ ἐστι). (*Ep. Serap.* 1. 25, PG 26. 589B)

He then cites a number of New Testament passages to show that the Spirit, although 'of God', is not another Son but is the Son's Spirit of adoption, and concludes:

In him, then, the Logos glorifies creation, and deifying and adopting it brings it to the Father (θεοποιῶν δὲ καὶ υἱοποιῶν προσάγει τῷ Πατρί). That which unites creation to the Logos cannot itself belong to the created order. And that which adopts creation cannot be foreign to the Son. Otherwise it would be necessary to seek another Spirit that this too might be united in him with the Logos. But that would be absurd. Therefore the Spirit does not belong to the created order, but is proper to the Godhead of the Father, in whom the Logos also deifies created things. And he in whom creation is deified cannot himself be outside the divinity of the Father. (*Ep. Serap.* 1. 25, PG 26. 589B)

Deification is a work of the Son in conjunction with the Spirit. Adoption is synonymous with deification.

Anathasius returns again to the topic of deification in the period of his third exile, when he was in hiding in the desert monasteries. In *De Decretis* 14 he says:

the Word was made flesh, not only to offer up this body for all, but that we, partaking of his Spirit, might be deified (καὶ ἡμεῖς ἐκ τοῦ πνεύματος αὐτοῦ μεταλαβόντες θεοποιηθῆναι δυνηθῶμεν), a gift which we could not otherwise have gained than by his clothing himself in our created body; for hence we derive our name of 'men of God' and 'men in Christ'. And as we, by receiving the Spirit, do not lose our own proper substance, so the Lord, when made man for us, and bearing a body, was no less God; for he was not lessened by the envelopment of the body, but rather deified it and rendered it immortal (ἀλλὰ καὶ μᾶλλον ἐθεοποιεῖτο τοῦτο καὶ ἀθάνατον ἀπετέλει). (*De Decr.* 14, PG 25. '448' (440)D; trans. Newman/Robertson, modified)

Athanasius' fondness for symmetrical statements is apparent in this passage. The Word was made flesh that we might become gods. This we experience through partaking of the Spirit in baptism. But we do not cease to be human by receiving the Spirit any more than the Word ceases to be divine by assuming a body. On the contrary, his assumed body becomes divine and immortal. The statements may be symmetrical but the relationship is not one between equal parties. Christ in his incarnation deifies a human body, and makes available the Spirit, who in turn deifies believers, though without swamping their humanity.

In the *De Synodis*, after reproducing among the creeds the fifth confession of Antioch, with its condemnation of the followers of Paul of Samosata, 'who say that after the Incarnation he was promoted to be God (ἐκ προκοπῆς τεθεοποιῆσθαι) from being a mere man by nature' (*De Syn.* 26, PG 26. 729C), he rehearses his familiar teaching that the Son cannot deify if he is himself deified:

And again, if, as we have said before, the Son is not such by participation, but, while all things originated have by participation the grace of God, he is the Father's Wisdom and Word of which all things partake, it follows that he, being the deifying and enlightening power of the Father in which all things are deified and quickened (ὧν τὸ θεοποιὸν καὶ φωτιστικὸν τοῦ πατρός, ἐν ᾧ τὰ πάντα θεοποιεῖται καὶ ζωοποιεῖται), is not alien in essence from the Father but co-essential. For by partaking of him we partake of the Father; because the Word is the Father's own. Therefore, if he was himself too from participation, and not from the Father as his essential godhead and image, he would not deify, being deified himself (οὐκ ἂν ἐθεοποίησε θεοπιούμενος καὶ αὐτός). For it is not possible that he who merely possesses from participation should impart of that partaking to others, since what he has is not his own but the Giver's; and what he has received is barely the grace sufficient for himself. (*De Syn.* 51, PG 260 784BC; trans. Newman/Robertson, modified)

Again the deifying power of the Son is taken for granted and is used as an argument to prove his full divinity. The Son can deify because he is not the Son by participation (μετουσία), which entails subordination in relation to that which is participated. In this context μετουσία is contrasted with ἴδιος, with being proper to the Father, or the Father's 'own'. But elsewhere ἴδιος is equivalent to a superior kind of participation (τὸ ... ὅλως μετέχεσθαι) (*CA* 1. 16, Bright 17). The Son participates wholly in the essence of the Father, not in something external to him. By implication deification here is equivalent to baptism, for the Son is a power who is deifying, enlightening, and life-giving. The deification which the Son brings is participation in the light and life of the Father.

Finally, Athanasius mentions deification in two anti-Arian letters. To Adelphius he writes that Christ 'became man that he might deify us in himself' (γέγονε γὰρ ἄνθρωπος ἵν᾽ ἡμᾶς ἐν ἑαυτῷ θεοποιήσῃ), enabling us to become a holy race and partakers of the divine nature (*Ep. Adelph.* 4, PG 26. 1077A). And to Maximus he says: 'we are deified not by partaking of the body of some man, but by receiving the body of the Word himself (ἀλλὰ αὐτοῦ τοῦ Λόγου σῶμα λαμβάνοντες θεοποιούμεθα) (*Ep. Max.* 2, PG 26. 1088C). The last phrase seems to be a veiled reference to the Eucharist. If so, it is the only specific mention of the role of the Eucharist in deification.

To sum up, the technical vocabulary of deification is used much more frequently by Athanasius than by his predecessors. It is also used in a different way. In the first place Clement, Origen, and Eusebius use θεοποιέω neat, as it were, allowing the context to supply the meaning, whereas Athanasius frequently couples it with an explanatory synonym. This may simply be a stylistic trait but nevertheless the list is revealing: υἱοποίησεν ... καὶ

ἐθεοποίησε (*CA* 1. 38, Bright 40)—υἱοποιήθησαν καὶ ἐθεοποιήθησαν (*CA* 1.
39, Bright 41)—ἀνακαινισθῆναι καὶ θεοποιηθῆναι (*CA* 2. 47, Bright 117)—ἡ
σωτηρία καὶ ἡ θεοποίησις (*CA* 2.70, Bright 140)—ἁγιάσῃ καὶ θεοποιήσῃ (*CA*
3. 39, Bright 194)—θεοποίησις καὶ χάρις (*CA* 3. 53, Bright 206)—
ὑπεραναβαῖνον . . . καὶ θεοποιούμενον (*CA* 3. 53, Bright 206)—θεοποιῶν καὶ
υἱοποιῶν (*Ep. Serap* 1. 25, PG 26. 589B)—τὸ θεοποιὸν καὶ φωτιστικόν (*De Syn.*
51, PG 26. 784B)—θεοποιεῖται καὶ ζωοποιεῖται (ibid.). Adoption, renewal,
salvation, sanctification, grace, transcendence, illumination, and vivification
are all presented as equivalents to deification. Although the concept itself is
not controversial, Athanasius may well be intending to exclude any possibility of misunderstanding.

Secondly, Athanasius brings deification into line with post-Nicene orthodoxy. Origen and Eusebius had both characterized the Son as deified by the
Father, Origen also holding that the Son is θεὸς λόγος . . . θεοποιός (*Sel. in
Ez.* 1. 3, PG 13. 769B). Athanasius believed the second proposition to be
inconsistent with the first. The Son can only deify if he is not himself the
recipient of deification; it is simply his flesh that is deified. Henceforth, the
need to place the Son on one side or the other of the 'genetic'/'agenetic'
divide will force theologians to align themselves either with Athanasius or
with Arius.

Thirdly, the subject of human deification is now no longer *nous* but the
flesh. Origen could speak of the *nous* or the *diathesis* being deified (*In Jo.* 32.
27. 339, GCS iv. 472. 34; *Orat.* 25. 2, GCS ii. 358. 23), but with Athanasius it is
always the 'body', 'flesh', or 'man'. Origen had also said, however, that the
Logos 'deified the human nature which he assumed' ('deificavit quam sus-
ceperat humanam naturam') (*In Matt.* ser. 33, GCS xi. 61. 7 f.). This notion is
the foundation of the whole of Athanasius' thinking. It enables him to apply
the concept of deification consistently both to the Son and to men. This
double application accounts for the two aspects or 'moments' of deification
which we find in his writings.[13] The first is the deification of the flesh by the
Logos in the Incarnation: the Logos deified that which he put on; he made
the body immortal; he renewed and exalted human nature. The second is the
deification of men by the Son. It arises from the first because in the Incarnation it is 'we' who have been assumed by the Logos through his flesh, for the
flesh is a generic reality in which all men share. But this deification, which in
principle is a deification of all men, has to be appropriated by individual
believers. It is through baptism that the Son is encountered as the deifying
and enlightening power of the Father. The Spirit also plays an essential role,
for only those in whom the Spirit comes to dwell are deified. The Spirit
enables us to receive the deifying body of the Word.

---

[13] The expression 'moment' is that of Bilaniuk (1973: 351). Bilaniuk also identifies a third 'moment',
viz. 'divinization (as a result of the first two) of the whole cosmos'. This last 'moment', however, is not
associated by Athanasius with the term θεοποιέω.

Lastly, Athanasius expands the content of deification, moving the emphasis away from immortality and incorruption to the exaltation of human nature through participation in the life of God. Deification is certainly liberation from death and corruption, but it is also adoption as sons, the renewal of our nature by participation in the divine nature, a sharing in the bond of love of the Father and the Son, and finally entry into the kingdom of heaven in the likeness of Christ. The most recent writers on Athanasius are rightly united in finding his idea of deification complex and rich.[14] Dalmais, moreover, detects a development from the divine knowledge and incorruptibility of the *De Incarnatione* to a less intellectualist conception in the later, anti-Arian writings (1954–7: 1380–1). The evidence seems to support this view. In struggling with the Arian objections from Scripture, Athanasius develops the dynamic aspects of deification, the perfecting and transcending of human nature. These aspects are not absent from earlier writers. Irenaeus in particular had already identified deification with adoption and had stressed humanity's participation in the life of God. Origen had developed the nature of this participation as a reaching out of God to man together with man's free response to God. In Athanasius Irenaeus' teaching on adoption has been combined with Origen's doctrine of a dynamic participation in the Trinity to produce a concept of deification as the penetration and transformation of mortal human nature by the eternal Son which enables it to participate in the light and life of the Father.

(d) Immanence and Transcendence

Nevertheless, it cannot be denied that there are aspects of Athanasius' concept of deification which cause unease to the modern mind. Those who are particularly struck by his emphasis on the transmission of incorruption and immortality through the Incarnation to the rest of humanity as a result of

---

[14] Demetropoulos (1954: 118) sees adoption, redemption, sanctification, renewal, and perfection as equivalent to deification but temporally prior to it; i.e. he reserves the term θεοποίησις for the eschatological fulfilment of deification. For Roldanus (1968: 166–9) the chief elements of deification are (i) an incorruptibility which implies a sharing in the divine life; and (ii) a liberation from sin and death which results from man's re-creation. Norman (1980: 139–71), arguing that deification is more than a Greek attainment of immortality and also more than an ethical attainment of likeness, lists eight different aspects: (i) the renewal of humankind in the image of God; (ii) the transcendence of human nature; (iii) the resurrection of the flesh and immortality of the body; (iv) the attainment of incorruptibility, impassibility, and unchangeableness; (v) participation in the divine nature and qualities of Godliness; (vi) attainment of the knowledge of God; (vii) the inheritance of divine glory; and (viii) ascent to the heavenly kingdom. Hess (1993: 371) sees divinization as one of a cluster of eight closely related motifs: renewal, divinization, partaking of God, union, adoption as sons, exaltation, sanctification, and perfection in Christ. He notes the anti-Arian polemical purpose of the divinization motif and its absence from Athanasius' Festal Letters, which he takes as evidence that deification is not a 'central or controlling motif'. But cf. Cyril of Alexandria, who does not refer to deification in his Festal Letters either.

the solidarity of the human race have spoken of an unsatisfactory 'physical' doctrine of redemption.[15] When he discusses redemption, Athanasius speaks of the body or the flesh of Christ but not his soul. The deification of man therefore seems to ignore the soul, our solidarity with Christ resting simply on the basis of the body. Another problem which has been discussed is whether Athanasius' soteriology is compatible with his ontology, that is to say, whether he has shown convincingly how mortal man can share in an utterly transcendent God (Norman 1980: 178–80, 199–203). The two questions are related, for in Athanasius' view the deified flesh of Christ is the very means by which mortal man does actually approach God. In order to form a judgement on these questions it will be helpful to examine briefly the place of deification within the wider framework of Athanasius' anthropology and soteriology.

Athanasius considers creation specifically only in his earliest work, where he gives two accounts of it, both of which may be considered a commentary on Genesis 1: 26. In *Contra Gentes* 3 God, who is beyond every substance (ὑπερέκεινα πάσης οὐσίας), is said to have created man after his own image. Unlike Origen, Athanasius distinguishes not between image and likeness but only between ἐικών and κατ᾽ εἰκόνα, man having been created in the image of the Image, who is the Logos. In his original state man possessed a contemplative understanding of intelligible reality (τῶν ὄντων), a conception and knowledge of God's eternity, a power to converse with God, and an idyllic and truly blessed immortal life. Adam's life in Paradise was characterized by *parrésia* and *theôria*, his soul being able to contemplate God through its purity. The Fall took place when the *nous* turned away from intelligible reality and began to cleave to the body and its desires, preferring its own apparent good to the contemplation of the divine. The result was the imprisoning of the soul in the pleasures of the body. The interior mirror, in which the soul was able to contemplate the image of the Father (i.e. the Logos), became obscured by the complexity of fleshly desires (cf. Louth 1981: 77–80). Hence the rise of idolatry.

The second account in *De Incarnatione* 3 has been described as historical and biblical in comparison with the timeless, Platonic account in the *Contra Gentes*, but in fact the perspective is very similar.[16] Perhaps in the description

---

[15] The opinion that Athanasius taught a one-sidedly 'physische Erlösungslehre' was first expressed by Harnack, although he did temper it somewhat: 'Yet the view of Athanasius was not simply naturalistic; incorruptibleness rather included the elements of goodness, love, and wisdom; a renewal affecting the inner nature of man was also involved. But it was not possible for Athanasius to expound this systematically' (1894–7: iii. 292 n. 3). Harnack's opinion, in spite of having been disputed by Bornhäuser, Roldanus, and others, remains the text-book judgement on Athanasius (cf. Tixeront 1910–16: ii. 150; Kelly 1977: 377–80).

[16] Louth 1975: 227–31. While endorsing his analysis, Louth no longer accepts his conclusion that Athanasius flirted with Neoplatonism in the *CG* only to reject it outright in the *De Inc.* (cf. Louth 1981: 77 n. 7).

of the effects of the Fall in the second account there is less emphasis on the loss of contemplation and more on the loss of immortality. In Paradise man had the promise of incorruption in heaven. He had been created from nothing and was therefore by nature mortal. But his natural corruption was offset by his contemplation of God, and had he not fallen he would have remained incorruptible and, as Psalm 82: 6–7 declares, would have lived as a god: 'I said you are gods and all of you sons of the Most High, but you die like men and fall as one of the princes.'

The recovery of the divine life lost by the Fall was made possible when the Logos became incarnate, ascribing to the flesh the properties of his own divine life. Through participation in this deified flesh men may once again be called gods. Unlike Clement and Origen, however, Athanasius calls men gods infrequently and always with reference to Psalm 82: 6 or John 10: 35.[17] In response to the Arian claim that the perfect become exactly like Christ he is careful to explain the biblical references to men as gods in a way which plays down any implication that men really are transformed into gods. Gods in the Christian sense are those who on the ontological level have been united to the Logos by the grace of adoption, while on the moral level they have become like God through imitation and progress in virtue.[18]

In the *Contra Arianos* Athanasius declares that only the Logos is θεὸς ἀληθινός, whereas those referred to as gods in Scripture are gods simply by grace, a grace which they receive from the Father by participation through the Spirit in the Logos (*CA* 1. 9, Bright 9). If there are sons and gods in Scripture it is because they were adopted and deified by the Logos (*CA* 1. 39, Bright 40–1). Such gods by deification are not to be identified with God himself, whether God be the Father or the Son. The Lord does tell us to be perfect as our heavenly Father is perfect (Matt. 5: 48), but this does not mean we become the same as the Father, for we are creatures who have been created out of nothing. There is one Son and God by nature; we become sons and gods by grace (*CA* 3. 19, Bright 173–4). The Logos is God, and eternal life and truth, 'but we become virtuous and sons by imitation' (cf. Eusebius, *De eccles. theol.* 3. 19, PG 24. 1044A). And so 'we are sons, but not as the Son; and gods but not as he is' (*CA* 3. 20, Bright 174–5). When the Lord prays to his Father that 'they may become one as we are one' (John 17: 21) it is therefore an analogous unity which he desires for men. The Father and the Son are united by essence and nature; the Son and believers are united by adoption and grace.

In Athanasius' other writings, too, when he refers to the scriptural designa-

---

[17] *De Inc.* 4. 32, Thomson 144; *CA* 1. 9, Bright 9; *CA* 1. 39, Bright 40; *CA* 3. 19–20, Bright 173–4; *Ep. Serap.* 1. 4, PG 26. 613C; *Ep. Afros* 7, PG 26. 1041C.
[18] The two levels are juxtaposed in *Ep. Afros* 7, PG 26. 1041BC.

tion of men as gods it is to stress the dissimilarity between men and God. To Serapion he writes: 'If some have been called gods, this is not by nature but by participation in the Son' (*Ep. Serap.* 2. 4, PG 26. 613C). And to the bishops of Egypt and Libya: 'calling gods those who, though creatures, have become partakers of the Word' . . . (*Ep. Afros* 7, PG 26. 1041C). The designation of men as gods was used by the Arians to minimize the difference between the perfect and the Son. Athanasius, unlike Origen, is therefore always cautious in ascribing divinity to men.

With this stress on the radical dissimilarity between God and men, how is it that we are deified? The answer, as already indicated in the last two quotations, is by participation.[19] In the *Letter to the bishops of Egypt and Libya* Athanasius states, like Justin and Origen, that the participant is by definition different from the participated, but in his anxiety to counter Arianism he goes on to deny that there is even any similarity between them (*Ep. Afros* 7, PG 26. 1041C; cf. *Ep. Serap.* 1. 23, PG 26. 584C). If this were strictly so, it is difficult to see how participation could take place at all. To Serapion, however, he declares that all things receive the characteristics of that in which they participate (*Ep. Serap.* 1. 23–4, PG 26. 584B–588B). By participating in the Spirit we become holy; by participating in the Logos we are able to contemplate the Father.

In his earliest work Athanasius refers to a participation which is purely ontological, all rational creatures participating in the Logos by virtue of their rationality (*De Inc.* 6. 13, Thomson 148). In his anti-Arian writings, however, he makes no further reference to this, preferring instead to appeal to the dynamic form of participation which had been developed by Origen, though rejecting the notion that the Son participates in the Father, because of its subordinationism. In the *De Decretis* Athanasius argues against the opinion he had heard Eusebius express that the Son alone participates in the Father while we participate in the Son (*De Decret.* 9–10, PG 25. 432CD). If that were so, we would then be the Son's sons. Rather, we are sons of the same Father as the Son is, our sonship being granted to us in accordance with our virtue, so that some sit on the twelve thrones, while others occupy lower places. Yet in a deeper sense the Son does participate in the Father. In the *Contra Arianos* Athanasius equates a complete participation in the Father (τὸ . . . ὅλως μετέχεσθαι τὸν θεόν) with the Father's begetting (*CA* 1. 16, Bright 17). Since the essence of God cannot be divided, his begetting the Son means that he communicates himself wholly to the Son. When men partake of God, they therefore partake of the Son, 'for that which is partaken of the Father is the Son' (*CA* 1. 16, Bright 17; cf. *De Syn.* 51, PG 26. 784AB; *De Decret.* 24, PG 25. 460AB). Thus when men are said to 'participate

---

[19] On participation in Athanasius the most extensive treatment is in Anatolios 1998 (see esp. 104–9). See also Bornhäuser 1903: 29–30; Bernard 1952: 32–9, 116–22; Balás 1966: 11–12; Norman 1980: 101–6, 113–15; Kolp 1982; Williams 1987: 215–29; and Pettersen 1995: 173–5.

in the divine nature' (2 Pet. 1: 4), it means that the Son communicates himself to them.[20]

This dynamic participation in the Logos is only possible because of the Incarnation. When the Logos assumed a human body, he became the subject (by the *communicatio idiomatum*) of what the body experienced. 'For what the human body of the Logos suffered, this the Logos, being united to the body, ascribed to himself in order that we might be enabled to participate in the deity of the Logos' (*Ep. Epict.* 6, PG 26. 1060c). By participating in the deified humanity of the Logos we participate in his impassible divinity, because the flesh has been endowed with divinity, just as the divinity has been endowed with humanity. This is the incorruption and immortality in which, according to Paul, we clothe ourselves (1 Cor. 15: 53) (cf. *CA* 3. 33, Bright 188).

The image of 'clothing' alludes to baptism. Athanasius refers directly to baptism infrequently.[21] But when the occasion demands the rite can provide him with an argument for the *homoousion* of the Son from ecclesiastical practice. In the first book of *Contra Arianos* he questions how the Arians can call God 'agenetic' (ἀγένητος) in preference to 'Father'. It is contrary to the way Christ taught us to baptize (cf. Matt. 28: 19). For it is only when God is called 'Father' that we, through his Logos, can become 'sons' (*CA* 1. 34). This idea is developed more fully in the second book. It is only because the Son co-operated with the Father in creating in the first place (as indicated by the first person plural in Gen. 1: 26) that he also has a role with him in the renewal of creation through 'the holy bath of baptism'. If God had made Christ a Son, asks Athanasius, why does he not make us sons too in the same way without need of the baptismal formula invoking the Son and the Spirit as well? It is a fact of the Church's life that naming the Father in the baptismal rite also entails naming the Son. If the purpose of baptism is to join us to the Godhead (ἵνα συναφθῶμεν τῇ θεότητι), what point is there in our being made one with the Son (ἵνα ἐνωθῶμεν τῷ υἱῷ) if he is a creature like ourselves? If God had made the Son a son, then he could have made us sons too in the same way. Our access to the Godhead through Christ in baptism depends on his being the Father's 'only own and true Son deriving from his essential being' (ὁ μόνος ἴδιος καὶ γνήσιος ἐκ τῆς οὐσίας αὐτοῦ ὢν

---

[20] 2 Peter 1: 4 had been cited previously by Origen, but in a different way to buttress the idea of becoming like God by the attainment of virtue. Athanasius cites the text six times: *CA* 1. 16, Bright 17; *CA* 3. 40, Bright 194; *Ep. Serap.* 1. 23, PG 26. 585B; *Ep. Serap.* 1. 24, 585C; *V. Ant.* 74, 945C; *Ep. Adelph.* 4, 1077A. The NPNF translation also detects an allusion in the Festal Letters (which are preserved only in a Syriac version) at *Ep.* 5. 5. On each occasion Athanasius uses the text to support the notion of the believer's dynamic participation in God. This participation was made possible by the Incarnation (*V. Ant.* 74), which transferred our nature to the Logos (*Ep. Adelph.* 4). It is appropriated by baptism (*Ep. Serap.* 1. 23 and 1. 24) and brings with it possession of the Son (*CA* 1. 16) and power over demons (*CA* 3. 40). Cf. Kolp 1982; Russell 1988.

[21] *De Decr.* 31; *CA* 1. 34; *CA* 2. 41; *Ep. Serap.* 4. 9, 12, 13. Allusions, however, to being born again and restored in the image (cf. *De Inc.* 14) are relatively common.

Υἱός), which is why he is named along with the Father in the baptismal formula (*CA* 2. 41, Bright 110–11).

Our union with the Son through baptism is made possible by the Spirit. The Spirit is the chrism and the seal with which the Logos anoints and seals us, making us thus through the holy oil the fragrance of Christ (*Ep. Serap.* 1. 23, PG 26. 585A). Another way of putting it is to say that the Son is life-in-itself (αὐτοζωή), the Spirit is life-giving (ζωοποιόν), and the faithful are made-alive (ζωοποιούμενοι) (*Ep. Serap.* 1. 23, 584B). Because the Spirit is himself fully divine he is able to make us 'partakers of the divine nature' (2 Pet. 1: 4), that is, of Christ. Through him we are called partakers of Christ and partakers of God (μέτοχοι Χριστοῦ καὶ μέτοχοι Θεοῦ) (*Ep. Serap.* 1. 24, 585C).

The Eucharist, like baptism, belongs to the Christian's ecclesial life. But Athanasius does not draw on it for anti-Arian arguments. We find it referred to, rather, in the Festal Letters which he sent each year to his suffragan bishops to be read to the faithful at the beginning of Lent. The divine Word is a heavenly food which nourishes our souls (*Ep.* 1. 7; 4. 4; 5. 5). The coming feast of Easter is the fulfilment of the types and shadows of the Jewish Passover (*Ep.* 4. 3). We no longer eat the flesh of a lamb but Christ's own flesh (*Ep.* 4. 4). Yet the Christian Eucharist is itself a symbol of 'the great and heavenly supper to which we are called if we are spotless within and without' (*Ep.* 40; trans. Payne Smith, NPNF). In the letter for the year 373, the last of his episcopate, Athanasius declares that 'as all the old things were a type of the new, so the festival that now is, is a type of the joy which is above' (*Ep.* 45; trans. Payne Smith, NPNF). It is with its eschatological fulfilment in mind that we are to approach the celebration of Easter.

The fruits of participation in Christ are the communication of divine life and the contemplation of the Father.[22] Exactly how the divine life is transmitted to us through the *communicatio idiomatum* of the incarnate Logos, we becoming the Son's 'own' as the Son is the Father's 'own', is explained in a passage of the *Contra Arianos*:

When the flesh was born from Mary the Theotokos, he [the Logos] is said to have been born, who furnishes to others an origin of being, in order that he may transfer our nature into himself (ἵνα τὴν ἡμῶν εἰς ἑαυτὸν μεταθῇ γένεσιν), and we may no longer, as mere earth, return to earth, but as being joined to the Logos from heaven, may be carried to heaven by him. In a similar manner he has therefore not unreasonably transferred to himself the other affections of the body also, that we, no longer as being men, but as proper to the Logos, may have a share in eternal life (ἵνα μηκέτι

---

[22] Cf. Anatolios: 'With reference to the humanity of Christ, Athanasius's point is that we are able to be saved and deified because Christ has securely received grace in a human way on our behalf, and has thus rendered us receptive of the Spirit by his own human reception of it ... Our deifying reception of the Spirit is thus derived from Christ's human receptivity' (1998: 159).

ὡς ἄνθρωποι, ἀλλ᾿ ὡς ἴδιοι τοῦ Λόγου, τῆς αἰωνίου ζωῆς μετασχῶμεν). (*CA* 3. 33, Bright 187–8; trans. Newman/Robertson, modified)

This transcendence of human nature is not, as in Origen, because we have become pure *noes*, but because we come to be wholly directed by the Logos and therefore receive his characteristics, characteristics which may be summed up in the expression, 'life-in-itself'. The enjoyment of this life is presented in eschatological terms, when we shall have ascended into heaven. There we shall sit on thrones. There too we shall contemplate the Father, for that which participates in the Logos joins the angels in the everlasting contemplation of God (*CA* 3. 51).

The eschatological nature of deification does not mean that its beginnings are not discernible in this life. We are fortunate in having from Athanasius a portrait of a man whom he considers a model of ascetic discipline and evangelical perfection.[23] Antony is a man in whom we might expect to observe the experiential effects of deification. Yet Athanasius never calls him θεοποιούμενος. In his disputation with the Greeks Antony says that the Logos assumed a human body and participated in human nature 'that he might make men participate in the divine and spiritual nature' (cf. 2 Pet. 1: 4) (*V. Ant.* 74, PG 26. 945C). But in Antony's case this participation in the divine nature is described in purely ethical terms, in his moral perfection, his humility, his graciousness, and the unperturbedness of his soul reflected in the joyful expression of his countenance (*V. Ant.* 67, 940A). Also important is his asceticism, which was manifested in his self-control and immunity to demonic attack through the subjugation of the body (*V. Ant.* 7, 852AD). After twenty years of solitude, he emerged from his hermitage 'initiated into the mysteries and inspired by God' (μεμυσταγωγημένος καὶ θεοφορούμενος) (*V. Ant.* 14, 864C). This state did not manifest itself in any extremes but in his conformity to a rational mean, his body being between corpulence and emaciation, and his unblemished soul between laughter and dejection, 'neither contracted by grief, nor relaxed by pleasure' but 'as if guided by reason' (ὡς ὑπὸ τοῦ λόγου κυβερνώμενος) (*V. Ant.* 14, 865A).

There are in Athanasius two parallel lines along which the concept of deification is developed, the ontological and the ethical. Ontologically deification is a participation in the personal life of God made possible by the Incarnation and brought into effect by baptism. Ethically the man of his own time whom Athanasius thought had come closest to perfection had

---

[23] The Athanasian authorship of *V. Ant.* has been challenged by Barnes (1986) largely on linguistic grounds. Barnes argues for a Coptic original to the Greek text. Louth (1988) and Brakke (1994), however, have shown convincingly that there are insufficient grounds for rejecting the traditional authorship. It may be added that from the point of view of deification there is nothing in the *V. Ant.* that contradicts the relevant material in Athanasius' unchallenged writings, as the ethical approach to deification is found there too, while the ontological approach is strictly eschatological. Roldanus (1968: 347–8) is right to agree with Dörries (1949: 389) that Antony represents the perfect model Christian, but to disagree with him that humanity's true destination has already been achieved in Antony's case.

become *theophoroumenos* through the purity attained by the subjugation of the body and the practice of the virtues. Such a man ascends after death to heaven where he enjoys the uninterrupted contemplation of God.

These two lines of thought represent the two traditions which Athanasius inherited. If he is not entirely consistent in the way in which he relates them to each other, that is hardly surprising, for his writings are not systematic expositions but treatises designed to counter specific threats to orthodox doctrine. When he is opposing the Arian denial of the full divinity of the Son, he stresses the ability of the Logos to transform not only the flesh which he assumed, but also, because of our kinship with that flesh, the whole of humanity as well. When he is looking at the same question from the human side and is opposing the Arian willingness to place the perfect alongside Christ as equal to him, he tends to deny that men have any likeness to the Logos and plays down the designation of men as gods. It is only when arguing on the former tack that he employs the technical terminology of deification.

The fact that all the passages in which he uses such terminology refer to the communication of divine life by the Logos, first to the flesh which he assumed and then to all believers who unite themselves to him, points to an essential feature of the deification of the believer in Athanasius, namely, its sacramental character. What is often described as 'physical redemption' is actually transmitted sacramentally. The synonyms for deification which Athanasius uses—adoption, renewal, salvation, sanctification, grace, illumination, and vivification—all refer to the effects of baptism. But it was not until the following century, with the work of St Cyril, that the sacramental aspect of deification was worked out fully and integrated in a satisfactory way with the ethical aspect. Hence the impression that some have gained that Athanasius teaches that the gifts of immortality and incorruption are conveyed to the believer in a crudely mechanical manner.

Underlying Athanasius' conception of deification, and indeed absolutely crucial to it, is his characteristically Alexandrian christology.[24] Humanity was created originally to live 'as a god', which means not subject to corruptibility, as is proved by Psalm 82: 6 (*De Inc.* 4. 30–3, Thomson 144). But this attribute, together with the divine image entailed by it, was lost through disobedience (*De Inc.* 6. 1–4, Thomson 146). Only God himself could remedy the situation, which he did through his divine Word, the sole source of salvation. By fashioning for himself a 'temple' (*naos*) from the body of the Virgin and appropriating it for his own as an 'instrument' (*organon*), the Word was able to recreate human nature in the divine image and then offer this restored humanity to the Father through his sacrifice on the cross, with benefits that accrued to the entire human race, for 'we all die in him' (*De Inc.* 8. 23–35,

[24] The argument of this paragraph is indebted to the seminal article of Frances Young (1971).

Thomson 152; cf. Rom. 6: 8). 'The organon-concept,' as Grillmeier says, 'allows [Athanasius] to stress the living power of the Logos in redemption and at the same time to emphasize his transcendence, without relinquishing any of the closeness of the community of Logos and sarx' (1975: 318). The 'agenetic' Word makes 'genetic' humanity the instrument of salvation by making it his own. But Grillmeier does not allow 'sarx' its full force.[25] 'Sarx' in Athanasius stands for the totality of human nature, soul as well as body. If the role of Christ's soul is not emphasized, it is because the human characteristic central to Athanasius' viewpoint is its receptivity (Young 1971: 113–14). The humanity of Christ could only have a passive role. Passivity, however, implies not incompleteness but perfection. The sin of ordinary human beings lies precisely in their failure to be receptive. Christ, by contrast, was *totally* receptive to the Word, so that we can say that the Word was the single subject of all Christ's saving acts.

The organon-concept enables Athanasius to think of the whole of humanity as deified in principle through the Incarnation. Beyond their natural ontological participation in Christ, however, men also have access to a participation which is supernatural and dynamic. As a result of the *communicatio idiomatum*, human beings linked by nature to the flesh of Christ are able to participate by grace in the divinity of Christ. The latter participation takes place through the union with Christ accomplished by baptism, in which men are promoted and exalted. Having received in baptism the attributes of the Logos, they transcend their human nature; they are no longer under the power of sin, death, and corruption but share in the divine nature. There is no question, however, of their ceasing to be human beings and becoming the same as God. Indeed, Athanasius holds a radically apophatic view of God. The participation in God which human beings enjoy is the divine life and light which the Father deigns to communicate to them by adoption and grace. They are sons and gods only in name (Demetropoulos 1954: 121; Roldanus 1968: 165).

The ethical aspect of deification supports the ontological, or sacramental. The main emphasis in Athanasius, however, no doubt because of his struggle with Arianism, is on the transformation of human life affected by the Incarnation. K. E. Norman has rightly said that 'his focus on the connection between the Incarnation and our participation in the divine nature tends to obscure the relationship of virtue to divine participation' (1980: 157). But the element of moral striving is not absent. Indeed, it is given a soteriological context by the deification of the flesh by the Logos. We are deified in principle by baptism, but we have to make this efficacious in

---

[25] Grillmeier's Logos–sarx model has been widely criticized, e.g. by Torrance 1995: 189–90; Anatolios 1998: 70–2. Note also Anatolios's warning against simply relating Christ's divinity to subjectivity and his humanity to instrumentality (1998: 140).

our own lives by moral effort. 'To actualize participation in the divine nature, the believer must imitate him who was divine by nature: the Logos of God' (Norman 1980: 110). The realistic and ethical aspects of deification must be kept in balance.

Finally, although deification begins in principle in this life, its fulfilment is eschatological. In spite of Adam's beatitude in Paradise, this fulfilment is more than simply a return to origins. He who was the Image itself came to renew him who was merely 'in the image', thereby endowing him with a still 'greater grace' (*CA* 2. 67, Bright 137). The immortality and contemplation of God which Adam enjoyed in Paradise are transferred to heaven and augmented, for the incarnation of the Logos has made the freedom from corruption which Adam enjoyed in Paradise more secure and his intimacy with God even closer. In imagery drawn largely from the biblical tradition, those who have at last been deified are described as seated on thrones contemplating the Father through the Son in the bond of love, having transcended their mortality through participation in the light and life of God.

(e) Conclusion

The struggle with Arianism provides the context for the development of Athanasius' doctrine of deification. Throughout his writings his use of θεοποιέω is bound up not with the attainment of moral excellence but with salvation. The 'agenetic' status of the Son is proved by his ability to deify; the Son can only make men gods if he himself is of the same essence as the Father. At times Athanasius makes use of the titular and ethical approaches to deification (he is unwilling to call men 'gods' except in name) but it is the realistic approach which serves his purposes best.

His development of the realistic approach to deification represents a modification of Origenism. The deification of the eternal Logos is rejected; it is only the flesh of the Logos that is deified. Origen's speculative anthropology is likewise rejected. Men are not fallen *noes*, who can rise up the scale of *logika*. Moreover, they are separated from God by a deep ontological divide. If men cannot participate in the eternal Logos, emphasis will naturally fall on the deified flesh of the incarnate Logos.

Two aspects of Origen's doctrine are of fundamental importance to Athanasius: his belief that the Logos deified the human nature which he assumed, and his understanding of man's dynamic participation in God. The solidarity of the human race is such that when the Logos deified the human nature which he assumed, 'we' too were deified, at least in principle. Origen's dynamic understanding of participation is taken up and focused on the incarnate Logos. It is through participation in the flesh of the Logos that we are raised to participate in the immortal and incorrupt divine life. Athanasius uses the concept of participation but is unwilling to admit a likeness or kinship between human beings and God. Moreover, participation in the deified flesh demands the development of the sacramental side of deification, which will only be accomplished by Cyril.

The unsatisfactory aspects of Athanasius' doctrine of deification reflect the undeveloped aspects of his christology. The silence of Athanasius with regard to the soul makes it difficult for him to relate the attainment of virtue to deification. The flesh of Christ is the *organon* with which the Logos brings about salvation: salvation comes through the embodied life. This physical emphasis was perhaps required as an antidote to the intellectualism of Origen, but it needed the refinement and completion which Cyril of Alexandria was to bring to it.

3. Apollinarius of Laodicea

When Athansasius returned to the East from his second exile in 346, he was received at the Syrian port of Laodicea (modern Latakia) by the presbyter Apollinarius and his son, also called Apollinarius. The two Apollinarii were excommunicated by their bishop, George, for the hospitality they had shown to the arch-enemy of the Arians. Undeterred, they persevered in their friendship with Athanasius, the younger Apollinarius becoming one of his strongest allies in the fight against Arianism.

Although the younger Apollinarius (*c.*310–*c.*390) was born in Berytus (modern Beirut), his father was of Alexandrian origin, which in itself probably accounts for the son's life-long commitment to the Alexandrian rather than the Antiochene christological tradition. In about 360 he became bishop of Laodicea, and for the next twenty years enjoyed a considerable reputation as an exponent of a rigorous christology 'from above'. In 371, as Apollinarius reveals in a letter to Serapion of Thmuis (Lietzmann, frags. 159–61), Athanasius sent him his *Letter to Epictetus* 'for his approval and comment' (Raven 1923: 105). At this stage there is no suggestion that Apollinarius' christology was suspected of unorthodoxy. Athanasius clearly regarded him as an expert he could consult with confidence.

Apollinarius' christology rests on two principles: first that Christ is fully divine: he is not a god by adoption (frag. 81, Lietzmann 224. 15), or by participation (*Kata meros pistis* 25, Lietzmann 176. 9); secondly that Christ is a single subject: he is one nature because he is one person (*Ep. ad Dion.* 1, Lietzmann 257. 15–16). By these principles Apollinarius sought to exclude both the subordinationism of the Arians and what he considered to be the adoptionism of the school of Diodore of Tarsus. Against the former he taught that there is no middle term between God and man (*Anacephalaeosis* 18, Lietzmann 244. 9), against the latter, the chief target of his polemical writings, that there is no mere indwelling of the divine in Christ (ibid. 28, Lietzmann 245. 20). '*Sarkôsis kenôsis*' (frag. 124, Lietzmann 237. 30): the

Incarnation is a self-emptying by which the divine Logos accommodates himself to human life, becoming in this way capable of suffering and of effecting our salvation.

Thus far Apollinarius and Athanasius were in perfect agreement. Where they parted company was on the nature of Christ's human soul. By remaining silent on the matter, Athanasius left the way open for what was to become the christology of Chalcedon. Apollinarius, however, took the step of denying that Christ had a human *nous* at all, the highest part of the soul being replaced by the Logos.[26] Salvation was effected by a Logos who remained transcendent, clothing himself in human flesh in an essential manner (i.e. forming a real unity, with the Logos as the soul's directing principle) so that the rest of humanity might have the opportunity to unite itself to the Godhead by participation or grace. The deification of the flesh of Christ and through that flesh the deification of the believer was the corollary to the condescension of the Logos at the Incarnation.

(a) Vocabulary

Apollinarius' vocabulary is wider than that of Athanasius. Besides θεοποιέω (*Kata meros pistis* 1, 31, Lietzmann 167. 4; 179. 8) and θεοποιός (*Kata meros pistis* 27, Lietzmann 177. 1), he also uses θεόω (frag. 147, Lietzmann 246. 26, 28) and ἀποθεόω (frag. 98, Lietzmann 230. 6) for the deification of the flesh by the Logos, though for the deification of the Christian he confines himself to θεοποιέω.

(b) The Deification of Christ

Most of Apollinarius' instances of the use of deification terms occur in his christological discussions. He insists that the Son is not deified by grace. Those who say that he is (οἱ δόσει καὶ χάριτι θεοποιεῖσθαι λέγοντες τὸν υἱόν) are outside the apostolic faith (*Kata meros pistis* 1, Lietzmann 167. 4). Nor is the Son a mere man who is deified at some stage in his life. For 'how could he say "I and the Father are one" (John 10: 30) before having been united and deified' (πῶς δὲ καὶ πρὶν ἑνωθῆναι καὶ ἀποθεωθῆναι λέγει 'ἐγὼ καὶ ὁ πατὴρ ἕν ἐσμεν')? (frag. 98, Lietzmann 230. 5–6). In order to exclude the idea that the baptism of Christ promoted him to divine sonship, one of Apollinarius' disciples adds that Christ was the same from the first appearance of his body, not deified later in the course of his career (οὐχ ὕστερον ἀποθεωθείς) (*De inc. Dei Verbi* 4, Lietzmann 307. 11–12). As a result of his incarnation he is said to be embodied God and deified body (λέγεται θεὸς σεσωματωμένος καὶ σῶμα τεθεωμένον) (frag. 147, Lietzmann 246. 26). In so far as he is embodied God, he is man; in so far as he is deified body, he is God. Apollinarius is fond of such symmetrical statements. The Logos becomes embodied without

---

[26] Cf. Raven 1923: 174. Only the innermost faculty in Christ was not human.

undergoing any change (for that would compromise his divinity) and the body becomes deified with the Logos taking the place of the *nous* as its unifying and directing principle. The Spirit is described as sanctifying and deifying (ἁγιαστικὸν καὶ θεοποιόν) because, like the Son, it is of the substance of God (*Kata meros pistis* 27, Lietzmann 176. 22–177. 1).

(c) *The Deification of the Believer*

The deification of human beings through Christ is the doctrine which this christology is designed to support. Apollinarius maintains that if the arguments of his adoptionist adversaries are accepted, the saints could not be called 'gods and sons and spirits' as they are in the Scriptures (*Kata meros pistis* 5, Lietzmann 169. 14–15). They cannot become like the Son. 'But we say that the Word of God became man for our salvation, that we may receive the likeness of the heavenly man and be deified in conformity with the likeness of him who is by nature the true Son of God' (καὶ θεοποιηθῶμεν πρὸς ὁμοιότητα τοῦ κατὰ φύσιν ἀληθινοῦ υἱοῦ τοῦ θεοῦ) (*Kata meros pistis* 31, Lietzmann 179. 8). Recovery of the divine likeness is only possible because he became man without undergoing any change himself. Indeed, in Apollinarius' view the Logos could not have become man without losing his divine immutability unless he had taken the place of the *nous* (frag. 97, Lietzmann 229). Recovery of the likeness, however, does not make human beings the same as Christ: the Logos 'became man, while remaining God, that he might show men to be gods while remaining men', as the author of the *De incarnatione Dei Verbi* put it (*De inc. Dei Verbi* 4, Lietzmann 307. 2–3). Receiving God does not make men true gods, 'for then there would be many gods, since many receive God' (frag. 83, Lietzmann 224. 32–3). This is where those who say that the Logos assumed a human being go wrong: they do not differentiate sufficiently between Christ and the faithful who receive him. Such a reception is not simply by faith. It includes the sacramental life of the Church, for the flesh of Christ saves us when we receive it as our food specifically because it is united to the Godhead (frag. 116, Lietzmann 235; cf. frag. 155, Lietzmann 249).

The concept of deification which Apollinarius employs is titular and analogous. Men do not become gods in any real sense. The gulf between the Logos and a normal human being is still immense after the Incarnation because the Logos remains transcendent in spite of his kenotic self-emptying. The deification of Christ's flesh, however, enables Apollinarius to make for the first time an explicit link between the believer's deification and the Eucharist. This corporeal aspect of participation in Christ was to receive a much fuller treatment from Cyril of Alexandria.

4. Cyril of Alexandria

The four occupants of the episcopal throne of Alexandria after Athanasius all had close personal connections with him. A few days before his death on 2 May 373, Athanasius appointed Peter, one of his senior presbyters and a companion in his vicissitudes, to succeed him. Peter (373–80) was succeeded by his brother Timothy, Timothy (380–4) by Theophilus, who had been Athanasius' secretary, and Theophilus (384–412) by his nephew Cyril. Cyril (412–44) was the first not to have known Athanasius personally, but the great man had been a benefactor of his family. He had taken Theophilus and his young sister, Cyril's mother, under his wing when they arrived in Alexandria from Memphis in about 362, seeking baptism in the Christian metropolis. Athanasius had placed the little girl with a community of virgins to be brought up by them until the time came for her to marry, and had groomed the boy for high office in the Church. In view of this, and the enormous prestige of Athanasius in the last years of his life, it is not surprising that Cyril should have held him in the deepest veneration, regarding him as the greatest of the Fathers of the Church.

Cyril took over Athanasius' scheme of salvation, the descending and ascending movement between the poles of human createdness and divine uncreatedness that Athanasius had derived from Irenaeus. The Word became human that humanity might become divine. The eternal Son condescended to adapt himself to the conditions of human life that by transforming the flesh through the Incarnation and promoting it to union with God he might bring it from corruption to incorruption, from human imperfection 'to a dignity that transcends our nature' (*In Jo.* 1. 9. 91c). We can benefit from this exaltation of the flesh, not by following Christ as an example in an external manner, but by participating personally in the new life which he inaugurated.

Our participation in God has a twofold aspect, an ontological one in which we are raised from non-existence to createdness, and a dynamic one in which we advance from createdness to transcendence. Our dynamic participation begins when we receive the Spirit in baptism. By receiving the Spirit to dwell within us, we become adopted sons of God and gods through grace. The Spirit and the Son together bring about our sanctification and filiation, which enable us to mount up to incorruptibility. With the Son and the Spirit we also have the Father. Cyril thus distinguishes between a corporeal and a spiritual aspect to our dynamic participation in God. Through the Eucharist the Son dwells within us in a corporeal sense, while the Spirit renews us and transforms us spiritually. The role of the moral life is not neglected in this inward transformation. This is because the divine image lies primarily in the human will. Human beings can choose the good, and when they do so they participate in the divine, for 'the divine (τὸ θεῖον) is in everything that is beautiful, and is the very source, root and origin of all virtue' (*Resp. Tib.* 14,

Wickham, 174. 15–16). Participation in the divine nature therefore also implies the acquisition of virtue, which is indispensable in the task of recovering our lost likeness to God.

Cyril's work thus represents a considerable advance on Athanasius. First, the deified Christian has a closer relationship with the whole Trinity. Cyril's stress on the one divine nature leads him to associate the Spirit with the Son and the Father so closely that he can say that when we have the Spirit and the Son, we have the Father. We do not merely become images of the Image. Nor do we simply participate in the divinity possessed by the Son. Secondly, the relationship of virtue to divine participation is brought out more strongly by Cyril. The due weight which he is able to give to the human soul in Christ has its effect on his anthropology in general. The recipient of salvation is not simply the 'flesh' but a unity of body and soul that images God in his or her will. Athanasius' insights into the transformation of human nature as a result of the Incarnation are thus combined with a conviction that moral progress plays a vital role in restoring our likeness to God. Thirdly, the role of the Eucharist is given more emphasis, with its power to assimilate to Christ spelled out fully for the first time. With his understanding of the trinitarian dimension and his integration of the Eucharist and the moral life into how human beings participate in the divine nature, Cyril brings the doctrine of deification, as Dalmais has said, to full maturity (1954–7: 1385).[27]

(a) Vocabulary

Cyril's new emphases are reflected in his vocabulary. In his earliest works he uses θεοποιέω/θεοποίησις in both a christological and an anthropological sense, much like Athanasius, to express on the one hand the deification of the temple which the Word assumed (*Thes.* 28, PG 75. 428C; *Dial. Trin.* v. 567e), and on the other the transforming effect on the believer of the incarnate Word (*Thes.* 15, PG 75. 284B) and the Holy Spirit (*Thes.* 4, 45A; 33, 569C; *Dial. Trin.* VII. 640a, 644c). Such usage is sparse, however, occurring chiefly in the works most clearly dependent on Athanasius.[28] In his biblical commentaries Cyril prefers to use the language of participation, supported by frequent reference to 2 Peter 1: 4, 'partakers of the divine nature', a text which Cyril cites on more occasions than any other ecclesiastical writer. Indeed in Cyril the language of participation replaces that of deification as a means of expressing the goal of human life.

The reason for this is not easy to determine. In 429 Cyril responded angrily to Nestorius' caricature of the deification of the flesh assumed by the Word at the Incarnation as an apotheosis:

---

[27] For a sensitive study of Cyril's doctrine of deification see Keating 2004.

[28] Keating (2004: 10–11) locates only about twenty texts that use the technical vocabulary of deification.

For we deny that the flesh of the Word became the Godhead, but we do say that it became divine in virtue of its being his own. For if the flesh of a man is called human, what is wrong with saying that that of the Word of God is divine? Why do you mock the beauty of the truth and call the deification (θεοποίησιν) of the sacred flesh an apotheosis (ἀποθέωσιν) all but scolding those who have chosen to hold an orthodox view for professing this? (*C. Nest.* 2. 8, Schwartz 46. 34–7)

But it was not the controversy with Nestorius that caused Cyril to change his approach. Five years previously, in his thirteenth Festal Letter (written towards the end of 424 to announce the Easter of 425), he had already denied in similar language that Christians believed in a deified man: 'Therefore he was God who became man; in no way was he a man who was deified' (θεὸς οὖν ἄρα ὑπάρχων γέγονεν ἄνθρωπος, τεθεοποίηται γὰρ οὐδαμῶς ἄνθρωπος ὤν) (*FL* 13. 4. 89–91, SC 434. 114). Here the assertion is made in the context of anti-Jewish polemic. But there are other overtones too. Marie-Odile Boulnois, in her commentary on the text, detects a possible allusion to Apollinarianism earlier in the same section ('he became a perfect man like us' (4. 65)) and it may be that Cyril already has Antiochene christological teaching in mind when shortly after his reference to deification he says: 'Of course, the divine is impalpable and invisible, but the Logos came to dwell with us openly, without being someone other than his flesh and the temple taken from the Virgin' (4. 96–9). It was perhaps the Jewish claim that Christians worshipped a deified man, reinforced on the one hand by hostility to Apollinarianism, and on the other by a sensitivity to possible objections from orthodox Christians not of his own tradition, that led Cyril to be wary of the θεοποιέω/θεοποίησις terminology he had inherited from Athanasius. The controversy with Nestorius simply confirmed this tendency.

Certainly, in his later works Cyril uses the technical language of deification only to deny that Christians believe in a deified man (e.g. *C. Nest.* 1. 10 and 2. 11, Schwartz 32. 1 and 49. 8; *Resp. Tib.* 7 and 9, Wickham 158. 23 and 162. 9; *Chr. un.* 742d, de Durand 396). Throughout his writings he much prefers to use biblical language, in particular the Psalmist's 'gods and son of the Most High' (Ps. 82: 6), which he refers to the adopted sonship of the baptized, a number of Pauline phrases drawn from passages expressing the mutual coinherence of Christ and the believer (esp. Rom. 8: 15; Gal. 4: 6 and 19) or the progress of the believer from glory to glory (2 Cor. 3: 18), and, above all, the phrase from 2 Peter 1: 4: 'partakers of the divine nature', which he takes to be correlative to Christ's partaking of our human nature (cf. Heb. 2: 14).

(b) The Key Texts

Cyril does not lend himself to easy excerption. His remarks on deification, at least in his later more discursive works, are always embedded within broader theological structures. The earliest significant passages are from the *Thesaurus* and the *Dialogues on the Trinity*, which belong to the first years of Cyril's episcopate (412–20), long before he became embroiled with Nestorius in 429.[29] His opponents in both these works are Arians, who continued to be influential in the Roman empire even if there is little evidence of their presence in Egypt.[30] In the fourth tractate of the *Thesaurus* Cyril offers an argument, closely modelled on that of Athanasius (cf. *CA* 1. 39), for the true divinity of the Son 'by nature' on the basis of biblical evidence for the deification of believers 'by participation'. If the Word had been begotten in time, and was therefore God and Son and Wisdom 'by participation', he would not have differed from ordinary rational beings, whom Scripture addresses as 'gods and sons of the Most High' (Ps. 82: 6):

For we have been adopted through entering into a relationship with God and have been deified by him (σχέσει γὰρ τῇ πρὸς θεὸν υἱοποιηθέντες παρ' αὐτοῦ θεοποιούμεθα). For if we are called sons of God through having participated in God by grace, what kind of participation do we attribute to the Word, that he should become Son and God? We are [sons and gods] by participation in the Holy Spirit; to think this of the Son would be absurd.   (*Thes.* 4, PG 75. 45A; cf. 15, 284B; 33, 569C)

Even in this early work, 'participation' is the key to the understanding of our relationship with God. It expresses a derivative mode of being, analogous to the relationship between heat and a fire or between fragrance and a flower. The latter image becomes a favourite one with Cyril (cf. Boulnois 1994: 159–70), aptly conveying the sense of a dependent reality which is distinct from its source and yet has no meaning apart from it. The Son does not depend on the Father by participation, because he is from his substance. But we do. We become partakers of the divinity of the Son through the indwelling of the Holy Spirit (*Thes.* 13, PG, 75. 225C).

Cyril returns to the role of the Spirit a number of times in the *Thesaurus* and the *Dialogues on the Trinity*. In the seventh book of the *Dialogues*, for example, among the arguments he puts forward for the divinity of the Holy Spirit, the chief one is the Spirit's power to raise the believer to participation in the divine life:

We are called 'temples of God' and indeed 'gods', and so we are.[31] Why is that? Enquire of our opponents whether we are really sharers in a bare grace without subsistence. But that is not the case. For we are temples of the real and subsisting Spirit. And it is through him that we are called 'gods', since by union with him (τῇ πρὸς αὐτὸ συναφείᾳ) we have become partakers of the divine and ineffable nature (cf. 2 Pet. 1: 4). But if the Spirit who deifies us by his own agency (τὸ θεοποιοῦν ἡμᾶς Πνεῦμα δι' ἑαυτοῦ) is different in kind from the divine nature and distinct from it in

---

[29] For the dating see de Durand, SC 231. 40–1.

[30] Socrates *HE* 1. 9 records the presence of two Arian bishops from Cyrenaica at the Council of Nicaea.

[31] Cf. Ps. 82: 6; John 10: 34; 1 Cor. 3: 16; 6: 19; 2 Cor. 6: 16.

terms of substance, we have failed to attain our hope, having been adorned with splendours which somehow lead to nothing. For how are we gods and temples, as the Scriptures say, through the Spirit that is within us? For if he lacks being God, how can he endow others with that name? No, we are indeed temples and gods. We should not pay the slightest attention to those in error. The Spirit of God is therefore not different in substance from him.   (*Dial. Trin.* VII. 639e–640b, de Durand iii. 166).

A little further on Cyril returns to the same argument. The divinity of the Spirit is proved by his ability to endow the believer with the characteristic attributes (τῆς ἰδίας ἰδιότητος) of God. It might be argued that it is possible to participate in a creature:

But it is inconceivable that created being should have the power to deify (θεοποιός). This is something that can be attributed only to God, who through the Spirit infuses into the souls of the saints a participation in his own property. When we have been conformed by the Spirit to him who is Son by nature, we are called gods and sons on account of him. And because we are sons, as Scripture says, 'God has sent the Spirit of his Son into our hearts, crying "Abba! Father" ' (Gal. 4: 6). If the power to deify by one's own agency (τὸ θεοποιεῖν δύνασθαι δι' ἑαυτοῦ) greatly exceeds that which belongs to the nature of a creature, how will anyone assign the Holy Spirit to the class of contingent existences, unless he has completely gone out of his mind? Or how will he who produces gods be declared a created being (πῶς ἂν λέγοιτο γενητὸν τὸ θεοὺς ἀποτελοῦν)?   (*Dial. Trin.* VII. 644de, de Durand iii, 180; cf. *In Jo.* 9. 1. 810e)

Cyril does not specify at this point what the special attribute of God is in which the deified participate. It is only in his exegetical works, and especially his *Commentary on John* (written in 425–8), that he develops his teaching on the progressive nature of Christian sanctification, which culminates in the recovery of the divine image, the acquisition of incorruption, and the attaining of transcendence. The first of the following passages shows how Christ reverses the effects of the Fall, not only as the agent of redemption, but also as the pattern imprinted upon us by baptism for our progress towards the recovery of the divine image:[32]

Since they received the Son through faith, they receive the privilege of being counted among the children of God. For the Son gives what belongs properly to him alone and exists by nature within him as a right, setting it out in common, as if making the matter an image of the loving kindness inherent within and of his love for the world. There was no other way for us who have borne the image of the man of dust to escape corruption, unless the beauty of the image of the man of heaven is imprinted upon us through our having been called to sonship (cf. 1 Cor. 15: 49). For having become partakers of him through the Spirit (cf. Heb. 3: 14; 6: 4), we were sealed into likeness to him and mount up to the archetypal form of the image, in accordance with which divine Scripture says we were also made (cf. Gen. 1: 27). For

---

[32] The dual aspect is well brought out by Keating 2004: 119–43. See also Keating 2003.

scarcely do we thus recover the ancient beauty of our nature, and are conformed to that divine nature, than we become superior to the evils that arose from the Fall.

We therefore ascend to a dignity that transcends our nature on account of Christ, but we shall not also be sons of God ourselves in exactly the same way as he is, only in relation to him through grace by imitation. For he is a true Son who has his existence from the Father, while we are sons who have been adopted out of his love for us, and are recipients by grace of the text, 'I have said, you are gods and all of you sons of the Most High' (Ps. 82: 6). Beings of a created and dependent nature are called to a transcendent status by the mere nod and will of the Father. But he who is Son and God and Lord does not acquire his being God the Son because God the Father has decreed it, or in virtue of the divine will alone, but because he has shone forth from the very essence of the Father and thus procures for himself by nature the distinctive good of that essence. Once again the Son is seen to be a true son when contrasted with ourselves. Since the status of 'by nature' is different from that of 'by adoption', and the status of 'in reality' different from that of 'by imitation', and since we are called sons by adoption and imitation, it follows that what he is by nature and in reality we who have attained these things become in a relative sense, for we have acquired this blessing by grace rather than by natural status. (*In Jo.* 1. 9. 91a–e)

Those who are called to sonship by adoption and grace have transcended the limitations of their human nature and, while still remaining creatures, have come to participate in the life of the Trinity itself:

For the descendants of Israel had 'a spirit of slavery inducing fear', while Christians have 'a spirit of sonship' eliciting freedom, 'which enables us to cry "Abba! Father!"' (Rom. 8: 15). Therefore the people who were destined to attain adoption as sons through faith in Christ were depicted beforehand in Israel in symbolic form, so that, for example, we understand our spiritual circumcision to have been prefigured originally in their physical version. To put it briefly, everything concerning us was already present in them typologically. Moreover, we can also say that Israel was called to attain sonship typologically through the mediation of Moses, with the result that they were baptized into him, as Paul says, 'in the cloud and in the sea' (1 Cor. 10: 2) and were restored from idolatry to the law of slavery, the written commandment being supplied by angels (cf. Gal. 3: 19). But those who have attained adoption as sons of God through faith in Christ are baptized not into anything belonging to the created order but into the Holy Trinity itself, through the mediation of the Word, who on the one hand joined what is human to himself by means of the flesh that was united to him, and on the other was joined by nature to him who had begotten him, since he was by nature God. Thus what is servile rises up to the level of sonship through participation in him who is Son in reality, called and, as it were, promoted to the rank which the Son possesses by nature. That is why we are called offspring of God and are such, for we have experienced a rebirth by faith through the Spirit. (*In Jo.* 1. 9. 92e–93b)

Our adoptive sonship is brought about by the Holy Spirit, who must himself be fully divine in order to effect it:

We must admit that either the Evangelist is totally mistaken, or if he is right and the matter is precisely as he says, that the Spirit is God and from God by nature, and indeed that we who are deemed worthy to participate in Christ through faith are made 'partakers of the divine nature' (2 Pet. 1: 4) and are said to be born of God. We are therefore called gods, not simply by grace because we are winging our way towards the glory that transcends us, but because we already have God dwelling and abiding within us, in accordance with the prophetic text, 'I will live in them and move among them' (2 Cor. 6: 16). (*In Jo.* 1. 9. 93d)

Cyril's perspective is profoundly Pauline as well as Johannine. We share in the life of Christ because Christ is 'in us' and we are 'in Christ'. Christ emptied himself to accommodate our human nature and by his subsequent exaltation we are exalted too:

You should not think that the Word was transformed into flesh, but rather that he dwelt in flesh, using as his own particular body the temple that is from the holy Virgin. 'For in him the whole fullness of deity dwells bodily', as Paul says (Col. 2: 9). Nevertheless, the assertion that the Word dwelt in us is a useful one because it also reveals to us a very deep mystery. For we were all in Christ. The common element of humanity is summed up in his person, which is also why he was called the last Adam: he enriched our common nature with everything conducive to joy and glory, just as the first Adam impoverished it with everything bringing corruption and gloom. This is precisely why the Word dwelt in all of us by dwelling in a single human being, so that through that one being who was 'designated Son of God in power according to the Spirit of holiness' (Rom. 1: 4), the whole of humanity might be raised up to his status so that the verse, 'I said, you are gods and all of you sons of the Most High' (Ps. 82: 6) might through applying to one of us come to apply to us all. Therefore 'in Christ' that which is enslaved is liberated in a real sense and ascends to a mystical union (εἰς ἑνότητα τὴν μυστικήν) with him who put on the form of a servant, while 'in us' it is liberated by an imitation of the human union with the One through our kinship according to the flesh. (*In Jo.* 1. 9. 96c–e)

Cyril's approach to deification is not mystical in a speculative sense but deeply theological, drawing on Paul, John, Irenaeus, and Athanasius for its leading ideas. Worked out in a polemical context as Cyril elaborated his arguments against Arianism, it was already fully developed by the time of the Nestorian crisis. Indeed, it accounts for the passion with which he opposed Nestorius. Any attack on his understanding of Christ was by implication also an attack on his vision of salvation.

(c) The Christological Basis for Deification

Cyril's spirituality, centred on the exaltation and transformation of human nature, rests squarely on his single-subject christology. The Word condescended to accommodate himself to human life. Christ was not a human being promoted to divine status through union with the Word, but was the Word himself incarnate. The enfleshed Word is the subject of all the acts of

Jesus Christ. The Word deified the temple in which he dwelt. He made the body his 'own'. The self-emptying of the Incarnation did not effect any change in the Word. He did not suffer any diminution of his deity. But the union of Word and flesh was so intimate that St John could say 'the Word became flesh' (John 1: 14):

> He was not content to claim that he came to be *in* the flesh but went so far as to say that he *became* flesh, in order to represent the union. We do not, of course, say that God the Word who is from the Father was transformed into the nature of flesh, or that the flesh changed into the Word. For each remains what it is by nature and Christ is one from both.   (*In Jo.* 4. 2. 363b)

In virtue of this mutual interpenetration of humanity and divinity, the acts of Christ as recorded in the Gospels cannot be assigned separately to his humanity (i.e. those which arise from fear or ignorance) or to his divinity (i.e. those which manifest divine power) (cf. *In Is.* 1. 4, PG 70. 181c); *Resp. Tib.* 9, Wickham 162). The Word is the single subject of all his acts whether before the Incarnation (τῆς ἐνανθρωπήσεως γυμνός) or after. Yet the body is not simply a passive instrument. The soul of Christ informs his humanity—and experiences emotions—but in constant interaction with the Word, which is the governing principle. In his exegesis of John 12: 27, 'Now is my soul troubled', Cyril attempts to follow the psychological vacillation implied by the text:

> For the thought of death that has slipped in attempts to agitate Jesus, while the power of the divinity at once masters the emotion that has been aroused and immediately transforms that which has been conquered by fear into an incomparable courage.   (*In Jo.* 8. 703d)

It is a complete human nature that the Word has assumed. If this were not so he could not have brought salvation to humankind. For he was not only the enfleshed Word but at the same time *the* representative human being:

> In Christ as the first-fruits, human nature was restored to the newness of life. And in him we have gained also that which transcends nature. That is also why he was called a second Adam in the divine Scriptures (cf. 1 Cor. 15: 45). Just as he experienced hunger and weariness as a man, so too he accepts the disturbance that comes from the emotions as a human characteristic. He is not, however, disturbed in the way that we are, but only insofar as he needs in order to experience the perception of the thing, and then immediately he reverts to the courageous attitude that is appropriate to him.   (*In Jo.* 8. 704ab)

The Word in his fullness and a human nature in its entirety together constitute the Saviour, the mediator, who recapitulates the whole of human existence in 'the second Adam' and presents it to the Father. An Arian Christ who occupies a lower grade of divinity, who is on our side of the 'agenetic'/ 'genetic' divide, cannot be an adequate mediator. Christ is transcendent,

sharing a community of being with God who is *hyperousios*—beyond being—
and at the same time is immanent, experiencing the limitations of human life.
Nor will a Nestorian Christ do. Nestorius put forward the idea of prosopic
union—two different πρόσωπα, or roles, the human and the divine, forming
a union by conjunction (συνάφεια) in the single πρόσωπον of Christ. This
too was rejected by Cyril. The human πρόσωπον seemed to him an individual
human hypostasis who had been promoted to divine status by a merely
extrinsic union with the Word. Such a Christ could not recapitulate the whole
of humanity in his person and transform it by divine power. Indeed, in
Nestorius' Antiochene tradition there was no place for the deification of
the Christian. Without a single-subject christology salvation must be seen
primarily in moral and exemplarist terms.

Salvation for Cyril is participation in the divine life. It can only be procured by one 'who has shone forth from the very essence of the Father' (*In
Jo.* 1. 9. 91d), one who is a son 'in reality' and not 'by imitation'. 'Father' and
'Son' are not metaphorical terms, as Eunomius claimed. They express an
ontological relationship. Nor is a nominal community created between them
by the word 'god', as Nestorius held (*C. Nest.* 2. 4, Schwartz 39 = Loofs 289.
6–15). It is only the Christian believer who is a 'god' in a nominal sense, in
virtue of the text, 'I said, you are gods and all of you sons of the Most High'
(Ps. 82: 6).

Christ as the divine Son is therefore the agent of redemption. Cyril took
over from Irenaeus and Athanasius the exchange formula: Christ became
what we are that we might become what he is:

Do you hear how the Only-begotten Word of God became like us, that we too might
become like him so far as is possible for human nature and to the extent that may be
ascribed to the renewal through grace? For he humbled himself that he might raise
up that which is humble by nature to his own stature, and he put on the form of a
servant although he was by nature Lord and Son, that he might transfer what was
servile by nature to the glory of adopted sonship, according to his own likeness and
with regard to him. Therefore he became like us, that is, a human being, that we
might become like him, I mean gods and sons. On the one hand he accepts what
belongs to us, taking it to himself as his own, and on the other he gives us in
exchange what belongs to him. (*In Jo.* 12. 1. 1088bc)

Our relationship with Christ is reciprocal but asymmetrical. 'Just as the Word
made his own the human condition which does not properly belong to him,
so humanity can make its own the divine mode of life which does not
properly belong to it' (Anatolios 1998: 174). Yet Christ does both the giving
and the taking. He is the pattern of our progress but in more than an
exemplary way. His submission to baptism, marked, according to the testimony of John, by the descent of the Holy Spirit in the form of a dove, is
the model for our own baptism, which is also to be accompanied by the

reception of the Spirit. The Spirit received by Christ on that occasion was also received in a sense by 'us' as represented in Christ.

When the Word of God became man he received the Spirit from the Father as one of us, not receiving anything specifically for himself—for he himself was the supplier of the Spirit—but that receiving as man he might save by nature, and establish again in us the grace which had departed, he who had known no sin. (*In Jo.* 2. 1. 123c)

Other events of Christ's life also have an intimate connection with us. His transfiguration is a glimpse vouchsafed to Peter, James, and John of the eschatological transfiguration awaiting every believer (*In Luc.* Frag. on Luke 9: 32 f., TU 34. 4. 3: 81). Cyril connects the Transfiguration with Paul's assurance that our bodies of humility will be transformed and made to conform to Christ's body of glory (Phil. 3: 21).

The resurrection of Christ is a pledge of the rising from the dead of all who through baptism have come to be 'in Christ' and through the practice of the moral life have maintained the restoration of the image. This appropriation of the divine life in a dynamic sense is the work of the Holy Spirit.

(d) The Role of the Holy Spirit

The Son's work of salvation is carried out through the Spirit, which must therefore also be fully divine (*In Jo.* 9. 1. 810a). The Spirit is of the substance of the Father, but is not a second Son because he is the 'Spirit of the Father and the Son' (*In Jo.* 9. 1. 809d). Cyril has no doubt that the Spirit has his principle of origin from the Father. The verb 'proceeds' (ἐκπορεύω) is never used of the Spirit in relation to the Son. Yet the Spirit is at the same time 'not alien to the Son' (οὐκ ἀλλότριον τοῦ υἱοῦ) (*In Luc.* Frag. on Luke 10: 21a, TU 34. 3. 4: 105. 18). The Spirit is operative together with the Son in baptism, in the Eucharist, and in the moral life.[33] He makes us temples of God and 'partakers of the divine nature'. He 'becomes in us some quality, as it were, of the Godhead' (*In Jo.* 9. 1. 811a). He bestows on believers the dignity of adoption as sons. And when we have the Spirit of the Son in our hearts we can cry, 'Abba! Father!' (*In Jo.* 9. 1. 811c). Participation in the Spirit conforms us to Christ, and enables us to be 'described as children of God and gods' (*In Jo.* 11. 9. 970c).

(e) The Use of 2 Peter 1: 4

Cyril's favourite way of expressing this is through 2 Peter 1: 4: 'partakers of the divine nature'. This text, which had previously been cited, but very sparingly, only by Origen, Athanasius, and Theophilus, becomes in Cyril his

---

[33] After the beginning of the Nestorian controversy Cyril became wary of language which might suggest that Christ co-operated with the Spirit as if with an external agency. Cf. his Anathema 9 in his *Explanation of the Twelve Chapters*.

preferred means of expressing how human beings appropriate the divine life.[34] The frequency of his citation of the text is quite remarkable. He uses it on numerous occasions to suggest succinctly the trinitarian dimensions of salvation. The active role of the Spirit is particularly prominent: 'for we are justified by faith and are proved to be partakers of the divine nature by participation in the Holy Spirit' (*In Jo.* 9. 766b). Christ revealed the Holy Spirit, but it is the Holy Spirit that makes Christ's indwelling in the believer possible: 'through him and in him we are conformed to the archetypal beauty, reborn in this way into newness of life and re-formed into divine adoption' (*In Jo.* 2. 1. 147a). Baptism into Christ through the Spirit enables us to participate in the divine nature not in an ontological sense but morally. It is the moral aspect of our kinship with Christ which is emphasized by the reference to 'the archetypal beauty'. The ugliness of sin is left behind as we are remodelled according to the standard of moral beauty set by Christ. But that is not the end of the matter. Through Christ we have access to the Father. 'Partakers of the divine nature' always implies a dynamic relationship *through* the Spirit *in* Christ *with* the Father.

Cyril rarely comments directly on 2 Peter 1: 4. The following passage is perhaps the closest he comes to an exegesis of the text:

How are we 'God's offspring' (Acts 17: 29)? In what way are we 'partakers of the divine nature' (2 Pet. 1: 4)? We do not limit our boast merely to the fact that Christ wished to take us into an intimate relationship with him. No, the truth of the matter is evident to us all. For 'the divine nature' is God the Word together with the flesh. And we are his 'offspring' even though he is God by nature, on account of his taking the same flesh as ourselves. Therefore the mode of the relationship rests on likeness (οὐκοῦν ἐμφερὴς ὁ τῆς οἰκειότητος τρόπος). For just as he is intimately related to the Father, and the Father through the identity of nature is intimately related to him, so we too are intimately related to him—in that he became man—and he to us. We are united (συναπτόμεθα) to the Father through him as through a mediator. For Christ is, so to speak, a frontier (μεθόριον) between supreme divinity and humanity, since both are present within him. And containing within himself, as it were, these two vastly discrete things, he is united (συνάπτεται) on the one hand to God the Father, since he is God by nature, and on the other to human beings, since he is truly human. (*In Jo.* 6. 1. 653de)

Cyril's fundamental conviction is that God is encountered in the person of the incarnate Word, Jesus Christ, who unites within himself the 'two vastly discrete things' (τὰ τοσοῦτον διῳκισμένα) of the human and the divine. In Christ our common humanity is raised to intimacy (εἰς οἰκειότητα) with God the Father. But in order to 'partake of the divine nature' as individuals, to assimilate ourselves personally to the Word made flesh who is the agent of

---

[34] On Cyril's use of 2 Pet. 1: 4 see Keating 2004: 144–90. For a brief account of the history of its exegesis see Russell 1988; in addition to the references given there, Theophilus of Alexandria alludes to 2 Peter 1: 4 twice in his homily (formerly attributed to Cyril) *In mysticam coenam*, PG 77. 1021B and 1025D.

our salvation, we need to become like Christ morally through baptism and obedience to the commandments. When we are 'in Christ' and he 'in us' in this manner, we can participate through him in his relationship with the Father.[35] But we do not cross the 'frontier' separating humanity from divinity.

(f) The Sacramental Life

The change wrought in us is qualitative rather than quantitative but it does have a corporeal dimension, which is expressed through participation in the Eucharist. The Holy Spirit accomplishes in us in principle the work of salvation, a work which is completed by our participation in the Eucharist. The Eucharist 'restores man wholly to incorruption' (*In Jo.* 3. 6. 324c). It is endowed with the qualities of the Word, 'or rather, is filled with his energy, through which all things are given life and maintained in being' (*In Jo.* 3. 6. 324e). Those who abstain out of a mistaken reverence cut themselves off from the source of life. The Eucharist transforms those who partake of it and endows them with the Word's own proper good, that is, immortality (*In Jo.* 4. 2. 362a). Just as water heated in a kettle acquires something of the quality of fire, so we acquire something of the quality of the Eucharist. Through our 'mingling with Life' we are transformed by its property. 'For it was absolutely necessary not only that our soul should be recreated into newness of life by the Holy Spirit, but also that this coarse and earthly body should be sanctified by an analogous participation and called to incorruption' (*In Jo.* 4. 2. 362b). If we abstain from the Eucharist, we forego having 'the provider of immortality' active within ourselves (*In Jo.* 4. 2. 365c). The Eucharist causes the passions to atrophy and dispels death and disease.

(g) The Restoration of the Image

The Eucharist does not effect a change in us in a mechanical way. Along with the participation in the eucharistic flesh of Christ, moral progress is required, which is brought about by our participation in the Spirit:

Therefore the Son does not change the least thing belonging to the created order into the nature of his own deity (for that would be impossible) but there is imprinted in some way in those who have become 'partakers of the divine nature' (2 Pet. 1: 4) through participating in the Holy Spirit a spiritual likeness to him and the beauty of the ineffable deity illuminates the souls of the saints. (*C. Nest.* 3. 2, Schwartz 60. 16–20)

The Eucharist brings incorruption (ἀφθαρσία) in a physical sense, which means stability with regard to the composite nature of the human person (Wickham 1983: 201 n. 15). Such stability also has a moral dimension which Cyril expresses in terms of our recovering the image and likeness of God.

---

[35] On participation in the incarnate Christ see Meunier 1997: 161–213; Keating 2004: 144–90; Keating 2003.

He makes no distinction between the two. Image and likeness, so far as he can see, are perfectly synonymous (*Dogm. Sol.* 4, Wickham 193). They are manifested in the human capacity for goodness, righteousness, and holiness (ἀγαθότητος καὶ δικαιοσύνης καὶ ἁγιασμοῦ) (*Dogm. Sol.* 3, Wickham 192. 19–20). Our having been created with this capacity entitles us to be called 'gods' (*C. Jul.* 2. 35–6, PG 76. 592C–592A). But the community with God which this signifies is purely nominal. We fell away from our original state through sin, but now Christ has restored us to it. Christ, the second Adam, has recapitulated in his person the whole of humanity, turning it away from the pole of death and disintegration and reorientating it towards the pole of divine life:

What then is the image of our first ancestor? It is to be prone to sin and subject to death and decay. And what is the image of the heavenly man? It is not to be conquered by passion in any way; it is to be ignorant of transgression and free from subjection to death and decay; it is holiness, righteousness and whatever is brother to these and like them. In my view these qualities are appropriately possessed by that nature which is divine and undefiled. For holiness and righteousness are superior to both sin and decay. The Word of God includes us in this, for he makes us partakers of his divine nature through the Spirit (cf. 2 Pet. 1: 4). (*C. Nest.* 3. 2, Schwartz 60. 6–12)

Recreated in Christ by the Spirit, human beings can come to share in the divine attributes of holiness, righteousness, and freedom from decay. These attributes cannot be attained by an external imitation of God or any mere effort of the will. They are freely given to those who are prepared to co-operate with the Son and the Spirit and thus 'mount up to the archetypal form of the image' (*In Jo.* 1. 9. 91b), which is the Father himself.

(h) Conclusion

With Athanasius and Cyril the roles of the charismatic teacher and the hierarchical guardian of apostolic doctrine meet in a single person. This episcopal tradition, fundamentally biblical and Irenaean, with relatively little contributed by Clement or even Origen, will henceforth be identified with the great see of Alexandria. With regard to deification its main features may be summed up under four points:

First there is a strong emphasis on the convergence of transcendence and immanence in Christ and through him, as the representative first-fruits of the human race and also the pattern to be emulated, in the believer as well. This approach derives from Irenaeus and is supported in Cyril's writings by his development of Paul's ἐν Χριστῷ theme.

Secondly, there is a fundamental reliance on the theme of participation, which offers a way of understanding on the ontological level how Becoming can share in Being, or the created in the uncreated, without abandoning its contingent status, and on the dynamic level how the created and contingent can partake increasingly of the divine nature through the operation of the Holy Spirit, which enables it to attain eventually to the image and likeness of God. This develops an Origenian theme.

Thirdly, there is a firm rejection of any approach to bridging the gulf between created and uncreated by positing an inferior level of deity which can function as a mediator. Mediation is accomplished through the exaltation of Christ's humanity.

Lastly, a central place is given to the ecclesial context of deification. The emphasis moves away from divinizing contemplation towards the practice of the virtues and the reception of the Eucharist in the Christian *synaxis*. Charismatic or ascetic groups are not left with a monopoly of the means of deification. The transformation of the believer, which is initiated by the Holy Spirit in baptism, is confirmed by the Spirit and the flesh of Christ in the Eucharistic body gathered around the bishop.

5. The Legacy of Alexandria

Cyril was not the last great bishop of Alexandria in undisputed possession of his see—that honour belongs to his successor, Dioscorus—but he does mark the end of an era. Things had already begun to change during the episcopate of his energetic uncle and predecessor, Theophilus. The new direction taken by Theophilus when he launched his attack on the Origenism of the Nitrian monasteries in the spring or summer of 400 had far-reaching consequences. The end of the Catechetical School, for example, and the new approach to exegesis evident in Cyril's writings are probably not unconnected with it. After Didymus the exegetical and philosophical traditions of Origenism vanish from sight. Nor do we hear any more about the activities of the School. Moreover, the allegorical method characteristic of Clement, Origen, and Didymus, in which every detail of the biblical text is given a symbolic spiritual meaning, gives way to a predominately christological reading with only occasional recourse to allegory.

Manlio Simonetti has rightly observed that with Cyril Alexandrian exegesis 'followed a new path, sacrificing much of its traditional character' (1994: 110). Simonetti attributes this principally to 'the need to find a plausible line of defence against the anti-allegorical offensive of the Antiochenes' (1994: 81). This may have been a significant motive, but the 'new path' must also be connected with the increasingly monarchical role of the bishop of Alexandria. With Cyril all administrative and teaching authority is finally concentrated in the hands of the hierarch: the 'academic' tradition of the Alexandrian spiritual teachers is absorbed into the 'catholic' tradition of the successor of the apostles. This is evident in the kerygmatic tone of everything Cyril wrote. His commentaries and dialogues were not intended primarily for intellectual study circles. They had a didactic and often polemical purpose, setting forth the true faith in order to inoculate his hearers against the attractions of heterodox thought.[36]

After Cyril there is very little exegetical activity in Alexandria (cf. Simonetti 1994: 110–14). The christological controversies that occupied the entire period between Chalcedon (451) and Constantinople III (680) made extended meditations on the Scriptures an unaffordable luxury. The need was now for dogmatic works which sought to clarify the doctrine of Christ. In the aftermath of Chalcedon, at least in the eastern part of the empire, both the 'dyophysite' defenders of the conciliar Definition and its 'monophysite' opponents claimed Cyril as their chief authority. His christological writings were anthologized and discussed in great detail. But the spiritual implications of his vision of a humanity raised through Christ to participation in the divine life were not fully explored until taken up in the seventh century by Maximus the Confessor.

In summary, the Alexandrians used the metaphor of deification to indicate the glorious destiny awaiting human nature in accordance with the divine plan of salvation. The fundamental 'moment' is the deification by the Logos of the representative human nature he received at the Incarnation. This has implications for individual human beings. The believer can participate in the deified flesh of Christ—the Lord's exalted humanity—through baptism, the Eucharist, and the moral life. Such participation leads to deification, not as a private mystical experience but as a transformation effected within the ecclesial body. The details of this were to be worked out in relation to the spiritual life by Maximus the Confessor. It is Maximus who is the true heir not only of the Cappadocians but also of the entire Alexandrian tradition.

[36] It has been suggested very plausibly that the *Commentary on Isaiah*, for example, 'was originally a series of lectures given to the clergy of Alexandria in order to teach them how to read and interpret the biblical text' (Cassell 1992, cited by Welch 1994: 11 n. 39).

7

The Cappadocian Approach

Divine Transcendence and the Soul's Ascent

Brooks Otis, in a stimulating article now more than forty years old, defined the Cappadocians' achievement as the recovery of the angelogical and anthropological portions of Origen's heritage by accommodating them to the anti-Origenist theology of Athanasius (1958). With regard to deification this meant the accommodation of the recovery of the divine likeness and the ascent of the soul to God to the Athanasian distinction between the 'agenetic' Trinity and the 'genetic' created order. Athanasius' solution to the problem of how a fully divine Logos could be a mediator between the 'agenetic' and the 'genetic' was through the deification of the flesh which the Logos assumed. The Cappadocians took this over as part of their defence of Nicene orthodoxy and attempted to combine it with the Platonic tradition of the soul's attainment of likeness to God.

1. Basil of Caesarea

Like Athanasius and Cyril, Basil of Caesarea had a strongly episcopal sense of tradition. But he was not initially destined for an ecclesiastical career. Born in about 330, he came from a Christian landowning family of wealth and status.[1] His father was a professor of rhetoric who ensured that his eldest son received a first-class education. On completing his university studies at Athens, Basil was drawn to monasticism and made a tour of the monasteries of Syria, Mesopotamia, Palestine, and Egypt to gain first-hand experience of organized asceticism. He then retreated to a family property at Annesoi in Pontus with the intention of leading a 'philosophic' life. Only gradually did he come to conclude that he must play his part in the social life of the Church as a cleric and eventually, from 370, a bishop.

---

[1] For an account of Basil's life see Rousseau 1994.

Basil's approach to deification reflects his background. From the later perspective of his episcopacy he claimed that he had wasted his youth on 'the wisdom made foolish by God' (*Ep.* 223. 2). But his university studies left a lasting impression on him, and as a young Christian ascetic it was the Alexandrian Platonists, Philo, Clement, and Origen, who engaged his sympathy. From these he would have learned that the expression 'gods' is used in Scripture as an analogous term, and may be applied to those who, through the imitation of God, had attained an eminent degree of virtue.

In Basil's writings Philo is mentioned only once (*Ep.* 190. 3), but there is evidence of his influence elsewhere, particularly in the *Hexaemeron* (Runia 1993: 236–8). As Runia observes, Basil 'sees Philo as part of the Alexandrian tradition of biblical exegesis, and so feels free to draw on the material he offers, but sees no compelling reason to draw attention to his particular contribution' (1993: 241). The same may be said with regard to Clement, who is never alluded to but whose influence is nevertheless discernible. Origen's contribution is more readily apparent. Indeed, Basil may have regarded him as part of the tradition he had inherited, for Origen was the revered teacher of Gregory Thaumaturgus, the evangelist of Cappadocia, who had baptized Basil's grandmother, Macrina the Elder. Near the end of his life Basil wrote that he had never changed the conception of God which he had received from his mother and grandmother, but only developed it (*Ep.* 223). Yet even with regard to Origen it is not easy to be precise about the extent of his influence. At the beginning of his career as a serious Christian in his Pontic retreat, Basil spent many hours with his friend Gregory of Nazianzus going through the works of Origen and selecting passages for the *Philocalia*, the Origenian anthology that was their first publication.[2] But in all his subsequent writings Basil refers to Origen only on one other occasion (*De Sp. S.* 29. 73). Perhaps he felt as a bishop that it was not appropriate to cite Origen as an authority.

No such reservations would have attached to Athanasius, the undisputed leader in Basil's generation of the struggle to establish Nicene orthodoxy. Basil appealed to 'the physician of the maladies of the churches' (*Ep.* 82) in 371 for help in his international initiative to resolve the Antiochene Meletian schism and counter the errors of Marcellus of Ancyra (*Epp.* 61, 66, 67, 69, 80, 82). But some seven years previously he had already enlisted his aid, without acknowledgement, in his polemical début, the *Adversus Eunomium* (written 363–4). His proof of the divinity of the Holy Spirit from his power to deify is an argument clearly drawn from Athanasius' *Letter to Serapion*.

In Basil we thus find a limited use of the concept of deification which draws on several aspects of the Alexandrian tradition but makes no use of

---

[2] M. Harl (SC 302. 1–20) regards the tradition that Basil and Gregory collaborated on the compilation of the *Philocalia* as dubious. For a defence of Gregory's participation see McGuckin 2001: 103–4.

the Pauline theme of incorporation into Christ or the Irenaean interpretation of Psalm 82: 6.[3]

(a) Vocabulary

Basil uses θεοποιέω very rarely. In his undisputed works he uses it three times in pejorative metaphorical sense (*Reg. fus. tract.* 20. 2, PG 31. 972C; *Reg. brev. tract.* 63, PG 31. 1124D; *Ep.* 188. 1) and only twice, in Book III of *Adversus Eunomium*, for the destiny of the Christian (PG 29. 665C). He also calls human beings θεοί a number of times, occasionally without referring to the authority of Scripture.

(b) Texts

When Basil was pressed by the Praetorian Prefect Modestus to fall into line with Valens' pro-Arian policy, he is reported to have refused the emperor's request on the grounds that his Sovereign forbade it, adding: 'Nor can I submit to the worship of any creature, since I am a creature of God and called to be a god' (Greg. Naz. *Or.* 43. 48). A creature who becomes a god, as Basil understood the Arian Christ to be, does not differ in any significant way from ourselves, and therefore cannot save us.

'Becoming a god' for Basil has no ontological implications. Those who are called to be gods, he says, are the perfect in virtue (*Adv. Eun.* 3. 5). This does not mean that they are 'gods' in any real sense. The word is used analogically: the foolish are called wise in Scripture, just as those who are not gods by nature are called gods (*Hom. in Ps.* 48. 6, PG 29. 445A). Words and realities do not coincide. If that were so names and natures would be one and the same. 'Therefore since those who are perfect in virtue are deemed worthy of the title of god, men would be of the same nature (*homoousioi*) as the God of the universe. But this would be absurd' (*Adv. Eun.* 2. 4).

Nevertheless, even the titular or analogical deification of human beings can be used as an argument for the divinity of the Holy Spirit: 'Also, if we call gods those who are perfect in virtue and perfection is through the Spirit, how can that which lacks deity deify others? (πῶς τὸ ἑτέρους θεοποιοῦν αὐτὸ τῆς θεότητος ἀπολείπεται;) (*Adv. Eun.* 3. 5). The argument recalls Athanasius, but in Athanasius gods are those who have received the grace of adoption rather than those who are perfect in virtue. Yet, like Athanasius, Basil goes on to insist that it is impious to suggest that the Spirit's deity is not by nature but is participated as is the case with men. 'For he who is deified by grace is of a mutable nature (ὁ γὰρ χάριτι θεοποιούμενος τῆς μεταπτωτικῆς ἐστι φύσεως) and can fall away through negligence.' Here, as he goes on to explain, Basil regards deification as an effect of baptism (PG 29. 665C).

---

[3] There are two good summaries of Basil's approach to deification: Papadopoulou-Tsanana 1970, esp. 122–7, and Christou 1978*b*: 303–13.

The most famous reference to the divine destiny of human beings in Basil's writings is in the ninth chapter of *De Spiritu Sancto* (*c*.375). In this, the chief work of his maturity, he asks how the Spirit's intimate association with the soul (οἰκείωσις πνεύματος πρὸς ψυχήν) is achieved. The answer is by the soul's separation from the passions and its return to its natural beauty, its ancient royal image. Once this is achieved, we shall be able to behold in the Spirit the image of the invisible God, and in that image the beauty of the archetype:

Through the Spirit hearts are lifted up, the weak are led by the hand, and they who are advancing are brought to perfection. Shining upon those that are cleansed from every stain, he makes them spiritual by communion with himself. Just as when a sunbeam falls on bright and transparent bodies, they themselves become brilliant too, and shed forth a fresh brightness from themselves, so spirit-bearing souls (αἱ πνευματοφόροι ψυχαί), illuminated by the Spirit, themselves become spiritual, and send forth their grace to others. Hence comes foreknowledge of the future, understanding of mysteries, apprehension of what is hidden, distribution of good gifts, the heavenly citizenship, a place in the chorus of angels, joy without end, abiding in God, being made like God, and, the highest goal of all, becoming a god (τὸ ἀκρότατον τῶν ὀρεκτῶν, θεὸν γενέσθαι). (*De Sp. S.* 9. 23, PG 32. 109BC; trans. Jackson, modified)

The social aspect of this beatitude is striking and characteristic of Basil: bodies illuminated by the Spirit communicate that brilliance to others. This is no 'flight of the alone to the Alone'. Yet it is also very different from Athanasius. On the one hand, the imagery is more spiritualized and more Platonic as souls rendered πνευματοφόροι and πνευματικαί are lifted up, suffused with light, to the likeness of God; on the other, it is more eschatological: the 'gods' are not merely the baptized but those who have finally entered into the joy of God's presence in heaven.[4] Paul Henry, after a detailed comparison of this passage with Plotinus' *Enneads*, has concluded that Basil's 'becoming a god' (θεὸν γενέσθαι) was inspired by Plotinus' 'having become a god, or rather being one' (θεὸν γενόμενον, μᾶλλον δὲ ὄντα).[5] While it may be true that Plotinus has influenced the *De Spiritu Sancto*, there is also an established Christian tradition of which Basil would have been aware (quite apart from his own mention of θεόν γενέσθαι in connection with Heracles in *Ad aduluscentes* 5. 16). Hans Dehnhard, in his discussion of Henry's view of the indebtedness of *De Spiritu Sancto* 9. 23 to Plotinus, draws

---

[4] Cf., however, *V. Ant.* 14, PG 26. 864C, where Athanasius describes Antony as θεοφορούμενος after many years of ascetic effort. Here in a monastic setting Athanasius does refer to moral perfection as a means of deification.

[5] 1938: 180–2. Henry compares *De Sp. S.* 9. 23 with a number of Plotinian texts, including *Enn.* VI. 9. 9, 50–9. H. Dehnhard is much more reserved than Henry (1964: 80–4). J. M. Rist is more reserved still, judging that so striking a phrase as *Enn.* VI. 9. 9 'could have been familiar to the learned or fairly learned while its origins were unknown to the person using it' (1981: 199–202).

attention to connections with Methodius of Olympus, Clement of Alexandria, and Gregory of Nyssa (1964: 80–4). We may also, I suggest, add from Hippolytus: 'not being enslaved to desires or passions and moral diseases, you will enter into communion with God and become a fellow-heir with Christ. For you have become a god' (ἔσῃ δὲ ὁμιλητὴς θεοῦ καὶ συγκληρονόμος Χριστοῦ, οὐκ ἐπιθυμίαις ἢ πάθεσι καὶ νόσοις δουλόμενος. Γέγονας γὰρ θεός) (*Ref.* 10. 34, GCS 3. 292–3). Hippolytus, in particular, seems much closer to Basil than does Plotinus. In Plotinus the soul is only discovering its innate divinity, as the qualifying phrase indicates, whereas in Hippolytus and Basil the soul becomes something it was not before, in the former through conformity to Christ, in the latter through illumination by the Spirit and the attainment of likeness to God.

The manuscript tradition for the ascription of Books IV and V of *Against Eunomius* to Basil is weak. They are certainly anti-Arian but they do not address the arguments of Eunomius' *Apology*, as do the first three books. They have in the past been attributed first to Apollinarius, and then to Didymus (*CPG* ii. 2837), but more recent opinion has tended to regard them as genuinely Basilian after all (Christou 1978*b*: 150–2). Henry (1938) and Dehnhard (1964) think they are by Basil because of their Plotinian influence. Panayiotis Christou believes that Book V is so close to Basil's *De Spiritu Sancto* that it is possible that it was an early exercise in explaining biblical doctrine with the help of Greek thought, written in Pontus at the outset of his eremitical retreat in 360 (1978*b*: 152). In this book the Spirit is described as the sanctifying and deifying agent of creation (τὸ τῆς κτίσεως ἁγιαστικὸν καὶ θεοποιόν) who fills it with the divine energies (*Adv. Eun.* 5, PG 29. 732B). Later the author argues for the divinity of the Holy Spirit from Psalm 82: 6. If the saints are called gods in Scripture, the Spirit, as the cause of the saints, is also the cause of gods, and must therefore himself be God (*Adv. Eun.* 5, PG 29. 772AB).

Among the works attributed to Gregory of Nyssa in Migne is Homily I *On the Creation of Man* (*CPG* ii. 3215). H. Hörner, however, has argued that this sermon is a collection of notes that Basil left on the Hexaemeron (GNO, Suppl. 1972: vii–ix). The author of the sermon makes an un-Gregorian distinction between image and likeness. We have the image already, he says; let us acquire the likeness, first by the quality of our moral life and secondly by submission to baptism. Christianity is defined as 'likeness to God in the measure that human nature is capable' (θεοῦ ὁμοίωσις κατὰ τὸ ἐνδεχόμενον ἀνθρώπου φύσει) (PG 44. 273D; Hörner, 33. 5–6). To become like God is to put on Christ, and to put on Christ is to put on the garment of incorruption in baptism. The writer is addressing a person who appears unwilling to accept baptism. 'When I wish to make you like God,' he says, 'do you flee the Word that deifies you (τὸν λόγον τὸν θεοποιοῦντα σε), blocking up your ears so as not to hear the saving words?' (PG 44. 276A, Hörner 33. 12).

(c) How is Perfection Attained?

In his undisputed works Basil uses θεοποιέω for the destiny of the Christian only in Book III of *Adversus Eunomium*, where he argues, like Athanasius, for the full divinity of the Spirit from his power to deify. Elsewhere the Christian goal is described in different terms. The primary aim of the Christian life, says Basil, is to give glory to God (*Reg. fus. tract.* 20. 2, PG 31. 975A), but after that it is to attain likeness to God in so far as is possible for human nature (*De Sp. S.* 1. 2, PG 32. 69B). The language of participation is sometimes used by Basil, for we are sanctified by participation in the holiness of the Spirit (*Adv. Eun.* 3. 2, PG 29. 660BC). But he gives much more emphasis to imitation, or *mimesis*, through the practice of virtue. His definition of Christianity is the imitation of the incarnate life of Christ: οὗτος ὅρος χριστιανισμοῦ, μίμησις Χριστοῦ ἐν τῷ μέτρῳ τῆς ἐνανθρωπήσεως (*Reg. fus. tract.* 43. 1, PG 31. 1028C). It is this which enables us to fulfil the aim of our calling, which is to become like God. Our *telos* is the blessedness of life in heaven: ἡ μακαρία διαγωγὴ ἐν τῷ μέλλοντι αἰῶνι (*De Sp. S.* 1. 2, PG 32. 69B).

The Son became incarnate and performed his saving work in order to make the attainment of this *telos* possible, the purpose of the divine economy being 'our return to the likeness of God from the alienation brought about by disobedience' *Hom. in Ps.* 48. 1, PG 29. 432B). Our relationship to Christ is therefore seen not so much in terms of incorporation into him as in imitation of him: 'for perfection of life the imitation of Christ is necessary' (*De Sp. S.* 15. 35, PG 32. 128C). Such an imitation, which brings about a likeness to God through his Son, is twofold. It implies not only following Christ's example of gentleness, humility, and endurance of suffering, but also symbolically sharing in his death and burial through baptism (ibid., 129AB).

The role of the Holy Spirit is equally essential:

Through the Holy Spirit comes our restoration to paradise, our ascent into the kingdom of heaven, our return to the adoption of sons, our liberty to call God our Father, our being made partakers of the grace of Christ, our being called children of light, our participation in eternal glory, and, in a word, our being brought into a state of all 'fullness of blessing' both in this world and in the world to come. . . . (*De Sp. S.* 15. 36, PG 32. 132B; trans. Jackson, modified)

The Holy Spirit through his sanctifying power makes human beings spiritual, conforms them to the image of the Son, and raises them up to the archetypal beauty itself (*De Sp. S.* 9. 23, 109AB). The first fruits of this are found in baptism, but the full enjoyment is experienced only in heaven.

All this must be accompanied by moral effort. True to his monastic vocation, Basil never loses sight of the need for asceticism. The 'gods' are those who have attained perfection in virtue. Yet this perfection is not achieved without the Spirit. In the first place, no one can set out on the path to perfection without self-knowledge as a preliminary: 'be attentive to yourself so that you can be attentive to God' (πρόσεχε οὖν σεαυτῷ ἵνα προσέχῃς Θεῷ) (*Hom. Attende tibi ipsi* 8, PG 31. 217B). Moreover, the overcoming of the passions is necessary before the Spirit can be free to work: as an eye full of dirt cannot apprehend visible things, he says, so a heart stained with dirt cannot apprehend the truth (*Hom. in Ps.* 33. 3, PG 29. 357C). But once the foundations are laid, the Spirit works a gradual transformation in us as 'the inner man is renewed day by day' (*Hom. in Ps.* 44. 2, PG 29. 389C).

The highest degree of perfection results in the vision of God. There are two faculties in the *nous*, says Basil, an evil one which draws men towards apostasy, and a good or divine faculty 'which brings us to the likeness of God'. If the *nous* assents to this 'diviner part' and accepts the gifts of the Spirit, it becomes perceptive of the divine. Mingled with the deity of the Spirit, it then 'beholds the divine beauty, though only so far as grace imparts and its nature receives' (*Ep.* 233. 1). This may begin even in this life, as the examples of Moses and the three disciples on Mount Tabor witness (*Hex.* 1. 1, PG 29. 5C; *Hom. in Ps.* 44. 5, PG 29. 400CD). Indeed Basil himself had had experience of this, as Gregory of Nyssa suggests in his encomium on his brother (PG 46. 800D, 804BC, 808C).

(d) What is the Role of the Sacraments?

This experience is also described in terms of taste. The eucharistic bread is the bread of life through which the believer comes to enjoy communion with God. The Eucharist is a symbol and real pledge of the 'taste' of God in heaven (*Hom. in Ps.* 33. 6, PG 29. 364C).

In spite of this foretaste, however, Basil's view of deification is essentially eschatological. He mentions the deification in principle which takes place at baptism, but does not develop it. The 'gods' are those who have entered into the kingdom of heaven, whose beatitude Basil describes, in imagery combining Platonic and biblical elements, as vision of beauty, participation in light, and communion with the angels and with God. Yet there is a final stage of deification which also involves the body. Although in Basil's view the image of God resides in the *nous*, it is not the *nous* alone which is deified (*Ep.* 233. 1). In the end the whole man is transformed: first the psyche is rendered spiritual through purification and the ascent to God; then, at the resurrection, the body itself becomes like the body of Christ as death is finally defeated and corruption is swallowed up by incorruption.

(e) Conclusion

Although Basil was a friend of Athanasius and an admirer of Origen, his teaching on deification seems to owe more to Clement than to the more recent Alexandrians. Like Origen he presents deification as the gradual spiritualization of men and reserves the term 'gods' for their final state. Like Athanasius he proves the divinity of the Spirit from his power to deify. But the transformation of the flesh in the Athanasian manner does not appear in Basil's writings. Moreover, the 'gods' are not those who have been adopted by baptism but those who have become perfect through the practice of virtue. Basil is altogether more Platonic. In this, as in his apophaticism, he resembles Clement. In Basil's view, when men contemplate God, they look up into an incomprehensible beauty. They merely become 'like' God through imitating his moral excellence, the term 'gods' being used either in a titular sense or else with reference to man's eschatological state. How far this employment of a Platonizing tradition is able to provide a satisfactory bridge between the 'genetic' and agenetic' orders of reality can only be assessed after a consideration of the other two Cappadocians, Gregory of Nazianzus and Gregory of Nyssa.

2. Gregory of Nazianzus

Like his friend Basil, Gregory of Nazianzus belonged to the provincial aristocracy of Cappadocia.[6] He was born in 329/30 in the little city of Nazianzus, of which his father, also called Gregory, was the bishop. After an excellent education, crowned by a ten-year stay in Athens (348–58), where he studied with Basil under the Christian rhetorician Prohaeresius,[7] he returned to Cappadocia to live a life of ascetic retreat on his family estates. The 'philosophical life' remained his first love. He was forced into the priesthood by his father, reluctantly accepted an episcopal appointment from Basil, and was persuaded by his friends to think that he could make an important contribution to the Nicene cause as bishop of Constantinople. His clerical career, however, gave him little satisfaction. The happiest period of his life was probably the four years spent in contemplative seclusion at St Thecla's in Seleucia (375–8) before his call to Constantinople.

Gregory appeals to the deification of the Christian as theological support for the *homoousion* of the Son and the Spirit almost as frequently as Athanasius.[8] But whereas Athanasius dwells on the idea of participation in

---

[6] Gregory has been the subject of good modern biographies by Gallay (1943*a*), Bernardi (1995), and McGuckin (2001). He is also the first person in antiquity to leave us an autobiographical work, his poem *De vita sua* (*Carm.* II. 1. 11). Begun in 382 as an *apologia* for the failure of his episcopal mission in Constantinople, it offers us a unique insight into his inner life. Only Augustine in his *Confessions* (written *c.* 398–400) is as revealing.

[7] A few years later the pagan sophist Eunapius also became a student of Prohaeresius, whose powerful oratory and youthfulness of soul (he was 87 at the time) so impressed Eunapius that he says he hung on his words 'as he might [of] some god who had revealed himself unsummoned and without ceremony' (*V. Soph.* 485; trans. Wright).

[8] The most comprehensive study of deification in Gregory of Nazianzus is Winslow 1979. Although occasionally criticized (e.g. Ellverson 1981: 22–7) for interpreting Gregory's soteriology too much in terms of deification, it is still indispensable. See also Gross 1938: 244–50; Theodorou 1956: 87–90; Althaus 1972; Moreschini 1997: 34–6.

the divine life, Gregory shifts the emphasis to the imitation of Christ. The category of 'participation' is not important to him; nor does he ever appeal to 2 Peter 1: 4. But imitation does not mean following an external model. It means that by becoming like the incarnate Son through the sacraments and the practice of 'philosophy', human beings can eventually transcend their earthly limitations, with the result that they are transformed by 'mingling'— to use one of Gregory's favourite expressions—with the divine light. Yet deification is never something which human beings accomplish in any literal sense. The gap between uncreated and created is never bridged. Indeed so aware is Gregory of this gap, that there are indications in his writings of the concept of perpetual progress towards God which is developed so strikingly by Gregory of Nyssa.

(a) Vocabulary

Gregory has a distinctive vocabulary which appears particularly in his mature writings. Among the early Greek Fathers only Athanasius employs deification terms more frequently, yet Gregory's vocabulary is quite different. He uses θεοποιέω only once, in an early oration, preferring on three further occasions to resolve it into θεὸν ποιέω.[9] He also uses θεὸς γίγνομαι a number of times[10] and θεὸς ἔσομαι once (*Or.* 2. 17, PG 35. 481B), along with two poetic variations: θεὸν τεύχω (*Carm.* I. 1. 3. 4, PG 37. 408) and θεὸν τελέω (*Carm.* I. 2. 14. 92, PG 37. 762). His favourite verb, however, is θεόω, which he uses very frequently.[11] The only noun he uses is the neologism θέωσις. This word first appears in the *Fourth Oration*, the First Invective against Julian, which was delivered shortly after Julian's death in July 363, and is used again on nine further occasions.[12] The adjective θεοποιός is used twice (*Or.* 3. 1, PG 35. 517A; *Carm.* II. 2. 7. 69, PG 37. 1556A).

---

[9] Θεοποιέω: *Or.* 2. 73, PG 35. 481B, delivered shortly after Easter 362. Mason's text of *Or.* 31. 29 (1899: 184. 6), following the Benedictine reading (PG 36. 168A), has a further instance. Gallay and Jourjon (SC 250), however, following a better MS tradition, print θεοῦν here instead of θεοποιοῦν. Θεὸν ποιέω: *Or.* 2. 22, PG 35. 432B; *Or.* 30. 14, PG 36. 121C; *Or.* 31. 4, PG 36. 137B.

[10] *Or.* 1. 5, PG 35. 397C; *Or.* 7. 22, 784D; *Or.* 7. 23, 785B; *Or.* 14. 23, 888A; *Or.* 17. 9, 976D; *Or.* 25. 2, 1201A, *Or.* 29. 19, PG 36. 100A; *Or.* 30. 3, 105C; *Or.* 30. 21, 133A; *Or.* 36. 11, 277C; *Or.* 40. 5, 421B; *Or.* 42. 17, 477C.

[11] *Or.* 4. 59, PG 35. 581; *Or.* 31. 28, 165A; *Or.* 31. 29, 168A; *Or.* 34. 12, 252C; *Or.* 38. 11, 324A; *Or.* 38. 13, 325C; *Or.* 40. 42, 420A; *Or.* 41. 9, 441B; *Or.* 45. 9, 633D; *Ep.* 6. 3, PG 37. 29C; *Ep.* 101, 180A, 185C; *Carm.* I. 1. 10. 61, 469A; *Carm.* I. 2. 10. 630, 725A; *Carm.* I, 2. 17. 2, 781A; Carm. I, 2. 33, 934A. The Benedictine text has a further instance at *Or.* 30. 12, PG 36. 117C (θεωθέν, apparently speaking of the will of the divine Son as deified) which Mason reproduces even though it puzzled him (p. 126, n. 1). Gallay and Jourjon (SC 250) restore the correct reading: θεόθεν 'from God'.

[12] *Or.* 4. 71, PG 35. 593ᵇ; *Or.* 4. 124, 664C; *Or.* 11. 5, 837C; *Or.* 17. 9, 976D; *Or.* 21. 2, 1084C; *Or.* 23. 12, 1164C; *Or.* 25. 2, 1200B; *Or.* 25. 16, 1221B; *Or.* 39. 16, PG 36. 353B; *Carm.* I. 2. 34. 61, PG 37. 957A. Even Winslow does not appreciate the novelty of the term: 'We would point out first of all, that no Christian theologian prior to Gregory employed the term theosis (or the idea contained in the term) with as much consistency and frequency as did he' (1979: 179). For the dating of the Orations see Gallay 1943*a*: 252–3, and McGuckin 2001.

Gregory does not use θεοποιέω or θεὸν ποιέω in his christological discussions. Nevertheless, the reasons for his verbal preferences appear to be more stylistic than doctrinal. His style, as is well known, displays many of the characteristics of Second Sophistic, combining Attic diction with neologisms and archaisms for striking effect.[13] Θεὸν ποιέω is clearly an archaism. Θέωσις is a back-formation from Gregory's preferred verb, θεόω. It is first used when a homoeoteleuton is required: ἀναβάσεως καὶ θεώσεως (*Or.* 4. 71, PG 35. 593B; cf. 21. 2, 1084C). Later it is used for the sake of assonance: ἡ θεότης . . . ἡ θέωσις (*Or.* 25. 16, PG 35. 1221B). On a further occasion Gregory uses the word to present a striking oxymoron: τῇ θεώσει θεός (*Or.* 39. 16, PG 36. 353B).

Although θέωσις is the usual term by which deification came to be known among the Byzantines, it did not prove immediately popular. It was not taken up again until Dionysius the Areopagite used it in the late fifth century, and only became fully assimilated with Maximus the Confessor in the seventh.

(b) Texts

Gregory's first references to deification occur in the orations he delivered in 362 on his return to Nazianzus after his flight to Pontus. The situation was delicate. Gregory had fled to Annesoi to join Basil in a life of monastic retirement only a few days after his father had bullied him into ordination on Christmas day 361.[14] By the following spring Gregory the Elder was in serious difficulties, a group of ascetic dissidents in his diocese having rejected his authority on the grounds of heresy. He had apparently compromised himself doctrinally by making a public statement not acceptable to the strict Nicenes.[15] Gregory returned at his father's request to repair the damage. His task was twofold: to rehabilitate himself in the eyes of the people of Nazianzus (his flight must have looked like a repudiation of his ordination), and to defend his father's authority by establishing his own spiritual and intellectual credentials.

The fundamental purpose of the Christian life is set out in the *First Oration* (delivered on Easter Sunday 362) in terms of the exchange principle: 'Let us become as Christ is, since Christ became as we are; let us become gods for his sake, since he became man for our sake'.[16] The best gift that we can give

---

[13] On Gregory's style see Guignet 1911; Gallay 1943*b*; Ruether 1969, esp. 55–9.

[14] The date of Gregory's ordination, Christmas day 361, was deduced (by Gallay) from Gregory's statement in his *First Oration* that 'a mystery anointed me' and 'on a mystery I return' (*Or.* 1. 2). Easter 362 is secure as the date for the *First Oration*. But Bernardi's argument (SC 247: 16–17) that the first mystery was simply Gregory's ordination has been widely accepted. Here I follow McGuckin (2001: 101) in staying with Gallay's date. It is not certain whether Christmas day in this period in Cappadocia was 25 December or 6 January (McGuckin 2001: 101 n. 58).

[15] For a discussion of the problem see McGuckin 2001: 108–9.

[16] *Or.* 1. 5. Winslow comments: 'Was it a typographical error or an unconscious distrust of the vocabulary of theosis which led the *NPNF* to translate *theoi* in this passage as "God's"?' (1979: 91).

to God is ourselves, 'becoming for his sake all that he became for ours' (*Or.* 1. 5). The rest of the oration is devoted to commending his father to the people as a standard of virtue and perfection of the priesthood, who, like a venerable Abraham, brings his only son as a willing sacrifice.

More was needed, however, to explain Gregory's actions than a typological allusion to himself as an obedient Isaac. In the *Third Oration*, preached on the following Sunday to a half-empty church, he associates himself more closely with his father. His congregation is invited to renew their obedience and love for 'both the old and the new shepherd', Gregory the Elder and his son. Yet Gregory does not hide the fact that for him the attractions of the contemplative life are stronger than those of an ecclesiastical career. He describes the monastic solitude he had enjoyed in Pontus as 'co-worker and mother of the divine ascent and producer of deification' (σύνεργον καὶ μητέρα τῆς θείας ἀναβάσεως, καὶ θεοποιόν) (*Or.* 3. 1). It was from this that the call from Nazianzus had torn him away.

Throughout his œuvre Gregory celebrates the ascetic life in similar terms. Writing to Basil in Pontus in 361, he says (with reference to Job 29: 2): 'Who will bring back to me the intimacy and unanimity of the brethren who were by you being deified and exalted?' (τίς ἀδελφῶν συμφυΐαν καὶ συμψυχίαν, τῶν ὑπὸ σοῦ θεουμένων καὶ ὑψουμένων;) (*Ep.* 6. 3). A secluded life has the power to deify by bodily purification (*Carm.* 1. 2. 10. 630), and by not allowing the mind to be mingled with mundane things (*Carm.* 1. 2. 17. 1–2; cf. 1. 2. 33. 89–90). In the *Fourth Oration*, the *First Invective against Julian*, delivered at the end of 363 or in 364 (which marks the first appearance of the word θέωσις), Gregory holds up for admiration the Christian ascetics,

who are immortal through mortifying themselves; who are united (συνημένους) with God through release [from the body]; who are separated from desire and are joined to that love which is divine and dispassionate; to whom belongs the fountain of light and who enjoy even now its radiance; to whom belong the angelic psalmodies, the night-long services and the departure of the intellect to God, rapt up before its time (ἡ περὶ νοῦ πρὸς θεὸν ἐκδημία προαρπαζομένου);[17] to whom belong purification and being purified; who know no limit in ascending or in being deified (μηδὲν μέτρον εἰδότων ἀναβάσεως καὶ θεώσεως). (*Or.* 4. 71; cf. Origen, *C. Cels.* 6. 44)

Purification leading to ascent and deification recalls Origen, who speaks of the virtuous, after they have been purified like gold in the fire, 'progressing to the divine realm' and being 'drawn up by the Logos to the supreme blessedness of all' (*C. Cels.* 6. 44; trans. Chadwick). But the setting is monastic with its psalmodies and vigils. And the intellect being rapt up to God surely alludes to Paul.

---

[17] This is the first time that the theme of ecstasy has appeared in a Christian author since Paul. Cf. 2 Cor. 12: 2: ἁρπαγέντα τὸν τοιοῦτον ἕως τρίτου οὐρανοῦ. Cf. also Philo, *QG* 4. 140; *Opif.* 70–1 (though in Runia's judgement (1993: 243) it is not likely that Gregory owned or had easy access to a copy of Philo's works); Porphyry, *V. Plot.* 23 (though Porphyry uses ἐνωθῆναι rather than ἁρπάζεσθαι).

When Gregory touches on deification in these early orations, Pauline and Platonic strands of thought sometimes mingle together. In the funeral oration for his brother Caesarius (late 368 or early 369) Gregory describes the bliss of those whom death has separated from the body. Having shaken off the fetters which confine the intellect's wing (τὸ τῆς διανοίας πτερόν), the soul escapes from the harsh prison of this life and goes to share in God's glory. The 'prison', it should be noted, is 'this life', not specifically the body itself. Later the soul will receive back the body that has shared the philosophical life with it, and will communicate its joys to it, because the mortal and the transient will have been swallowed up by life (*Or.* 7. 21). Here the Platonic image of the soul winging its way to heaven is combined with the Pauline metaphor of death being swallowed up in victory (cf. 1 Cor. 15: 53–4).

In the next paragraph an allusion to Psalm 82: 6–7 is introduced. 'Should we not come to know ourselves?' asks Gregory. Should we not reject the things of sense (τὰ φαινόμενα) and fix our gaze on the things of the intellect (τὰ νοούμενα)? Should we not be grieved 'that we linger in the tombs [i.e. bodies] which we carry about because we die the death of sin like men (cf. Ps. 82: 7) when we have become gods (cf. Ps. 82: 6)?' (*Or.* 7. 22). Here Gregory refers to the Platonic *soma–sema* theme, the body as a tomb, but it is not simply the fact of being embodied that is at issue. Our bodies are tombs only because they house souls which are dead through sin. And although Gregory expresses a Platonizing desire to escape from the body, it is not the escape itself that makes us gods. We linger in the body when we have *already* become gods (which indicates that Gregory is referring to the effects of baptism) but we can die like men (which means we can succumb to post-baptismal sin).

And a little later, when Gregory reflects on the nature of the human state, his understanding of our dual nature is expressed in more openly Pauline terms:

'What is man that thou art mindful of him' (Ps. 8: 5)? What is this new mystery concerning me? I am small and great, lowly and exalted, mortal and immortal, earthly and heavenly. I share one condition with the lower world, and another with God; one with the flesh, the other with the Spirit. I must be buried with Christ (cf. Rom. 6: 4), rise with Christ (cf. Rom. 6: 8; Col. 2: 12), be joint heir with Christ (cf. Rom. 8: 17), become a son of God (cf. Rom. 8: 14), a god myself.   (*Or.* 7. 23; cf. *Or.* 14. 23)

In this passage, which concludes a meditation on the Pauline theme of putting to death the 'earthly members' (Col. 3: 5), the Irenaean interpretation of the gods of Psalm 82: 6 as those made sons of God through baptism is not far below the surface. Dying and rising with Christ in baptism so that we come to be 'in Christ' makes us sons and gods. The new creation we have become enables us to shed the earthly side of our existence and realize our heavenly potential. But the philosophical life, the life of asceticism and contemplation, is also needed to bring about such a realization.

In his panegyric on Athanasius, Gregory pronounces blessed whoever through the exercise of reason and the practice of contemplation has separated himself from the veil or cloud of the flesh and

has become akin to God and mingled himself with the purest light, so far as is permissible for human nature. Such a man is blessed both through his ascent from this world and through his deification in the next (τῆς τε ἐντεῦθεν ἀναβάσεως, καὶ τῆς ἐκεῖσε θεώσεως), which is conferred by true philosophy and by rising above the duality of matter through the unity which is perceived in the Trinity.   (*Or.* 21. 2)

This paragraph embodies the same understanding of the human struggle for self-realization as does Gregory's funeral oration on his brother, but, as befits the philosophical life, expresses it in a more Platonic idiom. The purpose of the ascetic life is to become like God so far as possible. The means are separation, purification, and ascent. But the goal is different. The One of Neoplatonism has become the Trinity of Christian doctrine, and what is to be achieved is not *henôsis*, or union, but the transformation of the self expressed by the new Christian term, *theôsis*.

Such a programme was not for the ordinary faithful. To return to Gregory at Nazianzus in 362, the *Second Oration*, which discusses the philosophical life in some detail, was probably not delivered as a Sunday sermon in his father's church. More of a treatise than a homily, it has been described as an 'open letter' intended for a small circle of readers (Moreschini 1997: 241). Gregory's purpose is to justify to the clergy of Nazianzus his flight and return, to balance the superiority of the contemplative life against the duties of the priesthood and integrate them, so far as possible, in a single perspective. The Christian pastor is therefore presented as someone called to lead his people to a higher life:

Our aim is to endow the soul with wings, to snatch it up from the world and give it to God, and to watch over that which is in the image of God if it remains, or to lead it by the hand if it is in danger, or to restore it if it is ruined, and to make Christ dwell in the heart through the Spirit, and in short to deify (θεὸν ποιῆσαι) and bestow heavenly bliss on whoever has promised heavenly allegiance.   (*Or.* 2. 22)

Although the passage begins with a commonplace of Platonic teaching, the endowing of the soul with wings (cf. in particular Plato, *Phaedr.* 251b), it ends with an oblique reference to baptism.[18] The priest deifies as a spiritual guide, but he also procures the deification of the faithful through the administration of baptism.

---

[18] Bernardi has drawn attention to the allusion in the word *syntaxis*, which I have translated as 'heavenly allegiance', to the baptismal formula of renunciation of Satan and promise (*syntaxis*) to follow Christ (SC 247: 120 n. 1).

The priest's sacramental and liturgical role is made more explicit later in the treatise, when Gregory discusses the awesome vocation of the Christian priest, who

will make the sacrifices ascend to the altar on high, who will exercise the priesthood together with Christ, who will remodel the creature, who will present the image, who will create for the world above, and most of all, who will become a god and make gods (θεὸν ἐσόμενον καὶ θεοποιήσοντα). (*Or.* 2. 73)

The Liturgy complements the spiritual life as a parallel mode of raising human life to the level of the divine. The priest is a mediator, deified and deifying, through sharing in Christ's priesthood.

The relationship between priest and philosopher is portrayed vividly in one of the early orations delivered in Constantinople. Gregory was duped by a charlatan called Maximus, whom he took to be a philosopher who had suffered for the Nicene cause. At the beginning of the oration he calls him up to the altar: 'Come, stand close to the sacred things, to this mystical table, and to me who through these things lead you into the mystery of deification' (κἀμοῦ τοῦ διὰ τούτων μυσταγωγοῦντος τὴν θέωσιν), to which your words and life and purification through suffering have brought you' (*Or.* 25. 2). In the presence of God and the angels and the entire body (πλήρωμα) of the Church Gregory will crown him like the president of some spiritual games, since Maximus has 'defeated the falsehood of heresy for the honour of the living God who teaches us how to suffer with his own sufferings, the prize of which is the kingdom of heaven and to become a god through having risen above suffering' (*Or.* 25. 2). The philosopher's asceticism and witness to the faith are crowned by deification— but through the ministry of the priest.

Gregory had come to Constantinople in 379 at the invitation of the Nicene party.[19] The year was a critical one both politically and ecclesiastically. The previous year Valens had led the Roman army to a catastrophic defeat at the hands of the Goths at Adrianople, and had himself perished in the disaster. The new emperor Theodosius, unlike his Arian predecessor, was an upholder of Nicene orthodoxy. All through 379 he was occupied with the Gothic war. The Nicene party knew that the political ascendancy of the Arians was over, but they still needed to win over the educated administrative class of the capital. Hence the invitation to Gregory. A villa was placed at his disposal by a wealthy cousin, Theodosia, where he established a church, the Anastasia. It was there that he delivered most of his sermons, including the five *Theological Orations*, until in November 380 he was installed by Theodosius in the Church of the Holy Apostles as de facto bishop of Constantinople.

[19] On Gregory's links with Meletius of Antioch and the circumstances of his departure for Constantinople see McGuckin 2001: 235–8.

The concept of deification, or theosis as we may now call it, provided Gregory with his best way of explaining the condescension of the divine in the Incarnation without compromising the *homoousion* of the Son. Theosis is the goal and fulfilment of human life. Adam was created as a synthesis of opposites, earthly and heavenly: 'a living being placed here and transferred elsewhere, and, to complete the mystery, deified by its inclination towards God' (ζῶον ἐνταῦθα οἰκονομούμενον, καὶ ἀλλαχοῦ μεθιστάμενον, καὶ πέρας τοῦ μυστηρίου, τῇ πρὸς τὸν θεὸν νεύσει θεούμενον) (*Or.* 38. 11). This paradoxical duality is mirrored in Christ, the second Adam, who is 'a union of two opposites', flesh and spirit, 'of which the latter actively deified, while the former was the recipient of deification' (ὧν τὸ μὲν ἐθέωσε τὸ δὲ ἐθεώθη), with a rational soul mediating between the two (*Or.* 38. 13 = *Or.* 45. 9).[20]

In Christ that which assumed and that which was assumed are both God (θεὸς γὰρ ἀμφότερα) (*Or.* 37. 2), but it is only the flesh that is deified. Countering the Arian argument from Luke 2: 52 that Christ advanced progressively to divine status, Gregory insists that the Son is Son and God from the beginning, for in Christ's case there is no growth into divinity (οὐδὲ ἐκ προκοπῆς ἡ θέωσις) (*Or.* 25. 16).

Gregory could not entertain any christological approach which compromised the eternity of the Son. Otherwise the purpose of the Incarnation—the exaltation of man—would have been frustrated. The nature of the Son is without cause or beginning

but afterwards he was born for a cause (and that was to save you who insult him, whose Godhead you despise on account of this, because he accepted your grosser nature) and came into contact with flesh by means of *nous*, and man here below became God,[21] since he was mingled with God and became one, the higher nature having prevailed, that I might become a god in the same measure that he became a man. (*Or.* 29. 19)

The 'double metathesis' enables Gregory to say that the eternal Son filled the human nature which he assumed through the mediation of the *nous* with divine life, so that human nature in general might be deified in principle, thus enabling the individual believer to be deified in an analogous fashion by union of his or her *nous* with Christ.[22] The intellectual nature of this union is sometimes emphasized. On one occasion Gregory suggests that the incomprehensible transcendence of God can act as a spur to wonder and desire and thence to a purification which makes us gods (*Or.* 38. 7). But the

---

[20] Cf. *Or.* 39. 16, where it is the *sôma* of Christ that is deified, and *Carm.* I. 1. 10. 61 where Christ's soul and *nous* are differentiated.

[21] Mason punctuates: καὶ γενόμενος ἄνθρωπος, ὁ κάτω θεός. I follow Gallay (SC 250): καὶ γενόμενος ἄνθρωπος ὁ κάτω, θεός. Cf. Maximus, *Amb. Th.* 3, PG 91. 1040C.

[22] Cf. Maximus' comment on this passage, *Amb. Th.* 3, PG 91. 1040CD, discussed below (p. 283).

incarnational context of deification is never lost sight of. Christ makes us gods 'by the power of his Incarnation' (*Or.* 30. 14). 'What greater destiny can befall our humility than that humanity should be intermingled with God, and by this intermingling should become divine (θεόν)?' (*Or.* 30. 3). This new deified humanity is appropriated by us through baptism, which is another indication that the Son is simultaneously both wholly man and wholly God: 'If I now worshipped a creature, or were baptized into a creature, I would not have been deified, nor would I have changed my first birth' (*Or.* 40. 42).

With the dual nature of the Son as a principle vital for our salvation, we must be on our guard against those who would divide the Son into two separate entities, as well as those who would fuse them into one. In the *Letter to Cledonius* (*Ep.* 101), written after his resignation and departure from Constantinople, Gregory focuses chiefly on Apollinarian claims, but he does not neglect opposite errors. Attacking the notion of two sons (the Son of God and the son of Mary), he insists that both the human and the divine form a single entity: 'For both [natures] are one by mingling, God inhominated and man deified (τὰ γὰρ ἀμφότερα ἐν τῇ συγκράσει, θεοῦ μὲν ἐνανθρωπήσαντος, ἀνθρώπου δὲ θεωθέντος), or however one should express it' (*Ep.* 101. 21). Against the Apollinarians it is the duality that must be emphasized. The humanity that the Logos assumed was complete in every respect, 'for the unassumed is the unhealed'. By a neat use of Exodus 7: 1 Gregory suggests how the higher part of the human soul of Christ, the *nous*, was not crowded out by the Logos. Just as Moses was a god to Pharaoh but a servant of God, so our mind commands the body but does not share in God's honour (*Ep.* 101. 45). The effects of the Incarnation, however, were more far-reaching than the deification of the 'clay' of human nature. The 'image', residing in the human mind, was also leavened and mingled with God, deified by his divinity (θεωθεῖσα διὰ τῆς θεότητος) (*Ep.* 101. 46). Our destiny is not simply a return to our original beatitude, but something greater: the image is not only restored, but in attaining the goal for which Adam had been created is deified.

During Gregory's time in Constantinople it was not the Apollinarians that preoccupied him but the Arians. These, like the orthodox, were divided into factions, one of which was the Macedonian (named after the former bishop of Constantinople, Macedonius, deposed in 360), which, while prepared to accept the *homoousion* of the Son, denied it of the Spirit. To have the *homoousion* of the Spirit formally accepted by the Church as orthodox became one of the aims of Gregory's preaching campaign.

If the Son cannot deify us unless he is consubstantial with the Father, the same principle applies to the Spirit: 'If he is to be ranked with me, how can he make me a god, or how can he unite me with the Godhead?' (*Or.* 31. 4; cf. 34. 12). The Spirit is both 'God above me' and 'makes me a god here below' (*Carm.* 1. 1. 3. 4). He perfects, sanctifies, and deifies and therefore cannot himself be perfected, sanctified, and deified (*Or.* 41. 9). The fact that he deifies us through baptism proves that he is to be worshipped as God (*Or.* 31. 28). Indeed, the Holy Spirit is not limited by the rite itself in making us gods: he both anticipates baptism and is to be sought after it (*Or.* 31. 29).

Gregory's orations were not without effect. The council of bishops that met in Constantinople in May 381 confirmed that the Holy Spirit was to be worshipped with the Father and the Son, but did not explicitly endorse the *homoousion* of the Spirit. Disappointed at his failure to persuade the bishops to do so, and outmanoeuvred politically by his enemies, he resigned his see. In the course of his farewell address to the council he presents a carefully nuanced summary of his trinitarian doctrine. If one wishes to devise distinctive attributes for the Trinity, he favours 'ungenerated' (ἀγέννητον), 'generated' (γέννητον), and 'proceeding' (ἐκπόρευτον) (*Or.* 42. 17). These maintain the fundamental divide between God and the creature: 'A creature may be said to be "of God", and that too is a great thing for us. But it may never be called "God". Otherwise I shall admit that a creature is God, if I too become a god in the proper sense of the term' (ὅταν κἀγὼ γένομαι κυρίως θεός). For that is how things are. Either God or creature. In our case creature, for we are not gods' (*Or.* 42. 17). In spite of our deification through the contemplative life or through baptism, in the last analysis we become gods only by analogy.

From these texts it is clear that in his approach to deification Gregory follows the Athanasian pattern with an additional emphasis on the soul's separation from the body and ascent to God in the Platonic manner. On the theological level the Son is represented in the Incarnation as both deifying and deified, God deifying the body, or 'man', which he assumed and through this 'man' deifying the human race as a whole. The Spirit, for his part, is not deified but only deifies. Together with the Son, the Spirit deifies human beings through baptism. The Eucharist is also said to lead them to deification. The Christian priest, as the dispenser of the sacraments, is thus an agent of deification. But he is also an agent of deification as a spiritual guide. For the first time in a Christian writer the monastic life is presented as the setting which enables human beings to attain divine status. Deification in this sense, the *telos* of every serious Christian, is conceived of in accordance with the ethical approach. Christian ascetics are those who are struggling to ascend to God through leaving the body and its needs behind. Theosis on its first appearance is linked with *anabasis* (ascent), and this connection is repeated on other occasions. Although the transformation of the human race by the Incarnation is mentioned as the basis of a deification in the realistic sense, it is the ethical approach of Philo and Clement which Gregory chooses to develop.

The word *theos* applied to human beings has as many as five different senses, all of which are in some measure metaphorical, for the creature cannot become god literally (*Or.* 42. 17). The first sense is related to the Incarnation: 'man' becomes 'god' through intermingling with God; human nature is deified in the person of Christ through the incarnation of the Son (*Or.* 1. 5; 29. 19; 30. 3). The second is baptismal: the gods are the saved, those who have attained equality with the angels through having become sons of God and gods, yet still linger in the body (*Or.* 7. 22). The third is ethical: men become gods and akin to God even in this life by moral purification (*Or.* 30. 4). The fourth is eschatological: the soul that has escaped from the world becomes a god when it is reunited with its now spiritualized body (*Or.* 7. 21). And the fifth is purely analogous: magnanimity deifies because it imitates the divine *philanthropia* (*Or.* 17. 9; 36. 11). With regard to the human *telos*, the 'gods' for Gregory are thus on the one hand those who have begun through baptism to appropriate the deified humanity of the Son, and on the other those who have freed themselves from the material world through the ascetical struggle, both approaches leading to the angelic life in heaven. Gregory's perspective, like that of Basil, is at once both eschatological and Platonic.

(c) How is Deification Related to the Incarnation?

Gregory draws some of his christological arguments from Athanasius, maintaining that Christ is both deifier and deified, the Logos deifying the human nature which he assumed, which explains, for example, how Christ can be said to 'advance' (*Or.* 30. 12; 25. 16; cf. Athanasius, *CA* 1. 39). But whereas Athanasius worked with a christological model in which the Word is the subject of the life of the flesh, Gregory separates the two natures quite emphatically. He does sometimes speak of the flesh or the body or the will being deified, but more often it is 'man' (*Or.* 29. 19; 30. 3; 38. 13; 39. 16). The unity between God and man is explained by the Stoic *krasis* theory, whereby two natural substances interpenetrate each other while still retaining their separate identities. The 'man' which the Logos assumed is deified by 'intermingling' with the Logos through the mediation of the *nous*, which is why Apollinarianism must be resisted. Not only must Christ have a human soul because 'that which was not assumed was not healed', but, as Origen had taught, the mediation of the higher part of the soul, the *nous*, is essential if the Logos is to be united to the flesh (cf. Origen, *De Prin.* 2. 6. 3).

Gregory, it should be noted, avoids participation terms in his christological discussions. The union of the two natures takes place by σύγκρασις and μίξις rather than by μετουσία and μέθεξις. Nestorius was later to favour a similar terminology, though in his case he also rejected deification. What prevents Gregory's christology from tending towards Nestorianism is precisely the notion of deification. The God and the man in Christ are held in perfect union through the deification of the lower by the higher: the flesh, the will, the *nous*—the whole man—are wholly deified.

As Winslow has shown, the deification of the human nature of Christ is 'the principle upon which our analogous deification is based'.[23] The purpose of the Incarnation was the exaltation of man. For just as Christ is a synthesis of opposites, so is man, flesh and spirit being for Gregory separate creations. Man's *nous* has a certain kinship with God which his flesh lacks because it was his spiritual nature alone which was created in the image of God. By allowing the higher to prevail over the lower he is deified 'by his inclination towards God' (*Or.* 38. 11). As in his christology, Gregory tends to avoid the language of participation. Nowhere, for example, does he quote 2 Peter 1: 4. Nor is deification said to be equivalent to adoption. The believer is not so much incorporated into Christ as led to imitate him. The emphasis is thus inevitably on moral progress and the ascent of the soul, which is why Gregory stresses the metaphorical or analogous nature of man's divine status.

(d) Conclusion

In his study of Gregory's soteriology, Winslow presents 'theosis' as a fluid term descriptive of a dynamic relationship between God and man, which within the economy of salvation results 'in our progressive growth towards an adopted dignity of fulfilled creatureliness' (1979: 189). Rightly understanding theosis as fundamentally metaphorical, he suggests a sixfold dimension for it—as spatial (the ascent of the soul), visual (the illumination of the *nous* and the vision of God), epistemological (knowing God and being known by him), ethical (the ascetic endeavour), corporate (progressive union with God), and social (sharing in the divine life) (1979: 193 ff.).

I believe that Winslow's understanding of theosis is right. Not all the dimensions of the metaphor which he lists, however, are given equal prominence by Gregory himself. The realistic approach (which corresponds to Winslow's corporate and social dimensions) has a secondary place in Gregory's works, the emphasis being rather on the analogous and ethical approaches (which correspond to Winslow's spatial, visual, epistemological, and ethical dimensions). On the realistic level, theosis is the change wrought in 'man' by the Incarnation, the fruits of which are communicated to the individual believer by the Holy Spirit in baptism. On the analogous level theosis takes place through the imitation of God's *philanthropia*. On the ethical level it follows the escape of the soul from its bondage to matter and its ascent to God through ascetic endeavour and true philosophy.

The result of deification is that we become gods. This begins as a human response to the Incarnation, our ascent being a *mimesis* of Christ's descent. We have already become gods in principle in so far as we have been united with Christ by baptism, but our deification is only brought to fulfilment in

---

[23] Winslow 1979: 189. But cf. Strange 1985, who suggests that it was the other way round.

heaven after a long period of *ascesis*. Indeed, we can never become gods at all in the proper sense—that is to say, we can never overcome the generate/ingenerate divide. In heaven the image will be restored, the *nous* deified, and the flesh immortalized, but the gulf between the created and the uncreated will never be transcended. Nevertheless, the saved will be called gods, for Psalm 82: 1 says that God will stand in the midst of gods (cf. *Or.* 7. 22; 30. 4).

'Gregory', says Winslow, 'went far beyond his predecessors in his sustained application of theosis' (1979: 179). This is an exaggeration. Athanasius had already laid down the lines which Gregory was to follow: the deification of the human nature by the Incarnation, and then the believer's appropriation of this by accepting baptism and struggling to live the moral life. Gregory has much more to say on the moral life and makes much greater use of the Platonic tradition in saying it. But in the *Life of Antony* Athanasius had already adopted a similar approach. Where Gregory does go beyond Athanasius is in applying the terminology of deification to the ethical dimension. In this, as in his emphasis on the role of the *nous*, he reaches back to the tradition of Clement and Origen. On the other hand, he does not develop Athanasius' doctrine of participation. This is an aspect of deification which was taken up by Gregory of Nyssa.

3. Gregory of Nyssa

As a younger brother of Basil and a friend of Gregory of Nazianzus, Gregory of Nyssa collaborated closely with them in their struggle against Arianism. Unlike them he had not studied at one of the great schools, but he had still acquired a profound philosophical and theological formation. He was made bishop of the small town of Nyssa in 372 (the same year that Gregory of Nazianzus became bishop of Sasima) as part of Basil's campaign to maintain Caesarea's influence as an ecclesiastical metropolis. Although deposed under Arian pressure, he was restored when Valens met his death in 378. In 379 he was present at the Council of Antioch, the Nicene party's synod at which the idea of Gregory of Nazianzus going to Constantinople was probably first mooted. At the Constantinopolitan council of 381 he supported Gregory's efforts to win acceptance for the *homoousion* of the Holy Spirit. Even if his success at the council was limited, he impressed the emperor. Theodosius afterwards issued a rescript designating communion with him a sign of orthodoxy (*Cod. Theod.* 16. 1. 3).

Gregory's spiritual teaching has been the subject of intensive study since the Second World War.[24] Several writers have seen in Gregory a major

---

[24] The two seminal works for this study were von Balthasar 1942 and Daniélou 1944. Among the more significant publications since are Leys 1951, Völker 1955, and Jaeger 1966.

exponent of the doctrine of deification, but in fact he appeals to the doctrine very rarely.[25] Deification for the bishop of Nyssa refers primarily to the transformation of the flesh assumed by the Son at the Incarnation (and, by extension, to the operation of the sacraments), and secondarily to man's participation in the divine perfections. But 'deification' is not his favoured approach. He prefers in general to speak of 'participation' in the divine attributes and of the attainment of 'likeness' to God.[26]

(a) Vocabulary

As Balás has observed, Gregory 'uses the terminology of "deification" rather seldom' (1966: 159). In fact he uses θεοποιέω in a spiritual context only twice in two of his early works, and a neologism, συναποθεόω, also twice in a work of his maturity, the *Great Catechetical Oration*.[27] In this respect he presents a striking contrast with Gregory of Nazianzus.

(b) Texts

In his earlier works when Gregory mentions deification it is as a product of participation in the divine attributes. In the first, *On Virginity* (371), he presents virginity as a supreme attribute of God which deifies those who participate in it. Virginity signifies that which is pure and incorrupt.[28] 'What greater praise of virginity can there be,' says Gregory, 'than thus to be shown, so to speak, deifying those who share in her pure mysteries' (θεοποιοῦσαν τρόπον τινὰ τοὺς τῶν καθαρῶν αὐτῆς μυστηρίων μετεσχηκότας) so that they become partakers of the glory of the only truly holy and blameless God? (*De Virg.* 1, PG 46. 320D). Virginity is not a physical but a spiritual condition, a 'disengagedness of heart', as one writer has called it (NPNF 5. 342). It can therefore be acquired by the practice of philosophy.

How a human being may 'become a god' through the imitation of the characteristics of the divine nature is pursued in the exegetical work *On the*

---

[25] Gross describes Gregory's mystical theology at some length without pinpointing those aspects to which Gregory applies the terminology of deification (1938: 219–38). Völker's excellent study is the first to bring out the relationship between deification and participation in the divine perfections (1955: 274–82). Theodorou draws attention to the connection between the deification of Christ's body in the Incarnation and our own deification by analogy (1956: 78–81, 138–9). This aspect is developed in a fine study by Moutsoulas (2000; originally published in Greek in 1965) which roots Gregory's doctrine of deification firmly in his teaching on the Incarnation and the sacraments. The fullest treatment of how humanity shares in the attributes of the Godhead is still that of Balás's classic study of the idea of participation in Gregory (1966). Most recently Daley's penetrating analysis of divine transcendence and human immortality in Gregory (1997) has reaffirmed the christological context of his teaching on deification.

[26] Besides the fundamental studies of Merki 1952 and Balás 1966 see Leys 1951.

[27] Θεοποιέω: *De Virg.* 1, PG 46. 320D; *De Beat.* 5, PG 44. 1249A. Συναποθεόω: *Or. Cat.* 35, PG 45. 88A, Srawley 130. 4; *Or. Cat.* 37, PG 45. 97B, Srawley 152. 1. The second instance is from Srawley's emended text.

[28] *De Virg.* 1, PG 46. 321C; cf. Methodius of Olympus, *Symposium* 9. 4, where chastity is similarly presented as deifying.

Lord's Prayer. In order to approach God as Benefactor, one should become a benefactor oneself; in order to approach him as Good, one should become good, in order to approach him as Righteous, as Magnanimous and so on, one should acquire those attributes.

> And if a man is free from everything that comes under the idea of evil he becomes, so to speak, a god by his very way of life (θεὸς τρόπον τινὰ διὰ τῆς τοιαύτης ἕξεως γίνεται), since he verifies in himself that which reason finds in the divine nature. Do you realize to what height the Lord raises his hearers through the words of the prayer by which he somehow transforms human nature into what is divine? For he lays down that those who approach God should themselves become gods (θεοὺς γινέσθαι). (*Or. Dom.* 5, PG 44. 1177D; trans. Graef)

It is not clear which legislative text Gregory had in mind at this point. Perhaps he was thinking of Matthew 5: 48, 'You must be perfect as your heavenly Father is perfect.' His meaning, however, is clear. As in the treatise *On Virginity*, one is assimilated to God by participation in the divine attributes.

Among the divine attributes beatitude is the property of God par excellence (θεοῦ γὰρ ὡς ἀληθῶς ἴδιον ἡ μακαριότης ἐστιν) (*De Beat.* 5). Participation in the various beatitudes is therefore nothing other than communion with the Godhead (θεότητος κοινωνία). In the fifth homily *On the Beatitudes* Gregory expresses the opinion that through each beatitude the Lord deifies as it were (θεοποιεῖν τρόπον τινά) the person who hears him if that person understands the word rightly (*De Beat.* 5, PG 44. 1249A). The merciful, for example, become blessed because they receive mercy from God. 'If therefore the term "merciful" is suited to God, what else does the Word invite you to become but a god, since you ought to model yourself on the property of the Godhead?' (ibid., 1249B; trans. Graef).

It is also in the homilies *On the Beatitudes* that Gregory first alludes to the sacramental dimension of deification. In the seventh homily he stresses the immense gulf separating the divine nature from humanity. Nevertheless, man becomes akin to God and is received as a son by the Lord of the universe.

> How can one give thanks worthily for such a gift [i.e. of sonship]? With what words, what thoughts that move our mind can we praise this abundance of grace? Man transcends his own nature, he who was subject to corruption in his mortality becomes immune from it in his immortality, eternal from being fixed in time—in a word a god from a man (ἐκβαίνει τὴν ἑαυτοῦ φύσιν ὁ ἄνθρωπος ... θεὸς ἐξ ἀνθρώπου γινόμενος). (*De Beat.* 7, PG 44. 1280C; trans. Graef)

Man transcends his nature by becoming a son of God. It is the sacramental gift bestowed by baptism, rather than any ascent of the soul through philosophy, which Gregory seems to have in mind in this passage. Man does not transcend his nature by his own ascetical effort.

The spiritual meaning of baptism is expounded in the thirty-fifth chapter of the *Great Catechetical Oration* (*c.*385). Our salvation comes not simply from hearing the teaching of Christ but from what he achieved. Christ established a communion with man, becoming incarnate, 'in order that, through the flesh which he assumed and at the same time deified (διὰ τῆς ἀναληφθείσης παρ᾽ αὐτοῦ καὶ συναποθεωθείσης σαρκός) all that is akin to it and of the same nature with it might therewith be saved . . .' (*Or. Cat.* 35, PG 45, 88A, Srawley 130. 4). But this did not take place automatically without some action on the part of the individual believer. Baptism was devised so that the acts accomplished by Christ might be imitated, and thus appropriated, by the Christian.

When he turns to the Eucharist in the thirty-seventh chapter of the *Great Catechetical Oration*, Gregory extends the deification of Christ's body in the Incarnation to the rest of humanity in a similar fashion through the operation of this second sacrament. The union of divine and human in Christ endowed his flesh with true life.

Since, then, that flesh which was the receptacle of deity received this part also in order to maintain itself in being, and the God who manifested himself mingled himself with our mortal nature in order that by communion with his Godhead humanity might at the same time be deified (ἵνα τῇ τῆς θεότητος κοινωνίᾳ συναποθεωθῇ τὸ ἀνθρώπινον), he plants himself, in accordance with his plan of grace, in all believers by means of that flesh, which derives its subsistence from both wine and bread, mingling himself with the bodies of believers in order that, by union with that which is immortal, man also might participate in incorruption.   (*Or. Cat.* 37, PG 45. 97B, Srawley, 152. 1; trans. Srawley)

The humanity that was deified was the flesh of Christ. But that flesh is the same flesh that believers receive in communion. The Eucharist thus enables them to participate in the deifying effect of the Incarnation.

In striking contrast to Gregory of Nazianzus, Gregory does not use the operation of the sacraments as an argument for the *homoousion* of the Son. In fact the only occasion on which he uses any of the verbs 'to deify' in his anti-Arian works is when he faults the Eunomians on their logic. They place the Son on our side of the genetic/agenetic divide. Therefore if they call the Lord 'God' (as they do), they will also deify the rest of creation (καὶ τὴν λοιπὴν κτίσιν θεοποιήσουσιν) (*C. Eunom.* 4, PG 45 629D).

But creation does not partake of divinity. Gregory is never able to say that human beings become gods except in a qualified sense. In *The Life of Moses*, a work of his old age, Gregory discusses the transformation of Moses' right hand and the rod's changing into a snake (Exod. 4: 1–7) as figures of the Incarnation:

He who has some insight into these things right away becomes a god to those who resist the truth (θεὸς ἄντικρυς γίνεται τῶν ἀνθεστηκότων μὲν τῇ ἀληθείᾳ) who have been distracted to a material and unsubstantial delusion. (*V. Mos.* 2. 35, PG 44 336C; trans. Malherbe and Ferguson)

The person who has insight (*perinoia*) becomes a god in an analogous fashion, just as Moses was a god to Pharaoh (Exod. 7: 1).[29] Philo makes a similar point when he says that Moses was god to Pharaoh as a wise man is a god to a fool (*Det.* 162; cf. 3. 2 above).

Three points emerge from this rapid survey of Gregory's deification terms. First, deification for the bishop of Nyssa is primarily a christological term, expressing the transformation of the human nature of Christ by the divine, and it is only in this sense that it is used literally. Secondly, deification is extended to human beings through the sacraments, which bring about a participation in the deified body of Christ. Thirdly, the deification of human beings by participation in the divine attributes is deification in a strictly analogous sense. In all of Gregory's extensive spiritual writings he refers to such participation as θεοποιοῦσα only twice, and in both cases he qualifies it with τρόπον τινά, 'so to speak'.

(c) The Christological Basis of Deification

Gregory's christology, like that of Athanasius, is soteriologically driven.[30] Founded on the Irenaean-Athanasian exchange principle, it holds that the Word became incarnate 'so that by becoming as we are, he might make us as he is' (ἵνα ἐκ τοῦ γενέσθαι οἷος ἡμεῖς ἡμᾶς ποιήσῃ οἷος ἐκεῖνος) (*Antirrh.* 11, GNO III. 1. 146). The way in which this is brought about is expressed in a terminology very personal to Gregory. 'Mixture' language predominates. The Word was 'mingled with humanity' (κατεμίχθη τῇ ἀνθρωπότητι) (*Or. Cat.* 26, Srawley 101. 2–3). He 'infused himself into our nature' (πρὸς τὴν φύσιν ἡμῶν ἀνακιρναμένον) (*Or. Cat.* 27, Srawley 101. 10–11) in order that he should receive from us our human characteristics (ἰδιώματα) of finiteness and mortality, while we received from him his divine characteristics of eternity and incorruptibility. This mingling and communication of idioms does not imply a symmetrical interpenetration of two equal constituents. The divine swallows up the human, in Gregory's famous image, like a drop of vinegar absorbed by a boundless ocean (*Antirrh.* 42, GNO III. 1. 201; *Ad Theoph. adv. Apoll.*, GNO III. 1. 126; *C. Eunom.* 3. 4, GNO II. 150). Nor does it imply the annihilation of the human. The drop of vinegar in the ocean may no longer be perceptible, but nevertheless it still exists. The humanity taken up into the divinity may be transformed and endowed with incorruptibility but it is still human. Some have found this christology unsatisfactory because

---

[29] On *perinoia* as a term for a knowledge that 'is superior to that derived from the observation of material things', yet 'is not quite the same as the knowledge that comes from contemplation of God', see Malherbe and Ferguson, *Life of Moses* 163 n. 51.

[30] In what follows I depend heavily on Daley 1997.

it does not seem to do justice to the kenotic aspect of the Incarnation (e.g. Grillmeier 1975: 376). Others are impressed by Gregory's powerful vision of the saving reality of a God who, making humanity his own, transforms and exalts it (e.g. Daley 1997: 95).

The language of deification would have sat easily with such a christology but Gregory uses it very sparingly. The reason is probably connected with his struggle against Apollinarianism. Apollinarius' teaching on Christ as embodied deity and deified body (θεὸς σεσωματωμένος καὶ σῶμα τεθεωμένον), the Word taking the place of a human *nous* as Christ's directing principle, was totally unacceptable to Gregory because it depreciated both the divinity and the humanity of Christ. On the one hand, omnipotent divinity was reduced to being the directing principle merely of a circumscribed body. On the other, humanity was deprived of its highest principle, with the result that what was saved was no different in essence from a horse or an ox. Any language which suggested Apollinarius' σῶμα τεθεωμένον would therefore have been problematical to Gregory.

The transformation of human nature effected in Christ marks the beginning of a new glorified humanity in which each one of us can participate. Such participation is 'not through some connection conceived of in purely physical terms, or through sharing in some Platonic universal, but through human involvement with Christ in salvation history, especially through faith, baptism and a disciple's imitation'.[31]

(d) The Sacramental Life

Faith and baptism are the necessary means of our laying hold of the new humanity brought about in the risen and transfigured Christ because we are not disembodied spirits but twofold creatures 'compounded of soul and body' (*Or. Cat.* 37, Srawley 141. 1–2). Baptism inserts us into the saving action of Christ by our imitating in the threefold immersion the mystery of Christ's death and resurrection. It is described by Gregory as a recovery of 'the tunic of incorruption', a realization in the individual of the effects of Christ's defeat of death and corruption (*Bapt. diff.*, PG 46 420C). The Eucharist is expounded on similar lines. Since the sacramental elements are identical with the glorified flesh of Christ, they are the source of life for us, the remedy which makes our bodies immortal. Through the Eucharist our bodies participate in incorruption by mingling with Christ's body, for only in this way can the grace of immortality, which belongs properly to Christ alone, be transmitted to others (*Or. Cat.* 37, PG 45 97, Srawley 151–2).

---

[31] Daley 1997: 94. Daley draws attention to Hübner 1974, esp. 1–25 and 95–198 'for a careful discussion and refutation of the overly literal interpretation of Gregory's idea of human solidarity and "physical" redemption found in many histories of dogma' (1997: 94 n. 38). See also Moutsoulas 2000, esp. 99–128.

(e) The Ascent of the Soul to God

As Daniélou has pointed out, Gregory's spiritual doctrine is an extension of his sacramental theology (Musurillo 1961: 22). The soul's faculties, 'raised to the supernatural level by the sacraments', flower in the pursuit of the spiritual life. The flowering of these vivified faculties has a threefold aspect. The soul's purification from the passions and the multiplicity of earthly things raises it to the contemplation of God as true life, true beauty, and true goodness. But contemplation, or *theoria*, is not the goal of the soul's ascent. The soul will pass beyond contemplation into the immediate presence of God through divine love.[32] In his mature works, the *Homilies on the Song of Songs* and the *Life of Moses*, Gregory characterizes these three aspects under the images of light, cloud, and darkness.[33]

The way of light is the purificatory stage. The soul turns away from the deception of the sense to the reality which is God, and bathed in this divine light acquires the gifts of *apatheia* and *parresia*. The way of cloud, which corresponds to the Platonic *theoria*, the contemplation of intelligible reality, is the next stage. Beyond the way of cloud lies the way of darkness. The soul has now been cleansed of its corrosive deposits and has become a mirror reflecting the divine perfection. As Louth puts it, 'the mirror of the soul enables the soul to contemplate by possessing in itself in a created mode what God is in an uncreated mode' (1981: 92). The soul comes to be 'informed by the characteristics of the divine nature' (*Anim. et res.* 105A, trans. Callahan). It clings to the Good and mingles itself with it, having in this way the Trinity dwelling within. Yet God is not possessed. The way of darkness is a way expressing the transcendence and incomprehensibility of God yet at the same time his closeness to the soul. This utter inexhaustibility of God implies a perpetual advance of the soul as it is drawn ever more deeply into the experience of his presence. Gregory's account of Christ's *prokopé*, it should be noted, is a spiritualized one: Christ ever advances in our hearts. The doctrine of *epektasis* represents perfection as a process of constant advance as the soul reaches out to the infinite.

Gregory applies the terminology of deification to the operation of the sacraments and to an aspect of the way of darkness, the 'informing' of the soul with the characteristics of the divine nature. He prefers, however, to discuss the latter in his mature works in terms of participation rather than deification. God is absolute virtue (ἡ παντελὴς ἀρετή). Therefore 'whoever pursues true virtue participates in nothing other than God' (οὐδὲν ἕτερον ἢ Θεοῦ μετέχει) (*V. Mos.* 1. 7, PG 44. 301A). This is not to say that he possesses

---

[32] Cf. Daniélou 1944: 274: 'La vie mystique est faite, inséparablement ... d'un double élément d'intériorité et de transcendance, d'entrée et de sortie, d'instase et d'extase.'

[33] The best introduction to Gregory's doctrine of spiritual ascent is Louth 1981: 80–97. For fuller treatments see von Balthasar 1942, Daniélou 1944, Leys 1951, and Völker 1955.

God for 'since this good has no limit, the participant's desire itself has no stopping place but stretches out with the limitless' (ibid., trans. Malherbe and Ferguson).[34] Nor does the pursuer of virtue participate in the nature of God. It is the attributes or operations of God in which he participates. Gregory never quotes 2 Peter 1: 4. The most he will say is that the Christian *imitates* the nature of God: 'if man was originally a likeness of God, perhaps we have not gone beyond the limit in declaring that Christianity is an imitation of the divine nature' (*Prof. Chr.*, PG 46. 244D; trans. Callahan). This imitation restores the divine likeness in man, but does not allow him to become what God is. The concept of participation enables Gregory to uphold the unapproachable transcendence of God at the same time as man's closeness to him. That is why in his mature works he prefers to speak of 'participation' rather than 'deification'. He seems increasingly to have avoided anything that might tend to compromise God's uncreated transcendence.

(e) Conclusion

The youngest of the three Cappadocians therefore finds the concept of deification in the end inadequate for the paradoxical 'union' of man with God which he wishes to express.[35] Gregory of Nazianzus was able to use the concept of theosis as a frequent metaphor for man's growth towards fulfilment in God. Gregory of Nyssa appears to have been wary of the slightest tendency to compromise the utter transcendence and unknowability of God by the use of the terminology of deification. For him the terminology of participation provides an alternative means of expressing our ever deepening relationship with God through union with his energies, while his nature or essence remains totally beyond our comprehension.

4. The Cappadocian Achievement

The Cappadocians take the doctrine of deification from the Alexandrians and adapt it to a Platonizing understanding of Christianity as the attainment of likeness to God as far as is possible for human nature. They do not make much use of the terminology of the Alexandrians: θεοποιέω is used only twice by Basil, once by Gregory of Nazianzus, and twice by Gregory of Nyssa—Gregory of Nazianzus, the only Cappadocian to speak at all frequently of deification, much preferring to use θεόω and his own coinage,

---

[34] On Gregory's idea of *epektasis* see Daniélou 1944: 309–26.

[35] 'Union' is in inverted commas because *henôsis* is a term which Gregory uses only for the union of Christ with the Church (*Hom. 4 in Cant.*, PG 44. 836D) or the 'union with the immortal' attained by the believer in the Eucharist (*Or. Cat.* 37, PG 45. 97B, Srawley 152.5). As the goal of mystical ascent it is a characteristically Dionysian term. Cf. Meredith 1999: 101: 'The idea of union is peculiar to Denis, though foreign to Gregory.'

θέωσις. Nor do they base themselves on the realistic approach to deification. Only the body of Christ, the ensouled flesh which the Logos assumed, is deified in any literal sense, and even that becomes problematical in the struggle with Apollinarianism. Human beings are deified in a merely ethical or metaphorical sense, the emphasis being as much on the ascent of the soul to God as on the transformation of the believer through baptism.

The realistic approach to deification is important to the two Gregories as a way of holding together the human and the divine elements in their logos-man type of christology. It is this christology which makes it difficult for them to apply the realistic approach to human beings, for the latter would then be insufficiently distinguished from the Son. Basil and Gregory of Nazianzus stress the attaining of the divine likeness by imitation: for them Christianity is the imitation of the incarnate life of Christ. Christ deified the body which he assumed, the purpose of the Incarnation being to enable us to return to the likeness we have lost. But the imitation of God is not simply external. It consists in overcoming the passions and freeing the soul from the constraints of corporeal life, and also in putting on Christ in baptism. We imitate God through the practice of virtue; we also imitate him by clothing ourselves in Christ. Both baptism and the moral life are said to deify. In Gregory of Nyssa's case the concept of participation becomes important. Indeed, the language of participation tends to replace that of deification, man attaining his *telos* by participation in the divine attributes.

All three Cappadocians mention the role of the Eucharist in deification, but only Gregory of Nyssa develops it. In his realistic view of the Eucharist he anticipates Cyril of Alexandria, although he supports it with a different christology. The Godhead deifies the flesh at the Incarnation by commingling with it; this flesh in turn deifies believers by commingling with them when they receive it in eucharistic communion.

The Cappadocian concept of deification is conditioned by their Platonism and their apophatic approach to the Godhead. They took for granted that the attainment of likeness to God was the *telos* of human life. But God remains in his essence utterly beyond human grasp. The deification of the Christian is subordinated to this by being kept to the ethical and analogous levels. For Basil, *theos* is simply a title which God bestows on the worthy. It expresses man's eschatological fulfilment when the whole man, body and soul, will be spiritualized and rendered incorrupt that it may enjoy the vision of God. For Gregory of Nazianzus theosis is man's *telos* brought about on the one hand by the deifying power of the Holy Spirit in baptism, and on the other by the moral struggle in the ascetic life. But we can never become 'gods' in the proper sense, that is to say, we can never bridge the gap between the created and uncreated orders of reality. For Gregory of Nyssa a man becomes a god by imitating the characteristics of the divine nature, by participating in the divine attributes, by modelling himself on the properties of the Godhead. Ultimately he transcends his own nature and becomes immune from corruption and mortality, but Gregory of Nyssa is unwilling to call this 'deification'. Deification for him is fundamentally a christological concept, which by extension may also be applied to the Eucharist.

8

The Monastic Synthesis

The Achievement of Maximus the Confessor

By the early fifth century ecclesiastical writers, with rare exceptions, had ceased to speak of the deification either of the Christian or of the humanity of Christ. The movement away from the language of *deification* towards that of *participation*, which is observable in Gregory of Nyssa, is confirmed by Cyril of Alexandria. In these writers and their immediate successors deification is no longer perceived to be a helpful metaphor. This is probably because of the controversies about the legacies of Origen and Apollinarius that preoccupied many ecclesiastics in the late fourth and early fifth centuries. Basil and Gregory of Nazianzus had attempted to salvage whatever in Origen was compatible with Nicene orthodoxy. Their protégé Evagrius, however, developed the speculative side of Origen far beyond the master, elaborating a theory of the spiritual life as a process which culminated in the return of created intelligences to the divine source of their being. Later the more extreme adherents of Evagrius' version of Origenism were known as 'Isochrists' for believing that at the final apocatastasis the souls of the saved, having become pure intellects, would be equal to Christ himself (Cyril Scyth., *V. Sab.* 197). The Origenism of Evagrius and his fellow Nitrian monks was attacked bitterly by Cyril of Alexandria's uncle, Theophilus, who mounted a campaign against them in collaboration with Jerome and Epiphanius of Cyprus. Theophilus was also drawn by Gregory of Nyssa into the controversy over Apollinarianism (*Ad Theophil. adv. Apollinaristas*, GNO III. 1. 119–28). Evagrius had not spoken of deification by name. But for Apollinarius the deification of the flesh by the Word summarized his profoundly held conviction that the highest part of the soul in Christ had been replaced by the Word as its governing principle. His teaching was condemned by councils held in Rome (377), Antioch (379), and Constantinople (381) (cf. Raven 1923: 144–8). By Cyril's time it could well have been thought that the term θεοποίησις, even though sanctioned by the great Athanasius himself, no longer carried the right connotations.

Cyril's abandoning of the language of deification is all the more remarkable for the fact that he did so in spite of its impeccably Alexandrian provenance. Non-Alexandrians, with one possible exception, make no use of the technical terms except under the influence of Clement, Origen, or Athanasius.[1] Besides those treated in detail in the present study, mention may be made of Gregory Thaumaturgus, Methodius of Olympus, Eusebius of Caesarea, Cyril of Jerusalem, and Macarius Magnes. Gregory Thaumaturgus (d. *c.*270), who had been a pupil of Origen, referred to his master's teaching as a 'method for the attaining of a kind of apotheosis' (*Pan.* 11, PG 10. 1084C, Koetschau 27). Methodius of Olympus in Lycia (d. 311), commenting on the Jewish Feast of Tabernacles in an allegorical style very like Origen's, takes green branches of the booths to be the boughs of chastity, 'that deifying and blessed tree' (τῷ θεοποιῷ καὶ μακαρίῳ φυτῷ) (*Symp.* 9. 4, PG 18. 188A; GCS 27. 119). Chastity, bringing immortality to our souls, enables the pure to be made gods by God and contemplate him face to face, for only like can know like (*Symp.* 9. 3). Later Methodius was to turn against Origen, but there is no sign of this in the *Symposium* (cf. Patterson 1997*b*: 130). Eusebius of Caesarea (d. *c.*340) was a warm admirer of Origen (cf. *HE* 6). Under Origen's influence he declares that the Christ is the image of the invisible God deified by his Father (*Dem. Evang.* 5. 4, PG 22. 372BC, Heikel 225. 10. 13. 24). Although he does not mention the deification of the Christian, he comes near to it when he speaks of 'participation in the radiant splendour of the Godhead' (*De eccles. theol.* 3. 18, PG 24. 1041BC; GCS 4. 179. 34–6). Cyril of Jerusalem (d. *c.* 386) reveals a similar tendency. He describes the Holy Spirit as deifying in the manner of Athanasius (ἐν τὸ πνεῦμα τὸ ἅγιον, τὸ πάντων ἁγιαστικὸν καὶ θεοποιόν) (*Catech.* 4. 16, PG 33. 476A). But when he refers to the 'gods' of Psalm 82: 6, it is only to note that this is simply a titular appellation (*Catech.* Procatech. 6; cf. *Catech.* 11. 4). Macarius Magnes (fl. 400) is different. His intention was to answer Neoplatonist attacks on Christianity. Like other Platonizing writers, he speaks of the deification of the human intellect (*Apocrit.* 3. 23; 4. 26, Blondel 105. 28; 212. 21). After the Resurrection Christ exalted human nature, making what was mortal immortal, what was earthly unearthly, what was enslaved free, what was compounded uncompounded, in short, making man a god (*Apocrit.* 3. 14, Blondel 90. 10–13). This 'man' (ἄνθρωπος) was Christ's human nature. As far as the exaltation of the individual believer is concerned, Macarius says that he who honours his Maker deifies himself by participating in the Godhead (ἑαυτὸν δ' ἀποθεοῖ κοινωνῶν τῇ θεότητι) like someone basking in the sun or warming

---

[1] The exception is Hippolytus. Although nothing is known of his early life, it would have been strange if he had not had contact with Alexandria. Certainly his name was well known there. When Origen came to Rome in about 212, he made a point of going to hear him preach (Eusebius, *HE* 6. 14. 10). All other writers who use the language of deification can be shown to depend at least in this respect on the Alexandrian tradition.

himself by a fire (*Apocrit.* 4. 16, Blondel 186. 3–11). This participation in God in the Platonic manner is reminiscent of Origen (although the dynamic aspect characteristic of Origen is lacking), as is also Macarius' statement that the Logos makes rational beings gods in virtue of his being God, and christs in virtue of his being Christ (ὁ Θεὸς Λόγος τοὺς λογικοὺς θεοὺς ἐργαζόμενος, πῇ δὲ χριστοὺς ὡς Χριστός) (*Apocrit.* 4. 18, Blondel 197. 6).

The great Antiochene fathers never use the term 'deification' at all. That is not to say they repudiated the the Irenaean themes of divine sonship by grace and recapitulation in Christ. John Chrysostom (d. 407), for example, takes it for granted that the gods of Psalm 82: 6 refer to the baptized (e.g. *Hom. in Jo.* 3. 2; 14. 2). But we are gods only in a titular sense. Theodore of Mopsuestia (d. 428) spells this out very clearly. Although the baptized may be called gods (*Cat. Hom.* 3. 11; 4. 10; 11. 8; 14. 24), it is only at the resurrection that we will appropriate the divine attributes of immortality and immutability (*Cat. Hom.* 5. 20; 11. 7; 14. 24). The resurrection is a second spiritual birth that completes the first spiritual birth of baptism. Theodore uses an analogy from the human reproductive process (as understood in antiquity) to explain the relationship between the two. Our first physical birth from the male (the male semen having no human resemblance) is completed by our second physical birth from the female (in whom the human form is fashioned). Similarly, our first spiritual birth of baptism is completed by our second spiritual birth of resurrection, when we achieve our full human development through being transformed into an immortal and immutable nature (*Cat. Hom.* 14. 28). Without the Alexandrian soteriological perspective, deification can only be presented as a remote eschatological event.[2]

With Cyril's death in 444 deification disappears from view. In the search after Chalcedon to find a way of making the council's Definition acceptable to the monophysites, only Leontius of Jerusalem refers to it. Deification was perhaps felt to give too much away to Apollinarianism and Eutychianism. It reappears at the beginning of the sixth century with Dionysius the Areopagite, through whom an influence from the pagan Neoplatonist Proclus also enters into the Christian tradition, and is then used with great frequency by Maximus the Confessor in the seventh century. Maximus' achievement was to reclaim deification for the Byzantine Church. He abandoned the christological use of the term and developed it in a completely new way, making it central to his teaching for a monastic audience on the ascent of the soul. In so doing, he built on the work of Cyril and the Cappadocians, drawing also on Evagrius Ponticus, the Macarian Homilies, Diadochus of Photice, and Dionysius the Areopagite. These last four merit attention before we turn to Maximus himself.

---

[2] On the Antiochene approach to deification in general, see Gross 1938: 253–75; and on Theodore of Mopsuestia in particular, Keating 2004: 206–27.

1. Evagrius Ponticus

The reputation of Evagrius Ponticus (346–99), the chief theoretician of the monastic life in the late fourth century, suffered after his death from his thoroughgoing Origenism. His condemnation in 553 by the anti-Origenist Fifth Ecumenical Council has meant that those of his works that have come down to us survived under various pseudonyms. In his lifetime, however, he had many admirers. Rufinus, who met him on the Mount of Olives, calls him 'a most learned man, wonderful in every way' (*Hist. Mon.* 22, PL 21. 448). Palladius, who was his disciple in his last years, calls him a 'spirit-bearing and discerning man' (*HL* 11. 5). Socrates thought him an excellent man and the writer of books of a very valuable nature (*HE* 4. 23).

According to Palladius (*HL* 38. 2), Evagrius was born in Ibora in Pontus, the son of a chorepiscopus.[3] He became a disciple of the Cappadocians, being ordained reader by Basil and deacon by Gregory of Nazianzus, to whom he attached himself after Basil's death. He accompanied Gregory to Constantinople in 379, but in the capital had an experience that shipwrecked a potentially brilliant ecclesiastical career. He fell in love with a highly placed married woman, as he himself told Palladius, and the attachment seems to have been reciprocated. Delivered from his infatuation by the vision of an angel, he fled to Palestine, where he stayed with Melania at her monastery on the Mount of Olives. A critical illness, more psychological than physical, made him decide to adopt the eremitical life. On being nursed back to health by Melania, he left Jerusalem for Nitria in 383. After two years there he withdrew to the more secluded settlement of Kellia, where he lived an ascetic life for a further fourteen years.

Although Evagrius regarded himself as a disciple of Gregory of Nazianzus, he did not adopt Gregory's approach to deification. Nor does the technical language of deification appear in his writings. When he refers to the gods of Psalm 82: 6 in his dogmatic letter on the Holy Trinity (Ps.-Basil, *Ep.* 8), it is merely to emphasize that in the Bible human beings are called gods in a metaphorical sense only (κατὰ χάριν—here contrasted with the demons, who are gods ψευδῶς). The divine is not simply humanity writ large. It is of a different order of reality altogether, for which human language is totally inadequate: 'the ineffable must be worshipped in silence' (*Gnostikos* 41, SC 356. 166). And in order to approach the ineffable, a full programme of spiritual training is necessary: first the passions must be eliminated and then the mind purified of all material images.

This programme, leading to the ascent of the mind of God, is mapped out by Evagrius in the letter to Anatolius, which stands as the prologue to his

---

[3] On the life of Evagrius see Guillaumont, SC 170: 21–8.

trilogy on the monastic life, the *Praktikos*, the *Gnostikos*, and the *Kephalaia gnostika*:

Faith, children, [the desert fathers say,] is confirmed by the fear of God, and the fear of God in turn by continence, and continence is made unswerving by patience and hope, from which dispassion is born, the fruit of which is love, and love is the door to natural science (γνώσεως φυσικῆς) which is succeeded by theology (θεολογία) and the ultimate blessedness (ἡ ἐσχάτη μακαριότης). (*Praktikos*, Prol. 8, SC 171. 492)

The first stage is *praktikê*, the struggle against the passions, which has love as its goal, the second *gnôsis*, which aims at the attainment of theology (*Praktikos* 84). The first stage is dominated by the combat against the demons, the false gods of the Old Testament, each of whom is a specialist in some vice or other. On the opposite side are the angels, who assist us by inspiring us with good thoughts (*Praktikos* 80) and by suggesting the spiritual pleasures that are the source of our felicity (*Praktikos* 24). They rejoice when evil diminishes, acting as ministers to us of mercy and love (*Praktikos* 76). Senior monks perform a similar role: 'Our elders should be honoured as angels; it is they who anoint us for combat' (*Praktikos* 100).

The second stage, parallel to the first rather than consecutive to it, takes place against the background of this spiritual warfare. The struggle against the passions prepares the monk for contemplation (θεωρία) (*Praktikos* 36), but so long as he is still in the world the struggle must not be abandoned. *Gnôsis* begins as the contemplation of the essential natures of created things and rises through insight into incorporeal natures to the contemplation of God himself. Gradually the higher part of the soul is stripped of all images as it ascends to its ultimate goal. 'Knowledge of incorporeals', says Evagrius, 'raises the mind and presents it before the Holy Trinity' (*Ad monachos* 136; trans. Driscoll). The vision of God is the final beatitude (cf. *Gnostikos* 13). But the divine is not susceptible of definition (*Gnostikos* 27). The vision is a purely intellectual joy beyond any expression in words (*Gnostikos* 41) or images (Ps.-Basil, *Ep.* 8. 7). Any attempt to attain a sensory experience even of the angels or of Christ will only lead to demonic delusion (Ps.-Nilus, *De Orat.* 115, PG 79. 1192D–1193A). Moreover, the ultimate felicity is available only as an eschatological reality (Ps.-Basil, *Ep.* 8. 7). True prayer may assimilate the monk to the angelic life—ἰσάγγελος γίνεται μοναχὸς διὰ τῆς ἀληθοῦς προσευχῆς (Ps.-Nilus, *De Orat.* 113, PG 79. 1192D)—but 'the knowledge beyond which no other knowledge exists' transcends even the attenuated materiality of the angels and is attainable only on the 'last day', when the intellect sheds its covering of clay and makes the final transition from material knowledge to immaterial contemplation. 'For only then is our mind arisen, and awakened to sublime felicity, when it shall contemplate the "Oneness" and the "Alone-ness" of the Word' (ὁπηνίκα ἂν θεωρήσῃ τὴν ἑνάδα καὶ μονάδα τοῦ Λόγου) (Ps.-Basil, *Ep.* 8. 7; trans. Deferrari), which is the Father.

Although Evagrius never mentions Origen, the influence of Origen's more speculative writings is profound. This influence may have come to him through his patron Gregory of Nazianzus, whose decisive role in his intellectual development he acknowledges (*Praktikos*, Epil.; *Gnostikos* 44; cf. Socrates, *HE* 6. 30) and also through his older contemporary Didymus the Blind, whom he calls 'the great Gnostic teacher' (*Gnostikos* 48). In the latter part of his life he was, with one of the Tall Brothers, Ammonius, who was famous for having committed to memory many thousands of lines of Origen, Pierius, and Didymus (Palladius, *HL* 11. 4), the leader of an Origenist group at Kellia (Palladius, *HL* 24. 2). The radical Origenism promoted by this group provoked Theophilus' anti-Origenist campaign, which resulted in the condemnation of Origenism by an Alexandrian synod in 400. By then Evagrius was dead but his more speculative ideas continued to be influential in monastic circles through the dissemination of his *Kephalaia gnostika*.

The Origenist controversy resurfaced again in the sixth century in a struggle between rival monastic groups that culminated in the condemnation of Origenism at the Fifth Ecumenical Council of 553. In 543 the Emperor Justinian had already issued an Edict against Origen which had condemned nine propositions drawn from the *De Principiis*. The anathemas of 553 were directed more against the radical Origenism developed by Evagrius in his *Kephalaia gnostika*. What disturbed the fathers most were Evagrius' speculations concerning the pre-existence, fall, and restoration of souls together with the christology that this scheme entailed. According to the fifteen anathemas the Origenists held that all intelligent beings—Christ, the angels, human beings, and demons—formed a spiritual continuum which pre-existed the Fall and would one day be restored to its first state. These created intelligences (*noes*) lost their original unity when divine love grew cool in them. Those whose ardour diminished the least, namely, the angels, have the most subtle bodies. Those who grew cooler than the angels became human souls enclosed in material bodies.[4] Those who grew coldest of all became the demons. Only a single *nous* remained steadfast in the contemplation of God and that unfallen *nous* became Christ. The divine Word did not take a human body endowed with a rational soul. On the contrary, this unfallen *nous* (*Nous* as opposed to the *noes*) united himself to the Word and became Christ through the knowledge of the Monad conferred on him by the union. At the end of time matter will cease to exist. Only the *noes* will be left, now rendered purely spiritual and thus able to return to their original undifferentiated unity. By implication all human beings would become the same as Christ, contemplating the Monad as *Nous* without any intermediary.[5]

---

[4] Cf. Origen, who connects ψυχή with ψύχεσθαι, to grow cold (*De Prin.* 2. 8. 3). Origen's etymology is derived from Aristotle, *De Anima* 1. 2. 405^b.

[5] See also Evagrius' *Letter to Melania*, where he presents the *noes* as flowing back to God like rivers to the sea (*Ep. Melan.* 6).

This gnosticizing approach to deification, which sees the goal of the spiritual life as total assimilation to Christ through the shedding of the material element that accounts for individuation, was decisively rejected by the fathers of the Fifth Ecumenical Council.

2. The Macarian Writings

A very different outlook informs the Macarian writings, an outlook based not on Platonic intellectualism but on a Spirit-centred immanentism. These texts, which survive in three collections comprising homilies, *erotapocriseis* (Questions and Answers), and a short ascetical treatise (the *Epistula Magna*), are by an unknown author writing probably in the 380s, perhaps in Mesopotamia or the eastern part of Asia Minor.[6] In the Greek tradition they have always circulated under the name of Macarius.[7] This was not a deliberate pseudonym but probably reflects the use of *makarios* as an ecclesiastical title, which was then taken to be a personal name and identified with Macarius of Egypt. The environment in which the writings were produced, however, was that of Syrian monasticism. The language is full of the rich poetic imagery characteristic of Syriac literature, and also exhibits many of the traits of the Syrian encratite tradition. In view of this background, the relationship of the texts to Messalianism has been much debated. The consensus today is that Messalianism was not a self-conscious heresy but represents one extreme at the end of the broad spectrum of Syrian monasticism. The Macarian texts perhaps deliberately offer a corrective to the Messalian position, mitigating its dualist tendencies and its disdain of the sacraments (Stewart 1991: 9–11).

The Messalians, so far as we can tell (they left no texts of their own), believed that the soul at birth was occupied by a demon. Baptism alone did not suffice to dislodge it. The only sure remedy was continuous prayer.[8] Everything which hindered such prayer was rejected. This meant that in their understanding of the monastic life manual labour was excluded. The emphasis fell entirely on attaining a personal experience of the Holy Spirit, an experience which manifested itself in ecstatic forms of devotion. For it was only the experience of the Spirit that guaranteed salvation.[9]

Macarius also emphasizes the experiential side of the spiritual life and the role of the Holy Spirit, but without the hostility to normal ecclesial structures that seems to have marked out the Messalians. He presents the spiritual

---

[6] On the three collections see Stewart 1991: 70–4.

[7] In the Arabic tradition they are assigned to Symeon of Mesopotamia.

[8] Hence the name 'Messalians' from a Syriac word meaning 'the praying ones', which Greek writers also Hellenized as 'Euchites'.

[9] For the sources that enable us to reconstruct Messalian belief see Stewart 1991: 52–69.

life as a process which may be thought of as consisting of three stages. In the first, although we have turned to God, the heart is still dominated by sin. In the second the heart becomes a battleground between the divine power on the one hand and sin on the other. In the third stage sin is driven out by the co-operation of the human will with the power of the Holy Spirit. This final stage, in which the perfect Christian is raised to a state higher than that enjoyed originally by Adam, is described by Macarius on occasion as 'deification'.

(a) Vocabulary

The Homilies apply θεοποιέω once (Coll. I, *Hom.* 2. 12. 6) to the deified body of Christ by which believers are saved, and ἀποθεόω twice (Coll. II, *Homs.* 15. 35. 496 and 26. 2. 19) to the effect on the believer of participation in the Holy Spirit. Believers are also sometimes called 'gods' (Coll. II, *Homs.* 17. 1. 8; 27. 3. 47; 34. 2. 29) in the context of the final fulfilment of the eschatological life, in which the Father is revealed as Lord of lords, King of kings, and God of gods.

A notable feature of the Homilies is their frequent use of metaphors of both mingling and participation, although without sensitivity to their different philosophical backgrounds.[10] Citations of 2 Peter 1: 4 ('partakers of the divine nature') appear, uniquely in patristic literature, alongside discussions using the vocabulary of mixing and mingling.[11] With regard to the relationship between the human and the divine in the spiritual life, Macarius seems to have been equally happy with metaphors both of interpenetration and of transformation.

(b) Deification Texts

For Macarius the deification of the human person signifies his or her eschatological fulfilment through the sanctifying power of the Holy Spirit. The Spirit restores us not merely to what was lost by the Fall but to a state superior to that of Adam. An *erotapocrisis* sums this up as follows:

Question: Is it not so that when the Holy Spirit comes, the natural desire is uprooted along with the sin?

Answer: I have already said that not only is the sin uprooted but humankind also receives again the first creation of the pure Adam. By the power of the Spirit and the spiritual regeneration, humankind in this way comes to the measure of the first Adam and becomes greater than him. For humankind is deified (ἀποθεοῦται). (Coll. II, *Hom.* 26. 2)

---

[10] On the language of mingling and participation in the homilies see Stewart 1991: 170–88, 285–7.

[11] 2 Peter 1: 4 is quoted in Collection I (Berthold) in *Hom.* 40. 1. 99 and *Hom.* 44. 5. 6; in Collection II (Dörries, Klostermann, and Kroeger) in *Hom.* 25. 5; 39. 1; 44. 9 (bis); and 49. 3; and in Collection III (Klostermann and Berthold) in *Hom.* 8. 2 and 16. 6.

The process by which this takes place is through the struggle to overcome the sin that is lodged in the soul. For from the time of Adam the soul has become the dwelling place of the serpent. It is only when one renounces one's own will that the soul is brought under control:

Such a person is counted worthy to arrive at the good measure of the Spirit and receives through the divine power a pure humanity (τὸν καθαρὸν ἄνθρωπον) and becomes greater than himself. For such a person is deified (ἀποθεοῦται) and becomes a son of God, receiving the heavenly imprint in his soul. For God's elect are anointed with sanctifying oil and become officeholders and kings. (Coll. II, *Hom.* 15. 35)

Their being anointed with oil makes them christs (Coll. II, *Hom.* 17. 1; 34. 2; 43. 1). And their becoming christs means that they have been regenerated by the Spirit and re-formed into a new humanity, for 'all are transformed into a divine nature (εἰς θεϊκὴν γὰρ φύσιν ἅπαντες μεταβάλλονται), having become christs and gods and children of God' (Coll. II, *Hom.* 34. 2). 'All in joy, in gladness and in peace are kings and lords and gods. For it is written: "King of kings and Lord of lords"' (Coll. II, *Hom.* 27. 3).[12]

The perfect sovereignty of God over the redeemed implies that they attain, as it were, a community of being with him. Macarius expresses this on several occasions through participation language. When the soul receives the sanctification of the Spirit through faith and prayer, it becomes 'a partaker of the divine nature' (2 Pet. 1: 4) (Coll. II, *Hom.* 44. 9). The gift of participation given by God is 'from the hypostasis of his Godhead' (ἐκ τῆς ὑποστάσεως τῆς θεότητος αὐτοῦ) (Coll. II, *Hom.* 39). It is given when we have attained the likeness of the Lord, when we have been wounded by divine love (Coll. II, *Hom.* 25. 5). For then our souls are changed and re-created (Coll. II, *Hom.* 44. 9; 49. 3), having communed with the Holy Spirit and been commingled with him (Coll. II, *Hom.* 32. 6).

(c) The Perfect Christian

For Macarius participation, blending, and mingling are images expressing intimacy with the divine without any implications, on the philosophical level, about the ontological status of the believer. Who is the perfect Christian? It is the person who, in Pauline terms, has put on the perfect man, the τέλειος ἄνθρωπος, namely Jesus Christ (Coll. II, *Hom.* 2. 4; cf. Rom. 13: 14; Eph. 4: 13, 24). This enables the believer to recover the heavenly image which was lost in Adam. But such perfection is provisional. The struggle against evil must continue right up to death.

Some think they are perfect because of their celibacy and detachment from material things (Coll. II, *Hom.* 17. 13). They are mistaken. These

---

[12] The quotation is from 1 Timothy 6: 15, but the 'kings and lords and gods' implies an allusion to 1 Enoch 9: 4.

achievements are merely external matters. There is still evil in the heart which even the greatest ascetic must guard against (ibid.; cf. Coll. II, *Hom.* 8. 5; 15. 16). A saint, says Macarius, is a person who has been sanctified in his or her inner self (κατὰ τὸν ἔσω ἄνθρωπον) (Coll. II, *Hom.* 17. 13) as a result of unceasing dedication to the cross of Christ (Coll. II, *Hom.* 17. 1). Moreover, there are degrees of perfection (μέτρα τελειότητος) (ibid.). In a remarkable passage, which seems to draw on personal experience, Macarius speaks of twelve steps 'as it were' that a person must pass through in order to reach perfection (Coll. II, *Hom.* 8. 4). The twelfth step, however, is experienced only in a fleeting way. Grace comes from time to time and then recedes again. Otherwise the mystic would simply sit in a corner permanently enraptured and intoxicated (μετέωρον καὶ μεμεθυσμένον) and would cease to attend to his practical responsibilities (Coll. II, *Hom.* 8. 4; cf. *Hom.* 18. 7). No one is perfect in the sense of enjoying an uninterrupted communion with God.

These observations are made in the course of answering a series of questions. The next question probes further: 'Tell us about yourself. In what grade do *you* find yourself?' The author in his reply refers to a personal experience of the sign of the cross, 'which appeared as light and penetrated the inner man' (Coll. II, *Hom.* 8. 3). After this experience he felt a deep peace spread throughout his being and sensed a profound love for all men, including pagans and Jews. A person who has had such an experience puts his whole trust in Christ,

and doors are opened to him and he enters into many mansions, and the further he goes in the more doors are opened to him. From a hundred mansions he enters into another hundred, and becomes enriched, and the more he becomes enriched, again other newer wonders are shown to him, and things are entrusted to him as a son and heir which may not be expressed by human nature or uttered by mouth or tongue. (Coll. II, *Hom.* 8. 6)

This is the *epektasis*, the never-ending progress into the mysteries of the spiritual life, that we also find in Gregory of Nyssa. In Gregory, however, the progress is from light through the cloud into darkness. In Macarius it is towards an ever-increasing perception of divine light.

The experiential side of the spiritual life is brought out with dramatic effect by Macarius in his exegesis of Ezekiel's vision of the throne-chariot of God (Ezek. 1: 1–28). He does not say that he ascended personally into heaven to participate in the vision himself, in the manner of the *yored merkavah*, but he does suggest how the biblical text may be appropriated by the believer and made part of his or her own experience:

And that which the prophet actually saw was true and certain. But it was signifying something else and prefiguring a mystical and divine reality, a 'mystery truly hidden for ages and generations' (Col. 1: 26) and revealed in these last days with the coming of Christ. For the prophet was contemplating a mystery of the soul that was to receive its own Lord and become a throne of glory to him. For a soul that is counted worthy to participate in the Spirit of his light and is illuminated by the beauty of his ineffable glory, seeing that he has prepared it for himself as a throne and dwelling, becomes wholly light, and wholly face, and wholly eye. And there is no part of it that is not full of the spiritual eyes of light. That is to say, no part of it is in darkness, but has been turned entirely and completely into light and spirit. And it is wholly full of eyes since it has no backward or rear part, but faces forward in every way, seeing that the ineffable beauty of the glory of the light of the face of Christ has mounted it and sat upon it [. . .]. Thus the soul is illuminated perfectly by the ineffable beauty of the glory of the face of Christ and has participated perfectly in the Holy Spirit, and has been counted worthy to become a throne and dwelling of God. (Coll. II, *Hom.* 1. 2)

The theophany of Ezekiel's vision is linked with that of Christ's transfiguration, and in a remarkable spiritual exegesis, which perhaps owes something to the Jewish Merkabah tradition, the throne-chariot becomes the human soul which God takes possession of and makes his dwelling.

We may therefore say that the deification of the believer takes place in three stages. In the first the soul participates in divine glory even in this life through sharing in the Holy Spirit, having been born from above from God and become a child of God (Coll II, *Hom.* 5. 4). But on the experiential level this gives us only a fleeting foretaste of what is to come. The second stage occurs when the soul is resurrected and glorified at the time of death (Coll II, *Hom.* 34. 2; 36. 1). When we lay aside the body we will not be naked because we shall be clothed by the Holy Spirit (Coll II, *Hom.* 5. 8). The third stage occurs at the end of time when the body, too, will share in the glory of the soul:

But at the resurrection of bodies, the souls of which were previously raised and glorified, the bodies will also be glorified and illuminated with them by the soul which has already been illuminated and glorified. For the Lord is their house and tabernacle and city. They will put on the heavenly dwelling not made by human hands (cf. 2 Cor. 5: 1–2), the glory of divine light, since they have become children of light. They will not regard each other with a wicked eye. For wickedness has been rooted out. 'There is neither male nor female there, neither slave nor free' (Gal. 3: 28), for all have been transformed into a divine nature and have become christs and gods and children of God. (Coll II, *Hom.* 34. 2; cf. 5. 12)

All, however, will still retain their individuality, otherwise 'there will be no Peter or Paul' but 'everything will be God' (Coll. II, *Hom.* 15. 10). The absorption of the individual into the Godhead, condemned by Timothy of Constantinople as a Messalian proposition (No. 11, PG 86. 49c), is specifically excluded.

3. Diadochus of Photice

In Diadochus, who became bishop of Photice in Old Epirus some time
between 451 and 458,[13] the ascetical theory of Evagrius Ponticus is combined with the experiential emphasis of Macarius to produce an impressive
exposition of the stages of the spiritual life leading up to the final consummation of deification.

(a) Vocabulary

The technical vocabulary of deification appears only in the *Sermon on the
Ascension*. Diadochus reserves it for the eschatological state of the human
person, which is not discussed directly in his major work, the *Gnostic Century*.
In the *Sermon* there is a single instance of the otherwise unrecorded verb
θεωθέω, which, if the manuscript tradition is correct, is Diadochus' own
intensified form of the verb θεόω (*Ascen.* 6, SC 5 ter. 1145D).

(b) Progress from Image to Likeness

Diadochus makes a distinction between image and likeness. The image of
God resides in the higher part of the soul and belongs to us in virtue of our
creation (*Perf.* 78). This image was darkened by the Fall, which not only
produced 'wrinkles' on the soul but also made the body subject to corruption. The Word of God became incarnate in order to remedy this situation.
Through his baptism he granted us the waters of salvation. Baptism regener-
ates us by the operation of the life-giving Spirit, purifying us in body and
soul. Against the Messalians Diadochus says that 'it is not possible for the
soul, since it is a unity and of a simple character, to have two *prosopa* in it, as
some have thought' (*Perf.* 78). There are no warring principles in the soul of
good and evil. Baptism, the 'bath of incorruption', drives out the serpent.
But it does not follow that we no longer have to engage in the moral struggle.
The 'bath of holiness' may remove the 'wrinkle' of sin but it does not change
the duality of our will. The ascetic struggle is still necessary. Nevertheless,
baptism refurbishes the image of God within us and makes possible our
subsequent spiritual development

Growth in the spiritual life is represented by Diadochus as an ascent from
the image to the likeness, as a recovery through the acquisition of the virtues,
of humanity's original closeness to God. Diadochus conveys the nature of
this ascent by a striking simile. The difference between the image and the
likeness resembles the difference between a cartoon and a finished portrait.
First the artist draws an outline in a single colour. This is the image. Then he
paints in the flesh tones and renders the effect of the hair, giving the portrait

---

[13] Diadochus was not present at the Council of Chalcedon in 451 but he did respond to the
questionnaire the Emperor Leo I sent out in 458, the answers to which are recorded in the *Codex encyclius*.

its resemblance to the sitter, even down to the way he or she smiles. This is the likeness (*Perf.* 89). In more analytical terms the progress from image to likeness may be divided into three stages. Baptism merely conceals grace in the soul of the baptized. The first stage of its operation is when the whole person turns to the Lord. It is then that grace first makes itself felt in the heart as a sensible warmth. The second stage is when a person begins to advance in his or her observance of the commandments, ceaselessly calling upon the name of the Lord Jesus. In this stage divine grace is perceived as a fire burning up the tares growing on the soil of the human heart. The third stage is when a person has clothed himself or herself in all the virtues, and especially in perfect detachment from possessions. In this final stage grace illuminates the believer's entire nature, being experienced as a profound feeling firing him or her with an intense love for God (*Perf.* 85).

Diadochus' use of the imagery of light and fire is particularly noteworthy. Through the acquisition of virtue we advance 'from glory to glory' (*Perf.* 89; cf. 2 Cor. 3: 18). Each degree of glory is accompanied by a greater intensity of illumination. We shall know when we have reached perfection, says Diadochus, because 'we shall recognize the perfection of the likeness from the illumination' (*Perf.* 89). In the final stages, when the intellect begins to come frequently under the influence of the divine light, it becomes entirely transparent, with the result that it can see its own light in abundance (*Perf.* 40) (cf. Polyzogopoulos 1985: 96/198).

(c) Arrival at Perfection

To be perfect is to be permeated with the light and love of God. Indeed, the person who has reached perfection is wholly transformed by such love:

Such a person is present in life and at the same time not present. For although he is dwelling in his own body, he is dwelling out of it through love, in virtue of the ceaseless movement of the soul towards God. For henceforth, his heart burning with love, he steadfastly cleaves to God by a compelling desire, as if stepping outside (ὡς ἐκστάς) love of self through the love of God. (*Perf.* 14)

Yet even this exalted state is not called deification. God always remains hidden so long as we are still living the embodied life. It is only at the end of time that the perfect enter into the fullest communion with God. Of particular significance in this context is the dual nature of the incarnate Word. In a passage critical of monophysite christology, Diadochus emphasizes the corporeal character of the ascension of the Lord. He was 'taken up in glory' (1 Tim. 3: 16) as man, in order not to violate the laws of human nature, which is why the saints will be caught up in the clouds to meet the Lord in the air (1 Thess. 4: 17).

For it is fitting with regard to God who was made incarnate through the body, that this should also be the experience of those who are to be deified (τοῖς θεωθησομένοις) through the abundance of his grace, God having generously decided to make men gods. (*Ascen.* 6, 1145D)

This transformation, although only possible as an eschatological reality, is nevertheless only a return to what we once enjoyed: 'We are changed not into what we were not, but into what we were, having been renewed in glory by the transformation' (*Ascen.* 6, 1148A).

4. Dionysius the Areopagite

'Dionysius the Areopagite', the unknown Syrian of about 500 CE who, to commend himself to as wide a public as possible, adopted the name of St Paul's Athenian convert (Acts 17: 34) is, after so many centuries, the first to offer a definition of deification: 'theosis is the attaining of likeness to God and union with him so far as possible' (ἡ δὲ θέωσίς ἐστιν ἡ πρὸς θεὸν ὡς ἐφικτὸν ἀφομοίωσις τε καὶ ἕνωσις) (*EH* 1. 3, PG 3. 376A). The Platonism underlying this definition is immediately apparent, but the relationship between Dionysius and his philosophical sources is far from simple. E. R. Dodds's unsympathetic characterization of Dionysius' thought as the philosophy of Proclus dressed in Christian draperies with results that are 'not infrequently grotesque' (1963: xxvi, xxviii) represents a view at one end of the spectrum. At the other, Endre von Ivánka sees Dionysius as a Christian apologist who has merely clothed his thoughts in the fashionable language of the day in order to attract an educated audience (1949). As Andrew Louth has said in a perceptive comment, 'the Dionysian corpus is a landscape that presents very different aspects when looked at in different perspectives . . . [that of the *Ecclesiastical Hierarchy*] is the perspective that dominates the Byzantine reception of Dionysius, but it is undeniable that the corpus looks quite different when perceived from the perspective of the *Divine Names*' (1997: 713). It is within the perspective of the *Ecclesiastical Hierarchy* that Dionysius has set most of his discussions of deification. Surprisingly, perhaps, the more Procline perspective of the *Divine Names*, in which Dionysius sums up the Christian programme as the unification of the whole created order with God through a movement of return effected by a process of purification, illumination, and perfection, is not a perspective in which deification is a central metaphor.[14]

---

[14] Dionysius' dependence on Proclus was proved more than a century ago by J. Stiglmayr and H. Koch. Recently attention has focused on his subsidiary debt to Origen. A. Golitzin (1994), for example, 'makes a very good case for Dionysios' theology as "Neoplatonized Origenism" '(Louth 1997), though without developing his arguments. Some of the more detailed work has been done by I. Perczel (1999 and 2001), who argues with great ingenuity that in many places in *EH* Dionysius has clothed Origenian thought in the language of Proclus. My own findings (cf. 4 (f) below) support the idea of a 'Neoplatonized Origenism'. Dionysius discusses deification in contexts similar to Origen's but gives it a Procline slant.

(a) Vocabulary

Dionysius' usual terms for deification are θέωσις, the noun coined by Gregory of Nazianzus, together with the correlative verb θεόω.[15] This is perhaps remarkable in view of the much closer relationship that is usually noted (e.g. by de Andia 1996: 56–61) between Dionysius and Gregory of Nyssa. Dionysius also uses the Procline terms ἐκθέωσις, ἐκθεόω and ἐκθεωτικός, but these occur only in the *Divine Names*.[16] The adjective θεοποιός is used, but not the correlative noun θεοποίησις or the verb θεοποιέω.[17] Human beings are called θεοί on a number of occasions, chiefly with reference to the biblical 'God of gods' (Deut. 10: 17).[18] Although the concept of participation is important to him, Dionysius makes no appeal to 2 Peter 1: 4.

(b) The Texts

We shall review the texts in the order recommended by Louis Bouyer (1989: 180) and Paul Rorem (1993: 6) and begin with the letters, moving on to the two parallel works on the celestial and ecclesiastical hierarchies, and concluding with the *Divine Names* and its summary, the *Mystical Theology*.

Dionysius introduces the theme of deification in his second letter, addressed to the monk Gaius:

How is it that he who is beyond all things transcends both the source of deity and the source of goodness—if you understand deity and goodness as the substance itself of the gift which makes us good and deifies us (θεοποιοῦ δώρου) and that inimitable imitation of him who transcends deity and goodness by which we are deified and made good (καθ᾽ ὃ θεούμεθα καὶ ἀγαθυνόμεθα)? For if this is taken as the beginning of the deification and becoming good of those who are being deified and made good (εἰ τοῦτο ἀρχὴ γίνεται τοῦ θεοῦσθαι καὶ ἀγαθύνεσθαι τοὺς θεουμένους καὶ ἀγαθυνομένους), then he who is utterly beyond every beginning also transcends what is described here as deity and goodness, since he is the source of deity and goodness. By the same token, he who is inimitable and beyond relations transcends imitations and relations as well as those who imitate and participate. (*Ep.* 2, 1068A –1069A)

Dionysius here summarizes his teaching on deification. It is equivalent to imitating God, to participating in him, and to becoming good. But God transcends these activities and goals. Deification is merely our participation in one of the divine attributes, that of deity, as we strive towards an ultimately unattainable goal.

---

[15] Θέωσις: *CH* 1. 3, 124A; 7. 2, 208C; *EH* 1. 2, 373A; 1. 3, 376A; 1. 4, 376B (bis); 1. 5, 376D; 2. 2, 1, 393A; 2. 2, 6, 404A; 3, 424C; 3. 3. 4, 429D; 3. 3. 7, 433C (bis), 436C; 6. 3. 5, 536C; *DN* 2. 7, 645B ; 2. 8, 645C; 2. 11, 649C; 8. 5, 893A. Θεόω: *Ep.* 2, 1069A (bis); *EH* 1. 2, 372D; 1. 3, 376A (bis); 1. 4, 376B (bis).

[16] Ἐκθέωσις: *DN* 9. 5, 912D; 12. 3, 972A.
Ἐκθεόω: *DN* 1. 5, 593C; 8. 5, 893A.
Ἐκθεωτικός: *DN* 2. 7, 645A.

[17] Θεοποιός: *Ep.* 2, 1068A; *CH* 1. 1, 121A; *DN* 2. 1, 637B; 11. 6, 956B.

[18] Θεοί: *CH* 12. 3, 293B; *DN* 1. 6, 596B; 2. 8, 645C (tris); 2. 11, 649C, 649 D (bis); 12. 1, 969B; 12. 4, 972B.

From this summary we might expect to find the concept of deification restricted to a Platonic attaining of likeness to God. But in fact it is used most frequently in relation to the operation of the sacraments. This theme is developed in the *Ecclesiastical Hierarchy*. But before we review Dionysius' handling of the theme there we must examine another motif which is introduced at the beginning of the *Celestial Hierarchy*.[19] This is the motif of descent and return which had already been developed in elaborate detail by the non-Christian Neoplatonist, Proclus. Dionysius begins not with a philosophical analysis, however, but with a biblical text: 'Every good endowment and every perfect gift is from above, coming down from the Father of lights' (Jas. 1: 17). These divine gifts have the power to unify us and raise us up, returning us 'to the unity and deifying simplicity ($\dot{\epsilon}\nu\dot{o}\tau\eta\tau\alpha$ $\kappa\alpha\grave{\iota}$ $\theta\epsilon\sigma\pi\sigma\iota\grave{o}\nu$ $\dot{\alpha}\pi\lambda\dot{o}\tau\eta\tau\alpha$) of the Father who brings us together' (*CH* 1. 1, 120B).

The way we return is not simply by contemplation. We are embodied beings and need material means to raise us up to contemplate the heavenly hierarchies. On the earthly level, the Father 'brings us together' in the eucharistic assembly. Our earthly hierarchy imitates the heavenly. Lights and incense are images of immaterial light and of the diffusion of concepts like fragrances. The reception of the most divine Eucharist symbolizes our participation in Jesus. The Eucharist is the 'benevolent source of consecration' ($\phi\iota\lambda\dot{\alpha}\nu\theta\rho\omega\pi\sigma\varsigma$ $\tau\epsilon\lambda\epsilon\tau\alpha\rho\chi\dot{\iota}\alpha$) which has been bestowed on us 'on account of our analogous deification' ($\dot{\epsilon}\nu\epsilon\kappa\alpha$ $\tau\hat{\eta}\varsigma$ $\dot{\eta}\mu\hat{\omega}\nu$ $\dot{\alpha}\nu\alpha\lambda\dot{o}\gamma\sigma\upsilon$ $\theta\epsilon\dot{\omega}\sigma\epsilon\omega\varsigma$) (*CH* 1. 3, 124A). In the Eucharist our symbolic deification corresponds to our ascent to angelic unity and simplicity in the noetic sphere.

The celestial analogues of these human participants in the Eucharist are the highest ranks of the angels. They are the pure, the contemplative, the perfect in a real sense because they are filled with a primary and transcendent deification ($\pi\rho\dot{\omega}\tau\eta\varsigma$ $\kappa\alpha\grave{\iota}$ $\dot{\upsilon}\pi\epsilon\rho\chi\sigma\dot{\upsilon}\sigma\eta\varsigma$ $\theta\epsilon\dot{\omega}\sigma\epsilon\omega\varsigma$), that is, they are assimilated to the divine mind through the acquisition of an intuitive rather than a discursive knowledge, which gives them a direct understanding of the heavenly operations (*CH* 7. 2, 208C).

Their corresponding order on earth is the eucharistic community gathered round its bishop. In the opening chapter of the *Ecclesiastical Hierarchy* Dionysius refers to his exposition of the angelic hierarchy and says he will now discuss how the same principles govern the functions of its human analogue. The hierarch and his subordinates present in the liturgy a series of sensory images through which the faithful can rise to the contemplation of the divine. This ascent to God is described as a deification corresponding to unity ($\dot{\epsilon}\nu\sigma\epsilon\iota\delta\hat{\eta}$ $\theta\dot{\epsilon}\omega\sigma\iota\nu$) (*EH* 1. 2, 373A).[20] The hierarch receives deification

---

[19] In Rorem's view the first three chapters of the *Celestial Hierarchy* form a preface to both the *Celestial* and the *Ecclesiastical Hierarchies* (Rorem 1993: 59).

[20] Ἐνοειδής ('of single form' or 'unified') is equivalent in Dionysius to θεοειδής ('deiform' or 'deisimilar'). Cf. Proclus, below.

directly from God and imparts this to those below him according to merit. This hierarchy (a word invented by Dionysius) draws its perfection and inspiration from the hierarch (the bishop). But the source of hierarchy is the Trinity itself, the fount of life and the cause of all that is.

> We should therefore say that the blessedness of the Godhead, that which is deity by nature, that which is the fountainhead of deification (ἀρχὴ τῆς θεώσεως), from which derives the deification of those who are being deified (ἐξ ἧς τὸ θεοῦσθαι τοῖς θεουμένοις) has in its divine goodness bestowed the gift of hierarchy for the salvation and deification of all rational and spiritual beings .... (*EH* 1. 4, 376B)

The first leaders (καθηγέμονες) of the hierarchy (i.e. the apostles), being themselves filled with the divine gift, communicated it in abundance 'like divine beings for the lifting up and deification (ἀναγωγῆς καὶ θεώσεως) of those who came after them. In their written and unwritten initiations (μυήσεσι) they accommodated in a suitable way the divine to the human, the immaterial to the material, the transcendent to the familiar (*EH* 1. 5, 376D).

These symbolic earthly representations of transcendent realities were primarily baptism and the Eucharist. The role of the hierarch is to proclaim to all who desire to be saved that God in his love for humanity (διὰ φιλανθρωπίαν) 'has deigned to come down to us, and, by union with him which is like fire, to assimilate those things which have been unified according to their capacity for deification (πρὸς θέωσιν ἐπιτηδειότητα) "For to all who received him he gave authority to become children of God, who believed in his name, who were born not of blood or of the will of the flesh, but of God" ' (cf. John 1: 12–13) (*EH* 2. 2. 1, 393A).

The baptized initiate is then anointed in preparation for the trials to come. Following in the footsteps of the athletes who preceded him, he overcomes the obstacles that prevent him from attaining deification, for, to put it mystically, in baptism he has died with Christ to sin (*EH* 2. 2. 6, 404A).

After baptism the initiate is ready for the Eucharist 'the supreme sacramental rite' (τελετῶν τελετή) (*EH* 3, 424C). Like the other sacraments, one of its functions is 'to draw our divided lives together into a deification which endows us with unity' (τὰς μεριστὰς ἡμῶν ζωὰς εἰς ἐνοειδῆ θέωσιν συναγούσης) (*EH* 3, 424C). At the Eucharist the participant hears the reading of the scriptures, which culminate, for those who have been made fit for deification, in the transcendent theology of Jesus (i.e. the discourses of St John's Gospel) (τὴν ὑπερκόσμιον Ἰησοῦ θεολογίαν τοῖς πρὸς θέωσιν ἐπιτηδείοις) (*EH* 3. 4, 429D).

The catechumens, the penitents, and the possessed are then dismissed. Those who remain are the baptized in good standing who will participate in the central mystery of the Christian faith:

> For there is no equality, in my view, between someone who is entirely uninitiated and has not even begun to participate in the divine sacraments and someone who has

participated in one or other of the most sacred rites but is still in the grip of charms and disturbances that draw him in the opposite direction. From such people the sight of the most sacred things and communion with them is withheld, and rightly so. For if it is true that the completely divine man (ὁ καθόλου θεῖος ἀνήρ), the man who is worthy to partake of divine things, who has been lifted up to the summit of that which is deiform in itself through complete and perfecting deifications (ἐν παντελέσι καὶ τελειωτικαῖς θεώσεσιν), will not perform what belongs to the flesh except the things which are most necessary in accordance with nature, and then only if he happens to do them in an incidental fashion – such a man will be both a temple and an attendant of the thearchic Spirit through the very intensity of the deification (τῇ κατ' αὐτὸν ἀκροτάτῃ θεώσει) wrought by it, since like dwells in like. (*EH* 3. 3. 7, 433BC).

The final mention of deification in connection with the Eucharist refers to the sacraments in general working a sacred deification (τελεταὶ τὴν ἱερὰν τῶν τελουμένων θέωσιν ἱερουργοῦσαι) (*EH* 3. 7, 436C). Beyond that there is only one other occurrence of the term in the theological commentary on the consecration of a monk. Dionysius, referring to clerical ordination in general, says that all the sacred orders participate proportionately in the most divine gift of communion 'for their own lifting up and perfection of deification' (πρὸς τὴν οἰκείαν αὐτῶν τῆς θεώσεως ἀναγωγὴν καὶ τελείωσιν) (*EH* 6, Theoria 5, 536C).

When we turn to the *Divine Names* we encounter for the first time the vocabulary characteristic of Proclus, the *ek*- forms ἐκθεόω, ἐκθέωσις and ἐκθεωτικός. This is connected with the philosophical interests of the *Divine Names*, which are centred on the relationship of the unity of God to the multiplicity of created beings. Dionysius' fundamental principles are first that God is the supreme cause of all that is, secondly that all things resemble their cause but are not identical with it, and thirdly that their destiny and fulfilment lies in their returning to their cause as fully as is consistent with their separate identity and created status. Deification (ἐκθέωσις) represents the process of return to the supreme cause conceived of as *theos*. God is the θεαρχία of the θεούμενοι, just as he is the illumination (ἔλλαμψις) of the illuminated (τῶν φωτιζομένων), the sacramental principle (τελεταρχία) of those receiving the sacraments (τῶν τελουμένων), the principle of simplicity (ἁπλότης) of those undergoing simplification (τῶν ἁπλουμένων), the unity (ἑνότης) of those being unified (τῶν ἑνιζομένων), the source of life (ζωή) of the living (τῶν ζώντων), and the ultimate reality (οὐσία) of all that is (τῶν ὄντων) (*DN* 1. 3, 589C). The same point is made many times. Τὸ θεοποιόν, the principle of deification, is one of the attributes of God that can stand for the deity as a whole—like τὸ καλόν, τὸ σοφόν, τὸ φῶς, etc.—because God is not apportioned amongst his characteristics (*DN* 2. 1, 637B). The transcendent hiddenness of God may be expressed in such positive terms as θεός, ζωή, or οὐσιά, or σοφία, of which the corresponding active powers (δυνάμεις) are the ἐκθεωτικαί, the ζωογόνοι, the οὐσιοποιοί and the σοφοδώροι (*DN* 2. 7, 645B). As Deity God deifies, as Life he vivifies, as Light he illuminates, as Unity he unifies, as Reality he realizes. The different names of God stand for the whole of God seen in terms of his different powers. All beings strive to return to him as the principle and source of their existence (*DN* 8. 5, 893A; 9. 5, 912D; 11. 6, 956B).

On five occasions the principle of return is referred to by Dionysius by the Procline term ἐκθέωσις or one of its cognate forms (*DN* 1. 5, 593C; 2. 7, 645A; 8. 5, 893A ; 9. 5, 912D; 12. 3, 972A). In the most striking of these Dionysius refers to the 'union of deified minds (τῶν ἐκθεουμένων νοῶν) with light beyond deity' taking place 'when all intellectual activity ceases' (*DN* 1. 5, 593C). The precise extent of Dionysius' reliance on Proclus will be considered below.

Finally, we come to the *Mystical Theology*, a short text appended to the *Divine Names*, which summarizes Dionysius' entire spiritual teaching. As with Gregory of Nyssa, to whose *Life of Moses* the *Mystical Theology* is closely related, Moses' ascent of Mount Sinai is presented as the paradigm of the soul's ascent to God. And also as with Gregory, the technical language of deification is not used in this context.

Our survey of the texts has revealed that although Dionysius is a writer generally recognized to be the most strongly Neoplatonic of the later Greek ecclesiastical authors, his use of the concept of deification occurs more frequently in his discussions of the sacraments than in any other context. Deification belongs to the earthly liturgy rather than to the ascent into the divine darkness, to the operation of the sacraments rather than to the intellectual work of the philosopher. Only in the *Divine Names* does he use Proclus' characteristic vocabulary. This emphasis on deification as an aspect of the efficacy of the sacraments shows him to stand in the tradition of Origen, Athanasius, and Cyril, even if he uses a different vocabulary.

(c) The Ecclesiastical Dimension of Deification

Baptism for Dionysius is 'a divine birth' which raises the believer to 'a divine level of existence': (τὸ εἶναι θείως ἐστὶν ἡ θεία γέννησις (*EH* 2. 1, 392B). The descent into the water is a symbolic death, which for Christians is not a dissolution but a re-forming of their constituent parts. They descend into the water and rise from it filled with illumination (425B) in imitation of the death and resurrection of Christ (*EH* 2. 3. 7, 404B). The putting on of new clothes symbolizes the putting on of a new form, of a likeness to God, by which 'intelligent beings cleave to the immutability of the divine state' (*EH* 2. 3. 5, 401C). At the Liturgy after the reading of the Scriptures, the catechumens, the penitents, and the possessed are excluded from the *synaxis*. Those who remain are the baptized in good standing, 'those who are worthy of the vision of divine things and of communion with them' (*EH* 3. Mysterion, 425C). In his *theoria* Dionysius explains the symbolic meaning of the prayers and actions that follow. First the hierarch incenses the whole church. The spreading fragrance and the movement of the bishop from the altar to the end of the church and back again symbolize the reaching out of God to communion with the holy who participate in him without leaving 'his essentially motionless stability and fixity' (*EH* 3. Theoria 3, 429A). The covered bread and wine are placed on the altar and the kiss of peace is exchanged. This leads to a meditation by Dionysius on how the oneness of God moves towards multiplicity in the symbols on the altar, while the multiplicity of the faithful tends towards oneness in the kiss of peace. Then the commemorative diptychs are read and the hierarch washes his hands. The symbolic purification makes the human hierarch one with himself, having shed all traces of the delusions of the soul (*EH* 3. Theoria 10, 440A), and being conformed to God in this way he can turn towards him who is One. The eucharistic prayer that follows rehearses the saving acts of God. The human race was created for immortality but turned away from its glorious destiny and incurred the risk of destruction and dissolution of being (εἰς ἀνυπαρξίας ... καὶ ἀπωλείας κίνδυνον) (*EH* 3. Theoria 11, 441A). The final remedy was the Incarnation. This point in his exegesis of the eucharistic prayer gives Dionysius the opportunity to set down the christological basis for deification.

As Ysabel de Andia has shown, the terminology expressing God's relationship with his creation is peculiar to Dionysius (1996: 289). In place of the usual θεολογία/οἰκονομία distinction, Dionysius works with θεαρχία/φιλανθρωπία. Thearchy is God as he is in himself; philanthropy is the lovingkindness of God which goes out from him in the act of creation, reaches its fullness in the incarnation of the Word, and returns to him in the deification of the believer. 'Dionysius develops his christology precisely in the seven texts in which he mentions the "philanthropy" of Jesus' (de Andia 1996: 289). He avoids speaking of 'natures'. His Christ is the dynamic expression of God's love for his creation:

The supremely infinite loving-kindness of the thearchic goodness did not cease to lavish on us the efficacious blessings of its providence. It truly participated in all that appertains to humanity with the exception of sin; it united itself with our lowliness without losing anything of its own nature, without experiencing any confusion or suffering any injury . . .

It transformed the whole of what belongs to us beneficently into its opposite. It filled our mental darkness with a blessed and most divine light and adorned what was formless with deiform beauties. It delivered the dwelling-place of the soul, so far as our essence was not yet fully fallen, in complete salvation from accursed passions and corrupting defilements. It taught us the ascent that transcends this world and the way of life that is in conformity with God through our sacred assimilations to it so far as is possible. (*EH* 3. Theoria 11, 441ABC)

The incarnation of the Word *transforms* human nature in principle, giving it [IN CARNATION]
a new godlike form. It also *reveals* the way in which salvation may be
appropriated—by the ascent of the mind to a supramundane level and by the
imitation of God in the will—and *makes this possible* by supplying us with
grace in terms of light and beauty. Here the Platonic programme of attaining
likeness to God so far as is possible is integrated into a meditation on the
significance of the Eucharist. The reception of the divine gifts requires the
co-operation of the human will 'so far as is possible'.[21] The divine Word may
have accommodated himself to human life but

> It is necessary for us, if we seek communion with him, to have our attention fixed
> on his most divine life in the flesh, and by making ourselves resemble it to ascend
> from a sacred sinlessness to a deiform and integral state. For it is in this way that
> communion with what is like us will be granted in a harmonious way.   (*EH* 3.
> Theoria 12, 444B)

The moral life is complementary to our participation in the Eucharist.
Deification is not brought about by human effort. Its source is the divine
philanthropy (de Andia 1996: 292). And its point of departure is always Jesus
Christ, who manifests divine love in the mystery of the Incarnation, the
redemption, and the institution of the Eucharist. 'For the divinization of
man, which is based on the incarnation and redemption of Christ, is effected
in the sacraments of the Church' (de Andia 1996: 292).

(d) The Philosophical Dimension of Deification

Dionysius' teaching on deification, although centred on the work of Christ
and the efficacy of the sacraments, is inseparable from his Neoplatonic
ontology and ethical theory. He defines theosis, it will be recalled, as the
attaining of likeness (ἀφομοίωσις) to God and union (ἕνωσις) with him (*EH*
1. 3, 376A). Similarity and unity are not the result of two separate activities.
They are the fruit of a concentrated effort to return to the source of being
and thus attain the highest realization of the self. This programme is set out
most fully in the *Divine Names*, the work in which Dionysius comes closest to
the thought and language of Proclus.

Proclus (*c*.411–85) was for fifty years Diadochus of the Platonic Academy
of Athens. He was born in Constantinople, the son of a successful lawyer,
and studied philosophy first at Alexandria, during the episcopate of Cyril,
and then after 430 at Athens, where he became a disciple of Syrianus, succeeding him as Diadochus in about 436.[22] He is the first non-Christian writer

---

[21] As de Andia points out (1996: 290), Gross has missed this.
[22] We have a contemporary *Life of Proclus* by Marinus (ed. Cousin 1864; ET Edwards). See the discussion
in Siorvanes 1996: 1–6.

to use the technical language of deification with any frequency.[23] Deification, which in his usage is usually the past participle of ἐκθεόω (he very rarely uses the noun), is one of his key expressions for the reversion of things to their cause. The central problem addressed by his philosophical system was the perennial one of multiplicity. How are unity and divinity related to each other? The answer lay in the application of two principles, the rule that 'everything is in everything in a manner appropriate to each', and the rule that 'that which apprehends becomes like the object of cognition' (Siorvanes 1996: 57). These two principles, the one ontological, the other epistemological, complement each other.

On the ontological level the whole world forms a plenum or continuum. The supreme unifying principle underlying the existence of all that is cannot adequately be described by us. The best we can do is to call it 'the One' (τὸ ἕν). This transcendent Unity, however, has species in existence, the units or 'henads'. Each henad stands at the head of a further series. The reason for this is that all things, apart from the transcendent One, exist either in a causal mode, or in their own existence, or in participation. A cause produces an effect by the transmission of a property. Proclus uses three analogies to explain how the same property can exist both in the cause and in the effect. The first of these is the arithmetical (the monad causing other members by self-addition); the second is the emanative (the transmission of a property being like the radiation (ἔλλαμψις) of the sun, which leaves its source visibly undiminished); the third is the motive (the unmoved mover (τὸ ἀκίνητον) acting on that which is moved by an external source (τὸ ἑτεροκίνητον)) (Siorvanes 1996: 106–7). The emanative aspect of causality may also be expressed in terms of 'procession'. Such procession is not spatial or temporal. It is another way of suggesting how the same property may exist in both the cause and the effect. Procession belongs to a dynamic triad: remaining (μονή)—procession (πρόοδος)—reversion (ἐπιστροφή). For the effect always has the tendency to return to its cause or original state, that is to say, to a higher level of unity. The concept of participation is related to this, 'for participation (μέθεξις) emphasizes that an inferior cannot possess a superior entire' (Siorvanes 1996: 72). Participation is also connected with similarity: 'All participation is accomplished through kinship and likeness' (Proclus, *El. Theol.* 129; trans. Dodds). At the head of each series of participants stands a unit, a henad, which by virtue of its sharing in the One is divine. All things,

---

[23] Θεόω: *In Parm.* 1. 490, 491 (Cousin); *In Tim.* 3. 173e (Diehl ii. 111. 20). Ἐκθεόω: *Elements* 129 (Dodds 114. 12); 135 (Dodds 120. 2); 138 (Dodds 122. 7); 153 (bis) (Dodds 134. 30, 32); 160 (Dodds 140. 10); 161 (Dodds 140. 19); *In Remp.* (Kroll ii. 48. 10–12); *In Tim.* Prooem. 3ef (Diehl i. 11. 13); 2. 109ef (Diehl i. 360. 32); 2. 110d (Diehl i. 363. 21); 2. 111b (Diehl i. 365. 14–16); 3. 174b (Diehl ii. 113. 5); 4. 264c (Diehl iii. 83. 3); 5. 302b (Diehl iii. 205. 8); 5. 302de (Diehl iii. 207. 6–7); 5. 308d (Diehl iii. 226. 22); 5. 336a (Diehl iii. 315. 27). Ἐκθέωσις: *In Remp.* (Kroll i. 120. 17).

Ἐκθεωτικός: *Elements* 165 (Dodds 144. 2); *In Parm.* 4. 838 (Cousin); *In Tim.* 5. 302b (Diehl iii. 205. 6); 5. 302d (Diehl iii. 206. 26); 5. 302f (Diehl iii. 207. 25); 5. 306d (Diehl iii. 220. 12); 5. 313b (Diehl iii. 241. 19).

Θεοποιός: *In Tim.* 5. 308d (Diehl iii. 226. 28).

even material things, are in this way touched by the divine. However, only those entities with self-complete (αὐτοτέλειον) unity are divinities (Proclus, *El. Theol.* 64, 113, 114; cf. Siorvanes 1996: 73).

On the epistemological level, in Siorvanes' words,

We perceive physical qualities, and with our personal mind we formulate beliefs and theories about things: we try to match (*synarmosis*) our ideas to objects. However, we only have a 'partial' view and subjective knowledge of objects. To gain a more comprehensive picture, we have to bridge the gap between thinker and object. We have to travel out of our particular state, and exercise an intuitive intellective grasp. When thinker coincides with the object, conception is complete. But what we have is the sum total of the object's properties, not its essence. To grasp that, we have to apprehend its bare substance as one undifferentiated whole. At the centre of every coherent entity lies a pure unity, its selfhood. It is so unqualified by anything mental or physical that [it] cannot be touched even by intellect. It can only be reached by an act of union (*henôsis*).   (1996: 51)

Since unity is the character of divinity, the production of multiplicity from the One can only be seen as a gradual dilution of divinity as the original unity becomes more and more fragmented on the lower levels of reality (cf. *El. Theol.* 113). Conversely, reversion to the unity can be expressed as the acquisition of divinity through participation in even higher and more unified levels (*El. Theol.* 165; *In Parm.* 4. 838, Cousin). The ascending movement begins even on the level of the material world, for all things have a tendency to revert to their cause:

If Plato at once went on to call the world a god on account of the Soul, by virtue of its participation in Soul, we should not be astonished. For each thing is deified through what is immediately prior to it (ἕκαστον γὰρ ἐκθεοῦται διὰ τὸ πρὸ αὐτοῦ προσεχῶς), the corporeal world through Soul and Soul through Intellect. As the Athenian stranger said, by receiving divine Intellect soul becomes a god (*Laws* 10. 897b). Intellect becomes a god through the One, which is why Intellect is divine but not God.   (*In Tim.* 3. 174b; Diehl ii. 113. 3–9)

The return of the human soul is prompted first by an internal motion, which is the natural aspiration of an inferior principle for its superior. But is also drawn up by the influence of the henads (participated forms of the One), because deified things, even Soul and Intellect, can only bestow a mediated divinity. Only the One and the self-complete henads, such as the Demiurge, being gods in their own right, possess a deifying power which is not a participated property. Through asceticism and the acquisition of virtue, the human soul participates in the divine soul. Through philosophy it is able to participate in divine intelligence. The highest level of unification, however, is beyond philosophy and is accomplished by love—no doubt with the aid of theurgy—because love (ἔρως) is the unifying force par excellence (*In Tim.* 3. 173c; Diehl ii. 111. 13–23).

Dionysius took over much of Proclus' general scheme: God as a transcendent unity, the movement of procession and reversion, the scale of
being, the ascent of the human soul to increasing levels of unity, the ultimate
union with that which is beyond mind and being. But Dionysius also modified Proclus in important respects.[24] Proclus' system is fundamentally polytheistic. The procession from the One results in inferior divine entities, with
the result that the henads at the head of each series are divinities corresponding to the traditional gods. Moreover, the philosophical ascent of the human
soul, even if assisted by theurgy, is essentially an intellectual process. With
Dionysius the henads correspond to the attributes of God. These attributes
contain the whole of God—they are only conceptually separable from him.
It is through participation in these attributes that the believer rises up to
God. But they are not simply discovered by intellectual reasoning. They are
revealed by God. Dionysius' God is one who has manifested himself in the
Scriptures, who has descended through *philanthropia* at a particular point in
time, and who continues to be operative in the sacramental life of the
Church. The theurgical activity that enables the believer to benefit from this
is not, as in Proclus, the tapping into divine power by appropriate rituals, but
at its deepest level the very activity of the incarnate Christ that makes the
sacraments efficacious (Louth 1986: 432–8).

These points may be illustrated by the different ways in which Proclus and
Dionysius use the same *ek-* family of deification terms. In Proclus every
divine entity is deified by its immediate superior in the chain of being: the
unity deifies body through soul, soul through intellect, and intellect through
the unity's very being (*El. Theol.* 129).[25] The hierarchies in Proclus mediate
being; in Dionysius they mediate the 'light of divine revelation' (Louth 1989:
106). By the power of the Spirit, says Dionysius, in a manner transcending
speech and knowledge we achieve a union superior to that attained by our
own intellective power and energy (*DN* i. 1, 588A). God is hidden from our
minds. We can only know him through the Scriptures. It is the transcendent
knowledge (ὑπερούσιος ἐπιστήμη) we gain from them that draws us upward.
God may be the 'oneness that is the source of all oneness' (ἐνὰς ἐνοποιὸς
ἁπάσης ἐνάδος) (*DN* i. 1, 588B), but it is not by any innate oneness within
ourselves that we become like him. Proclus says that 'by the "one" in ourselves we apprehend the One, which by the brightness of its light is the cause
of all things' (*In Parm.* 7. 48, Klibansky; cited Siorvanes 1996: 197). Dionysius' perspective is different. God grants illumination from without, to which
we respond with a matching love (τῷ συμμέτρῳ . . . ἔρωτι) (*DN* i. 2, 589A).

---

[24] On the relationship between Proclus and Dionysius see Niarchos 1985; Louth 1989: 84–7; Rorem
1993: 164–5; Perl 1994.

[25] If one asks *how* the divine transmits its property to the participants, the answer is through the
περιουσία, the superabundance, of the divine. Divine qualities are not limited; they spill out and are shared
in by others. (I owe this observation to Lucas Siorvanes.)

Our starting-point is the Scriptures, where all the attributes of God are mentioned in his names and titles. By participation in these attributes, which are the beneficent emanations of the Godhead (ἀγαθουργοὺς τῆς θεαρχίας προόδους) (*DN* 1. 4, 589D) made accessible to us through the divine *philanthropia*, we are drawn up into divine unity. When we have received the gift of illumination we become like Christ. In scriptural terms, having become incorruptible and immortal we shall, in our eschatological fulfilment, be like the disciples at the Transfiguration, filled with the sight of God shining gloriously around us. We shall be 'equal to the angels and sons of God, being sons of the resurrection' (Luke 20: 36) (*DN* 1. 4, 592BC). In more philosophical terms, the minds that are *ektheoumenoi* are those that imitate the angels and, by a process of withdrawal from everything that tends to fragment and divide, become unified and thus able to attain union with a light that is beyond deity and transcends all intellectual activity (*DN* 1. 5, 593BC).

One of the expressions that Dionysius finds in the Bible to encapsulate this approach is the phrase 'God of gods' (Deut. 10: 17) (*DN* 1. 6, 596B). Dionysius makes no mention anywhere of Psalm 82: 6 and the exegetical tradition that makes the 'gods' addressed in that psalm the baptized. For him the word 'gods' expresses the aspect of unification. The 'gods' are those whose minds have become deiform or deisimilar (θεοειδεῖς) (*DN* 2. 8, 645C), who have replicated the unity of the one God (*DN* 2. 11, 649C). They are participants (μετέχοντες) in the imparticipable cause (ἀμέθεκτος αἴτιος) of unity (*DN* 12. 4, 972B). Even in the *Celestial Hierarchy* the aspect of unity is uppermost. There the name 'gods' is given both to the heavenly beings above us (the angels) and to those amongst us who are holy and most pleasing to God. 'For all spiritual and rational beings that turn wholly towards the unity of this [divine hiddenness] with all their strength and reach up ceaselessly towards its illuminations so far as possible are deemed worthy through their imitation of God with all their strength (if one may speak thus) of being called by the same divine title as God' (*CH* 12. 3, 293B).

(e) The Ascent of the Soul

The ascent of the soul is the leading metaphor for the attaining of the goal of human life in that most influential of spiritual tracts, the *Mystical Theology*. In this brief work the technical language of deification is not used. 'Theosis' is too cataphatic a word in this context. For the ascent is not to *theos* but to one who is beyond deity. 'Lay aside the faculties of the senses,' says Dionysius,

and reach up so far as is possible without the use of discursive reasoning (ἀγνώστως) to union with him who transcends all being and knowledge. For shedding all things and freed from all things, you will, by a wholly unqualified and absolute ecstasy that detaches you from yourself and from all things, be lifted up to the divine ray of the divine darkness. (*MT* 1. 1, 997B–1000A).

Ecstasy and union belong together as the two great characteristics of *erōs* (Louth 1981: 175; de Andia 1996: 150). The lover strives on the one hand to abandon self, on the other to be united with the object of his longing. And most remarkably, Dionysius holds that God himself goes out in ecstasy to meet the lover. The paradoxical 'ray' of divine darkness perhaps means to convey this sense of God's love being projected outside himself (cf. *DN* 4. 13, 712AB; Louth 1981: 176). Dionysius' biblical paradigm for the ascent of the soul is Moses' ascent of Mount Sinai:

> For not simply is the divine Moses bidden first of all to purify himself and then to separate himself from those not thus purified; but after all purification, he hears the many-sounding trumpets and sees many lights which flash forth pure and widely diffused rays. Then he separates himself from the multitude and with the chosen priests he reaches the summit of the divine ascents. But not even here does he hold converse with God Himself, nor does he behold Him (for He is invisible), but only the place where He is. And this, I think, means that the most divine and exalted of the things that are seen with the eye or perceived by the mind are but suggestions that barely hint at the nature of that which transcends any conception whatever, a presence which sets but its feet upon the spiritual pinnacles of its most holy places. And then Moses is cut off from both things seen and those who see and enters into the darkness of unknowing, a truly hidden darkness, according to which he shuts his eyes to all apprehensions that convey knowledge, for he has passed into a realm quite beyond any feeling or seeing. Now, belonging wholly to that which is beyond all, and yet to nothing at all, and being neither himself, nor another, and united in his highest part in passivity (ἀνενεργησία) with Him who is completely unknowable, he knows by not knowing in a manner that transcends understanding. (*MT* 1. 3, 1000C–1001A; trans. Louth 1981: 173)

This magnificent passage, which presents Moses lost in the vertiginous darkness of the presence of God—or rather of 'the place where he is' for God's presence eludes him—conveys in language that has never been sur-passed the paradoxical nature of the soul's union with God. The soul is simultaneously separated from God and united with him, disorientated and cut off from all sensation and thought, yet belonging wholly to something that transcends even being. Dionysius was clearly familiar with Gregory of Nyssa's *Life of Moses*. The similarities between the *Mystical Theology* and *the Life of Moses* have frequently been noted.[26] Both speak of a progression from purification to illumination. Both find a richness of meaning in the images of light, cloud, and darkness. But the differences are equally striking. The most significant of these concerns the nature of God. In Gregory's view God is true being. He is therefore supremely good by nature. And

---

[26] There is an exhaustive discussion in de Andia 1996: 303–73

because there is no limit to the good, there is no limit to the ascent towards it. Progress towards perfection never ceases. In Dionysius' view God is beyond being. And yet paradoxically the goal of the spiritual life is union with him. How can we conceive of a union between terms on such radically different levels of reality?

The idea of union in Dionysius is the subject of the major study by Ysabel de Andia to which I have already frequently referred. In the course of her discussion she takes issue with Jules Gross on his 'two ways' of deifying union, the 'way of ecstatic love' and 'the way of ecclesiastical hierarchy' (de Andia 1996: 281–8). For Gross the first way corresponds to the inward journey of Neoplatonism and consists of the attaining of unity within oneself, so that the 'one' of the soul can unite with the divine 'One' by a direct contact without the assistance of any intermediary. The second way is ecclesiastical, though of a rather peculiar kind, and is connected with the sacramental symbolism of the Eucharist (Gross 1938: 312–19). De Andia points out that Proclus' term, 'one of the soul', on which Gross bases his charge that Dionysius conceals 'the danger of pantheist reabsorption', is not found in the Dionysian corpus. Dionysius refers to τὸ ἓν ἑαυτοῦ, which, as de Andia shows, refers to the soul's return to its true self through unifying the multiplicity of the images and symbols it receives in a unitary vision which renders it deiform or godlike (de Andia 1996: 285). The union which such a soul achieves is not with the supraessential hidden reality of God but with the perceptible radiance (φανοτάταις μαρμαρυγαῖς) that reveals his presence, as it did on Mount Tabor (*DN* 1. 4, 592C). In de Andia's judgement, 'Denys does not refer the attributes of God to the soul but to the union: it is the union which is ineffable or unknowable and not the soul—which is what enables him to avoid the danger of fusion between God and the soul' (1996: 280).

(f) The Dionysian Understanding of Theosis

We began our enquiry with the definition of the *Ecclesiastical Hierarchy* that theosis signifies 'the attaining of likeness to God and union with him so far as possible' (*EH* 1. 3, 376A). Exactly the same definition is given in the *Celestial Hierarchy* for the σκοπὸς ἱεραρχίας (*CH* 3. 2, 165A). Theosis is therefore another term for the goal of hierarchy, and this identification of the two is the link that connects the ecclesiastical approach with the philosophical.

It is the ecclesiastical tradition that gives Dionysius much of the vocabulary of deification as well as the locating of deification in the sacramental life of the Church. Dionysius uses the technical language primarily in his exposition of the Liturgy. Remarkably, however, this language refers to the intellectual reception of the symbols rather than to corporeal participation in the body and blood of Christ. These symbols raise the mind to unity and simplicity, enabling it to participate in the divine attributes of goodness, wisdom, oneness, and deity.

In the noetic sphere ἐκθέωσις is the return to the supreme cause, conceived of as *theos*, a cause which is beyond all intellection and being. Proclus' influence is at its strongest here, but in Dionysius the return is not through successive levels of more and more integrated being, nor is it simply the result of purely intellectual processes. The return represents a direct reaching out to a personal, triadic God, who responds actively not only with the gift of the capacity for deification but also with the gift of himself, wholly present in each of his attributes.

5. Maximus the Confessor

Deification is a major theme in Maximus.[27] It informs the whole of his theological anthropology as a doctrine correlative to that of the incarnation of the Word. The Irenaean and Alexandrian principle that God became man in order that man might become god receives in his hands its greatest elaboration and most profound articulation. The kenosis of the Word is followed by the theosis of the believer, God's accommodation to the constrictions of human life by man's expansion, within the limitations of his creaturely capacity, to the infinity of the divine life. Deification is not simply another expression for salvation, the repair of the damage done by sin. It is the final end of salvation, the attainment of the destiny originally intended for humankind that Adam had in his grasp and threw away. It may be anticipated in some degree in this life, but it reaches its fulfilment in the next in the fullest possible union with the incarnate Word. It involves not only man but his whole world. For deification is in the end the goal, the *skopos*, of the entire cosmos.

The key to understanding Maximus is his monastic perspective. In his maturity he became a monk and accordingly the whole thrust of his writings is directed towards assisting his monastic or ascetically minded lay correspondents to advance in the spiritual life. Some doubt surrounds Maximus' origins. The Greek *Life* composed three centuries after his death by the Studite monk Michael Exaboulites (PG 90. 68–109), makes good its lack of information about Maximus' early life by borrowing from the *Life* of Theodore of Studios. A near-contemporary Syriac *Life*, discovered by

---

[27] The doctrine of deification in Maximus the Confessor has been the subject of intensive study since the Second World War. The pioneering work of von Balthasar (1941, 2nd edn 1961) and Sherwood (esp. 1955) was developed in important publications by Thunberg (1965, 2nd edn 1995) and Völker (1965) and has been brought to magnificent fruition in the penetrating studies of Blowers (1991) and Larchet (1996). For a review of recent work on Maximus see Thunberg 1995: 11–20.

Sebastian Brock in 1973, gives Maximus a Palestinian origin and locates his early years in the monastery of Chariton (the Palaia Lavra) (Brock 1973: 299–346). Most scholars, however, have not been persuaded of the reliability of the Syriac information (Larchet 1996: 8–12). Although it presents a plausible setting for the acquisition of Maximus' knowledge of Origenism, it does not account for the excellent education which he received, nor does it fit in with his well-attested career at the imperial court.

From the statement of his age at his trial in 655 (PG 90. 128C) we know that Maximus was born in 580. On completing his studies, he entered the imperial service, rising to be head of the imperial chancellery perhaps in 610. In 613 or 614 he resigned his post and entered the monastery of Philippicus at Chrysopolis (modern Üsküdar) on the Asian side of the Bosphorus. After some ten years there, in 624 or 625, he transferred to the monastery of St George at Cyzicus (modern Erdek) on the southern shore of the Propontis. It was at this monastery that he composed his earliest works, which include Letter 2 to John the Cubicularius and the *Quaestiones et dubia*. In 626, however, the Persian invasion of Asia Minor forced him to withdraw to North Africa, where he joined the monastery of Eucratas near Carthage. This marks the beginning of a very productive period, from which we have the *Commentary on the Lord's Prayer*, the *Mystagogia*, and the earlier part of the *Ambigua*, all from 628–30, the *Quaestiones ad Thalassium* from 630–3, the *Ambigua ad Thomam* (*Amb.* 1–5) from 633 or later, and the *Chapters on Theology* from 630–4. Towards the end of his time at the monastery of Eucratas he wrote a series of *opuscula* on christological themes. These date from the period in which Maximus had begun to be active in the Monothelite controversy, the controversy that was to take him to Rome in 646 and to his eventual martyrdom at Lazica in Georgia in 662.

The works mentioned above are the principal sources of Maximus' doctrine of deification. They are all occasional pieces written in response to requests from his correspondents. They reveal Maximus' reliance on his predecessors, principally on the Cappadocians, amongst whom Gregory of Nazianzus holds pride of place (cf. Berthold 1982), and also on Cyril of Alexandria (cf. Thunberg 1995: 40–8), Dionysius the Areopagite (cf. Bellini 1982), Evagrius Ponticus, Diadochus of Photice (cf. Des Places 1982) and the Macarian Homilies. But equally they demonstrate Maximus' ability to transform his sources and create a new synthesis of patristic teaching.

(a) Vocabulary

Maximus uses a broader vocabulary than any of his predecessors. His preferred terms by far, however, throughout his writings are the verb θεόω and the noun θέωσις, which link him firmly to his chief guide, Gregory of

Nazianzus.²⁸ He also makes some use, principally in the *Quaestiones ad Thalassium*, of the Procline noun ἐκθέωσις and adjective ἐκθεωτικός, which he has probably derived from the *Divine Names* of Dionysius the Areopagite.²⁹ Like his Alexandrian and Cappadocian predecessors, he uses the verb θεοποιέω in both a theological and a pejorative sense in roughly equal proportions.³⁰ The remaining verbs, with a single instance of each, are ἀποθεόω (used by Clement, Origen, and Apollinarius) and συνθεόω (used by Leontius of Jerusalem).³¹ Besides ἐκθεωτικός, Maximus also uses the adjectives θεοποιός (from Gregory of Nazianzus and the Alexandrians), θεοποιητικός (for the first time in a Christian writer), and his own neologism, θεωτικός.³²

None of these terms seems to differ significantly from any other in meaning. They all refer to the same process by which human beings are penetrated and transformed by the divine. Maximus also refers to Christians as gods through grace, usually without citing Psalm 82: 6.³³

---

²⁸ Θεόω: *Ep*. 2, PG 91. 401C; *Ep*. 12, PG 91. 468C, 504A; *Qu.D*. 81. 6, 124. 13, CCSG 10. 65, 92; *Myst*. 13, PG 91. 692C; *Amb. Th*. 3, PG 91. 1040C; *Amb. Io*. 7, PG 91. 1084C, 1088C, 1092B; *Amb. Io*. 20, PG 91. 1237B; *Amb. Io*. 31, PG 91. 1280B; *Thal*. 22, CCSG 7. 141. 78; *Thal*. 40, CCSG 7. 273. 110, schol. 2: 275. 8; *Thal*. 54, CCSG 7. 459. 285, schol. 15: 475. 136; *Thal*. 64, CCSG 22. 237. 785; *Opusc*. 1, PG 91. 36A; *Opusc*. 3, PG 91. 48B (octiens); *Opusc*. 7, PG 91. 77C, 80D, 81C, 81D (tris); *Opusc*. 20, PG 91. 233D, 236A, 236B (see p. 298 n. 3).

Θέωσις: *Ep*. 2, PG 91. 393B; *Ep*. 9, PG 91. 445C; *Ep*. 16, PG 91. 577C; *Ep*. 24, PG 91. 609C (= *Ep*. 43, 640B); *Qu.D*. 61. 9, CCSG 10. 48; *Pat*., CCSG 23. 29. 42, 29. 51, 34. 132, 55. 475–6, 56. 509, 71. 783; *Myst*. 5, PG 91. 680A, 680B; *Myst*. 24, 709C, 712A, 713A; *Amb. Th*. 3, PG 91. 1040D; *Amb. Io*. 7, PG 91. 1076C, 1084B, 1084C, 1088C; *Amb. Io*. 10/19, PG 91. 1200B; *Amb. Io*. 20, PG 91. 1237B (tris), 1241B; *Amb. Io*. 42, PG 91. 1345D; *Amb. Io*. 63, PG 91. 1389B (= *Amb. Io*. 10, PG 91. 1176A); *Thal*. intro., CCSG 7. 37. 344, 37. 348; *Thal*. 9, CCSG 7. 70. 10, 79. 25; *Thal*. 22, CCSG 7. 137. 33, 139. 3, 139. 52, 139. 64, 141. 93, 141. 96, 143. 116, schol. 5: 145. 30 (bis), 145. 35, schol. 6: 145. 39, schol. 7: 147. 48; *Thal*. 35, CCSG 7. 241. 42, 241. 43, schol. 2: 241. 5; *Thal*. 40, CCSG 7. 267. 22, 273. 109, 275. 137, schol. 3: 275. 12; *Thal*. 54, CCSG 7. 459. 281, 465. 391, schol. 15: 475. 133; *Thal*. 59, CCSG 22. 53. 140, 53. 141 (bis), 59. 221, schol. 5: 69. 32; *Thal*. 60, CCSG 22. 79. 119; *Thal*. 61, CCSG 22. 91. 108, 103. 304, schol. 14: 111. 71; *Thal*. 63, CCSG 22. 173. 441, 177. 488; *Thal*. 64, CCSG 22. 237. 801; *Opusc*. 1, PG 91. 33C, 36A; *Cap. Theol*. 1. 54, PG 90. 1104B; *Cap. Theol*. 1. 55, PG 90. 1104B; *Cap. Theol*. 1. 60, PG 90. 1105A; *Cap. Theol*. 1. 97, PG 90. 1124A; *Cap. Theol*. 2. 88, PG 90. 1168A.

²⁹ Ἐκθέωσις: *Thal*. 9, CCSG 7. 79. 16; *Thal*. 11, CCSG 7. 89. 15; *Thal*. 15, CCSG 7. 103. 39; *Thal*. 20, CCSG 7. 123. 57; *Thal*. 22, CCSG 7, schol. 2: 143. 9, schol. 3: 143. 11; *Thal*. 54, CCSG 7. 465. 379; *Thal*. 59, CCSG 22. 61. 242 (cf. suppl. schol. q59 244, q59 247, CCSG 22. 337); *Opusc*. 1, PG 91. 33B.

Ἐκθεωτικός: *Myst*. 22, PG 91. 697B; *Thal*. 2, CCSG 7. 51. 21; *Thal*. 9, CCSG 7. 69. 21; *Thal*. 13, CCSG 7. 95. 17; *Opusc*. 1, PG 91. 33B .

³⁰ Θεοποιέω: *Qu.D*. 124. 12, CCSG 10. 92; *Pat*., CCSG 23. 55. 475–6; *Myst*. 7, PG 91. 685D; *Myst*. 23, PG 91. 701C; *Amb. Io*. 10, PG 91. 1129D; *Thal*. Intro., CCSG 7. 37. 355; *Thal*. 22, schol. 8, CCSG 7. 147. 58; *Thal*. 64, CCSG 22. 285. 557.

Θεὸν ποιέω: *Ep*. 2, PG 91. 393C; *Thal*. Intro., CCSG 7. 43. 429.

³¹ Ἀποθεόω: *Opusc*. 1, PG 91. 36A; συνθεόω: *Cap. Theol*. 2. 88, PG 90. 1168A.

³² Θεοποιός: *Amb. Io*. 42, PG 91. 1348A; *Thal*. 15, CCSG 7. 101. 29; *Thal*. 25, CCSG 7. 161. 63.

Θεοποιητικός: *Amb. Io*. 21, PG 91. 1249B.

Θεωτικός: *Thal*. 15, CCSG 7. 103. 50; *Thal*. 47, CCSG 7. 325. 221.

The use of θεουργέω to mean 'to deify' may also be noted at *Amb. Thom*. 4, PG 91. 1044D.

³³ *Ep*. 2, PG 91. 393C; *Qu. D*. 61. 10, CCSG 10. 48; *Myst*. 21, PG 91. 697A; *Myst*. 24, PG 91. 704 D; *Amb. Io*. 7, PG 91. 1092C; *Amb. Io*. 20, PG 91. 1237A; *Amb. Io*. 42, PG 91. 1345D; *Thal*. 22, CCSG 7. 143. 107; *Thal*. 44, CCSG 7. 299. 23; *Cap. Theol*. 2. 25, PG 90. 1136B.

(b) Early Texts: the Primacy of Love

Maximus' earliest mention of deification is in his great letter on love written from Cyzicus in 624–5 to the palace official, John the Cubicularius. In this letter Maximus discusses the whole range of different forms of love, from the fissiparous nature of self-love to the unifying nature of the love of God. The latter is love's pinnacle, 'For nothing is more truly godlike than divine love, nothing more mysterious, nothing more apt to raise up human beings to deification (οὐδὲ ἀνθρώποις πρὸς θέωσιν ὑψηλότερον (*Ep.* 2, PG 91. 393B; trans. Louth 1996). The economy of salvation demonstrates this, for the law and the prophets 'were succeeded by the mystery of love, which out of human beings makes us gods, and reduces the individual commandments to a universal meaning (λόγος)' (ibid., 393C; trans. Louth 1996). This is not the natural yearning of the soul for union with God but a divine gift which subsumes every virtue and elevates humanity to the likeness of God (cf. Thunberg 1995: 309–12; Larchet 1996: 477–82). The saints manifested this love in a superlative degree. As an outstanding example Maximus cites Abraham, who through his ascetic struggle replicated the love of God within himself, giving God a human likeness. This convergence of the human and the divine through the unifying function of love makes love the greatest of goods, 'since through it God and man are drawn together in a single embrace, and the creator of humankind appears as human, through the undeviating likeness of the deified (τοῦ θεουμένου) to God in the good so far as is possible to humankind' (*Ep.* 2, PG 91. 401C; trans. Louth cf. Larchet 1996: 212–13).

A similar point is made in the *Chapters on Love*, which were also composed at Cyzicus at about the same time (624–5). In the third Century, for example, Maximus writes that when God created rational beings, he endowed them with four of his attributes: being, eternal being, goodness, and wisdom. The first two were granted to their essential nature (*ousia*), the second two to their volitive faculty, 'so that what he is in his essence the creatures may become by participation' (*Cap. Car.* 3. 25; trans. Palmer, Sherrard, and Ware). By attaining likeness to God 'so far as is possible to humankind', by participating in the divine attributes through the virtuous exercise of the will, human beings become what God is while still remaining creatures. This is more than just a moral achievement brought about by ascetic endeavour because the mystery of love in which the believer participates is that which has succeeded the law and the prophets—that is, Christ himself.

Finally in the same period (624–5) Maximus touches on deification in two of the *aporiai* in the *Quaestiones et dubia*. In the first he comments on Ephesians 1: 18–19: 'that you may know what is the hope to which he has called you, what are the riches of his glorious inheritance in the saints, and what is the immeasurable greatness of his power in us who believe according to the working of his great might'. The 'working of his great might', says Maximus, is 'the deification to be granted to those who are worthy (ἡ τοῖς ἀξίοις δωρηθησομένη θέωσις), which for those who participate in his attributes makes gods out of human beings' (*Qu.D.* 61, CCSG 10. 48). In the second he comments on the closing words of St Matthew's Gospel: 'I am with you always, to the close of the age' (Matt. 28: 20): 'The Lord says that he is with us in the present age and that the saints, having been deified by grace (τῇ χάριτι θεωθέντες), will be with him in the age to come' (*Qu.D.* 81, CCSG 10. 65). In both of these passages the focus is on the eschatological dimension of deification. Even if it is initiated in some sense in this life, deification by grace is fundamentally the final destiny of the saints.

(c) The Commentary on the Lord's Prayer: the Reciprocal Nature of Kenosis and Theosis

The main texts in which Maximus discusses deification belong to the early years of his sojourn in North Africa. From this period (628–34) we have *Letter* 24/43, the *Commentary on the Lord's Prayer*, the *Mystagogia*, the *Liber Ambiguorum*, the *Quaestiones ad Thalassium* and the *Chapters on Theology*, which together provide us with a profound meditation on the significance of deification from several different approaches.

Letter 24/43, addressed like Letter 2 to John the Cubicularius, contains a major statement of the place of deification in the divine scheme of things:

> Because he is truthful he will give us everything that he has promised. This is 'what no eye has seen, nor ear heard, nor the heart of man conceived, what God has prepared for those who love him' (1 Cor. 2: 9). For that is also why he made us, that we might 'become partakers of the divine nature' (2 Pet. 1: 4) and sharers in his eternity, and prove to be like him through the deification bestowed by grace. (*Ep.* 24, PG 91. 609C (= *Ep.* 43, 640BC)

Deification is presented in this passage as the goal for which human beings were created (cf. Larchet 1996: 84). It is achieved through attaining a likeness to God, not merely by moral effort but as a result of divine grace experienced as the gift of theosis. This gift is a participation in the divine attribute of eternity. Maximus (unlike Cyril) appeals only rarely to 2 Peter 1: 4. Perhaps he regarded it as potentially dangerous to draw his readers' attention to a participation in a *physis* that might have been understood in terms of *ousia*. For Maximus 'participation' does not seem to have had a clearly defined philosophical sense. Normally participation is in the attributes of God and his spiritual gifts (e.g. *Qu.D.* 180, CCSG 10. 123). But on one occasion Maximus can say that we become 'partakers of the divine nature' (2 Pet. 1: 4) without further qualification, so that 'what [God] is by essence the creature might become by participation' (*Cap. Car.* 3. 25, PG 90. 1024BC). And on another (an exegesis of Paul's 'fellow-heirs with Christ' (Rom. 8: 17)) he can say that we (humanity as a whole) receive the whole of Christ as God and man 'by an ineffable participation', corresponding to his descent 'by an unfathomable condescension' (*Thal.* 59, CCSG 22. 59. 230–2). That this does not imply participation in God's essence, however, is made clear in such passages as his discussion in *Ambiguum* 7 of what it means to become 'a part of God', to which we shall come shortly.[34]

It was probably shortly after the letter to John the Cubicularius that Maximus composed his *Commentary on the Lord's Prayer* (628–30), which he produced in response to a request from an unnamed correspondent. In the prologue he says that he will set down not his personal opinions but what God wills, 'for the Lord's counsel stands for ever' (Ps. 33: 11). Commenting on the word 'counsel', he says:

Perhaps the counsel of God the Father to which David here refers is the unfathomable self-emptying of the only-begotten Son which He brought about for the deification (ἐπὶ θεώσει) of our nature, and by which He has set a limit to the ages. (*Or. dom.* Prol., CCSG 23. 29. 41–4; PG 90. 873CD; trans. Palmer, Sherrard, and Ware)

Again, deification is the goal for which humanity was created. But an important new theme is also introduced, the reciprocal relationship between the incarnation of the Word and the deification of man. The kenosis of the divine Son took place in order to bring about the theosis of the human person. The fact that deification is the *skopos*, the salvific goal, of the divine counsel is the chief grounds for our learning the Lord's Prayer and putting it into practice (*Or. dom.* 1, CCSG 23. 29. 50–2, 873D). For the Lord's Prayer contains the seven great new mysteries of the New Dispensation. These are: 'theology, adoption as sons by grace, equality with the angels, participation in eternal life, the restoration of human nature when it is reconciled dispassionately with itself, the abolition of the law of sin, and the destruction of the tyranny that holds us in its power through the deceit of the evil one' (*Or. dom.* 1; trans. Palmer, Sherrard, and Ware).

The appropriation of each of these mysteries corresponds to a different aspect of the *processus* of deification:

Theology, or the knowledge of God, is an essential prerequisite. It is taught by the incarnate Word of God, since he manifests in his own person both the Father and the Spirit. None of the three Persons can be known in his essential being, but the Son's hypostatic union with the flesh has made him, and through him the Father and the Spirit, accessible to the human mind through their operations (876CD).

The second mystery, adoption as sons by grace, is brought about by baptism and is maintained with God's help by the pursuit of the moral life

---

[34] Cf. Larchet (1996: 600–1), who notes that Maximus does not develop a precise idea of participation and gives several examples. 2 Peter 1: 4 is cited perhaps three times by Maximus, at *Ep.* 12, PG 91. 468C, *Ep.* 24, PG 91. 609C (= *Ep.* 43, 640B) and *Or. dom.* 5, PG 90. 905D; cf. Russell 1988.

through the practice of the commandments. Maximus expresses the fruits of this by a variation on the exchange formula, man's kenosis with regard to the passions responding to God's kenosis with regard to divine power, thus drawing the human and the divine towards each other on convergent courses: 'by emptying themselves of the passions they lay hold of the divine to the same degree as that to which, deliberately emptying himself of his own sublime glory, the Logos of God truly became man' (*Or. dom.* 2, 877A; trans. Palmer, Sherrard, and Ware).

The third mystery is equality with the angels. This has been achieved in principle for humanity by Christ's sacrifice on the cross. The fundamental work of the atonement was to overcome divisions and bring about unity. One of these divisions is the one existing between heaven and earth, the reconciliation wrought by Christ 'making the festal assembly (πανήγυριν) of earthly and heavenly powers a single gathering for his distribution of divine gifts, with humankind joining joyfully with the powers on high in unanimous praise of God's glory' (*Or. dom.* 2, 877B; trans. Palmer, Sherrard, and Ware). In a more mystical sense he united heaven and earth in his own person, so that those who participate in him spiritually participate in the unity he has restored.

The fourth mystery enters more deeply into this mystical dimension: The Word 'enables us to participate in divine life by making himself our food, in a manner understood by himself and by those who have received from him a noetic perception of this kind. It is by tasting this food that they become truly aware that "the Lord is good" (Ps. 34: 8), for he transmutes those who eat it with a divine quality, bringing about their deification (ποιοτῆτι θείᾳ πρὸς θέωσιν μετακιρνῶν τοὺς ἐσθίοντας) since he is clearly the bread of life and of power both in name and in reality' (*Or. dom.* 2, 877C; CCSG 23. 34. 129–33; trans. Palmer, Sherrard, and Ware, modified). The Word is received as spiritual food through a 'noetic', or intellectual, appropriation of the divine, but the eucharistic allusion is no doubt also intentional.

The fifth mystery is the unification of human nature. Here Maximus is referring to the healing of the will of fallen humanity, which pulls us in contrary directions. Christ's voluntary acceptance of his passion has broken down the dividing wall (cf. Eph. 2: 14). That is to say, on one level he has removed the barrier between Jews and Gentiles, and on the other he has abolished the interior conflicts of the human will, for 'our will is no longer opposed to the principle of nature, but we adhere to it without deviating in either will or nature' (*Or. dom.* 2, 880A; trans. Palmer, Sherrard, and Ware).

The sixth mystery is the abolition of the law of sin. Again Christ accomplishes something in his own person which affects the rest of humanity. His virginal conception and birth gave Christ a human nature unencumbered by sensuality. He frees human nature in principle from the bonds of sin. Those who are willing can share in the benefits of this, 'for the mystery of salvation

belongs to those who choose it, not to those who are compelled by force'
(*Or. dom.* 2, 880B; trans. Palmer, Sherrard, and Ware).

The final mystery is the destruction of the tyranny of the evil one. The
flesh defeated in Adam proves victorious in Christ, Adam's captor himself
being captured. The flesh of Christ thus becomes poison to the devil but life
to humankind.

These seven mysteries are the benefits wrought by the Word's incarnation.
Change is brought about in human nature in principle by Christ, and then
appropriated by the individual believer through a free act of faith. This
appropriation of the work of Christ by the believer is manifested as theosis,
which is presented in a series of ascending unities as equivalent to adoption,
unification with the angels, and participation in divine life (cf. *Amb. Io.* 41,
PG 91. 1308B). The underlying sacramental symbolism is there even if
not made explicit. Baptism and the Eucharist are implied as our means of
sharing in the divine life through the free exercise of the will.

After the Prologue, Maximus returns to deification by name in the *Commentary on the Lord's Prayer* only on two further occasions. The first occurs at
the end of his long discussion of the petition 'Thy kingdom come'. The
coming of the kingdom is 'the perfection of the person created according to
Christ'. A person who is gentle and humble 'moves incessantly towards God'
(πρὸς θεὸν ἀεικίνητος) (*Or. dom.* 4, 893C; trans. Palmer, Sherrard, and Ware).
Such a person practises self-denial:

For he does not regard what is painful in the senses as a privation of pleasure: he
knows only one pleasure, the marriage (συμβίωσιν) of the soul with the Logos. To
be deprived of this marriage is endless torment, extending by nature through all the
ages. Thus when he has left the body and all that pertains to it, he is impelled towards
union with the divine; for even if he were to be master of the whole world, he would
still recognize only one real disaster: failure to attain by grace the deification for
which he is hoping (τῆς προσδοκωμένης κατὰ χάριν θεώσεως). (*Or. dom.* 4, 893D;
trans. Palmer, Sherrard, and Ware)

The second occasion occurs in the peroration to the work. Maximus refers
again to the angelic state to which the believer is raised by Christ when in
fulfilment of the Father's will he has set aside the passions and allowed
himself to be led only by an insatiable desire for Christ. But the attainment
of the angelic life is not the ultimate goal. A still higher level awaits us:

Then he leads us up still further on the supreme ascent of divine truth to the Father
of lights, and makes us share in the divine nature (cf. 2 Pet. 1: 4) through participation by grace in the Holy Spirit. By virtue of this participation we are called children
of God and, cleansed from all stain, in a manner beyond circumscription, we all
encircle him who is the author of this grace and by nature the Son of the Father.
From him, through him and in him we have and always will have our being, our
movement and our life (cf. Acts 17: 28).

When we pray, let our aim be this mystery of deification, which shows us what we were once like and what the self-emptying of the only-begotten Son through the flesh has now made us .... (*Or. dom.* 5, 905D–908A; trans. Palmer, Sherrard and Ware)

In these two passages from the main body of the text of the *Commentary on the Lord's Prayer* it is the eschatological dimension of deification on which Maximus concentrates. In a manner reminiscent of Origen and Gregory of Nyssa, he presents the journey towards God as a dynamic *diabasis* without end. The moral life orients us towards God. But it is in virtue of our having come to participate in the Holy Spirit through our baptism that Christ bestows on us the grace to live in the closest companionship (συμβίωσις) with him, and takes us up still further to share in the attributes of the Father. Deification is an ascent towards successively higher levels of unity and ever greater intimacy with God. In a sense it is therefore also a return to our origins. The divine likeness lost in Adam was restored to humanity in Christ, and is acquired by believers in a personal way through their seeking their destiny in Christ (cf. Madden 1982: 149–50).

(d) The Mystagogia: the Ascent to God through Contemplation

The *Mystagogia*, or Commentary on the Liturgy, comes from the same period (628–30). In the Prologue Maximus mentions Dionysius' commentary (the *Ecclesiastical Hierarchy*) but says that he will follow a different plan. He begins by considering the church building first as an image of God, then of the world, and finally of a human being. It is in his discussion of the church as an image of a human being and of how we attain unity from multiplicity, how we reintegrate the many faculties and virtues of the soul so as to arrive at a oneness that assimilates us to God, that he first makes mention of theosis. A glance at Maximus' psychology, as briefly set out by Maximus himself in Chapter 5 (PG 91. 672D–676A), will help us to understand this. Not only is the human being a composite creature consisting of body and soul, but the soul itself is also twofold.[35] Its dual aspect, contemplative and active, reflects its two fundamental powers, the one intellectual (νοερά), the other vital (ζωτική). These powers lead to a system of linked faculties and virtues, the syzygies of the soul: mind (*nous*) and reason (*logos*), wisdom and prudence, contemplation and action, knowledge and virtue, enduring knowledge and faith, the first element of each pair representing the intellectual aspect, the second the vital. The first elements, considered as an independent series, have truth as their goal (*telos*), the second elements, goodness. Goodness and truth together reveal God. By joining goodness to truth, the soul reduces the decad (the five syzygies) to a monad. This is the oneness that unites it to God. It is thus that Maximus is able to say of the soul:

---

[35] This is the basic dichotomy on which Maximus builds his normally trichotomist psychology. Cf. Thunberg 1995: 169–79.

It will be beautiful and splendid, having become as like him as possible by the perfecting of the four principal virtues which reveal the divine decad in the soul and include the other blessed decad of the commandments. For the tetrad is the decad in potency, joined together in a progressive series from the monad.[36] And, moreover, it is itself a monad which combines to embrace the good as a unity and which by being itself shared without division reflects the simplicity and indivisibility of the divine activity. It is through them that the soul vigorously keeps its own good inviolable and bravely repels what is alien to it as evil, because it has a rational mind, a prudent wisdom, an active contemplation, a virtuous knowledge, and along with them an enduring knowledge which is both very faithful and unchangeable. And it conveys to God the effects discretely joined to their causes and the acts to their potencies, and in exchange for these it receives the deification that creates simplicity (τὴν ποιητικὴν τῆς ἁπλότητος θέωσιν). (*Myst.* 5, PG 91. 680AB; trans. Berthold, modified)

Maximus returns several times to the unifying, and therefore deifying, effect of the contemplative or active operations of the virtuous mind. The syzygies of the soul, as pairs of causes and effects, produce an ingrained disposition towards goodness and truth. This disposition is 'the divine science and precise knowledge, the love and peace, in which and through which theosis arises' (*Myst.* 5, PG 91. 680BC). The person who wishes to be pleasing to God must pay diligent attention to his soul, 'which is immortal and divine and destined to be deified as a result of the virtues' and hold the flesh in contempt (*Myst.* 7, PG 91. 685D).

The remaining mentions of deification are set more precisely in an ecclesiastical context in the various reprises of the liturgical action given by Maximus in the course of his commentary. The first occurs in chapter 13, where Maximus rapidly reviews the chants and actions involving the whole body of the faithful after the reading of the Gospel and the closing of the church's doors. In a series of allusions to ascending levels of unity reminiscent of his commentary on the Lord's Prayer, he passes from the kiss of peace (reconciliation with each other and with God), to the recitation of the Creed (thanksgiving for salvation), to the singing of the Sanctus (unity with the angels), to the recitation of the Lord's Prayer (adoption in the Spirit), and finally, at the climax of the rite just before communion, to the acclamation 'One is holy', which symbolizes the ascent of the faithful 'in a manner beyond knowledge to the unknowable monad, deified by grace, and made like the monad by participation in an indivisible identity so far as this is possible' (τῇ χάριτι θεωθέντας καὶ κατὰ μέθεξιν πρὸς αὐτὴν ὁμοιωθέντας τῇ κατὰ δύναμιν ἀδιαιρέτῳ ταυτότητι) (*Myst.* 13, PG 91. 692C).[37]

---

[36] Maximus is referring here to the Pythagorean tetractys. Cf. Iamblichus, *Theology of Numbers*, who says that the decad 'is consummated by the tetrad along with the numbers which precede it' (trans. Waterfield 55), i.e. 10 is the product of 1+2+3+4.

[37] θεωθέντας is the reading given by Sotiropoulos. Combefis has ἑνωθέντας, 'unified'.

When the sacrament is distributed, those who receive it worthily are transformed into it, for the sacrament, as pure goodness, is a powerful cause
which produces a like effect. Nothing of this good is lacking in the participants so far as is humanly possible. 'As a result, they have the ability to be
gods by adoption through grace both in reality and in name, because the
whole of God fills them entirely and leaves no part of them empty of his
presence' (*Myst.* 21, PG 91. 697A).

Maximus concludes his *Mystagogia* with two extended meditations on the
same liturgical events as symbolic of the mystical ascent of the soul. The first
occurs in the twenty-third chapter. The entrance of the clergy and people
into the church represents the recollection of the senses and the withdrawal
of the mind from external appearances. The divine chants kindle an ardent
desire for God. The hearing of the Gospel, coming after the Law and the
Prophets, brings the mind into unity with itself. The bishop's descent from
his throne after the readings to go to the altar symbolizes the descent of the
Word from heaven. The dismissal of the catechumens is the separating out
of those thoughts that are bound up with the senses. The closing of the
doors after their departure signifies the attaining of a knowledge of intelligibles which is immaterial, simple, immutable, and godlike through entering
into unutterable mysteries. In this final stage of recollection the mind
encounters the Word himself. By the kiss of peace the soul brings
together the ineffable principles and modes of salvation, while the Word
teaches it to give thanks through the Symbol of Faith. Now the soul
attains the mind (νόησιν) of the angels, so far as this is possible for
human beings. It encompasses the spiritual principles of sensible things
and even penetrates to the nature of the monad and the triad, the oneness and threeness of God. Abstracted from all things and focusing
entirely on the unity of the Godhead, it is taken up by God, in a way
entirely appropriate to himself 'as he infuses himself into it without
passion and deifies it completely' (ἀπαθῶς ἑαυτὸν ἑνίεντος, καὶ ὅλην
θεοποιήσαντος) (*Myst.* 23, PG 91. 701C).

In the first part of the following chapter Maximus considers the ascent of
the soul once more, this time from the perspective of the work of the Holy
Spirit. Again we are taken through the readings, the closing of the doors, the
kiss of peace, the reciting of the Creed, and the entry into the central
mystery of the rite. Through the singing of the Sanctus the soul is raised up
to union and equality of honour with the angels as it joins with them in the
sanctifying glorification of God. Through the praying of the Our Father it
receives adoption by the grace of the Holy Spirit. And 'through the holy
reception of the spotless and life-giving mysteries it receives all possible
communion and identity with him [i.e. God] by participation through having
attained likeness to him, on account of which man is deemed worthy to
abandon his human status and become a god' (*Myst.* 24, PG 91. 704D).

The peroration of the Mystagogy is a brief recapitulation, as Maximus says (705A), of what he has been discussing up to this point. He touches again on the symbolic meanings of the first entrance of the people and the clergy, the readings, the divine melodies of the chants, the descent of the bishop from his throne, the closing of the doors, the kiss of peace, the singing of the Sanctus and the recital of the eucharistic prayer. The climax, as before, is the communion of the faithful:

The blessed invocation of the great God and Father and the acclamation of the 'One is holy', etc., and the reception of the holy and life-giving mysteries signify the adoption, the union and intimacy, and the divine likeness and deification (θέωσιν) that is in every case to come upon all who are worthy through the goodness of our God. (*Myst.* 24, PG 91. 709C; trans. Berthold, modified)

Maximus likes to build up his arguments by setting up corresponding triads. In this passage calling God Father is linked with adoption, the acclamation 'One is holy' with union and intimacy, and the reception of the sacrament with attaining the divine likeness and deification. In the next paragraph there are further sets of triads. The faithful, the virtuous, and the gnostics correspond to beginners, those making progress, and the perfect, who in turn correspond to the biblical triad of slaves, hired servants, and sons. In these triads the sons belong to the highest grade, as do the perfect and the gnostics:

A son is the one to whom it was said: 'Son you are always with me, and all that is mine is yours, (Luke 15: 31). Through deification by grace (κατὰ τὴν ἐν χάριτι θέωσιν)[38] they are so far as possible what God is and is believed to be by nature and cause. (*Myst.* 24, PG 91. 712A)

In the last analysis deification is not a private mystical experience, the result of a self-centred cultivation of the soul's development in isolation from other people. Deification is the fruit of love, and that is something that precludes the neglect of one's neighbour. A good disposition must manifest itself in an altruistic love that imitates and reciprocates the divine philanthropy:

For a work is proof of a disposition. Nothing brings us more easily either to justification or to deification (if I may speak thus), nothing is more apt to bring about closeness to God, than mercy towards the needy offered from the soul with pleasure and joy. (*Myst.* 24, PG 91. 713A)

Thus Maximus can ask:

Who is therefore so slow and unresponsive with regard to virtue as not to desire deity (μὴ ἐφίεσθαι θεότητος) when the acquisition of it is so cheap, easy, and effortless? (*Myst.* 24, PG 91. 713C)

---

[38] Larchet (1996: 602–3) prefers to read κατὰ θέσιν (with Combefis) rather than κατὰ θέωσιν (with Sotiropoulos).

(e) The Liber Ambiguorum: *the Mutual Interpenetration of the Human and the Divine*

When he was writing the *Mystagogia*, Maximus had before him the *Ecclesiastical Hierarchy* of Dionysius the Areopagite. In the *Liber Ambiguorum*, the earlier part of which belongs to the same period (628–30), he set himself the task of explaining difficulties in Dionysius and Gregory of Nazianzus (PG 91. 1032B). The first collection of *Ambigua* is addressed to John, archbishop of Cyzicus. In this collection *Ambiguum* 7, which is devoted to the refutation of Origenism, contains one of Maximus' most important discussions of deification. The second part of the *Ambiguum* comments on a passage from Gregory of Nazianzus' *Fourteenth Oration* which seems to imply that originally we fell from heaven (cf. Greg. Naz. *Or.* 14. 7, PG 35. 865C). At issue here is the doctrine of the *logoi*, by which Origen accounts for the participation of beings in God. The later Origenists, according to the anathemas of 553, had made the fall of the soul from its original perfection one of their principal doctrines. In their view spiritual beings had originally enjoyed repose (στάσις), but through satiety (κόρος) had experienced a fall (κίνησις), which had brought them into a condition of corporeal existence (γένεσις). Against this descending triad, repose—fall—corporeal birth (στάσις—κίνησις—γένεσις), Maximus opposes an ascending triad, being—well being—ever being (εἶναι—εὖ εἶναι—ἀεὶ εἶναι), an extraordinarily rich idea which implies a progressive acquisition of the likeness of God through a triple birth of the believer (naturally in the double birth of soul and body, sacramentally in baptism, and eschatologically in the resurrection) which corresponds to a triple birth of Christ not only in his incarnate life (birth as man, baptism, resurrection) but also in his life as the eternal Word (Christ becoming incarnate typologically in the Scriptures, historically in the flesh, and spiritually in the believer) (cf. Thunberg 1995: 368–73).

The biblical basis on which Maximus develops these themes is the Pauline conviction that we are in Christ and Christ is in us. Paul says: 'It is no longer I who live, but Christ who lives in me' (Gal. 2: 20). We should not be perplexed by this, says Maximus. The saying does not imply the destruction of our free will, but rather our relationship to what is by nature stable and immutable, or the free surrender of our will (ἐκχώρησιν γνωμικήν). It is from this that we take our idea of being and movement,

like the image ascending to the archetype or like the impression of a stamp faithfully reflecting the archetype that henceforth has neither the inclination nor the ability to be borne elsewhere. Or to put it more clearly and more accurately, that does not have the power to will, because it has received the divine energy, or rather, because it has become a god by deification, and moreover has been pleased to separate itself from the things and concepts that naturally belong to it, through the grace of the Spirit which has conquered it. It has shown that it has only God operating, so that there is a single energy throughout all, an energy both of God and of those worthy of God, or rather of God alone, as wholly indwelling (περιχωρήσαντος) all who are worthy in a manner befitting goodness. (*Amb. Io.* 7, PG 91. 1076BC)

Christ is in us, raising us from being to well being and even to ever being by the grace of the Spirit. But we are also in Christ, for 'in him we live and move and have our being' (Acts 17: 28). This phrase from Paul's speech before the Areopagus (quoting Epimenides of Knossos) gives Maximus the opportunity to present a portrait of the deified man:

He comes to be in God through attentiveness, since he has not corrupted the *logos* of being that pre-exists in God, and he moves in God in accordance with the *logos* of well being that pre-exists in God, since he is activated by the virtues, and he lives in God in accordance with the *logos* of ever being that pre-exists in God. In this life, because he has made a highly impassible habit of mind his own, he is already immovable, and in the life to come, because of the deification which will be given to him, he will lovingly accept and embrace the *logoi* mentioned above that pre-exist in God, or rather, he will accept and embrace God himself in whom the *logoi* of the good are established. And he is 'a part of God' (μοῖρα θεοῦ), as one who exists, on account of the *logos* of his being which is in God, as one who is good, on account of the *logos* of well being which is in God, and as a god, on account of the *logos* of his ever being which is in God. He has respected these and operated in accordance with them. By these he has inserted himself totally into God alone, and has imprinted the stamp and form of God alone totally upon himself so that he himself may be a god by grace and be called such, just as God is a man by condescension and is called such on his account, and also so that the power of this reciprocal arrangement (ἀντιδιδομένης ἐπὶ τούτῳ διαθέσεως) may be revealed that deifies man for God through his love for man, and by this beautiful correspondence (καλὴν ἀντιστροφήν) makes God man, for the sake of man's divinization, and man God for the sake of God's humanization (ποιοῦσαν . . . τὸν μὲν θεὸν ἄνθρωπον, διὰ τὴν τοῦ ἀνθρώπου θέωσιν, τὸν δὲ ἄνθρωπον θεόν, διὰ τὴν τοῦ θεοῦ ἀνθρώπησιν). (*Amb. Io.* 7, PG 91. 1084BC)

This is a very full statement of the principle of reciprocity which we shall encounter again in *Ambiguum* 10. By cultivating the likeness of God through the practice of the virtues and the exercise of love in virtue of God's condescension to man at the Incarnation, a human being can live with the life of God alone and share in his attributes. This is what it means to attain well being.

Maximus continues his portrait of the deified man with the following passage:

The whole of the rational creation of angels and men—those of them that have not corrupted through negligence any of the divine *logoi* naturally united to them by the Creator for the sake of the final end in accordance with the movement, but rather have prudently kept themselves whole and unperverted, as instruments of divine nature, and possess knowledge now and in the future—these he treats as he sees fit, to whom the whole of God has adhered altogether in the manner of a soul, since they have become suitable and useful to the Master like members of a body. He fills them with his own glory and beatitude, giving them and granting them that life which is eternal and unutterable and in every way free from every mark constitutive of the present life, which is made up of decay, for it does not breathe air nor is it made up of blood vessels running from the liver. No, the whole of God is participated by the whole of them, and he becomes to their souls like a soul related to a body, and through the soul he affects the body, in a way that he himself knows, that the former might receive immutability and the latter immortality, and that the whole man might be deified, raised to the divine life (θεουργούμενος) by the grace of the incarnate God, the whole remaining man in soul and body by nature, and the whole becoming god in soul and body by grace and by the divine brightness of that blessed glory altogether appropriate to him, than which nothing brighter or more exalted can be conceived. For what is more desirable to the worthy than deification, by which God makes the whole of himself through goodness united to those who have become gods? (*Amb. Io.* 7, PG 91. 1088BC)

The best comment on this doctrine of the mutual interpenetration of the human and the divine in the person who has attained both well being and ever being is provided by Maximus himself in his first *Opusculum*:

With regard to the single operation (μίας ἐνεργείας) treated in the seventh chapter of the great Gregory's *Ambigua*, the argument is clear. In my description of the future state of the saints I said that there is a single operation of God and of the saints which has the power to deify all the saints, the operation of the beatitude that is hoped for, which exists in essence in God and is brought about by grace in the saints. 'Or rather, of God alone', I added (cf. PG 91. 1088A), since the deification of the saints by grace, the potentiality for which we do not have implanted in us by nature, is a consequence of the divine operation alone. Neither the potentiality (δύναμιν) for these things nor the accomplishment (πρᾶξιν) of them belongs to us, for the latter is complementary to a natural capacity. It is a fact that accomplishment depends on potentiality, and potentiality on substance (οὐσίας). For accomplishment derives from potentiality and potentiality derives from substance and is inherent in substance. These are therefore said to be three things dependent upon each other: the empowered (δυνάμενον), potentiality (δύναμις), and the practicable (δυνατόν). 'The empowered' is a term applied to substance, 'potentiality' to that by which we have the power of movement, and 'the practicable' to that which lies within our power to bring about. If something is naturally within our power to bring it about, we have it by a natural potentiality. Deification does not belong to what lies within our potentiality to bring about naturally, since it is not within our power. For no *logos* of that which transcends nature lies within nature. Therefore deification is not an accomplishment that belongs to our potentiality: we do not possess the potentiality for it by nature, but only through the divine power, since it is not a reward given to the saints in requital for righteous works, but is proof of the liberality of the Creator, making the lovers of the beautiful by adoption that which he has been shown to be by nature, according to the *logoi* which he himself knows, so that he may both be perfectly known and also remain completely beyond comprehension. I therefore did not abolish the natural activity of those who will experience this, an activity that they naturally cease from and manifest only the experience of enjoying the good things, but simply indicated the supernatural power that brings about deification and produces what it does for the sake of the person deified. (*Opusc.* 1, PG 91. 33A–36A)

Maximus is anxious to exclude any idea that theosis is the product of human effort or that it destroys a person's identity. But one who experiences it voluntarily lays aside normal human functions and manifests only what is divine.

The role of the body is examined a little further on in *Ambiguum* 7 where Maximus comments on Gregory Nazianzen's statement in his *Fourteenth Oration*, that we become a 'part of God' when the body is trained to be a co-worker with the soul (PG 35. 865C):

What he [Gregory] means is something like this: God in his goodness made man to consist of soul and body, in that he gave him a soul endowed with reason and intelligence. As the soul is in the image of him who made it, on the one hand it cleaves closely to God intellectually in desire and in total love with all its power, and receives in addition deification in accordance with the likeness (τὸ καθ᾽ ὁμοίωσιν προσλαβοῦσαν θεωθῆναι). On the other, it cleaves to the body wisely with intelligent forethought for that which supports it and in accordance with the commandment to love one's neighbour as oneself, and it reckons to reconcile it [the body] through the virtues to God as a fellow-servant, itself mediating to procure for it the indwelling of its Maker, and to make him who has bound them together the indissoluble bond of the immortality which he has given to it. This is so that what God is to the soul, the soul might become to the body, and that God should be proved to be the unique Creator of all things, that he might occupy all beings in proportion through the human race, and that the many that are by nature separated might come into one with each other, converging upon each other around the one nature of man. It is also so that God himself might become all in all, embracing all things and making them subsist in himself, by the fact that no being possesses any longer any movement independent of him, nor is without a share (ἄμοιρον) in his presence. It is in this sense that we are 'gods' and 'children' and 'body' and 'members' and 'part' (μοῖρα) of God in name and in reality, by virtue of the reference of the divine plan (σκοπός) to the end (τέλος). (*Amb. Io.* 7, PG 91. 1092BC)

In this passage deification is related to man's role as mediator, Maximus explaining Gregory's characterization of man as a 'part' of God and in doing so correcting an Origenistic version of the apocatastasis. Although all human beings have the potentiality to be saved—'the unique divine power will manifest itself in all things, in a vivid and active presence proportioned to each one' (*Myst.* 7, PG 91. 685C; trans. Berthold)—they are saved in virtue of the orientation of their will, not through their ontological make-up (Larchet 1996: 652–62).

The next *Difficulty* in which deification is mentioned is the tenth. The passage under discussion is drawn from Gregory's *Twenty-first Oration*. Here Gregory is at his most Platonist (cf. Blowers 1991: 102–6). The person who is blessed is one who has escaped from matter through the exercise of reason and the practice of contemplation, which raise that person, so far as is permissible for human nature, to assimilation to God and union with light. The ascent from this world to deification in the next is achieved by true philosophy and by transcending the duality of matter through the unity perceived in the Trinity (*Or.* 21. 2, PG 35. 1084C). Maximus first tackles the apparently Origenistic suggestion that deification might be attained by intellectual effort alone without the work of asceticism. He excuses Gregory for not mentioning the latter because the ascetic struggle does not create virtue; it only manifests it. True philosophy is a divine power which makes us participators in the Good and 'parts of God'. Those who have been drawn into the closest possible relationship with God do really transcend matter (PG 91. 1108B). But how? Through withdrawing from practical activity and devoting themselves to the contemplation of God. Maximus draws on Dionysius' teaching about three different kinds of motion of the soul to suggest the different ways in which we can know God (PG 91. 1112D–1113A; cf. *DN* 4. 8–9, PG 3. 704D–705B). The first, corresponding to Dionysius' circular movement, is a direct intuition of God by the mind without any intermediary. The second, corresponding to Dionysius' linear movement, is the intellectual activity of the deduction of causes. The third, corresponding to Dionysius' spiral movement, is the contemplation of the images provided by the senses. It is as a result of these different approaches that we gain knowledge of God:

Thus they raise the mind, freed and pure of any motion around any existing thing and at rest in its own natural activity, to God, so that in this way it is wholly gathered to God, and made wholly worthy through the Spirit of being united with the whole Godhead, for it bears the whole image of the heavenly, so far as is humanly possible, and draws down the divine splendour to such a degree, if it is permitted to say this, that it is drawn to God and united with him. For they say that God and man are paradigms of one another, that as much as God is humanized to man through love for mankind, so much has man been able to deify himself to God through love (τοσοῦτον τῷ ἀνθρώπῳ τὸν θεὸν διὰ φιλανθρωπίαν ἀνθρωπίζεσθαι, ὅσον ὁ ἄνθρωπος ἑαυτὸν τῷ θεῷ δι᾽ ἀγάπης δυνηθεὶς ἀπεθέωσε), and that as much as man is caught up by God to what is known in his mind, so much does man manifest God, who is invisible by nature, through the virtues. (*Amb. Io.* 10, PG 91. 1113BC; trans. Louth, lightly modified)

The exchange formula brings out the analogous nature of the divine in man. Human beings are able to deify themselves by the practice of the virtues because God has already presented them with an exemplary humanity—the 'image' which is Christ. They 'draw down the divine splendour' not by a Neoplatonic practice of theurgy (even if the language is similar) but by restoring the image of God in themselves through responding in love to the divine *philanthropia* manifested in the Incarnation. Those minds which have thus come to bear 'the whole image of the heavenly' achieve a transition from the sensible to the intelligible, from being to well being (the life of virtue) and ultimately to ever being (the eschatological fulfilment in God), though even now there are 'natural reflections of the divine dwelling within them'.

One of those who transcended the material in this way was Abraham, on whose attempted sacrifice of Isaac Maximus offers a spiritual meditation. The meaning behind the biblical text (Gen. 22: 1–19) is

> that there can be no divine offspring in the mind of the free understanding in the spirit, if it is attached to the enslaved seed of the flesh, but that it can happen by the blessed promise, that is, the grace of deification laid up in hope for those who love the Lord, which already exists figuratively and can be received in advance. (*Amb. Io.* 10, PG 91. 1200B; trans. Louth)

Abraham is a historical example of a mind which has been drawn up to God. He has transcended the passionate aspect of the soul (represented by his natural attachment to his son) and has received even in this life in symbolic form the eternal well being which is the ultimate fruit of the love of God.

In *Ambiguum* 20 another opportunity for the discussion of deification is presented by a difficulty concerning Gregory of Nazianzus' statement in his *Second Theological Oration* that Paul was taken up into the third heaven (2 Cor. 12: 2) by his own advance (πρόοδος), or ascension (ἀνάβασις), or assumption (ἀνάληψις) (*Or.* 28. 20, Mason 51). In his response Maximus assigns Gregory's three equivalent expressions to three different categories. The first term, 'advance', belongs to the category of substance ('man'), the second, 'ascension', to the category of relation ('good man'), and the third, 'assumption', to the category of grace (as when a man is called a 'god'), for

> the man who has in all things become obedient to God, in accordance with the text, 'I said, you are all gods' (Ps. 82: 6), is not a god, nor is he called such, in accordance with [the category of] nature or relation, but he has become a god and is called such in accordance with [the category of] adoption and grace. (*Amb. Io.* 20, PG 91. 1237A)

Grace is not correlative to a natural faculty capable of receiving it, otherwise it would not be grace but a natural power.

In that case, again, the fact would not be strange if deification was in accordance with a faculty capable of receiving nature. For deification would not be a gift of God but appropriately a work of nature, and such a person would be capable of being a god by nature and of being called such in a proper sense. (*Amb. Io.* 20, PG 91. 1237B)

Having established that point, Maximus declares: 'How, then, deification makes the deified person go out from himself, if it is contained within the bounds of nature, I am unable to conceive.' Paul was able to ascend to the third heaven only because his deification enabled him to transcend the limitations of human nature.

In the rest of his discussion Maximus speculates on the nature of Paul's ascent to the third heaven on the basis of the fundamental principle he has established that such an ascent is a gift of grace and not a natural intellectual accomplishment. The three expressions put forward by Gregory, coupled with the three heavens traversed by Paul, offer Maximus a perfect opportunity to present his interpretation as a series of linked triads. 'Advance', 'ascension', and 'assumption' correspond to three ascending levels of knowledge (the ethical, the contemplative, and the theological) which correspond in turn to three ascending levels of being or modes of existence (the moral life, the intellectual life, and the divine life). The highest level or mode in ontological terms is a return (ἀποκατάστασις) by grace of all things to the Creator 'from whom and through whom and in whom they exist' as to the goal or consummation (πέρας) of their being (1240A). Or alternatively, in epistemological terms, it is 'an ineffable initiation into true and theological wisdom' (1240B). The attainment of this level or mode enables the person thus taken up to be called by the name of God, or to become a god by analogy (1240A).

The third heaven is not a place, for by his ascent the believer transcends both time and place (1240A). Maximus conjectures (κατὰ στοχασμόν) that the boundaries of the third heaven are provided by the *logoi*, the inner principles, of his three epistemological approaches, 'practical philosophy, natural contemplation and theological mystagogy' (1240B). Or alternatively, in more biblical (and Dionysian) terms, it refers to the three orders of angels above us (1240C). Paul, rapt out of the body in a way that surpasses words and knowledge, received in the third heaven words communicated to him in silence by a supernatural initiation (κατὰ μύησιν ὑπερκόσμιον). In conclusion, Maximus offers a final triad corresponding to Gregory's three expressions, namely, the Pauline faith, hope, and love:

The perfect practice of virtue, in accordance with what is termed 'advance', is brought about, as the experts say, by correct faith and the genuine fear of God; the faultless contemplation of nature, in accordance with 'ascension', is brought about by confident hope and an untroubled conscience; and deification, in accordance with 'assumption', is brought about by perfect love and a mind voluntarily blind to all existent things in a superlative degree.   (*Amb. Io.* 20, PG 91. 1241B)

The connection of deification with love is also underlined in the next *Ambiguum*, where Maximus (attempting to read a deeper meaning into Gregory's slip of the pen in attributing the Evangelist's words at John 21: 25 to the Baptist) presents love as ecstatic and unifying and therefore deifying (θεοποιητική) (*Amb. Io.* 21, PG 91. 1249B). This is a theme that Maximus had already sketched out in his letter to John the Cubicularius (*Ep.* 2). Here, drawing on the theoretical work of Evagrius Ponticus, he develops it in systematic detail (1248A–1249B). The five senses form a series parallel to the five faculties or aspects of the soul, sight, hearing, smell, taste, and touch with regard to the sensible world corresponding, respectively, to the intelligent (νοερά), the rational (λογική), the incensive (θυμική), the appetitive (ἐπιθυμιτική), and the vital (ζωτική) aspects of the soul with regard to the spiritual world. When the corresponding faculties in each series function together in harmony, they produce the four general virtues, prudence (φρόνησις) being derived from the combination of sight with intelligence and hearing with reason, courage (ἀνδρεία) from the combination of smell with the soul's incensive faculty, moderation (σωφροσύνη) from the combination of taste with the appetitive faculty, and justice (δικαιοσύνη) from the combination of touch with the vital faculty. The four general virtues combine in turn to form two still more general virtues, prudence and justice linking to produce wisdom (σοφία), the goal of knowledge (πέρας τῶν γνωστῶν), and courage and moderation linking to produce serenity (πραότης) or dispassion (ἀπάθεια), the goal of action (πέρας τῶν πρακτῶν). Love (ἀγάπη) is finally a combination of σοφία with πραότης. It therefore brings to its possessor a deisimilar unity, not because it makes the other virtues superfluous, as in Evagrius, but because it is the compendium of all the virtues, the fruit of the correct functioning of the whole human person in both its corporeal and its spiritual aspects (cf. Thunberg 1995: 309–22; Larchet 1996: 477–88).

The remaining allusions to deification in the *Ambigua* all occur in the context of discussions of the broader divine *skopos* of creation. In *Ambiguum* 31 Maximus offers a series of meditations on Gregory of Nazianzus' statement: 'The laws of nature are dissolved; the world above must be filled' (*Or.* 37. 2). In one of these he takes the dissolution of the laws of nature to refer to the Incarnation, when the Word became perfect man without abandoning his own nature in the slightest degree, 'and deified us perfectly without in any way denying our own nature by the slightest change' (*Amb. Io.* 31, PG 91. 1280B). In *Ambiguum* 41 Maximus returns to the same theme in greater detail. His discussion is prompted by another variant of the same statement of Gregory of Nazianzus: 'And natures are instituted afresh, and God becomes man' (*Or.* 39. 13, PG 36. 348D). On this occasion he dwells on the human person's return to unity with its cause through transcending the five divisions dividing everything that has come into being. In descending order, the first division is between uncreated and created, the second between intelligible and sensible, the third between heaven and earth, the fourth between paradise and the inhabited world, and the fifth between male and female. The human person transcends these divisions one by one in reverse order as it ascends to ever greater levels of unity. The last division is transcended by that same love which, as we have seen, unites all the human faculties and all the virtues:

And finally, beyond all these, the human person unites the created nature with the uncreated through love (O the wonder of God's love for us human beings!), showing them to be one and the same through the possession of grace, the whole [creation] wholly interpenetrated (περιχωρήσας) by God, and become completely whatever God is, save at the level of being, and receiving to itself the whole of God himself, and acquiring as a kind of prize for its ascent to God the most unique God himself . . .   (*Amb. Io.* 41, PG 91. 1308B; trans. Louth)

The next *Ambiguum* comments on Gregory's three births, 'namely, the natural birth, that of baptism and that of the resurrection' (*Or.* 40. 2). Baptism prepares the believer for his third birth into the divine life by enabling him to attain the likeness of God:

Those who treat of divine things in a mystical way . . . say that humanity first came into existence in the image of God assuredly so as to be born of the Spirit by choice and receive in addition the likeness which comes upon it through the keeping of the divine commandment, so that the same human being should be the creation (πλάσμα) of God by nature and also the son of God and a god through the Spirit by grace. For it was not possible in any other way for a created human being to be proved a son of God and a god through deification by grace (κατὰ τὴν ἐκ χάριτος θέωσιν) unless first he had been born in the Spirit by choice, through the independent power of self-determination that naturally dwells within him. This deifying (θεοποιόν) and divine and non-material birth was neglected by the first human being through his preferring sensible and discernible pleasure to goods that are for the time being spiritual and invisible.   (*Amb. Io.* 42, PG 91. 1345D–1348A)

If the second birth of baptism is connected with the baptism of Christ, participation in which raises the believer in principle to divine sonship, the third birth is connected with his resurrection, which marks the definitive transition to divine glory. Commenting on Gregory's 'more sublime than the sublime or more wonderful than the wonderful' from his sermon 'On the New Sunday' (*Or.* 44. 5), Maximus says:

And again the first Sunday is a symbol of the future natural resurrection and incorruption, the second bears the image of the future deification by grace. If indeed the enjoyment of goods is on a higher level than the state of purification from evils, the state of perfection in accordance with true knowledge on a higher level than the healthy exercise of free will in accordance with virtue, and the re-formation by grace after the divine model in accordance with deification (ἡ ἐν χάριτι πρὸς τὸν θεὸν κατὰ τὴν θέωσιν μεταποίησις), on a higher level than natural incorruptibility, of which things the first Sunday is a type and the second a symbol, the teacher [Gregory], moved by the Spirit, rightly calls the new Sunday more sublime than the sublime.   (*Amb. Io.* 63, PG 91. 1389B (duplicated in *Amb. Io.* 10, PG 91. 1176A))

The second collection of *Ambigua*, written shortly after 633, is addressed to an enquirer called Thomas. The third difficulty concerns a passage from Gregory's *Third Theological Oration*, delivered in Constantinople in 380, in which Gregory deals with the problems raised by the Eunomians. He states that through Christ's assumption in the flesh 'man here below became god, since he was mingled with God and became one, the higher nature having prevailed that I might become a god in the same measure as he became a man' (*Or.* 29. 19, PG 36. 100A; Mason 103. 3–4). Commenting on the last phrase, 'that I might become a god in the same measure as he became a man', Maximus says to his respondent:

It does not refer to my situation, for I am sullied by sin and completely without an appetite for what is life in the true sense. It refers to yours, for through the perfect recovery of nature you are distinguished by grace alone and are destined by the power that derives from this to be proved a god in the same degree as he who is God by nature partook of our weakness when he became incarnate, the deification (theosis) of those who are being saved by grace being measured out in a manner known only to himself against his own self-emptying (kenosis). They will become wholly godlike and receptive of the whole of God and him alone. For this is the perfection towards which those who believe that they are truly following the promise hasten. (*Amb. Th.* 3, PG 91. 1040CD)

Maximus reproduces Gregory's *tosouton . . . hoson* construction, bringing out more fully the reciprocity between kenosis and theosis by emphasizing the contrast between the deity by nature of God, which he 'contracts' by his self-emptying in order to accommodate himself to the conditions of human life, and the deity by grace of man, by which we are 'expanded' so as to be able to receive God. The analogous nature of Gregory's model of deification recedes. The 'mingling' between God and man refers not only, as in Gregory, to the body of Christ, but more explicitly to the believer in relation to God. The human and the divine penetrate each other as a result of grace (cf. also *Amb. Th.* 4, PG 91. 1044D; Larchet 1996: 629–30).

(f) *The* Quaestiones ad Thalassium: *the Fulfilment of the Coming Age*

The *Quaestiones ad Thalassium* was written in North Africa in 630–3 shortly after the earlier *Ambigua*. The occasion of writing was a request from a monastic superior called Thalassius for the resolution of a number of scriptural difficulties,[39] some of them genuine cruxes, such as the cursing of the barren fig tree (Matt. 21: 18–22; Mark 11: 12–14), others passages from the Old and New Testaments which seemed to call for an extended spiritual exposition. The question and answer exchange between Thalassius and Maximus, as Paul Blowers has demonstrated, indicates a specifically monastic setting (1991: 56–69). Maximus' use of the plural 'you' (e.g. Intro., CCSG 7. 21. 70–1) seems to suggest that the difficulties had arisen in the context of discussions amongst the brethren of Thalassius' community. On the

---

[39] Thalassius, it should be noted, had requested an *anagogical* (i.e. a spiritual or mystical) interpretation of Scripture (*Thal.* Intro.; CCSG 7. 17. 19–7. 19. 29).

narrowly monastic level, Maximus seeks (as in the *Ambigua*) to correct the Origenism of the Evagrian tradition. In more general terms, his intention is to defend the integrity of the biblical text and its value for spiritual reading, 'to show that all of scripture – including, indeed especially, its difficult passages, its ἀπορίαι – is indispensable to the soul in its struggle to attain to deification' (Blowers 1991: 14).

One of these *aporiai*, the nature of the mysterious tree of the knowledge of good and evil, is taken up in the Introduction to the *Quaestiones ad Thalassium*. Why are good and evil bracketed together as the fruit of the same tree? And why is the fruit forbidden? The answer is that knowledge can be either good or evil: good when it is interpreted spiritually, evil when it is taken in a corporeal sense, the latter being a teacher of the passions.

That is why, perhaps, God forbade it to the man for a while, postponing its consumption so that first, as was most just, having come to know his own cause through participation in it by grace, together with the immortality given to him in accordance with grace, and having been trained by such participation for dispassion and immutability, as if he had already become a god by deification (ὡς θεὸς ἤδη τῇ θεώσει γενόμενος), he might safely examine God's creatures with God's permission and receive the knowledge of them as a god, not as a man, possessing by grace and with wisdom the same knowledge of beings as God, through the re-forming of the mind and the senses for deification (διὰ τὴν πρὸς θέωσιν τοῦ νοῦ καὶ τῆς αἰσθήσεως μεταποίησιν). (*Thal.* Intro., CCSG 7. 37. 338–49)

But instead of fulfilling his vocation and being deified as God intended, the first man himself deified creation (τὴν κτίσιν ἐθεοποίησεν) (*Thal.* Intro., CCSG 7. 37. 355; cf. 43. 429). This misuse of knowledge was the essence of the Fall (cf. Blowers 1991: 172 n. 155; Larchet 1996: 190–4).

A number of the questions that follow touch upon the subject of humanity's failed destiny and the steps needed to recover it. The second question concerns a text in John, 'My father is working still, and I am working' (John 5: 17). If the Father completed the work of creation in six days (cf. Gen. 2: 1–3), what work is he doing now? The answer is that God is working not only for the preservation (συντήρησις) of his creatures, but also for their advance (πρόοδος) and their providential attainment of the divine likeness (ἐξομοίωσις). Such an attainment is a movement towards unity and well being, a movement from the partial and divided to the complete and universal: 'the one and the same *logos* will be observed in all things, not divided into the modes in which it is equally predicated, and thus will manifest the grace in action that deifies all things' (ἐνεργουμένην τὴν ἐκθεωτικὴν τῶν ὅλων ἐπιδείξηται χάριν) (*Thal.* 2, CCSG 7. 51. 18–22).

In the ninth question Thalassius asks Maximus to reconcile the Johannine 'Brethren, we are God's children now, and it does not yet appear what we shall be' (1 John 3: 2) with the Pauline 'For the Spirit searches everything, even the depths of God' (1 Cor. 2: 10). In his reply Maximus makes a distinction between our knowledge on the one hand of the divine *skopos* and our ignorance on the other of precisely what our future state will be. John says that he did not know 'the mode of the future deification of those who become in this life children of God through the virtues in accordance with faith' because the reality of the form of future goods has not yet been revealed. For the present we walk with faith. Paul speaks about the revelation of God's plan with regard to future goods, but not because he himself knows 'the mode of deification according to the divine plan' (*Thal.* 9, CCSG 7. 79. 15–16). Which is why he says: 'I press on toward the goal for the prize of the upward call of God' (Phil. 3: 14). That is, he wishes 'to know from experience the mode of the actual fulfilment of the *skopos* (which is divine and known to him in this life through revelation) of the power that is capable of deifying those who are worthy' (τῆς ἐκθεωτικῆς τῶν ἀξιουμένων δυνάμεως) (*Thal.* 9, CCSG 7. 79. 18–21). The apostles agree with one another (they 'sing the same tune') because they are moved by the same Spirit. 'The one confesses his ignorance of the mode of the future deification according to grace (τοῦ τρόπου τῆς μελλούσης κατὰ τὴν χάριν θεώσεως), the other magnanimously introduces the knowledge of the goal' (τοῦ σκοποῦ . . . τὴν εἴδησιν) (ibid. 24–6).

The eleventh question enquires into the fall of the angels, which is given prominence in the Epistle of Jude: 'What is the principle [ἀρχή – RSV: "position"] the angels did not keep and what is their dwelling which they left (Jude 6)?' Maximus forgoes the opportunity to expatiate on angelology. He contents himself with stating that the angels were created for the same *skopos* as human beings and were equipped with more formidable means for attaining it: The 'principle' is the *logos* according to which they were created, 'or the natural power (δυναστεία) given to them by grace for their deification (πρὸς ἐκθέωσιν)' (*Thal.* 11, CCSG 7. 89. 15–16).

The thirteenth question is on the 'eternal power and deity' that may be observed in the phenomenal world (cf. Rom. 1: 20). This refers to the providence (πρόνοια) that maintains all things and the deifying operation (ἐκθεωτικὴ . . . ἐνέργεια) of that providence upon them (*Thal.* 15, CCSG 7. 95. 16–17). Power is correlative to providence and deity to deification.

The fifteenth question investigates the operation of the Holy Spirit. According to Maximus the biblical passages adduced (Wisd. 1: 4 and 12: 1) indicate the three activities of the Spirit: the sustentive (συνεκτικόν), the legislative (νομοθετικόν) and the deifying (θεοποιόν). These spheres of operation become increasingly more focused. The first activity follows from the presence of the Holy Spirit in all things as the natural principle or *logos* of their being. The second alludes to his operation under the Old Covenant, supplying moral law and the typological adumbration of the mystery of Christ in the Scriptures. The third is restricted to the baptized. For in addition to the first two modes of operation the Holy Spirit is also in all those who through faith have been allotted the divine and truly deifying (θεοποιὸν) name of Christ. He is present in them not only as guardian and providential motivator of the natural principle of beings, as demonstrator of the transgression of the commandments and protector thereof, as proclaimer of the prophecy of Christ, but also as creator of the sonship given them by grace through faith. For as worker of wisdom he comes into those who alone have been cleansed in body and soul by the exact observance of the commandments. He converses with them as his own, by simple and immaterial knowledge, and stamps their minds with the undefiled grasp of ineffable realities, leading to deification (πρὸς ἐκθέωσιν ἐντυποῦν). (*Thal.* 15, CCSG 7. 101. 28–103. 40; trans. Blowers 1991: 167–8)

The work of the Holy Spirit begins with baptism but must be maintained by the keeping of the commandments, for the Spirit's deifying indwelling (θεωτικὴ ἐνοίκησις) is dependent upon a devout way of life (*Thal.* 15, CCSG 7. 103. 50).

In the twentieth question Thalassius raises the problem of the barren fig tree (Matt. 21: 18–22; Mark 11: 12–14). 'What is to be made of the incontinence of [Jesus'] hunger in seeking fruit out of season? And what is meant by the curse of something that is senseless?' (*Thal.* 20, CCSG 7. 121. 2–5; trans. Blowers 1991: 33). Maximus' reply is that Christ is here addressing the vainglory of the Scribes and the Pharisees. His appetite is for the salvation of all men and he hungers for their salvation (πεινῶν αὐτῶν τὴν ἐκθέωσιν). In cursing the one that does not bear fruit he is cursing the hypocrite. The real meaning must be the symbolic one.

With the twenty-second question we come to a *locus classicus* of deification. Thalassius' enquiry concerned the meaning of Ephesians 2: 7: 'that in the coming ages he might show the immeasurable riches of his grace in kindness towards us in Christ Jesus'. For Maximus the 'coming ages' are the two ages of sarkosis and theosis, of the humanization of the divine and the divinization of the human, which meet in the person of Jesus Christ:

He who, by the mere inclination of his will, laid the foundation of all creation, visible and invisible, had in an ineffable manner a supremely good plan (βουλὴν) for created beings before all ages and before the creation of those beings. The plan was for him to mingle, without change on his part (ἀτρέπτως ἐγκραθῆναι), with human nature by true hypostatic union (διὰ τῆς καθ᾽ ὑπόστασιν ἀληθοῦς ἑνώσεως), to unite human nature to himself while remaining immutable (ἀναλλιώτως), so that he might become a man, as he alone knew how, and might make humanity divine in union with himself. Also, according to the plan, it is plain that God wisely divided and distinguished the ages between those intended for the purpose of God becoming a man, and those intended for the purpose of man being made a god. (*Thal.* 22, CCSG 7. 137. 4–16; trans. Blowers 1991: 128–9, modified)

With regard to the two ages, one of the scholia (Laga and Steel (1980: xii) think it probable that Maximus was his own scholiast) summarizes the difference as follows:

Of the ages, the former are revelatory of the divine incarnation, and have reached their term with us; the latter are indicative of our deification (ἐκθεώσεως) the richness of whose glory has not yet been revealed. (Scholion 2, CCSG 7. 143. 7–10)

Humankind is now at some point in its passage through the second age. The first age not only makes the second one possible through the redemptive work of Christ but is its pledge and guarantee:

For if he has fulfilled the goal of his mystical effort for becoming a man, having become like us in every respect save without sin, and even descended into the lower regions of the earth where the tyranny of sin was pressing humanity, then God will also completely fulfil the goal of his mystical effort to deify humanity (ἐπὶ τῷ θεωθῆναι τὸν ἄνθρωπον μυστικῆς ἐνεργείας λήψεται πέρας), in every respect, of course, short of an identity of essence with God, and assimilate humanity to himself and elevate it to a position above all the heavens. It is to this exalted position that the greatness of God's grace, and of his infinite goodness, summons lowly humanity. (*Thal.* 22, CCSG 7. 139. 37–46; trans. Blowers 1991: 129)

As an exegesis of Ephesians 2: 7 this is the literal or historical sense. In a further comment Maximus makes use of a 'katagogic' christological perspective drawn from Cyril of Alexandria in order to summarize the nature of the relationship of the two ages: 'In short, the former have to do with God's descent (καταβάσεως) to human beings, while the latter have to do with humanity's ascent (ἀναβάσεως) to God' (*Thal.* 22, CCSG 7. 139. 54–6; trans. Blowers 1991: 130). Divine incarnation and human ascent are intimately related and indeed correlative to each other.[40]

At this point Maximus turns to the spiritual sense of the two ages, the sense that may be applied to the inner life of the believer. The two ages on this level represent a principle of activity (τὸ ποιεῖν) on the one hand and a principle of passivity (τὸ πάσχειν) on the other. The former may be regarded as the age of the flesh, 'characterized by activity', that is to say, by the struggle of the ascetic life, and the latter as the age of the Spirit, 'characterized by the transformation of humanity in its passivity':

Existing here and now, we arrive at the ends of the ages precisely as active agents and reach the end of the exertion of our power and activity. But in the coming ages, we shall undergo the transformation of deification by grace (τὴν πρὸς τὸ θεοῦσθαι χάριτι μεταποίησιν) and be no longer active but passive; and for this reason we shall not cease from being deified (οὐ λήγομεν θεουργούμενοι). At that point our passivity will be supernatural, and there will be no limit to the divine activity in infinitely deifying those who are passive (ἐπ' ἄπειρον τῶν τοῦτο πασχόντων θεουργίας). (*Thal.* 22, CCSG 7. 141. 74–82; trans. Blowers 1991: 130, lightly modified)

---

[40] Larchet remarks that there is a risk that in subordinating the Incarnation to divinization the former on the one hand is made a necessary *processus*, and on the other is reduced to an instrumental function (1996: 86). He believes Maximus is aware of the danger, however, for elsewhere he underlines the voluntary nature of the Incarnation.

The passivity of this transformation emphasizes its gifted nature:

> For nothing created is by nature productive of deification, any more than it is capable of comprehending God. It is a natural property of divine grace alone to grant beings deification in a proportionate manner, and to illuminate their nature by the light that transcends nature, enabling it to rise above their limitations through the abundance of glory.   (*Thal.* 22, CCSG 7. 141. 93–8)

The fifth scholion drives this point home:

> Thus we passively experience deification by grace as something which is above nature, but we do not actively accomplish it; for by nature we do not have the capacity to attain deification.   (*Thal.* 22, schol. 5, CCSG 7. 145. 28–30; trans. Palmer, Sherrard, and Ware)

The mystery of Christ as the context in which the spiritual transition is made from the limitations of this life to the transcendent glory of the next is the subject of the thirty-fifth question. The texts under discussion concern the flesh, bones, and blood of Christ (John 1: 14; 6: 53; 19: 31–6; cf. Exod. 12: 46). Maximus offers several allegorical interpretations of these in which the flesh and blood stand for various aspects of the spiritual life that are accessible to the believer, while the bones represent the mystery of a divinity that remains hidden. Thus:

> It could perhaps be said as well that the flesh of the Logos is the return and restoration of human nature to itself through virtue, while his blood is the future deification that will sustain human nature by grace unto eternal well-being. His bones are the unknown power itself that sustains human nature, through the process of deification, unto that eternal well-being.   (*Thal.* 35, CCSG 7. 241. 39–44; trans. Blowers 1991: 148)

In terms of Question 22 the flesh is the active life of the pursuit of virtue, the blood the passive life in which we are transformed by divine glory.

The fortieth Question, on the significance of the six stone jars at the wedding feast at Cana (John 2: 6), gives Maximus the opportunity to discuss the divine plan of salvation once again through a symbolic interpretation of the details of the biblical narrative. Humanity was created with all that it needed to do God's will. The six jars stand for the effective power that made it possible for it to keep the divine commandments. They were empty at the feast because humanity had squandered their contents in the pursuit of material goals. When the Creator appeared as Saviour he refilled them with the power of the natural knowledge that enabled humanity again to fulfil what was required of it. But when the water was changed into wine, humanity was able to receive a knowledge that transcended nature. This is why 'the good wine, that is the wine productive of deification' comes last of all. It stands for the eschatological transformation of nature by direct divine action into something productive of supernatural joy.

Two further details of the story are developed in a way that reinforces this interpretation: the servants who drew the water, and the mother of the Word who bade her Son perform the miracle. With regard to the first:

The drawers ... are the ministers of the Old and New Testaments ... through whom the water of knowledge was drawn and was returned again to nature. This water was changed into the grace of deification by him who had in his goodness created nature, and was deified by the Word by grace through his love for humanity. (*Thal.* 40, CCSG 7. 273. 103–10)

With regard to the second detail, the mother of Jesus stands for faith. For just as Mary gave birth to the Word historically in the flesh, so faith engenders the Word spiritually in our hearts. Accordingly, just as his mother was present with Jesus at the wedding feast, so it is the Word together with faith that restores the knowledge lost to us through sin 'and changes it into the deification that banishes the mind from the genesis of beings, strengthening the knowledge of nature, and, as it were, putting sinews in it in order to make it immutable, like spiritual water strengthened with the quality of wine' (*Thal.* 22, CCSG 7. 275. 136–50).[41]

The fifty-fourth Question is on the significance of Zerubbabel, who led the exiles out of Babylon and back to Jerusalem (1 Esdras 4: 58–60). Zerubbabel, of course, is a type of Christ, who unlike the first Zerubbabel did not lead the captives from one land to another, but from earth to heaven, from evil to virtue, from ignorance to knowledge, from corruption to incorruption, from death to immortality, from the phenomenal to the real, from transience to permanence (*Thal.* 54, CCSG 7. 457. 244–59). This transition brought about by Christ is actually an improvement on the original creation. The Incarnation took place

in order to save the image and immortalize the flesh and, having utterly banished the principle of the serpent which had been introduced into nature, to present nature pure again as from a new beginning, with an additional advantage through deification over the first creation (τῇ θεώσει πλεονεκτοῦσαν τὴν πρώτην διάπλασιν), and, as if by a new beginning giving substance to something not previously existing, to restore to health that which had thus collapsed, having strengthened it so as to be immune to falling through its immutability, and to fulfil all the will of God the Father with regard to it, having deified it by the power of the Incarnation. (*Thal.* 54, CCSG 7. 459. 278–86)

It is not only the humanity assumed by Christ that is deified through the Incarnation. Among the spiritual meanings suggested by the various details of the biblical allusions to Zerubbabel is an account of how Christ deifies the devout Christian. Zechariah's vision of Zerubbabel mentions the plummet – in the Septuagint, the plummet of tin – with which Zerubbabel laid

---

[41] Cf. *Qu.D.* 54 (CCSG 10. 465. 379) where faith + the moral life = deification (ἐκθέωσις).

the foundations of 'this house' (the second Temple) and with which he will complete it (the Church) (Zech. 4: 9–10). 'Some say,' says Maximus, 'that tin is an alloy of silver and lead' (*Thal.* 54, CCSG 7. 465. 368–9). Lead is symbolic of training and punishment and the weight of punishment, silver of brightness and glory and splendour. The alloy of the two thus represents faith, which on the one hand punishes and disciplines, but on the other 'brightens and glorifies and illuminates and leads those who have attained excellence in it to deification (ἐκθέωσιν) through the keeping of the commandments' (*Thal.* 54, CCSG 7. 465. 378–80).

There is another possible interpretation of the plummet from a christological viewpoint: 'Some have taken the plummet of tin to refer to the Lord Jesus Christ' (*Thal.* 54, CCSG 7. 465. 383–4). In this case the plummet symbolizes the twofold operation of Christ in the believer, on the one hand (as lead) training the soul and disciplining the flesh, on the other (as silver) 'illuminating the mind with the virtues and glorifying it with knowledge and turning it into light by theosis, since he is the representation of the first light' (cf. Heb. 1: 3) (*Thal.* 54, CCSG 7. 465. 389–91).

Questions 59, 60, and 61, in which Maximus comments on a series of verses of the First Epistle of Peter, highlight the relationship between theosis and salvation. The subject of Question 59 is the verse: 'As the outcome (τέλος) of your faith you will obtain the salvation of your souls' (1 Pet. 1: 9). Maximus has already dwelt on faith as the essential prerequisite for deification (in Questions 22 and 54). Here the end of faith is salvation, which enables him by a chain argument to make it equivalent to deification and link it, moreover, to 'participation in divine things that transcend nature', to attainment of likeness to that which is participated, and even to arrival at identity with it, for theosis 'is in outline the boundary and limit of times and ages and of everything within times and ages' and thus marks the transition to eternity (*Thal.* 59, CCSG 22. 53. 1040–3). Those who have striven to attain this are the saints. With the spiritual eye of the soul fixed on their goal, they sought 'after the resurrection of their will the incorruption also of their nature'. They did not still need the resurrection of the will because they had already received it from the Spirit in accordance with their pursuit of the practical life: 'They sought the incorruptibility they did not have, and searched out the modes and principles of the deification that accompanied it' (*Thal.* 59, CCSG 22. 59. 219–21; cf. *Thal.* 59, CCSG 22. 61. 240–3). Salvation is thus 'the fullest grace of deification that will be given to the worthy by God' (*Thal.* 61, CCSG 22. 103. 303–4).

In Questions 60 and 61 Maximus gives particular attention to the role of Christ in the work of salvation and consequently deification. Christ is both the creator and the redeemer of humanity, playing an active part first in our coming into existence (being), then in our transition through baptism to the moral life (well being), and ultimately in our entry into eternity (ever well being): 'He who was the creator of the substance which beings possess by nature also personally effected (αὐτουργὸν) the deification of creatures by grace, so that the giver of well being should also be proved to be the bestower of ever well being' (*Thal.* 60, CCSG 22. 79. 117–20). The work of Christ undoes that of Adam by giving humanity the possibility of a second birth. The 'undoing' is emphasized by a series of paradoxical juxtapositions. By his passion Christ brought about dispassion, by his death eternal life, and by his natural sarkosis a supernatural theosis.

In Questions 63 and 64 Maximus returns to the exegesis of the christo-logical and spiritual senses of select passages from the Old Testament. The first text is Zechariah 4: 2–3, the vision of the lampstand and the two olive trees. In his usual manner Maximus presents several possible interpretations. In one of them the two trees represent providence and justice, providence on the right (the hypostatic union of the Word with ensouled flesh, which we can see only by faith), and justice on the left (understood by us 'in the mystery of the life-giving sufferings endured by the incarnate God for our sake') (*Thal.* 63, CCSG 22. 173. 429–30): 'The right-hand tree is therefore the providential mystery of the incarnation of the Word, as effective (ἐνεργητικὸν) of the supernatural deification by grace of those being saved, a deification predestined before the ages, which no principle in beings will be able to attain in the least degree by nature' (*Thal.* 63, CCSG 22. 173. 439–43). The left-hand tree is the mystery of the passion, as effective of the return to obedience. Thus providence/judgement is presented as equivalent to Incarnation/passion.

Alternatively, the two trees stand for the two peoples, Jewish and Gentile, for out of them is created a single people, the 'sons of fatness' (Zech. 4: 14, LXX). 'Fatness' suggests the oil of baptism, which makes men sons of God 'by birth in the Spirit and by the grace of adoption for deification' (τὴν πρὸς θέωσιν χάριν τῆς υἱοθεσίας) (*Thal.* 63, CCSG 22. 177. 487–9). The lampstand in the middle is God incarnate.

Question 64 comments on the last verse of Jonah on God's pity for Nineveh, 'in which there are more than a hundred and twenty thousand persons who do not know their right hand from their left' (Jonah. 4: 11), which gives Maximus the opportunity to set out at length his thinking on the relationship between the natural law, the written law, and the law of grace. He presents these three kinds of law in terms of three ascending degrees of love. The natural law promotes rational behaviour. It is that to which Christ refers when he urges us to treat others as we would wish to be treated ourselves (cf. Matt. 7: 12; Luke. 6: 31). The written law encourages the fear of God and the formation of habits of virtue. It is summed up in the com-mandment to love one's neighbour as oneself (cf. Matt. 22: 39; Mark 12: 31). The law of grace, which was inaugurated by the Incarnation, teaches us to imitate God. It represents the degree of love that Christ expresses by loving us more than himself, for he made our condemnation his own 'and deified us by grace in the same degree that he became man by nature in accordance with the economy of salvation', that we might learn the truly spiritual love summed up in the verse: 'Greater love has no man than this, that a man lay down his life for his friends' (John 15: 13).

Therefore the law of nature, to put it briefly, is a natural rational principle which takes control of the senses in order to banish irrationality, which divides that which is naturally united. The written law is a natural rational principle, which, after the removal of the irrationality of the senses, bestows in addition a spiritual desire, which brings about a reciprocal relationship with that which is kin to us. But the law of grace has been established as a supernatural rational principle that refashions nature in an immutable manner for the sake of deification, that reveals, as if in an image, in a manner incomprehensible to the nature of men, the archetype that transcends substance and nature, and that bestows the permanent possession of eternal well being. (*Thal.* 64, CCSG 22. 237. 794–804)

(g) *The* Gnostic Centuries: *the Perfection of the Saints*

The eschatological aspect of deification is also treated in the two *Centuries on Theology and the Incarnate Dispensation of the Son of God*, the so-called *Gnostic Centuries*, which belong to about the same period as the *Quaestiones ad Thalassium* (630–4). The first occasion is in the course of a discussion on the significance of the eighth day, the day following the seven days of creation. Historically the eighth day is the day of the resurrection of Christ. In the inner life of the devout Christian the eighth day stands for the attainment of the fullness of life. The six days of creation symbolize the stages of the moral or philosophical life, culminating on the sixth day with the contemplation of the inner principles of everything subject to nature and time. The seventh day stands for the intellect's transcendence of created things, when the Christian enters into the repose of God.

But if he is also found worthy of the eighth day he has risen from the dead – that is, from all that is sequent to God, whether sensible or intelligible, expressible or conceivable. He experiences the blessed life of God, who is the only true life, and himself becomes a god by deification. (*Cap. Theol.* 1. 54, 1104AB; trans. Palmer, Sherrard, and Ware, modified; cf. *Cap. Theol.* 1. 55, 1104B; 1. 60, 1105A)

That the eschatological fulfilment of the eighth day may be anticipated even in this life by those who are advanced in spiritual knowledge is illustrated by the Transfiguration. Christ was and is experienced in two forms. As he was perceived in the normal state of his earthly life, he is the Christ of the *praktikoi*, the beginners. As he was perceived by Peter and John and those who have become like them, he is the Christ of the *gnostikoi*, the spiritually advanced:

The first is an image of the Lord's initial advent, to which the literal meaning of the

Gospel refers, and which by means of suffering purifies those practising the virtues. The second prefigures the second and glorious advent, in which the spirit of the Gospel is apprehended, and which by means of wisdom transfigures and deifies those imbued with spiritual knowledge (τῆς διὰ σοφίας τοὺς γνωστικοὺς μεταμορφούσης πρὸς θέωσιν): because of the transfiguration of the Logos within them 'they reflect with unveiled face the glory of the Lord' (2 Cor. 3: 18). (*Cap. Theol.* 1. 97, 1124A; trans. Palmer, Sherrard, and Ware)

This second advent is the angelic state, which is characterized by dispassion and incorruptibility (*Cap. Theol.* 1. 98).

Towards the end of the second Century Maximus speculates on the state of perfection of the saints, whether it involves progress and change or is a fixed condition. He draws an analogy with the physical development of the human person towards full maturity: food is taken first for growth and then for sustenance.

In the same way the reason for nourishing the soul is also twofold. While it is advancing along the spiritual path it is nourished by virtue and contemplation, until it transcends all created things and attains 'the measure of the stature of the fullness of Christ' (Eph. 4: 13). Once it has entered this state it ceases from all increase and growth nourished by indirect means and is nourished directly, in a manner which passes understanding. Having now completed the stage of growth, the soul receives the kind of incorruptible nourishment which sustains the godlike perfection granted to it, and receives a state of eternal well being. Then the infinite splendours inherent in this nourishment are revealed to the soul, and it becomes a god by participation in divine grace (γίνεται θεὸς τῇ μεθέξει τῆς θεϊκῆς χάριτος), ceasing from all activity of intellect and sense, and at the same time suspending all the natural operations of the body. For the body is deified along with the soul through its own corresponding participation in the process of deification (συνθεωθέντος αὐτῇ κατὰ τὴν ἀναλόγουσαν αὐτῷ μέθεξιν τῆς θεώσεως). Thus God alone is made manifest through the soul and the body, since their natural properties have been overcome by the superabundance of his glory. (*Cap. Theol.* 2. 88, 1165D–1168A; trans. Palmer, Sherrard, and Ware, modified)

After the *Gnostic Centuries* Maximus' attention came to be fully absorbed by the monothelite question. In this connection he comments several times on what he takes to be Gregory of Nazianzus' mention of the will of Christ as θεωθὲν ὅλον, but never returns to the role of deification in the spiritual life.

(h) The Maximian Vision

Deification for Maximus is central to his theological vision. It provides the purpose and goal of creation. It presupposes and supports his neo-Chalcedonian christology. It expresses the transition in principle of the serious Christian from the flesh to the spirit. And finally, it sums up the entry of the saints into the eternity of the age to come. In presenting his vision Maximus is anxious to exclude both a Eutychian fusion of the divine and the human and an Origenistic ascent of the pure intellect to an undifferentiated assimilation to Christ. Deified human beings become god in the same measure that God became man, but although penetrated by divine energy they retain their created human status.

Deification was the goal for which humanity was created. This is spelled out by Maximus in his interpretation of the details of the Wedding Feast at Cana. Our first ancestors lacked nothing to prevent them from fulfilling the will of God. The commandment prohibiting them from tasting of the tree of the knowledge of good and evil was not arbitrary. It was for their own good: the knowledge of evil exposes us to the passions, and the passions deify creation. The six jars of the Wedding Feast were empty as a result of the Fall, their contents squandered. The Saviour refilled them with the teaching of the law and the prophets. When he changed the water into wine, a new era was introduced that transcended nature. The law and the prophets were now superseded by the mystery of love in the person of Christ.

Maximus' understanding of the Incarnation is Chalcedonian and Cyrillian. Cyril's single-subject christology 'from above' governs Maximus' presentation of the two natures. The divine Word who created us also effected our salvation. He descended in order that we might ascend. He emptied himself in order that we might be filled with divine glory. *Katabasis* is followed by *anabasis*, kenosis by theosis. Christ brought about a situation which excelled that of the original creation. He gave humanity a new beginning: through the hypostatic union of the Word with ensouled flesh, which deified us in principle, through the mystery of the passion, which effected our return to obedience, and through the resurrection, which has inaugurated the age of the Spirit.

In his own person Christ united heaven and earth, created and uncreated. The life of the Christian is an ever-increasing appropriation of the unity achieved by Christ through a transition from the life of the flesh to the life of the spirit. In practical terms a considerable ascetic effort is required. Our understanding of the process is helped by the symbolic value of the various triads by which Maximus discusses the human situation. Our ontological status is presented in terms of being, well being, and ever being. This fundamental trichotomy corresponds to other triads – to the moral life, the intellectual life, and the divine life, to existing as a human being, a good human being, and a god, to faith, hope, and love. The ascetic life is concerned with attaining a moral likeness to God. Through the renunciation of sensual gratification the soul strives to attain a *symbiôsis* with Christ. The human and the divine begin to interpenetrate each other as we appropriate immortality, stability, and immutability.

But deification is not something that can be attained in isolation without the social dimension. The ecclesial life is also needed. Baptism deifies us in a nominal sense by endowing us with the name of Christ. Baptism also bestows the Holy Spirit. And it is the Spirit in its threefold sustentive, legislative, and deifying activity that raises us up to share in the attributes of God. The reception of the Eucharist consolidates this process, which Maximus expresses in terms of further triads. Our life in the ecclesial community is a progress from slaves to hired servants to sons, from beginners to the advancing to the perfect, from the faithful to the virtuous to the gnostics. The final term in each of these triads is equivalent to 'gods'. But this attaining of the status of 'gods' is not the fulfilment of a natural capacity. It is a gift of grace.

The only real disaster that can befall us, says Maximus, is the failure to attain deification. While baptism and the moral life initiate it, the transformation of deification by grace will only take place in the age to come. After the active life of this earthly existence will come the life of passivity, when we shall be transformed by divine glory. Maximus conveys this teaching through the symbolism of the Eighth Day, of which the vision of the Transfiguration was a foretaste.

Maximus, for all the intensity of his conviction, still maintains a distance between the human and the divine in his teaching on deification. God and man are *paradigms* of each other. The emphasis falls on imitation rather than participation. The exchange formula preserves a Chalcedonian distinction between the human and the divine, a perfect coinherence without change of natures. Deification, as Thunberg says, 'is as it were simply the other side of Incarnation' (1995: 432). In appropriating it, human beings attain a deification which is analogous and nominal rather than realistic.

But there is a strong experiential side, too, which we can glimpse from time to time. Maximus is reticent about himself in his writings. He speaks with authority about the contemplative life, but when he gives us his portrait of the deified man, he writes impersonally. Nor does he make any claim for himself when he discusses Paul's ascent to the third heaven. Deification for Maximus is not to be located in private mystical experiences. Where he does seem to write with personal intensity is in his exposition of the Liturgy. The divine chant kindles an intense desire for God. The hearing of the Gospel brings the mind to union with itself. The singing of the Sanctus raises the worshippers to union with the angels. And the reception of 'the spotless and life-giving mysteries' fills them with God 'and leaves no part of them empty of his presence'. It is here in the eucharistic celebration that we can best sense Maximus himself as a contemplative filled with the grace of theosis.

9

Epilogue

With Maximus the Confessor, deification entered the Byzantine monastic tradition as the goal of the spiritual life. Its theological basis, however, did not become a topic of discussion again until the fourteenth century, when it was challenged seriously for the first time by the opponents of Palamism. The final victory of Palamism in 1368 gave official approval to the doctrine of theosis as an authentic part of the Orthodox theological tradition. But with the fall of Constantinople in the following century and the subsequent ascendancy of scholasticism and Latin influence, deification went underground, only to re-emerge with the 'Philokalian renaissance' of the eighteenth century. Even then, its importance only came to be recognized in academic theological circles in the latter half of the twentieth century. Today it has regained its central position in Orthodox thought and has also attracted the interest of Western theologians. The purpose of this final chapter is to outline these developments.

1. Leontius of Jerusalem

Little is known of Leontius of Jerusalem except that he was the author of two polemical treatises, *Against the Monophysites* and *Against the Nestorians*. From these works it is clear that he saw himself as a defender of Chalcedonian orthodoxy against its enemies on both flanks. He has long been thought to belong to the first half of the sixth century, but recently a convincing argument has been made for reassigning him to the early seventh century (Krausmüller 2001). More specifically, his *Against the Nestorians* contains a reference to a massacre of Christians in Jerusalem that seems to place the work between the ferocious conquest of the city by the Persians in 614 and its bloodless surrender to the Arabs in 638 (Krausmüller 2001: 654–6). If *Against the Nestorians* does belong to this period, it finds its historical context in Heraclius' drive to restore religious unity to the empire after his triumphant campaign against the Persians. At this time the Nestorians (who lived mostly in Persian territory) came into prominence in Byzantine affairs. The

Nestorian Catholicos Isho'yahb II twice led a Persian embassy to Heraclius' headquarters in Armenia (628) and Syria (631). On the first occasion he celebrated a Liturgy at which the emperor and his court received communion (Meyendorff 1989: 342–3). Leontius might well have felt that a refutation of the christology of the Church of the East (as the Nestorian church is properly called) was opportune.

In his argument against the Nestorians Leontius finds deification a useful concept because he is anxious to deny hypostatic status to Christ's humanity. Interpreting Chalcedon's 'one hypostasis in two natures' in the light of Cyril's single-subject christology, he identifies the subject of Christ's life and salvific activity as the Word, who 'having himself in these latter times clothed with flesh his hypostasis and nature, which existed before his human nature, and which, before the ages, was without flesh, hypostatized human nature— not the nature of a mere man—into his own hypostasis ($\tau\hat{\eta}$ ἰδίᾳ ὑποστάσει . . . ἐνυπέστησεν)' (*Adv. Nest.* 5. 28, PG 86. 1748D; trans. Meyendorff 1975: 74, modified). This generic human nature taken into the hypostasis of the Word yet retaining its own identity, is described as 'deified' in order to assimilate it to the Word as closely as possible.

The vocabulary which Leontius uses, however, is not Cyrillian, but resembles that of Dionysius the Areopagite. His nouns are θέωσις (*Adv. Nest.* 1. 18, 3. 1, 3. 8, PG 86. 1468D, 1605A, 1632BC) and ἐκθέωσις (*Adv. Nest.* 1. 18, PG 86. 1468C); his verbs are θεοποιέω (*Adv. Nest.* 3. 8, PG 86. 1632B), θεόω (*Adv. Nest.* 1. 44, PG 86. 1504C) and his own neologism, συνθεόω (*Adv. Nest.* 1. 44, PG 86. 1504C). He also mentions the biblical references to human beings as gods in Psalm 82: 6 and Daniel 2: 47 (*Adv. Nest.* 3. 6 and 3. 8, PG 86. 1621C and 1636C) to demonstrate that without a double consubstantiality Christ would not differ from ordinary human beings.

Leontius begins his treatise by listing the complaints of the Nestorians against the 'monophysites', whether Chalcedonian or otherwise. The first of these is 'that we do not correctly honour the "synthesis" of the divine and human natures' (*Adv. Nest.* Prooem., PG 86. 1400A). Leontius sets himself the task of explaining the 'synthesis' in terms which do justice to the humanity of Christ but do not compromise the leading role of the divinity. To accomplish this he has to show that the hypostasis of the union is the pre-existent hypostasis of the Word. The humanity had no existence before the union. A true account of the union therefore has to respect the integrity of each of the natures but not present the Incarnation as a union between two equals.

Leontius called the product of the union κυριακὸς ἄνθρωπος—'dominical man', a bold expression not generally approved by the orthodox.[1] For

---

[1] Κυριακὸς ἄνθρωπος is first attested in Athanasius, *Exp. Ps.* 40: 6 (see *PGL* s.v. ἄνθρωπος 1. 5), but was regarded as dubious. Gregory of Nazianzus treats it as Apollinarian (*Ep.* 101, PG 37. 177B), but Cyril of Alexandria reports it as used by Nestorius to suggest a specially privileged human being who advanced in wisdom to full divinity (*Dial. Nest.*, PG 76. 252B). (Augustine also used the expression *homo dominicus* but

humanity was taken into the divine hypostasis by an *ektheôsis*: 'Only through the greatest benefaction on the part of [the divine nature] towards us did its incarnation take place, so that to the dominical man there accrued the wealth of deification (τὸν πλοῦτον τῆς ἐκθεώσεως) (*Adv. Nest.* 1. 18, PG 86. 1468C). Grillmeier comments: 'The sluice gates are opened for the flowing of the divine wealth over into the humanity of Christ (the *aparchê* for us) by the recognition of the fact that the human being has now become the "proper nature" of the God-Logos' (1995: 310). If Christ were consubstantial only with us, if he were a God-bearing man, he would not be sufficiently differentiated from us, for we too are called 'gods' in Scripture, having been deified by the grace of adoption (*Adv. Nest.* 3. 6, PG 86, 1621C; 3. 8, 1625D, 1632B). The 'dominical man', however, has special gifts (ἴδια χαρίσματα) which make him the unique Son of God, namely, that he has been set apart from all things visible and invisible like a son born in the purple or even crowned in the womb of his mother,[2] for he has no independent existence: 'He has been united with the God-Logos from his first creation, and is Son not by adoption as we are, but by being united to the Logos for the sake of his manifestation' (*Adv. Nest.* 3. 8, PG 86. 1628D–1629A).

In the early seventh century *theôsis* and *ektheôsis* thus become part of the technical vocabulary of neo-Chalcedonian christological debate. They are used by Leontius to express the 'giving' and 'receiving' of the *communicatio idiomatum*, to maintain the oneness of the hypostasis but keep the difference of the natures by 'attributing the natural properties (ἴδια) to the recipient and the deified properties to the deifier' (καὶ τοῦ θεωθέντος πρὸς τὸν θεώσαντα) (*Adv. Nest.* 1. 44, PG 86. 1504C). Only a few years later Maximus the Confessor uses a similar argument from deification against the Monothelites. For if the human will of Christ is deified, as Gregory of Nazianzus seemed to teach, the fact that there is a deified, and therefore a deifier, implies a duality of natures.[3] The emphasis is different from Leontius, but both theologians find deification useful for expressing the idea of simultaneous unity and duality.

---

later retracted it (*Retract.* 1. 19. 8).) Perhaps for apologetic purposes Leontius was using a term which Nestorians would have found acceptable, but qualifies it by describing such assumed humanity as deified.

[2] For a plausible explanation of this image with reference to contemporary events see Krausmüller 2001: 652–4.

[3] In *Opusculum* 20, 'by 640' according to Sherwood (1952: 41–2), Maximus responds to a set of questions from a priest called Marinus, who was puzzled by certain passages in the works of Anastasius I of Antioch (patriarch 559–70, 593–9). One of these, a quotation from Gregory of Nazianzus' *Fourth Theological Oration* (*Or.* 30. 12), 'his willing is not opposed to God since it is wholly from God', seemed to support the Monothelite position. In his response (PG 91. 233B–236B) Maximus argues that some manuscripts read θεωθέν (deified) rather than θεόθεν (from God). This he believes to be the correct reading because it ties Christ's will in with his divine nature, 'maintaining both the difference and the closest possible union' (PG 91. 236A), and he later uses the same argument in other *Opuscula* (e.g. 3, 48B; 15, 172A, 176A, and 177C). In fact Gregory is arguing against the Eunomian claim that the Son's will being different from the Father's proves that Father and Son are not consubstantial. Although Mason and the Benedictine edition print θεωθέν, the most recent critical editions prefer Anastasius' alternative reading, θεόθεν.

2. John Damascene

With John Damascene (d. *c.*750), we return to the sacramental and eschato-logical dimensions of deification.[4] John, like his father before him, had been in the service of the Caliph at Damascus, but early in the eighth century, perhaps in around 706, resigned his office and became a monk at a monas-tery near Jerusalem. It was there that he composed his compendious *Fountain Head of Knowledge* and his treatises in defence of the holy images, in which he sums up the teaching of his predecessors on deification.

As with Maximus, St Gregory of Nazianzus is his supreme guide, provid-ing him with his theological anthropology and his understanding of the goal of human life. John elaborates his anthropology in his exegesis of the description of Paradise in Genesis. The human person was created as a composite nature consisting of matter and spirit, therefore dwelling simul-taneously both in the realm of the senses and in the realm of the soul. The soul's realm is symbolized by the tree of life, 'where God makes his home, and where he wraps man about as it were with a glorious garment, and robes him in his grace, and delights and sustains him like an angel with the sweetest of all fruits, the contemplation of himself'. By this tree 'the sweetness of participation in the divine is imparted to all who share it' (*De fid. orth.* 2. 11; trans. Salmond).

Such was the original state of humanity. Man was created perfect, 'glori-fied with every virtue', a microcosm of the larger world (*De fid. orth.* 2. 12). His sinlessness did not mean that he was incapable of falling; it meant that sin was the result of the misuse of free will, not an integral part of his nature. John distinguishes between image and likeness. The image resides in the mind and the will; the likeness is the attaining of 'likeness in virtue so far as possible' (*De fid. orth.* 2. 12). The likeness that makes humankind godlike was possessed by it at the beginning. It was ironic that the enemy ensnared it by holding out the hope of divinity (Gen. 3: 5: 'you will be like God, knowing good and evil') (*De fid. orth.* 3. 1).

The Fall lost us the likeness but left the image intact. This provides the basis for the return. Christ 'took on himself a share in our poor and weak nature to cleanse us and make us incorruptible, and establish us once more as partakers of his divinity' (cf. 2 Pet. 1: 4) (*De fid. orth.* 4. 13). The way we avail ourselves of this is through baptism and the Eucharist. The sacraments are adapted to our composite nature. That is why they are both physical and spiritual. We are incorporated into Christ by water and the Spirit, who deifies because he is not himself deified (θεοῦν, οὐ θεούμενον) (*De fid. orth.* 1. 8; cf.

---

[4] There are accounts of John's doctrine of deification in Bornhäuser 1903 and Gross 1938: 328–38. See also Louth 2002: 175, 184, 251.

Greg. Naz., *Or.* 41. 9, PG 36. 441B). The bread and wine of the Eucharist are in reality 'the deified body of the Lord' (*De fid. orth.* 4. 13). For the bread is united with Christ's divinity like Isaiah's burning coal, which is no longer ordinary wood, but wood that is all fire. We receive communion ('partake of the divine coal', as John says) 'that our sins may be consumed and our hearts illumined, that we may be deified by participation in the divine fire' (*De fid. orth.* 4. 13). By communion 'we partake of the divinity of Jesus', we anticipate in this life our future state. For deification is ultimately an eschatological reality. In this life our mode of existence necessarily has much in common with any creature that shares in animal life. 'But elsewhere, that is, in the age to come, [man] is changed and—to complete the mystery—becomes deified, in the sense of participating in the divine glory, not in the sense of changing into divine being' (*De fid. orth.* 2. 12). The sacraments as composites of matter and spirit will then be left behind, for they are simply antitypes of future things, 'not as though they were not in reality Christ's body and blood, but because now we partake of Christ's divinity through them, while then we shall partake intellectually, through the vision alone' (*De fid. orth.* 4. 13).

Our partaking of Christ's divinity through the Eucharist makes us superior to the angels (*Imag.* 3. 26). They participate in divine energy and grace, but are not, as we are through the reception of Christ's body and blood, 'partakers of the divine nature' (2 Peter 1: 4). Originally, man was created little less than the angels (Ps. 8: 5, LXX). Now, in virtue of the hypostatic union of humanity and divinity in Christ, he has been promoted above them. The angels will not reign with Christ or be glorified with him. But we shall, because in the Eucharist we partake of both natures of Christ, 'of the body in a bodily way, of the divinity spiritually, or rather, of both in both ways, not because they are hypostatically identified . . . but through the commingling of the body and the blood' (*Imag.* 3. 26. 55–62).

Those who have entered into the eschatological reality are the saints. In his defence of the holy images, John protests against those who will allow icons of Christ and the Theotokos but not of the saints. The saints, after all, are called gods by Scripture (Ps. 82: 1). Because grace has come upon them in the person of Christ, they are like iron mingled with fire. Although John is applying to the saints an image referring to the union of the human and the divine in Christ that goes back to Origen, could it be that he also has in mind the apophthegmata of the desert fathers describing such ascetics as Pambo (no. 12), Sisoes (no. 14) and Silvanus (no. 12) as transfigured with light?

In his iconophile works, however, John was not writing specifically for monks. For an exponent of deification within a monastic context, we must move on to Symeon the New Theologian.

3. Symeon the New Theologian

Symeon was born in 949, according to the most widely accepted dating,[5] to a noble provincial family. Having embarked on a career in the imperial service, he resigned in 977 and entered the Stoudion monastery in Constantinople. Shortly afterwards he transferred to the Monastery of St Mamas, also in the capital, becoming *hegoumenos* in 981. In 1005 he was forced to resign and afterwards lived in seclusion until his death in 1022.[6] His writings not only discuss deification in the traditional theological terms, but also present us with remarkable personal accounts of the experience of participation in the divine light.[7] In his emphasis on the vision of divine light Symeon reaches back to Gregory of Nazianzus and looks forward to the fourteenth-century hesychasts. He is thus a pivotal figure in the Byzantine monastic tradition.

Deification is mentioned frequently in his writings. As with many of his predecessors, it is part of the essential structure of his soteriology. The deification of humanity was the purpose of the Incarnation. 'Why did God become man?' asks Symeon. 'So that man might become god' (*Eth.* 5. 31–4). 'God wants to make gods out of human beings ... He wants this so much that he ... descends and appears on earth for this purpose' (*Eth.* 7. 598). Strikingly, in one of his hymns—like Gregory of Nazianzus he was a poet— Symeon makes the deification of humanity brought about by the Incarnation in principle apply to himself personally:

> The Word remained immutable in his divinity
> And yet he became man by assumption of the flesh;
> In the same way he kept me a man, immutable in flesh and soul,
> And yet he made me wholly a god,
> When he assumed my condemned flesh
> And clothed me in divinity.
> For when I was baptized in Christ, I put on Christ ...
> How is he not a god by grace and adoption (χάριτι καὶ θέσει)
> Who has put on the Son of God
> In assurance, knowledge and contemplation ...?
> God became wholly man,
> And so you should think in an orthodox way
> That I became wholly god by communion with God,
> In assurance and knowledge, not in essence but by participation.
> (*Hymn* 50. 184–202; trans. Alfeyev 2000: 263, lightly modified)

Putting on the divinity of Christ takes place through baptism, which makes

---

[5] The suggested chronologies are 949–1022 (Hausherr), *c.*965–*c.*1042 (Kroll) and 956–1036 (Christou). For details see Alfeyev 2000: 28–9.

[6] For the *Life of Symeon* by his disciple, Nicetas Stethatos, see Hausherr and Horn 1928; cf. Alfeyev 2000: 27–42.

[7] On Symeon's approach to deification see Krivocheine 1986: esp. 383–90, and Alfeyev 2000: esp. 255–70. In what follows I rely heavily on Alfeyev.

us gods by grace and adoption, and is nurtured by the Eucharist. The 'wondrous new exchange' (συνάλλαγμα) between God and man that occurred at the Incarnation is sustained by Christ's eucharistic gift of himself to the faithful: 'God received his human flesh from the Virgin Mary and gave her divinity instead; now he gives his flesh to the saints to deify them' (*Eth.* 1. 10. 118–24).

Deification is properly eschatological. In *Hymn* 27 Symeon celebrates the glory of the saints:

> Not only does God repose in the saints
> But also the saints live and move in God . . . .
> O wonder! Like angels and like sons of God
> Will they be after death, gods united with God:
> Those who are gods by adoption, being like him who is God by nature.
> (*Hymn* 27. 90–5; trans. Alfeyev 2000: 264, modified)

Yet this eschatological fulfilment has its beginning in this life. In the hymn quoted above, Symeon says that the gods by adoption who have become united with God after death are those who have attained a likeness to him. Elsewhere he describes this, like St Maximus, as an anticipation of the Eighth Day. A foretaste of Paradise and a pledge of the Kingdom are given in this life to the worthy (cf. *Hymn* 1. 73 ff.; 17. 851–4; 19. 107–46). Indeed, only those who have become 'heavenly and divine' through moral improvement in the course of their earthly life will enter the Kingdom after death (*Hymn* 44. 405–24).

Deification is thus the recovery of the original likeness to God. In a passage which alludes to the serpent's promise, 'you will be like God' (Gen. 3: 5), Symeon says that God 'does not envy mortals when they become equal to him by grace . . . but is glad and rejoices when he sees us, who from being human become by grace what he is by nature' (*Hymn* 44. 384–93).

The supreme image of deification as a result of spiritual progress is that of illumination and participation in the divine light. In claiming this, Symeon acknowledges his debt to Gregory of Nazianzus:

> Perfection is endless (ἀτελὴς ἡ τελειότης)
> For its beginning is its end.
> How is it its end? As Gregory said, speaking as a theologian:
> 'Illumination is the end
> Of all who desire;
> And the divine light
> Is the term of all contemplation.'
> (*Hymn* 23. 413–20, citing Greg. Naz. *Or.* 39. 8; trans. Alfeyev 2000: 265, modified)

And in one of his sermons he says, 'God is light, and to those who have entered into union with him, he imparts of his own brightness to the extent that they have been purified' (*Cat.* 15. 68–70). That this was not simply a theoretical matter for Symeon is indicated in a number of passages, especially his autobiographical descriptions of ecstasy. It is worth quoting one of these at length, for the fervour and intensity of his spirituality can best be conveyed in his own words:

The person inwardly illumined by the light of the Holy Spirit cannot endure the vision of it, but falls face down on the earth and cries out in great fear and amazement, since he has seen and experienced something that is beyond nature, thought or conception. He becomes like someone suddenly inflamed with a violent fever: as though on fire and unable to endure the flames, he is beside himself, utterly incapable of controlling himself. And though he pours forth incessant tears that bring him some relief, the flame of his desire kindles all the more. Then his tears flow yet more copiously and, washed by their flow, he becomes even more radiant. When, totally incandescent, he has become like light, then the saying is fulfilled, 'God is united with gods and known by them' (Greg. Naz. *Or.* 45. 3), in the sense perhaps that he is now united to those who have joined themselves to him, and revealed to those who have come to know him. (*Cap.* 68; trans. Palmer, Sherrard, and Ware)

To become light does not imply that one has become totally spiritualized. The body too shares in the transformation. Symeon follows St Maximus in this respect, but he goes beyond him in the realism of his teaching. In his notorious fifteenth *Hymn*, he says that we become Christ's members, and Christ becomes each of our members—even our private parts will be 'adorned with the beauty of his divinity and glory' (*Hymn* 15. 141–57). Deification is the state of the total transformation of both men and women in every detail of their persons.[8] No aspect of humanity will be left unsuffused with divine glory. Thus it is not only the life of beatitude after death, but even the fullness of life after the resurrection that can be anticipated here below.

Symeon's teaching was so bold and so forcefully expressed that it is not surprising that he encountered opposition. This centred on his devotion towards his spiritual father, Symeon the Studite, and his veneration of him as a saint immediately after his death (cf. Alfeyev 2000: 136–42). Symeon's critics were unhappy about contemporary saints, especially if they were charismatic figures regarded as sources of authority independent of the hierarchy. They wanted to push the saints back into the Church's distant past. The same critics were also unhappy about deification as participation in the divine light, wanting to restrict it to the remote future, the eschatological state. This opposition to the experiential aspects of deification was to come to a head in the fourteenth century.

---

[8] Symeon specifically mentions also the female parts deified by the emergence of the Saviour from the womb of the Theotokos.

4. Gregory Palamas

The hesychast controversy of the fourteenth century centred on the powerful figure of Gregory Palamas.[9] Born in 1296 of a noble provincial family, he received an excellent education in the capital. Unlike most young men of his background, he did not enter the imperial service but at the age of twenty became a monk. His forcefulness and charisma even in his youth may be judged from the fact that he persuaded his widowed mother and his brothers and sisters to join him in the monastic life. In about 1318 he went with his two brothers to Mount Athos, where he came into contact with the hesychastic life, the life of prayer and withdrawal whose goal was participation in the uncreated energies of God. Turkish raids on the Athonite monasteries forced him to spend some time in the safety of Thessalonica and Beroea in the 1320s, but by 1331 he was back on the Holy Mountain. It was there, at his hermitage of St Sabbas, that he first heard of the *succès d'estime* in Constantinople of the 'philosopher' Barlaam of Calabria. He began a correspondence with Barlaam on the problem of the knowledge of God, which resulted in 1337 in the publication of the first of his 'Triads' in defence of the Holy Hesychasts.

Barlaam had maintained, in the course of an argument against the Latin doctrine of the *filioque*, that the nature of the procession of the Holy Spirit lay outside human cognizance because God was beyond knowledge. But as Palamas pointed out, if God was not knowable, the Orthodox position on the *filioque* was no more secure than the Latin. There was another approach which maintained the supra-transcendence of God (Palamas and Barlaam were both keen students of Dionysius the Areopagite) and yet allowed him at the same time to be accessible to human thought and experience. That was the distinction between the essence and the energies of God. In his essence (*ousia*) God was beyond even Godhead but in his operations or energies (*energiai*) he came into an intimate relationship with the contingent order, so that the worthy could participate in him through attaining a vision of the divine light.

Barlaam was shocked by the claim that human beings could participate in God. In response he wrote a treatise, *Against the Messalians*, in which he accused the hesychasts of the same error as that of the fourth-century heretics who believed that through ascetic effort and uninterrupted prayer they could achieve a corporeal vision of the divine essence. Palamas responded to this in 1341 with his third *Triad*, the first treatise of which was subtitled *On Theosis*.

This treatise on deification was the first work to defend the doctrine

---

[9] On Palamas and his spiritual teaching, the standard work is Meyendorff 1959a. His doctrine of deification is the subject of detailed studies by G. Mantzaridis (1984) and A. N. Williams (1999).

explicitly against hostile criticism. In the previous *Triads* Gregory had already laid emphasis on deification as an experiential reality. Knowledge of God may be fundamentally apophatic, but that does not imply that God is inaccessible to human beings. The contemplation of the divine light by the monks is the contemplation of God's glory (*Triad* 1. 3. 5). This glory is not the essence of God but it is nevertheless divine. For it transforms the body as well as the soul, communicating its own splendour to it. Moses the lawgiver, Stephen the protomartyr, and Arsenius the desert ascetic are examples from the Bible and the Fathers of men who were visibly transformed by divine light (*Triad* 2. 3. 9). God transcends the senses yet the knowledge of God is experiential. The monks know this. They see the hypostatic light spiritually—in reality not in a symbolic fashion. They know that they experience 'an illumination immaterial and divine, a grace invisibly seen and ignorantly known. *What* it is, they do not pretend to know' (*Triad* 2. 3. 8, Meyendorff 403. 17–20; trans. Gendle).

In the third *Triad* Palamas goes on to discuss the theory of deification and the scriptural and patristic basis for it. The true monk has not only tasted deification but follows experienced teachers who, drawing on the monastic tradition, are able to give him expert guidance. Barlaam, by contrast, is an αὐτόπλαστος μοναχός, a self-made monk; he has simply worked out his opinions for himself for he regards deifying grace as created (*Triad* 3. 1. 5, Meyendorff 567. 15–20). These opinions may be summed up as follows. The light which the monks see is not divine; it is a created symbol of divinity (*Triad* 3. 3. 11 and 13). It is therefore grace, not God, that is experienced. What the hesychasts call deifying grace is the perfection of human beings as rational creatures. Deification is virtue and wisdom; that is to say, it is created and natural (*Triad* 3. 1. 31). Against this Palamas maintains that the deifying light is essential, not symbolic, but is not itself the essence of God. The grace which is experienced by those who see this light is not a *thing* but a *relationship* (*Triad* 3. 1. 29). At the same time it goes beyond relationship. For although God unites himself with man, he remains wholly other. Deification therefore goes beyond natural perfection. It refers to the transformation of our nature by divine action.

Palamas does not ignore the well-established patristic teaching on the doctrinal context of deification.[10] The divine transformation of human nature (ἡ μεταστοιχείωσις τοῦ ἡμετέρου φυράματος καὶ ἡ κατ᾽ αὐτὸ θεουργία καὶ ἡ θεϊκὴ ἀναμόρφωσις) was effected in principle by the Incarnation. Was this 'not accomplished in Christ from the start, from the moment in which he assumed our nature'? (*Triad* 3. 1. 15, Meyendorff 587. 23–4; trans. Gendle). Yes, it was. But it also needs to be appropriated and realized by the individual through baptism: the divine light is 'the pledge of the future

---

[10] On Maximus' influence on Palamas see Savvidis 1997: 174–97.

promise, the grace of adoption, the deifying gift of the Spirit' (*Triad* 3. 1. 6, Meyendorff 569. 4–5). Our transformation also has an eschatological dimension, for the grace of adoption bestowed through baptism is identical with 'the light of ineffable glory seen by the saints, the enhypostatic, uncreated light, eternally issuing from the eternal in a manner beyond our understanding, now perceived in part but in the life to come revealed to the worthy more perfectly and himself revealing God to them' (*Triad* 3. 1. 6, Meyendorff 569. 5–10). Yet although the vision of the divine light is crowned by its eschatological fulfilment, it can only be the fruit of spiritual progress made in this life. The 'philosopher' (Barlaam) knows nothing of this.

What, then, is the light that the ascetics see? The hermeneutic key is provided by the Gospel account of the transfiguration of Christ (Matt. 17: 1–9; Mark 9: 2–9; Luke. 9: 28–36). The light seen on Mount Tabor was 'not just a phantom without substance' (*Triad* 3. 1. 14, Meyendorff 585. 27). But neither was it an independent reality (*Triad* 3. 1. 17). That is why Gregory calls it 'enhypostatic', i.e. without any hypostasis of its own (*Triad* 3. 1. 28). For its hypostasis is Christ; he himself is the deifying light (*Triad* 3. 1. 16). Thus Gregory does not add a fourth person to the Trinity, as his critics maintained. Nor does he follow Barlaam in seeing the energies merely as the attributes of God. The deifying light pertains to God's essence but is not itself the essence of God (οὐσιῶδες ἐστίν, ἀλλ᾽ οὐκ αὐτὸ οὐσία θεοῦ) (*Triad* 3. 1. 23, Meyendorff 601. 28–9).

The proof of the divine nature of the Taboric light is in the effects it produces in the hesychast. Deification goes beyond natural perfection, for if it simply perfected the rational creature qua rational creature, the deified would not be 'born of God' (*Triad* 3. 1. 30). All men, together with the angels, would have been gods by virtue of their rationality. Deification is more than the achievement of moral excellence. It is a supernatural gift that transforms both mind and body, making divinity visible (*Triad* 3. 1. 33). For what Christ is by nature the Christian can become by grace:

> So, when the saints contemplate this divine light within themselves, seeing it by the divinising communion of the Spirit, through the mysterious visitation of perfecting illuminations—then they behold the garment of their deification, their mind being glorified and filled by the grace of the Word, beautiful beyond measure in his splendour; just as the divinity of the Word on the mountain glorified with divine light the body conjoined to it. For 'the glory which the Father gave him', he himself has given to those obedient to him, as the Gospel says, and 'he willed that they should be with him and contemplate his glory' (John 17: 22, 24). (*Triad* 1. 3. 5, Meyendorff 115. 16–26; trans. Gendle)

The saints henceforth live with the life of God (*Triad* 3. 1. 35). Their souls cease to give way to evil pleasures and passions and acquire inner peace and stillness (*Triad* 3. 1. 33).

The Athonite monks supported Palamas in 1340 by subscribing to a statement known as the *Hagioritic Tome*. This was followed in 1341 by a formal endorsement of Palamite doctrine by the Home Synod of Constantinople. In the same year Barlaam returned to Italy, but opposition to Palamas still continued, for not all were convinced of his orthodoxy. In the second phase of the controversy, from 1341 to 1347, his leading opponent was Gregory Akindynos.

Akindynos was a monk of possibly Bulgarian origin who had established himself in Thessalonica.[11] He had become acquainted with Palamas before 1330, perhaps at Beroea. In the early stages of the controversy he had tried to mediate between Palamas and Barlaam from a position which he believed to lie midway between the two. He wrote to Barlaam early in 1341 criticizing equally Palamas's 'uncreated god or divinity next to the divine nature and lower than it and visible in itself (if that is what he says), and your theory that the divine grace is created (if you, too, say this), which to me are a new and strange theology' (*Letter* 10. 197–200; trans. Hero). Two years later, in February 1343, he attacked Palamas again on what seemed to him the innovative distinction between the essence and the energies:

the 'new theologian' not only in long written discourses but also by word of mouth has been proclaiming two uncreated divinities, not to say actually a great many, 'one higher and the other infinitely lower'; one invisible and the other visible even to the bodily eyes of certain men; one activating and the other activated; one nameless and the other having a name; one being the essence and the other not; one incapable of being shared and the other capable of being shared. The latter he calls deification (θέωσιν) and power and energy and grace and illumination and form and essential and natural glory of God, being separate, as he says, from his essence and nature. (*Letter* 27. 81–91; trans. Hero, modified)

Akindynos does not use the term 'theosis' anywhere else in his letters.[12] The concept seems unfamiliar to him. Indeed, the desire to become a god was associated by him more with the fall of Lucifer and the temptation of Adam than with the spiritual life:

it is the madness from which the first apostate from God suffered, and though he was the morning star, he became darkness along with an untold multitude. And he transmitted it to our Forefather in return for that wondrous hope by which he excited him—the hope of divinity, that is (cf. Gen. 3: 5)—and deprived him even of immortality, which he had by the grace of his maker. Just as the present apostates do, no less, to those who trust in them, both boasting that they have themselves become uncreated gods without beginning and promising that they will make such those who are obedient to them. (*Letter* 49. 45–52; trans. Hero)

---

[11] For biographical details see Hero, *Letters of Gregory Akindynos* ix–xxxiii.
[12] He does, however, like Palamas, describe the Holy Spirit as 'deifying not deified' (θεοῦν οὐ θεούμενον) (*Letter* 66. 31).

This, of course, is a caricature of what Palamas really taught. When he came to write his *One Hundred and Fifty Chapters* in 1349 or 1350 he went out of his way to emphasize that the saints are gods simply 'by participation', and then only in that aspect of God which is participable:

Those who have pleased God and attained that for which they came into being, namely, divinization (τουτέστι τῆς θεώσεως)—for they say that it was for this purpose that God made us, in order to make us partakers of his own divinity (cf. 2 Pet. 1: 4)—these then are in God since they are divinized by him and he is in them since it is he who divinizes them. Therefore, these too participate in the divine energy, though in another way, but not in the substance of God. And so the theologians maintain that 'divinity' (θεότητα) is a name for the divine energy.   (*Cap.* 105; trans. Sinkiewicz)

By now Palamas was well aware that his speaking of higher and lower θεότητες was a source of difficulty to his opponents. He sought to answer them more fully in his *Defence Against Barlaam and Akindynos*, a collection of three treatises, the last of which is entitled *On Divine and Deifying Participation*. In the course of exploring the notion of human participation in the divine, he considers a new issue, whether the deification of the human person abrogates his or her individuality. Only the saints properly participate in God (*On Deif. Part.* 16). They do not simply improve their nature but receive the divine energy itself. The uncreated gift of the Spirit restores them to the likeness of Christ. They put on Christ's glory and radiance, 'so that they are no longer recognized by their own characteristics', but (quoting Maximus' *Ambiguum* 7, PG 91. 1076c) become like pure air wholly suffused by light, or like pure gold made molten by divine fire, because they have become 'gods by theosis' (*On Deif. Part.* 21). They nevertheless retain their individuality because the Christ they have put on became incarnate as an individual. The word 'divinities' does not divide the divine nature; it simply signifies the uncreated energies in which the saints participate. But the Akindynists saw the divinities as evidence of polytheism. They were not persuaded that Palamas's new terminology could be interpreted in an orthodox way because there was no room in their radically apophatic theology for any human participation in the divine.

For a while, during the civil war of the 1340s, Akindynos was in the ascendancy as principal theological adviser to the anti-Palamite patriarch, John Calecas. But the victory in 1347 of the Emperor John VI Cantacuzene, a strong Palamite supporter, ensured that Palamism would receive official approval. At Constantinopolitan councils held in 1347 and 1351 the Church condemned Akindynos and accepted the teaching of Gregory Palamas as Orthodox doctrine. In 1347 Palamas was appointed Metropolitan of Thessalonica, a post he held until his death twelve years later.

The council of 1351 did not, however, put an end to the dispute. In its third phase, opposition to the hesychasts was led by the lay polymath Nicephorus Gregoras. But it was the Palamites who had popular support. When Gregoras died the mob sacked his house and dragged his corpse through the streets.

The fourth and final phase of the dispute was dominated by the affair of Prochorus Cydones.[13] Prochorus, the brother of the famous statesman and Catholic convert Demetrius, became a monk at the Athonite monastery of the Great Lavra in about 1350. In the early 1360s we find him leader of a small anti-Palamite faction. He did not follow his brother into the Latin Church but he did participate in his programme of translations from Thomas Aquinas and the Latin Fathers and these deeply influenced the way he presented his theological views. In his *Refutation of the Tome of 1351* he denied that God can be divided into essence and energies or that human beings can participate in him.[14] To divide the energies from the essence of God is to reify his attributes. God, for example, does not *have* light; he *is* light. Light is therefore a synonym or analogy for the essence of God, not an independent entity. If there are no 'real' energies, God cannot be divided into 'participable' and 'imparticipable'. What then is the nature of theosis? Prochorus did not refuse to use the term, but he insisted that it must refer to a qualitative rather than a substantial change in us. The vision of the apostles on Mount Tabor, after all, signified a change in the beholder, not in the reality of Christ. 'Theosis' is therefore a relational term. We become 'gods' only by title or analogy.

Prochorus Cydones was condemned by the Home Synod of Constantinople in 1368. His trial was also the occasion for the official canonization of Gregory Palamas, whose proclamation as a saint enshrined the hesychast doctrine of deification as the Orthodox Church's noblest expression of the content and purpose of the spiritual life. This doctrine was to have enormous influence, especially in the Slavic world.

5. The Dissemination of Hesychast Spirituality

The chief centre from which hesychasm spread northwards was not Mount Athos but the monastery of Paroria in south-east Bulgaria.[15] This monastery

---

[13] For a detailed account of the Prochorus affair see Russell 2004a.

[14] The full title of Prochorus' work is *A Refutation of the Misinterpretation of texts quoted in the tome against Ephesus and Gregoras*. This is a work of six books, of which the first is reproduced under the title *De Essentia et Operatione*, in Migne, PG 151. 1191–1242, where it is attributed to Gregory Akindynos, and the sixth has been published by M. Candal (1954).

[15] On the spread of hesychasm among the Slavs, see Obolensky 1971: 389–97; Meyendorff 1981: 96–118; Bouyer 1968: iii. 5–53.

had been founded in about 1330 by Gregory of Sinai (*c.* 1265–1346).[16]
Gregory does not seem to have been influenced by his younger contemporary, Gregory Palamas, but the two men were on Mount Athos and in Thessalonica together and probably knew each other. Gregory's main sources
seem to have been St John Climacus and St Symeon the New Theologian.
Like Symeon he understood deification as participation in the divine light,
but in his case he treats it chiefly as an eschatological state. At the resurrection the body will be transmuted into a spiritual body; it will recover its
original prelapsarian state through being conformed to the image of the Son
of Man 'through full participation in his divinity' (*On Commandments and
Doctrines* 46). But there are hints that the beginnings of this are experienced
in the present life. The place in heaven that will be allotted to each will be
'according to their virtue, their knowledge and the degree of deification that
they have attained' (*On Commandments and Doctrines* 44). This will not depend
simply on our own efforts, for baptism gives us a foretaste of the Spirit and
implants within us the Word who 'deifies us in his superabundant beauty' (*On
Stillness* 3).

Gregory's foundation did not long survive his death, but his work was
continued by his disciple, St Theodosius of Trnovo, who established his own
monastery at Kilifarevo, not far from Trnovo, in about 1350. The life at
Kilifarevo was modelled on that of Paroria, and from this second foundation
the hesychastic ideal spread among the Slavs.

The end of the fourteenth century was a period of decline on Mount
Athos, with a number of monasteries abandoning the coenobitic life and
adopting an idiorhythmic rule. Russia too experienced a decline but a revival
was begun by St Sergius of Radonezh (*c.*1314–92), who in about 1354
founded the Great Lavra of the Holy Trinity just north of Moscow. He went
to Constantinople for his monastic rule, which he received from the Patriarch Philotheus, a disciple of Gregory Palamas. From the mother house of
the Holy Trinity St Sergius founded a total of some forty monasteries, all of
them stamped with the character of the hesychastic life. As the Russian
monasteries began to acquire vast estates, however, the contemplative
tradition went into decline. Hesychasm owed its revival to St Nil Sorsky
(1433–1508), a monk of St Cyril at Beloozero, who after a stay on Mount
Athos re-established the eremitical life in the north Russian forest near his
former monastery. He does not seem to have known the writings of Gregory
Palamas, but was familiar with Symeon the New Theologian and Gregory of
Sinai, whose teaching he promoted. His spiritual descendants were the great
starty of the nineteenth century.

The flowering of the hesychastic life in nineteenth-century Russia was
stimulated by the 'Philokalian renaissance' on Mount Athos, which itself was

---

[16] On the life of Gregory of Sinai, see Balfour 1982: 59–91.

a product of the 'Kollyvades' movement. The 'Kollyvades' monks, scandalized by the lax practices prevalent on Athos in the eighteenth century, wanted to return to a more ancient observance. One of their number, St Nicodemus of the Holy Mountain, together with Macarius Notaras, Metropolitan of Corinth, conceived the idea of making an ample anthology of spiritual texts from the manuscripts in the monastic libraries of Athos and having it printed at one of the Greek presses in Venice. The resulting *Philokalia of the Neptic Fathers* (Venice 1782) was a landmark in the dissemination of hesychastic teaching. Within a few years it had been translated into Slavonic by St Paisy Velichkovsky at the monastery of Neamt in Moldavia. The monks of Neamt took the *Philokalia* and its teaching into Russia, where in the following century it was translated into the vernacular by St Theophan the Recluse.

Maximus the Confessor, Symeon the New Theologian, Gregory of Sinai, and Gregory Palamas figure prominently in the *Philokalia*. Their teaching on deification through participation in the divine light became familiar to a wide monastic readership. St Seraphim of Sarov, the best-known of the Russian nineteenth-century mystics, was seen by more than one of his disciples transfigured by an intense light. 'Remember the transfiguration of the Lord on Mount Tabor', the *staretz* is reported to have said. 'When Moses and Elijah came to him then, in order to hide the shining light of divine grace which blinded the disciples, a cloud, it is said, overshadowed them. In this manner the grace of the All-Holy Spirit of God manifests itself in an indescribable light to all those in whom God manifests its action' (Bolshakoff 1977: 135). In more recent times a remarkable testimony to the continuity of the same teaching and experience of transfiguration has been borne by St Silouan of Mount Athos and his disciple, Archimandrite Sophrony.[17] If the repentant sinner perseveres and 'consciously abides in the Holy Spirit', says Sophrony, 'the vision of immortal glory and undying light is vouchsafed to him' and he becomes a participant in the life of Christ, having become "without beginning" (not in essence but by grace)' (Sophrony 1988: 45). Such perseverance is directed not towards the pursuit of mystical experience but to making Christ fully effective in the Christian's life.[18]

---

[17] Archimandrite Sophrony came to England in 1959 and founded an Orthodox monastery at Tolleshunt Knights in Essex. His books on St Silouan have circulated widely. Less well known is his spiritual testimony (Sophrony 1988) in which he vividly describes his own experience of uncreated light. Interestingly, this is balanced by the equally powerful experience of the mind's descent into hell.

[18] A curious early twentieth-century aberration in the development of the hesychastic tradition may be mentioned here, the heresy of the name-worshippers, which arose from treating the name itself of God as a separate hypostasis. That the Orthodox Church pronounced it a heresy underlines its opposition to the multiplication of hypostases in the Godhead. For further information see Papoulides 1977.

6. Modern Approaches to Deification

Archimandrite Sophrony discusses the doctrine of deification and his experience of the divine light in the language of the hesychastic monastic tradition. But the desire of human beings to transcend their finitude is not only monastic; it is universal. In his recent book *Immortal Longings*, subtitled *Versions of Transcending Humanity*, Fergus Kerr (1997) has reflected on a number of thinkers from Karl Barth to Martha Nussbaum who have explored (or more often deplored) the ways in which we seek to liberate ourselves from the limitations of our existence. It is striking how Plato still looks over the shoulder of so many philosophers and theologians. Diotima's speech in the *Symposium* on the ascent of love continues to exercise a powerful fascination, even among those hostile to any notion of transcendence that appears to deprive us of our human nature. 'We must divest ourselves', says Barth, 'of the idea that limitation implies something derogatory or even a kind of curse or affliction' (*Church Dogmatics* III/4. 567, cited Kerr 1997: 23). Far from finding our true identity in an ascent to something more than human, it is our very finitude that provides us with the necessary conditions for our highest fulfilment. In Kerr's words,

> In differentiating creatures from himself, God of course limits them to be only his creatures; but in so doing he gives them precisely their specific genuine reality. In differentiating human beings from other creatures he limits them to be only human beings—and thus distinguishes them from all other creatures. In differentiating *this* human being from all others, God limits him or her, in relation to all others, to be only *this* particular human being. In so doing, he treats him or her as a soul, as a subject, as this unique and irreplaceable particular individual, as an 'I' to be addressed as 'Thou'. (1997: 37)

It is this conviction that a personal relationship with God must entail our finitude that lies behind the frequently repeated statement: 'Our destiny is not that we might be made divine but rather that we might at last become truly human.' Without the particularity of finitude we are not free to love God or to be loved by him.

Yet Barth also held that Jesus Christ is the authentic pattern of our humanity. Herein lies the key to a satisfactory modern approach to deification. Jesus Christ is the pattern of our humanity, as a model to be imitated not externally but ontologically. There are two aspects to this: as the second Adam, Christ has recreated humanity in the image and likeness of God; as the Son of the Father, he has revealed that true being is relational. The two aspects are closely connected. This was understood more than a century ago by J. R. Illingworth, whose 1894 Bampton Lectures, *Personality, Human and Divine*, have proved a fruitful starting-point for the modern study of theological anthropology. It was Illingworth's conviction that our personality 'is essentially triune' because self-consciousness depends on 'a subject, an object, and their relation' (1903: 39). But 'it is a potential, unrealized triunity, which is incomplete in itself, and must go beyond itself for completion' (1903: 41):

If, therefore, we are to think of God as personal, it must be by what is called the method of eminence (via eminentiae) the method, that is, which considers God as possessing, in transcendent perfection, the same attributes which are imperfectly possessed by man. He must, therefore, be pictured as One whose triunity has nothing potential or unrealized about it; whose triune elements are eternally actualized, by no outward influence, but from within; a Trinity in Unity; a social God, with all the conditions of personal existence internal to himself.   (1903: 41–2)

Human personhood is triune and therefore fundamentally relational because that is the structure of the ultimate reality we call God—not a God locked in inaccessible unicity, but a social God, and hence a personal God. This is what made the Incarnation possible. A God 'within whose Being are personal distinctions, can at once be conceived as essentially, eternally, absolutely Love' (1903: 101):

And this new insight into the divine nature, threw a new light upon the destiny of man, as capable, through the Incarnation, of being made holy in the Beloved, and so raised . . . to be a partaker of the eternal love of God. Thus the actual Trinity of God explains the potential trinity of man; and our anthropomorphic language follows from our theomorphic minds.   (1903: 101)

To become partakers of the divine nature is therefore to share fully in the relationship of love between the Father and the Son that was made accessible to us through the Incarnation. Only in this way do we realize the full potentiality of our personhood.

Illingworth refers to some of the early Fathers, but the typical precursors he mentions for his conception of personhood are Augustine, Luther, and Kant (1903: 16). It was not until after the First World War that the attention of Western scholars was drawn to the Orthodox tradition by emigré Russian theologians such as Bulgakov, Florovsky and Krivocheine. The influence of the Russians has been remarkable, not only on Anglicans and Roman Catholics, but latterly also on the Greeks themselves. Among the Anglicans who owe a debt to the Russians one of the most distinguished is Eric Mascall. In his *Christ, the Christian and the Church* (1946) Mascall puts forward an understanding of deification not unlike that of Illingworth (essentially the participation of the baptized in the love of the Son for the Father) but expressed in traditional theological terms rather than in the language of philosophical idealism.[19] Drawing on the Fathers and the Spanish mystics, he summarizes

[19] Anglican interest in the patristic teaching on deification goes back to the Tractarians, on whom see Louth 1983*b*.

the consequences of the Christian's incorporation into Christ through filial adoption in the following words:

We receive—of course in a way adapted to our mode of existence as creatures, for *quidquid recipitur recipitur ad modum recipientis*—a real participation in the life of the Holy Trinity; through our union with Christ we are caught up into the act whereby he eternally adores the heavenly Father. We are made, in the New Testament phrase, 'partakers of the divine nature' (2 Pet. 1: 4). . . . It is this participation in the life of God, this sharing in the response which the eternal Son makes to the Father's love, that is the basis of the teaching of both the fathers and the mystical theologians about the 'divinization' or 'deification' of man in Christ.   (1946: 96–7)

But Mascall was aware how unfamiliar such language was to his readers. Anxious to remove any danger of misunderstanding, he goes on:

It is absolutely essential to remember the conditions under which it takes place if we are to avoid serious heresy. . . . It is through our adoptive union with Christ and the hypostatic union of his human nature with his divine Person that we are caught up into the life of union which he essentially shares with God the Father. And . . . one of the characteristics of our adoptive union with Christ is that our personal identity is preserved. Even if, in a strictly guarded sense, we can say, with some of the mystics that Christ and God are *what* we become, we can never say that they are *who* we become.   (1946: 97)

This emphasis on sharing in the divine life through participation by baptism in the restored humanity of the incarnate Son reflects the realistic approach to deification that goes back to Irenaeus. In articulating its ecclesial dimension Mascall is helped by the Russians. He quotes with approval Florovsky's remark that 'the Church is the living image of eternity within time' and Bulgakov's that in its liturgical services the Church 'makes actual for us the mystery of the Incarnation' (1946: 116–17).

The conviction that elevation to the divine life far from dehumanizing us actually makes us more fully human is elegantly set out in *The Importance of Being Human* (1959). Starting from the conviction that openness to God belongs to the essence of human nature, and that the human reality is relational, Mascall argues for a supracosmic destiny for humanity which effects a real transformation of our nature, perfecting it without destroying it. 'Christian tradition, in East and West alike', he says, 'has found only one word adequate to denote [this supernaturalization of nature]—the word "deification" '(1959: 63). Human nature is capable of deification first because of its rationality. It is as a rational creature that man bears the stamp of God's image. And it is because rationality reflects the nature of God that human beings can be raised to the supernatural order. But this is not something that they can attain as isolated individuals. The human race is restored and recreated in Christ. Christians are taken into this renovated human nature by being incorporated into the glorified humanity of Christ through baptism. They become sons through the Son, who lifts them into the life of the Trinity. And in the Eucharist they have a prefiguration and foretaste of the glory that is to come.

Mascall believes in a real transformation of nature by grace. He appeals for support to Vladimir Lossky, whose *Mystical Theology of the Eastern Church* had recently appeared in English. But the distinction between the essence and the energies of God, advocated by Lossky, troubled him: 'I must confess that I find the Palamite doctrine very difficult to follow and still more difficult to accept' (1959: 70). A decade later, having encountered Meyendorff's study of Gregory Palamas, he was much more positive: 'The impression which one derives is, surprisingly enough, that, whatever may be true as regards verbal idiom and the strictly philosophical setting, there is a fundamental *dogmatic* and *religious* agreement between St Gregory Palamas and St Thomas Aquinas' (1971: 221). Indeed, Meyendorff's study was a landmark, stimulating many scholars to reconsider their view not only of Palamas's essence/energies distinction but also of his doctrine of deification.

Roman Catholic writers have not, on the whole, had any difficulty with the patristic doctrine of deification. Louis Bouyer, in particular, in his *History of Christian Spirituality* and his study on *The Christian Mystery* has done much to disseminate an awareness of deification as 'nothing but the reality of our sharing in the divine sonship recognized as proper to Jesus, the Son of God made man precisely to offer us that possibility' (1989: 227). But they have had difficulties with Palamism. Bouyer himself, while admitting that the essence/energies distinction raises the thorniest of metaphysical problems, accepts that all Palamas 'sought to affirm was the possibility of a real and immediate contact between man and God in divine grace, while rejecting any sort of pantheism or "divinisation" which would make us "gods" in the pagan or hellenistic sense' (1968: 588). Hans Urs von Bathasar, on the other hand, with his insistence on the apophaticism of God within his self-disclosure was not prepared to accept that there was another apophaticism lying behind that self-disclosure. This seemed to him altogether too Neoplatonic. The Trinitarian God of Christian revelation was not a penultimate reality, but ultimate reality itself (cf. Gawronski 1995: 56–60, with refs.). He also had his reservations about the participation of the Christian in the divine light of Tabor (Gawronski 1995: 60). But he was too steeped in the Greek Fathers not to share their perspective on the goal of the Christian life. Humankind is to reflect the glory of God and be transformed into his image, not as a passive spectator 'but rather taken up by God's Glory and love to become "a co-worker of Glory" ' (Gawronski 1995: 167). Although von Balthasar does not use the language of deification, he does present the content of the doctrine from his own perspective, in which God's mystical gifts are not to be sought as sensual experience, ecstatic or otherwise, but as 'a loving obedience to

God's will which leads the one who is formed in Christ to a full insertion in the silent Word of adoring love' (Gawronski 1995: 180).

Another leading Roman Catholic theologian who conveys the essence of deification without making much use of the vocabulary is Karl Rahner. Rahner is opposed to a naturalistic concept of human nature. Grace is not something added on, 'justifying and divinizing' human nature and thus turning 'the vocation to the supernatural end into man's inner goal' in a merely extrinsic fashion (Rahner 1961: 299). The divine destiny is 'an ontological constituent of his concrete quiddity' because an accidental reality cannot be divinizing (Rahner 1961: 310 n.). That is to say, God creates man in such a way that he can receive the Love which is God himself as an unexpected and unexacted gift: 'The capacity for the God of self-bestowing personal Love is the central abiding existential of man as he really is' (Rahner 1961: 312). The question then arises, how can a supernatural end be set for man without anulling his nature? (Rahner 1961: 317). The answer lies in our participation in uncreated grace. Uncreated grace (God's self-communication to man) implies a new relationship with God. Man is actually re-created *by* the divine self-communication. He is not just 'deemed' to be justified. Created grace follows as a consequence to this. The life of future glory is 'the definitive flowering (the "manifestation", the "disclosure") of the life of divine sonship already possessed and merely "hidden" for the moment' (Rahner 1961: 326). Yet the beatific vision is 'not *just* "growth" to a final stage arising out of an inner impulse'. It is also 'a new eschatological intervention of God' (Rahner 1961: 335). Man is called to share in God's transfiguring glory. In other words, our supreme end is the fulfilment of our adopted sonship through being taken up into the source of our being. This is the classic doctrine of deification in all but name. The recipient of glory remains a finite creature yet at the same time is blessed with the infinite self-communication of God himself (Rahner and Vorgrimler 1965: 51, 430).

As might be expected, Greek theologians have made more explicit use of both the language and the content of deification.[20] This has not always been so. The great Orthodox *Dogmatics* of Panayiotis Trembelas, published in three volumes from 1959 to 1961, devotes only two of its 1,505 pages to theosis. A fundamental change occurred in the 1960s, stimulated by Panayiotis Christou's publication of the complete works of Gregory Palamas. One of the early fruits of this enterprise was the 1963 thesis of Christou's research student and editorial collaborator, Georgios Mantzaridis, Ἡ περὶ θεώσεως τοῦ ἀνθρώπου διδασκαλία Γρηγορίου τοῦ Παλαμᾶ, which Christos Yannaras has described as the turning-point of Greek theology in

---

[20] For detailed reviews of the work of contemporary Greek theologians see Yannaras 1992: 436–89, and Spiteris 1992: 255–462. Other Orthodox have also written on deification. On Dumitru Stăniloae, the eminent Romanian theologian, see Bartos 1999.

the twentieth century.[21] Manztaridis speaks of the Incarnation's twofold effect, the regeneration and deification of human nature by Christ, made accessible to all through the Church's sacraments. The Church is the 'communion of deification', through which the believer can receive a share of the divine energies and become what God is 'save in identity of essence', for the 'uncreated and imperishable grace of God dwelling in man renders him, too, imperishable, eternal, and unoriginate' (1984: 42, with refs to Palamas and Maximus).

Mantzaridis' important study sought to interpret the theological and anthropological context of deification as experienced in the Orthodox tradition. This tradition, as the author rightly saw, was not monolithic: 'Man's deification during the age of the great Fathers was dominantly a Christocentric experience, while during the hesychast period the same reality was experienced more in a Spirit-centred manner' (1984: 128). The Christocentric aspect is well brought out by another member of the renewal movement, Panayiotis Nellas, who emphasizes the Pauline roots of the doctrine:

The real anthropological meaning of deification is Christification. It is no accident that in his Letter to the Colossians, where he hymns Christ as 'the image of the invisible God, the first-born of all creation' (Col. 1: 15), St Paul calls on 'every man' to become 'mature in Christ' (Col. 1: 28), and adds that the faithful 'have come to fullness of life in him' (Col. 2: 10). When he urges the faithful to show that they are attaining 'to mature manhood, to the measure of the stature of the fullness of Christ' (Eph. 4: 13), and to acquire 'the mind of Christ' (1 Cor. 2: 16), the heart of Christ (cf. Eph. 3: 17), and so on, St Paul does not do so for reasons of external piety and sentiment; he speaks ontologically. He is not advocating an external imitation or a simple ethical improvement but a real Christification. For as St Maximos says, 'God the divine Logos wishes to effect the mystery of his incarnation always and in all things' (*Amb. Io.* 7, PG 91. 1084D). (1987: 39)

Nellas was concerned that the doctrine of deification should not be isolated as an independent strand of spiritual teaching but be fully integrated into christological and anthropological thought. In this way it can define the human goal and the means of attaining it, that is to say, the whole of the ecclesiastical and spiritual life, relating all its elements intimately to Christ.

Nellas died prematurely in 1986. But his work has been continued by two of Greece's most distinguished theologians, John Zizioulas and Christos Yannaras. Zizioulas has meditated for many years on the anthropological implications of christology. In a notable article published in 1975 he brings modern philosophical thought to bear on the Greek patristic teaching on

---

[21] Yannaras 1992: 447. The 1960s was an important decade for theological renewal in Greece. Besides rediscovering Palamas, the Greeks were also influenced by emigré Russians, such as Berdyaev, Florovsky, and Meyendorff, and Western patrologists, such as Daniélou, de Lubac, von Balthasar, Congar, and Bouyer. Mantzaridis' thesis was published in Thessalonica in 1963, reissued in his *Palamika* in 1973, and translated into English in 1984.

man (1975: esp. 434–47; cf. 1985: 27–65). The individual is not a static, self-contained entity. Personhood implies openness of being. It is therefore a *relational* category, expressed through communion in freedom and love. The paradigm of true humanity is Christ. A human being 'in Christ' becomes a true person through entering into the same filial relationship that constitutes Christ's being. Humanity only attains its true stature when united with God. '*Theosis*, as a way of describing this unity in personhood, is, therefore, just the opposite of a divinisation in which human nature ceases to be what it really is' (1975: 440). Indeed, 'personhood' becomes with Zizioulas a way of re-expressing what the Fathers meant by 'participation'. For in virtue of its relational nature, personhood implies difference from God without division, as well as communion with him without confusion (1975: 446–7). When Zizioulas returns to the same topic ten years later, it is to emphasize this unity-in-distinction:

> The eternal survival of the person as a unique, unrepeatable and free 'hypostasis', as loving and being loved, constitutes the quintessence of salvation, the bringing of the Gospel to man. In the language of the Fathers this is called 'divinization' (theosis), which means participation not in the nature or substance of God but in His personal existence. The goal of salvation is that the personal life which is realized in God should also be realized on the level of human existence.   (1985: 49–50)

The most complete theological synthesis of these themes is found in the work of Christos Yannaras. We know from revelation that God exists as a Triad of Persons, a community of personal freedom and love. God does not *have* love as an attribute; He *is* love, because his life is actualized as communion. Human beings, by contrast, are constituted as potentialities. They have the potential to stand opposite another, the 'potential to say "I" addressed to "you" '. The human person therefore 'exists only as a self-conscious otherness, consequently only in *comparison with* every other existence, only in relation to, in connection with' (1991: 30). For Yannaras, the overcoming of this otherness is the true function of the erotic impulse.[22] This is equally true of our relationship with God. Because we are in the image of God, we can either respond to the erotic call of God, which is life, or reject it, which is death. Our being in the image of God has further implications. Not only does it imply the potentiality to respond to God's call, but also the potentiality to live with the life of Christ:

> For man to be an image of God means that each one can realize his existence as Christ realizes life as love, as freedom and not as natural necessity. Each can realize his existence as a person, like the Persons of the triadic Divinity. Consequently, man

---

[22] This is one of Yannaras's most distinctive theological ideas. See his *Τὸ Πρόσωπο καὶ ὁ Ἔρως* (1987). The erotic impulse is placed in nature for its natural end and purpose. 'It serves the imaging in nature of the triadic mode of life—the personal co-inherence of life within limits of created nature. It intends finally the deifying union of man with God' (1991: 72).

can realize his existence as eternity and incorruptibility, just as the divine life of triadic co-inherence and communion is eternal and incorruptible. (1991: 59)

The alternative is an autonomy and existential self-sufficiency that imprisons us in our own inadequacies. This reflects the self-deification accepted by Eve when she yielded to the serpent's temptation to seek equality with God (cf. Gen. 3: 1–6). Its rejection brings about the Church. The Church is not an instrument of individual salvation. That would be to restrict salvation to 'an unlimited kind of survival after death in some "other" world', whereas '*salvation* for the Church is the liberation of life from corruption and death, the transformation of survival into existential fullness, the sharing of the created in the mode of life of the uncreated' (1991: 48). Immortality, consequently, is not the avoidance of personal extinction but the transcendence of death through a personal relationship with God. And not only with God. We are all related to and responsible for one another, for 'in reality the Church entrusts to everyone the enormous honour to be responsible for the salvation of the whole world, of this world whose flesh is our flesh and whose life is our life' (1991: 48).

One of the chief means of expressing this belonging to each other and to God is through the Eucharist. In the Eucharist the desire for individual survival is transformed into a loving relationship:

The existential change which is completed by the descent of the Holy Spirit in the Eucharist refers neither to objects in themselves nor to individuals in themselves, but to the relationship of individuals with the objects, a relationship of reference and offering of creation to God by man, a relationship which transfigures the mode of life changing the existence both of individuals and of things in the eucharistic communion with God into a participation in the triadic fullness of life. (1991: 129)

Deification in this profoundly patristic approach is the actualization of life as communion, enabling us to participate in the Son's loving relationship with the Father and thus attain the true fulfilment of our humanity.

Latterly, theologians of the reformed traditions have also come to take a sympathetic view of deification. In this they have been influenced not only by the scholars of the Russian diaspora, but also by the Greeks. Wolfhart Pannenberg, for example, speaks of the life-giving power of the Spirit which raises human beings above their finiteness (1985: 524). Citing Yannaras and Zizioulas, as well as Maximus and Dionysius, he sets out his understanding of a cosmic eros

that is at work in the ecstatic self-transcendence characteristic of all life and especially human life, as an expression of the redemptive love of the biblical God, who has put eros into the hearts of his creatures so that 'through their own nature he might draw to himself those set in motion by his call.' The movement of eros reaches beyond the transient to the permanent or, in biblical terms, to a future life that will no longer be separated from its source in the spirit but will be permeated by the spirit and therefore be immortal.   (1985: 526)

A recent publication on the supranatural fulfilment of the human person, *Persons Divine and Human* (Schwöbel and Gunton 1991), takes up many of the points made by Illingworth a century previously. Of particular interest for our theme is the dialogue between John Zizioulas and Christoph Schwöbel. Commenting on Zizioulas's insistence that the two natures of the Son 'have no independent existence apart from their personal particularization in the *hypostasis* of the Son', Schwöbel agrees that

Human persons can participate in this primacy of the personal by being included in the relationship of 'sonship' to the Father in Baptism, so that their identity is no longer defined in terms of the possession of general properties of created natures, but through the sacramental participation in the Father–Son relationship.   (1991: 15)

In this way, by applying modern insights into the relational nature of person-hood to the patristic teaching on deification, we can deepen our understand-ing of what it is to be human. To attribute to ourselves an independent and autonomous existence is to make what the Fall symbolizes personally our own. The true fulfilment of our humanity is expressed by the doctrine of theosis, which teaches us how, by sharing in the divine sonship of Christ with all that that implies in ecclesial and ascetical terms, our identity can be redefined as 'gods by grace' destined to be transformed by divine glory through participation in the triadic fullness of life.

Deification in the Syriac and Latin Traditions

The Christian understanding of deification was not confined to the Greek-speaking provinces of the Roman empire. Its fundamental tenet, the Irenaean principle that the Son of God became as we are that we might become as he is, came to be more widely diffused. Among Latin speakers we encounter it for the first time in Tertullian (d. *c.* 225), and among Syriac speakers in Ephrem the Syrian (d. 373). But it never became a prominent theme. Nor do we find in Latin and Syriac writers the careful elaboration of a doctrine of deification of the spiritual life, such as we have studied in Maximus the Confessor. We do find, however, a conviction that the Christian's destiny is to go beyond the recovery of what was lost in Adam and share in the life of God himself.

1. The Syriac Tradition[1]

The Syriac-speaking homeland was east of the Syrian desert in northern Mesopotamia and the adjoining district east of the Tigris. The chief cities of this region were Edessa, Nisibis, and Seleucia-Ctesiphon, the first two of which developed important schools. That of Edessa flourished in the fourth century, lasting until the Emperor Zeno closed it in 489 for its opposition to his religious policies. It was succeeded by the School of Nisibis, which in the fifth and sixth centuries became a centre of 'Nestorian' learning and contributed much to the intellectual life and missionary expansion of the Church of the East.

A striking feature of Syriac theological literature is its poetic character. Many writers produced metrical hymns and rhythmic prose of great beauty. This reliance on poetry is reflected in the extensive use Syriac writers make of symbolism and typology. When deification is mentioned, it is as a poetic image rather than as a concept to be discussed and analysed. The one exception is a heterodox work attributed to Stephen bar-Sudhaile which treats of the ascent of the soul.

(a) Ephrem the Syrian

One of the oldest of Syriac texts, the *Odes of Solomon*, speaks of our putting on Christ (7. 4; 13. 12), or clothing ourselves in his holiness (13. 3), or his name (39. 3).

---

[1] I am indebted to Sebastian Brock for all the references and most of the translations from the Syriac in this section. On deification in the Syriac tradition see esp. Brock 1990: 72–4; 1992: 148–54.

But it is Ephrem the Syrian, an exact contemporary of Athanasius (they both died in 373), who first introduces the exchange formula: 'He gave us divinity, we gave him humanity' (*H. de Fid.* 5. 7).[2] Ephrem even extends the idea of exchange in an original way to include God's self-communication in the anthropomorphic images of Scripture: 'He clothed himself in our language, so that he might clothe us in his mode of life' (*H. de Fid.* 31; trans. Brock). In the very text of the Bible the eternal intersects with the temporal, so that the temporal might be taken up into the eternal (cf. Young 1997: 155–7). In his account of the state of our first parents, Ephrem dwells on their failed opportunity. Adam and Eve in Paradise were created with free will for a divine destiny. But they misused their freedom by trying to seize divinity prematurely (cf. Gen. 3: 5) when they ate of the forbidden Tree of Knowledge. They therefore forfeited the divinity that would have been bestowed on them by the Tree of Life and passed on mortality to their descendants. But God in his mercy undid the effects of the Fall through the incarnation of the Word: 'Divinity flew down to draw humanity up', with the result that now man 'has become a god just as he desired' (*C. Nis.* 48. 17–18; trans. Brock).

Yet divinity in this life is merely titular: 'God in his mercy called mortals "gods by grace"' (*H. de Fid.* 29. 1; trans. Brock). It is only at the resurrection that we shall be crowned with glory. Nevertheless, we can begin to purify our eye here on earth and in so doing can become more able to behold God's incomparable Glory (*H. de Par.* 9. 26). Our model is Moses, who ascended to the mountain summit: 'Nourished with the divine glory, he grew and shone forth' (*H. de Par.* 9. 22; trans. Brock). At the resurrection our bodies will be spiritualized and our souls furnished with wings, enabling us to mount up to union with God:

> For bodies shall be raised
> to the level of souls
> and the soul
> to that of the spirit,
> while the spirit will be raised
> to the height of God's majesty
> (*H. de Par.* 9. 21; trans. Brock)

This ascent to sharing in God's glory is the winning of the crown that Adam had failed to achieve. But it is not yet called deification. The precise term was not used until deification came to play a part in the christological controversies of the fifth and sixth centuries.[3]

(b) The West Syriac Tradition (Syrian Orthodox)

The West Syriac tradition is bound up with the miaphysite resistance in Syria to the Chalcedonian definition of Christ 'made known in two natures'.[4] Two of the leading

---

[2] Ephrem probably knew no Greek. But it is possible that by this time Irenaeus was already translated into Syriac (cf. Murray 1975: 306).

[3] In Syriac the expression *etallah* ('he was deified') only came into existence after the verbal form *etbarnash* ('he was inhominated') had come into use in the late fifth century. (I owe this information to Sebastian Brock.)

[4] By this time (the late fifth century) the old Antiochene christology of divine and human *prosopa*, or roles, held together by a moral union in a symmetrical relationship had all but disappeared.

theologians of this movement, which resulted in the establishment of a separate hierarchy in the sixth century creating the Syrian Orthodox Church, were Philoxenus of Mabbug (d. 523) and Jacob of Serug (d. 521). Both were educated at the great School of Edessa. Philoxenus became bishop of Mabbug (Hierapolis) in 485. Although he wrote only in Syriac, he was conversant with the Greek intellectual tradition, and became with Severus of Antioch one of the principal leaders of the miaphysite opposition to imperial religious policy. Jacob of Serug became bishop of Batnae in Osrhoene in 519. Unlike Philoxenus, he avoided theological controversy. Renowned for his verse homilies (*memre*), mostly on biblical themes, he was known as 'the flute of the Holy Spirit'. He mentions deification, alluding to the exchange formula, in a homily in which he says that God 'became the Son of Man and made human beings into gods' (*Verse Hom.* 3. 597; ed. Bedjan).

It is Philoxenus, however, who develops this theme in his *Tractatus tres de Trinitate et Incarnatione*. Philoxenus declares that the purpose of the Incarnation is 'to make us children of the Father and gods in heaven' (229. 15; Vaschalde's Latin trans.). He became man so that we should become sons and gods, and we become sons and gods by baptism. 'Because the Word, who is God, wished to make humans into children of God, we confess that he was emptied, became flesh, and was completely inhominated, in order to recreate the entire human being in himself, and because he became human in us, we too have been deified and become children of the Father' (229. 15 = 129. 9–15; Latin trans.) who said that the flesh was made and then the Word dwelt in it. 'We have all become children in the Son who became human; we have all been deified in the One God who became human' (243. 7–8). Christ redeemed and renovated human nature, not a particular human being as the heretics claim. What we lost in Adam, the (head) of our race, has been recovered. All have been made sons by the Son, who was made man, and we have all been deified by the one inhominated God. The heretics make Christ 'grow in grace' and develop like one of us (243).

Philoxenus' understanding of the Incarnation entered into the liturgical texts of the Syrian Orthodox Church. The *Fenqitho* (or Festal Hymnary) says: 'Your divine body became the heaven of Life and it deified our entire mass so that it should not be seduced any more into corruption and mortality' (v. 447b). 'You became human and deified us' (vi. 169b = 455a). 'He gave divinity to Adam as he had previously asked' (vii. 454a). The Maronite *Shehimto* (Weekday Office), Friday Nocturns, also says: 'Our Lord Jesus Christ, source (lit.: head) of divinity of those who are divinized, and divinizer and sanctifier of those who serve perfectly as priests . . .', which occurs in a slightly adapted form in the Syrian Orthodox burial rite for priests.

(c) The East Syriac Tradition (Church of the East)

The East Syriac tradition was formed beyond the Roman frontier in Persian territory. Christians of this tradition did not recognize the Council of Ephesus of 431, not because they were 'Nestorians' but because they lived outside Roman jurisidiction. They use *barnasha* (*anthropos*) with the generic sense of 'humanity', and salvation is conceived as being achieved through Christ's humanity 'deified' at the moment of conception. One of their great teachers was Babai, abbot of a monastery at Mount Izla, near Nisibis (d. 628). His book *On the Union* (of the natures of Christ) was an anti-monophysite work refuting an opponent called Henana, the then head of the School of Nisibis. He says: He assumed that which is human 'personally' not 'naturally'. The form of God assumed the form of a servant. There is no distance in Christ between the divine and the human. It is not like Paul putting on Christ. For Christ and Paul were not one Paul. But Christ is one Son, 'God who became Man, who took the likeness of a servant and dwelt in him unitedly, and the Man who was divinized, who took the name more excellent than all names', in a single adhering, in a single person of the one Lord Jesus Christ (*Lib. De Unione* 299 = 241; Vaschalde's Latin trans.).

Two writers of the early seventh century, Isho'yahb II and Sahdona, mention deification. Isho'yahb II, the Catholicos of Seleucia-Ctesiphon entrusted with the embassies to Heraclius, speaks of 'the man who was divinized in the Virgin', and alludes to the exchange formula with 'God who became man for our salvation, and the man who was divinized for our exaltation . . .' (*Lettre christologique* 107, 186). Sahdona (in Greek 'Martyrius') was an important spiritual writer. He was educated at the School of Nisibis, became a monk in 615/20 and bishop of Mahoze (near Kirkuk) in *c.* 635/40. He was forced out of his see by a synod of the Church of the East and took refuge in Edessa. It was there that he probably wrote his masterpiece, *The Book of Perfection*, in which he refers to 'the man' who 'was truly united in his nature to God the Word, and had been divinized . . .'. The deification of human nature in Christ had consequences for the believer: 'let us sculpt out the beauty of our rules by gazing on the likeness of his glory (cf. 2 Cor. 3: 18), so that we may be seen to be glorious statues of his divinity within creation' (*Perf.* 62; trans. Brock 1987: 228). This is nothing other than the recovery of our original dignity: 'for this is how we were established by him in the world: we were smelted down from dust (cf. Gen. 2: 7), just like other natural beings, but when we were poured out he clothed us in the beauty of his own image (cf. Gen. 1: 27) and caused us to acquire the the radiance of his likeness, adorning us with the glory of his divinity—or rather, making us secondary gods on earth, giving us an authority of his own within creation' (*Perf.* 63; trans. Brock 1987: 228). In the eighth century another spiritual writer, John of Dalyatha, says: 'You, O man, are the image of God. Do you want the image to take on the likeness of the model? . . . Carry continually in your heart the yoke of your Lord, and (carry) wonder in your mind at his majesty, until it shines out in its glory and is changed into the likeness, until you become a god in God, having acquired the likeness of the Creator by the union which assimilates to him' (*Letter* 29. 1).

As in the Western Syrian tradition, liturgical texts also refer to deification. In the *Hudra* (Festal Hymnary) we read: 'O Being who became man, and man who became God' (1. 137); and: 'O he who lowered himself to a humble state in order to raise up our low estate to the exalted rank of his divinity' (1. 147).

(d) A West Syriac Esoteric Text

The Book of Hierotheos is a curious spiritual work of the sixth century. Although the author does not give his name, the manuscript tradition attributes the work to 'Hierotheos', the supposed teacher of Dionysius the Areopagite. It purports to have been translated from the Greek, but all the indications are that it was composed in Syriac. Strongly influenced by the Pseudo-Dionysian writings, it also draws on Gnostic teaching and apocryphal scriptures.

Its subject is the ascent of the mind to God. The author, referring to Paul's ascent to the third heaven (2 Cor. 12: 2–4), claims himself to have had experience of ascent to the 'universal Essence'. The text's editor, F. S. Marsh, thinks the author's sources are literary rather than personal (1927: 247). Nevertheless he believes that the work 'hints at the existence of strictly private monastic "study-circles" ' which shared mystical experiences and were prepared to guide spiritual searchers (1927: 248).[5]

The beginning of the ascent is to respond to God, who calls us to our state of original unity with supreme Goodness. The next stage is to seek Christ, which is expressed in Pauline terms—'seek to be in Christ and that Christ may be in you'. The mind must become like Christ, which implies that we must reproduce the life and particularly the passion of Christ in our own experience. For Paul says, if we suffer with Christ we shall be glorified with him (cf. Rom. 8: 17), and that we must put to death the old man (cf. Eph. 4: 22; Col. 3: 9). Christ was crucified between two thieves. The triple crucifixion reflects the fact that human beings are made up of three essences: mind, soul, and body. We must crucify the mind on the middle cross, with the soul on its right hand and the body on its left (*Disc.* 2. 21). Without the purifying and cleansing power of the Cross there is no unification.

Two ascents and descents follow, but eventually the mind must pass beyond Christ, for Christ is only a 'mansion' on the way to the Father. The mind must rise above all duality to a 'commingling' with the Universal Essence. This means that it must transcend vision or anything to do with the senses. It must transcend the name of 'god'. It must transcend even love, for love, too, implies a duality: the lover and the beloved. When it has passed beyond every duality, even beyond unification, when all distinction is removed, it reaches its fulfilment—the summit of its ascent—which is complete identity with the Good (*Disc.* 4. 18–21).

The author of this work has been identified as very probably Stephen bar-Sudhaile, who Philoxenus of Mabbug tells us had spent some time in a monastery near Jerusalem, where he had claimed to have received visions and revelations, and on that basis had produced some fanciful exegesis of Scripture. Philoxenus also reports that 'certain reliable men' from whom he had heard the story, went to Stephen's cell and were horrified to find on the wall the inscription: 'Every species (or "nature" or "substance") is consubstantial with the divine Essence' (Marsh 1927: 222–32). Stephen's work is an interesting example of an esoteric text coming from the same milieu that nurtured the sixth-century Origenists. According to Marsh, it continued to be read and copied until the mid-nineteenth century (1927: 248).

2. The Latin Tradition

Deification is also found in the Latin tradition, but, with the exception of St Augustine, very sparsely.[6] The West knew of the Greek exegesis of Psalm 82: 6, and, from

---

[5] A recent monograph on Hierotheos (Pinggéra 2002) has not been available to me.

[6] Among the Latin writers not discussed below may be mentioned Novatian (*De Trin.* 15. 7), Cassian (see Casiday 2003), and Boethius (see Chadwick 1981: 211, 236). For the later Latin tradition (notably Bernard, Bonaventure, and Thomas Aquinas) see *DS* iii. 1399–1445; Williams 1999.

the mid-fourth century, of the exchange formula, but only Augustine reflects on what it means to participate in the divine.

(a) Tertullian

The earliest Latin author to use deification terms in a Christian context is Tertullian (*c.* 155–*c.* 220).[7] Like the Greek apologists he takes a Euhemeristic view of contemporary polytheism, but goes further in turning the argument neatly to the advantage of monotheism: if a deifying power exists, it suggests the activity of a supreme God (*Apol.* 11. 10). The supremacy of God is not compromised by the references to 'gods' in Psalm 82: 1 and 6. In *Against Marcion* Tertullian refutes an objection that his rational argument for the oneness of God is undermined by the Psalmist. The sharing of the same *name* as God by those addressed by him in the 'assembly of the gods' does not prove that they share in the *reality* of divinity (*Adv. Marc.* 1. 7. 1, PL 2. 253C; CSEL 47. 298. 30–299. 2).

The supremacy of God, however, does not mean that divinity is something totally inaccessible to human beings. Tertullian appeals to Psalm 82: 6 on two further occasions as a text with which to counter erroneous ideas about God. On the first he cites it in his polemical work against the Carthaginian Gnostic Hermogenes, who taught a dualist system in which God and matter were two equal and exclusively divine eternal principles. But we ourselves possess something of the divine, Tertullian argues. 'For we shall be even gods, if we shall deserve to be amongst those of whom he declared, "I have said, you are all gods" (Ps. 82: 6) and "God stands in the congregation of the gods" (Ps. 82: 1). But this comes of his own grace, not from any property in us, because it is he alone who can make gods' (*Adv. Herm.* 5, CSEL 47. 132. 7–10; trans. Holmes, ANF 3. 480). On the second occasion Tertullian uses the same text against the modalist Monarchianism of Praxeas. Arguing a fortiori (in the way the text is used in John 10: 35) he claims that 'if Scripture has not been afraid to pronounce to be gods those men who by faith have been made sons of God, you may know that much more has it by right applied the name of God and Lord to the only true Son of God' (*Adv. Prax.* 13; Evans 1948: 103. 16–18; trans. Evans 147). This and all but one of the other biblical quotations used in the same chapter of *Against Praxeas* are also found together in a single passage of Irenaeus (*AH* 3. 6. 1), which proves conclusively that Tertullian drew his material from the bishop of Lyons (Evans 1948: 263).

Tertullian's interpretation of the gods of Psalm 82: 6 as the adopted sons of God who have become gods through grace may have come from Irenaeus, but in *Against Marcion* there seems to be an allusion to 2 Peter 1: 4 that is without parallel in contemporary Greek literature, anticipating Origen's use of the text in the *De Principiis* by more than a decade. Adam's fall, says Tertullian, was not a disaster without some mitigation. Hope was held out to him 'by the Lord's saying, "Behold, Adam is become one of us" (Gen. 3: 22), that is, in consequence of the future taking of humanity into divinity' ('de futura scilicet adlectione hominis in diuinitatem') (*Adv. Marc.* 2. 25, CSEL 47. 370. 25–7). What is meant by taking humanity into divinity is perhaps explained in the following book of the same work, where Tertullian is discussing the final consummation of the world after the millennium, when 'we shall

---

[7] Tertullian uses 'deificari', 'deificatio', and 'deificus' (Oroz Reta 1993: 372).

be changed in a moment into the substance of angels, even by the investiture of an incorruptible nature, and so be removed to that kingdom in heaven of which we have now been treating' (cf. 1 Cor. 15: 52–3) (*Adv. Marc.* 3. 24, CSEL 47. 420. 10–13; trans. Holmes, ANF).

(b) Hilary of Poitiers

With respect to deification Tertullian has no immediate successors. The next Latin writer to touch on the theme is Hilary of Poitiers (*c.* 315–367/8), 'the Athanasius of the West', who on account of his anti-Arian views spent four years in exile in Phrygia (356–60).[8] There he learned Greek, which gave him access to Eastern writers, and in particular to Origen.[9] During his years of exile Hilary occupied himself with the writing of his *De Trinitate*. It is not thought that he made direct use of Athanasius or any other Greek writer in the composition of this great work, but the later books do exhibit a use of the exchange formula that is characteristic of Irenaeus and Athanasius. At the Incarnation the Word 'did not resign his divinity but conferred divinity on man' (*Trin.* 9. 4, PL 10. 284A; CCSL 62A, 375. 26–7). 'for the object to be gained was that man might become god' (*Trin.* 9. 38, PL 10. 310A; CCSL 62A. 412. 13–14). Spelled out in greater detail:

When he emptied himself of the form of God and took the form of a servant, the weakness of the assumed humanity did not weaken the divine nature, but that divine power was imparted to humanity without the virtue of divinity being lost in the human form. For when God was born to be man the purpose was not that the Godhead should be lost, but that, the Godhead remaining, man should be born to be god. (*Trin.* 10. 7, CCSL 62A. 464. 5–11; trans. Gayford, NPNF, modified)

Hilary aligns himself in this passage with the kenotic model of the Incarnation characteristic of Irenaeus and the Alexandrian tradition. But this was not a model which he acquired through his contact with the East. Even in his *Commentary on Matthew*, which preceded his exile, he was able to refer to Christ, 'through whom, because God came into man, man in turn becomes a god' (*In Matt.* 5. 15, PL 9. 950CD). This, of course, implies no more than the deification of the whole of humanity in Christ in principle. As Hilary says in the *De Trinitate*, God became flesh 'that by the assumption of the flesh of one, he might dwell within all flesh' ('assumptione carnis unius interna universae carnis incoleret') (*Trin.* 2. 25, PL 10. 67A; CCSL 62. 61. 15). Christ became a representative human being, taking on the weakness of our nature without himself being changed into that weakness (*Tract. Ps.* 138. 3, PL 9. 793C–794A; CSEL 22. 746. 15–18; Wild 1950: 65). How the new humanity embodied by him is appropriated by the believer depends on two further stages. First, Christ's humanity needs to be perfectly deified as a result of his Resurrection. Secondly, we need to share in that deification ourselves by being conformed to Christ's now glorious human nature, which takes place as a result of our own resurrection (Wild 1950: 65).

---

[8] Hilary's doctrine of deification has been the subject of a monograph by P. Wild (1950), on which the following section relies.

[9] Hilary's debt to Origen (cf. E. W. Watson, NPNF 2nd series 9, xlii–xliv) has been challenged by Hanson (1988: 473), but the consensus of opinion remains that Hilary knew some of Origen's works. Jerome says explicitly that in his *Commentaries on the Psalms* Hilary imitated Origen (*De vir. ill.* 100).

In this further development the influence of Origen is discernible. Origen had spoken about a progressive deification of the lower levels of reality in Christ by those superior to them. Thus the flesh of Christ is deified by his soul, and his soul by the Logos (cf. Chapter 5. 5 (d) above). With Hilary, Christ's human nature only became truly divine when it was glorified after the Resurrection (Wild 1950: 59). The human experience parallels that of Christ. Deification is initiated not by the spiritual rebirth of baptism (Hilary does not equate deification with adoptive sonship) but by the second rebirth of our resurrection, when we shall come to participate in the glorified body of Christ. Deification is an eschatological event. Christ 'will hand over to his Father as a kingdom those who are resplendent with the honour of divinity' ('quos iam diuinitatis honore claros') (*Tract. Ps.* 139. 17, PL 9. 824A; CSEL 22. 788. 27–9). We are changed by our resurrection from corruption to immortality from human weakness to divine glory. In the language of the exchange formula 'we lay hold of that for which Christ once laid hold of us' (cf. Phil. 3: 12):

For if God, who was born man, lays hold of us through a bodily nature, though his nature is entirely different, and was made what we are, it is up to us to try to lay hold of what he is now, so that our hastening may join itself in that glory in which he put off the nature of this corruption. And so we shall lay hold of that for which we were laid hold of if we attain the nature of God, since God previously attained the nature of man ('si naturam dei consequamur, deo ante naturam hominum consequente'). It is to be seized by discipline and entered upon by a sort of embrace and by a physical bond lest it slip away or perish. (*Tract. Ps.* 2. 47, PL 9. 290A; CSEL 22. 73. 12–20; trans. Wild, modified)

It is only in our eschatological fulfilment that we shall be like Christ. Hilary does not distinguish between image and likeness. Our recovery of the image lost by Adam takes place when we attain to the glorified humanity of Christ. Only rarely does Hilary mention the role of the Spirit, 'whom we receive as a pledge of immortality and as a participation of God's incorrupt nature' ('quem ad inmortalitatis pignus et ad diuinae incorruptae naturae consortium sumeremus') (cf. 2 Pet. 1: 4) (*Trin.* 1. 36, PL 10. 48C; CCSL 62. 35. 11–13). His emphasis is usually not on baptism and the life in the Spirit but on the resurrection and the life in Christ. St Paul's terminology is understood in an eschatological context. 'In Christ' refers to our being conformed to Christ's glorious body in the world to come. It is then, rather than in our sacramental union with Christ, that we shall be 'concorporales' and 'comparticipes' with him (cf. Eph. 3: 6) (Wild 1950: 119).

Deification as the glorification and spiritualization of the whole human person is brought out most clearly in the *Tractatus super Psalmos*, a late work thought to be influenced by Origen. In this treatise Hilary reflects on the expression 'God of gods' (Pss. 136: 2; 138: 1). In his view this must have a merely titular meaning: Many are called gods in heaven and on earth as the Apostle taught (*Tract. Ps.* 135. 6, PL 9. 771A; CSEL 22. 716. 25–6), but as there is only one true God, the others are gods in a nominal sense only (Wild 1950: 149). Unlike Irenaeus and Athanasius, for whom the 'gods' are those who have been incorporated into Christ by baptism, Hilary attributes a purely eschatological meaning to the expression. Human beings can be called gods when they have been glorified, which means when they have been assimilated to the angelic life. 'I said, you are gods and all of you sons of the Most High' (Ps. 82: 6) refers to the heavenly court of men and angels. Deification thus takes place only when human beings have been fully spiritualized, for the name 'gods' belongs properly to the angels.

(c) Augustine of Hippo

Augustine of Hippo (354–430) refers more frequently than any other Latin Father to the doctrine of deification.[10] Its biblical basis in Psalm 82 seemed to him incontrovertible. Moreover, it was sanctioned by the tradition of the Church. Unlike Tertullian and Hilary, however, Augustine knew very little Greek. Aware of his limitations, he wrote to Jerome asking him for Latin translations of biblical commentaries by Greek authors, especially Origen (*Ep.* 28. 2). But Jerome was already on the point of embarking on his campaign against Origenism, so the translations never came. It is interesting to speculate what might have happened if Augustine had been exposed more fully to Origen. His approach to deification might have been enriched by Origen's discussions of participation, though it is unlikely that Origen's optimistic anthropology would have made any inroads on his deeply pessimistic commitment to predestination.

Augustine's first love was philosophy. As a student of rhetoric at Carthage he had read Cicero's *Hortensius*, which had fired him with an enthusiasm for the pursuit of wisdom. His first reference to deification is directly inspired by his philosophical studies. In 388 or 390 his friend Nebridius wrote to him asking him to join him in Carthage so that they could lead a monastic life together. At the time Augustine was living at his birthplace of Thagaste. At Cassiciacum in northern Italy he had attempted to lead a life of philosophical seclusion. Now as a baptized Christian he was living a converted life in Numidia with a group of *servi Dei*, serious laymen dedicated to living the Christian life in its fullness. In reply to Nebridius he says that the planning of troublesome journeys ill befits those who are preparing for 'that last great journey we call death'. Such men avoid burdening themselves with public office and seek to deify themselves in a state of freedom from worldly affairs (*Ep.* 10. 2). The phrase 'deificari in otio' (to attain deification in a life of scholarly seclusion) has been shown to derive from Porphyry's *Sententiae ad intelligibilia ducentes* (Folliet 1962; Bonner 1986a: 371–2). Porphyry was the first non-Christian to speak of the conformity of the soul to God in terms of deification. Not that Augustine is likely to have made an independent study of Porphyry. The *Sententiae* were intended to be a resumé of the thought of Plotinus. Augustine probably came across them in Marius Victorinus' Latin version as an introduction to his translation of the *Enneads*. They therefore do not represent an influence separate from that of Plotinus (O'Connell 1968: 20–1).

Augustine's engagement with Plotinus forced him to rethink his earlier attachment to Manichaeism. As a Manichee he would have believed that the soul was a fragment of the God of light trapped in a hostile world of darkness. As a Christian

---

[10] Several studies have been made of Augustine's approach to deification: see esp. Bonner 1986a; also Stoop 1952; Capanága 1954; Oroz Reta 1993; and Casiday 2001. I am indebted to Henry Chadwick for sending me a brief paper on deification in Augustine, in which he drew my attention to several references that had escaped the attention of previous scholars (esp. *Vera rel.* 46 (86); *De nat. et grat.* 33. 37; and *C. Adim.* 93. 2), besides the exegesis of Psalm 82 (81) in Dolbeau's Mainz sermons. References to Chadwick forthcoming are to this personal communication, which is to appear in finished form in the Strasbourg *Revue des Sciences Religieuses*.

Neoplatonist he still held that the soul was fundamentally divine in the sense that God was always present to it. Man participated in God's being simply by existing. The soul may be alienated from God by sin but it cannot escape from his presence, even if it is an angry presence. The 'divinity' of the soul thus expresses God's omnipresence (O'Connell 1968: 32–3). As a priest and then a bishop (from 396) Augustine moved away from his Platonic opinions, relying more on traditional biblical exegesis (Rist 1994: 95). The fundamental spiritual insights of Platonism, however, were never repudiated. In the early *De vera religione* (of 390/1), probably following Porphyry, he says that God does not envy his rational creation but confers the supreme dignity of divine status upon it: 'non illi ergo invidet [deus] ut sit quod ipse est' (*De vera rel.* 46 (86). 7–8). Even in the great work of his maturity, *De Civitate Dei*, Augustine quotes Plotinus and Porphyry with approval. They are right to speak of attaining the divine likeness as the goal of human life: 'We must fly to our beloved *patria . . .* our way is to become like God' (*De Civ. Dei* 9. 17, CSEL 40(1). 434. 21–4; cf. *Enn.* 1. 6. 8 and 1. 2. 3). Our whole life should, as Porphyry says, become a prayer to God through enquiring into and imitating his nature, for 'imitatio deificat affectionem ad ipsum operando' (*De Civ. Dei* 19. 23. 4, CSEL 40(2). 416. 15–16). Imitation and deification are two aspects of the same process. The reward for those who imitate God is that like the spirits they come to be penetrated by intelligible light and enjoy perfect happiness in the participation of God (*De Civ. Dei* 10. 2, CSEL 40(1). 448–9).

Platonism, however, needed to be corrected and completed by the Scriptures. The spirits may participate in a noetic light that brings them into direct contact with God; but human beings need a divine mediator if they are to enjoy such a relationship, and that mediator is Christ:

The grace of God came to you and 'gave you the power to become the sons of God' (John 1: 12). Hear the voice of my Father saying, 'I have said, you are gods and all of you children of the Most High' (Ps. 82: 6). Since then they are men, and the sons of men, if they are not the children of the Most High, they are liars, for, 'all men are liars' (Ps. 116: 11). If they are the sons of God, if they have been redeemed by the Saviour's grace, if purchased with his precious blood, if born again of water and of the Spirit, if predestinated to the inheritance of heaven, then indeed they are children of God. And so thereby are gods. What then would a lie have to do with you? For Adam was a mere man; Christ, man and God; God, the Creator of all creation. Adam a mere man, the man Christ, the mediator with God, the only Son of the Father, the God-man. You, O man, are far from God, and God is far above man; between them the God-man placed himself. Acknowledge Christ and by him as man ascend up to God. (*Serm.* 81. 6, PG 38. 503; trans. Macmullen, NPNF)

In this passage Augustine interprets Psalm 82: 6 in conjunction with an exegesis of Psalm 116: 11, 'all men are liars', that we also find in Didymus of Alexandria. If, according to Scripture, all men are liars, those who have ceased to be liars are no longer men. They have been promoted, as it were, to be gods, which in Christian tradition means they have been baptized. The gods are those, as Origen had said, to whom the Word of God came. They are called gods, not by nature but by grace, through the Son by the gift of the Holy Spirit (*De Fid. et Symbol.* 16). Augustine links these points with the Pauline concept of justification:

See in the same psalm those to whom he says, 'I have said, You are gods and all of you sons of the Most High; but you shall die like men, and fall like one of the princes.' It is evident, then, as he has called men gods, that they are deified by his grace, not born of his substance. For he who justifies someone is just through his own self and not through another; and he who deifies someone is a god through himself, not by partaking of another. He who justifies is the same as he who deifies, in that by justifying he makes us sons of God ('Ille enim justificat, qui per semetipsum non ex alio justus est; et ille deificat, qui per seipsum non alterius participatione Deus est. Qui autem justificat, ipse deificat, quia justificando, filios Dei facit.'). 'For he has given them the power to become sons of God' (John 1: 12). If we have been made sons of God, we have also been made gods: but this is the effect of grace adopting, not of nature generating. For only the Son of God [is] God. . . . The rest that are made gods are made by his own grace, are not born of his substance, that they should be the same as he, but that by favour they should come to him, and be fellow heirs with Christ. (*Enar. in Ps.* 49. 2, CCL 38. 575. 5–576. 20; trans. Cleveland Coxe, NPNF, modified)

An interesting light is thrown on Augustine's exposition of Psalm 82(81) by one of the newly discovered Mainz sermons.[11] In the thirteenth (= Dolbeau 6) he comments on the first verse of the psalm: 'Deus stetit in synagoga deorum',

which his people chanted with the wording 'congregatione' for the Greek 'synagoga'. Some of his people understood Greek, he explains, but not all. (Their command of Greek no doubt came from trade between Hippo and the East; some of them may have been Orientals employed by merchants.) There in the exposition of the psalm we read: 'Vult enim deus non solum uiuificare sed etiam deificare nos' ('for God wishes not only to make us alive but even to deify us'). If this is met with incredulity, Augustine answers that God is faithful to his promises and is omnipotent. And it is more incredible that God became man in the Incarnation. He is not by nature mortal, nor are we naturally immortal. If God can become man, then surely he can deify mortals. (Chadwick forthcoming)

For Augustine, as for his contemporary, Cyril of Alexandria, the deification of human beings is the purpose for which the Word became incarnate and is appropriated by them through baptism. The ecclesiastical dimension of deification is emphasized further by the exchange formula: 'The Son of God became the Son of Man that he might make the sons of men sons of God' (M 13. 1). 'He descended that we might ascend' (*Ep.* 140). 'He became a partaker in our weakness, bestowing on us a participation in his divinity' ('particeps nostrae infirmitatis, donans participationem suae divinitatis') (*Enar. in Ps.* 58). 'He both brought down his majesty to human affairs and raised human lowliness to the realm of the divine, that he might be a mediator between God and man, being made a man by God above men' (*Ep. ad Gal. Exp.* 24. 8). Christ is not simply a model to be emulated, but the agent of a new creation, for in him human nature is re-fashioned in conformity with the divine image (*De Trin.* 14 and 15).

For all his earlier Platonism Augustine's understanding of deification as a Catholic bishop is firmly incarnational and sacramental. A number of Platonic themes are recast in biblical terms. In *De Civitate Dei*, for example, he was able to refer to the ascent of the soul to God in purely Plotinian terms (*De Civ. Dei* 9. 17, quoted above). But in his *Enarrationes in Psalmos* the ascent is re-expressed as an interior pilgrimage.

[11] For a review of these sermons see Chadwick 1996. The text of M 13 on Psalm 81(82) was discovered by François Dolbeau in 1990 in the Stadtsbibliothek of Mainz and published by him in Dolbeau 1993: 88–106. For a good English translation see also Casiday 2001.

The steps of ascent are in the human heart. For heaven is not up in the sky. It is the totality of all holy souls, in whom God is enthroned (*Enar. in Ps.* 122. 3). The future happiness is already present in the saints, but its fulfilment is eschatological (*De Trin.* 14. 25; cf. Bonner 1986*a*: 381). 'We experience mortality, we endure infirmity, we look forward to divinity' ('Gerimus mortalitatem, toleramus infirmitatem, expectamus diuinitatem') (M 13. 1). Our divinity will only be achieved with the beatific vision, when the promise of the serpent, 'You shall be as gods' (Gen. 3: 5) is brought to its true fruition by God 'who would have made us as gods, not by deserting him, but by participating in him' (*De Civ. Dei* 22. 30).

Augustine frequently refers to the concept of participation to convey the relationship between the contingent and the self-existent. Thus the ability not to sin is a participated divine quality, a gift dependent on God, not a natural human attribute; 'for it is one thing to be God, another thing to be a partaker of God. God by nature cannot sin, but the partaker of God receives this inability from God' (*De Civ. Dei* 22. 30). Although the holy are 'participes Dei', Augustine does not appeal to 2 Peter 1: 4 ('divinae consortes naturae'). His wariness of the text would have been confirmed by the use of it made by the Pelagians. In his analysis of the proceedings of the Council of Diospolis, at which the Eastern bishops acquitted Pelagius of heresy, Augustine comments on the claim of Pelagius, or at least of Coelestius, one of his more radical disciples, that 'people cannot be called sons of God unless they have become entirely free from sin' (*De Gest. Pel.* 42 and 65). Coelestius had appealed to 2 Peter 1: 4 in support of his opinion: for 'from what Peter says, that "we are partakers of the divine nature," it must follow that the soul has the power of being without sin, just in the way that God himself has' (*De Gest. Pel.* 65). Coelestius' accusers took this to imply that he considered the soul a part of God. But Coelestius himself was probably only stating an extremely optimistic view of human nature. Augustine expresses his satisfaction that this, among other opinions, was repudiated by Pelagius at the council. For him human nature could never be entirely free from sin. The children of God were the baptized, not those who had become literally like God. The Coelestian doctrine deprived human beings of dependency on God's grace and made the sacraments superfluous.

'Participation in the divine is for Augustine the heart of redemption' (Chadwick forthcoming). But such participation is qualified. We cannot be the same as God, even if we can become one with his flesh through the sacraments. 'The creature will never become equal with God even if perfect holiness were to be achieved in us. Some think that in the next life we shall be changed into what he is; I am not convinced' (*De nat. et grat.* 33. 37; trans. Chadwick). Augustine was aware that there were those among his hearers whose reservations were deeper than his own. But he was confident that his teaching had the authority of Scripture and tradition behind it. He does not try to justify it in the language of Platonism. In the end deification is beyond human explanation: 'That he should make men gods is to be understood in divine silence' ('Ut deos homines faciat, divino est intelligenda silentio') (*C. Adim.* 93. 2). It may be said to be analogical, to be appropriated through baptism and the Eucharist, to be experienced fully only eschatologically, but it still remains a mystery.

APPENDIX 2

The Greek Vocabulary of Deification

With the exception of a few references to human beings or angels as 'gods' (Exod. 7: 1; Deut. 10: 17; Ps. 82: 6; John 10: 34), none of the Greek expressions for deification is used in the Septuagint or the New Testament. Linguistically, deification appears at first sight to have impeccably pagan credentials. The situation, however, is more complex, as the following survey shows. I have attempted to examine all the Greek terms for deification used in inscriptions, papyri, and literary texts. This task has already been performed in an admirable way with regard to the earlier material by C. Habicht (1970). Here I propose, so far as possible, to complete his account to about 500 CE.

(i) Ἀποθεόω/ἀποθειόω

The characteristic terminology of deification first appears in the Hellenistic age. It is uncertain exactly when it began to be used. Aristoxenus, a pupil of Aristotle, is reported by Athenaeus to have mentioned the deification of personified Justice (ἀπεθεώθη δὲ καὶ αὐτὸ τὸ τῆς Δίκης ὄνομα), but Athenaeus (who was writing at the end of the second century CE) is likely at this point to have been using his own words.[1] There is also a reference to the deified Ganymede (Γανυμήδης οὗτος ἀποθεούμενος) by Nicolaus, a dramatist of the New Comedy of uncertain date, perhaps of the second century BCE.[2]

The first certain occurrence of the verb, ἀποθεόω, however, is in Polybius (c. 200 – after 118 BCE), who mentions that Alexander's court historian, Callisthenes, 'wished to deify (ἀποθεοῦν) Alexander' (*Hist.* 12. 23. 4). At about the same time, in 118 BCE, a decree of Ptolemy VII refers to the king's deified predecessors as the ἀποτεθεωμένοι (*P. Tebt.*, eds Grenfell and Hunt 5. 78; cf. note *ad loc.*). Not long

---

[1] Aristoxenus, frag. 50 (ed. Wehrli, 24. 14) = Athenaeus 12. 546b. Cf. Habicht 1970: 175. From Aristoxenus' time we have a use of θεοποίητος by Isocrates to mean 'made by the gods' or 'a divine creation' (*Or.* 7. 62 [Areopagiticus]). Apart from this there is only the isolated word θεοποιούς from Aristophanes (frag. 786/7), which, as Julius Pollux tells us, means 'makers of statues of the gods' (*Onomasticon* 1. 12–13).

[2] Nicolaus, frag. 1 35 (ed. Kock, *Comicorum Atticorum Fragmenta*, iii. 384). Habicht 1970: 175 says that Nicolaus is certainly not older than the second century BCE. Körte (ed. Pauly, Wissowa, and Kroll, *Real-Encyclopädie*, Nikolaos [19] 362) thinks it likely that this dramatic poet is to be identified with the adviser and confidant of Herod the Great, Nicolaus of Damascus (end of the first century BCE).

afterwards ἀποθεόω is used in the *Alexander Romance* of Ps.-Callisthenes. An oracle tells Alexander that when he has been deified (ἀποθεωθείς) his body will be venerated and many kings will send gifts to his tomb, which will be the city of Alexandria itself which he has founded.[3]

The earliest surviving instance of the noun ἀποθέωσις is in a dated inscription. Ἀποθέωσις and ἐκθέωσις appear together in the Canopus Decree of 238 BCE as equivalent terms for the incorporation of Berenice, the deceased daughter of Ptolemy III, into all the temples of Egypt.[4] A century later, a *psephisma* for a gymnasiarch at Pergamon speaks of a public gift of unguent 'after the apotheosis of the royal couple'.[5]

It will be seen that these early instances of ἀποθεόω and ἀποθέωσις are all connected with the Hellenistic ruler-cult. There seems to be little doubt that the terms originated in the chanceries of the royal courts. Later, Euhemerism will also play a significant role, but at this stage its influence is apparent only in the Jewish writer, Ps.-Aristeas. This cultivated Alexandrian (fl. *c.*200 BCE) ridicules polytheism and popular religion, even if they are defended from a Euhemeristic point of view, on the grounds that it is 'empty and vain to deify one's equals' (διὸ κενὸν καὶ μάταιον τοὺς ὁμοίους ἀποθεοῦν) (*Ep. ad Phil.*, SC 89. 170).

The Roman period is marked by a widening of applications of ἀποθέωσις. The first metaphorical use is by Cicero, who says in a letter to Atticus of July 61 BCE that the consulship which Curio used to call an apotheosis will be worth nothing if Afranius gets in.[6] Cicero's friend, the Epicurean rhetorician Philodemus, personifies rhetorical persuasion, saying, perhaps under the influence of Euhemerism, that if she had been considered divine because of her practical usefulness she would have been deified (ἀπεθεώθη) by philosophy (*Rhet.* 5. 32. 5 ed. Sudhaus I. 269). Diodorus of Sicily, who was certainly influenced by Euhemerism, explains in his *World History*, written between 60 and 30 BCE, how Ouranos, the inventor of urban life, was accorded immortal honours (ἀθάνατους τιμάς) after his death because the accurate way in which he predicted the movements of the heavenly bodies to his ignorant subjects convinced them that he 'partook of the nature of the gods'. Titaea, the mother of the Titans, was also deified (ἀποθεωθῆναι) after her death because of her 'many good deeds for the peoples' and was renamed Ge (*Bibl.* 3. 57. 2).

Diodorus, like many of his contemporaries, was fascinated by the strange customs of the Egyptians. In his discussion of the Egyptian worship of animals he remarks that they deified the he-goat (τὸν δὲ τράγον ἀπεθέωσαν) because of his generative

---

[3] Ps.-Call. 1. 33. 11. Ps.-Callisthenes cannot be dated with certainty, the possible period of composition ranging from the first century BCE to the second century CE.

[4] *OGI* 56. 53 and 56. Another equivalent expression is ἐπεὶ εἰς θεοὺς μετῆλθεν (55). M. Radin 1916: 44–6 argues for a difference in nuance between ἀποθέωσις and ἐκθέωσις but the evidence, here at least, does not bear this out. Cf. Habicht 1970: 174 n. 24.

[5] *Ath. Mitt.* 33 (1908) 381, no. 3. 9–10, corrected by H. Hepding, *Ath. Mitt.* 35 (1910) 419–20: μετὰ δὲ τὴν τῶν β]ασιλέων ἀποθέωσιν δημοσίαι ἐτίθετο τὸ ἄλειμμα. Cf. *OGI* 308. 2–4: ἐπεὶ βασίλισσα ['Ἀπ]ολλωνὶς Εὐσεβής (the wife of Attalus I, 241–197 BCE) μεθέστηκεν εἰς θεούς and *OGI* 339. 16: τῶν τε βασιλέων εἰς θεοὺς μεταστάντων (after the death of Attalus III in 133 BCE).

[6] *Att.* 1. 16. 13: 'Sed heus tu! Videsne consulatum illum nostrum, quem Curio antea ἀποθέωσιν vocabat, si hic factus erit, fabam mimum futurum?' As D. R. Shackleton Bailey has pointed out (*Cicero's Letters to Atticus*, i (Cambridge 1965) 325), 'consulatum illum nostrum' is the consular office which Cicero is always talking about, not Cicero's own consulship.

member (*Bibl.* 1. 88). This seems to him comparable to the Greeks' deification of Priapus, but the deification of crocodiles he finds too bizarre for his taste (λείπεται δ' ἡμῖν εἰπεῖν περὶ τῆς τῶν κροκοδείλων ἀποθεώσεως) (*Bibl.* 1. 89). Surviving inscriptions and papyri provide us with further examples of the apotheosis of animals in Egypt. In this connection our stock of terms is augmented by the verb ἀποθειόω. An inscription from the crocodile necropolis at Theadelphia (Batn-Herit), dated 57/ 6 BCE, mentions the tombs τῶν ἀποθειουμένων ἱερῶν ζώων.[7] Two papyri of the second century CE refer to the apotheosis of the holy bulls, Apis at Memphis and Mnevis at Heliopolis.[8] A papyrus of the third century uses ἀποθεόω to signify the killing of a lizard by drowning for use in a magic spell.[9]

The application of these terms to the imperial cult is well known but less frequent than might be expected. The Latin *consecratio*, the official proclamation of the deceased emperor or member of his family as a *divus*, was rendered in Greek by ἀποθέωσις.[10] Thus the people of Samos date their official decrees from the apotheosis of Augustus in 14 CE, the best preserved example being from 85 (ἔτους οά τῆς ἀποθεώσεως).[11] Similarly, *consecro* was represented by ἀποθεόω. A decree of Paullus Fabius Persicus of about 44 CE, checking abuses in the financial administration of the Artemision at Ephesus, expresses the deification of Livia, the consort of Augustus and mother of Tiberius, by the emperor Claudius in the words: ἀπεθέωσεν αὐτ[ὴν ἥ τε σύγκλητος κ]αὶ θεὸς Σεβαστ[ός.[12] Seneca's satire on the deification of Claudius in 54 CE, the *Apocolocyntosis*, had the alternative and less offensive title of the Ἀποθήοσις (*sic*) (Schanz and Hosius 1935: ii. 471–2). The equivalence of *consecratio* and ἀποθέωσις becomes so well established that eventually even the consecration of the new city of Constantinople can be called an apotheosis.[13]

In imperial times the literary use of ἀποθεόω and ἀποθέωσις is not very frequent.

---

[7] Mitteis and Wilcken, *Chrestomathie*, no. 70. III. 17. On the Egyptian deification of animals cf. Plutarch, *De Iside* 71–5, and Cicero, *De natura deorum* 1. 36. 'The correct attitude', says Plutarch (*De Iside* 71), 'is that of the Greeks, who regard certain animals as sacred to certain gods.' Both Cicero and Plutarch find the Egyptian attitude absurd, but account for it in a rationalistic way by appealing to the usefulness or strength of the animals deified.

[8] Schubart and Uxkull-Gyllenband, *Aegyptische Urkunden* 5. [89] 203: Οἱ [μὴ] πέμ[ψ]αντες στολίσματα [εἰ]ς ἀπο[θέ]ωσιν Ἄπιδος ἢ Μνέ[υι]δος κατακρίνοντ[αι πρόσ]τειμον. (This is the Gnomon of the Idios Logos, dated between 151 and 160 CE. The editors note that although in Ptolemaic times the kings often bore the cost of the burial, in the imperial period every Egyptian temple was required to deliver byssos (fine linen) to Memphis and Heliopolis for wrapping the mummified holy bulls.) Mitteis and Wilcken, *Chrestomathie*, no. 85. 15–20: Παπήνεγκα καὶ παρέδωκα ὑπὲρ τοῦ προκειμένου ἱεροῦ ὑπὲρ ἀποθεώσεως Ἄπιδος Θαώϊτος βύσσου στολίσματος πήχεις δέκα. (This is *P. Genev.*, no. 201, dated 170 CE. Wilcken (p. 112) notes that Apis only becomes Osorapis after 70 days. The deification is not immediately at death but after the period of official mourning.)

[9] Kenyon, *P. Lond.*, no. 121. 628–9: λαβων καλαβωτην απ[ο υγ]ρου εασον αυτον εις κρινον εως αν αποθεωθη. (Cf. A. D. Nock 1931: 235–87).

[10] Diodorus, *Bibl.* 4. 2. 1: ἔθος γάρ ἐστι Ῥωμαίοις ἐκθειάξειν βασιλέων τοὺς ἐπὶ παισὶ διαδόχοις τελευτήσαντες τήν τε τοιαύτην τιμὴν ἀποθέωσιν καλοῦσι.

[11] *IGR* iv. 1732. Cf. 1704: ἐν τῷ ρμ [.έτει] (uncertain figure between 140 and 146, i.e. a year between 154 and 160 CE); 1726: [ἔτους . . . τῆς Καί]σαρος ἀποθεώσε[ως.

[12] *Die Inschriften von Ephesos* (ed. H. Wankel) Ia (Bonn 1979), no. 17–19. 66. Cf. D. Magie 1950: 545–6.

[13] John Lydus, *On Powers, or the Magistracies of the Roman State*, 30: Ὥσπερ ἀρχέτυπον εἶδος ἡ μονάς, παράδειγμα δὲ μονάδος ἕν, οὕτως ἐν προοιμίοις ἡ καθ' ἡμᾶς εὐδαίμων πόλις τῆς τότε πᾶσαν ὑπεροχὴν ἐκβεβηκυίας Ῥώμης ἐνομίσθη. ὅθεν ὁ Κωνσταντῖνος οὐδαμοῦ πρὸ τῆς ἐπ' αὐτῇ κωνσεκρατίωνος (οὕτω δὲ τὴν ἀποθέωσιν Ῥωμαῖοι προσαγορεύουσιν) Ῥώμην νέαν δείκνυται καλῶν, κάστρα δὲ καὶ αὐτὴν ἴσα ταῖς ἄλλαις τῶν χωρῶν (ed. Bandy (Philadelphia 1983) 128. 8–13). Lydus was born in 490.

Strabo (64/3 BCE to after 21 CE) mentions that the Veneti call the death of Diomedes an apotheosis (*Geog.* 6. 3. 9). Plutarch (before 50 CE to after 120) refers to the deification of Romulus without comment in his life of Numa (*Numa* 6. 3). In his life of Demetrius, however, we encounter the first pagan criticism of deification. The extravagances of Demetrius prompt him to declare that the value of statues, paintings, and apotheoses is to be measured by the actions that called them forth (*Demetrius* 30. 4–5). There is a further use by Plutarch of the verb ἀποθεόω which seems to take up a point made by Longinus. In his essay *On the Glory of the Athenians* Plutarch says that Demosthenes in an oblique way had deified those who had fallen at Marathon by swearing oaths by them.[14] Longinus treats this theme in some detail. He comments on the skill of Demosthenes in stirring up the emotions of his hearers by swearing 'by those who had risked their lives at Marathon', and says that the orator thus 'deifies his audience's ancestors'.[15] Finally, a spurious text included in the *Moralia* speaks of the honouring of Agesilaus by the Thasiotes 'with temples and apotheoses'.[16]

From the second century onwards there are further extensions of meaning. First, ἀποθέωσις and ἀποθεόω are no longer reserved to heroes and emperors but at least in the Greek cities of Asia Minor can refer simply to the burial of ordinary citizens.[17] Secondly, metaphorical applications continue to be made. We have from the Hadrianic period a use of ἀποθειόω in a metaphorical sense by the paederastic poet Straton to express the heightened senses of someone who has fallen in love.[18] Thirdly, philosophical uses appear for the first time. A Stoic text probably of the second century, which has been adapted to Christian use, refers to the *nous* as the apotheosis of the soul, and speaks of the fool who is unable to look up and know God, 'who has made all things for the salvation and apotheosis of man'.[19] At about the same time two tractates of the Hermetic Corpus make use of ἀποθεόω. In the fourth tractate the rejection of the corporeal and the choosing of the spiritual is described as the correct choice which deifies a man (τὸν ἄνθρωπον ἀποθεῶσαι) (*CH* IV. 7). In the tenth tractate escape from the body and the contemplation of the Good are similarly represented as the appropriate condition for deification (*CH* x. 7).

---

[14] *Moralia* 350c: τούτους ἀπεθέωσε τοῖς ὅρκοις ὁ ῥήτωρ ὀμνύων οὓς οὐκ ἐμιμεῖτο.

[15] *On the Sublime* 16. 2: τοὺς μὲν προγόνους ἀποθεώσας, ὅτι δεῖ τοὺς οὕτως ἀποθανόντας ὡς θεοὺς ὀμνύναι παριστάνων.

[16] Ps.-Plutarch, *Apoph. Lakon.*, Agesilaus 25 (*Moralia* 210cd).

[17] *CIG* ii. 2831 (Aphrodisias): ἑτέρῳ δὲ οὐδενὶ ἐξέσται κηδευθῆναι ἐν τῇ σορῷ ἢ μόν[ῳ] Ἀχιλλεῖ καὶ Ἀχιλλεί[ᾳ] τέκνῳ αὐτοῦ ἐὰν δέ τις μετὰ τὸ ἀποθεωθῆναι τοὺς προδηλουμένους τολμή[σῃ] ὀστέα ἢ ἕτερόν τινα ἐνθάψαι, ἢ ἐκκόψαι [τὴν] ἐπιγραφὴν, ἐ[ξ]ώλη[ς] ἀπόλοιτο σὺν τέκνοις καὶ παντὶ τῷ γένει. 2832 (Aphrodisias): μετὰ δὲ τὴν τούτων ἀποθέωσιν οὐδεὶς ἐξ[ου]σ[ίαν] ἕξει ἐνθάψαι ἕτερον. Keil and von Premerstein, 1908: 85, no. 183 (Kula, Lydia): ὅταν δ᾿ἀπ[ο]θεωθῇι Λυκῖνος, ὑ[π]άρχε[ιν] τοῖς ἐκγόνοις αὐτοῦ τό τε γέρας ὁμοίως, ὅταν [γε] ἐπιδημῶσ[ι]. Cf. the verbs ἀφηρωΐζω and ἀποϊερόω used in exactly the same way at Aphrodisias in *CIG* ii. 2827, 2845.

[18] *Anth. Pal.* 12. 177: εἰ δὲ μὲ καὶ πεφίληκε τεκμαίρομαι· εἰ γὰρ ἀληθές, πῶς ἀποθειωθεὶς πλάζομ᾿ ἐπιχθόνιος;

[19] *Philokalia* (eds Nicodemus of the Holy Mountain and Macarius of Corinth), i: *Parainesis*, 135: Ὁ νοῦς ἐν τῇ ψυχῇ φαίνεται, καὶ ἡ φύσις ἐν τῷ σώματι. Καὶ ὁ νοῦς μὲν τῆς ψυχῆς ἀποθέωσίς ἐστίν ἡ δὲ φύσις τοῦ σώματος, διάχυσις ὑπάρχει. 168: τὸν θεὸν τὸν τὰ πάντα εἰς σωτηρίαν καὶ ἀποθέωσιν ἀνθρώπου ποιήσαντα. Cf. I. Hausherr, 'Un écrit stoïcien sous le nom de Saint Antoine Ermite', *OCP* 86 (Rome 1933): 212–16.

The use of ἀποθέωσις in a pagan philosophical context does not occur again until the fifth century, when the Neoplatonist Hierocles refers twice to apotheosis as the result of the attainment of virtue (*In Carmen Aureum*, 27. 2, ed. Koehler, 119. 13); 27. 4, (120. 12). Among Christian authors Clement of Alexandria (d. *c.*213), Origen (d. *c.*253), Gregory Thaumaturgus (d. *c.*270), Apollinarius (d. *c.*390), Didymus the Blind (d. *c.*398), Macarius Magnes (fl. 400), Nestorius (d. after 450), Ps.-Macarius (fifth century), and Maximus the Confessor (d. 662) employ these terms. Clement refers six times to the deification of outstanding men in a Euhemeristic fashion (*Prot.* 10. 96. 4; *Strom.* 1. 105. 1, 3, and 4; 1. 137. 3; 3. 5. 2). Origen uses ἀποθεόω twice in the same way (*Hom. Jer.* 5. 3; *C. Cels.* 4. 59). But he also uses the verb in a manner not unlike that of the Hermetists to denote the deification of those who choose to live according to virtue rather than according to the flesh (*Com. Matt.* 16. 29; *In Psalm.* 81). Gregory, Origen's pupil, claims in a similar way that the virtue of prudence reflects the divine mind and produces 'a kind of apotheosis' (*Panegyric* 11). Didymus applies ἀποθεόω in a novel way to the effect on the believer of baptism, which 'immortalizes and deifies us' (ἀπαθανατοῖ καὶ ἀποθεοῖ ἡμᾶς) (*De Trin.* 2. 14). Apollinarius uses the same verb to denote the deification of the flesh assumed by the Logos, a usage which Nestorius reproduces only to condemn (Frag. 98; cf. Loofs, *Nestoriana*, pp. 265, 275). Macarius Magnes says that when a man honours his Maker, 'he deifies himself by sharing in the Godhead' (ἑαυτὸν δ᾽ ἀποθεοῖ κοινωνῶν τῇ θεότητι) (*Apocriticus* 4. 16). The Macarian homilies refer to a man's being deified and becoming a son of God when he has undergone spiritual regeneration: ἀποθεοῦται γὰρ λοιπὸν ὁ τοιοῦτος καὶ γίγνεται υἱὸς θεοῦ (*Mac. Hom.* (Coll. II) 15. 35). When a man has been deified in this way he becomes greater than the first Adam (*Mac. Hom.* (Coll. II) 26. 2). Maximus uses ἀποθεόω on a single occasion to express the exchange formula: 'Man's ability to deify himself through love for God's sake is correlative to God's becoming man through compassion for man's sake' (*Amb. Io.* 10, PG 91. 1113B). Finally, we may note in Gregory of Nyssa a new compound form, συναποθεόω to denote the deification of the human nature of Christ contemporaneously with the Incarnation (*Orat. Cat.* 35, 37). The first Christians to use ἀποθεόω and ἀποθέωσις, Clement and Origen, thus follow a recognizable contemporary usage which their successors extend to embrace the operation of baptism and the transformation of the flesh at the Incarnation. This Christian usage, however, remains rare.

(ii) Θεοποιέω—θεοποιΐα—θεοποίησις—θεοποιός

The earliest instance of θεοποιέω occurs in an inscription of between 27 and 11 BCE in which the citizens of Mytilene promise to look out for any honours that can deify Augustus even more than those they have already voted him.[20] This is the only pagan use of θεοποιέω with reference to the ruler-cult.

---

[20] *OGI* 456. 44–50: εἰ δέ τι τούτων ἐπικυδέστερον τοῖς μετέπειτα χρόνοις εὑρεθήσεται, πρὸς μη[δὲν] τῶν θεοποιεῖν αὐτὸν ἐπὶ [πλέ]ον δυνησομένων ἐλλείψει[ν] τὴν τῆς πόλεως προθυμίαν καὶ εὐσέβειαν. Cf. Habicht 1970: 176–7; S. R. F. Price 1980: 34–5.

The first appearance of θεοποιέω in a literary text occurs in about 7 BCE when Dionysius of Halicarnassus states that the peculiar circumstances of the death of Romulus lend support to those who 'deify mortal things' (τοῖς θεοποιοῦσι τὰ θνητά) (*Ant. Rom.* 2. 56. 6). In the second century Lucian says with some irony in the first chapter of *The Scythian* that the enrolment of Toxaris among the heroes in Athens shows that 'it is also possible for the Athenians to deify Scythians in Greece, (ἀλλὰ καὶ Ἀθηναίοις ἐξεῖναι θεοποιεῖν τοὺς Σκύθας ἐπὶ τῆς Ἑλλάδος) *Scyth.* 1. The only other pagan author to use θεοποιέω is Sextus Empiricus (fl. *c.*200 CE), who says that the Pythagoreans used to treat Pythagoras as a god (τοῦτον γὰρ ἐθεοποίουν) (*Adv. Math.* 7. 94), that the Stoic sage 'was in all respects considered a god because he never expressed a mere opinion' (κατὰ πάντα ἐθεοποιεῖτο διὰ τὸ μὴ δοξάζειν) (*Adv. Math.* 7. 423), and that 'Euhemerus declared that those considered gods were certain men of power, which is why they were deified by the rest and reputed to be gods' (καὶ διὰ τοῦτο ὑπὸ τῶν ἄλλων θεοποιηθέντας δόξαι θεούς) (*Adv. Math.* 9. 51).

Θεοποιέω, while remaining uncommon among pagan writers, became the preferred verb among Christians to denote both pagan and Christian deification. The Apologists use the verb a number of times to denote the pagan deification of inanimate things.[21] Clement is the first to apply it to Christian deification.[22] Thereafter the verb is used by Hippolytus (*Ref.* 10. 34), Origen[23] and Eusebius of Caesarea,[24] then by Athanasius (with great frequency),[25] and subsequently by Didymus the Blind,[26] the three Cappadocians,[27] and Apollinarius of Laodicea[28] in the fourth century, Macarius Magnes,[29] Ps.-Macarius,[30] and Cyril of Alexandria[31] in the fifth century, Leontius of Jerusalem[32] in the sixth century, and Maximus the Confessor[33] in the seventh century. In terms of frequency of use, θεοποιέω, largely through the influence of Athanasius, becomes by the fourth century a word with a primarily Christian range of meanings. Towards the end of the patristic age, however, it tends to be replaced by θεόω.

The earliest witness to the noun θεοποιΐα is the scholar Julius Pollux (second century CE), who defines it as the art of making statues of the gods (*Onomast.* 1. 13). A century later (*c.*270) Porphyry uses it to denote the Egyptian deification of animals (*De Abstin.* 4. 9). In the following century Athanasius[34] and Eusebius[35] use it in a similar way for the invention of gods by the pagans in general. In the fifth century Hierocles is able to use the word for deification by progress in virtue, but no

[21] Aristides, *Apol.* 7. 11; 13. 1; Athenagoras, *Legat.* 22. 9, 10, 12; Tatian, *Orat.* 18.
[22] *Prot.* 9. 87. 1; 11. 114. 4; *Strom.* 6. 125. 4.
[23] For references, see p. 141.
[24] But comparatively rarely; see p. 236.
[25] For references, see p. 167.
[26] *Com. Gen.* (SC 244, p. 248); *De Trin.* 2. 4, 25; 3. 2, 16.
[27] Basil, *Adv. Eun.* 3. 5; Greg. Naz. *Or.* 2. 73; Greg. Nys. *De Virg.* 1; *C. Eun.* 4. 629D.
[28] *Quod unus sit Christus* 1; *Kata meros pistis* 1, 31.
[29] *Apocrit.* 4. 18, 26.
[30] *Mac. Hom.* (Coll. I) 2. 12. 6.
[31] *Thes.* 4. 15, 33; *Dial. Trin.* VII. 640a, 644d.
[32] *Adv. Nest.* 3. 8; 5. 25.
[33] *Ep.* 31; *Myst.* 7.
[34] *CG* 12. 21, 29.
[35] *Praep. evang.* 1. 5; 2. 6; 3. 3, 5, 13; 4. 17; *Dem. evang.* 1. 2; *Is.* 19. 1; 41. 15.

Christian ever uses it in this sense.[36] Instead, Christians use the form θεοποίησις, which is first encountered in the writings of Athanasius,[37] and appears again in Didymus[38] and Cyril of Alexandria.[39]

The adjectival noun θεοποιός survives in a fragment from Aristophanes (frag. 786/7). Without a context its meaning is uncertain, but it probably means 'a maker of statues of the gods'. This is the sense it has in Lucian's *Lover of Lies* (*Philopseudes* 20), and is also the definition given by Julius Pollux (*Onomasticon* 1. 13). The first Christian author to use the word, Clement of Alexandria, follows the same usage, but alongside this he also gives it a new adjectival sense, namely, 'deifying' (*Prot.* 4. 51. 6; *QDS* 19). It remains a rare word, being used once by Origen (*Sel. in Exod.* 1. 3), Methodius (*Symposium* 9. 4), Athanasius (*De Syn.* 51), Apollinarius (*Kata meros pistis* 27), Ps.-Basil of Caesarea (*Adv. Eunom.* 5. 732B), and Cyril of Jerusalem (*Catech.* 4. 16), twice by Gregory of Nazianzus (*Or.* 3. 1; *Carm.* II. 2. 7), and Cyril of Alexandria (*Dial. Trin.* v. 567e; vii. 644d), and four times by Ps.-Dionysius (*CH* 1. 1. 120B; *DN* 2. 1. 637B; 11. 6. 956B; *Ep.* 2. 1068A). We find it taken up in the sense first attested by Clement of Alexandria, however, by the late Neoplatonists Proclus (*In Tim.* 5. 308d, (ed. Diehl, iii. 226. 28), Hierocles (*In Carm. Aur.* 19. 10 (84. 1)), and Damascius (*V. Isidori*, ed. Zintzen, 207. 8).

(iii) Ἐκθεόω/ἐκθειόω—ἐκθέωσις—ἐκθεωτικός

Dionysius of Halicarnassus, the earliest literary author to use θεοποιέω is also the first witness to ἐκθειόω. In offering a rationalistic explanation of how Pistis or Fides came to be worshipped in Rome, he says that Numa added Pistis to Dike, Nemesis, and Erinyes, which had already been deified (ἐκτεθειῶσθαι), so as to strengthen the force of contracts which had been made without a witness (*Ant. Rom.* 2. 75. 2). Our next witness is the Jewish Platonist Philo of Alexandria (fl. 39 CE), who uses ἐκθειόω several times in his references to the pagan deification of animals, men, and heavenly bodies.[40] At the end of the first century Plutarch uses ἐκθειόω in his discussion of how Herodotus has cheapened the story of Io, 'whom all Greeks consider to have been deified' (ἣν πάντες Ἕλληνες ἐκτεθειῶσθαι νομίζουσι) by the barbarians (*Moralia* 856e).

Ἐκθεόω occurs for the first time in Appian, who uses it to signify the dedication of an altar.[41] The first witness to its use with the meaning 'to deify' is Clement of Alexandria, who uses it in both a pagan and a Christian context.[42] Origen also uses the word but only once and with a pejorative sense.[43] Christian writers, however, did

---

[36] *In Carmen Aureum* 27. 5 (ed. Koehler, 120. 16).

[37] *CA* 1. 39; 2. 70; 3. 53.

[38] *On Genesis* (SC 233, p. 109. 12).

[39] *C. Nest.* 2. 8.

[40] *Decalogue* 8, 53, 70, 79; *Spec. Leg.* 1. 10, 344; *Conf.* 173.

[41] *The Civil Wars* 3. 3: τὴν ἀγορὰν οὖν καταλαβόντες ἐβόων καὶ τὸν Ἀντώνιον ἐβλασφήμουν καὶ τὰς ἀρχὰς ἐκέλευον ἀντὶ Ἀματίου τὸν βωμὸν ἐκθεοῦν καὶ θύειν ἐπ' αὐτοῦ Καίσαρι πρώτους.

[42] *Prot.* 2. 26. 5; *Paed.* 1. 98. 3; *Strom.* 1. 105. 1.

[43] *Hom. Jer.* 5. 2; cf. Aelian (who was a younger contemporary of Clement's and an older contemporary of Origen's), *De nat. anim.* 10. 23: σέβουσι δὲ ἄρα οἱ αὐτοὶ Κοπτῖται καὶ θηλείας δορκάδας καὶ ἐκθεοῦσιν αὐτάς, τοὺς δὲ ἄρρενας καταθύουσιν. Cf. Preisendanz, *P. Graec. Mag.* i. 2455–9: λαβὼν μυγαλὸν ἐκθέωσον πηγαίῳ ὕδατι.

not adopt the term. By contrast, it does become important among the Neoplatonists. Porphyry (232/3–*c.* 305) says that a man deifies (ἐκθεοῖ) himself by attaining likeness to the divine.[44] Proclus (*c.* 410–83) uses ἐκθεόω frequently, particularly in his *Commentary on the Timaeus*, to express the divinity which is acquired by participation in the divine. Only the One and the demiurge are gods per se; the rest are ἐκθεούμενοι.[45] Ps.-Dionysius betrays a Procline influence with two instances of ἐκθεόω (*DN* 1. 5. 593B; 8. 5. 893A). Hermias refers to Dionysus as one of the ἐκθεούμενοι (*Schol. in Phaedr.* 135a, (ed. Couvreur, 138. 24). Damascius, the last head of the Academy in the sixth century, takes it for granted that only the ὑπερούσιος θεός is God in the true sense; the others are ἐκθεούμενοι (*Dub. et sol.* 100, (ed. Ruelle, 1. 258. 3).

For the origins of ἐκθέωσις we must probably go back to Callimachus (*c.* 305–*c.* 240 BCE). On the deification of Arsinoe I of Egypt in 270 BCE he wrote a celebratory poem which the later summary of his works, the *Diegesis*, entitles the Ἐκθέωσις Ἀρσινόης (*Dieg.* 10. 10, Callimachus (ed. Pfeiffer, 1. 218, frag. 228). It always remained a rare noun. It appears with ἀποθέωσις without any discernible difference of meaning in the Canopus Decree of 238 BCE (*OGI* 56. 53). It is the term used by Philo for the setting up of false gods in general and for the self-deification of Caligula in particular (*Leg.* 77, 201, 332, 338, 368; *Dec.* 81). But it does not seem to be used again until the fifth century CE, when we find it in Proclus (*In Remp.*, ed. Kroll, i. 120. 17). Proclus also uses an adjectival form, ἐκθεωτικός, which he seems to have coined himself.[46] The first author to find a Christian use for ἐκθεόω, ἐκθέωσις, ἐκθεωτικός is Ps.-Dionysius.[47]

(iv)   Θεόω—θέωσις

Θεόω appears first in Callimachus, the earliest writer to have used any of the technical terms of deification. He represents Heracles as still gluttonous among the gods 'although his flesh had been deified [i.e. by self-immolation] beneath a Phrygian oak' (οὐ γὰρ ὅ γε Φρυγίῃ περ δρυὶ γυῖα θεωθεὶς/παύσατ᾽ ἀδηφαγίης)(*Hymn III to Artemis* 159–60). Not long afterwards another Alexandrian, the Jewish writer Ps.-Aristeas, uses θεόω in his comments on the absurdity of pagan deification (*Ep. ad Phil.*, SC 89, p. 170).

Thereafter there is silence until the verb is revived in the second century CE by the Cynic philosopher Oenomaus of Gadara (fl. *c.* 120), to pour scorn on the notion that one of the gods had deified a certain olive trunk.[48] Θεόω appears in the *Poemandres* of the Hermetic Corpus to express the state of the soul that has stripped away the passions through true knowledge and, assimilated to the Powers, has entered the

---

[44] *To Marcella* 17: αὐτὸς δὲ ἑαυτὸν καὶ εὐάρεστον ποιεῖ θεῷ καὶ ἐκθεοῖ τῇ τῆς ἰδίας διαθέσεως ὁμοιότητι τῷ μετὰ ἀφθαρσίας μακαρίῳ.

[45] *El. Theol.* 129, 135, 138, 153, 160; *In Remp.* (ed. Kroll, ii. 48.10–12); *In Tim.*, prooem. 3ef.

[46] *El. Theol.* 165; *In Parm.*, 4. 838 (ed. Cousin); *In Tim.* 5. 302b (ed. Diehl, iii. 205. 6); 5. 302d (iii. 206. 26); 5. 302f (iii. 207. 25); 5. 306d (iii. 220. 12); 5. 313b (iii. 241. 19).

[47] These all occur in the most philosophical of his works. Ἐκθεόω: *DN* 1. 5. 593C; 8. 5. 893A; ἐκθέωσις: *DN* 9. 5. 912D; 12. 3. 972A; ἐκθεωτικός: *DN* 2. 7. 645A.

[48] Cited by Eusebius, *Prep. evang.* 5. 34: καίτοι εἰ ἀσφαλὲς ἦν, οὐκ ἂν ἦν ἐπιβατὸν ληρῷ οὐδ᾽ ἂν εἷς τις τῶν Ὀλυμπίων εἰς τοῦτο ἦλθεν παρανοίας ὡς ἐλαῖνον κορμὸν θεῶσαι.

eighth sphere (*CH* I. 26; cf. *CH* XIII. 10). Clement of Alexandria at about the same time also uses the verb to indicate deification through the eradication of the passions in a way which is not dissimilar (*Strom.* 4. 152. 1). In the third century the Neoplatonist Iamblichus (*c.*250–*c.*325) uses θεόω to signify the deifying power of the doctrine contained in the Pythagorean symbols.[49]

Although Proclus also uses θεόω several times in his commentaries on the *Parmenides* and the *Timaeus* (*In Parm.* 1. 34, 35, ed. Cousin, 490, 491); *In Tim.* 3. 173e, (ed. Diehl, ii. 111. 20), it is in fact in Christian usage that the verb becomes established. Apollinarius uses it twice (Frag. 147, ed. Lieztmann, 246), and Gregory of Nazianzus no fewer than twenty-one times to express both the deification of the human nature of Christ and the *telos* of the Christian believer.[50] Θεόω is next found in Macarius Magnes, where it simply means to 'dedicate' or 'consecrate' the mind (*Apocriticus* 3. 23), but is not used in Gregory's sense until it is taken up by Ps.-Dionysius,[51] Diadochus of Photice (*Hom. Ascens.* 6), Leontius of Jerusalem (*Nest.* 3. 5; 4. 37; 5. 10 G 25), Maximus the Confessor[52] (largely in his exegesis of Gregory), and John Damascene.[53] From these it passes into the Byzantine tradition.

Θέωσις, the correlative noun to θεόω, was coined by Gregory of Nazianzus. It first appears in the Fourth Oration, the *First Invective against Julian*, which was composed shortly after Julian's death in July 363.[54] Although this became the standard term for deification in Byzantine theology, it is the rarest of the various expressions employed by the earlier Fathers. Like θεόω it appears again in Ps.-Dionysius,[55] Leontius of Jerusalem (*Adv. Nest.* 1. 18), Maximus the Confessor,[56] and John Damascene.[57] The only pagan writer to have used the term was the Athenian Neoplatonist Damascius. The multiplicity of suprasubstantial henads, he says, implies not that they are self-subsistent hypostases, but that they are granted illuminations and θεώσεις (*Dub. et sol.* 100, ed. Ruelle, i. 258. 5).

(v) Ἀποθειάζω—ἐκθειάζω

The verb ἐκθειάζω, which Plutarch is the first to use, remains comparatively rare. Plutarch says that Sertorius κατὰ μικρὸν ἐξεθείαζε his pet fawn to impress the Lusitanians who formed the bulk of his troops (*Sert.* 11. 3). The grammarian Heraclitus gives it a metaphorical turn when he says that the whole world has 'deified' the

---

[49] *V. Pyth.* 23. 103: τὰς τῶν Πυθαγορικῶν συμβόλων ἐμφάσεις καὶ ἀπορρήτους ἐννοίας [. . .] ὑπὲρ ἀνθρωπίνην ἐπίνοιαν θεωθεῖσαι.

[50] For references see p. 214 above.

[51] For references see p. 249 above.

[52] *Thal.* 40, 44, 64; *Opusc.* 4, 7. (PG 91. 60B, 81D); *Epp.* 12, 31; *Ambig.* (PG 91. 1040CD, 1088B, 1237B, 1336A).

[53] *De fid. orth.* 2. 12; 3. 17; *C. Jac.* 52; *Anacr.* (PG 96. 854B). For other writers of the seventh and eighth centuries, see Lampe, *PGL*, s.v.

[54] *Or.* 7. 71; for a complete list, see above, p. 214.

[55] *CH* 1. 3; 7. 2; *EH* 1. 2. 3, 4; 2. 2. 1; 2. 3. 6; 3. 1; 3. 3. 4; 3. 3. 7; 6. 3. 5; *DN* 2. 8, 11; 8. 5.

[56] *Thal.* 9, 22, 40, 44, 59, 60, 61, 63; *Orat. Dom.* 873C, 877C, 893D, 905D; *Cap. Theol.* 1. 54, 55, 60, 97; 2. 25, 88; *Opusc.* 33C; *Epp.* 2, 9, 43; *Myst.* 680C; *Ambig.* 1040D, 1088C, 1237B.

[57] *De fid. orth.* 3. 17; 4. 18; *C. Jac.* 52; *Carm. Theog.* 93. Cf. also Ps.-Cyril (7th cent.), PG 77. 1152C.

wisdom of Homer.[58] In the second century Lucian uses ἐκθειάζω as a synonym for θεοποιέω to refer to the way that Orestes and Pylades are rendered divine honours in Thrace (*Toxaris* 2, 8). Iamblichus says that Pythagoras in his lifetime was 'deified' by his admirers and followers.[59] In the third century Herodian, applying the term to the imperial cult, writes: 'it is the custom with the Romans to deify (ἐκθειάζειν) emperors who die leaving behind them children as their successors' (*Hist.* 4. 2. 1). In the next century Julian accuses the Christians of deifying a quality in God which they find blameworthy in men, namely, jealousy (*C. Gal.* 155d). Finally in the late fifth century Hermias claims that Plato ἐκθειάζει τοὺς Αἰγυπτίους ὡς ἀρχαίους, that is to say, treats them as divine oracles (*Schol. in Phaedr.* 199a).

The few Christian authors who use this verb do not apply it to the human *telos*. Clement of Alexandria uses it frequently along with θειάζω.[60] Origen and Athanasius also use it but only twice each.[61] In every case ἐκθειάζω is employed in a pagan context with a pejorative sense.

There is only a single witness to the verb ἀποθειάζω. In the fourth century CE Themistius coined it on analogy with ἐκθειάζω to denote the deification of Heracles (*Orat.* 20. 239d).

(vi) Conclusion

The pattern which emerges from this survey is that of a group of more or less synonymous words which from the third century BCE to the sixth century CE express in some way, either literally or metaphorically, the transference of people or animals or abstractions from the transient world below to the everlasting world above. The words, however, are not entirely synonymous. It is significant that Christian writers adopt some in preference to others and coin new forms for their own use. Jewish writers in Greek, unlike Christians, never apply these terms to the human *telos*.

In the Hellenistic period the vocabulary is small, comprising the verbs θεόω and ἀποθεόω and the nouns ἐκθέωσις and ἀποθέωσις and is used exclusively in the context of the deification of heroes and rulers. Whether Euhemerus himself used any of these terms is not known, but in the first century BCE it is mainly in Euhemeristic writers that we find them. Dionysius of Halicarnassus augments the number of verbs, introducing ἐκθειόω and θεοποιέω, the latter with a slightly pejorative sense but otherwise without any extension of meaning. Ἀποθειόω also appears contemporaneously in an Egyptian inscription.

In early imperial times we find ἀποθέωσις used as the equivalent of the Latin *consecratio*. Moreover, a Greek community can use θεοποιέω for its awarding of divine honours to the living emperor. By the second century ἀποθέωσις has become synonymous with solemn burial and can be used of ordinary citizens.

Philosophical uses of the vocabulary begin with Plutarch in the late first century. Plutarch also introduces the term ἐκθειάζω. In the second century there is a revival

---

[58] *Homeric Problems* 79 (ed. Oelmann, p. 106. 5): τὴν δ᾿Ομήρου σοφίαν ἐκτεθείακεν αἰὼν ὁ σύμπας.
[59] *V. Pyth.* 2. 11: τὸν νεανίαν ἐπευφημοῦντες ἐξεθείαζον καὶ διεθρύλουν.
[60] For references see p. 122 above.
[61] Origen: *Hom. Jer.* 7. 3; *Com. Jo.* 10. 34. Athanasius: *CG* 8, 9.

of θεόω and the first appearance of ἐκθεόω, verbs which come to be taken up strongly by the Neoplatonists. Among the Neoplatonists the words with the prefix *apo-* are on the whole avoided. A distinction in meaning between ἀποθέωσις and ἐκθέωσις was first proposed by M. Radin in 1916 (Radin 1916: 44–6). Habicht rejects Radin's arguments, but in doing so he only has in mind the earlier material, in which the distinction does not yet seem to have developed (Habicht 1970: 174 n. 24). But the distinction which Radin wished to make does seem to be valid later. Ἀποθέωσις was applied particularly to the imperial cult and by extension to the dead generally; in its wider use it implies a 'return to origins', an ascent of the soul to the place whence it came. It is in this sense that we find ἀποθεόω used in the Hermetic writings and in Origen. The Neoplatonists, however, wished to express the descent of divine power into lower levels of being and the transformation of entities on those levels through participation in the divine. For this purpose ἐκθέωσις and its derivatives are more appropriate, the prefix *ek-* conveying the sense of 'making completely'.

Before the later Neoplatonists—and Proclus in particular—the terminology of deification was used much more frequently by Christians than by pagans. Until the beginning of the Christian era there are only seventeen surviving instances of the use of the terms. By the end of the third century the number of instances has risen to sixty-eight, which is more than equalled by the Apologists, Clement, Origen, and Hippolytus, who use the term more often by the middle of the third century than all of their pagan contemporaries and predecessors put together.[62] There seem to be two fundamental reasons for this. The first is that the imperial cult, although diffused throughout the empire, was not much discussed. It was not problematical (except to Jews and Christians) and therefore did not excite much comment. The second is that in Platonism there was no true deification until Iamblichus began to develop the concept of theurgy. Plotinus, for example, never once uses any of the expressions of deification for the simple reason that if the human soul is already divine in essence, it does not need to be deified.[63] When Christian authors wished to speak about deification they therefore had to hand a relatively unexploited set of terms with a wide range of meaning which they could adapt to their own purposes without much difficulty.

Christian authors show a marked preference for the verbs θεοποιέω and θεόω and the nouns θεοποίησις and θέωσις, both nouns being late coinages found almost exclusively in Christian writers. The second-century Apologists use θεοποιέω with some frequency, but only with reference to pagan deification. Clement is the earliest writer to apply θεοποιέω to Christian deification, along with θεόω and several other terms which he uses in a manner indistinguishable from that of his pagan contemporaries. The first verb is taken up by Athanasius, who is the first witness to the noun, θεοποίησις, and the second by Gregory of Nazianzus, who produces the noun, θέωσις. Cyril of Alexandria follows Athanasius' terminology, while Ps.-Dionysius and Maximus the Confessor follow Gregory's. It is therefore the latter set of terms that comes to predominate in Byzantine usage.

---

[62] The Apologists use the terms 6 times (all of them in a pagan context), Clement 39 times (15% in a Christian context), Hippolytus 4 times (25% in a Christian context), and Origen 20 times (50% in a Christian context), making a total of 69. For detailed references see the relevant chapters.

[63] He does say θεὸν γενόμενον but at once corrects it with μᾶλλον δὲ ὄντα (*Enn.* VI. 9. 9. 58).

Appendix 2

Of the other terms, ἀποθεόω and ἀποθέωσις are found in an approving Christian context only in Origen, Gregory Thaumaturgus, Didymus, Apollinarius, Macarius Magnes, Ps.-Macarius, and Maximus the Confessor. Even before the beginning of the Nestorian controversy, 'apotheosis' had begun to acquire perjorative connotations. Nestorius confirmed these when he protested vigorously against the 'apotheosis' of the humanity of Christ by the 'innovators'. Nor did 'ektheosis' take root in the Church. Ἐκθεόω occurs only once after Clement, in Ps.-Dionysius, and ἐκθέωσις only three times, in Maximus the Confessor. Yet these are the terms that were most popular among the later pagan Neoplatonists. Christian writers were thus successful in evolving their own distinctive terminology for deification.

Bibliography

Texts and Translations

ALCINOUS. *Alcinoos, Enseignement des doctrines de Platon.* Ed. John Whittaker. French trans: Pierre Louis. Collection des Universités de France. Paris: Belles Lettres, 1990.
—— *Alcinous: The Handbook of Platonism.* ET John Dillon. Oxford: Clarendon Press, 1993.
APOLLINARIUS OF LAODICEA. *Apollinaris von Laodicea und seine Schule.* Texts ed. Hans Lietzmann. Tübingen: J. C. B. Mohr (Paul Siebeck), 1904.
APULEIUS OF MADAURA. *Apuleius of Madauros: The Isis Book.* Ed. with English trans. J. Gwyn Griffiths. Études préliminaires aux religions orientales dans l'empire romain 39. Leiden: Brill, 1975.
—— *Lucio Apuleio. Metamorfosi.* Ed. Federico Roncoroni. Italian trans. Nino Marziano. Milan: Garzanti, 2002.
—— *The Transformations of Lucius otherwise known as The Golden Ass.* ET Robert Graves. Harmondsworth: Penguin, 1950.
ARISTOTLE. *Aristotelis Metaphysica.* Ed. W. Jaeger. OCT. Oxford: Clarendon Press, 1957.
—— *Aristotelis De Anima.* Ed. W. D. Ross. OCT. Oxford: Clarendon Press, 1956.
—— *Aristotelis Ethica Nicomachea.* Ed. I. Bywater. OCT. Oxford: Clarendon Press, 1890.
—— *The Complete Works of Aristotle: The Revised Oxford Translation.* ET ed. Jonathan Barnes. 2 vols. Bollingen Series 71.2. Princeton, NJ: Princeton University Press, 1984.
ATHANASIUS OF ALEXANDRIA. *Athanasius Werke.* Ed. H. G. Opitz *et al.* Berlin: Walter de Gruyter, 1934–.
—— *The Orations of St Athanasius Against the Arians.* Ed. William Bright. Oxford: Clarendon Press, 1873.
—— *Athanasius: Contra Gentes and De Incarnatione.* Ed. with English trans. Robert W. Thomson. OECT. Oxford: Clarendon Press, 1971.
—— *Vita di Antonio.* Ed. G. J. M. Bartelink. Italian trans. Pietro Citati and Salvatore Lilla. Scrittori Greci e Latini. Milan: Fondazione Lorenzo Valla, Arnaldo Mondadori editore, 1974.
—— *Select Writings and Letters of Athanasius, Bishop of Alexandria.* Trans. J. H. Newman *et al.*, ed. Archibald Robertson. NPNF, Second series, 4. Edinburgh: T & T Clark; Grand Rapids, Mich.: William B. Eerdmans, repr. 1995.
ATHENAEUS. *Athenaeus. Deipnosophistae.* Text with English trans. C. B. Gullick. 7 vols. LCL. Cambridge, Mass.: Harvard University Press, 1927–41.

AUGUSTINE OF HIPPO. *Sancti Augustini episcopi opera omnia.* Ed. the Maurists. PL 32–47.

—— *Sancti Aurelii Augustini episcopi De civitate Dei libri XXII.* Ed. Emanuel Hoffmann. 2 vols. CSEL 40. Vienna, Prague, and Leipzig: F. Tempsky and G. Freytag, 1899–1900.

—— *Sancti Aurelii Augustini Enarrationes in Psalmos.* Ed. D. Eligius Dekkers, OSB, and Johannes Fraipont. 3 vols. CCSL 38–40. Turnhout: Brepols, 1956.

—— *The Works of Aurelius Augustine, Bishop of Hippo.* Trans. ed. Philip Schaff. NPNF, First series, 1–8. Edinburgh: T & T Clark; Grand Rapids, Mich.: William B. Eerdmans, repr. 1994–8.

—— *Sermons.* Trans. Edmund Hill, OP. 11 vols. The Works of Saint Augustine. A Translation for the 21st Century. III. 1–11. New York, NY: New City Press, 1979–97.

—— *Expositions of the Psalms 33–50.* Trans. Maria Boulding, OSB. The Works of Saint Augustine. A Translation for the 21st Century. I. 16. New York, NY: New City Press, 2000.

BABAI. *Liber de Unione.* Ed. with Latin trans. A. Vaschalde. CSCO, Scriptores Syri, ser. 2, tom. 61. Rome: Karolus de Luigi; Paris: J. Gabalda, 1915.

BASIL OF CAESAREA. *S. P. N. Basilii Caesareae Cappadociae archiepiscopi opera omnia quae extant.* Ed. J. Garnier, OSB and P. Maran, OSB. PG 29–32.

—— *The Book of Saint Basil the Great, Bishop of Caesarea in Cappadocia, On the Holy Spirit, written to Amphilochius, Bishop of Iconium, against the Pneumatomachi.* Ed. C. F. H. Johnston. Oxford: Clarendon Press, 1892.

—— *Basilio di Caesarea. Sulla Genesi (Omelie sull' Esamerone).* Ed. with Italian trans. Mario Naldini. Scrittori Greci e Latini. Milan: Fondazione Lorenzo Valla, Arnaldo Mondadori editore, 1990.

—— *Homilia i de creatione hominis.* Ed. H. Hörner. GNO Supplementum. Leiden: E. J. Brill, 1972.

—— *Saint Basil: The Letters.* Text with English trans. Roy J. Deferrari. 4 vols. LCL. Cambridge, Mass.: Harvard University Press, 1926–34.

—— *The Treatise De Spiritu Sancto, the Nine Homilies of the Hexaemeron, and the Letters of Saint Basil the Great, Archbishop of Caesarea.* Trans. Blomfield Jackson. NPNF, Second series, 8. Edinburgh: T & T Clark, 1895 (repr. 1996).

—— *Saint Basil the Great: On the Holy Spirit.* Trans. David Anderson. Crestwood, NY: St Vladimir's Seminary Press, 1980.

CICERO. *M. Tullii Ciceronis De Natura Deorum.* Ed. W. Ax. Stuttgart: B. G. Teubner, 1961.

—— *Cicero: The Nature of the Gods.* ET Horace C. P. McGregor. Harmondsworth: Penguin, 1972.

CLEMENT OF ALEXANDRIA. *Clemens Alexandrinus.* Ed. O. Stählin, L. Früchtel, and U. Treu. 4 vols. GCS. Berlin: Akademie-Verlag, 1960–80.

—— *Clement of Alexandria.* Selections with English trans. G. W. Butterworth. LCL. Cambridge, Mass., and London: Harvard University Press and William Heinemann, 1919.

—— *Alexandrian Christianity.* Selected English trans. of Clement and Origen by J. E. L. Oulton and Henry Chadwick. LCC. London: SCM Press, 1954.

—— *Clement of Alexandria.* ET Alexander Roberts and James Donaldson. ANF 2.

Edinburgh: T & T Clark; Grand Rapids, Mich.: William B. Eerdmans, repr. 1994: 171–567.

—— *Clément d'Alexandrie. Extraits de Théodote.* Ed. with French trans. F. Sagnard, OP. SC 23. Paris: Éditions du Cerf, 1948.

CYRIL OF ALEXANDRIA. *S. P. N. Cyrilli, Alexandriae Archiepiscopi, Commentarius in Isaiam Prophetam.* Ed. Jean Aubert. PG 70. 9–1450.

—— *S. P. N. Cyrilli, Alexandriae Archiepiscopi, Thesaurus de sancta et consubstantiali Trinitate.* Ed. Jean Aubert. PG 75. 9–656.

—— *Sancti Patris nostri Cyrilli archiepiscopi Alexandrini in D. Ioannis Evangelium.* Ed. Philip Edward Pusey. Oxford: Clarendon Press, 1872.

—— *Contra Nestorium.* Ed. Eduard Schwartz. *Acta Conciliorum Oecumenicorum*, 1. 1. 6. Berlin and Leipzig: Walter de Gruyter, 1927–9: 13–106.

—— *Cyrille d'Alexandrie. Deux dialogues christologiques.* Ed. with French trans. Georges Matthieu de Durand, OP. SC 97. Paris: Éditions du Cerf, 1964.

—— *Cyrille d'Alexandrie. Dialogues sur la Trinité.* Ed. with French trans. Georges Matthieu de Durand, OP. 3 vols. SC 231, 237, 246. Paris: Éditions du Cerf, 1976–8.

—— *Cyrille d'Alexandrie. Lettres Festales*, vol. iii. Ed. W. H. Burns with French trans. M.-O. Boulnois and B. Meunier. SC 434. Paris: Éditions du Cerf, 1998.

—— *Cyril of Alexandria: Select Letters.* Ed. with English trans. Lionel R. Wickham. OECT. Oxford: Clarendon Press, 1983.

—— *Cyril of Alexandria.* Selected English trans. Norman Russell. London: Routledge, 2000.

CYRIL OF SCYTHOPOLIS. *Cyril of Scythopolis. Lives of the Monks of Palestine.* Trans. R. M. Price. Introduction and notes John Binns. CSS 114. Kalamazoo, Mich.: Cistercian Publications, 1991.

DIADOCHUS OF PHOTICE. *Diadoque de Photiké. Oeuvres spirituelles.* Ed. with French trans. Édouard des Places, SJ. SC 5 ter. Paris: Éditions du Cerf, 1966.

DIDYMUS THE BLIND. *Didyme l'Aveugle. Sur la Genèse.* Ed. with French trans. Pierre Nautin. 2 vols. SC 233 and 244. Paris: Éditions du Cerf, 1976 and 1978.

—— *Didyme l'Aveugle. Sur Zacharie.* Ed. with French trans. Louis Doutreleau, SJ. 3 vols. SC 83, 84, and 85. Paris: Éditions du Cerf, 1962.

—— *Didyme l'Aveugle. Traité du Saint-Esprit.* Ed. with French trans. Louis Doutreleau, SJ. SC 386. Paris: Éditions du Cerf, 1992.

DIO CASSIUS. *Dio Cassius: Roman History.* Text and English trans. E. W. Cary. 9 vols. LCL. Cambridge, Mass.: Harvard University Press, 1914–27.

DIODORUS SICULUS. *Diodorus Siculus. Library of History.* Text with English trans. C. H. Oldfather *et al.* 12 vols. LCL. Cambridge, Mass.: Harvard University Press, 1933–67.

TO DIOGNETUS. *The Apostolic Fathers.* Text with English trans. J. B. Lightfoot, ed. and completed J. R. Harmer. London: Macmillan, 1926: 487–511.

—— *À Diognète.* Text and French trans. H.-I. Marrou. SC 33 bis. Paris: Éditions du Cerf, 1965.

DIONYSIUS THE AREOPAGITE. *Corpus Dionysiacum*, i: *Pseudo-Dionysius Areopagita. De Divinis Nominibus.* Ed. Beate Regina Suchla. Berlin and New York: Walter de Gruyter, 1990; ii: *Pseudo-Dionysius Areopagita. De Coelesti Hierarchia, De Ecclesiastica Hierarchia, De Mystica Theologia, Epistulae.* Ed. Günter Heil and Adolf Martin Ritter. Berlin and New York: Walter de Gruyter, 1991.

—— *Pseudo-Dionysius: The Complete Works.* ET Colm Luibheid and Paul Rorem. CWS. London: SPCK, 1987.

EMPEDOCLES OF ACRAGAS. *Empedocles: The Extant Fragments.* Text with English trans. and commentary M. R. Wright. 2nd edn Bristol Classical Press. London: Duckworth; Indianapolis, Ind.: Hackett, 1995.

EPHREM THE SYRIAN. *Saint Ephrem:. Hymns on Paradise.* Trans. Sebastian Brock. Crestwood, NY: St Vladimir's Seminary Press, 1990.

EUNAPIUS. *Philostratus and Eunapius: Lives of the Sophists.* Text with English trans. Wilmer C. Wright. LCL. Cambridge, Mass., and London: Harvard University Press, 1921 (repr. 1989).

EUSEBIUS OF CAESAREA. *Demonstratio Evangelica.* Ed. I. A. Heikel. GCS. Berlin: Akademie-Verlag, 1913.

—— *Historia Ecclesiastica.* Ed. E. Schwartz and T. Mommsen. 2 vols. GCS. Berlin: Akademie-Verlag, 1903–8.

—— *Ecclesiastical History.* Text with English trans. Kirsopp Lake and J. E. L. Oulton. 2 vols. LCL 153, 265. Cambridge, Mass., and London: Harvard University Press and William Heinemann, 1926–32.

EVAGRIUS PONTICUS. *The 'Ad monachos' of Evagrius Ponticus: Its Structure and a Select Commentary.* Greek text with English trans. Jeremy Driscoll. Studia Anselmiana 104. Rome: Pontificio Ateneo S. Anselmo, 1991.

—— *Évagre le Pontique. Le Gnostique.* Greek fragments of the *Gnostikos* and French trans. by Antoine and Claire Guillaumont. SC 356. Paris: Éditions du Cerf, 1989.

—— *Évagre le Pontique. Traité pratique ou le moine.* Greek text of the *Praktikos* and French trans. Antoine and Claire Guillaumont. SC 170–1. Paris: Éditions du Cerf, 1971.

—— *Les six centuries des 'Kephalaia Gnostica' d'Evagre le Pontique.* Syriac text with French trans. Antoine Guillaumont. PO 28. 1. Paris: Firmin-Didot, 1958.

—— *Epistula fidei.* Text and English trans. as Ps.-Basil, *Ep.* 8, Roy Deferrari, *Saint Basil: The Letters,* i. 46–93.

—— *Epistula ad Melaniam.* ET Martin Parmentier, 'Evagrius of Pontus' "Letter to Melania" '. *Bijdragen, tijdschrift voor filosofie en theologie* 46 (1985): 2–38.

—— *De oratione.* Ps.-Nilus of Ancyra, PG 79. 1165–1200.

—— *Evagrius Ponticus: The Praktikos; Chapters on Prayer.* ET John E. Bamberger. CSS 4. Kalamazoo, Mich.: Cistercian Publications, 1981.

GALEN. *Galen: Selected Works.* Trans. P. N. Singer. The World's Classics. Oxford and New York: Oxford University Press, 1997.

GOSPEL OF PHILIP. *The Gnostic Scriptures.* ET Bentley Layton. London: SCM Press, 1987: 325–53.

—— 'The Gospel of Philip', ET Wesley W. Isenberg, in *The Nag Hammadi Library in English.* Ed. James M. Robinson. Leiden: E. J. Brill, 1988: 139–60.

GREGORY AKINDYNOS. *Letters of Gregory Akindynos.* Ed. with English trans. Angela Constantinides Hero. Corpus Fontium Historiae Byzantinae XXI. Washington, DC: Dumbarton Oaks, 1983.

GREGORY OF NAZIANZUS. *S. P. N. Gregorii Nazianzeni opera omnia.* Ed. C. Clémencet, OSB, and A. B. Caillau, OSB. PG 35–8.

—— *The Five Theological Orations of Gregory of Nazianzus.* Ed. Arthur James Mason. Cambridge Patristic Texts. Cambridge: Cambridge University Press, 1899.

—— *Grégoire de Nazianze. Discours.* Orations 1–12 and 20–43 ed. with French trans. J. Bernardi, M. A. Calvet-Sebasti, P. Gallay, M. Jourjon, G. Lafontaine, C. Moreschini, J. Mossay. SC 247, 250, 270, 284, 309, 318, 358, 384, 405. Paris: Éditions du Cerf, 1978–95.

—— *Grégoire de Nazianze. Lettres théologiques.* Ed. with French trans. P. Gallay and M. Jourjon. SC 208. Paris: Éditions du Cerf, 1974.

—— *Gregorio di Nazianzo. Tutte le Orazioni.* Ed. Claudio Moreschini with Italian trans. Chiara Sani and Maria Vincelli. Bompiani, Il Pensiero Occidentale. Milan: R. C. S. Libri, 2000 (conveniently prints in a single volume the critical texts issued by SC with the remaining *Orations* from PG).

—— *Select Orations of Saint Gregory Nazianzen, sometime Archbishop of Constantinople.* ET Charles Gordon Browne and James Edward Swallow. NPNF, Second series, 7. Edinburgh: T & T Clark; Grand Rapids, Mich.: William B. Eerdmans, repr. 1996: 203–482.

GREGORY OF NYSSA. *Contra Eunomium.* Ed. W. Jaeger. 2 vols. GNO I–II. 2nd edn, Leiden: E. J. Brill, 1960.

—— *Opera Dogmatica Minora.* Part 1. Ed. F. Mueller. GNO III. 1. Leiden: E. J. Brill, 1958.

—— *Oratio catechetica.* Ed. E. Mühlenberg. GNO III. 4. Leiden: E. J. Brill, 1996.

—— *De Vita Moysis.* Ed. H. Musurillo. GNO VII. 1. Leiden: E. J. Brill, 1964.

—— *De Oratione Dominica, De Beatitudinibus. Ed. J. F. Callahan.* GNO VII. 2. Leiden: E. J. Brill, 1992.

—— *Grégoire de Nysse. Traité de la virginité.* Ed. with French trans. M. Aubineau. SC 119. Paris: Éditions du Cerf, 1966.

—— *The Catechetical Oration of Gregory of Nyssa.* Ed. James Herbert Srawley. Cambridge Patristic Texts. Cambridge: Cambridge University Press, 1903.

—— *Gregorio di Nissa. La Vita di Mosè.* Ed. with Italian trans. Manlio Simonetti. Scrittori Greci e Latini. Milan: Fondazione Lorenzo Valla, Arnaldo Mondadori editore, 1984.

—— *Select Writings and Letters of Gregory, Bishop of Nyssa.* ET William Moore and Henry Austin Wilson. NPNF 5. Edinburgh: T & T Clark; Grand Rapids, Mich.: William B. Eerdmans, repr. 1995.

—— *The Lord's Prayer; The Beatitudes.* ET Hilda C. Graef. ACW 18. Westminster, Md.: Newman Press; London: Longmans, Green & Co., 1954.

—— *Saint Gregory of Nyssa: Ascetical Works.* ET V. W. Callahan. Fathers of the Church 58. Washington, DC: Catholic University of America Press, 1967.

—— *Gregory of Nyssa: The Life of Moses.* ET Abraham J. Malherbe and Everett Ferguson. CWS. New York, Ramsey, and Toronto: Paulist Press, 1978.

—— *St Gregory of Nyssa: The Soul and the Resurrection.* ET Catharine P. Roth. Crestwood, NY: St Vladimir's Seminary Press, 1993.

GREGORY PALAMAS. *Grégoire Palamas. Défense des saints hésychastes.* Text and French trans. Jean Meyendorff. Spicilegium Sacrum Lovaniense. Études et documents 30. Louvain: 'Spicilegium Sacrum Lovaniense' Administration, 1959.

—— *Saint Gregory Palamas: The One Hundred and Fifty Chapters.* Text and English trans. Robert E. Sinkewicz, CSB. Toronto: Pontifical Institute of Mediaeval Studies, 1988.

—— *Gregorio Palamas. Scritti filosofici e teologici.* Text of selected treatises and Italian trans. Ettore Perella. Bompiani, Il Pensiero Occidentale. Milan: R. C. S. Libri, 2003.

—— *Gregory Palamas: The Triads.* ET selected texts Nicholas Gendle. CWS. London: SPCK, 1983.

HERACLITUS. *Heraclitus.* Ed. with English trans. M. Marcovich. Merida, Venezuela: Los Andes University Press, 1967.

—— *Heraclitus.* ET Philip Wheelright. Oxford: Oxford University Press, 1959.

HERMETICA. *Corpus Hermeticum.* Text and French trans. A.-J. Festugière. 4 vols. Collection des Universités de France. Paris: Belles Lettres, 1946–54.

—— *Hermetica.* ET Brian P. Copenhaver. Cambridge: Cambridge University Press, 1992.

HERODIAN. *Herodian.* Text and trans. C. R. Whittaker. 2 vols. LCL. London and Cambridge, Mass.: William Heinemann and Harvard University Press, 1970.

'HIEROTHEOS'. *The Book of the Holy Hierotheos.* Syriac text and English trans. F. S. Marsh. London: Williams & Norgate, 1927.

HILARY OF POITIERS. *S. Hilarii Episcopi Pictavensis Tractatus Super Psalmos.* Ed. Antonius Zingerle. CSEL 22. Vienna, Prague, and Leipzig: F. Tempsky and G. Freytag, 1891.

—— *Sancti Hilarii Pictavensis Episcopi De Trinitate Libri* I–XII. Ed. P. Smulders. CCSL 62, 62A. Turnhout: Brepols, 1979–80.

—— *Hilaire de Poitiers. Sur Matthieu.* Ed. with French trans. J. Doignon. 2 vols. SC 254, 258. Paris: Éditions du Cerf, 1978–9.

—— *St Hilary of Poitiers: Select Works.* ET E. W. Watson, L. Pullan, *et al.* NPNF, Second series, 9. Edinburgh: T & T Clark; Grand Rapids, Mich.: William B. Eerdmans, repr. 1997.

HIPPOLYTUS OF ROME. *Hippolytus Werke.* Ed. H. Achelis, G. Bonwetsch, *et al.* GCS. 4 vols. Leipzig and Berlin: J. C. Hinrichs and Akademie-Verlag, 1897–1955.

—— *Contra Noetum.* Ed. with English trans. R. Butterworth, SJ. Heythrop Monographs 2. London: Heythrop College, 1977.

IAMBLICHUS. *Giamblico. La vita pitagorica.* Greek text and Italian trans. Maurizio Giangiulio. Milan: Rizzoli, 1991.

—— *Iamblichus: On the Pythagorean Life.* ET Gillian Clark. Translated Texts for Historians, Greek Series 8. Liverpool: Liverpool University Press, 1989.

—— *The Theology of Arithmetic: On the Mystical, Mathematical and Cosmological Symbolism of the First Ten Numbers.* ET Robin Waterfield. Grand Rapids, Mich.: Phanes Press, 1988.

IGNATIUS OF ANTIOCH. *The Apostolic Fathers.* Greek text and English trans. J. B. Lightfoot, ed. J. R. Harmer. London: Macmillan, 1926, 97–162.

IRENAEUS OF LYONS. *Sancti Irenaei episcopi Lugdunensis Libros quinque adversus Haereses.* Ed. W. Wigan Harvey. 2 vols. Cambridge: Typis Academicis, 1857.

—— *Irenaeus: Against Heresies.* ET Alexander Roberts and James Donaldson. ANF 1. Edinburgh: T & T Clark; Grand Rapids, Mich.: William B. Eerdmans, repr. 1996.

ISHO'YAHB II. *Lettre christologique.* Ed. L. Sako. Rome: n.p., 1983.

JACOB OF SERUG. *Homiliae Selectae.* Ed. P. Bedjan. 5 vols. Paris: and Leipzig: Harrassowitz, 1905–10.

John of Dalyatha. *La Collection des lettres de Jean de Dalyatha.* Ed. with French trans. R. Beulay, OCD. PO 39. Turnhout: Brepols, 1978, 253–538.

John Damascene. *Die Schriften des Johannes von Damaskos.* Ed. Bonifatius Kotter, OSB. 5 vols. Patristische Texte und Studien 7, 12, 17, 22, 29. Berlin and New York: Walter de Gruyter, 1969–88.

—— *John of Damascus: Exposition of the Orthodox Faith.* Trans. S. D. F. Salmond. NPNF, Second series, 9. Edinburgh: T & T Clark; Grand Rapids, Mich.: William B. Eerdmans, repr. 1997.

—— *John of Damascus: On the Divine Images.* ET David Anderson. Crestwood, NY: St Vladimir's Seminary Press, 1980.

Justin Martyr. *Apologiae pro Christianis, Iustini Martyris.* Ed. Miroslav Marcovich. Patristische Texte und Studien 38. Berlin: Walter de Gruyter, 1994.

—— *Dialogus cum Tryphone, Iustini Martyris.* Ed. Miroslav Marcovich. Patristische Texte und Studien 47. Berlin: Walter de Gruyter, 1997.

—— *Justin. Dialogue avec Tryphon.* Text and French trans. G. Archambault. 2 vols. Textes et documents pour l'étude historique du christianisme 8. Paris: Picard, 1909.

—— *Dialogue of Justin, Philosopher and Martyr, with Trypho, a Jew.* Trans. Alexander Roberts and James Donaldson. ANF 1. Edinburgh: T & T Clark; Grand Rapids, Mich.: William B. Eerdmans, repr. 1996, 194–270.

—— *St Justin Martyr: The First and Second Apologies.* ET Leslie William Barnard. ACW 56. New York and Mahwah, NJ: Paulist Press, 1997.

—— *Justin Martyr: The Dialogue with Trypho.* ET A. Lukyn Williams. London: SPCK, 1930.

Leontius of Jerusalem. *Adversus Nestorianos.* PG 86. 1399–1768.

Macarius. Collection I. *Makarios/Symeon. Redern und Briefe. Die Sammlung des Vaticanus Graecus 694* (B). Ed. H. Berthold. 2 vols. GCS. Berlin: Akademie-Verlag, 1973.

—— Collection II. *Die 50 geistlichen Homilien des Makarios.* Ed. H. Dörries, E. Klostermann, and M. Kroeger. Patristische Texte und Studien 6. Berlin: Walter de Gruyter, 1964.

—— *Pseudo-Macarius: The Fifty Spiritual Homilies and the Great Letter.* ET George A. Maloney, SJ. New York and Mahwah, NJ: Paulist Press, 1992.

Macarius Magnes. *Apocriticus ad Graecos.* Ed. C. Blondel. Paris, 1876.

Maximus the Confessor. *S. P. N. Maximi Confessoris opera omnia.* Greek text and Latin trans. François Combefis and Franz Oehler. PG 90 and 91.

—— *Maximi Confessoris Quaestiones ad Thalassium,* i: *Quaestiones I–LV una cum latine interpretatione Joannis Scotti Eriugenae.* Ed. Carl Laga and Carlos Steel. CCSG 7. Turnhout: Brepols; Louvain: University Press, 1980.

—— *Maximi Confessoris Quaestiones ad Thalassium,* ii: *Quaestiones LVI–LXV.* Ed. Carl Laga and Carlos Steel. CCSG 22. Turnhout: Brepols; Louvain: University Press, 1990.

—— *Maximi Confessoris Quaestiones et Dubia.* Ed. José Declerck. CCSG 10. Turnhout: Brepols; Louvain: University Press, 1982.

—— Ἡ Μυσταγωγία τοῦ Ἁγίου Μαξίμου τοῦ Ὁμολογητοῦ. Ed. Charalambos Sotiropoulos. Athens, 1978.

—— *The Philokalia*, vol. ii. Selected English trans. G. E. H. Palmer, P. Sherrard, and K. Ware. London: Faber & Faber, 1981.

—— *Maximus Confessor: Selected Writings*. ET George C. Berthold. CWS. Mahwah, NJ: Paulist Press, 1985.

—— *Maximus the Confessor*. Selected English trans. Andrew Louth. London: Routledge, 1996.

NESTORIUS. *Nestoriana: Die Fragmente des Nestorius*. Ed. F. Loofs. Halle: Max Niemeyer, 1905.

NUMENIUS. *Numénius. Fragments*. Text and French trans. Édouard des Places. Collection des Universités de France. Paris: Belles Lettres, 1973.

ORIGEN. *Origenes Werke*. Greek and Latin texts ed. P. Koetschau *et al.* 12 vols. GCS. Leipzig: J. C. Hinrichs; Berlin: Akademie-Verlag, 1899–1955.

—— *The Philocalia of Origen*. Ed. J. Armitage Robinson. Cambridge Patristic Texts. Cambridge: Cambridge University Press, 1893.

—— *The Philocalia of Origen*. ET George Lewis. Edinburgh: T & T Clark, 1911.

—— *Entretien d'Origène avec Héraclide*. Text and French trans. Jean Scherer. SC 67. Paris: Éditions du Cerf, 1960.

—— *Origene. Omelie sul Cantico dei Cantici*. Latin text and Italian trans. Manlio Simonetti. Scrittori Greci e Latini. Milan: Fondazione Lorenzo Valla, Arnoldo Mondadori editore, 1988.

—— *Origen: Contra Celsum*. ET Henry Chadwick. Cambridge: Cambridge University Press, 1953 (repr. with corrections 1965).

—— *Origen on First Principles*. Trans. G. W. Butterworth. Gloucester, Mass.: Peter Smith, 1973.

—— *Alexandrian Christianity*. Selected English trans. J. E. L. Oulton and Henry Chadwick. LCC 2. London: SCM Press, 1954, 180–455.

—— *Origen's Commentary on the Gospel of John*. Trans. Allan Menzies. ANF 10. Edinburgh: T & T Clark; Grand Rapids, Mich.: William B. Eerdmans, repr. 1995, 297–408.

—— *Origen's Commentary on the Gospel of Matthew*. Trans. John Patrick. ANF 10. Edinburgh: T & T Clark; Grand Rapids, Mich.: William B. Eerdmans, repr. 1995, 412–512.

—— 'The Commentary of Origen upon the Epistle to the Ephesians'. Ed. J. A. F. Gregg. *JTS* 3 (1902): 554–76.

PALLADIUS OF HELENOPOLIS. *Palladio. La Storia Lausiaca*. Text ed. G. J. M. Bartelink with Italian trans. Marino Barchiesi. Scrittori Greci e Latini. Milan: Fondazione Lorenzo Valla, Arnoldo Mondadori editore, 1974.

PANEGYRICI LATINI. *Panégyriques latins* i–iii. Ed. E. Galletier. Collection des Universités de France. Paris: Belles Lettres, 1949–55.

PHILO OF ALEXANDRIA. *Philo*. Text with trans. F. H. Colson and G. H. Whitaker. 10 vols with 2 supplementary vols by R. A. Markus. LCL. London and Cambridge, Mass.: William Heinemann and Harvard University Press, 1929–62.

—— *Philo of Alexandria: The Contemplative Life, the Giants, and Selections*. Trans. David Winston. CWS. Ramsay, NJ: Paulist Press, 1981.

PHILODEMUS. *Philodemi Volumina Rhetorica*. Ed. S. Sudhaus. 3 vols. Leipzig: B. G. Teubner, 1892–6.

PHILOSTRATUS. *Philostratus: The Life of Apollonius of Tyana, the Epistles of Apollonius and the Treatise of Eusebius.* Text with trans. F. C. Conybeare. 2 vols. LCL. Cambridge, Mass.: Harvard University Press, 1912.

PHILOXENUS OF MABBUG. *Tractatus de Trinitate et Incarnatione.* Text ed. with Latin trans. A. Vaschalde. CSCO, Scriptores Syri, 9. Paris: Firmin-Didot, 1907.

PLATO. *Platonis Opera.* Ed. J. Burnet. 5 vols. OCT. Oxford: Clarendon Press, 1900–7.

—— *The Collected Dialogues of Plato, including the Letters.* Trans. ed. Edith Hamilton and Huntingdon Cairns. Bollingen Series 71. Princeton, NJ: Princeton University Press, 1961.

PLOTINUS. *Plotini Opera.* Ed. Paul Henry and Hans-Rudolf Schwyzer. OCT. 3 vols. Oxford: Clarendon Press, 1964–82.

—— *Plotinus.* Text and trans. A. H. Armstrong. 7 vols. LCL. Cambridge, Mass., and London: Harvard University Press and William Heinemann, 1966–88.

PLUTARCH. *Moralia.* Text with English trans. F. C. Babbitt *et al.* 15 vols. LCL. Cambridge, Mass., and London: Harvard University Press, 1922–69.

PORPHYRY. *Porphyry: On the Life of Plotinus and the Order of his Books.* Text and trans. A. H. Armstrong in *Plotinus: Enneads,* i. 2–85. LCL. Cambridge, Mass., and London: Harvard University Press and William Heinemann, 1966.

—— *Porphyry the Philosopher: To Marcella.* Text and trans. Kathleen O'Brien Wicker. SBL Texts and Translations 28. Graeco-Roman Religion Series 10. Atlanta, Ga.: Scholars Press, 1987.

PROCLUS. *In Platonis Parmenidem.* Ed. V. Cousin. Paris: Durand, 1864 (repr. Hildesheim: Olms, 1961).

—— *Procli commentarium in Parmenidem. Pars ultima adhuc inedita interprete Guilielmo de Morbeke.* Ed. R. Klibansky and L. Labowsky. London: Warburg Institute, 1953 (repr. 1973).

—— *Commentary on Plato's Parmenides.* Trans. J. M. Dillon and G. R. Morrow. Princeton: Princeton University Press, 1987 (repr. 1992).

—— *In Platonis rem publicam commentarii.* Ed. W. Kroll. 2 vols. Leipzig: B. G. Teubner, 1899–1901.

—— *In Platonis Timaeum commentaria.* Ed. E. Diehl. 3 vols. Leipzig: B. G. Teubner, 1903–6.

—— *Proclus: The Elements of Theology.* Text and trans. E. R. Dodds. 2nd edn Oxford: Clarendon Press, 1963 (repr. 1992).

—— *Neoplatonic Saints: The Lives of Plotinus and Proclus by their Students.* Trans. with notes Mark Edwards. Translated Texts for Historians 35. Liverpool: Liverpool University Press, 2000.

SAHDONA. *Oeuvres spirituelles.* Ed. with French trans. A. de Halleux, OFM. CSCO, Scriptores Syri, 86–7, 90–1, 110–13. Louvain: Peeters, 1960–5.

SENECA. *Petronius, The Satyricon and Seneca, the Apocolocyntosis.* Trans. J. P. Sullivan. Harmondsworth: Penguin, 1974.

SEXTUS EMPIRICUS. *Sextus Empiricus.* Text with trans. R. G. Bury. 4 vols. LCL. Cambridge, Mass.: Harvard University Press; London: William Heinemann, 1933–49.

SOCRATES SCHOLASTICUS. *Socrates' Ecclesiastical History.* Ed. William Bright. Oxford: Clarendon Press, 1878.

—— *The Ecclesiastical History of Socrates Scholasticus*. ET A. C. Zenos. NPNF, second series, 2. Edinburgh: T & T Clark; Grand Rapids, Mick.: William B. Eerdmans, repr. 1997.

SYMEON THE NEW THEOLOGIAN. *Syméon Le Nouveau Théologien. Hymnes.* Ed. J. Koder, with French trans. J. Paramelle. 3 vols. SC 156, 174, 196. Paris: Éditions du Cerf, 1969–73.

—— *Syméon Le Nouvean Théologien. Kephalaia.* Ed. with French trans. J. Darrouzès. SC 51. Paris. Éditions du Cerf, 1957.

—— *Syméon Le Nouveau Théologien. Traités théologiques et éthiques.* Ed. with French trans. J. Darrouzès. 2 vols. SC 122, 129. Paris: Éditions du Cerf, 1966–7.

—— *The Philokalia*, vol. iv. Selected English trans. G. E. H. Palmer, P. Sherrard, and K. Ware. London: Faber & Faber, 1995.

TALMUD. *Sifre: A Tannaitic Commentary on the Book of Deuteronomy.* ET Reuven Hammer. Yale Judaica Series 24. New Haven and London: Yale University Press, 1986.

TATIAN. *Tatian: Oratio ad Graecos and Fragments.* Text and trans. Molly Whittaker. OECT. Oxford: Clarendon Press, 1982.

TEACHING OF SILVANUS. *The Teachings of Silvanus: A Commentary (Nag Hammadi Codex VII, 4)*. Coptic text with English trans. J. Zandee. Egyptologische Uitgaven 6. Leiden: E. J. Brill, 1991.

—— 'The Teaching of Silvanus'. Trans. Malcolm L. Peel and Jan Zandee, in *The Nag Hammadi Library in English*, ed. James M. Robinson. Leiden: E. J. Brill, 1988, 379–95.

TERTULLIAN. *Quinti Septimi Florentis Tertulliani Opera.* Ed. Aemilius Kroyman. Pars III. CSEL 47. Vienna and Leipzig: F. Tempsky and G. Freytag, 1906.

—— *Tertullian's Treatise Against Praxeas.* Text and English trans. Ernest Evans. London: SPCK, 1948.

THEODORE OF MOPSUESTIA. *Les Homélies Catéchétiques de Théodore de Mopsueste.* Text and French trans. Raymond Tonneau, OP, and Robert Devreesse. Studi e Testi 145. Vatican City: Biblioteca Apostolica Vaticana, 1949.

THEODOTUS. *Clement d'Alexandrie. Extraits de Théodote.* Text and French trans. F. Sagnard, OP. SC 23. Paris: Éditions du Cerf, 1948.

THEOPHILUS OF ANTIOCH. *Theophilus of Antioch: Ad Autolycum.* Ed. with English trans. R. M. Grant. OECT. Oxford: Clarendon Press, 1970.

TREATISE ON THE RESURRECTION (EPISTLE TO RHEGINUS). *The Gnostic Scriptures.* ET Bentley Layton. London: SCM Press, 1987, 316–24.

—— 'The Treatise on the Resurrection (1, 4)'. ET Malcolm L. Peel, in *The Nag Hammadi Library in English*, ed. James M. Robinson. Leiden: E. J. Brill, 1988, 52–7.

VALENTINUS. *Quellen zur Geschichte der christlichen Gnosis.* Ed. W. Völker. Sammlung ausgewählter kirchen- und dogmengeschichtlicher Quellenschriften, N. F. 5. Tübingen: J. C. B. Mohr (Paul Siebeck), 1932, 57–60.

—— *The Gnostic Scriptures.* ET Bentley Layton. London: SCM Press, 1987, 217–64.

—— 'The Gospel of Truth (1, 3 and XII, 2)'. ET Harold W. Attridge and George W. MacRae, in *The Nag Hammadi Library in English*, ed. James M. Robinson. Leiden: E. J. Brill, 1988, 38–51.

Studies

ABEGG, MARTIN G. (1997). 'Who Ascended to Heaven? 4Q491, 4Q427 and the Teacher of Righteousness', in Evans and Flint 1997: 61–73.

ALBRIGHT, W. F. (1968). *Yahweh and the Gods of the Canaan*. London: SCM Press.

D'ALÈS, A. (1916). 'La doctrine de la récapitulation en saint Irénée'. *RechSR* 6: 185–211.

—— (1924). 'La Doctrine de l'Esprit en S. Irénée'. *RechSR* 14: 497–538.

ALEXANDRINA (1987). *Hellénisme, judaisme et christianisme à Alexandrie. Mélanges offerts à P. Claude Mondésert*. Paris: Éditions du Cerf.

ALFEYEV, HILARION (2000). *St Symeon the New Theologian and the Orthodox Tradition*. Oxford: Oxford University Press.

ALLCHIN, A. M. (1988). *Participation in God*. London: Darton, Longman & Todd.

ALLEN, R. E. (1965). 'Participation and Prediction in Plato's Middle Dialogues', in R. E. Allen (ed.), *Studies in Plato's Metaphysics*. London: Routledge & Kegan Paul, 43–60.

ALTERMATH, F. (1975). 'The Purpose of the Incarnation according to Irenaeus'. *StPat* 13 (=TU 116): 63–8.

ALTHAUS, H. (1972). *Die Heilslehre des heiligen Gregor von Nazianz*. Münster: Aschendorff.

ALVIAR, J. JOSÉ (1993*a*). 'Continuous and Discontinuous Figures in Origen'. *StPat* 26: 211–16.

—— (1993*b*). *KLESIS. The Theology of the Christian Vocation according to Origen*. Blackrock: Four Courts Press.

ANATOLIOS, KHALED (1996). 'The Soteriological Significance of Christ's Humanity in St Athanasius'. *St Vladimir's Theological Quarterly* 40: 265–86.

—— (1998). *Athanasius: The Coherence of His Thought*. London and New York: Routledge.

ANDIA, YSABEL DE (1986). *Homo Vivens. Incorruptibilité et divinisation de l'homme selon Irénée de Lyon*. Paris: Études Augustiniennes.

—— (1996). *Henosis. L'Union à Dieu chez Denys l'Aréopagite*. Philosophia Antiqua 71. Leiden: E. J. Brill.

—— (1997). 'Mystères, unification et divinisation de l'homme selon Denys l'Aréopagite'. *OCP* 63: 273–332.

ARMSTRONG, A. H. (ed.) (1970). *The Cambridge History of Later Greek and Early Medieval Philosophy*. Cambridge: Cambridge University Press.

—— (1976). 'The Apprehension of Divinity in the Self and Cosmos in Plotinus', in R. Baine Harris (ed.), *The Significance of Neoplatonism*. Norfolk, Va.: International Society for Neoplatonic Studies, 187–98. (Reprinted in Armstrong 1979.)

—— (1979). *Plotinian and Christian Studies*. London: Variorum.

—— (ed.) (1986). *Classical Mediterranean Spirituality: Egyptian, Greek, Roman*. London: Routledge & Kegan Paul.

ARNOLD, D. W. H. (1991). *The Early Episcopal Career of Athanasius of Alexandria*. Notre Dame, Ind.: University of Notre Dame Press.

ATTRIDGE, HAROLD W. (1989). *The Epistle to the Hebrews*. Hermeneia. Philadelphia, Pa.: Fortress Press.

AUBINEAU, M. (1956). 'Incorruptibilité et divinisation selon saint Irénée'. *RechSR* 44: 25–52.

BAERT, E. (1965). 'Le Thème de la vision de Dieu chez S. Justin, Clément d'Alexandrie et S. Grégoire de Nysse', *Freiburger Zeitschrift für Philosophie und Theologie* 12: 439–97.

BAGNALL, ROGER S. (1993). *Egypt in Late Antiquity.* Princeton, NJ: Princeton University Press.

BALÁS, D. L. (1966). Μετουσία θεοῦ. *Man's Participation in God's Perfections according to Saint Gregory of Nyssa.* Studia Anselmiana 55. Rome: Libreria Herder.

—— (1975). 'The Idea of Participation in the Structure of Origen's Thought: Christian Transposition of a Theme of the Platonic Tradition', in *Origeniana,* premier colloque internationale des études origéniennes. Quaderni di 'Vetera Christianorum' 12: 257–76.

BALFOUR, DAVID (1982). *Saint Gregory the Sinaite: Discourse on the Transfiguration.* Athens: reprinted from *Theologia* 52/4–54/1, 1981–3.

BALTHASAR, HANS URS VON (1942). *Présence et pensée. Essai sur la philosophie de Grégoire de Nysse.* Paris: Beauchesne.

—— (1961). *Kosmische Liturgie. Das Weltbild Maximus des Bekenners* (2nd edn). Einsiedeln: Johannes-Verlag.

BARDY, G. (1937). 'Aux origines de l'école d'Alexandrie', *RechSR* 27: 65–90.

—— (1942). 'Pour l'histoire de l'école d'Alexandrie', *Vivre et Penser* (= wartime *Revue biblique*) 2: 80–109.

BARNARD, LESLIE WILLIAM (1997). *St Justin Martyr: The First and Second Apologies.* Translated with introduction and notes. ACW 56. New York/Mahwah, NJ: Paulist Press.

BARNES, TIMOTHY D. (1986). 'Angel of Light or Mystic Initiate? The Problem of the *Life of Antony*'. *JTS* n.s. 37: 353–68.

—— (1993). *Athanasius and Constantius: Theology and Politics in the Constantinian Empire.* Cambridge, Mass., and London: Harvard University Press.

BARRETT, C. K. (1962). 'The Theological Vocabulary of the Fourth Gospel and the Gospel of Truth', in W. Klassen and G. F. Snyder (eds), *Current Issues in New Testament Interpretation.* Festschrift Otto A. Piper. London: SCM Press, 210–23.

BARTOS, EMIL (1999). *Deification in Eastern Orthodox Theology: An Evaluation and Critique of the Theology of Dumitru Stăniloae.* Foreword by Kallistos Ware. Paternoster Biblical and Theological Monographs. Carlisle: Paternoster Press.

BAUER, W. (1971). *Orthodoxy and Heresy in Earliest Christianity* (1934). Trans. R. Kraft. London: SPCK.

BAUR, L. (1916–20). 'Untersuchungen über die Vergöttlichungslehre in der Theologie der griechischen Väter'. *Theologische Quartalschrift* 98 (1916): 467–91; 99 (1918): 225–52; 100 (1919): 426–46; 101 (1920): 28–64, 155–86.

BEAUJEU, J. (1973). 'Les Apologètes et le culte du souverain', in Den Boer 1973: 103–42.

BEBAWI, GEORGE (1988). 'St Athanasius: The Dynamics of Salvation'. *Sobornost* 8/2: 24–32.

BEIERWALTES, W. (1965). *Proklos: Grundzüge seiner Metaphysik.* Frankfurt am Main: Klostermann.

BELL, H. IDRISS (1953). *Cults and Creeds in Graeco-Roman Egypt*. New York: Philosophical Library.

BELLINI, ENZO (1982). 'Maxime interprète de pseudo-Denys l'Aréopagite', in Heinzer and Schönborn 1982: 37–49.

BERCHMANN, R. M. (1984). *From Philo to Origen: Middle Platonism in Transition*. Brown Judaic Studies 69. Chico, Calif.: Scholars Press.

BERNARD, R. (1952). *L'Image de Dieu d'après Athanase*. Paris: Aubier.

BERNARDI, JEAN (1995). *S. Grégoire de Nazianze. Le théologien et son temps*. Paris: Éditions du Cerf.

BERTHOLD, GEORGE C. (1982). 'The Cappadocian Roots of Maximus the Confessor', in Heinzer and Schönborn 1982: 51–9.

BEVAN, E. (1927). *A History of Egypt under the Ptolemaic Dynasty*. London: Methuen.

BICKERMAN (BIKERMAN), E. J. (1938). *Institutions des Séleucides*. Haut-Commissariat de la République Française en Syrie et au Liban. Service des Antiquités. Bibliothèque archéologique et historique, 26. Paris: P. Geuthner.

—— (1973). 'Consecratio', in Den Boer 1973: 3–37.

—— (1988). *The Jews in the Greek Age*. Cambridge, Mass., and London: Harvard University Press.

BIELER, LUDWIG (1935). *Theios Anêr. Das Bild des 'göttlichen Menschen' in Spätantike und Frühchristentum*. Vienna: Oskar Höfels.

BIGG, CHARLES (1913). *The Christian Platonists of Alexandria: The 1886 Bampton Lectures* (2nd edn). Oxford: Clarendon Press (repr. 1968).

BIGGER, CHARLES P. (1968). *Participation: A Platonic Inquiry*. Baton Rouge, La.: Louisiana State University Press.

BIKERMAN, E. J. *see* BICKERMAN, E. J.

BILANIUK, P. B. T. (1973). 'The Mystery of Theosis or Divinisation', in D. Neiman and M. Schatkin (eds), *The Heritage of the Early Church: Essays in Honor of Georges Vasilievich Florovsky*. OCA 195. Rome: Pontificium Institutum Orientalium Studiorum, 337–59.

BILLINGS, T. H. (1919). *The Platonism of Philo Judaeus*. Chicago, Ill.: University of Chicago Press.

BINNS, JOHN (1994). *Ascetics and Ambassadors of Christ: The Monasteries of Palestine 314–631*. Oxford: Clarendon Press.

BLACK, MATTHEW (1976). 'The Throne-Theophany Prophetic Commission and the "Son of Man" ', in Hamerton-Kelly and Scroggs 1976: 57–73.

—— (1985). *The Book of Enoch or First Enoch: A New English Edition with Commentary and Textual Notes*. Leiden: E. J. Brill.

BLOWERS, PAUL M. (1991). *Exegesis and Spiritual Pedagogy in Maximus the Confessor*. Christianity and Judaism in Antiquity 7. Notre Dame, Ind.: University of Notre Dame Press.

—— (1997). 'Realized Eschatology in Maximus the Confessor, *Ad Thalassium* 22'. *StPat* 32: 258–63.

BOCCACCINI, GABRIELE (1998). *Beyond the Essene Hypothesis: The Parting of the Ways between Qumran and Enochic Judaism*. Grand Rapids, Mich.: William B. Eerdmans.

BOCKMUEHL, MARKUS N. A. (1990). *Revelation and Mystery in Ancient Judaism and Pauline*

Christianity. Tübingen: J. C. B. Mohr (Paul Siebeck). (Repr. Grand Rapids, Mich., and Cambridge: William B. Eerdmans 1997.)

BOLSHAKOFF, SERGIUS (1977). *Russian Mystics*. CSS 26. Kalamazoo, Mich.: Cistercian Publications.

BONNER, GERALD (1986*a*). 'Augustine's Conception of Deification'. *JTS* n.s. 37: 369–86.

—— (1986*b*). *St Augustine of Hippo: Life and Controversies* (2nd edn). Norwich: Canterbury Press.

BORNHÄUSER, K. (1903). *Die Vergottungslehre des Athanasius und Johannes Damascenus*. Beiträge zur Föderung christlicher Theologie 2. Gütersloh: C. Bertelsmann.

BORNKAMM, GÜNTHER (1971). *Paul*. Trans. D. M. G. Stalker, London: Hodder & Stoughton.

BOSTOCK, GERALD (2001). 'Osiris and the Resurrection of Christ'. *Expository Times* (May): 265–71.

BOTTERILL, STEVEN (1994). *Dante and the Mystical Tradition: Bernard of Clairvaux in the Commedia*. Cambridge Studies in Medieval Literature 22. Cambridge: Cambridge University Press.

BOULNOIS, M.-O. (1994). *Le paradoxe trinitaire chez Cyrille d'Alexandrie. Herméneutique, analyses philosophiques et argumentation théologique*. Collections des Études Augustiniennes, Série Antiquité 143. Paris: Institut d'Études Augustiniennes.

BOUTTIER, M. (1966). *Christianity according to Paul*. Trans. F. Clarke. London: SCM Press.

BOUYER, LOUIS (1968). *A History of Christian Spirituality*, vol. i: *The Spirituality of the New Testament and the Fathers*. Trans. M. Ryan *et al.* London: Burns & Oates.

—— (1989). *The Christian Mystery: From Pagan Myth to Christian Mysticism*. Trans. Illtyd Trethowan. Edinburgh: T & T Clark.

BOWERSOCK, G. W. (1973). 'Greek Intellectuals and the Imperial Cult in the Second Century A.D.', in Den Boer 1973: 177–212.

BOWMAN, ALAN K. (1996). *Egypt after the Pharaohs 332 BC–AD 642* (2nd edn). London: British Museum Press.

BRADLEY, D. J. M. (1974). 'The Transformation of the Stoic Ethic in Clement of Alexandria'. *Augustinianum* 14: 41–66.

BRAKKE, DAVID (1994). 'The Greek and Syriac Versions of the *Life of Antony*'. *Le Muséon* 107: 29–53.

—— (1995). *Athanasius and Asceticism*. Baltimore and London: Johns Hopkins University Press.

BRÉHIER, E. (1950). *Les Idées philosophiques et religieuses de Philon d'Alexandrie*. Études de philosophie médiévale 8. Paris: J. Vrin.

BROCK, SEBASTIAN (1973). 'An Early Syriac Life of Maximus the Confessor'. *Analecta Bollandiana* 91: 299–346.

—— (1987). *The Syriac Fathers on the Spiritual Life*. CSS 101. Kalamazoo, Mich.: Cistercian Publications.

—— (1990). *Saint Ephrem: Hymns on Paradise*. Crestwood, NY: St Vladimir's Seminary Press.

—— (1992). *The Luminous Eye: The Spiritual World Vision of Saint Ephrem the Syrian* (revised edn). CSS 124. Kalamazoo, Mich.: Cistercian Publications.

BROOKE, A. (1912). *The Johannine Epistles*. ICC. Edinburgh: T & T Clark.

BROWN, PETER (1967). *Augustine of Hippo: A Biography*. London and Boston: Faber & Faber.

—— (1971). *The World of Late Antiquity*. London: Thames & Hudson.

—— (1972). *Religion and Society in the Age of Saint Augustine*. London: Faber & Faber.

—— (1982). *Society and the Holy in Late Antiquity*. London: Faber & Faber.

—— (1987). 'Late Antiquity', in Veyne 1987: 235–95.

—— (1988). *The Body and Society: Men, Women and Sexual Renunciation in Early Christianity*. New York, NY: Columbia University Press.

BROWN, R. E. (1966–70). *The Gospel According to John*. Anchor Bible 29, 29A. New York, NY: Doubleday.

—— (1979). *The Community of the Beloved Disciple*. London: Geoffrey Chapman.

BUCKLEY, M. J. (1963). 'Saint Justin and the Ascent of the Mind to God'. *Personalist* 44: 89–104.

BULTMANN, R. (1952). *Theology of the New Testament*, vol. i. Trans. K. Grobel. London: SCM Press.

—— (1956). *Primitive Christianity in its Contemporary Setting*. Trans. R. H. Fuller. London: Thames & Hudson.

BURKERT, WALTER (1972). *Lore and Science in Early Pythagoreanism*. Trans. E. L. Minar. Cambridge, Mass.: Harvard University Press.

—— (1985). *Greek Religion*. Trans. J. Raffan. Cambridge, Mass.: Harvard University Press.

—— (1987). *Ancient Mystery Cults*. Cambridge, Mass.: Harvard University Press.

BURNETT, F. W. (1984). 'Philo on Immortality: A Thematic Study of Philo's Concept of *palingenesia*'. *CBQ* 43: 447–70.

BUTTERWORTH, G. W. (1916). 'The Deification of Man in Clement of Alexandria'. *JTS* 17: 157–69.

—— (1973). *Origen on First Principles*. Being Koetschau's text of the *De Principiis* translated into English, together with an Introduction and Notes. Introduction by Henri de Lubac. Gloucester, Mass.: Peter Smith.

CAGNAT, R. (1914). *Cours d'epigraphie latine*. Paris: Fontemoing.

CANDAL, M. (1954). 'El libro VI de Prócoro Cidonio (sobre la luz tabórica)'. *OCP* 20: 247–96.

CAPÁNAGA, VICTORINO (1954). 'La deificación en la soteriologia agostiana'. *Augustinus Magister* 2: 745–54.

CASIDAY, AUGUSTINE (2001). 'St Augustine on Deification: His Homily on Psalm 81'. *Sobornost* 23/2: 23–44.

—— (2004). 'Deification in Origen, Evagrius and Cassian', in L. Perrone (ed.), *Origeniana Octava*. Louvain: Peeters, 995–1002.

CASSELL, J. DAVID (1992). 'Cyril of Alexandria and the Science of the Grammarians: A Study in the Setting, Purpose, and Emphasis in Cyril's *Commentary on Isaiah*'. Ph.D. dissertation. University of Virginia.

CERFAUX, L. and TONDRIAU, J. (1957). *Un concurrent du christianisme: le culte des souverains dans la civilisation gréco-romaine*. Bibliothèque de Théologie, 3, 5. Tournai: Desclée.

CHADWICK, HENRY (1965). 'St Paul and Philo of Alexandria'. *BJRL* 48: 286–307.

—— (1966). *Early Christian Thought and the Classical Tradition: Studies in Justin, Clement, and Origen.* Oxford: Oxford University Press.

—— (1970). 'Philo and the Beginnings of Christian Thought', in Armstrong 1970: 137–57.

—— (1981). *Boethius: The Consolations of Music, Logic, Theology, and Philosophy.* Oxford: Clarendon Press.

—— (1991). *Saint Augustine: Confessions.* Oxford: Oxford University Press.

—— (1996). 'New Sermons of St Augustine'. *JTS* n.s. 47: 69–91.

—— (forthcoming). Article on Augustine's doctrine of deification to appear in the *Revue des Sciences Religieuses.*

CHARLESWORTH, M. P. (1935). 'Some Observations on the Ruler Cult, Especially in Rome'. *HTR* 28: 5–44.

—— (1939). 'The Refusal of Divine Honours'. *PBSR* 15: 1–10.

CHRISTOU, PANAYOTIS (1978*a*). Ἑλληνικὴ πατρολογία, vol. ii: Γραμματεία τῆς Περιόδου τῶν Διωγμῶν. Thessalonica: Patriarchikon Idruma Paterikon Spoudon.

—— (1978*b*). Ὁ Μέγας Βασίλειος. Βίος καὶ πολιτεία, συγγράμματα, θεολογικὴ σκέψις. Analecta Vlatadon 27. Thessalonica: Patriarchikon Idruma Paterikon Spoudon.

—— (1982). 'Maximos Confessor on the Infinity of Man', in Heinzer and Schönborn 1982: 261–71.

CLARK, Elizabeth A. (1977). *Clement's Use of Aristotle: The Aristotelian Contribution to Clement of Alexandria's Refutation of Gnosticism.* New York and Toronto: Edwin Mellen Press.

—— (1992). *The Origenist Controversy: The Cultural Construction of an Early Christian Debate.* Princeton, NJ: Princeton University Press.

CLAUS, D. B. (1981). *Toward the Soul.* New Haven, Conn., and London: Yale University Press.

COLLINS, ADELA Y. (1995). 'The Seven Heavens in Jewish and Christian Apocalypses', in Collins and Fishbane 1995: 59–93.

COLLINS, JOHN J. (1974*a*). 'Apocalyptic Eschatology and the Transcendence of Death'. *CBQ* 36: 21–43.

—— (1974*b*). 'The Son of Man and the Saints of the Most High in the Book of Daniel'. *JBL* 93: 55–8.

—— (1984). *The Apocalyptic Imagination: An Introduction to the Jewish Matrix of Christianity.* New York, NY: Crossroad.

—— (1995). 'A Throne in the Heavens: Apotheosis in Pre-Christian Judaism', in Collins and Fishbane 1995: 43–58.

COLLINS, JOHN J. and CHARLESWORTH, JAMES H. (1991). *Mysteries and Revelations: Apocalyptic Studies since the Uppsala Colloquium.* Journal for the Study of pseudepigrapha, Supplement Series 9. Sheffield: Sheffield Academic Press.

COLLINS, JOHN J. and FISHBANE, MICHAEL (1995). *Death, Ecstasy and Other Worldly Journeys.* Albany, NY: State University of New York Press.

CONGAR, M.-J. (1935). 'La déification dans la tradition spirituelle de l'Orient'. *La Vie Spirituelle* 43, suppl. 91–107. (Repr. in *Unam Sanctam* 50, Paris, 1964.)

CONZELMANN, HANS (1965). 'Paulus und die Weisheit', *New Testament Studies* 12: 231–44.

—— (1969). *An Outline of the Theology of the New Testament.* Trans. John Bowden. London and New York: SCM Press.

CORRINGTON, GAIL PATERSON (1986). *The 'Divine Man': His Origin and Function in Hellenistic Popular Religion.* American University Studies Series VII. Theology and Religion 17. New York, Berne, and Frankfurt am Main: Peter Lang.

CORWIN, VIRGINIA (1960). *St Ignatius and Christianity in Antioch.* New Haven, Conn.: Yale University Press.

COX, PATRICIA (1983). *Biography in Late Antiquity: The Quest for the Holy Man.* The Transformation of the Classical Heritage 5. Berkeley, Calif.: University of California Press.

CROUZEL, H. (1955). 'L'Anthropologie d'Origène dans la perspective du combat spirituel'. *Revue d'ascétique et de mystique* 31: 364–85.

—— (1956). *Théologie de l'image de Dieu chez Origène.* Théologie 34. Paris: Aubier.

—— (1961). *Origène et la 'connaissance mystique'.* Museum Lessianum, section théologique 56. Bruges and Paris: Desclée de Brouwer.

CUMONT, FRANZ (1903). *The Mysteries of Mithra* (2nd edn). Trans. T. J. McCormack. New York, NY: Open Court.

—— (1949). *Lux Perpetua.* Paris: P. Geuthner.

DALEY, BRIAN E. (1997). 'Divine Transcendence and Human Transformation: Gregory of Nyssa's Anti-Apollinarian Christology'. *StPat* 32: 87–95.

DALMAIS, I.-H. (1954–7). 'Divinisation—patristique grecque'. *DS* iii: 1376–89.

—— (1972). 'Mystère liturgique et divinisation dans la "Mystagogie" de saint Maxime le Confesseur', in *Epektasis. Mélanges patristiques offerts au cardinal Daniélou.* Paris: Beauchesne, 55–62.

DANIÉLOU, JEAN (1944). *Platonisme et théologie mystique. Essai sur la doctrine spirituelle de Saint Grégoire de Nysse.* Théologie 2. Paris: Aubier.

—— (1973). *Gospel Message and Hellenistic Culture.* A History of Early Christian Doctrine Before the Council of Nicaea 2. Trans. John Austin Baker. London: Darton, Longman & Todd.

DANIÉLOU, JEAN and MARROU, HENRI (1964). *The Christian Centuries,* vol. i: *The First Six Hundred Years.* Trans. Vincent Cronin. London: Darton, Longman & Todd.

DAUMAS, FRANÇOIS (1982). 'Le Fonds Égyptien de l'Hermétisme', in Julien Ries *et al.* (eds), *Gnosticisme et monde hellénistique.* Actes du Colloque de Louvain-la-Neuve (11–14 mars 1980). Louvain-la-Neuve: Centre d'histoire des religions, 3–25.

DAVIES, JON (1999). *Death, Burial and Rebirth in the Religions of Antiquity.* Religion in the First Christian Centuries. London and New York: Routledge.

DAVILA, JAMES, R. (1999). 'Heavenly Ascents in the Dead Sea Scrolls' in Flint and VanderKam 1999: ii. 461–85.

DEAN-OTTING, MARY (1984). *Heavenly Journeys: A Study of the Motif in Hellenistic Jewish Literature.* Judentum und Umwelt. Frankfurt am Main: Peter Lang.

DECHOW, JON F. (1988). *Dogma and Mysticism in Early Christianity: Epiphanius of Cyprus and the Legacy of Origen.* North American Patristic Society, Patristic Monograph Series 13. Macon, Ga.: Mercer University Press; Louvain: Peeters.

DEHNHARD, HANS (1964). *Das Problem der Abhangigkeit des Basilius von Plotin.* Patristische Texte und Studien 3. Berlin: Walter de Gruyter.

DEISSMANN, ADOLF (1957). *Paul* (1926, 2nd edn). Trans. W. E. Wilson, London: Hodder & Stoughton.

DEMETROPOULOS, P. Ch. (1954). *Ἡ ἀνθρωπολογία τοῦ Μεγάλου Ἀθανασίου*. Athens.

DEN BOER, W. (ed.) (1973). *Le Culte des souverains dans l'empire romain*. Entretiens sur l'antiquité classique 19. Geneva: Fondation Hardt pour l'Étude de l'Antiquité Classique.

DES PLACES, E. (1969). *La Religion grecque. Dieux, cultes, rites et sentiment religieux dans la Grèce antique*. Paris: Picard.

—— (1982). 'Maxime le Confesseur et Diadoque de Photicé', in Heinzer and Schönborn 1982: 29–35.

DEUTSCH, NATHANIEL (1995). *The Gnostic Imagination: Gnosticism, Mandaeism and Merkabah Mysticism*. Brill's Jewish Studies 13. Leiden: E. J. Brill.

DILLISTONE, F. W. (1985). *Christianity and Symbolism* (2nd edn). London: SCM Press.

DILLON, JOHN (1983). 'The Nature of God in the *Quod Deus*', in John Dillon and David Winston, *Two Treatises of Philo Judaeus:* De Gigantibus *and* Quod Deus. Chico, Calif.: Scholars Press.

—— (1996). *The Middle Platonists* (2nd edn), London: Duckworth.

DILLON, J. M. and LONG, A. A. (eds) (1988). *The Question of 'Eclecticism': Studies in Later Greek Philosophy*. Berkeley, Los Angeles, London: University of California Press.

DODD, C. H. (1953) *The Interpretation of the Fourth Gospel*. Cambridge: Cambridge University Press.

DODDS, E. R. (1963). *Proclus: The Elements of Theology. A Revised Text with Translation, Introduction and Commentary* (2nd edn). Oxford: Clarendon Press (repr. 1992).

—— (1965). *Pagan and Christian in an Age of Anxiety*. Cambridge: Cambridge University Press.

DODWELL, H. (1689). *Dissertationes in Irenaeum*. Oxford.

DOLBEAU, FRANÇOIS (1993). 'Nouveaux sermons de saint Augustin pour la conversion des païens et des donatistes (V)'. *Revue des Études Augustiniennes* 39: 57–108.

DÖRRIES, HERMANN (1949). 'Die *Vita Antonii* als Geschichtsquelle', in *Nachrichten der Akademie der Wissenschaften in Göttingen*, Philologisch – historische Klasse, 357–410. (Repr. in his *Wort und Stunde*, vol. i. Göttingen: Vandenhoeck & Ruprecht, 1966, 145–224.)

DREWERY, BENJAMIN (1960). *Origen and the Doctrine of Grace*. London: Epworth Press.

—— (1975). 'Deification', in Peter Brooks (ed.), *Christian Spirituality: Essays in Honour of Gordon Rupp*. London: SCM Press, 33–62.

DUPUIS, J. (1967). '*L'Esprit de l'homme'. Étude sur l'anthropologie religieuse d'Origène*. Museum Lessianum, section théologique 62. Brussels: Desclée de Brouwer.

DU TOIT, DAVID S. (1997). *Theios Anthropos. Zur Verwendung von theios anthropos und sinnverwandten Ausdrücken in der Literatur der Kaiserzeit*. Wissenschaftliche Untersuchungen zum Neuen Testament 2/91. Tübingen: J. C. B. Mohr (Paul Siebeck).

EICHRODT, WALTHER (1967). *Theology of the Old Testament*. 2 vols. London: SCM Press.

ELLVERSON, A.-S. (1981). *The Dual Nature of Man: A Study in the Theological Anthropology of Gregory of Nazianzus*. Uppsala: Almqvist & Wiksell International.

ERMONI, V. (1897). 'La Déification de l'homme chez les Pères de l'église'. *Revue du clergé français* 11: 509–19.

EVANS, CRAIG A. and FLINT, PETER W. (eds) (1997). *Eschatology, Messianism and the Dead Sea Scrolls*. Grand Rapids, Mich., and Cambridge: William B. Eerdmans.

EVERY, GEORGE (1968–9). 'Theosis in Later Byzantine Theology'. *Eastern Churches Review* 2: 243–52.

FALLER, OTTO (1925). 'Griechische Vergottung und christliche Vergottlichung'. *Gregorianum* 6: 405–35.

FARNELL, L. R. (1921). *Greek Hero Cults and Ideas of Immortality*. Oxford: Oxford University Press.

FEDWICK, P. J. (ed.) (1981). *Basil of Caesarea: Christian, Humanist, Ascetic*. 2 vols. Toronto: Pontifical Institute of Medieval Studies.

FESTUGIÈRE, A.-J. (1932). *L'Idéal religieux des grecs et l'évangile*. Paris: Gabalda.

—— (1939). 'Divinisation du chrétien'. *La Vie spirituelle, ascetique et mystique* 59: 90–9.

—— (1943–54). *La Révélation d'Hermès Trismegiste*. 4 vols. Paris: Gabalda.

—— (1954). *Personal Religion among the Greeks*. Berkeley and Los Angeles, Calif.: University of California Press.

FILORAMO, GIOVANNI (1990). *A History of Gnosticism*. Trans. Anthony Alcock. Oxford: Blackwell.

FISHBANE, MICHAEL (1995). 'The Imagination of Death in Jewish Spirituality', in Collins and Fishbane 1995: 183–208.

FITZMYER, JOSEPH A. (1999). 'Paul and the Dead Sea Scrolls', in Flint and VanderKam 1999: ii. 599–621.

FLINT, PETER W. and VANDERKAM, JAMES C. (1999). *The Dead Sea Scrolls After Fifty Years: A Comprehensive Assessment*. 2 vols. Leiden: E. J. Brill.

FLOYD, W. E. G. (1971). *Clement of Alexandria's Treatment of the Problem of Evil*. Oxford: Oxford University Press.

FOERSTER, WERNER (1972). *Gnosis: A Selection of Gnostic Texts*. Ed. and trans. R. McL. Wilson. Oxford: Clarendon Press.

FOLLIET, GEORGES (1962). '*Deificari in otio*. Augustin, *Epistula* 10.2'. *Recherches Augustiniennes* 2: 225–36.

FOWDEN, GARTH (1982). 'The Pagan Holy Man in Late Antique Society'. *JHS* 102: 33–59.

—— (1993). *The Egyptian Hermes: A Historical Approach to the Late Pagan Mind* (2nd edn). Princeton, NJ: Princeton University Press.

FRANKFURTER, DAVID (1996). 'The Legacy of Jewish Apocalypses in Early Christianity: Regional Trajectories', in VanderKam and Adler 1996: 129–200.

—— (1998). *Religion in Roman Egypt: Assimilation and Resistance*. Princeton, NJ: Princeton University Press.

FRASER, P. M. (1972). *Ptolemaic Alexandria*. 3 vols. Oxford: Oxford University Press.

GALLAY, PAUL (1943*a*). *La Vie de S. Grégoire de Nazianze*. Paris: Vitte.

—— (1943*b*). *Langue et style de S. Grégoire de Nazianze dans sa correspondance*. Paris: J. Monnier.

GAMBLE, HARRY Y. (1995). *Books and Readers in the Early Christian Church: A History of Early Christian Texts*. New Haven and London: Yale University Press.

GAWRONSKI, RAYMOND (1995). *Word and Silence: Hans Urs von Balthasar and the Spiritual Encounter between East and West*. Grand Rapids, Mich.: William B. Eerdmans.

GOLITZIN, A. (1994). *Et introibo ad altare dei: the Mystagogy of Dionysius Areopagita, with special reference to its predecessors in the Eastern Christian tradition.* Thessalonica: Patriarchikon Idruma Paterikon Meleton.

GOODENOUGH, E. R. (1928). 'The Political Philosophy of Hellenistic Kingship'. *Yale Classical Studies* 1: 55–102.

—— (1935). *By Light, Light: The Mystic Gospel of Hellenistic Judaism.* New Haven, Conn.: Yale University Press.

—— (1953). *Jewish Symbols in the Greco-Roman Period.* 3 vols. Bollingen Series 37. New York: Bollingen Foundation.

GRANT, R. M. (1954). 'The Heresy of Tatian'. *JTS* n.s. 5: 62–8.

—— (1956). 'Aristotle and the Conversion of Justin'. *JTS* n.s. 7: 246–8.

—— (1957). 'Tatian and the Bible'. *StPat* 1 (=TU): 297–306.

—— (1970). *Theophilus of Antioch Ad Autolycum.* Oxford: Oxford University Press.

—— (1979). 'Place de Basilide dans la théologie chrétienne ancienne'. *Revue des Études Augustiniennes* 25: 201–16.

—— (1997). *Irenaeus of Lyons.* London and New York: Routledge.

GRAY, J. (1970). *I and II Kings.* London: SCM Press.

GRAY, P. T. R. (1979). *The Defense of Chalcedon in the East (451–553).* Studies in the History of Christian Thought. Leiden: E. J. Brill.

GRESE, W. (1979). *Corpus Hermeticum XIII and Early Christian Literature.* Leiden: E. J. Brill.

GRIFFITHS, J. GWYN (1986a). 'The Faith of the Pharaonic Period', in Armstrong 1986: 3–38.

—— (1986b). 'The Great Egyptian Cults of Oecumenical Spiritual Significance', in Armstrong 1986: 39–65.

GRILLMEIER, ALOYS (1975). *Christ in Christian Tradition*, vol. i: *From the Apostolic Age to Chalcedon (451)* (2nd edn). Trans. John Bowden. London and Oxford: Mowbrays.

—— (1995). *Christ in Christian Tradition*, vol. ii: *From the Council of Chalcedon (451) to Gregory the Great (590–604)*, pt. ii: *The Church of Constantinople in the Sixth Century.* In collaboration with Theresia Hainthaler. Trans. John Cawte and Pauline Allen. London: Mowbrays.

GROSS, JULES (1938). *La Divinisation du chrétien d'après les Pères grecs. Contribution historique à la doctrine de grace.* Paris: Gabalda. (Trans. Paul A. Onica, *The Divinisation of the Christian According to the Greek Fathers*, Anaheim, Calif.: A & C Press, 2000.)

GRUBE, G. M. A. (1980). *Plato's Thought* (2nd edn). London: Athlone Press.

GRUBER, G. (1962). *ZOE. Wesen, Stufen und Mitteilung des wahren Lebens bei Origenes.* Münchner theologische Studien 23. Munich: M. Huber.

GRUENWALD, ITHAMAR (1988). *From Apocalypticism to Gnosticism: Studies in Apocalypticism, Merkavah Mysticism and Gnosticism.* Frankfurt am Main: Peter Lang.

GUIGNET, M. (1911). *Saint Grégoire de Nazianze et la rhétorique.* Paris: Alphonse Picard.

GUILLAUMONT, A. (1962). *Les 'Kephalaia Gnostica' d'Évagre le Pontique et l'histoire de l'origenisme chez les Grecs et les Syriens.* Patristica Sorboniensia 5. Paris: Éditions du Seuil.

HAAS, CHRISTOPHER (1997). *Alexandria in Late Antiquity: Topography and Social Conflict.* Baltimore and London: Johns Hopkins University Press.

HABICHT, CHR. (1970). *Gottmenschentum und griechische Städte* (2nd edn). Zetemata 14. Munich: C. H. Beck.

HALL, ROBERT G. (1990). 'The Ascension of Isaiah: Community Situation, Date and Place in Early Christianity'. *JBL* 109: 289–306.

HALPERIN, DAVID (1988). *The Faces of the Chariot: Early Jewish Responses to Ezekiel's Vision.* Texte und Studien zum antiken Judentum 16. Tübingen: J. C. B. Mohr (Paul Siebeck).

HAMERTON-KELLY, R. and SCROGGS, R. (eds) (1978). *Jews, Greeks and Christians.* Leiden: E. J. Brill.

HAMMER, REUVEN (1986). *Sifre: A Tannaitic Commentary on the Book of Deuteronomy.* Yale Judaica Series 24. New Haven and London: Yale University Press.

HANSON, R. P. C. (1988). *The Search for the Christian Doctrine of God: The Arian Controversy 318–381.* Edinburgh: T & T Clark.

HARNACK, ADOLF von (1896–9). *History of Dogma.* 7 vols. Trans. N. Buchanan. London: Williams & Norgate. (Reprinted New York: Russell & Russell, 1958; page refs are to this edn.)

HARTMAN, LOUIS F. and DI LELLA, ALEXANDER A. (1978). *The Book of Daniel.* Anchor Bible 23. Garden City, NY: Doubleday.

HAUSHERR, I. and HORN, G. (1928). *Un grand mystique byzantin. Vie de Syméon le Nouveau Théologien (942–1022) par Nicétas Stéthatos.* OCA 12. Rome: Pontificium Institutum Orientalium Studiorum.

HEINZER, F. and SCHÖNBORN, C. (eds) (1982). *Maximus Confessor. Actes du Symposium sur Maxime le Confesseur, Fribourg, 2–5 septembre 1980.* Paradosis 27. Fribourg: Éditions universitaires Fribourg Suisse.

HELLEMAN, WENDY E. (1990). 'Philo of Alexandria on Deification and Assimilation to God', in D. T. RUNIA (ed.), *Studia Philonica Annual* 2: 51–71.

HENGEL, MARTIN (1974). *Judaism and Hellenism: Studies in their Encounter in Palestine During the Early Hellenistic Age.* 2 vols. Trans. John Bowden. London: SCM Press.

HENRY, PAUL (1938). *Études plotiniennes*, vol. i: *Les états du texte de Plotin.* Museum Lessianum, section philosophique 20. Brussels: L'Édition Universelle.

HESS, HAMILTON (1993). 'The Place of Divinization in Athanasian Soteriology'. *StPat* 26: 369–74.

HIMMELFARB, MARTHA (1991). 'Revelation and Rapture: The Transformation of the Visionary in the Ascent Apocalypses', in Collins and Charlesworth 1991: 79–90.

—— (1993). *Ascent to Heaven in Jewish and Christian Apocalypses.* New York and Oxford: Oxford University Press.

—— (1995). 'The Practices of Ascent in the Ancient Mediterranean World', in Collins and Fishbane 1995: 121–37.

HOLLADAY, CARL R. (1977). *Theios Aner in Hellenistic Judaism: A Critique of the Use of This Category in New Testament Christology.* SBL Dissertation Series 40. Missoula: Society for Biblical Literature.

HÜBNER, R. M. (1974). *Die Einheit des Leibes Christi bei Gregor von Nyssa: Untersuchungen zum Ursprung der 'physischen' Erlösungslehre.* Philosophia Patrum 2. Leiden: E. J. Brill.

HUSSEY, J. M. (1986). *The Orthodox Church in the Byzantine Empire.* Oxford: Clarendon Press.

IDEL, MOSHE (1988). *Kabbalah: New Perspectives.* New Haven, Conn.: Yale University Press.

ILLINGWORTH, J. R. (1903). *Personality, Human and Divine*. The Bampton Lectures for 1894. London: Macmillan.

IVÁNKA, ENDRE. von (1949). 'La Signification historique du *Corpus Areopagiticum*'. *RechSR* 36: 5–24.

JACOBSON, HOWARD (ed.) (1983). *The Exagoge of Ezekiel*. Cambridge: Cambridge University Press.

JAEGER, W. (1947). *The Theology of the Early Greek Philosophers*. Oxford: Oxford University Press.

—— (1966). *Gregor von Nyssa's Lehre vom heiligen Geist* (ed. H. Dörries). Leiden: E. J. Brill.

JAKAB, ATTILA (2001). *Ecclesia alexandrina. Évolution sociale et institutionnelle du christianisme alexandrin (IIᵉ et IIIᵉ siècles)*. Christianismes anciens 1. Bern: Peter Lang.

JOHNSON, A. R. (1942). *The One and the Many in the Israelite Conception of God*. Cardiff: University of Wales Press.

—— (1964). *The Vitality of the Individual in the Thought of Ancient Israel* (2nd edn). Cardiff: University of Wales Press.

JONES, W. H. S. (1913). 'A Note on the Vague Use of *theos*'. *CR* 27: 252–5.

KADUSHIN, M. (1965). *The Rabbinic Mind*. New York: Jewish Theological Seminary of America.

KANNENGIESSER, CHARLES (1983). *Athanase d'Alexandrie évêque et écrivain: une lecture des traités contre les Ariens*. Théologie historique 70. Paris: Beauchesne.

—— (1986). 'Athanasius of Alexandria vs. Arius: The Alexandrian Crisis', in Pearson and Goehring 1986: 204–15.

KEATING, DANIEL A. (2003). 'Divinization in Cyril: The Appropriation of Divine Life', in Thomas G. Weinandy and Daniel A. Keating (eds), *The Theology of St Cyril of Alexandria*. London and New York: T & T Clark.

—— (2004). *The Appropriation of Divine Life in Cyril of Alexandria*. Oxford Theological Monographs. Oxford: Oxford University Press.

KEIL, J. and PREMERSTEIN, A. von (1908), *Bericht über eine Reise in Lyiden und der Südlichen Aiolis*. Denkschriften der Wiener Akademie, phil.-hist. Klasse 53, 2 Abh. Vienna.

KELLY, J. N. D. (1977). *Early Christian Doctrines* (5th edn). London: Adam & Charles Black.

KENNEY, J. P. (1991). *Mystical Monotheism: A Study in Ancient Platonic Theology*. Hanover and London: Brown University Press.

KERR, FERGUS (1997), *Immortal Longings: Versions of Transcending Humanity*. London: SPCK.

KOLARCIK, MICHAEL (1991). *The Ambiguity of Death in the Book of Wisdom 1–6: A Study of Literary Structure and Interpretation*. Rome: Editrice Istituto Pontificio Biblico.

KOLP, A. L. (1982). 'Partakers of the Divine Nature: The Use of II Peter 1: 4 by Athanasius'. *StPat* 17: 1018–23.

KRAUSMÜLLER, DIRK (2001). 'Leontius of Jerusalem, a Theologian of the Seventh Century'. *JTS* n.s. 52: 637–57.

KRIVOCHEINE, ARCHBISHOP BASIL (1986). *In the Light of Christ: Saint Symeon the New Theologian (949–1022): Life—Spirituality—Doctrine*. Trans. A. P. Gythiel. Crestwood, NY: St Vladimir's Seminary Press.

KUYT, ANNELIES (1991). *Heavenly Journeys*. Leiden: E. J. Brill.

LAMBERT, R. (1984). *Beloved and God: The Story of Hadrian and Antinous*. London: Weidenfeld & Nicolson.

LANE FOX, ROBIN (1986). *Pagans and Christians*. New York and Harmondsworth: Viking.

LARCHET, JEAN-CLAUDE (1996). *La Divinisation de l'homme selon saint Maxime le Confesseur*. Cogitatio Fidei 194. Paris: Éditions du Cerf.

LATTEY, C. (1916). 'The Deification of Man in Clement of Alexandria: Some Further Notes'. *JTS* 17: 257–62.

LAWSON, JOHN (1948). *The Biblical Theology of Saint Irenaeus*. London: Epworth Press.

LAYTON, BENTLEY (1987). *The Gnostic Scriptures*. London: SCM Press.

LE BOULLUEC, A. (1987). 'L'École d'Alexandrie. De quelques aventures d'un concept historiographique', in *Alexandrina. Hellénisme, judaïsme et christianisme*. Paris: Éditions du Cerf, 403–17.

LEIPOLDT, JOHANNES (1923). *Sterbende und Auferstehende Götter*. Leipzig.

LEWY, H. (1929). *Sobria Ebrietas*. Giessen: A. Töpelmann.

LEYS, R. (1951). *L'Image de Dieu chez saint Grégoire de Nysse*. Museum Lessianum, section théologique 49. Brussels: L'Édition Universelle; Paris: Desclée De Brouwer.

LIESKE, ALOISIUS. (1938). *Die Theologie der Logosmystik bei Origenes*. Münsterische Beiträge zur Theologie 22. Münster: Aschendorff.

LIEU, JUDITH M. (1996). *Image and Reality: The Jews in the World of the Christians in the Second Century*. Edinburgh: T & T Clark.

LILLA, SALVATORE R. C. (1971). *Clement of Alexandria: A Study in Christian Platonism and Gnosticism*. Oxford: Oxford University Press.

LINFORTH, IVAN M. (1941). *The Arts of Orpheus*. Berkeley and Los Angeles, Calif.: University of California Press.

LLOYD, A. C. (1982). 'Participation and Procession', in H. J. BLUMENTHAL and A. C. LLOYD (eds), *Soul and the Structure of Being in Late Neoplatonism*. Liverpool: Liverpool University Press, 18–42.

—— (1990). *The Anatomy of Neoplatonism*. Oxford: Clarendon Press.

LOSSKY, VLADIMIR (1957). *The Mystical Theology of the Eastern Church*. London: James Clarke & Co.

—— (1963). *The Vision of God*. Trans. Ashleigh Moorhouse. Preface by John Meyendorff. Leighton Buzzard: Faith Press.

—— (1978). *Orthodox Theology: An Introduction*. Trans. Ian and Ihita Kesarcodi-Watson. Crestwood, NY: St Vladimir's Seminary Press.

LOT-BORODINE, MYRRHA (1932–3). 'La Doctrine de la "déification" dans l'Église grecque jusqu'au XIᵉ siècle', *Revue d'histoire des religions*. (Reprinted in Lot-Borodine 1970: 19–183.)

—— (1970). *La Déification de l'homme selon la doctrine des Pères grecs*. Preface by Cardinal Jean Daniélou. Paris: Éditions du Cerf.

LOUTH, ANDREW (1975). 'The Concept of the Soul in Athanasius, *Contra Gentes—De Incarnatione*'. *StPat* 13: 227–31.

—— (1981). *The Origins of the Christian Mystical Tradition*. Oxford: Clarendon Press.

—— (1983a). *Discerning the Mystery: An Essay on the Nature of Theology*. Oxford: Clarendon Press.

—— (1983*b*). 'Manhood into God: The Oxford Movement, the Fathers and the Deification of Man', in K. Leech and R. [D.] Williams (eds), *Essays Catholic and Radical*. London: Bowerdean Press, 70–80.

—— (1986). 'Pagan Theurgy and Christian Sacramentalism in Denys the Areopagite'. *JTS* n.s. 37: 432–8.

—— (1988). 'St Athanasius and the Greek *Life of Antony*'. *JTS* n.s. 39: 504–9.

—— (1989). *Denys the Areopagite*. London: Geoffrey Chapman.

—— (1997). Review of Hieromonk Alexander (Golitzin), *Et Introibo ad Altare Dei: The Mystagogy of Dionysius Areopagita, with Special Reference to Its Predecessors in the Eastern Tradition*. *JTS* n.s. 48: 712–14.

—— (2002). *St John Damascene: Tradition and Originality in Byzantine Theology*. Oxford Early Christian Studies. Oxford: Oxford University Press.

MacCormack, Sabine G. (1981). *Art and Ceremony in Late Antiquity*. The Transformation of the Classical Heritage I. Berkeley, Calif.: University of California Press.

McFague, Sallie (1983). *Metaphorical Theology: Models of God in Religious Language*. London: SCM Press.

McGuckin, John (1986). *The Transfiguration of Christ in Scripture and Tradition*. Studies in the Bible and Early Christianity 9. Lewiston and Queenston: Edwin Mellen Press.

—— (2001). *Saint Gregory of Nazianzus: An Intellectual Biography*. Crestwood, NY: St Vladimir's Seminary Press.

Madden, Nicholas (1982). 'The Commentary on the Pater Noster: An Example of the Structural Methodology of Maximus the Confessor', in Heinzer and Schönborn 1982: 147–55.

Magie, D. (1950). *Roman Rule in Asia Minor*. Princeton, NJ: Princeton University Press.

Mahé, J.–P. (1982). *Hermès en Haute-Égypte*, vol. ii: *Le fragment du Discours Parfait et les Définitions hermétiques arméniennes*. Bibliothèque copte de Nag Hammadi, 'textes' 7. Quebec: Université Laval.

—— (1991). 'La Voie d'immortalité à la lumière des *Hermetica* de Nag Hammadi et de decouvertes plus récentes', *VigChr* 45: 347–75.

Malherbe, Abraham J. (1989). *Paul and the Popular Philosophers*. Minneapolis, Minn.: Fortress Press.

Mantzaridis, Georgios I. (1984). *The Deification of Man: St Gregory Palamas and the Orthodox Tradition*. Trans. Liadain Sherrard with a foreword by Bishop Kallistos of Diokleia. Crestwood, NY: St Vladimir's Seminary Press. (First published in Greek in 1963.)

Marcovich, M. (1967). *Heraclitus*. Merida, Venezuela: Los Andes University Press.

Marsh, H. G. (1936). 'The Use of *Mystêrion* in the Writings of Clement of Alexandria with Special Reference to his Sacramental Doctrine'. *JTS* 37: 64–80.

Martin, Annick (1996). *Athanase d'Alexandrie et l'Église d'Égypte au IVe siècle (328–373)*. Collection de l'École Française de Rome 216. Rome: École Française de Rome.

Martin, Luther H. (1987). *Hellenistic Religions: An Introduction*. New York and Oxford: Oxford University Press.

Mascall, E. L. (1946). *Christ, the Christian and the Church: A Study of the Incarnation and its Consequences*. London: Longmans.

—— (1959). *The Importance of Being Human: Some Aspects of the Christian Doctrine of Man*. London: Oxford University Press.

—— (1971). *The Openness of Being: Natural Theology Today*. The Gifford Lectures in the University of Edinburgh 1970–1. London: Darton, Longman & Todd.

MAYER, A. (1942). *Das Gottesbild im Menschen nach Clemens von Alexandrien*. Studia Anselmiana 15. Rome: Herder.

MAZZANTI, ANGELA MARIA (1998). *Gli uomini dèi mortali. Una rilettura del Corpus Hermeticum*. Origini, Nuova Serie 2. Bologna: Edizioni Dehoniane.

MEEKS, WAYNE A. (1967). *The Prophet-King: Moses Traditions and the Johannine Christology*. Leiden: E. J. Brill.

—— (1968). 'Moses as God and King', *Studies in the History of Religions* 14: 354–71.

—— (1983). *The First Urban Christians: The Social World of the Apostle Paul*. New Haven and London: Yale University Press.

MÉHAT, A. (1966). *Études sur les 'Stromateis' de Clément d'Alexandrie*. Patristica Sorboniensia 7. Paris: Éditions du Seuil.

MEIJERING, E. P. (1974). *Orthodoxy and Platonism in Athanasius: Synthesis or Antithesis?* (2nd edn). Leiden: E. J. Brill.

MEREDITH, ANTHONY (1999). *Gregory of Nyssa*. London: Routledge.

MERKI, H. (1952). Ὁμοίωσις θεῷ. *Von der platonischen Angleichung an Gott zur Gottähnlichkeit bei Gregor von Nyssa*. Fribourg: Paulusverlag.

MEUNIER, BERNARD (1997). *Le Christ de Cyrille d'Alexandrie. L'humanité, le salut et la question monophysite*. Théologie historique 104. Paris: Beauchesne.

MEYENDORFF, JOHN (1959*a*). *Introduction à l'étude de Grégoire Palamas*. Patristica Sorbonensia 3. Paris: Éditions du Seuil.

—— (1959*b*). *St Grégoire Palamas et la mystique orthodoxe*. Maitres spirituels. Paris: Éditions du Seuil.

—— (1975). *Christ in East Christian Thought*. Crestwood, NY: St Vladimir's Seminary Press.

—— (1981). *Byzantium and the Rise of Russia: A Study of Byzantino-Russian Relations in the Fourteenth Century*. Cambridge: Cambridge University Press.

—— (1989). *Imperial Unity and Christian Divisions: The Church 450–680 AD*. Crestwood, NY: St Vladimir's Seminary Press.

MIGLIORINI FISSI, ROSETTA (1982). 'La nozione di *deificatio* nel *Paradiso*'. *Letture classensi* 9/10: 39–72.

MILLAR, FERGUS (1973). 'The Imperial Cult and the Persecutions', in Den Boer 1973: 143–75.

—— (1992). *The Emperor in the Roman World* (2nd edn). London: Duckworth.

MOFFAT, JAMES (1924). *A Critical and Exegetical Commentary on the Epistle to the Hebrews*. ICC. Edinburgh: T & T Clark.

MONDÉSERT, CLAUDE (1944). *Clément d'Alexandrie. Introduction à l'étude de sa pensée religieuse à partir de l'écriture*. Paris: Aubier.

MOORE, G. F. (1927). *Judaism in the First Centuries of the Christian Era: The Age of the Tannaim*. 3 vols. Cambridge, Mass.: Harvard University Press.

MORENZ, SIEGFRIED (1973). *Egyptian Religion*. Trans. Ann E. Keep. London: Methuen.

MORESCHINI, CLAUDIO (1997). *Filosofia e letteratura in Gregorio di Nazianzo*. Collana Platonismo e filosofia patristica. Studi e testi 12. Milan: Vita e Pensiero.

MORRAY-JONES, C. R. A. (1992). 'Transformational Mysticism in the Apocalyptic-Merkabah Tradition'. *Journal of Jewish Studies* 43: 1–31.

MORTLEY, R. (1973). *Connaissance religieuse et herméneutique chez Clément d'Alexandrie*. Leiden: E. J. Brill.

MOUTSOULAS, ELIAS D. (2000). *The Incarnation of the Word and the Theosis of Man according to the Teaching of Gregory of Nyssa*. Trans. Constantine J. Andrews. Athens: n.p.

MOWINCKEL, S. (1967). *The Psalms in Israel's Worship*. 2 vols. Oxford: Basil Blackwell.

MULLEN, E. T. (1980). *The Assembly of the Gods*. Harvard Semitic Monographs 24. Chico, Calif.: Scholars Press.

MURPHY-O'CONNOR, JEROME (1996). *Paul: A Critical Life*. Oxford: Clarendon Press.

MURRAY, ROBERT (1975). *Symbols of Church and Kingdom: A Study in Early Syrian Tradition*. Cambridge: Cambridge University Press.

MUSURILLO, HERBERT (1961). *From Glory to Glory: Texts from Gregory of Nyssa's Mystical Writings*. New York, NY: Charles Scribner's Sons. (Repr. 1979.)

—— (1972). *The Acts of the Christian Martyrs*. Oxford: Oxford University Press.

MYLONAS, G. E. (1961). *Eleusis and the Eleusinian Mysteries*. Princeton and London: Princeton University Press.

NELLAS, PANAYIOTIS (1987). *Deification in Christ: Orthodox Perspectives on the Nature of the Human Person*. Contemporary Greek Theologians 5. Trans. Norman Russell with a foreword by Bishop Kallistos of Diokleia. Crestwood, NY: St Vladimir's Seminary Press. (First published in Greek in 1979.)

NEMESHEGYI, P. (1960). *La Paternité de Dieu chez Origène*. Tournai: Desclée.

NEWMAN, J. H. (1881). *Select Treatises of St Athanasius in Controversy with the Arians*. 2 vols. London: Pickering.

NIARCHOS, K. (1985). 'The Concept of "Participation" according to Proclus, with reference to the Criticism of Nicolaus of Methone', *Diotima* 13: 78–94.

NICKELSBURG, GEORGE W. E. (1972). *Resurrection, Immortality and Eternal Life in Intertestamental Judaism*. Cambridge, Mass.: Harvard University Press.

NIKIPROWETZKY, V. (1977). *Le Commentaire d'Écriture chez Philon d'Alexandrie: son caractère et sa portée, observations philologiques*. Leiden: E. J. Brill.

NILSSON, M. P. (1925). *A History of Greek Religion*. Oxford: Oxford University Press.

—— (1935). 'Early Orphism and Kindred Religious Movements'. *HTR* 28: 181–230.

—— (1948). *Greek Piety*. Oxford: Oxford University Press.

—— (1953). 'The Bacchic Mysteries of the Roman Age'. *HTR*: 46: 175–202.

NOCK, A. D. (1928). 'Notes on the Ruler-Cult I–IV'. *JHS* 48: 21–43 (= *Essays*, 134–59).

—— (1930). 'Synnaos theos'. *Harvard Studies in Classical Philology* 41: 1–62 (= *Essays*, 202–51).

—— (1931). 'The Lizard in Magic and Religion'. *Proceedings of the British Academy* 17: 235–87 (= *Essays* 271–6).

—— (1944). 'The Cult of Heroes'. *HTR* 38: 141–7 (= *Essays*, 575–602).

—— (1957). 'Deification and Julian'. *JRS* 47: 114–23 (= *Essays*, 832–46).

—— (1964). *Early Gentile Christianity and its Hellenistic Background*. New York: Harper & Row (= *Essays*, 49–133).

—— (1972). *Essays on Religion and the Ancient World* (ed. Z. Stewart). Oxford: Oxford University Press.

NOEL, VIRGINIA L. (1992). 'Nourishment in Origen's *On Prayer*', in Robert J. Daly (ed.), *Origeniana Quinta*. Louvain: Peeters, 481–7.

NORMAN, K. E. (1980). 'Deification: The Content of Athanasian Soteriology'. Ph.D. thesis. Duke University.

OBOLENSKY, DIMITRI (1971). *The Byzantine Commonwealth 500–1453*. London: Weidenfeld & Nicolson.

O'CONNELL, ROBERT J. (1968). *St Augustine's Early Theory of Man, AD 386–391*. Cambridge, Mass.: Harvard University Press.

ODEBERG, HUGO (1928). *3 Enoch, or The Hebrew Book of Enoch*. Cambridge: Cambridge University Press.

ORPHANOS, MARKOS (1974). *Ἡ ψυχὴ καὶ τὸ σῶμα τοῦ ἀνθρώπου κατὰ Δίδυμον Ἀλεξανδρέα (τὸν Τυφλόν)*. Thessalonica: Patriarchikon Idruma Paterikon Meleton.

OROZ RETA, JOSÉ (1993). 'De l'illumination à la déification de l'âme selon saint Augustin'. *St Pat* 27: 364–82.

OSBORN, ERIC (1957). *The Philosophy of Clement of Alexandria*. Cambridge: Cambridge University Press.

—— (1973). *Justin Martyr*. Tübingen: J. C. B. Mohr (Paul Siebeck).

—— (1981). *The Beginning of Christian Philosophy*. Cambridge: Cambridge University Press.

—— (1997). *The Beginning of Christian Theology*. Cambridge: Cambridge University Press.

—— (2001). *Irenaeus of Lyons*. Cambridge: Cambridge University Press.

OSBORNE, CATHERINE (1987). *Rethinking Early Greek Philosophy*. London: Duckworth.

OTIS, BROOKS (1958). 'Cappadocian Thought as a Coherent System', *DOP* 12: 95–124.

PAGELS, ELAINE (1973). *The Johannine Gospel in Gnostic Exegesis: Heracleon's Commentary on John*. SBL Monograph Series 17. Nashville and New York: Abingdon Press.

—— (1975). *The Gnostic Paul: Gnostic Exegesis of the Pauline Letters*. Philadelphia: Trinity Press International (repr. 1992).

—— (1979). *The Gnostic Gospels*. New York, NY: Random House. (Page references are to the Penguin edition of 1990.)

PANAGIOTOU, S. (1984). 'Empedocles on His Own Divinity'. *Mnemosyne* 36: 276–85.

PANNENBERG, WOLFHART (1985). *Anthropology in Theological Perspective*. Trans. Matthew J. O'Connell. Edinburgh: T & T Clark.

PAPADOPOULOU-TSANANA, O. (1970). *Ἡ ἀνθρωπολογία τοῦ Μεγάλου Βασιλείου*. Thessalonica: Patriarchikon Idruma Paterikon Meleton.

PAPOULIDES, K. K. (1977). *Οἱ Ρῶσοι ὀνοματολάτραι τοῦ Ἁγίου Ὄρους*. Thessalonica: Institute for Balkan Studies.

PATTERSON, L. G. (1997*a*). 'The Divine Became Human: Irenaean Themes in Clement of Alexandria'. *StPat* 31: 497–516.

—— (1997*b*). *Methodius of Olympus: Divine Sovereignty, Human Freedom, and Life in Christ*. Washington: Catholic University of America Press.

372   *Bibliography*

PEARSON, BIRGER A. (1986). 'Earliest Christianity in Egypt: Some Observations', in Pearson and Goehring 1986: 132–59.

—— (1990). *Gnosticism, Judaism, and Egyptian Christianity*. Studies in Antiquity and Christianity. Minneapolis, Minn.: Fortress Press.

PEARSON, BIRGER A. and GOEHRING, JAMES E. (1986). *The Roots of Egyptian Christianity*. Studies in Antiquity and Christianity. Philadelphia, Pa.: Fortress Press.

PERCZEL, ISTVÁN (1999). 'Le Pseudo-Denys, lecteur d'Origène', in W. A. Bienert and U. Kühnweg (eds), *Origeniana Septima*. Louvain: Peeters, 673–710.

—— (2001). ' "Théologiens" et "magiciens" dans le *Corpus dionysien*'. *Adamantius* 7: 54–75.

PERL, E. D. (1994). 'Hierarchy and Participation in Dionysius the Areopagite and Greek Neoplatonism', *American Catholic Philosophical Quarterly* 68/1: 15–30.

PETTERSEN, ALVYN (1995). *Athanasius*. Oustanding Christian Thinkers Series. London: Geoffrey Chapman.

PINGGÉRA, K. (2002). *All-Erlösung und All-Einheit. Studien zum 'Buch des heiligen Hierotheos' und seiner Rezeption in der syrisch-orthodoxen Theologie*. Wiesbaden: Reichert.

PODSKALSKY, GERHARD (1988). *Griechische Theologie in der Zeit der Türkenherrschaft 1453–1821*. Munich: C. H. Beck.

POLYZOGOPOULOS, THEODORITUS (1985). *The Anthropology of Diadochus of Photice*. Athens: Offprint from *Theologia* 55 (1984) 772–800, 1071–1101; 56 (1985) 174–221.

POPOV, I. V. (1906). 'Ideia obozhenia v drevne-vostochnoi tserkvi'. *Voprosy filosofii i psikhologii* 97: 165–213.

PREISS, TH. (1938). 'La Mystique de l'initiation et de d'unité chez Ignace d'Antioche'. *Revue d'histoire et de philosophie religieuses* 18: 197–241.

PREUSS, K. F. A. (1894). *Ad Maximi Confessoris de Deo hominisque deificatione doctrinam adnotationum pars I*. Schneeberg: C. M. Gärtner.

PRICE, S. R. F. (1980). 'Between Man and God: Sacrifice in the Roman Imperial Cult'. *JRS* 70: 28–43.

—— (1984a). 'Gods and Emperors: The Greek Language of the Roman Imperial Cult'. *JHS* 104: 79–95.

—— (1984b). *Rituals and Power: The Roman Imperial Cult in Asia Minor*. Cambridge: Cambridge University Press.

PROCTER, EVERETT (1995). *Christian Controversy in Alexandria: Clement's Polemic against the Basilideans and Valentinians*. American University Studies, Series VII, no. Vol. 172. New York: Peter Lang.

RAD, G. VON (1972). *Genesis*. London: SCM Press.

RADIN, M. (1916). 'Apotheosis', *CR* 30: 44–6.

RAHNER, K. (1961). *Theological Investigations*. vol. i: *God, Christ, Mary and Grace*. Trans. Cornelius Ernst, OP. London: Darton, Longman & Todd; New York: Seabury Press.

RAHNER, K. and VORGRIMLER, H. (1965). *Concise Theological Dictionary*. Ed. Cornelius Ernst, OP. Trans. Richard Strachan. Freiburg: Herder; London: Burns & Oates.

RAVEN, CHARLES E. (1923). *Apollinarianism: An Essay on the Christology of the Early Church*. Cambridge: Cambridge University Press.

REESE, J. M. (1970). *Hellenistic Influences on the Book of Wisdom and its Consequences*. Rome: Pontificio Istituto Biblico.

REGNAULT, L. (1971). 'Irénée de Lyons'. *DS* vii: 1938–69.

RIORDAN, WILLIAM (1991). 'Divinization in Denys the Areopagite'. Doctoral thesis. Rome: Pontificia Studiorum Universitas a S. Thoma Aq. in Urbe.

RIST, J. M. (1962). 'Theos and the One in Some Texts of Plotinus'. *Medieval Studies* 24: 169–80.

—— (1964*a*). 'Mysticism and Transcendence in Later Neoplatonism'. *Hermes* 92: 213–25.

—— (1964*b*). *Eros and Psyche: Studies in Plato, Plotinus and Origen.* Toronto: University of Toronto Press.

—— (1967*a*). 'Integration and the Undescended Soul in Plotinus'. *American Journal of Philosophy* 88: 410–22.

—— (1967*b*). *Plotinus: The Road to Reality.* Cambridge: Cambridge University Press.

—— (1981). 'Basil's "Neoplatonism": Its Background and Nature', in Fedwick 1981: 139–222.

—— (1994). *Augustine: Ancient Thought Baptized.* Cambridge: Cambridge University Press.

RITSCHL, D. (1959). 'Hippolytus' Conception of Deification'. *SJT* 12: 388–99.

RIUS-CAMPS, J. (1968, 1970*a*, 1972). 'Comunicabilidad de la naturaleza de Dios segun Origenes'. *OCP* 34: 5–37; 36: 201–47; 38: 430–53.

—— (1970*b*). *El dinamismo trinitario en la divinizacion de los seres racionales segun Origenes.* OCA 188. Rome: Pontificium Institutum Orientalium Studiorum.

ROBERTS, C. H. (1979). *Manuscript, Society and Belief in Early Christian Egypt.* The Schweich Lectures 1977. London: Oxford University Press for the British Academy.

ROBERTSON, ARCHIBALD and PLUMMER, ALFRED (1914). *A Critical and Exegetical Commentary on the First Epistle of St Paul to the Corinthians* (2nd edn). ICC. Edinburgh: T & T Clark.

ROBINSON, JAMES M. (ed.) (1988). *The Nag Hammadi Library in English* (rev. edn). Leiden: E. J. Brill.

ROGERSON, J. W. (1970). 'The Hebrew Conception of Corporate Personality: A Re-Examination'. *JTS* n.s. 21: 1–16.

ROLDANUS, J. (1968). *Le Christ et l'homme dans la théologie d'Athanase d'Alexandrie.* Leiden: E. J. Brill.

ROREM, PAUL (1993). *Pseudo-Dionysius: A Commentary on the Texts and an Introduction to Their Influence.* New York and Oxford: Oxford University Press.

ROUSSEAU, PHILIP (1994). *Basil of Caesarea.* Berkeley, Calif.: University of California Press.

—— (1999). *Pachomius: The Making of a Community in Fourth-Century Egypt.* Berkeley, Los Angeles, and London: University of California Press.

ROWLAND, CHRISTOPHER (1982). *The Open Heaven: A Study of Apocalyptic in Judaism and Early Christianity.* London: SPCK.

RUDOLPH, KURT (1987). *Gnosis: The Nature and History of Gnosticism.* Trans. R. McL. Wilson. San Francisco, Calif.: Harper & Row.

RUETHER, ROSEMARY R. (1969). *Gregory of Nazianzus: Rhetor and Philosopher.* Oxford: Oxford University Press.

RUNIA, DAVID T. (1988). 'God and Man in Philo of Alexandria'. *JTS* n.s. 39: 48–75.

—— (1990). *Exegesis and Philosophy: Studies on Philo of Alexandria*. Aldershot: Variorum.

—— (1993). *Philo in Early Christian Literature: A Survey*. Compendia Rerum Iudaicarum ad Novum Testamentum 3. Assen and Minneapolis: Van Gorcum and Fortress Press.

RUSSELL, D. S. (1964). *The Method and Message of Jewish Apocalyptic*. London: SCM Press.

RUSSELL, NORMAN (1988). ' "Partakers of the Divine Nature" (2 Peter 1: 4) in the Byzantine Tradition', in J. Chrysostomides (ed.), *Kathegetria: Essays presented to Joan Hussey on her 80th Birthday*. Camberley: Porphyrogenitus, 51–67.

—— (2003). 'Palamism and the Circle of Demetrius Cydones', in Ch. Dendrinos, J. Harris, E. Harvalia-Crook, and J. Herrin, (eds), *Porphyrogenita: Essays in Honour of Julian Chrysostomides*. Aldershot and Burlington, Vt.: Ashgate, 153–74.

—— (2004*a*). 'Prochoros Cydones and the Definition of Orthodoxy', in A. Louth (ed.), *Byzantine Orthodoxies?* Aldershot: Ashgate.

—— (2004*b*). 'Theophilus and Cyril of Alexandria on the Divine Image: A Consistent Episcopal Policy towards the Origenism of the Desert?' in L. Perrone (ed.), *Origeniana Octava*. Louvain: Peeters, 939–46.

SACCHI, PAOLO (1994). *Storia del Secondo Tempio. Israele tra VI secolo a.C. e I secolo d.C.* Turin: Società Editrice Internazionale.

SANDERS, E. P. (1977). *Paul and Palestinian Judaism: A Comparison of Patterns of Religion*. London: SCM Press.

—— (1991). *Paul*. Oxford: Oxford University Press.

SAVVIDIS, KYRIAKOS (1997). *Die Lehre von der Vergöttlichung des Menschen bei Maximos dem Bekenner und ihre Rezeption durch Gregor Palamas*. Veröffentlichungen des Instituts für Orthodoxe Theologie 5. St Ottilien: EOS Verlag.

SCHÄFER, PETER (1981). *Synopse zur Hekhalot-Literatur*. Tübingen: J. C. B. Mohr (Paul Siebeck).

—— (1986). 'The Aim and Purpose of Early Jewish Mysticism', 12th Sacks Lecture, Oxford. (Reprinted in *Hekhalot-Studien*: 277–95.)

—— (1988). *Hekhalot-Studien*, Texte und Studien zum antiken Judentum 19. Tübingen: J. C. B. Mohr (Paul Siebeck).

—— (1992). *The Hidden and Manifest God: Some Major Themes in Early Jewish Mysticism*. Trans. Aubrey Pomerance. New York, NY: State University of New York Press.

SCHANZ, M. and HOSIUS, C. (1935). *Geschichte der Römischen Literatur bis zum Gesetzgebungswerk des Kaisers Justinian*. Munich: C. H. Beck.

SCHLIER, H. (1929). *Religionsgeschichtliche Untersuchungen zu den Ignatiusbriefen*. Beihefte zur *ZNTW* 8. Giessen.

SCHNURR, G. M. (1969). 'On the Logic of the Ante-Nicene Affirmations of the Deification of the Christian'. *Anglican Theological Review* 51: 97–105.

SCHOEDEL, WILLIAM R. (1985). *Ignatius of Antioch: A Commentary on the Letters of Ignatius of Antioch*. Philadelphia: Fortress Press.

SCHOLEM, GERSHOM (1955). *Major Trends in Jewish Mysticism* (3rd edn). London: Thames & Hudson.

—— (1960). *Jewish Gnosticism, Merkabah Mysticism and Talmudic Tradition*. New York, NY: Jewish Theological Seminary of America (repr. 1965).

SCHÜRER, E., VERMES, G., MILLAR F. and GOODMAN, M. (1979–86). *The History of the Jewish People in the Age of Jesus Christ*. 3 vols. Edinburgh: T & T Clark.

SCHWEITZER, ALBERT (1957). *The Mysticism of Paul the Apostle*. (1931). Trans. W. Montgomery. London: Adam and Charles Black.

SCHWÖBEL, CHRISTOPH (1991). 'Human Being as Relational Being: Twelve Theses for a Christian Anthropology', in Schwöbel and Gunton 1991: 141–70.

SCHWÖBEL, CHRISTOPH and GUNTON, COLIN E. (eds) (1991). *Persons Divine and Human: Kings College Essays in Theological Anthropology*. Edinburgh: T & T Clark.

SCOTT, ALAN (1991). *Origen and the Life of the Stars: A History of an Idea*. Oxford: Clarendon Press.

SCOTT, JAMES M. (1992). *Adoption as Sons of God: An Exegetical Investigation into the Background of υἱοθεσία in the Pauline Corpus*. Tübingen: J. C. B. Mohr (Paul Siebeck).

—— (1997). 'Throne-Chariot Mysticism in Qumran and in Paul', in EVANS and FLINT (1997).

SCOTT, K. (1928). 'The Deification of Demetrius Poliorcetes'. *American Journal of Philology* 49: 137–66, 217–39.

—— (1929). 'Plutarch and the Ruler-Cult'. *Transactions and Proceedings of the American Philological Association* 60: 117–35.

—— (1932). 'Humour at the Expense of the Ruler-Cult'. *Classical Philology* 27: 317–28.

—— (1936). *The Imperial Cult under the Flavians*. Stuttgart and Berlin: W. Kohlhammer.

SCURAT, K. E. (1973). 'The Doctrine of Saint Athanasius the Great on Deification' (in Russian). *Review of the Patriarchate of Moscow* 5: 61–4 and 8: 63–8. Romanian trans. in *Mitropolia Olteniei* 26 (1974): 938–44 (inaccessible to me).

SEGAL, ALAN F. (1977). *Two Powers in Heaven: Early Rabbinic Reports about Christianity and Gnosticism*. Leiden: E. J. Brill.

—— (1995). 'Paul and the Beginning of Jewish Mysticism', in Collins and Fishbane 1995: 95–122.

SHERRARD, PHILIP (1992). *Greek East and Latin West* (2nd edn). Athens: Denise Harvey.

SHERWOOD, POLYCARP (1952). *An Annotated Date-List of the Works of Maximus the Confessor*. Studia Anselmiana 30. Rome: Orbis Catholicus, Herder.

—— (1955). *The Earlier Ambigua of St Maximus the Confessor*. Studia Anselmiana 36. Rome: Orbis Catholicus, Herder.

SHOTWELL, W. A. (1965). *The Biblical Exegesis of Justin Martyr*. London: SPCK.

SIMONETTI, MANLIO (1994). *Biblical Interpretation in the Early Church: An Historical Introducton to Patristic Exegesis*. Trans. John A. Hughes. Edinburgh: T & T Clark.

SIORVANES, LUCAS (1996). *Proclus: Neo-Platonic Philosophy and Science*. Edinburgh: Edinburgh University Press.

—— (1998). 'Proclus on Transcendence'. *Documenti e studi sulla tradizione filosofica medievale* 9: 1–19.

SKARSAUNE, OSKAR (1987). *The Proof from Prophecy: A Study in Justin Martyr's Proof-Text Tradition: Text-Type, Provenance, Theological Profile*. Supplements to *Novum Testamentum* 56. Leiden: E. J. Brill.

SKEMP, J. B. (1973). 'Plato's Concept of Deity'. *Zetesis* (E. de Strycker Festschrift). Antwerp: Nederlandsche Boekhandel, 115–21.

SMITH, MORTON (1958). 'The Image of God: Notes on the Hellenization of Judaism, with Especial Reference to Goodenough's Work on Jewish Symbols'. *BJRL* 40: 473–512.

—— (1981). 'Ascent to the Heavens and the Beginning of Christianity'. *Eranos-Jahrbuch* 50: 403–29.

—— (1990). 'Ascent to the Heavens and Deification in 4QM^a', in Lawrence H. Schiffmann (ed.), *Archaeology and History in the Dead Sea Scrolls*. Sheffield: Sheffield Academic Press.

SOPHRONY (SAKHAROV), ARCHIMANDRITE (1988). *We Shall See Him as He Is*. Trans. Rosemary Edmonds. Tolleshunt Knights: Stavropegic Monastery of St John the Baptist.

SOSKICE, JANET MARTIN (1985). *Metaphor and Religious Language*. Oxford: Clarendon Press.

SPARKS, H. F. D. (ed.) (1984). *The Apocryphal Old Testament*. Oxford: Oxford University Press.

SPITERIS, YANNIS (1992). *La teologia ortodossa neo-greca*. Bologna: Edizioni Dehoniane.

—— (1996). *Palamas: la grazia e l'esperanza. Gregorio Palamas nella discussione teologica*. Rome: Lipa Edizioni.

STĂNILOAE, D. (1974). 'La Doctrine de saint Athanase sur le salut', in C. Kannengiesser (ed.), *Politique et théologie chez Athanase d'Alexandrie*. Théologie Historique 27. Paris: Beauchesne.

—— (1981). 'The Procession of the Holy Spirit from the Father and His Relation to the Son, as the Basis of our Deification and Adoption', in L. Visscher (ed.), *Spirit of God, Spirit of Christ: Ecumenical Reflections on the Filioque Controversy*. Faith and Order Paper 103. London: SPCK; Geneva: WCC.

STARR, JAMES M. (2000). *Sharers in Divine Nature: 2 Peter 1: 4 in its Hellenistic Context*. Coniectanea Biblica New Testament Series 33. Stockholm: Almqvist & Wiksell International.

STEAD, G. C. (1981). 'Individual Personality in Origen and the Cappadocian Fathers', in U. Bianchi and H. Crouzel (eds), *Arche e Telos*. Milan: Vita e Pensiero.

—— (1985). Review of C. Kannengiesser, *Athanase d'Alexandrie évêque et écrivain*. *JTS* n.s. 36: 220–9.

STEEL, C. G. (1978). *The Changing Self: A Study of the Soul in Later Neoplatonism: Iamblichus, Damascius and Priscus*. Brussels: Koninklijke Academie voor Wetenschappen, Letteren en Schone Kunsten van België.

STEWART, COLUMBA (1991). *'Working the Earth of the Heart': The Messalian Controversy in History, Texts, and Language to A.D. 431*. Oxford Theological Monographs. Oxford: Oxford University Press.

STOOP, J. A. A. (1952). 'Die deificatio Hominis in die Sermones en Epistulae van Augustinus'. Ph.D. thesis. University of Leiden.

STRÄTER, H. (1894). *Die Erlösungslehre des hl. Athanasius*. Freiburg im Breisgau: Herder.

STRANGE, C. R. (1985). 'Athanasius on Deification'. *StPat* 16: 342–6.

STROUMSA, GUY G. (1995). 'Mystical Descents', in Collins and Fishbane 1995: 139–54. (Reprinted in Stroumsa 1996: 169–83.)

—— (1996). *Hidden Wisdom: Esoteric Traditions and the Roots of Christian Mysticism.* Studies in the History of Religions 70. Leiden: E. J. Brill.

SWARTLEY, WILLARD M. (1973). 'The Imitatio Christi in the Ignatian Letters'. *VigChr* 27: 81–103.

TELFER, W. (1952). 'Episcopal Succession in Egypt'. *JEH* 3: 1–12.

THÉODORIDÈS, ARISTIDE (1982). 'De l'assimilation à la divinité dans la sagesse de l'ancienne Égypt', in Julien Ries *et al.* (eds), *Gnosticisme et monde hellénistique.* Actes du Colloque de Louvain-la-Neuve (11–14 mars 1980). Louvain-la-Neuve: Université Catholique de Louvain, Institut Orientaliste, 26–37.

THEODOROU, A. (1956). *Ἡ περὶ θεώσεως τοῦ ἀνθρώπου διδασκαλία τῶν Ἑλλήνων πατέρων τῆς Ἐκκλησίας μέχρις Ἰωάννου τοῦ Δαμασκηνοῦ.* Athens: n.p.

THUNBERG, LARS (1985). *Man and the Cosmos: The Vision of St Maximus the Confessor.* Crestwood, NY: St Vladimir's Seminary Press.

—— (1995). *Microcosm and Mediator: The Theological Anthropology of Maximus the Confessor* (2nd edn). Chicago and La Salle, Ill.: Open Court.

TIEDE, DAVID L. (1972). *The Charismatic Figure as Miracle Worker.* SBL Dissertation Series 1. Missoula, Mont.: Society of Biblical Literature.

TIGCHELER, JO (1977). *Didyme l'Aveugle et l'exégèse allegorique.* Nijmegen: Dekker & Van der Vegt.

TINSLEY, E. J. (1957). 'The Imitatio Christi in the Mysticism of St Ignatius of Antioch'. *StPat* 2: 553–60.

TIXERONT, JOSEPH (1910–16). *History of Dogmas.* Trans. H. L. B. 3 vols. St Louis, Mo.: Herder.

TOLLINTON, R. B. (1914). *Clement of Alexandria: A Study in Christian Liberalism.* 2 vols. London: William & Norgate.

TORJESEN, KAREN JO (1986). *Hermeneutical Procedure and Theological Method in Origen's Exegesis.* Patristische Texte und Studien 28. Berlin and New York: Walter de Gruyter.

TORRANCE, THOMAS F. (1995). *Divine Meaning: Studies in Patristic Hermeneutics.* Edinburgh: T & T Clark.

TOYNBEE, J. M. C. (1971). *Death and Burial in the Roman World.* London: Thames & Hudson.

TREMBELAS, P. (1959–61). *Δογματικὴ τῆς Ὀρθοδόξου Καθολικῆς Ἐκκλησίας.* 3 vols. Athens: Adelphotês Theologôn 'Ho Sôtêr'.

TREVETT, CHRISTINE (1992). *A Study of Ignatius of Antioch in Syria and Asia.* Studies in the Bible and Early Christianity 29. Lewiston, Queenston, and Lampeter: Edwin Mellen Press.

TRIGG, JOSEPH W. (1983). *Origen: The Bible and Philosophy in the Third-Century Church.* Atlanta: John Knox Press. (British edn London: SCM Press, 1985.)

—— (1998). *Origen.* London and New York: Routledge.

TURNER, H. E. W. (1952). *The Patristic Doctrine of Redemption: A Study of the Development of Doctrine during the First Five Centuries.* London: A. R. Mowbray.

TURNER, JOHN D. (1980). 'The Gnostic Threefold Path to Enlightenment', *Novum Testamentum* 22: 325–51.

VAN DEN HOEK, ANNEWIES (1988). *Clement of Alexandria and His Use of Philo in the Stromateis.* Leiden: E. J. Brill.

VanderKam, James C. (1984). *Enoch and the Growth of an Apocalyptic Tradition*. Washington: Catholic Biblical Association of America.

—— (1996). 'I Enoch, Enoch Motifs, and Enoch in Early Christian Literature', in VanderKam and Adler 1996: 33–101.

VanderKam, James C. and Adler, William (eds) (1996). *The Jewish Apocalyptic Heritage in Early Christianity*. Compendia Rerum Iudaicarum ad Novum Testamentum 4. Assen: Van Gorcum; Minneapolis: Fortress Press.

Vermaseren, M. J. (1976). *Liber in Deum: l'apoteosi di un iniziato Dionisiaco*. Leiden: E. J. Brill.

Vermes, Geza (1995). *The Dead Sea Scrolls in English* (4th edn). Harmondsworth: Penguin.

Veyne, Paul (ed.) (1987). *A History of Private Life*, vol. i: *From Pagan Rome to Byzantium*. Trans. A. Goldhammer. Cambridge, Mass.: Harvard University Press.

Völker, Walther (1931). *Das Vollkommenheitsideal des Origenes: eine Untersuchung zur Geschichte der Frömmigkeit und zu den Anfängen christlicher Mystik*. Beiträge zur historischen Theologie 7. Tübingen: J. C. B. Mohr (Paul Siebeck).

—— (1952). *Der wahre Gnostiker nach Clemens Alexandrinus*. TU 57. Berlin and Leipzig: Akademie-Verlag and J. C. Hinrichs.

—— (1955). *Gregor von Nyssa als Mysiker*. Wiesbaden: Franz Steiner Verlag.

—— (1958). *Kontemplation und Ekstase bei Pseudo-Dionysius Areopagita*. Wiesbaden: Franz Steiner Verlag.

—— (1965). *Maximus Confessor als Meister des geistlichen Lebens*. Wiesbaden: Franz Steiner Verlag.

—— (1968). *Scala Paradisi. Eine Studie zu Johannes Climacus und zugleich eine Vorstudie zum Symeon dem neuen Theologen*. Wiesbaden: Franz Steiner Verlag.

—— (1974). *Praxis und Theoria bei Symeon dem neuen Theologen*. Wiesbaden: Franz Steiner Verlag.

—— (1977). *Die Sakramentsmystik des Nikolaus Kabasilas*. Wiesbaden: Franz Steiner Verlag.

Waelkens, M. (1983). 'Privatdeifikation in Kleinasien und in der griechischrömischen Welt: zu einer neuen Grabinschrift aus Phrygien', in R. Donceel and R. Lebrun (eds), *Archéologie et religions de l'Anatolie ancienne. Mélanges en l'honneur du professeur Paul Naster*. Louvain-la-Neuve: Centre d'histoire des religions, 259–307.

Wahba, Matthias F. (1988). *The Doctrine of Sanctification in St Athanasius' Paschal Letters*. Cairo and Rhode Island: Holy Virgin Coptic Orthodox Church and St Mary and St Mena Coptic Orthodox Church.

Walker, Susan and Bierbrier, Morris (1997). *Ancient Faces: Mummy Portraits from Roman Egypt*. London: British Museum Press.

Wallis, R. T. (1972). *Neoplatonism*. London: Duckworth.

Ware, Kallistos (1983). 'Salvation and Theosis in Orthodox Theology', in *Luther et la Reforme Allemande dans une Perspective Oecuménique*. Geneva: Éditions du Centre Orthodoxe, 167–84.

Warne, Graham J. (1995). *Hebrew Perspectives on the Human Person in the Hellenistic Era: Philo and Paul*. Lewiston, Queenston, and Lampeter: Edwin Mellen Press.

Weinstock, S. (1971). *Divus Julius*. Oxford: Oxford University Press.

Weiser, A. (1962). *The Psalms*. London: SCM Press.

WELCH, LAWRENCE J. (1994). *Christology and Eucharist in the Early Thought of Cyril of Alexandria*. San Francisco: International Scholars Press.

WELLES, C. B. (1934). *Royal Correspondence in the Hellenistic Period*. New Haven, London, and Prague: Yale University Press.

WESTERMANN, CLAUS (1984). *Genesis 1–11*. London: SCM Press.

WHEELWRIGHT, PHILIP (1959). *Heraclitus*. Oxford: Oxford University Press (repr. 1999).

WHITELEY, D. E. H. (1964). *The Theology of St Paul*. Oxford: Basil Blackwell.

WHITTAKER, M. (1982). *Tatian: Oratio ad Graecos and Fragments*. Oxford: Oxford University Press.

WICKHAM, Lionel R. (1983). *Cyril of Alexandria: Select Letters*. Oxford: Clarendon Press.

WIDDICOMBE, PETER (1994). *The Fatherhood of God from Origen to Athanasius*. Oxford: Clarendon Press.

WILD, PHILIP T. (1950). *The Divinization of Man according to Saint Hilary of Poitiers*. Pontificia Facultas Theologica Seminarii Sanctae Mariae ad Lacum. Dissertationes ad Lauream 21. Mundelein, Ill: Saint Mary of the Lake Seminary.

WILDUNG, DIETRICH (1977). *Egyptian Saints: Deification in Pharaonic Egypt*. Hagop Kevorkian Series on Near Eastern Art and Civilization. New York: New York University Press.

WILLIAMS, A. N. (1999). *The Ground of Union: Deification in Aquinas and Palamas*. New York and Oxford: Oxford University Press.

WILLIAMS, ROWAN (1987). *Arius: Heresy and Tradition*. London: Darton, Longman & Todd.

WINSLOW, DONALD F. (1965). 'The Idea of Redemption in the Epistles of St Ignatius of Antioch'. *Greek Orthodox Theological Review* 11: 119–31.

—— (1979). *The Dynamics of Salvation: A Study in Gregory of Nazianzus*. Patristic Monograph Series 7. Philadelphia: Philadelphia Patristic Foundation.

WINSTON, DAVID (1979). *The Wisdom of Solomon*. Anchor Bible 43. New York, NY: Doubleday.

—— (1985). *Logos and Mystical Theology in Philo of Alexandria*. Cincinatti: Hebrew Union College Press.

WITT, R. E. (1931). 'The Hellenism of Clement of Alexandria'. *Classical Quarterly* 25: 195–204.

WOLFSON, E. (1974). *Through a Speculum that Shines: Vision and Imagination in Medieval Jewish Mysticism*. Princeton, NJ: Princeton University Press.

WOLFSON, H. A. (1947). *Philo*. 2 vols. Cambridge, Mass.: Harvard University Press.

WRIGHT, M. R. (1995). *Empedocles: The Extant Fragments* (2nd edn). London and Indianapolis: Bristol Classical Press.

WYBREW, HUGH (1989). *The Orthodox Liturgy: The Development of the Eucharistic Liturgy in the Byzantine Rite*. London: SPCK.

YANNARAS, CHRISTOS (1987). *Τὸ Πρόσωπο καὶ ὁ Ἔρως* (4th edn). Athens: Ekdoseis Domos. (German edition: *Person und Eros*. Göttingen: Vandenhoeck & Ruprecht, 1982).

—— (1991). *Elements of Faith: An Introduction to Orthodox Theology*. Trans. Keith Schram. Edinburgh: T & T Clark.

—— (1992). Ὀρθοδοξία καὶ Δύση στὴ Νεώτερη Ἑλλάδα. Athens: Ekdoseis Domos.

YOUNG, FRANCES M. (1971). 'A Reconsideration of Alexandrian Christology'. *JEH* 22: 103–14.

—— (1997). *Biblical Exegesis and the Formation of Christian Culture*. Cambridge: Cambridge University Press.

YOUSIF, PATROS (1989). *An Introduction to the East Syrian Spirituality*. Rome: Centre for Indian and Inter-religious Studies.

ZIESLER, JOHN (1989). *Paul's Letter to the Romans*. Trinity Press International New Testament Commentaries. London: SCM Press.

—— (1990). *Pauline Christianity* (rev. edn). Oxford and New York: Oxford University Press.

ZIZIOULAS, JOHN D. (1975). 'Human Capacity and Human Incapacity: A Theological Exploration of Personhood'. *SJT* 28: 401–47.

—— (1985). *Being as Communion: Studies in Personhood and the Church*. Contemporary Greek Theologians 4. Crestwood, NY: St Vladimir's Seminary Press.

—— (1991). 'On Being a Person: Towards an Ontology of Personhood', in Schwöbel and Gunton 1991: 33–46.

ZUNTZ, GÜNTER (1971). *Persephone: Three Essays on Religion and Thought in Magna Graecia*. Oxford: Clarendon Press.

Index of References

New Testament

OTHER ANCIENT AUTHORS

MODERN AUTHORS

General Index